Danny Gwira

GOJU

The Roar of the Tigress

The real self-defense for women only

Editions Dedicaces

GOJU: THE ROAR OF THE TIGRESS.
THE REAL SELF-DEFENSE FOR WOMEN ONLY
by DANNY GWIRA (Founder of African Goju© & South American Goju©)

Copyright © 2015 by Editions Dedicaces LLC

All rights reserved. No part of this book may be used or reproduced in any form whatsoever without written permission except in the case of brief quotations embodied in critical articles or reviews.

Published by:
　　Editions Dedicaces LLC
　　12759 NE Whitaker Way, Suite D833
　　Portland, Oregon, 97230
　　www.dedicaces.us

Library of Congress Cataloging-in-Publication Data
　　Gwira, Danny.
　　Goju: The Roar of the Tigress/ by Danny Gwira.
　　p. cm.
　　ISBN-13: 978-1-77076-485-9 (alk. paper)
　　ISBN-10: 1-77076-485-2 (alk. paper)

Danny Gwira

The Roar of the Tigress

The real self-defense for women only

DEDICATED TO:

Evelyn my very first female martial arts student (1975) and to every single female who reads this book. I love you all!

Content

Chapter One - What is the real self-defence for women? 11

Chapter Two - The value of a man 22

Chapter Three - In the nightclub – Beware! 32

Chapter Four - Date Rape 50

Chapter Five - Mental Rape 73
    1. Emotional blackmail 74
    2. Silent treatment 76
    3. Sexual blackmail 78
    4. Emotional starvation 79
    5. Belittlement & verbal insults 82
    6. Fear of reprisals 84
    7. Imbalance in a relationship 87
    8. Financial blackmail & bribery 94
    9. Abuse of your feelings 99
    10. The workplace 105

Chapter Six - Armed Robberies – *"Why me"?* 111
    A. Money/valuables 114
    B. Flaunting wealth 115
    C. Debts, swindling and offending 117
    D. Security 118

Chapter Seven - Outside your home… How safe? 121
    1. Shopping/Bag snatching 122
    2. Dressing/Male attention 124
    3. Witness to a crime 126
    4. Going out… 128
    5. Public relations… 133
        (a). Reception 133
        (b). Shop 134
        (c). Restaurant 134
        (d). Office 136
        (e). Public transport 138
        (f). Double-dealing 141

6. Driving 143
   (a). Accidents..143
   (b). Road rage 146
   (c). Safety Measures 147
7. In a crowd..149
8. Abroad 153

Chapter Eight - Is your abode a fortress? 159
   1. Young children 159
   2. Fire safety..162
   3. Burglary...164
   4. Security tricks 167
   5. Business premises 170
   6. Strangers...171
   7. Friends/flatmates..173
   8. Boyfriends/lovers & one night stands 174

Chapter Nine - People! – Can you trust them? 179
   1. Patronising men 180
   2. I'm as good as any man...184
   3. Sexism...189
   4. Dating…...193
      (a) The Internet..193
      (b) Dating agencies 195
      (c) Speed-dating 196
      (d) How do you get rid of a boring date? 196
   5. The Police 198
      (a) The Police Station 199
      (b) The Courts 201
      (c) In Prison 202

Chapter Ten - Beware of the Conman 205
   1. Confidence tricks as an art form..205
      (a) Pressure sales 205
      (b) Hole-in-the-wall scams 210
      (c) Credit card theft..211
      (d) Identity theft..213
      (e) Simple scams...214
      (f) Investment fraudsters..215
      (g) Loan sharks..216
      (h) Religious conmen...217
      (i) Voodoo 219
      (j) Third World Scams 220

- 2. Counterfeit...223
  - (b) Electronic Equipment 224
  - (c) Credit cards, Traveller's Cheques, Notes, Coins and Tickets............225
  - (d) Designer attire, perfumes and jewellery...............................229
  - (e) Food and Drink..231
  - (f) Property..233
  - (g) 'Rogue Traders'...235
- 3. Christmas: Season of goodwill (or is it?)................................236

Chapter Eleven - With friends like these… 242
- 1. Keeping secrets..242
- 2. Family members..245
- 3. Misogyny 248
- 4. Racism 251
- 5. Taking advantage..254
- 6. The plunderer 259
- 7. Success through fame or wealth 264
- 8. Blackmail 269
- 9. Infidelity 272
  - (a) Only a fling!..272
  - (b) Affairs 273
  - (c) Experimentation 275
- 10. Female Fun 276
  - (a) Toy boys...276
  - (b) Sugar Daddies 280
  - (c) Gigolos 282
- 11. Pressure persuasion 283
- 12. Betrayal 288

Chapter Twelve - Children: How safe are they? 293
- 1. Potential dangers...293
- 2. Disappearance 297
- 3. Strangers 300
- 4. Peer pressure..302
- 5. The Internet...305
- 6. Bullying, teasing & gossip 308
- 7. Gangs, weapons and fights 312
  - (a) Gangs 312
  - (b) Weapons..314
  - (c) Fights 318
- 8. Intoxicants 321
  - A. Cigarettes..321
  - B. Alcohol 323
  - C. Illegal drugs...326

9. Sex, pregnancy, abortions, diseases and homosexuality 337
    (a) Sex 337
    (b) Pregnancy 338
    (c) Abortion 340
    (d) Diseases 341
    (e) Homosexuality 342
10. Give the youth a chance! 343

Chapter Thirteen - Senior citizens – Protect them! 347
1. Ageism: 348
2. Robbers & Con artists: 350
3. Disappearance: 352
4. Security: 352
5. Exercise: 354

Chapter Fourteen - The impossible situation (Part 1) Battle of the sexes 355
A. THE SEX WEAPON 357
B. MARITAL RAPE 365
C. WIFE BEATING 371
D. AFFAIRS 380
    1. Mental affairs 383
    2. Physical affairs 392

Chapter Fifteen - The impossible situation (Part 2) Dilemmas 403
1. Substance abuse 404
    (a). Alcohol 405
    (b). Drugs 411
2. Addictions 418
    (a). Gambling 418
    (b). Cigarettes 422
    (c). Sex 424
    (d). Gluttony 427
    (e). Exercise addiction 431
3. Crime 434
4. Work/family life balance 439
5. The Break-up 446
    (a). ultimatum 451
    (b). dismissal 451
    (c). separation 452
    (d). divorce 452

Chapter Sixteen - The impossible situation (Part 3) Life or Death 457
A. Murder and Manslaughter 461
B. Kidnapping 466
C. Armed robbery 474

D. Stalking 479
  E. Miscarriage of justice 484
    1. Wrongful accusation 484
    2. Police brutality 487
    3. Torture 489
    4. Societal malpractices 491
    5. Religious groups, clubs and organisations 496

Chapter Seventeen - The impossible situation (Part 4) Terrorism 501
  1. Air Rage 527
  2. Hijacking 528
  3. Hostage-taking 530
  4. Suicide-bombing 533
  5. Explosions 536
  6. High-profile Murders 537
  7. Spying and Sabotage 538
  8. Illegal Strikes, Riots, Looting and Rape 540
  What can we do? 542

Chapter Eighteen - The real self-defence is common sense 547
  1. What does this book mean for women? 547
  2. Goju Real Self-defence is the modern way to go! 550
  3. The top 50... 552

Appendix 571

Chapter One
What is the real self-defence for women?

Self-defence for women! Ha! Ha! Ha! Yes, most men will have a chuckle; because like it or not, we still live in a male-orientated society. Although there has been some improvement in the female situation over the years; it is still not easy being a woman. Many are regularly used and abused by their male partners and opportunists; not to mention attacks by rapists, muggers and thieves. What I say is; there is no need for any of these attacks to happen! Most self-defence books only explain the physical side of self-defence: a kick here...a punch there...a throw, hold or choke where it hurts! That may work in some cases; but a high standard of martial arts is needed, and most women don't have that. These books also fail to mention that a lot of the techniques are illegal. If for example, you kicked a man in the groin or poked him in the eye; he could sue and you might find yourself in the dock, accused of attacking him! *"But he started it!"* you might proclaim with indignation. All very well but; did you have to blind him or ruin his marital life? To you, he was just a drunken groping nuisance who needed to be taught him a lesson; but to his possible wife and children, you are the bitch that hurt their dear father and husband!

Although few women are equal to men in the physical sense; it is possible that after many years of training, a woman can become as tough and as strong as many a man. Some have even been known to beat up men in fights; but that is not the norm. Women have other and probably more effective ways to defend themselves; because their best self-defence is their sex. By nature; men will always go to the aid of a woman in trouble. Some countries do not even allow a woman on the front lines in a battle; mainly because it would distract the attention of the men if she were shot or wounded. No nation wants to see their mothers, sisters and daughters arriving home in body bags! Society has much more sympathy for women who are attacked, than they do for men; and many hardened criminals would prefer not to injure women, when committing crimes. In all prisons; a convict is never safe from the other inmates...if it is found out he attacked, injured or raped a woman. He may have to be put into protective custody; in case he is stabbed, cut up or even killed! So you see ladies; you still have a lot going for you! You have to realise this and use everything to your advantage; because in this *Goju* system, anything goes!

Realistically; self-defence for women is mostly common sense and following a set of rules. Problems usually arise when these rules are either broken or not taken seriously. Fighting only works, if she is able to escape or receive help after hurting her attacker. This means her attack must work at the first attempt; or she could be seriously injured. Beating up an attacker is one thing; but trying to fight an angry or embarrassed opponent whom she has tried to injure, is a completely different proposition. Only a seasoned martial artist will be able to deal with such a scenario! The best female martial artists usually have a father, husband, boyfriend, brother or close male relative who is also in the martial arts; and introduced her to the art. Not many women are so lucky! For the majority of females; self-defence is something that other women need. Attacks and rapes are what you read about in the papers or see on the news! This is why many women have a nonchalant attitude to life and its dangers. *"Oh, I can defend myself easily when I'm attacked. Just gouge his eyes out or kick him in the balls. If that fails I'll scream till the cops come!"* That may work and it may not. What if it doesn't? In some areas; where are the police when you need them? If it does work and you do hurt him seriously; are you prepared to go through life looking over your shoulder for possible revenge from his loved ones? Statistics have shown that women are attacked as often, if not more than men; therefore sooner or later, most women might become or know someone who will become a victim of a rape, a mugging or an attack.

A lot of martial arts teachers deceive women and let them believe they can beat up men; so that they continue to pay the somewhat exorbitant fees some clubs charge to teach techniques they know will not realistically work. So I say; why take the chance of fighting a man, when you can beat him more effectively without touching him? The fit woman kicking the punching bag looks good on the television and in magazines; but it sends out the wrong message and causes a lot of amusement amongst men, who will always believe that it will never work on them! The male pride will never accept a beating from a woman; and that makes him more dangerous because he feels he has to come out the winner, by any means at his disposal. Many women are beaten up and raped; simply because of this factor. They tried to physically fight back! Confused? Welcome to the real self-defence for women!

If a woman cannot beat a man physically; other methods will have to be used and that is the purpose of this book. There really are 'other methods'…lots of them! Men in the worldwide sense; are still richer and more powerful than women and therefore have a great advantage over them. In most walks of life; men get what they want by the sheer power of their affluence and influence. The aptly-named 'boys club' or 'gentleman's gang', is a fact of life; because when push comes to shove, men will stick together and team up against any woman trying to break into their arena. The few women, who do manage to get in, still have to play by rules laid down by men. It is a harsh and competitive world in which we live in; and that is why most women have so far, done nothing about their plight. Some would rather fight each other, in order to gain the approval of the male; rather than join forces and fight him! Men devised most of the laws, without real consideration for the female; and there is still an on-going struggle by women, to get even the archaic ones changed. Those men who cannot get what they want by pressure or money; will resort to force and (sometimes armed) violence. As if that is not enough; some women have to endure rape, mental humiliation and physical beatings. Few women are brave enough to report their mistreatment; because to do so, will rock the very foundations of their existence and alter their way of life for ever.

The real self-defence for women is not only about the obvious attacks like rape and bag snatchers; but also about defence from less visible threats like those from a loved one, usually boyfriends and husbands. For example; you need money for the children or to buy food for the house. He refuses to give it to you; but would gladly spend it elsewhere, with the boys in the pub or God forbid, with one of his numerous girlfriends! What do you do if he is richer than you; and you have to demean yourself by begging him for every cent? In most countries he is legally the 'man' of the house; so you cannot argue with him. If you do; you will be branded a troublemaker and you'd be surprised at how many of your own female 'friends' could turn against you. *"It could be worse! At least he does not beat you up! You don't know how lucky you are; he bought you a brand new car for your birthday didn't he?! Look at all the jewellery you've got from him!"* Etc. You dare not use sex as a weapon; because he could and most probably, will rape you. (Remember; not all rapes are physical. I will discuss mental rape later on in this book).

With very little chance of prosecution; husbands literally get away with whatever they want, in a marital home. A wife finds herself bending over backwards, just to please her man; at the expense of her own dignity, self-esteem and happiness. There is not much any woman can do about her marital woes; without baring her whole life and soul to public scrutiny and possible ridicule. She can refuse to cook; but he will simply waste the money in restaurants. Even worse; he could go to his girlfriend, who will be only too glad to cook for him and listen to his tales of what an 'evil wife' he has at home. If she stops washing his clothes; he will just buy new ones. Doesn't clean the house; and she would be shooting herself in the foot because her friends would visit and blame her for keeping an untidy house. Her own female instincts would eventually force her to clean up the mess! Yes, it can be horrible being female; and because most women are loving and kind-hearted, they don't complain and just 'get on with it' for the good of the family! I am now telling you; it is not good self-defence to sacrifice personal integrity, self-esteem, dignity and happiness for altruism. You should never put up with anything that hurts you or feels wrong when you do it; because you will always live to regret it. Once you fall into a muddy ditch; it will be very hard to get yourself out, without getting dirty! This book will help make sure you do not fall in!

Most of the examples mentioned in the above paragraph, might not necessarily refer to the financially independent woman or one who lives alone; but don't throw this book away just yet. It does not matter how wealthy, successful or 'independent' a woman is; because her problems could be worse. Ninety percent of women in the world; are not self-sufficient and still depend on their husbands, boyfriends, fathers and lovers for financial or emotional support. A rich, controlling father is as bad, if not worse, than a boyfriend; because the threat to write her out of his will, can reign in even the most rebellious female. The toughest financially independent woman will still have female instincts; which means she has a heart! The clever male or female in her life could take advantage of this; and inflict the most horrendous mental rape on her, that would make the physical rape seem like a walk in the park! Financial independence always leads to emotional dependence; because the richer and more successful a woman is, the greater her emotional insecurities. She will always need someone she can trust and depend on; and it is that same person who could hurt her the most.

Some of you will be forgiven for asking the question, *"Defence against what? I am in control of my life! Who cares about anyone else?"* That could be true; but the few women who are really in control of their lives, arrived there through bitter experience. I would hate for you to go through that as well. This book will help you avoid most of the pitfalls that can make your life hell; but more importantly, it will put you into a frame of mind that will allow you to enjoy your life and never be taken for granted, used and abused. The real self-defence is about defending you from the daily hassles in life. You know; men with groping arms; those with their brains between their legs; over-zealous con men; bag-snatchers; drunks in nightclubs; philandering husbands; calculating 'friends' pretending to help you with all your problems; troublesome teenagers etc. Never a dull moment being female! Every man thinks he is a brilliant lover; and would like to prove it in the only way he knows how. What makes it funny is that some of them have such big potbellies and look so unhealthy and unfit; that you must wonder what they are bragging about! They probably need a mirror, in order to see the instrument they intend to satisfy you with! This belief in their sexual prowess can make men behave in stupid and childish ways; which can really amuse and sometimes annoy the female. Sorry girls; I must apologise for my sex. Our brains really are between our legs. This book is your chance to give it a good kick when we misbehave!

Don't get me wrong; because not all men are like that. Some are polite and decent; but with a general lack of understanding of the female by most men, the so-called 'perfect man' is a myth. Men always have a hidden agenda. They are usually nice to you, until they find they cannot get what they want from you; and then they will move on to their next prey. Married men who cannot easily move on; (because they are stuck with you by marriage and the kids) will sulk and behave like spoilt children, until you cave in to their selfish wishes. Just go shopping and you will notice the 'polite' shop assistant, who is more interested in you than selling you things; and quickly acts like you don't exist, when you refuse to give him your phone number. A female hitchhiker will have come across the lecherous rat, who stops to give her a lift and then insults her; dropping her by the wayside, because she refused to go to that 'nice hotel' for a drink. The insults to the female integrity are numerous. While most women have their own ways of dealing with each situation, the cancer will never go away; so long as men continue to believe that a smile from a woman means more than it really does, and a *"No!"* means *"Yes"*. This book is an attempt to defuse the war of the sexes; with simple, sometimes humorous, sometimes emotionally violent ways of 'letting him down gently'! In the end; there will be only one winner in your life...you!

I will try to deal with most of the mental and physical attacks experienced by the female population. I will also show you simple tactics against people who, more often than not, are friends of yours; who just want to get friendlier. Most physical self-defence techniques will not work; unless you have been practising them for many years. They may also be illegal; and that is why this book will not show any. If you want to learn the martial arts in the conventional sense; it would be better for you to join a club. I'm sure if you look hard enough; you will find some good ones around, which won't deceive you. This book however; can be useful because you do not have to fight to defend yourself! It is to help you make sure the attack never takes place! Fight without fighting is how women can be at their most dangerous; but in order to succeed, a drastic change in her way of thinking might have to be made by some of the women reading this book. You only need to watch television or pick up the newspapers to be told of attacks made, not only in lonely places but also in the cities and in private homes; to understand the need for knowledge of the real self-defence.

There is one basic principle in self-defence. *You must use your most effective weapon, as quickly as you can; against the most vulnerable part of your opponent.* This can be divided into three categories. Firstly, your most effective weapon is your female sense and intuition; through which you can avoid trouble, before it is allowed to happen. If it doesn't feel right...it isn't right; and nobody should convince you otherwise! Women are very clever at 'feeling' if something is wrong. How many times have you got dressed to go out; only to go back and change because the dress doesn't 'feel' right? Everyone else seems to think the dress is nice; but nothing will make you go out in it! That is the feeling I am talking about; so respect it, and it will save your life! Always rely on your gut feminine instinct, which can never be wrong; simply because an instinct is based on who you are and would make you feel terrible, if you go against it. Believe me; if something is not right for whom you are, it will hit you like a ton of bricks and you should never go against it! Secondly, you need speed and timing, so that you act before it can happen; and if it does, knowing how to react quickly and effectively. Finally; you have to know the place to attack or counterattack your opponent, where it hurts most. In most cases; this will be first on his ego. If he does not get the message, the next step will be in the police station with the law firmly on your side; so that he does not even think of trying anything on you again.

The real self-defence for women will not only teach you to avoid trouble; but will also show you what to do when trouble will not leave you alone. It will serve as a guideline for you to devise your own tactics; and help you make the world a safer place for yourself. At the end of the day, it is your life; so love and defend it any way you can, because nobody will do it for you. A kick in the groin might work for you; while on another occasion, a few choice words, screams or tears will suffice in calming down and defeating the opponent. This can only happen; if he leaves you alone and will not bother you anymore. If you live in the States or Europe; you will obviously have to act differently than if you lived in a Third World country, where rights for women are still in their infancy. There are times you will travel, so your tactics might have to change slightly to suit the environment; but the end-result remains the same...your mental and physical self-preservation. I will try to show as much as I can in this book; bearing in mind that you do not have a high standard in the martial arts and you do not want to go through the many years of training required, in order to achieve it. The rest will be up to you!

If you are ever attacked; it is usually your fault, I am sorry to say. You see, with women more so than with men, an attack is usually coerced; which means she consciously or unconsciously attracts the attack. Very few men attack women for the hell of it. No man jumps on or attacks a woman on the streets for no good reason; because he will feel the full force of the law! (Women probably have more to fear from random physical attacks from other females; than they do from a male!) The attacker usually knows the woman; even though she may not remember ever coming across him. Failing to act on your suspicions of a man you felt uncomfortable with, to either a friend or the police; is why I insist it is usually your fault! There are always subtle patterns and warning signs before any attack; and you have to train yourself to spot them before they are allowed to hurt you. Once you begin to understand and value your self-defence; they become easier to spot. If you are about to cross the road, you still look left then right and left again; even though it may seem safe enough to cross. That is what you were taught as a youngster; and it has stuck with you ever since and become part of you. You are instinctively aware that if a car knocks you over; you will be seriously injured or may even die! I want you to value yourself in the same way; so that protecting yourself becomes of the utmost importance and nothing should detract you from that aim.

The real self-defence concerns a lot more things than you could ever imagine. It concerns your body; your property; your loved ones; your reputation; your integrity; your self-esteem; your dignity; your job; your country; and anything else you care about; which, were you to lose or damage, would drastically change your way of life and in some cases, make your life not worth living. If you ever feel your life is not worth living; it is as bad as, if not worse than, a physical beating. Physical violence could soon be a thing of the past; because of the legal problems it would cause the attacker. Nobody wants to go to prison; so new ways have to be devised, in order to beat an opponent! If someone arranges for your house to be robbed; harms your children; dupes you of your hard-earned cash; spreads a vicious rumour against you; denigrates and insults you in public; causes you to lose your job; abuses your religion or ethnic origin; then he would have as good as beaten you up...without touching you! The main drastic change in your way of thinking has to be that with this new meaning of self-defence in mind; you have to take full responsibility for the things you care about and be ruthless in making sure you will not be intimidated or beaten. You would not allow someone to grab your hand and slowly break your fingers, without a fight; would you? In the same way; you should not let anyone steal your property; harm your family; damage your reputation; bully your integrity; trample on your self-esteem; mock your dignity; ridicule your job; or insult your country; because it hurts. Yes ladies...it really hurts!

There are millions of beautiful, honest and upright women who go through their lives unmolested; simply because they know the A-Z of staying safe. There is no luck or bad luck in self-defence. You dig your own grave. The police in every country tell women what to do and what not to do in their area; with pamphlets and leaflets (don't go out alone at night – make sure your doors are always locked – don't get too drunk – don't allow anyone into your house after a night out, if you have no intention of sleeping with him - etc.). Therefore, if after a night out she is raped, either at home or in a dark alley; why should she blame anyone but herself? Nobody forces drink onto you; so why would you want to get blindingly drunk? Blaming a man for raping you after the event; isn't much help to you, is it? You cannot expect the police to be everywhere at once; just to look after you! If you take a job; don't just look at the salary. Think! And weigh up all the pros and cons. On occasions; will you have to walk home alone at night? What precautions are you going to take? Etc. Treating self-defence as a lifestyle; is the way to prevent unwanted attacks and molestations. Learning to fight properly may take too long and requires a discipline few women have the time for; so the only option is to plan each day like a military campaign and leave nothing to chance. Besides; fighting is so ungainly and unladylike isn't it? Not really twenty-first century!

In this world; a lot of trouble can be avoided, if only you use your head. Basic common sense is all that is required! Being female; you still have the advantage of people rushing to your aid, if you are ever molested on the street. A scream, a few tears at the right moment or a report to the police station; can scare off most molesters on a busy street. You are female! Nobody will call you a coward; if you report someone to the police. However, I must stress again that it would be better to avoid trouble; than be forced to act after it has happened. In a scenario, where you cannot walk away from trouble; you will have to be smart and leave no stone unturned. Like a chameleon; a woman has to be able to blend in with her environment and the situation at hand. This means she has to know how, where, why and when to be intelligent; deliberately stupid; devious; cunning; clever; manipulative; strong; weak; slow; fast; compliant and sexy; in order to defend herself. She does not need to apologise for using what will work for her; in order to keep her safe! She has to learn how to swerve, bob and weave herself out of everyday situations; without getting entangled. Above all; she must be true to herself and allow no one to upset her apple cart. That is the secret to *the real self-defence for women only*; and this book will show her how.

I will discuss many things, which might seem obvious to you; because they are simple common sense advice. But you would be surprised at the number of (especially younger) women, who take life for granted; and do not bother to follow, what the police call basic safety rules. Every woman is different; and it is no use pretending otherwise. I have therefore deliberately generalised in the following chapters; because I know you are clever enough to realise which parts of this book concern you, and which parts don't. By taking only what will work for you; you should easily be able to formulate your own self-defence strategy. If you add this recipe to what you already know; it will make you one helluva tough cookie to crack! You will also notice that I have repeated certain advice, several times in this book. Please don't get bored; because it is to make sure it sinks deep into your consciousness and becomes part of you. That way you will never forget it! *("Look left, look right and look left again!")* I have also used terms and language; which some women might find offensive, rude, patronising or sexist. I apologise in advance; but I am not a diplomat and this book is not a fairground ride. It embodies many serious topics; and drastic ways to deal with them! A rapist about to rape a victim; is going to think of and use derogatory language like *"bitch"* or *"whore"* on her. Bearing that in mind; you will notice that such language is only used to make a point and is nothing personal. After all; a 'bitch in suspenders' can be a sexy turn-on for any hot-blooded man! *"Pant... Pant... Yes please!!!"*

The minute most men realise their partners are doing self-defence; there is a chuckle and a smile as if to say, *"Well it's okay, so long as she doesn't use it on me; and if she does, it won't work anyway!"* Men on the whole don't take female self-defence seriously; and that is the reason for the title of this book. *The Roar of the Tigress* is my way of telling these men that deep inside every woman, is a tigress waiting to explode; and when she is angry, she will roar and bite back in ways one can never predict. *"For women only!"* was designed for two reasons: To make women feel they have something for themselves; and to make men curious. When a man sees the title; he will wonder why it is *'for women only'* and will definitely take a peek. What he will see in this book; will not make comfortable reading for him. He will realise that behind that beautiful smile of yours; lurks a determined female who will not be messed with. It is okay for you to join a gym or try to lose weight; because he stands to benefit from the new-look, new shape and slimmer, healthier you. But now; you are doing self-defence. This is a threat to him; because the only reason a woman goes in for self-defence is to protect herself. If his woman is taking an interest in self-defence; it may not only be for robbers, unwanted suitors or thieves. It might just be for him; and the kind of self-defence I am talking about, is something he will not have bargained for! Here is a clear message for any man who dares to pick up this book. *"Be very careful in the way you treat your woman; because by the end of this book, you will not be able to get away with things you used to take so much for granted in your better-half. You have been warned!"*

For me however; keeping you safe from physical and mental harm is serious business. I will take it as a personal failure; if after reading this book, you ever encounter any attacks on your precious self that you cannot handle. Love me or hate me; I will tell it as it as I see it!

"Are you ready Tigress? Give me a smile and let's go for it!!!"

Chapter Two
The value of a man

Do women really need men? Although some may disagree; the answer has to be, *"Yes they do need men"* and in more ways than they may be aware of. The usefulness of a man is only valid if it helps you; and not hinders you. Last chapter, I mentioned that men have a huge advantage over women; because of their greater financial and political clout. It is still a man's world in many ways; so it makes sense to make use of any man who can help you in what you are trying to achieve. Anything; from carrying your bags for you to taking you to lunch when you are hungry and haven't got enough money on you, is fair game. Some women have perfected the 'damsel in distress' technique; and will not think twice about making a man to do things for them. The trick is being aware of the cut-off point; after which, a man will realise he is being used and will expect a payback! Modern society has raised so much suspicion amongst the sexes that many women will not ask for help from a man; in case he gets the wrong idea and thinks she fancies him. In the same vein; a man will not joke around with a woman, in case she accuses him of sexual harassment! This chasm between the sexes is the main reason why there is an increasing lack of sympathy by men; whenever a woman encounters problems. Some men deliberately go out of their way to hinder the progress of women; because it is still seen as a threat to the hegemony they have enjoyed over the centuries. Rapes, beatings, date-rapes and public groping are all done by certain men; who at one point or another in their lives, have been crushed by the sheer wit and power of the female and feel they can no longer talk to her. They therefore prefer to inflict their masculinity on her; in the only way they know how…sheer force.

Too many commercials and media outlets these days belittle men and make jokes at their expense; that some women actually believe they are now there for the taking. The fact that men don't seriously complain about male sexism; does not mean they don't feel it. There may one day be a serious backlash; because men are on the back foot and are in real fear of their virility being stripped off them by women. Statistics show that in schools, the girls are out-performing the boys; and many traditionally male jobs are now going to women. Very soon; men will only be good for manual labour and procreation! After many centuries of male domination; one can understand why some women are gleefully ready to jump on the bandwagon and crush the men while they are down. The drawback with this attitude is that the real power in this world is political and economic; which is still firmly under the control of men. Token positions and appointments aside; I doubt whether they are ready to hand over to women just yet! If things get too hot to handle; the men in real power will fight back and it won't be a pretty sight. It is a war I'm not sure the female can win because there are many women who would rather have a man run things than a woman; and would do anything to stop her becoming too powerful. For some reason, women are reluctant to support each other where it really matters; leaving the men literally laughing all the way to the bank, by earning salaries far in excess of the women. It seems as if women still have an inferiority complex; and will push each other out of the way, in order to get ahead and impress the men. Men however; tend to support each other where it counts...to the detriment of the female. Hence, there are relatively few women in positions of real political and economic power; as most countries and top companies are run by men. For this reason, a smart female will not bother to fight the status-quo; but will work around it and assimilate herself into it, in order to gain what she wants and make sure her life runs smoothly for her. The most successful women are those who know the value of each man to them; and handle him accordingly. From the odd-job man, to the boss in a male-dominated company, to the rich sugar daddy; every man has his uses. It is therefore is up to the woman to see this value and utilise it; in order to get the best out of any man she needs. To hate, fight or denigrate him serves no purpose to her at all.

The value of a man lies in his male instincts to protect what he considers weaker than him. If you are walking down the street and you trip and fall down; the chances are, a man will come to your rescue. If your boyfriend hits you in public; there will be no shortage of men queuing up to stop him doing further damage. On occasions; you might even get a man to open a door for you or offer you his seat on a crowded bus! All this seems nice and chauvinistic; but you should never have to feel you owe any man anything for helping you. He did it because he wanted to; and unless he is your relative or very good friend, there is always a hidden agenda...usually sexual. This involuntary action in helping the 'weaker sex'; is one of the reasons most armies do not like having women on the frontline in a war. It is not because the women cannot fight; as women are actually more vicious than men in war! It is simply because, were a woman fighting alongside men on the frontline to be shot; the men would involuntarily come to her aid and waste a lot more time and effort, than were a man to be wounded! A successful woman is often accused of *"sleeping her way to the top"*. In most cases, this is not strictly true. It is because this woman knows how to move around a man's world; and is acutely aware how a man's brain and feelings work. She gives as good as she gets in the opinion stakes; and she never gets offended by so-called 'sexist' jokes. She is well-versed in sports and politics and goes drinking with the boys; thereby ensuring their warmth and protection. She becomes a good friend to the men, who learn to trust her and love her like a sister; and would do anything for her. Although to the outsider looking in, she may seem over-friendly to the men and is *"definitely shagging the boss"*; all she has done is realise the value of a man and knows how to use him without his realising he is being used! I would say that is admirably clever; wouldn't you?

In reality, women are not the weaker sex; but in self-defence terms, it will serve you better to let men think you are. Even if you are dealing with a lowly clerk and you are the boss; a simple smile, a *"please"*, a *"thank you"* and even a *"sorry"* goes a long way in perpetuating the belief that you need him. You will then be able to get him to do anything for you! Yelling at him in front of others and throwing your weight around on any man causes deep resentment; and even if he does not show it in front of you, rest assured it will lie festering in his subconscious and he will find a way to pay you back. (How would you like a man to yell at you, in a room full of other women? Not so funny is it?) Self-defence is about making sure your life works well for you; which means you need people on your side to succeed. You should therefore try not to portray the *"I'm better than any man"* attitude; even if you are. Respect with anyone has to be earned; and is usually developed over many years. Trying too hard to prove you are better than a man, only shows that you are not; and he will quickly see through you and undermine you. A female does not need to tell the whole world she is tough; because she should already know she is *"intuitively cleverer than a man"* and the way she carries herself will let others know it too and respect her. Trying to fight men at their own game, may win you some short-term brownie points; but it will make you enemies amongst the male fraternity. If that were to happen; you will not survive long and could soon find yourself on the scrap-heap, shunned even by your own female counterparts. If you do manage to bully your way to the top of your profession, you will find it is much harder to stay there; and you will need on your side, the same men you trampled on to get there.

Seeing the value in a male is essential in everything you do; because by nature, men still want to and will help women…if really needed. You should therefore take advantage of this goodwill; and not feel ashamed to utilise a man, whenever necessary. Every smart woman knows a man's ego is easy enough to manipulate! When walking around town; the presence of any male accompanying you can put off 90% of potential troublemakers…especially the wisecracks and groping! This works as long as you make it obvious when walking with a man, that he is your protector; by holding his hand or gripping him by the arm. No man in his right mind would refuse a lady holding onto him in public; because it makes him feel all-powerful and content, sending out the signal to other men that he is ready to defend her against the world! If you don't hold on to him; it leaves a slight security gap for other men (thieves as well as suitors) to think they can move in. This is okay, if that is your intention; but for peace of mind in town, it is better to be safe than sorry. Having a man as your 'protector' is only a means to an end; and can go a long way in defending you from unwanted harassment and solicitations. Holding onto a man in public does not mean you cannot look after yourself; and it certainly does not make him your boyfriend. Besides; I'm sure you will know how to put him in his place, if he tries to take advantage of the situation! It is just a question of having the right attitude; and knowing that bad things do happen out on the streets. Having someone with you is always better than facing things on your own! Feeling you are so strong that you don't need anybody; is the kind of attitude that drives a wedge between the sexes. There are always some men who are secretly pleased when a lady is robbed or date-raped; because they believe it has brought her down a peg or two!

Some women might sniff at the mere suggestion of having a man as a protector and let's face it; some men look like they couldn't punch their way out of a paper bag! This is a good point; but although yours may not be the strongest man in town, his mere presence can delay an attack on you. This is because whoever goes for you or your possessions, will have to deal with him first; thereby affording you valuable seconds, which could save your life. In any threatening situation; the male instinct to protect you will come out on top. The man you thought was a weak skeleton could turn out to have more mental courage than even the toughest looking bodybuilder; so never judge a book by its cover. I do understand that it can be impractical to always have a man on stand-by for when you are going out; so you have to use your head. If you are just going to the shops in your area, where everyone from the local traffic warden to the shop assistant to the parking attendant knows you; then you could very easily go out without a man and feel perfectly safe. However; if you are going anywhere you are not familiar with, especially in the evenings, then you have to make an effort to protect yourself. I am assuming you do not know how to fight effectively; and are not willing to damage your nails, ruin your hair or smudge your make-up in a struggle with a molester or bag-snatcher. Even though you are an independent woman; you won't feel so tough if something happens to you on a night out and no one was there to help you!

If you are a nice-income earner with your own car and still want to go out, but cannot find an accommodating man; then go with a girlfriend (or preferably two). This could still be dangerous if your car breaks down on a lonely road; so make sure someone knows where you will be at all times. Confidence is obviously the key. Depending on where you live; you can assess whether to take precautions or not. Once you feel fine about preventing certain obstacles, including punctures on a lonely road if they occur; then you may go out alone. But I repeat; it is always safer to go with someone. Even when going out on a date with a boyfriend; you should always let him come and pick you up and never 'meet him there'. If he cannot come and pick you up without good reason; it means there could be an imbalance in your relationship and he does not value you enough to care about your safety. If you insist on going to meet up with him; you are better-off looking for a brother, cousin or platonic friend to accompany you, (who else is going to fix the puncture for you?) even if you have to buy him drinks (you have money; remember!) His male presence alone can save you a lot of hassles in the club, until you decide what you want to do; or until your boyfriend finally shows up. *"Where the hell have you been???"*

If at the end of the evening, you prefer to go to a lover's flat for the night and you don't want your 'bodyguard' tagging along; then at least he will know who you left with. If anything were to happen to you, (we all know about car snatchers and date-rape; but it always happens to someone else, thank God!) he will be able to tell the police what your last movements were. Even though you may end up giving him money for a taxi to go home, he should also tell you his exact intentions; just in case you have to send an SOS to him, if something goes wrong with your date. It seems like a lot of trouble because most times, a night out is perfectly safe; but in the final analysis, it is your life and I cannot really live it for you. I can only give you suggestions, based on the facts that date-rape, muggings, car-snatching, robberies etc do exist; and happen more times than we can ever imagine...usually to those who chose to go out alone. The newspapers only print the sensational stories. Most attacks are never reported; and even if they are, it is of no comfort after the event. Even if the perpetrators are caught, the legal punishment rarely fits the crime; leaving the victim feeling angry, cheated and humiliated. It's entirely your decision!

As a woman; you have to realise that by nature all men are cavemen in different guises. However hard he tries to be accommodating and nice to you, the caveman in him is always bubbling very close to the surface; and anything could trigger it off. Always be aware that a man is normally physically stronger than a woman; and were he to lose it and attack her, he could cause tremendous physical damage. The wrong word; a joke at an importune time; an insult; rebuke; public humiliation or rejection; could all set him off into reacting in a manner so uncharacteristic, that it will shock you he is capable of behaving in that way. A man could 'snap' at any moment; and it could be for something you said, did or didn't do, several weeks before. He could suddenly turn round and yell at or hit you; which as far as you are concerned, you did nothing to deserve. He could rape you, even in the marital bed; in order to prove he is not the wimp you think he is. The drip-drip-drip effect of snide remarks and belittling comments you have been heaping on him over the years; could suddenly explode back in your face. If a man were to hit you; it would be because he does not feel valued by you and as a result, loses respect for you. Although legally he is in the wrong; that will not stop a man attacking a woman he purports to love. It just happened! You can send him to counselling or anger management classes or even call the police; but the fact remains, he still attacked you. He might very well go to prison for hitting you or raping you; but that will not heal your broken jaw, swollen eye sockets, bruised vagina or wounded pride any quicker. In self-defence terms; you have failed to keep your man under control, thereby putting yourself in danger. The purpose of this book is to prevent such unfortunate incidents and not have to act after the event; so for the most part, you have take matters into your own hands and not take anything or anyone for granted.

A man has to feel he is valued; in order to get the best out of him. This does not mean you should acquiesce to everything he does or agree with everything he says; but there are good and bad ways of doing things. You have to know your man well enough by watching his eyes and facial reactions to certain things you say or do; and if you find they annoy him, you should try not to repeat them. The fact that he says nothing does not mean he enjoys being insulted or humiliated in front of his friends. *"I think you made a mistake darling"* said calmly, is much better than yelling, *"You stupid ignorant idiot. That is not how to do it!"* In any relationship; if you want things to run smoothly, you may have to use your head and let him be the man of the house…even though your ego might not like it. However; you should understand that there are many ways to remain in control, while letting him think he is in charge. Always ask his advice on family matters and don't impose your will on him; because he will silently resent it. Go with his ideas; even if you think yours are better. Sooner or later, he will get it wrong; and then you can quietly 'suggest' a better way. If you really are smarter than him; he will quickly realise that you always have the better ideas and will gladly cede the marital power over to you. Always let him believe it was his decision; and never tease him that his ideas never work! Just remember that a woman always knows best how to run her household; but it may take a little time for him to realise it!

If you are constantly nagging, challenging and belittling him; you win the battle but not the war. Beating you up may not be his style; but he can hurt you just as badly by secretly picking up prostitutes. He could even find himself a nice 'quiet' girlfriend on the side; who will love to be 'protected' by him. As smart as you think you are; you will always be the last person to find out! He could hurt you even more, if he suddenly stops sleeping with you for no apparent reason; always burying himself in his work and claiming 'tiredness'. An uncomfortable and unhappy home riddled with secrets; is not good self-defence. Most men are easy going; and the smart woman knows exactly how to 'fine tune' and keep her man on his toes. Fighting and arguing never works in a relationship. You have to use your female wiles; which means backing off when necessary and going for the jugular if need be. Once a man knows you are not to be messed with; you will be surprised at how nice he can be to you! If you live alone and you don't have a man; then marital politics may not apply to you. Go and find yourself one and value him! A man can be useful; especially for those lonely nights when the vibrator doesn't quite hit the spot and you need something to talk to and cuddle before you go to sleep! *Terrible aren't I?*

The value of a man to a woman; is in her knowing that a man's ego is very fragile and massaging it, instead of bruising it. The idea is to let him 'protect you', but not walk all over you; therefore, you occasionally have to go to war to put him in his place. But generally, if he thinks he is protecting you; you will get a lot more out of him. Be kind but firm to your man; and for God's sake, save the sarcastic comments for someone else. Humour goes a long way. *"Darling, you know the garden needs a haircut"* said with a smile and a hug; will work much better than *"Get the garden sorted, you lazy sod. I'm going to the hairdressers!"* He may be a lazy sod; but he does not need reminding! The only reason he spends so much time in the pub; is to get away from you! There is more truth to the drunk confiding in the barmaid; *"My wife doesn't understand me!"* than the cartoons suggest! Your self-defence always begins with you. Remove the ingredients that cause friction and the war of words; and ultimately, the battle of sexes cannot commence. It is very easy to get a man to do anything for you; if you handle him right! Although peace in a marital home is a two-way street; I am assuming you are the smart one and you want your household to run smoothly, in the way you would like it to. It is therefore up to you to take the initiative; and behave in such a way that he would never dream of harming or upsetting you. Not all men are good; but with a little patience and a brilliant sense of humour, any man can be trained to suit your needs. If you have a man you love; value him, fight to keep him and gently coax him into being perfect for you. Without your help and effort; he will remain the caveman nature endowed him. Good luck girls!

Men also have to be aware that a woman can cause a lot more trouble to a man; than vice-versa. The law is generally on the woman's side in marital arguments and divorces; therefore, a man should do his utmost to make sure his woman is happy. Few women would begin an affair, abuse, insult, yell at or belittle them; if their men paid more attention, listened more and performed their sexual responsibilities on a regular basis.

> *"A good lay once a day will be more than enough.*
> *To put a smile on her face and even make her laugh.*
> *A happy woman is a joy to see and makes the world go round.*
> *No more nagging, no more bitching, she won't even make a sound."* ©

The lines from this song are every husband's dream; one which is probably unattainable because most men believe a woman is so hard to please that whatever they do, she will never be satisfied. Women are more honest than men in the sense that they act more with their feelings; and when they love, they do so wholeheartedly. This means they are more dangerous when they feel they have been betrayed (a woman scorned!) They are also very tough and resilient; enabling them to handle problems a lot easier than men realise. It does not take much to make a woman happy! Attention, faithfulness, lots of hugs and kisses making her feel wanted and important to her man; are all she really needs. A comfortable home, money, children, clothes and jewellery; are all side-dishes to the main course of love. A lot of women are unhappy and angry; because they are tired, over-worked and under-valued. They are on the warpath; so the men had better watch out because this book is here to let them know that the jokes are over. A real empathy, honesty and commitment have to be made by men towards their female partners; or face the consequences. Domestic violence is not the sole capability of men; because women can be even more dangerous in a battle of the sexes. The following chapters will emphasise that!

"Come on Tigress, show me your claws! We're going to the nightclub!"

Chapter Three
In the nightclub – Beware!

Nobody is completely unbeatable; because even a martial arts expert cannot be certain he or she can be safe from a knife or gun attack. You must therefore keep in mind that any woman can be beaten up, robbed, drugged or raped; if she is lured into a false sense of security and puts her trust in the wrong person. I can however guarantee that if you follow my advice, you will greatly reduce the chances of your ever getting caught out; because I will put you into a frame of mind that will allow you to spot the signs that lead to trouble. Self-defence is like a game of chess; where you have to think several moves ahead, in order to defeat your opponent. I aim to turn you from being a victim to being in control of your own defence; which means, being the aggressor if necessary! The fact that you may be weaker physically than a man; does not mean you cannot beat him. Nowadays, mental tactics are much more effective than physical aggression! Women have their own role to play in the survival of the human race; so there is no shame in fighting 'dirty' to beat a man and preserve your chosen way of life. Women were made differently from men and are smarter in many ways; and this makes up for their lack of physical strength. It is imperative you fight differently; and believe that you won't allow anyone to beat you. You therefore have to take advantage of what men perceive you to be; in order to defend yourself from them. A female animal in the jungle always has an 'ace up her sleeve'; in order to defeat a male aggressor and protect her offspring. If a man thinks you are weak, let him believe that; and hit him hard where it hurts, when he least expects it. Making him think you are strong will alert him; and he will be much harder to beat, if his defences are up! If he cannot show you the respect your sex deserves, then he will be in for a bumpy ride; and rightly so. I will dwell on rape in more detail in the next two chapters; but for now I will discuss how to defend yourself when you go out to a nightclub.

The first thing you must realise is that a lot of men go to a club to pick up girls; and they all have their own (sometimes underhand) tactics to get a girl into bed. If you are one of those who want to be picked up, then all well and good; don't let me stop you. Go ahead, but be prepared to face the consequences of your night out; because few people will feel sorry for you if you are drugged, robbed, beaten up or raped. This means that whenever you do go out; your self-preservation should be more important than having a good time. You can have a much better time when you have blocked all the loopholes and you know you will be safe! There are a lot of 'nutters' and angry young men high on drugs and alcohol inside every nightclub, pub or bar; so you have to treat going out at night as if you are going to war and believe that anyone is capable of anything. If your boyfriend/partner does not have the decency or money to pick you up, take you out and bring you home safely; then why keep him? If you allow this imbalance in your relationship to perpetuate; you will slowly and surely become a doormat for him to stamp on and wipe his feet. You only have one life; so protect it! This means being with someone who loves, cherishes and respects you; otherwise don't bother. A good sex life does not compensate for love and respect. Anyone; who is prepared to leave you by yourself in a nightclub or anywhere else, is not worth having. I'm sure you can find someone better!

I have already explained that you should always go out with somebody, preferably a male; as a protection against amorous suitors. If that person is not your partner; it should be someone who will not interfere in your date, but cares enough to make sure you get home safely and observe who takes you home after the dancing. At least, if something were to happen to you; he would be able to furnish the police with a lead as to where you were last seen and with whom. The name, car number and address of your suitor should always be noted by your friend; if you decide to go home with a total stranger. Don't be afraid to ask him questions about where he lives and works; before going anywhere with a man. If he refuses to tell you or it looks like he is lying; then play it safe and refuse to go, even if he is the most handsome man in the world. If he knows that someone is looking out for you, it will curtail any bad intentions he has in store for you; because he knows he is less likely to get away with it. A clandestine shot from your friend's mobile phone will be most welcome to the police; if something did happen to you. As soon as you get to your destination; don't forget the obligatory text or phone call to your friend to let him know where and how you are. Another call first thing the next morning; will also be a good idea to put his mind at rest. Sounds like common sense doesn't it? But you would be surprised at how many girls either forget or are unaware of, the basic rules of going out!

Never go out to a nightclub; unless you have decided on how you can be taken in and out safely. If you have no car; then arrange a taxi to pick you up and drop you back home. This way; you won't have to compete with drunken yobs on the streets, looking for a taxi after closing time. If you can afford to go out; then I assume you have enough money to guarantee your transport! Try to go with friends and make sure one of you will stay completely sober all evening; in order to look after the rest of you. Always take enough money to have a good time in a nightclub or don't bother going at all; because there is always a price to pay when you depend on others for drinks. Never allow anybody you do not know well, to pay anything for you; whether you are in a group, or alone and waiting for somebody. Nobody likes to feel they have been used! If a man buys you a drink, he is expecting at least a lively conversation or a dance from you; which could lead on to his making a play on you. If someone else makes a move on you; in his mind he will feel he owns you, simply because he bought you a drink! He will try to thwart any potential suitor by putting his arm around you or by engaging in spurious chit-chat with you; in a somewhat desperate bid to send the signal out to other men to keep off. Sooner or later; you will have to burst his bubble and refuse to kiss him or go home with him. Make no mistake; even grown men can behave in childish ways and WILL fight over a woman because they still believe she is the weaker sex and needs protecting! If any man wants to buy you a drink; you have to make it very clear that you will leave him when your partner arrives and he should not get any ideas that you are free, single and willing to mingle with him! Nightclub fights are caused because one or the other of the basic rules is broken. A lot of times, it is the fault of the girl; by not being truthful and thinking she could get 'one over' on a guy.

The most important lesson, when arriving at a nightclub; is to have your own money and never allow anyone you do not know well, to pay the entrance fee for you. This means you have to try and avoid any conversation with anyone standing around the gate; by keeping a straight face and acting like you have more important things to do than engage in silly small-talk. This first signal of your independence will put the brakes on any thoughts a man might have that you are easy; and stop him coming to bother you later on in the evening by pretending he knows you very well...all because you smiled and said *"Hi"* to him at the gate. One can always tell when a girl is expecting a date; because she is constantly checking her mobile phone for messages. Why he could not pick her up and bring her; only he knows the answer. There are always guys around every entrance of a nightclub on the look-out for such an opportunity! Let's pretend you arrive alone at a club to meet your boyfriend on a prearranged date. You pay off the taxi, walk to the gate of the nightclub and there stand two handsome men. One of the handsome studs says, *"Hi Darling! Are you going in? Let me pay for your ticket"*. *"After all; what are friends for?"* continues the other. Now the gate fee is exorbitant, maybe fifteen or twenty dollars/euros; and you think to yourself, *'Why not let these idiots pay for my ticket and let me save the little money that I have'*. They pay and you all go in; which of course means they would like to sit with you and buy you drinks. *'Why not?'* you think; *'My boyfriend isn't here yet and they're rather cute as well'*!

That kind of scenario is precisely where the trouble starts! By allowing any man to pay your gate fee; you automatically become his property in the unwritten nightclub code of ethics. Enter your boyfriend; who comes over (from his other girlfriend?) and kisses you. All hell breaks loose. *"Who are you?"* shouts one of the drink buyers. *"And who the hell are you too?"* retorts your boyfriend. Depending on the backgrounds of the men involved, a fight could ensue; and you might end up getting pushed, slapped or beaten up. You could even be labelled a troublemaker; and banned from the club for good. The whole sorry episode was really your fault. Just because of a fifteen or twenty dollar/euro gate fee, look at the trouble it has caused; and it could easily have been so much worse. What if your boyfriend had not shown up for reasons best known to him? That means you would have had a good time drinking, eating and dancing all night; at the expense of your two suitors. At the end of the night; what do you do? You have no car; (because like most women you don't believe in drinking and driving) so they have to *"drop you home"*. You insist you can go home by yourself in a taxi; but you are too drunk to even see straight, let alone look for a cab by yourself. (What did they slip into your drink while you were out 'powdering your nose'? Rohypnol?). *"It's too dangerous on your own"*, says one of them. *"There are robbers out there"*, quips the other. *"Don't worry we will take you home!"* They have been *'nice'* to you all evening; so *'why not?'* You get inside their car... *"First let me drop my friend home"*, says one; and you mutter something about not taking your key and your mother waiting up for you. But what chance do you have of convincing someone speeding down the expressway, to alter course and drop you home first? You reach the friend's house and he invites you both in for a drink; but you refuse to get out of the car. They tell you there is something wrong with the car; and it cannot re-start. He opens the bonnet and fiddles around with the engine; to no avail. *"We'll have to look at it in the morning!"* *"Don't worry you can sleep here. I have a spare room!"* By then you are so tired, unnaturally drunk and all you want is a bed; but you still refuse to accept their 'kind' offer.

In your drunken state; you still think you are in control. *'I know what they are up to; but they won't get it'*. (A lot of people believe they are in control of their sobriety; after they have been drinking.) *"How about that drink?"* says the first guy. *"We can't sit out here all the time, while he's fixing the car."* Inside the house you go; and then you are trapped. If you fancy them and want to make love to them; then all well and good...but what if you don't? Could you really handle two of them? You can scream; but who will come and rescue you in the middle of the night? Any fighting skills you may have; will never be sufficient in your drunken (drugged?) condition. Even if you are raped; you can't go to the police and report it because it would be very difficult to prove. Remember; there will be witnesses in the nightclub to attest to what a good time you had with your 'rapists'. Besides; what were you doing in their house at that time of night? You were not forced into their car. You went on your own free will. Again; there will be witnesses in the club to say they even saw you kissing one of your 'abductors'. No Sweetheart, you have no case; unless you are prepared to have your sexual history dragged through the mud in a court of law. Do you even know the real names of the guys you claim *"raped you?"*...all because you did not pay the entrance fee yourself. This story may sound apocryphal; but the scenario in its different guises, happens more times than you can imagine. Please take care when you do go out to the pub, bar or nightclub; and trust no one. The prevention is better than the cure; is the point I am trying to make here. You will feel very stupid; if you are ever conned into doing something you never wanted to do. Most girls will not even admit to having been raped; as it would bring shame and dishonour to themselves, their friends and family. Many 'savvy' women will not fall for this scenario (again?); but there are a lot of young girls out there who are not yet experienced in the dos and don'ts of nightclub life. I therefore feel justified in emphasising it; even if it may not apply to you personally.

You have to be aware that there are many ways a man can seduce a woman. Most times it is okay, because the girl also enjoys being chatted up; and the final decision whether she allows herself to be seduced or not, rests with her. In order for you to be certain the guy chatting you up is the right man for you; it is imperative that you use your head. Look; Listen and Learn! You know who you are and what you want from a man; so try to study him. Behind the smooth talk and bravado, lies the real person; who might not be who you want. It is always better to find out sooner, in the safety of the club; rather than later in his house, where you cannot get away. The way you behave; counts a lot in the way a man will first look at you and later influence his attitude and intentions towards you. A lot of rapes and attacks after a night out; need never have happened, if the woman had kept her mouth shut a little while longer. This does not mean you have to keep as quiet as a mouse; but it would be better when meeting a man or men for the first time in a club, that you remain mysterious and say nothing until you have sized up the opposition. You should let him do all the talking; and then suddenly hit him with a sharp or witty riposte to let him know he is dealing with an intelligent woman. Look to see if his facial expression, angle of conversation or attitude changes; before going back to playing dumb, till you feel like saying something else to gauge his reaction. He will eventually give himself away; and if you like what you see then go for it girl! If not; just keep playing the sparring game until it's time to go home and then thank him for a *"wonderful evening"*! It can be fun being a woman; because the biggest seduction cards are all in your hand...you just have to know when and how to play them! Shouting and having an over-bearing attitude, in order to make your point with men; only shows you are so full of insecurities that you only feel good when you have held a man by the balls and crushed them. If you think that will impress him and make him respect you; please think again. Loud and opinionated women are a turn-off for men in nightclubs; because they have come for a good time, not a fight! There are even those who believe the only way to shut her up is with *"a good seeing to!"* He will then start making plans in his mind on how to shut you up; by fucking you as quickly as possible and then dumping you. Pretending to be nice to you; agreeing with what you say; drugging and date-raping you; cannot be discounted. You are so busy making your point to him, you may forget to watch your drink; and he could slip anything into it!

Whenever you are with the man you love; try not to show any interest in other males. I'm sure you would not like him ogling the feline beauties wandering around the club! Even if he is a husband or long-term partner; a man still likes to feel he is the king of his woman's world. If you doubt this; just look around at the facial reactions of any man, whenever he has a woman draped all over him...sheer bliss, contentment and pride! This is his way of telling other males that you are his; and they shouldn't bother trying anything! In public; a man's persona changes from his private attitude to you, where he might take you for granted. This is because at home, nobody is watching; and there is no competition for your affections. In a nightclub this public attitude can lead to problems; if he feels your attention waning or that you have eyes for some gorgeous hunk on the dance floor. He will feel pangs of jealousy; which he may not immediately show, but could get worse as the evening goes by. Your topic of conversation would then move out of the comfort zone to criticism. Before you know it, you are having an argument; which as far as you are concerned started out of nothing. Like the scent of a dead carcass to a vulture, there will be males in the club on the look out for cracks in the relationship; and will be ready to move in on you as soon as his back is turned. While he is in the toilet, they will pounce and strike up a conversation with you; and because you are angry with your boyfriend, you could end up giving a handsome hunk your phone number. The hunks will move away as soon as he returns; but the damage would have been done, because he might start accusing you of all sorts of things. Every disagreement you have ever had in the past; will resurface! Many a fight between couples has erupted in a nightclub; over seemingly innocuous reasons.

He might be too smart to attack you in a public place; but will wait till you get home and then unleash his anger on you. He could accuse you of behaving like a *"cheap whore"* and might end up yelling at, hitting or raping you; just to prove he is still in control of you. Some men will do the opposite; which could be just as hurtful to you. They will go into a sulk; refuse to sleep with you or show you any affection (which could last for days). Eventually, he might go into a huff and storm out of the house...in the middle of the night! It is obvious where he is going...to another girlfriend; who will soothe him and make him feel good again. Believe me; men have a way of making everything the woman's fault and then justifying it by betraying her! Don't forget; all this started in the nightclub where you did not pay him enough attention. If you reverse the process, whereby he does not pay you enough attention and starts ogling other girls; you could react in a similar way and the girls will pounce on him while you are in the toilet. It happens all the time in a nightclub; when a happy couple is having a whale of a time. Suddenly, one of them falls silent and insists he or she wants to go home; whilst the other insists on staying. They then start arguing and fighting; ending with the unhappy one walking out and leaving the other one behind. You can imagine what happens behind closed doors; when the other eventually arrives home! Either way; it is not good self-defence, if your relationship is damaged on a night out. This can easily happen; because once the alcohol starts flowing, you tend to forget the one you are with and other people appear more attractive than they really are. If you pay each other complete attention and concentrate on the positives; then a night out can be wonderful...the way it's meant to be. Why do you think nightclubs are so expensive? You are supposed to have a good time; so don't ruin it for each other, by forgetting why you are there!

If you are out in a group; then paying each other complete attention is not so important because you are all friends out to have a bit of fun and then go home. This does not mean you should neglect your partner completely. A little bit of sexy eye contact will let him know you are thinking of him; and can be good foreplay for the main event, when you get home. Most men will not mind if you are having a long girlie chat; but if you concentrate too much on a man, even if he is friends to both you and your partner, it can get a bit testing and the green-eyed monster will come bubbling up to the surface. If he has been suspecting something before; the nightclub will accentuate everything. In his alcoholic haze, he might have visions of you and him in bed together; which might produce insecure behaviour on his part. Be aware that the biggest threats don't always come from men. Yes ladies, your biggest threat could be from other women; some of whom are just as ready to fight each other, as they are to combat men. Just imagine how you would feel, if he spent all night talking to one of your girlfriends; completely ignoring you. Even if you keep convincing yourself you *'trust him completely'*; it cannot be easy, because you won't know what the girl is really up to! For your own self-defence; try not to encourage or spend too much time with someone else's man inside a nightclub, bar or pub, if he is there with his girl. If you fancy a man; make sure he is not there with any girl before you pounce! This is because the girl he is with, might have her own plans for him; even though as far as you are concerned, he is a free agent. Some girls are very brazen at picking up men; but there will come a day when you pick on the wrong man and his girl might not be so ready to let him go. You will then have a fight on your hands. A man may be too scared to hit you in public; but a woman will have no such qualms! With so much glass around; it would not be funny to have a drink poured on you, a bottle smashed over your head or a glass shoved into your face. Jealousy brings out the worst in people; and someone high on alcohol/drugs is capable of anything.

Women on women fights in nightclubs are a regular sight; and they are usually over men. *"Leave my man alone; you bitch!"* is as common as *"Get your filthy hands off me; you pervert!"* Men love to see two women having a go at each other; especially when the fight starts and their tits, asses and thighs are well-exposed in the mêlée. The men, who go in to try and separate the women usually enjoy a nice 'feel'; as they try to break them apart. All I can say is that there are enough men to go round; so there is no need to go after someone else's boyfriend in a nightclub, or anywhere else. Most times it is the man's fault for being untruthful and not telling the girl that he is in a relationship; because he wants both pieces of cake. Fighting over a man is unnecessary; and an insult to your sex. Men are supposed to fight over you...not the other way round! If you really need to have a particular man, you have to be a little more subtle; so the nightclub is not the place. Find a way to get him alone outside the gents' toilet; quickly exchange phone numbers and then go for him on a different day, when his girlfriend is not around. I must caution you that it is not a good idea to go for any man who clearly belongs to somebody else; because it is a recipe for trouble. If he leaves his girl for you; then he is obviously not trustworthy and will probably leave you as well, when the next willing woman comes along. If he decides to go in for you; you will make an enemy of his girlfriend. Once you acquire a reputation as a man-snatcher; it is very hard to erase. Eventually; everyone you know, will find out! A bad reputation is not good self-defence; because you could lose out on many things, without your realising why people are all of a sudden shunning you. It can be a very lonely existence for you; when the phone stops ringing and the invites to parties and weddings stop arriving on your doorstep.

The basic rules of decency are always broken in a nightclub; because most people will be drunk, high or both. Try to have a sense of humour and don't take amorous comments seriously. If a guy you don't know, comes up to you and compliments your beauty etc; don't be offended. If he puts his arm around you, gently remove it if you don't like it; but keep smiling and never get angry, because he is obviously intoxicated and is expecting you to say something. (For a drunk; any conversation is better than none and even a rebuke can be a turn-on!). Smile politely, thank him for the compliment and move away from him; if necessary, explaining that you have to go to the *'Ladies'*. The chances are; by the time you return, he would have found someone else to pester. Never insult anyone; because it could turn into a war of words, which could backfire and you could both be thrown out of the club. A fight could even ensue when other men rush to your aid; because to them, you are the poor defenceless female who needs protecting. Just maybe; you might thank them 'properly' for helping you! Remember; those coming to help you might be as bad, if not worse than the harmless drunk you insulted! Frying pan to fire scenarios could be easily avoided; if you have a sense of humour.

Most women have an arsenal of witty retorts to counter the growing menace of unoriginal chat-up lines. Here are a few ways to get rid of a man in whilst keeping your sense of humour. He says: *"Can I buy you a drink?"* You say: *"Actually I'd rather have the money"*. He says: *"I'm a photographer. I've been looking for a face like yours"*. You say: *"I'm a plastic surgeon. I've been looking for a face like yours"*. He says: *"Hi. Didn't we go on a date once? Or was it twice?"* You say: *"Must have been once. I never make the same mistake twice"*. If a guy keeps pestering you for your phone number and you want to get rid of him; try to memorise the number of your local police station. Smile sweetly and tell him you are a *"little busy tonight; but would love it if he called you soon"*. If you then give him the number; he will go away, very pleased with himself. When he does call; he will get the stern voice of the police sergeant on duty and will quickly hang up the phone! Don't worry; if he ever meets you again and asks you why you gave the number of the cop shop to him, smile just as sweetly and say; *"That is where my dad/husband works. He vets all my callers!"* He will never bother you again...perfect!

Many young girls will absorb a lot of unoriginal comments from a guy; just because he is buying the drinks. Hang tough ladies; don't ever feel you owe a man anything when he sucks up to you. He obviously has his own agenda and is nice to you for a reason; which is usually sexual. Just be careful to buy at least one round of drinks; even if he buys three. If after an hour of boring conversation, you want to get away from him; buy him a drink and excuse yourself politely. Never say you will be back; if you have no intention of doing so. The chances are; he will come looking for you, claiming he was *"concerned"* for your safety and thought something had happened to you! If that does happen; don't tell him to get lost but kindly apologise and explain that you were told your boyfriend was around and you were looking for him. Give him a gentle peck on his cheek to thank him for his kindness; and he will get the message, in a nice way. Men hate to be short-changed or made to look foolish; so you have to learn how to let them down gently. He bought you drinks; so he feels you at least owe him your allegiance for that evening. The only way to get out of this; is to make sure you buy at least one third of the amount of rounds he bought you. The police in all cities have their most difficult times at weekends; as a result of alcohol/drug consumption. Bad things do happen in pubs and nightclubs; so you have to be aware of your surroundings and act accordingly. You can tell a guy; *"No way José"* with a smile. You are quite capable of refusing an offer of a drink; with a joke. *"Are you trying to get me drunk and have your wicked way with me? I prefer sex when I'm sober!"* It is not so hard to tell a man you are uncomfortable with; *"I think you are cute; let me take your picture!"* How difficult is it to tell a problematic pest: *"I'd love to fuck you too, but not tonight; I'm flying the red flag. Anyway, here is my home phone number.* (the local cop shop or a wrong number) *please give me a call sometime!"* That is the main reason you should always go out with your friends. You can enjoy yourself; without the pressure of having to fend off unwanted suitors!

Although it is tempting to put a troublesome pest in his place, by yelling at him to leave you alone or even slapping his face; it is much more rewarding to hit him with your sharp tongue. I know every woman is capable of this; if she has to! Women tend to have sharper tongues than men; and have such an array of putdowns, that it takes a brave man to argue with a woman in public. He says, *"Fuck you, ugly bitch. I'll get myself some new pussy!"* And she counters, *"You could have had my pussy; if you had a few inches more!" If I'm so ugly; why are you sniffing around me? Woof Woof Bad doggie!"* The ripostes are not only aimed at men. She says, *"You cheap, lousy, fat pig of a whore!"* and she retorts, *"That reminds me; your Scrooge of a husband owes me €1000! Every time I shag him; he gives me a cream doughnut instead of paying me!"* Women are so cute that even a friendly comment said with the best intentions, can backfire. She says, *"Do you like my new dress?"* and she strikes, *"It looked better on you last year!"* The putdowns are too many to mention all in this book; but it goes to show that if you hate being embarrassed in public, then you have to mind your own business, say nothing, keep smiling and stick to your friends. After a few drinks, you may not even be safe from your friends; so the only way to defend yourself from wisecracks in a nightclub is to have a good sense of humour and learn to laugh, even if the joke is on you.

Don't take anything seriously; because whatever is said would probably be denied the next day, when the offender is sober. Be kind and friendly; but with the biggest pests, try to get rid of them in a smooth way. If you are with friends and the pest follows you around the club like a lovesick puppy; you should quickly grab hold of a female friend and hug her or kiss her full on the lips. The idea that you are a lesbian; will get rid of the most drunkenly amorous of pests! You can explain later to your friend; who might not be amused, but will have saved you. An ear-bashing from your girl friend is definitely preferable to the cheesy chat-up lines from your drunken suitor! Always keep in mind that a pest might have been a cool dude before he started drinking. While sober, he was so 'charming' you might have divulged some information to him like where you live and work; phone number; where you hang out etc; which you regretted, as soon as the alcohol revealed his darker side. If you feel really bad about this; then change your phone number. If he shows up at your house; contact the police and let him know in no uncertain terms, that you will have him cautioned for pestering you. Mobile phones that can take pictures are a godsend; because you can clandestinely take a picture of someone, while pretending to make a call. You can then forward the picture to a friend's mailbox for safe keeping; before you decide to go home with a guy you've met for the first time. There are many tools at your disposal to ensure you are safe, ladies…use them! If all else fails; the police remain your best bet. Always make sure you have enough info for them to do their job properly!

I'm sure you already know that ladies don't always go to the loo to do the obvious. The ladies toilet is your sanctuary; the place to catch up on the gossip, compare notes etc and come out looking better than when you went in. Because that is what ladies do! It is also the place to talk to your friend about how you are going to get rid of the jokes you have been lumbered with. It is the war room where strategy is planned. All very cosy girls; but don't forget that while you are away, the guys could be planning their own strategy. Who is watching over your drinks or food? A date-rape drug,

LSD, ecstasy and an assortment of things could easily be put into your drink while you are away; to make you more pliable later on. No matter how much the politicians claim they know what they are doing; drugs are here to stay and it is very easy to buy them. All nightclubs have an anti-drugs policy; but it is almost impossible to stop drugs entering a club. Any drug becomes twice as potent when mixed with alcohol. Even if he does not slip a pill into your drink; he might drug you legally by refilling your glass with even more alcohol, or buy you a cocktail that is so strong it would knock you out as quickly as any illegal drug. You might be too drunk or too polite to complain; because he has been buying you drinks all evening.

To avoid any suspicions; always make sure you are watching over your drinks, if you are with a stranger or someone you feel uncomfortable with. When going to the loo, carry your glass with you; or better still, finish your drink before going. You can then say something like, *"That was nice; I've had enough drink for a while. I'm off to the ladies. Back soon."* A nice peck on the cheek will keep him quiet until you return. This will deter him from buying you a drink while you are away; but if he does refill your glass against your wishes, be firm and refuse it. To make your point; get up and buy yourself a soft drink, because you don't owe him anything. If you want to be a little bit more devious, you can 'accidentally on purpose' knock the drink over; preferably onto his lap, and then say: *"Oops! Sorry! I told you I've had too much to drink!"* Your life is more valuable than any cocktail he might have bought you. If it comes to the critical and he is becoming nasty; give him back the money for the drink he bought for you and then leave his company or report him to the manager for pestering you. This will show him that the lovely girl who gave him a peck on the cheek before going to the toilet; can also be a horrible bitch, when crossed! He will surely get the message and leave you alone! He might be handsome and sexy etc; but *'wolf in sheep's clothing'* is too nice a description of some of the guys you might meet in a nightclub or bar.

Many women are too well-brought up and polite, not wanting to hurt a man's feelings; but that attitude does not pay. The greatest crime you can commit; is the crime against yourself. You know you are drunk; yet you accept more drink from a suitor, just to be nice and not offend him. Where is the sense in that? Ladies; you have to be tough in this modern age. Never ever do what you do not feel like doing. Alcohol is a legalised drug; and is the cause of more trouble in a nightclub than you or I will ever know. Anyone who tries to ply you with drink in the name of fun is up to no good. He might not even be thinking of having sex with you. If you are drunk; it would be much easier and safer for him to steal something from your bag and pass it on to a friend. You arrive back from the dance floor; and your credit card, cash or even mobile phone could be missing. It might genuinely not be your suitor. Some other guy could be quietly sitting nearby; watching you as you get more and more drunk. Many women put their bags on the floor while sitting in a nightclub; and after a few drinks, forget all about the bag as they chat and dance the night away. One trip to the dance floor and your life could be in ruins; depending on what was taken out of your bag!

Try to check your bag, before going to a nightclub; and leave anything you will not need, at home. I am not a woman; but from my experience, all a female needs to take to a nightclub is some lipstick/facial make-up; a legitimate ID card; a calculated amount of cash; a fully-charged mobile phone; a cash-point card with a withdrawal limit; and a single key that will get her back into her house. All of these could be safely carried in one of those purses that strap around the waist, covered by her clothes! If you live alone; try to keep a spare key hidden somewhere safe around your house (not under the front doormat, flower pot or on a window ledge) or with a trusted neighbour…in case you lose the key. There is no need to bring a bunch of keys; because if you lose it, you will be greatly inconvenienced. If you must carry a bag; make sure you are going out with friends. You will then be able to take turns watching over each other's stuff, when one goes on to the dance floor or to the toilet. Sometimes even friends are not safe. (I will discuss this in a later chapter). Depending on which nightclub you are going to; you should always plan accordingly. If you are on a blind-date in an unfamiliar place, or abroad; you have to be extra-security-conscious. The clubs frequented by the less affluent members of a society, will pose a different threat to those high-class places. There is really no safe nightclub; because the human being is multifaceted. A broke con-man could dress well, pretend he is rich and steal from you; whilst a millionaire who may not steal from you, could still drug and date-rape you.

On the dance floor, it is generally safe because most dancers will be dancing with a partner; but you might occasionally come across the mischievous types who will 'deliberately' bump into you or step on your toes. If another woman bumps you or accidentally steps on your toes; don't retaliate because a woman will see herself as your equal and will definitely give as good as she gets, if you accuse her of anything. The alcohol/drugs in her will start a war of words, which will lead to acerbic insults or a fight; so quietly slide away from where she is dancing and ignore her. If she has no dance partner and follows you around the floor, it means she deliberately wants to annoy you; (to impress one of your female enemies whose boyfriend you once seduced???) so either leave the floor or report her to the manager. A sense of humour is paramount, if a man steps on your toes; because it may be his sick way of getting a reaction from you, since he might feel he would otherwise have no chance of talking to you. *"You clumsy oaf!"* or *"You fucking idiot!"* might embarrass him and he will have to deny it; so just tap him on his shoulder and say something like, *"Ouch, that hurt; I hope you're not so clumsy in bed!"* quietly in his ear. If he is an ignorant idiot and does not apologise; then be sensible and move away from him. If you are really hurt; don't be afraid to sit right there on the dance floor, hold your ankle, start crying and make a meal out of it. The security will quickly come and ask what the matter is; and again, don't be scared to loudly point the guy out before they carry you off to be treated. The ankle-breaker will be severely reprimanded and embarrassed by the whole episode. If he starts aggressively denying it to the bouncers; he might even be banned from the club. Breaking a defenceless girl's ankle on the dance floor; will not do his reputation or street credibility any good. It's either he admits he did it on purpose; or lets everyone know he does not know how to dance. What a dilemma!

The worse thing to do is to start a fight or argument on the dance floor or anywhere else in the club. Every fight will cause some damage to your property, reputation and self-esteem; because you will most likely tear your dress, ruin your hair, break your nails and embarrass yourself. The security men always keep a sharp eye on what is going on; and you will be ignominiously thrown out and banned from the club. Is the person you are fighting, worth the value of your dress; which could easily have cost 500 dollars? Who is going to replace the broken heal on your expensive pair of shoes? It sounds very hollow to say you won a fight; when your gold watch is broken and you have to use your own money to buy medicine from a chemist to treat your cuts and bruises. Inevitably; you will also be charged with wilful destruction of property and made to pay for any damage caused; which could run into thousands of dollars, because the bill will definitely be padded!

Try to make friends with the bouncers and manager of any club you go to. Greet them by their first names, as soon as you arrive; crack a few jokes and take a genuine interest in what they have to say. Theirs is a thankless job; and you will be surprised at how friendly a bouncer can be, considering their reputation as hard, unemotional bullies. They will always know who you are, if you are a regular; which greatly helps, should you ever have an argument with a groping pest in the club. You should phone ahead of time and ask them to leave your name at the gate; so that you don't have a problem getting in. It is an easy way of jumping the queue and letting everyone around the entrance see that you are well-connected; so if they have any devious plans for you, they should forget it! Don't ever be afraid to go to the manager or the bouncer; if someone is really giving you a hard time. They will warn him to leave you alone; and if he continues, he will be thrown out. This will put a halt to any devious plan that may have been hatching in his mind; because he will know you have friends in the club. If it were to happen that someone is thrown out on your account; then make sure when you are leaving the nightclub, you are not alone. Ask a bouncer to escort you to a taxi; in case the pest is lurking around outside. There is nothing worse than a jilted pest; who is drunk and sore at a perceived injustice! If you feel funny and unnaturally drunk and you suspect your drink has been spiked; come right out and tell the manager and he will make sure you get to your home safely. It is very hard to prove who spiked your drink; so it is always better to be wrong and safe, than sorry. Around closing time is when someone is likely to slip a pill into your drink; because that is when everyone is told to quickly finish their drinks and leave. Most women will rush to the loo for their last minute freshening up routine; and will return to quickly down their drinks. The pill will take effect as he is taking you (his) home; and you may not have the strength to ward off his advances!

I do not intend putting you off going to a nightclub; because it is not all doom and gloom. It can be an enjoyable experience and a wonderful place to have fun and rekindle the love you have for each other; so I advise you and your partner to find time to have a good night out every couple of months. Many women have gone out for years without a hint of trouble; and some always get VIP treatment. Are they lucky, or smart? They are obviously doing something right; and probably don't need this chapter. Collaboration as opposed to confrontation and having enough money to take care of yourself; is the key to having a great time in a nightclub. Be kind and humorous but never ever betray your principles; because they are what make you the woman you are and you'd be damned, if some drunken pest is going to spoil your evening! With that attitude, you will earn the respect of men; which will prevent them going too far with you...unless you want them to! In nature, the female always calls the shots. I am only making you aware of that fact. (As if you didn't already know!)

"I love you Tigress. Fancy a quickie? No? .I thought not! In that case; the next chapter should be of interest to you."

Chapter Four
Date Rape

There is a saying, *"Man proposes and God disposes"*; but in self-defence terms, you have to go with the adage *"You get what you deserve!"* And that brings us to the title of this chapter. I am sorry to say this, especially to those of you who have been victims of rape in the past; but somewhere along the line you were probably at fault and it should not have happened. I make this statement without malice; only to stress that 90% of all rape situations need never have arisen. In this modern age of relative sexual equality; there are very few excuses left for a woman. She has to be responsible for her own actions; because no one else will be! A child or senior citizen will attract sympathy, if something bad happens; but when an able-bodied woman is raped, it is usually lip service that is paid. Society seems to protect the rapist; because rape is difficult to prove without the woman having to bare her sexual history to judicial scrutiny. Many women would rather not report a rape than have to go through that embarrassing ordeal! It does not help the female cause; when some unscrupulous women have been known to deliberately lead men on and then try to extort money by threatening to report them for rape, if they don't pay up. This clouds the genuine cases and no one knows who to believe anymore; so the man is usually given the benefit of the doubt. *"What a shame she was raped, poor thing...et cetera!"* But behind the public sympathy; will be the private nudge, wink and snigger. *"Serves her right; why did she lead him on?" "Who asked her to get drunk and go to his house/hotel room?!" "She's just a whore. She'll fuck anything in trousers, the dirty bitch!"* and so on. I want you to get angry enough to have a *'me against the world'* attitude; and assume total responsibility for your actions. You must make sure rape will never happen to you; by taking this chapter seriously.

What really is rape? Rape is sex without the consent of one or the other of the participants. This means that technically, a woman can rape a man; though few will take that accusation seriously. In many marriages, a wife is often raped by a violent or drunken husband; (returning home from a failed night on the town with the boys) but rarely is it ever reported, because most societies frown upon a wife accusing her husband of rape. She risks being shunned by her in-laws; and even members of her own family may try to get her to retract any statement she made to the police, in order to save the family's reputation. Whichever way you look at it; rape is very traumatic. It leaves a mental scar; long after the physical injuries have healed! The possibility of pregnancy or contracting a sexually transmitted disease from a rape; is enough to cause permanent damage to a woman's self-esteem, dignity, confidence and sexual existence. (Murder and kidnapping are probably the only other crimes worse than rape; but I will deal with those in Chapter 16.) I cannot tell you why a seemingly well-behaved gentleman suddenly becomes a rapist; and it would be an impossible task trying to explain to a horny man what constitutes as rape, when he has an erection and believes a woman's *"No"* most likely means *"Yes"*. I am only interested in your part of the equation and how to avoid it; because rape will always be with us. (Some women even fantasise being raped by their favourite movie heartthrob!). The reality however, is serious. It can ruin a woman for life; and the only thing you can do is make sure you are not one of the statistics. Now that we have a reasonable definition of rape; what can you do to prevent it ever happening to you?

There are not many lunatics in any society who go around physically dragging girls off the streets and raping them in broad daylight; because they would never get away with it. Most rapes occur under a roof; and are committed by so-called decent people on normal but somewhat naïve girls, who are often too petrified and ashamed to tell anyone about it. Most rapists are known to, and are sometimes former or even current lovers of the victim. Under normal circumstances, he should not have raped her; so why did he do it? He obviously got carried away in his 'amorous over-enthusiasm' for his victim. If you go deeper into it; why did he have this amorous over-enthusiasm for the girl? And there lies the answer...'the girl!' Could it have been the way she dressed? Her perfume...? Make-up...? Sexual magnetism...? Over-friendliness...? Enticement...? Men will always have an excuse for rape; so you have to take the bull by the horns and take personal responsibility for what happens to you. This means your self-defence begins at home and should always be part of your daily routine.

Critics will argue that it is not only cosmetically beautiful women who are raped; and no woman is safe from the clutches of a determined rapist. Whatever a girl wears will surely attract one lunatic or another; so what is the point of dressing conservatively? Even nuns, grannies, the mentally-challenged and homeless women have been raped before! The mere fact that a woman is desolate, flea-ridden and filthy; will turn on some perverts! It is very true that whatever one wears, will surely excite one person or another; but why increase the risk by exposing your tits and thighs for lust-crazed drunken males to leer at? It will only enable them to harbour improper thoughts; which could lead to disrespectful behaviour towards you. If you must dress provocatively; make sure you go with a group of friends, so that there is no chance of anyone breaking into your circle and annoying or attacking you.

If we assume that it is only a man who can rape a woman; then if you are never alone anywhere with a man, you can never be raped! It really is as simple as not putting yourself in a position or a situation, where rape or any other attack is possible. When going out at night; why do you have to wear that low-cut dress? Why that sexy perfume? Why go out alone? Why follow a stranger to his house; if you have no intention of sleeping with him? Why allow him to buy you drinks or pay the entrance fee for you; giving him a reason to try his luck with you? Why did you act in such a way that gave him the impression he had a good chance with you? Why were you so friendly; pouring your heart out to him in your chit-chats? Why did you let him think you did not really want to go back home because of certain domestic problems; making him assume you'd be better off coming to sleep at his house? Why did you go out with no independent money of your own; so that you had to depend on him to take you 'home'? *"Why? Why? Why do the bad things happen to me?"*

The questions are endless; and it is usually too late by the time one asks them. Although a few rapes occur in lonely fields and alleyways; it is still probably the girl's fault. She should not have been out walking alone in a secluded area at the wrong time; even if she had been using that route for years, without problems. This would have made it easy for someone to watch her movements over a period of time and bide his time to strike. If she had been alternating her route or walking with friends; then that would not have been possible. I am not here to criticise you, tell you what to wear or how to behave; because it is your life. But you have to be aware that the world is changing very quickly and becoming more dangerous; so you have to use your head and understand that there are bad people around who will harm you, if you allow them to. If however, you observe a few very simple rules; you can make your life a lot safer and not let yourself get messed up by ruthless and exploitative bastards.

There is nothing wrong with going out with a man; because only you will know why you are with him. I cannot live your life for you; I am only here to help you defend yourself, physically and mentally. I therefore have to make you aware of what *could happen;* and then you can decide for yourself, what you want to do. If any man asks you out anywhere, he may not reveal his real intentions; but be assured that he is up to something, even if you know him well and he is gay! (Remember the saying, *"there's no such thing as a free lunch!"*) A guy you have known for years may have a secret crush on you; so don't assume going to his house for a few drinks means you are safe from rape. Even your female friends can unwittingly cause you problems; because they can introduce you to a man by convincing you how *"wonderful"* he is. You go on a date with him on their recommendation; and end up being mistreated or even raped. Your boyfriend's best friend or brother could be the one who will try something, when you never expected him to; all because you considered him safe and let down your guard. It will be difficult to push him off you in a rape situation; because you will not be sure if he is serious or prancing around, until it is too late. You can now deduce that it is often those we consider harmless; who are the most dangerous!

"All this does not mean a man has a right to rape a woman!" No, it does not; but it is your life and you have to be in complete control of it. This means accepting responsibility, however painful; for the consequences of your actions or inactions. Women are being raped and abused every day, around the world; even amongst intelligent professionals, in so-called respectable marriages. You have to be honest with yourself and accept that it

could happen to you; if it is not already happening. We live in an age where the police in most countries are banging their heads against the wall trying to combat terrorism and other very serious crimes; whilst criminals are released after a few years in jail, even for some horrendous offences...only for them to re-offend. One can therefore empathise why the police don't really have the time or will to chase after and prosecute date-rape suspects; and usually place that particular crime, quite low in their list of priorities. Furthermore; politically correct do-gooders always seem to have an excuse for them: *"It's not his fault he became a rapist. He was abused by his father when he was young..."* and they end up being freed by sympathetic judges. This in turn makes the rape victim out to be a liar and puts her in real danger of reprisals from her attacker's family/friends; in addition to the pain and sense of betrayal she already feels from the rape. I apologise if it looks like I am being overtly insensitive; but nobody deserves to have to go through such an ordeal.

When a woman is accused of leading a man on; there is more truth in it than she realises. A simple smile can set off a series of unconscious motions; ending up with him in her bed. A man is by nature a hunter and will always look for sex; so you have to be careful how you interact with all men. Always assume that any man, who comes up to you, has something up his sleeve; and be on your guard. By all means talk and be nice to him; but you must know the 'cut-off' point when you have to make him aware that you are not interested in him or what he has to say. You then have to invent a quick excuse, like a husband/partner or an important appointment; in order to get away from him. It is very difficult to resist the charm of someone you are physically attracted to, but resist you must; because the more you follow his sexual magnetism, the easier it is for him to try anything on you. The more handsome and drop-dead gorgeous he is, the more likely that he is not used to rejection by a female. You will find it hard to say *"No!"* and stop him raping you; if he gets you into bed. You have to make sure you don't get carried away with how a man looks or anything he says or does; and always be prepared to tell him the truth, when you know he has no chance with you. *"Say what you mean...and mean what you say"* in order to save you a lot of hassles later on! If you notice a man coming on too strongly, you should never go home with him that night; unless you are determined to sleep with him on your terms. That initial eagerness can easily lead to over-enthusiasm and desperation, once you are alone in a room with him; and all sense of decorum and decency will go out of the window, as he tries to have his 'wicked way' with you. It is always safer to give any new man in your life, a few months to prove his commitment; before taking that leap of faith.

Even if you never talk to strangers, you are still not completely safe; because your social life would be non-existent, if you refused even to smile at a man. Sooner or later, you will get bored/lonely and be caught out. Don't forget; a man can see you on the street and follow you for weeks, without your knowledge…until he knows where you work, go to school, shop and live. One day while you are in the pub or walking down the street; he will come up to you, pretending to have met you before. Your own curiosity will want to know how he knows so much about you; and your never-talking-to-strangers rule will fly straight out of the window. *'He's quite cute'* you think! By that time, he would have managed to grab your attention; so a conversation could end up with you chatting to him like an old friend. This can easily lead to date-rape; because he already had an infatuation for you, before he came up to you. There is only one thing on his mind...and he will do anything to get it! If you don't remember ever meeting a man before; always trust your instincts and assume that he is up to something. Be on your guard; because men have all kinds of tricks they use to capture a girl's attention. I don't want to put you off men; but there are certain stages which lead up to all date-rapes. It is important that you know them all; and are constantly aware at which stage you are at, when being courted by any man.

Stage one: The greeting. (*"Hi, what's your name…etc"*)

Pre-ceded by eye contact; this usually happens to all women in public places and can be a lot of fun. There is no need to be afraid because he cannot harm you; and I'm sure every girl has her own way of dealing with this. It can be pretty depressing for the woman who never gets a pass from a man; so enjoy it while it lasts. The power is completely with you; whether to give him your real name, a false name, ignore him, tell him to mind his own business or keep moving away from him, claiming you are in a hurry. If you do give him a reason to chase after you; then he will be encouraged to move on to stage two.

Stage two: The compliment. (*"My, you are looking good...etc"*)

All compliments should be treated as frivolous and not taken seriously; but it can still be good to hear nice things said about you. Just enjoy it, but keep in mind that he is making a subtle move on you; so it is up to you to decide whether you want to hear more or cut him off right there, before he gets over-excited. A woman will usually be amenable to stage three, if the compliment showered on her is original and exciting; otherwise the man will be put into the same category as all the other losers and given no chance to continue. A handsome man with an original compliment usually works on a woman; and depending on her status or mood, (single, married, divorced, happy, sad or horny) she might even make a move on him!

Stage three: The move. (*"Can I buy you a drink?...etc"*)

The moves come in all kinds of disguises; but they all have one aim and that is, he would like to get to know you better. Most women are flattered by such attention and depending on what she is feeling at the time; she will either accept or refuse politely. If you do accept the invitation, you have to be aware that he thinks you like him; so be on your guard, because his idea of love might not be yours. A quiet coffee in the afternoon has a different connotation to a drink in the bar. You can therefore tell where his mind is at, by where he wants to take you. If you fancy him, you can go right ahead and accept; but it would be safer for you not to go to any place where alcohol is served, with someone you have just met. A couple of innocuous coffee or cinema dates would be preferable first; until you get to know him better. Unfortunately, you are only human; so you cannot resist him and agree to go for a drink with him. Be prepared for stage four.

Stage four: The probe. (*"Have you got a boyfriend?... I really like you...etc".)*

Try to understand that he might be more excited than you are; and might say things or act in an over-exuberant or inquisitive way, which should not be taken seriously. Play around with him and enjoy the fun, because such a person is not dangerous and can easily be handled by you; so don't worry about what he says or does. You have to beware of the brilliant conversationalist who makes you laugh, keeps his hands to himself and acts the perfect gentleman; all the time trying to find things out about you, in order to see how far he can go with you. If possible, try not to give him your phone number till you are sure you would like to see him again; and make sure you don't tell him things you might later regret, like where you live or work. Tell him something like your father is a policeman and you have six brothers who are all martial art experts; because this will let him think twice about any bad intentions he might have planned for you! You should swerve, bob and weave, while running him around in circles; because he will be doing his best to find your weak spot and catch you out. If he likes what you have to offer and thinks he can sleep with you that same day; he will move on to stage five. These first four stages are very safe because you are on neutral territory; and you can have a good time, laughing, joking and having fun. If you are in a club, pub or bar; don't forget to buy at least one round of drinks for every three of his!

Stage five: The charm offensive. *"You're so clever. I've never met a girl like you, etc"*

Stage five is the beginning of possible rape; and that is why I say it is the woman's fault if she is ever date-raped. The drinks are taking effect and you are both tipsy; so his compliments start to flow and you might actually begin to believe them. If you want to sleep with him, then all well and good; but if you don't, then this is the time to slow the pace down. You are still safe on stage five; if you are not tipsy and have sober friends with you. Every girl has a weak mental spot; and a good seducer will probe and prod till he finds it. It is a subtle process, during which your demeanour and mood slowly changes from trepidation to relaxation; and before you know it, he has said something to make you smile, giggle and laugh...he's actually made you happy! Once he notices this; he will harp on the same theme till you are like putty in his hands! Flattery; sympathy for your problems; politeness; kindness; consideration for your feelings; showing off how much money he has; applauding your intelligence and ideas; have all at one time or another, worked on even the most stubborn, intelligent and liberated women. This will be followed by attempts to touch you, feel you, hold you and kiss you. Most girls will rebuff these first attempts; but that will not stop him...so hang in there lady! If you like him; go ahead and kiss him back, while enjoying the attention...but don't allow his hands to wander too much! (It's a bit too early for him to discover your recent boob job or other bodily secrets you might be harbouring!) A good seducer knows what he wants and will do everything to get it. He is most likely to rape you, should he ever be in that position; because he is not used to being refused sexually. Get him in bed and change your mind at the last minute, will not do you any good; because he will have all kinds of tricks and excuses to have his sexual way with you.

Women love to be complimented; and men have used this tactic for years to first mentally and then physically rape a woman. By telling you how intelligent, beautiful, sexy etc you are and your believing him; he has already mentally raped you. This is because when the physical rape does occur; you will have a much harder time dealing with the fact that you thought he liked you. *'He even said I was beautiful, intelligent etc. How could he do such a thing to me?'* That horrible thought preying on a rape victim's mind; is much harder to erase than the bruises she has received from the physical rape. The minute stage five begins; you have to be on your guard and assume he could rape you, if you go too far with him...even if he seems like a genuine guy. You don't really need someone telling you how pretty or intelligent you are; because you should already know whether you are or not. Therefore, any compliment at this stage, should be shaken off like water off a duck's back; and not allow yourself to be complacent. *"You are so sexy and beautiful!"* should be politely repulsed with, *"Thank you; you're not so bad yourself".* This said without a smile, but with an air of one who is above such silly chitchat; will force him back to stage three. *"Like another drink?"* and you should respond with either, *"No thanks,"* or *"I think it's my round; let me buy **you** a drink!"* Once you get up to buy him a drink; it automatically diffuses the situation and pushes you back to stage two. The toilet trick is just as effective into pushing you back a couple of stages; so just get up, crack a joke about your *"weak bladder"* and move towards the toilet, anytime you feel him getting too heavy with you. If you do not allow him to move through the stages, there is nothing he can do; so try and stay in control of the situation. In reality; it is the female who, like a spider, snares the male into her web. Once there and she is raped; who else is to blame? You have a right to change your mind; but why put yourself in that position? Every woman knows that a man's brains are between his legs! Why would you expect him to behave in any other way; or have the sense to take *"No!"* for an answer?

The evening is still young; so inevitably he will regroup and you will soon be back to stage four. Remember; there are some very experienced men in the art of seduction. Are you prepared for the onslaught? He will move in 'for the kill'; which means if this does not work, he will move onto another girl. He will now slide his way back onto stage five; which means telling you what you want to hear and even agreeing with everything you say, to make you appear even more intelligent than you know yourself to be! You could be in a situation where you don't want to sleep with him yet; but you still like him and don't want to lose him. Sensing your uncertainty, he will now try and make you jealous by eyeing up other voluptuous females wandering around the club. He will pretend not to have any more interest in you and may even go to the toilet; but will make sure you see him chatting up another girl on his way back. It is at this point that you may become amenable to stage five; because you might feel a few pangs of jealousy and give in to his charms...just to send the message to the other girls that he is yours! Don't worry, you are still safe; but you are close to the cut-off point where you will have to make a major decision.

Now that he has made you aware you have competition; he will continue his charm offensive on stage five. If you are not resolute, you will find yourself laughing at his jokes and becoming friendlier. A gentle touch on your arm suddenly feels so good. *'Is it the drink or am I becoming attracted to him?'* Remember the chess game. STOP AND THINK SEVERAL MOVES AHEAD! You have to see things before they happen. Do you really want to sleep with him? If you don't; then now is the time to force him back to stage four. The real definition of a kiss is, 'permission at headquarters for position at base'; and that of a dance is, 'vertical expression of horizontal intention'. He will ask you to dance and try to kiss you during a steamy clinch. The further you go, the harder it is for you to come back. If you do kiss him, hug him, hold him etc and make him aware that you want him; then he will have every reason to assume you want to sleep with him. You are now at the halfway point of a possible rape situation; so you have to slow down on your drinking, watch your glass against spiking and keep your wits about you. One extra drink can make a big difference to your sobriety and tip you 'over the edge'; whereby you may not be able to prevent his advances! This is when he will try his luck with stage six and invite you to his place for a drink, a meal, a DVD or even a game of *Monopoly!* It does not matter if the date is in a pub, bar, nightclub, cinema, restaurant or anywhere else; because he will try any excuse to get you to come to his place. If you agree to go; make sure you want to have sex and are not going to change your mind at the last minute. No man has a right to rape you; but that does not mean you should lead him on. Convictions for date-rape are much fewer than acquittals; so please take responsibility for your actions.

Stage six: The invitation. (*"How about going back to my place?"*)

Flirting and going on a date is normally safe, if you like the guy and he likes you; but if you have no intention of going any further, you should never give him the chance to think so. Do not try to be over-friendly with a man; just because he paid for your drinks in a club or bought you dinner in a restaurant. This is the point where you have to clip his wings a bit because he is flying a little too close to the sun; and you should refuse to go back to his place. You should really make sure you don't get to stage six by slowing down proceedings during stage five; in order to save yourself any awkwardness and ruin a perfectly good evening. Kiss him by all means; but make it plain in no uncertain terms that you like him but are not ready to go to his place or anywhere else for sex. Do it in a nice way, if you like him; so that he does not give up on you completely. *"I'd love to go, but not tonight because I have to be up early tomorrow for a job interview."* Or even, *"Another time maybe; I did not tell my mother I would be staying out and she is sick. I have to take her to the hospital tomorrow".* You are a woman! You don't need me making up plausible excuses for you!

Refusing to go to his place does not make you safe from rape; because he will quickly change *"Why don't we go to my place"* to *"Can I see you again?"* If you accept this offer; he will be a gentleman and let you off this time. On your next date, you will not start on stage one but on stage two; and it may not be the nightclub, but a seemingly innocuous date to the cinema. He will cut to the chase and move swiftly; because he assumes a second meeting with him means you have indirectly acquiesced to sex. He has been dreaming of this moment; because your initial refusal has made him even more determined to fuck you. We are now faced with different versions of the stages! Let's assume you have accepted his offer of a date to the cinema, dinner, lunch or even football match etc. (It's not the date that is important. What really matters is that you are alone with him and how to prevent rape). Stages two, three and four will be repeated. He will still be the perfect gentleman and then move on to stage five with more compliments; but his mind would already be on stage six and how to get you to his (or your) place. In many ways, taking a man to your house is safer than going to his; because he will not be able to drug or rape you so easily, without knowing the way your house works. Nevertheless; if you have no intention of sleeping with someone, you must never tell him where you live, let alone invite him there. If you do and he rapes you; you will look very stupid having to explain why you allowed him in. He may also arrive at your house uninvited and cause you unnecessary problems in the future. (Before you let anyone inside where you live, I would like you to read Chapter 8.)

You have to keep on treating any compliment or flattery with the suspicion it deserves; because it will go a long way in not allowing yourself to be lulled into a false sense of security. He will still offer to buy you drinks and be very nice to you; but this time, stage five will be a little more forceful. His kisses will be more intense and so will yours, if you like him; but his mind will be far ahead of yours and will be thinking of what he is going to do with you in bed. He might not accept a refusal to his invitation so gracefully and will probably appeal to your conscience; *"Don't you trust me? I can't make you do anything you don't want to do"* or pretend to be hurt and upset by your refusal; *"I thought you liked me..."* Any compliment or suggestion to make you believe he loves you and cares for you; becomes mental rape when they are not fulfilled. *'He says he loves me and I am beautiful; so why can't he understand that I don't want sex right now?'* This deceit should ring the warning bells in your head that he cannot be trusted and will say anything to get you into bed; with a strong possibility of raping you, if you try to deny him what he believes is his due.

Once you rebuff his advances; he might go off in a huff and not call you for days. It's a common tactic to make you jealous; and many women continually fall for it. Relax and never ever chase after him; because you will lose your main trump card, which is your dignity. Something good is always worth waiting for; and if he cannot see that, then good riddance! Turn the tables on him, if he does call a few weeks later and asks you out. *"Sorry I am busy. I didn't hear from you; so someone else has asked me out!"* He will give all kinds of excuses (the longer the excuse…the bigger the lie!) as to why he did not call; when the real reason was that you refused to sleep with him! If you like him; you should still make him sweat a little and offer to fit him in *"sometime next week"*. If he does not pursue you, then thank your lucky stars; because someone like that (who only wants you for sex and not for who you are) would definitely have raped you, if you had gone to his place. He probably tried the same tactics with other girls and failed as well; and that is why he eventually remembered you. You have now become 'unfinished business' in his diary and he will keep trying sporadically, till he gets you; so it is better to kick him straight into touch before he does you any serious damage. A lot of men hate 'dick-teasers'; so *'teaching her a lesson'* becomes paramount and consumes any sense of decency he might have.

Most girls have an in-built mechanism for refusing sex on the first or second date; but the threat of losing him, usually forces her into having intercourse a little quicker than she originally intended.

The whole thing is like a cat and mouse game. He wants to get between your legs as quickly as he can; and you want to make sure he is for real before you give in. Girls are becoming very self-confident these days; and some will fuck a man on the first date and then tell him to get lost. One night stands are not the playing field of men alone! The majority of women however, still believe in love before sex; and anything but 'sex when she is ready', is rape. Even if she allows sex and he does not fulfil the promises he made in stages two and five; she will feel let down (mental rape). Since most rapes occur under a roof; you have to make sure you are never alone with a man, under a roof or anywhere else. Nobody forces you to go to a man's house alone! Okay; you are only human and you agree to stage six and go to his house. *'After all, he did take me to dinner and I am in the mood for a bit of romance'*. You now have to open your eyes wide and be concerned about your safety; because you are going into unknown territory, with much higher stakes.

Stage seven: The strike. *(Exploration of your body...)*

On the way to his house, keep your eyes open so that you can make a note of the town, street and house number. As soon as you arrive there; go to the loo and text a good friend as to your whereabouts and what you are up to. You should also make a call and let your date hear you loudly telling your friend the address where you are and with whom (even though he may have given you a wrong name). If he has any ill intentions towards you; he will realise that someone else knows where you are. You will once more be brought back to stage five; except this time, there is no need for stage six because you are already in his house. It is in this environment (stage seven) that you have to keep an eagle eye on him to make sure he does not slip something into your drink or food. If he goes into the kitchen; try to follow him, without making it obvious you are spying on him. Hold him round the waist and pretend you want to help him as he is mixing the drinks or preparing the snacks. Anything goes; so long as you can keep an eye on him!

This seems very paranoid; but if you do not know him well, you have to be cautious. Once you have been drugged; all your defences will go out of the window and there is nothing anyone can do to stop him doing whatever he likes to you. Sleeping tablets and other date-rape drugs are easily available. The girl hardly ever remembers what happened to her when she recovers; let alone prove she was (anal? gang?) banged. Once he believes getting you to his place means the hard work is already done, he might forget to tell you how beautiful you are; and if he does, it is usually after he has kissed you and there is a stirring in his loins. Stage five will become part of stage seven; and you will find your defences slowly falling. The deadly combination of a cool atmosphere; alcohol; telling you things to make you feel good; while stirring your sexual impulses; always works on a woman. Nice music, full stomach, horny as hell; *'why not?''*

STOP AND THINK! You had better let him know right there and then, in your most serious voice, that you are not going to sleep with him; and kissing is as far as you will go. That will cool him down for a while; but he will soon be back to stage seven and the kissing will start again. This time he will be a little more desperate; so you have to learn to recognise the signs. Like a drowning man clinging to a raft, he will grab you a little harder and kiss you much more forcefully; as if that would turn you on quicker. Most men have yet to learn that force hardly ever turns a woman on. When this happens; get up and go to the loo, telling him you have a running stomach. A smelly fart dropped at the right time will emphasise this and cool down the most amorous of intentions! He will not be too pleased with you for stinking up the air; but you can make a joke out of it, which will deflate his hard-on. It may seem funny; but the idea is self-defence in any way you know how. If breaking wind will put him off you momentarily and prevent a possible rape; why not? Slapping his face or getting angry is not always the best way to get out of such a sticky situation.

The dilemma is, you do like him; but you do not want to sleep with him yet! You must have a good sense of humour to bring him back to stage five. If he really is a gentleman, he might revert to stage four; which means in your mind, he respects you enough to leave you alone. However; in his language, he might have mentally given up on you and is thinking of ways to get rid of you and send you home, without it seeming like he is a spoilt brat. Losing with dignity is very important with all men; because he would not want you bad-mouthing him in town, in case he has to try his luck with other women. If he cannot wait until you are ready for sex and allows you to go home; you should thank your stars because someone like that would have fucked you and definitely dropped you after his conquest. A man who is not prepared to 'roll up his socks' to woo a woman; is not worth having! If you do not want to lose him; you will need to put in a little effort to get him back to stage five. You should explain that you do like him, but due to certain reasons, you would rather not sleep with him this time; but *"soon"*. These can range from being in your period; to your last boyfriend unceremoniously dumping you, after sleeping with you. You therefore find it hard to trust any man; until you really get to know him etc. Women are experts at making up convincing excuses not to have sex with a man; so you won't have any problems there!

Stage seven is the point you must try not to get to; unless you really want to have sex with him. It is much harder to get back to stage five, once you embark on stage seven. The kisses will be more intense and his brain will really be between his legs. He will try to remove your clothes and will be pushing his fingers into your vagina; fumbling around trying to find that elusive clitoris, which he assumes is his key to paradise. The force and speed of his movements can put a lot of women off; and it is at this point that she will pull his hands out from between her legs and decide she does not want to go further. By this time, he will have lost control of all his senses; and fucking you is all that matters. He will use force if he has to, in order to get what he wants; because you dared to arouse his sexual feelings. This is the grey area that gives men the benefit of doubt in rape cases. She says *"I told him to stop; but he wouldn't and raped me!"* He crudely counters, *"I fingered her cunt and she was mad for it; begging me to fuck her. I never forced her legs open did I?"* People will ask what she was doing by allowing him to probe her insides; if she did not want to do it. A few sniggers and snide remarks like, *"Did you enjoy it? Bet you loved it!"* and she will feel like she was the one on trial. It is a degrading and horrible feeling, I would not wish on anyone! Unless the rape is one where you were physically dragged off the streets in broad daylight or intruders broke into your home and attacked you; you have to bite the bullet and accept it is your fault for allowing any situation to reach stage seven. However; this book is not meant to poke fun at or denigrate anyone. It is simply an attempt to make sure date-rape or any other kind of rape never happens to you; so please don't be offended and read on.

When he first started kissing you; it obviously felt nice because he was well-behaved, attractive and kind to you. Unfortunately, that behaviour was only to lure you into his lair; and now that you are here, his real character will rise to the surface. The time it takes a woman to get turned on, is much different from the time it takes a man; and therein lies the problem. It is much harder for a man to turn off once he gets going; especially one hell-bent on fucking the woman. Again, it's only natural you couldn't help yourself; as many girls have fallen for the charm trap. Don't worry; it is still not too late to tell him to stop, except this time, action must speak louder than words. No sense in telling him to stop and then going back to kissing and being finger-fucked! Get up off the bed or sofa and use the weak bladder excuse to go to the loo. (Some girls will put on a tampon before they go out at night, even if they are not in their period; which is a very effective turn-off for men.) Once up; you should stay up and change the topic of conversation to try to get back to stage five. Being fingered or tongued might feel nice; but spare a thought for the man who is also worked up. If you love him but just don't want sex with him at that particular time; offer to play with him and try to masturbate him or give him head till he comes. The strength is immediately drained from a man, once he ejaculates. If you also manage to experience an orgasm whilst being pleasured, then you would have avoided a nasty rape situation; because he will be satisfied for the time being. Make a mental note never to let yourself get into that position again! It's getting serious girls. Welcome to stage eight.

Stage eight: Sex. *(He now wants to sleep with you... but you don't.)*

Mutual masturbation usually works; but is not full-proof. What if he insists on fucking you; rejecting your hand or blow job, because it is a poor substitution for the real thing? He wants sex and you don't! If you don't want sex, for reasons best known to yourself, and he does; then anything that happens forthwith, is physical rape and you have a fight on your hands. You are now in a position where he will fight back and you will get hurt; so you have to decide quickly whether to give in to sex or fight for your life. It should never have got this far, but it has; so what do you do? Even if you allow sex; it is still technically rape because the consent was given under duress. With little or no bruising around your private parts; you will have a hard time proving it, without baring your whole soul to public scrutiny. *'Might as well lie back and think of my favourite heartthrob...after all, I do like him. Why not make him wear a condom and I might actually enjoy it?* Sorry; how mischievously irresponsible of me! Even though the thought might cross your mind to give in; he has not actually raped you yet. You should consequently always cling to the belief that you will not allow him to have his way with you. There are still a few tricks you can use, in order to diffuse the situation; so don't make it easy for him. The following examples will usually work and kill his enthusiasm. He will not want to touch you with a bargepole!

1. Use the weak bladder or upset stomach trick and lock yourself inside the loo. You should refuse to come out till you feel he has calmed down.

2. Threaten to go to the police; if he hits you or tries to fuck you. Remind him that your friend knows where you are.

3. Quickly stick you fingers down your throat and vomit all over him when he next tries to kiss you. (This would be easy if you have had a few drinks).

4. Pee all over yourself and ruin his carpet, bed or sofa. (Desperate times call for desperate measures!)

5. Run around the room like a deranged woman screaming and shouting and he will fear you might have alerted the neighbours; but don't try to leave the room, in case he thinks you are trying to escape.

Most men will by now get the message and see that you are crazy and will not give in easily; so they will cool off and try damage limitation. *"I really am sorry, but I got carried away. It's because*

I love you so much, I couldn't help myself etc." Stay calm; tidy yourself up and tell him in your most polite vocal tone that you want to leave. He will see that you are not to be messed with and should oblige and be extra nice to you. Ring a friend and let him hear you telling her not to go to the police; because he did not rape you and he did not hit you. This will make him realise just how close he was to being arrested. Quickly leave his house and never ever let yourself get into such a situation again! An experience like this will make sure you are more careful in the future. It can be a good thing; because it is unlikely a man will ever be able to rape you, as you have just witnessed many of the rape signs first-hand. (A lot of women do not take date-rape seriously, because it has never happened to them. Just remember that it could!!!)

Stage nine: Rape! *(No way out!)*

If he refuses to see reason and there is a dangerous look in his eyes; then you really are in trouble. He may now feel he has gone too far and you will run to the police anyway. He will try to stop you; most probably violently! At this stage, you will see that he is not the gentleman you thought he was; so anything goes now. It's war! Welcome to stage nine. Keep your legs tightly closed and lie on your front; in order to make it difficult for him. If a girl is determined not to yield to a man's demands and has crossed her legs; it is almost impossible for him to prise them open. He will have to hit her or threaten her to get in. A black eye is bad enough; but do you really need a swollen lip, broken nose, smashed cheekbones and half your hair in his hands as well? *"Certainly not!"* Therefore, any aggressive move on his part will be enough incentive for you to go on to stage ten; because you will need something to show the police. There has to be some evidence of violence on you; in order to justify what you are about to do next. If he hits you or rips your clothes then he means business; so you have to change tactics!

Stage ten: Armageddon. *(What must be done must be done!)*

Stage ten is the last resort; because if you get it wrong, he will reach a point of no return. He will either kill you or beat you so badly, he will definitely be arrested and charged with murder, manslaughter or grievous bodily harm; in addition to kidnapping, rape and attempted rape. As soon as he hits you; quickly cool him down by agreeing to have sex. You must do so in a nice and convincing way, not out of fear; or he will not believe/trust you. Don't bother crying, because he will think you are pretending; and don't try to physically fight him or he will fight back and you might not be strong enough to cope with him. You are now to use your feminine wiles and try to win an *Oscar* for acting; because your life or virginity is in real danger. Be determined, stay calm and smile; even though you might be hurting inside. This is not easy to do; but refusing to concede will be much worse for you. *"It's okay, I'll do it! Relax!"* Hug him, give him a kiss and agree to have sex; but tell him you have to use the toilet first to get yourself ready for him. Once you are inside the toilet; quietly text your friend to call the police immediately to the address. (Don't phone the police yourself because he might hear you talking in the loo.) Don't panic if he takes your phone from you; because it will not change what you are about to do.

The following scenario is very difficult to do, but you must; because he will hurt you very badly, if you don't. Seductively remove some of your clothes and then slowly kiss him all over his body; until he is lulled into a false sense of security. When he gets comfortable; kiss him full on the lips and violently bite a sizeable chunk of his tongue or lip off! The amount of blood that will flow will shock you; but you must continue by grabbing something solid in the room and hitting him hard on his head with it. Start screaming and run out of the house or apartment; even if you are completely naked. Don't stop running till you get someone to help you and take you to the police to report what you did. By that time; the police alerted by your friend might have arrived at the scene. Your hysterical condition coupled with the bruises on your face; will convince them that he attacked you and it was all in self-defence. Once you decide to bite him, there is no going back; so don't be scared to really go for it. Depending on how badly he hit you or how mentally hurt you feel; you can dispense with the biting of his tongue and give him a blow job. As soon as he starts enjoying it; bite the tip of his penis off! He will be so shocked and in so much pain; you will be able to hit him with an object and then run off for help. If he manages to rape you before you are able to kiss him or give him a blow job; you can wait till he is asleep and either cut his penis completely off with a sharp knife or find some boiling water and pour it all over him!

Stage ten is drastic; but you should do it, if you have no other alternative. Taming a wild cat is a huge boost to a man's ego. You start off fighting and struggling, really making it hard for him; and a couple of punches to your face later, you have *'cooled down'* enough to see things his way. He will be at your mercy, as soon as you become pliable and seduce him; which would make it very easy to bite it off! Don't worry about him! If they find the chunk you bit off, a good doctor will be able to sew it back on; although it will never be the same again. The perfect reminder for any of his friends who think they can get away with rape! How do you know you will have the nerve to do it? It is easy to talk about it; but the reality is different. If you were about to be killed; I'm sure you would have no problems. If you are raped, you might as well be dead; because the quality of your life will never be the same again. Remember; you have to first pretend to want sex; hold him; hug him; kiss him; and then bite him! This is not so easy, if he is (was) your friend. It is therefore important he hits you or rips your clothes off first, before you go through with it; because there has to be a sense of justice in your actions. If you go around biting off men's penises without justification; you will one day land before a not too sympathetic judge and you will go to prison! Try biting off a partially frozen sausage from your freezer and you will realise it is quite hard to bite it completely off; so you have to practise biting the tip of the sausage! You may never have to use this tactic; but it is always good for your self-confidence to know that if push came to shove, you will be able to do it successfully!

Once you realise that anybody could turn out to be a rapist; then you will have a better chance to defend yourself against physical rape. If you make sure you never get to stage seven; you will be safe. That is the final cut-off point; where reason and logic are thrown out of the window. After that; it becomes a different scenario, whereby your life could really be in danger. When that happens; I'm afraid anything goes! After biting him; don't be scared to hit him with whatever is available in the room (chair, flower vase, mobile phone, lap-top computer, loud speaker, bottle, glass, ashtray etc.) It is very unlikely he will be able to withstand the double attack! However; I must stress the point that you have to use reverse psychology, before you will have the chance to do him damage. If you start off fighting and acting as if you are tough; he will be obliged to behave in the same manner and will be on his guard. Although a woman could be physically stronger than the man she is fighting; mentally, few women have that inner belief they can beat an angry man. Whereas, the man has been brought up to believe he is tougher than a woman; and this gives him a huge psychological advantage when the chips are down. He will make sure you don't get away with it and he will be so much more dangerous. If you knock him down and don't knock him out; he will get up and it would be like you were fighting two angry men… a struggle you are unlikely to win.

The tricks you learn from the fighting arts take years to perfect. If you tried them and they did not work; you would be in serious trouble. It is impossible to recreate in a martial arts club; how an angry, crazy man will act and react in a life or death situation. So for your sake; you have to play the part of a spider and draw him into your web. When his defences are down and he thinks he has 'won'; that is the time to Hit Him Hard! The three H's will always work, if his guard is down; but it must be accompanied by tears, screams and shouting, so that it would appear to everyone that you were the victim. You really are the victim. Believe it! He tried to rape you didn't he? Even though he would be the one covered in blood; looking for the piece of his lip, tongue or penis! However, blood attracts sympathy; and you would look bad in the eyes of the police and the public, if there was no visible damage done to you. If your clothes had been ripped off and you had a couple of black eyes or a broken cheekbone; the cops will take a much more sympathetic view of why you poured hot water over his genitals, stabbed him with the kitchen knife or bit the tip of his penis off! Self-defence is about fighting to win; which means winning not only the battle, but also the war. The best way to win the war is to have the police and the law on your side.

I'm sure you have noticed that this chapter is really for a woman going out on a blind date or with someone she does not know well; and ending up at his house. I am also aware that not all women are willing to cut off a man's prick or bite his tongue, whatever the provocation; simply because the rapist might be their husband or a boyfriend they are living with. When that happens, it becomes an impossible situation; therefore, other slightly less violent but just as effective ways have to be employed. This will be revealed to you in Chapter 14. So don't worry; you don't have to go cutting off every man's penis, just because he tried to rape you! Stage eight should be enough to stop most men in their tracks!

"Whew, Tigress; .if you think date-rape is bad, you might change your mind after reading the next chapter!"

Chapter Five
Mental Rape

Please don't assume that rape could never happen to you; because there are different kinds of rapes. Whether she is rich, poor, intelligent, stupid, beautiful or ugly; a man will always try to use a woman for his own ends. Even if he does not rape her physically; he could still rape her mentally and emotionally. Taking advantage of someone's feelings is a serious affront, which society has yet to deal with; simply because many women are not prepared to admit they are victims, in order to protect the children and family. Many live in abject fear of the men in their lives; men who can turn on the charm as quickly as they can yell an insult! They get away with all kinds of abuse; forcing their women into accepting and performing degrading acts. Friends who come to visit, have no idea what is going on; because most of the abuse is behind closed doors and there are no bruises to give the game away. No more; ladies! Self-defence is about your well-being. If you are ready to take real control of your life; you must stand up, be selfish and think of yourself first. If you are not happy; how can you make anyone around you happy? If you try to satisfy your partner at the expense of your own well-being; he will walk all over you.

Mental cruelty is a much more powerful weapon than physical brutality; and comes in so many disguises, that it is very difficult for a woman to even be aware she is being raped. When a woman gives in to her man; she is 'protecting' her way of life and does not want to rock the boat. Any man behaving like that; would be called names like 'wimp' or 'coward'! It works best when the female is compliant with the male's wishes and there is no rebellion; because it allows him to take her for granted. The abuse then becomes normal behaviour; whereby he does not even think he is doing something wrong and she is convinced he still loves her. The minute the woman decides she has had enough and openly questions her man's authority; she will be greeted with either a sound beating or emotional terror. Beatings are more common amongst the poorer less-educated sections of a society; because they know no other way of proving a point. However, amongst the intelligent and the well-off; examples of beatings are few and far between. Educated men have now realised that a beating causes too much trouble; because the bruises would have to be explained and word would soon get out that he is a wife-beater. This would not be good for his image or reputation! (The police would definitely not be amused!)

There are several aspects which fall under the title of mental rape. In order to make it easier for you to recognise them and realise it could be happening to you; I will put them under headings and offer a way to counter the threat. Please understand that I am not you! You will have to use your head; and either follow my advice or take bits of what I say and add them to what you already know of your situation, in order to formulate a strategy that will work best for you. I am sure there are psychology experts who have propounded their own theories on mental abuse; but as far as I am concerned, it falls under self-defence and it can be stopped. Although my methods might seem unorthodox; they will work, if you are not afraid to try them out. The important thing is that after reading this book, you stop mental rape happening to you; because nothing else matters, except your well-being. From prostitution to drug couriering, credit card fraud and other crime related shenanigans; there is no end to what an unscrupulous man can do to use and abuse a gullible and a not so gullible woman. Her only crime is that she falls in love with someone, she believes really cares for her; who in the end, takes complete and total advantage of her.

1. Emotional blackmail

Mental rape is everywhere; amongst the well-off and the not so well-off! *"Come here you bitch!"* shouts the man; and the frightened girl is seen running to do what her lord and master wants! There is not much difference between that and when a businessman orders his wife; *"I'm bringing an important client home for dinner; prepare something special for him!"* After slaving over a hot stove and making sure the house is spick and span, she then has to endure a few hours of crawling up the client's arse; laughing at his jokes and being utterly bored, all for her man. It would not be so bad, if she was getting something out of it; but it is a rare businessman, who gives his wife an equal share of his profits. Her pliability to the client could have earned her man millions in business revenue; but she would be lucky if she received more than a token present for her efforts. He will conveniently forget that she could have ruined everything, by making a nuisance of herself; but she did it because she was mentally blackmailed. She literally had to do it; because to refuse would rock the very foundations of their relationship. All men are aware of this fallibility in the female; and will take advantage of it when necessary!

No woman likes to be the cause of friction between herself and her man. This gives him licence to get her to do things, she would rather not have done; for comparatively little or no reward. The businessman did not bring his client home to meet his family for fun. He obviously wanted to impress him, in order to gain contracts and other privileges. A stable relationship is very important in the business world; because it somehow lets people believe he is reliable, honest and happy. A happy man works better! By bringing the client home to meet his 'dutiful' wife or partner; it shows he is in control. You can almost hear what is going through the impressed client's head. *'What a nice woman this man has got. Cooks well, interesting conversationalist and a sexy pair of tits as well!'* No doubt the businessman cajoled his partner into wearing something 'client friendly!' He probably sat at the dinner table with a huge smile on his face; watching the drunken client openly flirting with his not-too-amused wife. To warn him off; might ruin the business deal! It is not uncommon for certain ambitious men to make their wives sleep with an important client; in the name of business! Terrible but true!

The best way to thwart emotional blackmail is to be brazen and let him know you are aware of what he is up to! Even if you are wrong; it will let him realise that you will not lie down and die without a fight and you won't let him get away with his share of responsibilities. A lot of women stay out of their partner's business; which leaves her open to emotional blackmail. This is because he can get her to do things for him; claiming he is *"too busy trying to make a better life for both of us"*. It would then be easy to make her feel guilty, when she asks him to do something simple; like emptying the garbage or mowing the lawn. Before she realises; she is doing all the work in the house and he seems to always arrive home after 'working late at the office'… with the smell of alcohol on his breath. *"I stopped for a quick drink with a few friends after work..."*. Try to take an avid interest in what he does; so that he cannot use his work as an excuse to turn you into a domestic slave. Once you fall into a rut; it will be hard to get out of it! If he wants you to cook dinner for a client; ask him how much is he making out of it. Tell him you want your share; or you might ruin it for him! You can then come to an arrangement; whereby you can extract something commensurate with your efforts. (I'm sure you have a long list of things you would like from him). Any time a man asks you to do something out of the ordinary; ask him: *"Why? What's in it for me?"* You are not looking for a quarrel; so be nice but very firm and don't let him fob you off with excuses and platitudes. After a while, he will realise that honesty is the best policy; and he will involve you in all his decisions. A woman has to stop taking the blame for ruining a relationship; and pass the buck onto the man. Every smart man knows that the key to a peaceful home is to keep his better-half happy! Feisty and inquisitive women are sometimes given bad press; but it is a good thing in a relationship. Don't be afraid to stand up and be counted; because you are meant to be equal partners!

2. Silent treatment

The silent treatment is probably the most common form of mental rape and is far more effective than a beating, because it is never ending; whilst the damage done to one's feelings and self-esteem, is incalculable. It is very true that women enjoy a good 'natter'; and the highlight of many a woman's day, is to sit with the one she loves and just talk. (She talks and he supposedly listens!!!... *"Yes Dear..."*). *"Sorry girls!...Couldn't resist that one!"*. When a man refuses to talk to a woman and behaves as if she does not exist, it can be very painful to her; especially if she cannot fathom the reason why he is giving her the cold shoulder. At first she will try to brave it out and thinks; *'Sod him! If he won't talk to me, I won't talk to him either!'* Believe me; if they sleep in the same bed, the woman is more likely to crack under such a strain. Which woman doesn't enjoy a nice hug, kiss and sweet loving words in her ears as she falls asleep? When that is not forthcoming; she will really be upset. After a week of this; she will be the one to make a peace offering and try to get things back to normal. The only exception to this rule is when the man has done something extremely wrong, like sexual infidelity; and then it is because she cannot get herself to look at him, let alone touch or talk to him. In such a scenario; he will most likely come begging. Men however, can cruelly deliver the silent treatment for no apparent reason; and they are prone to childish acts like slamming the door and going off to the pub. It is usually for something petty, like she did not have his dinner ready on time; or was not eager to have sex with him on a particular occasion. The more he realises it is hurting her, the more he will use it in the future. Men know the silent treatment hurts women; and pretending it does not, only exacerbates matters.

To fight back against the silent treatment; I am afraid you have to resort to being a 'bitch', by showing him that you know exactly what he is doing and are not ashamed to admit it hurts. You therefore have to let him know that you can hurt him even more. Let him realise that you are a real person, not just a body; and you also represent everything that makes the household and his life tick. You are a wife/partner/mother; a cook; a cleaner; a dishwasher; a laundrywoman; a gardener; a sex machine; an adviser; a shoulder to cry on etc; and if he will not talk to you, then he also cuts off any links to everything else you represent. Stop cooking for him; cleaning the house; giving him news, advice or sympathy;...and sex should definitely be out of the question! It's not a good idea to use children as pawns; because they have done nothing wrong. The fight is between you and him; so you would obviously have to cook for the kids, but the ban on doing things for him or the house stays. When he runs out of underwear or shirts to wear or cannot find any milk for his breakfast cereal; he will have to find the time to wash his own clothes and walk (God forbid!) to the shops for groceries. If he comes home and his dinner is not even out of the freezer and the house is in a mess, whilst you are out having a drink with friends; he will very quickly understand your true value…which is the time you save him. When he realises that somehow you manage to do it all, whilst keeping down a job and looking after the children; there will be a renewed respect and fear for you. He will know that you don't actually need him; and using the silent treatment on you, is like cutting off his nose to spite his face. He will see sense and start talking to you; but you should never give in so easily. Let him beg for a few days before you 'reluctantly' decide to give him another chance; but with a severe warning that if he tries the silent trick again, you will not be so willing to come to the peace table. When you do make up; you will notice his lovemaking will be so much better. This is because he will finally appreciate who you really are!

3. Sexual blackmail

Silent treatment also means starving you sexually; and it does not necessarily mean he has another lover. He is most likely punishing you for something; so you have to try and find out what it is. All the excuses about working too hard should not wash with you. He is annoyed at something you have said, done or failed to do. It could be something silly; like your not being at home when he returned. (You might have hopped out to buy some groceries!) Men by nature like to rule the roost; and the very thought of your having a life and making independent decisions, can be a sexual turn-off. He comes home to find an empty house; with a note on the table telling him to cook his own supper, because you've gone to bingo or to see a friend. You come back home later after a good time and snuggle up to him in bed; expecting him to rise to the occasion. Forget it! How would you feel if he came back late one night; pissed out of his mind, expecting sex on demand? So you can see that even the slightest unintended mistake, can cause a man's libido to fail and trigger off the silent treatment; which could last for weeks, depending on how you react to it. It is a very potent weapon in his armoury; once he realises that a lack of sexual intercourse hurts you.

Don't fall for this kind of blackmail; because it takes two to tango. If he will not sleep with you; then you can have a well-earned rest! Ask him bluntly what the problem is; and if he is not forthcoming, (it can be a bit embarrassing for him to admit that he won't sleep with you because you did not have his dinner ready) you will have to treat him in the same way as the silent treatment…by going on a strike. This time however; you must go a step further by enjoying your life a bit more. Put on your make-up, get dressed in sexy attire and as soon as he arrives home…you go out and don't come back for a few hours. You can have fun in a bingo hall, join a dancing class, visit relatives or go for a drink with friends you have ignored for months; all because you were too busy looking after him. Whatever you do, you should not have an affair; because the sympathy vote will shift to him in any eventuality of a separation or divorce. There is however; no harm in letting him stew and wonder what you are up to! As soon as you arrive home; go straight to bed and ignore him completely. After a few days of this, he will get jealous and ask you where you are going; or where you have been. How can you answer him; if he is not talking to you? Oh dear; he will have to call a truce and then the cards will all be in your favour. He will have to admit the real reason for the sexual blackmail; which will enable the two of you to sort out the problem. Sex however, should still be out of the question; because you have gone off it, after not doing it for a while! He will then be forced to pull out all the stops; be nice to you and woo you all over again. Make it very difficult by hugging him, maybe even kissing him but stopping at full sex; until you are satisfied he has seen the error he made in trying to sexually blackmail you. You can then give him the best sex he has ever had! Knowing what he has to lose; he will never try that trick again. It's called 'pussy power' ladies! Use it wisely and you will have him eating out of your hands.

4. Emotional starvation

More and more men are resorting to emotional torture; as a less hassle way of controlling their loved ones. For example; how can you prove to anyone that your man refuses to hug you, talk to you, compliment you or starves you sexually? The obvious option of walking away or having an affair; is usually the hardest one. This is because you are not only walking away from him, but also from your way of life; which obviously has its rewards, otherwise you would not still be with him. Most men try and set the guidelines early on in a relationship; and if you are not careful, you will be swept along in a wave of euphoria which will be difficult to break out of. He starts off being kind to you, complimenting your every move and before you know it, you are a mental slave to his affection; which he can turn on and off like a tap, in order to keep you under his control. Like a drug, you will always be looking forward to your next 'compliment fix'; and will do anything to get it. Those halcyon days will soon be a distant memory, by the time you realise you are running after him like a love-sick puppy and looking after him as if he were a child. He will expect you to have his dinner ready on time and be available for sex whenever he wants; without a thought to how you are feeling. This usually happens a few years after you marry him!

Sadly, the female tends to blame herself when her man is not forthcoming with his emotions. You snuggle up to him on the sofa and he quickly picks up a newspaper to read; without reciprocating the love you are throwing at him. *'Why won't he hug me...?'* He stops kissing you when he arrives home from or leaves for work. *'He must be having an affair...'* He never initiates sex and when you do get it on, you are the one doing all the work; whilst he lies there like a stiff dummy. *'He doesn't love me anymore...!'* You sit at the dinner table in silence and he responds to your questions with monosyllables and grunts. *'Am I so boring that he doesn't like talking to me...?'* You get your hair done, go for a beauty treatment and put on a sexy new dress; but he doesn't even notice. *'Am I so unattractive that he won't even look at me...?'* So many kind and generous gestures he used to give you before; and now he won't do them anymore. *'What on earth have I done wrong...?'* It can be a horrible time for any woman who has to go through such an ordeal and can be a real test to her femininity and self-esteem; leaving her feeling low, dejected and at a loss as to what she should do to win back his love. She then makes the mistake of trying too hard to please him; thereby playing right into his hands. *'Yesss! Now I've got her where I want...!'*

It's hard to believe, but when a man tries to subjugate a woman with emotional and mental abuse; it's mostly because he loves her so much, he is actually scared of losing her. In his own twisted way, he thinks by keeping her under his control, she will be too scared to go anywhere; and that means no one else can have her. The best way to counter this threat is to turn the tables and make a life of your own; by playing it like a game you are determined to win at all costs. Find a hobby, join a gym or a club in order to take your mind off his lack of affection towards you; because it can be soul destroying to sit down and worry about him. This will let him know that you are capable of doing things without him. Deep down you still love him and therefore you don't really want to leave him; (you should not let him know that) but you just need to teach him a lesson in respect and set the blueprint for his future behaviour towards you. This means you have to use what they call 'tough love' and let him understand that you are not as weak as he thinks; and you will not be pushed around anymore by him or anyone else. Moreover; you are even prepared to leave him, if things don't change for the better!

He won't hold/hug you... *'Cool! I know someone who will be delighted with a hug from me!'*

He won't kiss you... *'Oh Dear; that means there will be no sex for him!'*

He won't talk to you... *'Phew! I have nothing to say to him either; the boring old fart!'*

He has no time for you... *'Thank God; now I don't have to cook and clean up after him!'*

Although it won't be easy; you must get on with your life as if he does not exist. Keep smiling and look happy when you come home; as if you've just had a great time. When he is within earshot, end your phone calls with *"...and I love you too darling!"* You may have to confide in one of your friends to play along and pretend you have an admirer; so that she can send you a few late night calls/saucy text messages. If you conveniently leave your mobile phone on the kitchen table when you go to the bathroom, he will most likely take a peek. He will definitely get jealous; and once he realises his emotional starvation trick is not working, he will try damage limitation and attempt to get close to you in order to find out what you are up to. That is when you turn around and play the same cruel trick on him. When he tries to hug you; walk away as if you are not interested. If he wants sex; lie there like a dummy and refuse to participate in any of his favourite positions, or better still, use the *"I'm not in the mood...I've got a headache"* tactic. If he talks to you; invent an excuse that you have to *"use the bathroom/go out/tend to the children"* in order to get away from him. Eventually; he will become frustrated and get the message that you are actually serious. *'Now hang on here. Maybe I've gone too far. I could actually lose her if I'm not careful'.*

Such a man is unlikely to lash out at you, because he is obviously intelligent enough to know that hitting you will bring too much trouble; and that is why he was using the emotional starvation technique. He will have to raise the white flag; because like it or not, he will realise that two can play at his game...and a woman can cause a lot more trouble for a man around the house than vice-versa. That is when you tell him that you are ready for a fresh start; but the domestic situation has to be changed because you will not put up with any more disrespect on his part. *"Yes, I do still love you; but I can live without you and I am prepared to take it further and walk out on you, if you give me any reason to...!"* Even if he is providing you with a fantastic lifestyle, which is the envy of your friends; he still has no right to treat you badly. Walking out on him, will be very damaging to his reputation; because he cannot stop you telling all his friends and business partners what he is really like. He will therefore do a lot of grovelling; to keep you from leaving him. In the influential worlds of business, media, entertainment, sports, finance or politics; any man whose wife walks out on him because of mistreatment, will be alienated. He will find it almost impossible to rebuild his reputation! You will have him where you want; but he will have a lot of making up to do. Make sure you squeeze every drop of humble pie out of him and enjoy it!

5. Belittlement & verbal insults

A very strong weapon in a man's armoury; is belittling your achievements. Most people are prepared to bend over backwards for someone; when a genuine favour is politely asked. In this case, he will shout at you to do something and then insult you for getting it wrong; even when the fault is either very minor or non-existent. *"Please"*, *"Thank you"* and *"Sorry"* are words which are never used by these men; who delight in reducing their women to nervous wrecks, who can never get anything right. This method of mental rape is very effective in controlling her; because she will continually strive to impress her man, in order to make him happy. The happiest day of her life is when he says, *"Well done!"* which is rarely forthcoming; because he knows that is the way to keep her subjugated. *"You are useless!"* *"Stupid cow!"* *"Can you never get anything right?"* These are just some of the nicer insults; which, over a period of time, will completely destroy her confidence. (Sorry to say this; but mental rape works both ways. Although in the minority; some men are also routinely abused by their women. Fortunately, this book is about self-defence for women; not against them!)

Firstly, you have to accept yourself for whom you are and know your limitations; because nobody is completely stupid or useless. If you feel you can improve certain aspects of your life, then do so for yourself; but never because he thinks you are hopeless. Once again; you have to stop doing things for him, if he will not appreciate what you do. Use a sense of humour to state your intentions, whenever he asks you to do anything for him; and never get angry. *"Sorry, I cannot iron your shirt/cook your dinner/get you a beer from the fridge/make love etc. because you said I was useless/called me stupid etc; and I don't want to make any more mistakes. Why don't you do it yourself?"* He may try to sweet-talk you by pretending he did not mean it; and might even 'apologise', in order to get what he wants...but don't fall for it. Rudeness has to be stamped out early; before it is allowed to get to the point where he is yelling requests at you and believes it is okay.

The soft-hearted nature of many women often lands them in trouble; and they wonder why their men never change for the better! Keep him at arms length for as long as it takes; till you feel there has been a definite change in his attitude towards you. If he does something wrong without apologising; you may have to remind him to say *"sorry"* (and mean it) or you will do nothing for him. When he wants you to do something for him; you should refuse to do it unless he asks nicely. If he does not thank you for something you've done; you have to warn him that you will not do anything else for him, without a show of gratitude. You see, *"Please"*, *"Thank you"* and *"Sorry"* are simple words; which help in making him realise that you are someone who should be appreciated and prevents belittlement in a relationship. You obviously have to set a good example, by using those three words whenever necessary; and this will make it harder for him to neglect them. Once he realises you will not change your mind and you will not do anything for him; he will have to reverse his attitude. If he continues with the insults; you may have to think about moving out for a while... till he begs you to return.

6. Fear of reprisals

A clever weapon a man will use on a woman is the threat of physical violence. Actual physical abuse will not work; because he will have to explain your bruises to friends or the police. If he yells at and frightens the life out of you with his sheer difference in physical size; he does not have to hit you, because a glare or certain facial expressions will be enough. It would be hard for you to prove to anyone that he has abused you; without physical proof. If he bangs his fist on the table, scattering everything and yells; *"Where's my fucking dinner, you lazy bitch...?"*, you will find yourself rushing to give him what he wants and then have to clear up the mess. The next time he comes home in a foul mood; you will make sure everything is just the way he likes it. He does not have to beat you to get you to be his slave; because the threat is constantly there. There was once a case about a husband who always went out in the evenings without his key; forcing his wife to stay up and be ready to open the door when he returned. This way; he would not have to wake her up for sex! The woman had to consent to his lustful wishes, even though she may have preferred to sleep; because she knew the consequences of refusing her drunken husband. He had literally made her a mental and sexual prisoner; raping her, without the law being able to do anything about it.

Which would you say is worse? Your man arrives home drunk and rips your clothes off; he then throws you onto the floor and sexually rapes you. Or; your man who has been systematically beating you up over the years, comes home drunk, gives you a certain look and takes his clothes off. Standing there with his erection; he shouts *"Now!"* and you find yourself taking off your night gown to obey his request. Whilst the first case would seem worse; it is actually much better because you could go to the police and charge him with rape, by using your bruises as evidence. With the second; you have no way of proving he raped you, because you consented to sex and he never physically forced you. The quicker the crime, the worse it seems; and that is why society sees the rapist or murderer as more evil than the alcohol or cigarette manufacturer, whose products slowly kill people with cancer, blood poisoning, liver, and lung diseases. Finally, there is the kind of violence on women which is obvious to everyone that you have been on the receiving end of a beating; but are forced to deny it, because you don't want to cause any problems for your man. He will hit you; but you will have to tell friends that you *"walked into a door!"* to explain a black eye. He will push you around until you fall and break a bone or twist a joint; but you will explain it away by saying *"you tripped and fell"*, otherwise he will hit you again for disgracing him.

Fear of reprisals is probably the hardest form of mental rape to overcome; because there are no signs of abuse and therefore, you will not get any sympathy from anyone...except maybe your closest friends. The above examples are really forms of legalised rape; and are difficult to defend yourself against, because the law is yet to recognise this form of mental abuse. Going to the police; because he yelled at you and insulted you...will not impress them. They are obviously very busy with more serious crimes; and may not have time for something that could not even be classified as domestic violence because he has not hit you and no one can prove he ever hit you, since you have refused to make a complaint. It does not help that many men who use this form of abuse are often rich, charming and pillars of society; so nobody is going to believe you. This perpetuity of abuse, making everyone else unaware it is happening to her and unable to do anything about it; is what makes it worse than the physical rape. A man who frightens the life out of you, insults you, threatens to hit you, hits you and then forces you to lie about what really happened; is a controlling manipulative bully and needs to be taught a severe lesson. Running away is useless because he will come looking for you; and you cannot be a fugitive for ever. You won't even be able to kick him out; because he will feel he has done nothing wrong and will refuse to leave. Leaving him is the hardest thing to do; because he will probably lay on the charm and you will find yourself coming back to forgive him. *"...he must love me to come looking for me!"*

Wake up Girl! Stop making excuses for him. If the law is not going to help you; then you will have to go on to Plan B and help yourself. Assuming you still love him; the first thing to do is make him aware that you don't like being yelled at or threatened. Don't cry or feel sorry for yourself; but be firm and let him know unequivocally every time he steps out of line. If he continues; try and confide in his friends or family members to talk to him and shame him into taking a long hard look at his behaviour. If that does not work; you have to go and seek advice from a professional counsellor, who will come and advise him about the implications of what he is doing to you. Stop doing things for him around the house; and refuse any requests you find abhorrent. Sooner or later, he will lose his rag; because his hold over you is based on the fact that you are afraid of what *might happen*. If you show you are not afraid of him; you will find that he is actually a coward and there is nothing he can do, except hit you. Once he sees that you are prepared to go to the police; then you would have dismantled his arsenal. You will have all the ammunition you want to prosecute him, if he dares touch you; because you now have potential witnesses in his and your friends who already know what has been happening, as do family members and your counsellor. He does not have a leg to stand on! His attitude will change very quickly; because he will realise that everyone knows what he is really like and he cannot pretend otherwise.

He will then have some serious wooing to do, in order to regain your love and confidence; but you have to make sure he has really changed. This could take six months or more; before you allow him back inside your heart. If you feel he deserves it; you can start doing the little things you used to do for him, one privilege at a time. You can start with cooking his dinner and talking to him, without arguing! Sex however; should be last on the agenda. It is the cherry on top of the cake; and he will not take you seriously, if he gets it too easily. He will try to be nice to you, in order to get into your bed; but you have to be strong and tell him, *"I'm not ready yet"*. This is when you will find out what he is really made of; because he will finally realise the extent of his cruelty to you. If he refuses to change, beats you up, tries to physically rape you or goes off with another girl; then you have all the reasons in the world to get a prosecution, barring order, separation or even a divorce. You may love him; but love cuts both ways. It would be better for you to give your precious self to someone else who will appreciate you; because life is too short to spend it in an unhappy environment.

7. Imbalance in a relationship

Imbalance in a relationship is when one party is being taken advantage of by the other; deliberately or not. If you find yourself doing all the work in the household, whilst he does nothing; it means you have well and truly spoilt him. Like a child; he will kick, scream and throw the toys out of the pram, if you dare suggest he lift a finger to help you. He will have a truckload of excuses why he cannot do something and will find refuge in his 'work' or in the pub; just to get away from doing his share of the chores. There has to be ground rules laid down early on in the relationship or there will surely be an imbalance; which easily leads to many other forms of mental rape. This is because, if he can get away with not doing something as essential as the housework, then he will feel he can get away with anything; including having an affair or disrespecting you with a rude, demeaning and insulting attitude. Since your hands are always full cleaning up after him/the kids, you will definitely not be looking your best; and he will have plenty of free time on his hands. Boredom will set in; and he will begin to regard you more as a cook and cleaning lady, than a wife or partner. It has to be up to you not to allow that to happen; because as a woman, you are supposed to be the intuitive and responsible one. If you want your marital life to run smoothly; you must keep a tight rein on him. Any man left to his own devices, will eventually become a disaster!

"He was so considerate and kind when I married him; and now look at him... the drunken, fat, lazy slob!" Every man is what you make him; so a woman whose husband has turned from a true gentleman into a potbellied drunken beast, has to shoulder a lot of the blame for allowing it to happen. A potbelly does not grow overnight; and to even allow it on top of you during sex, means you probably need your head examined! What were you feeding him with during all the years it took for the stomach to grow that big? Before you marry any man, you should study him for simple signs of nonchalance and put them right before it is too late; because you are going to spend the rest of your lives together. Of course you love him and he is lovely etc; but he could change for the worse. It would therefore be better; if you were aware of some of the things that could go wrong, several years down the line. Like all men, there are obviously a few distasteful hiccups in your

man; but don't be disheartened because they can be cured, if you catch them early enough. Depending on how repugnant a habit is; you must use any shock tactic means at your disposal, in order to make him stop/change. This may include; getting hysterical or angry; refusing to speak or sleep with him; breaking off the engagement; postponing or cancelling the wedding; and finally leaving him. I hope the following warning signs will give you an idea; so that you can imagine what it would be like if he carried any bad behaviour or habits into the marriage.

1. Telling you to go home by yourself after a night out in a club; because he cannot be bothered to make sure you get home safely.

(Even if it means pretending to be afraid of the dark, you have to teach or cajole him to care about your safety; otherwise like so many men, he will think you can take care of yourself. Maybe you can; but one day you could be molested, robbed or attacked on your way home and he won't be around to help. Would you not feel slightly betrayed?)

2. Making you pay for the date when he was the one who invited you out; without first warning you that he would have no money.

(There is no guarantee he will have money after you marry him; and he could end up thinking it is okay to take cash from your purse without asking. He won't be bothered to find a job; if he knows you earn enough. Can you support the two of you/the kids? Think long and hard before marrying anyone who has no intention of pulling his weight to support you. He could owe large sums of money to people who will cause you future problems.)

3. Not noticing; even when you have gone to great lengths to look good for him or cook him a fantastic meal.

(Do you realise how many times you will be cooking for him or making an effort to look nice; after you get married? Living under the same roof; how long can you keep it going without any sign of appreciation?)

4. Allowing someone to insult or attack you in public; without any attempt to defend you.

(Whether you are right or wrong is immaterial. Any man worth his salt should be ready to defend you in public; unless you tell him to back off. When you get home, give him a severe telling-off; if that ever happens to you. I'd hate to think what he would do; if a thief broke into your home in the middle of the night. Can you guarantee such a man will fight tooth and nail to protect you and the children?)

5. Drinking/drugging to excess; and refusing to listen when you warn him to slow down.

(Marriage is supposed to be a happy and peaceful time; so it would not be in your best interests to marry an alcoholic or a drug addict who refuses to seek help...because it leads to all kinds of problems. If he won't listen to you now; he will definitely not take any heed after he has put a ring on your finger. He will probably be imbibing even more than he does now; and may resort to lying to you in order to hide the fact. Alcoholism and drug dependency are both illnesses; which can only be cured by impartial professionals. Don't flatter yourself that you can change him; because you can't!)

6. Shouting at you and insulting you during an argument.

(This means he loses his temper easily; which is a short step away from using violence on you. Even if he has not done so yet; his temper could get worse as the years go by. Once you are married, you will definitely have problems; any of which could set him off and he could easily yell at, push or hit you.)

7. Lying to you; even when all the evidence points to the fact that you have caught him out.

(If you let him get away with lying to you; he will never stop. It will get worse when you are married and the stakes are higher; because he will have more to lose by admitting an unpalatable truth. Without trust there is no point in getting married.)

8. *Expecting sex on demand; and goes off in a sulk when you are not in the mood and "just want to hug, kiss and talk".*

(There will definitely be times in married life when you will not feel like sex; and if he cannot understand that, then he is likely to find himself a 'bit on the side'. Be careful of any man who cannot take a sexual refusal; because he might believe there is no such thing as rape in a marriage and try to force you.)

9. *Refuses to exercise and doesn't take good care of his health.*

(You wouldn't like him to drop dead at an early age and you become a widow with children to bring up; would you? Tease him into eating properly, going to the gym or taking up a sport. It wouldn't do any harm to leave magazines of hunky well-built men around your bedroom; as a not-so-subtle hint! Have your man medically checked up before you marry him and do the same for yourself; so that he doesn't think you are picking on him.)

10. *Spends a lot of time with his mates in the pub and ignores you when he is with them.*

(You will have to draw a boundary on the behaviour and the time he spends with his friends; but don't ban him completely. After you are married; you wouldn't like him to bring the guys around to your house to trash your living room with beer, crisps and kebab, whilst watching the game on your television! Boys will always be boys; so make sure you remind him and his pals you very much exist!)

11. *Tells you what to do and orders you around...*

(Be very careful if your man never asks for your opinion; always insisting and expecting you to do things his way. Being strong-willed and refusing to do his bidding will make no difference; because this form of control is in his character. It will only get worse when you are married, when he will feel he owns you. He will definitely use other forms of mental rape on you; possibly culminating in physical abuse, in order to subjugate you. Maybe it is better you don't marry him!)

12. Jealous rages and humiliating you in front of your friends.

(Jealousy brings out the worst traits in the human being; and will blind him from any sense of decency he may have. Trying to keep you away from your friends or family; losing his temper if you so much as glance at another man; censoring your opinions and snooping on your phone calls/Emails; are all behaviour patterns brought on by jealousy. In the beginning, it might seem harmless or even flattering; but it will suffocate you when you are married. It is an undeletable part of his character; and your options will be limited on how you can get away from him! My sincere advice would be not to marry anyone who will not allow you to be who you are. It would not be a marriage; but more of a prison!)

Even though the sex is great; you must understand that no marriage survives on sex alone. Few sex sessions last for more than an hour; whilst there are twenty-four hours in a day. What happens before and after the sex is more important than what happens during it; so you cannot be expected to carry him on your back and mollycoddle him. Once you are married or living together; you should immediately divide the household chores between you. If you feel the kitchen is your domain, because of his clumsiness; then make sure he does something with the same amount of drudgery to compensate...like cleaning the bathroom and toilet. There is a strong feeling amongst men that the women are slowly chipping away at their masculinity and the walls are about to crumble; so they will have to fight back. You therefore have to be tough but subtle in your dealings with your man; because he will try to regain his masculinity. Don't expect an easy ride; but keep smiling, even when telling him off! Find out what he likes best and within reason make sure it is always done; and then make sure he also knows what you like and he does it. If he falls short in one of his tasks that make your world go round; then you should immediately 'forget' to do one of his favourite things...like cooking his dinner. He cannot keep on eating in restaurants for ever, as it will eventually become too expensive for him; and he will long for some home cooking. This done with a smile and without malice early on in a relationship, would make sure it is never repeated; because he will know the consequences of his actions or inactions.

Preying on female kindness is so commonplace; that men have become used to having their partners do for them, things they could and should very easily have done themselves. Men have realised that playing the 'little boy lost' works; and the mothering instinct in women will always come to their rescue. *"Can you put the laundry in the washing machine please?"* would be answered by *"How does it work?"*... She says, *"You know damn well how it works!"*... He replies, *"What temperature? How much soap do I need?"*... She then says, *"Oh you are useless!"* and comes down to do it herself. Fantastic! Now she won't ask him again to do it! If however, she insists he does it; then he will deliberately ruin the wash by mixing the colours or knocking something over and breaking it. Deliberate calamity! *'Don't worry; Mummy will fix it!'* Don't let him get away with such obvious trickery. If he breaks something; refuse to replace it, unless he pays for it. It will soon become an expensive business for him to continue causing domestic havoc! If he forgets to empty the rubbish; you should gently remind him, but never do it for him. If it continues; it means he is doing it on purpose, hoping you will pick up the pieces. Remind him twice; and the third time it happens, you should suddenly 'remember' a prior appointment with the hairdresser and walk out of the house. When you return; you should insist you are too *"tired"* to cook the dinner or even indulge in his favourite sexual act!

If he is the type of man who will not do the baby duties and prefers to sleep while you are up five times a night to tend to the crying, feeding and nappy changing; then he needs to be taught a lesson. The best way to do this, is to wait till he is about to go to the pub, football match or out with the boys; and then ask him to hold the baby for a few minutes, while you go to the bathroom. Quickly call your friend to ring you back immediately; citing an emergency. Make sure he is within earshot; when you answer the phone with, *"Oh my God. You stay right where you are. I'm on my way."* Ignore his protestations, get into the car and drive off; and don't return for a couple of hours! He will be left holding the baby and unable to go out; whilst you get a well-earned gossip time with your friend. When you return; there must be no sign of sweet revenge on your part. You should even congratulate him on doing a *"great job"*; bonding and looking after the baby! There is nothing he can say or do; without attracting accusations of *"not caring for our child"* from you. If you have to go out in an emergency and cannot cook his dinner as agreed upon; a note for him to cook his own dinner is not enough. *"Please cook your own dinner this time and I'll make it up to you. Get ready for some action when I return. Love you"*. The 'sweetener' will make him feel you are not taking advantage of him; and he will overlook the fact that you could not fulfil your obligation. Always be convincing when paying him back; so that he feels you 'care' and he has not 'lost out'. It will keep the balance in the relationship on an even keel.

There has been a movement to glamorise the 'new man' attitude; which really belongs to the commercials. There are some men, who are naturally good at helping out at home, but most are not; and they only do it to have some peace in the house. As explained before; you have to tailor your man to suit your needs. If you cannot do that; then you have to blame yourself when things go wrong. You should never allow it to get to the stage where he is sitting in his favourite armchair watching the sports and drinking a beer; whilst you are cleaning up after him. It does happen...even in this modern age! Women, being kind and forgiving by nature, tend to overlook a man's foibles; and that is when he will definitely take advantage of you. However; if you enjoy being a doormat for people to wipe their feet on, then there is nothing I or anyone else can do. Believe me; there are some women who relish mothering their men. Their relationships survive; only because she is prepared to put up with his laziness and ineptitude. This is because in a strange way, it makes her feel in control of the domestic situation; and therefore, irreplaceable.

You have to work hard at balancing any relationship; and that also means not taking too much advantage of a man. If having his dinner ready is what makes him happy; why not make sure it is done? If you go out to work as well and are too tired; then you have to come to an arrangement and stick to it...only changing it with his approval. He also has to do certain things for you; and make sure you approve of any change of plan. It is all about treating each other equally and with respect. There are so many ways to get him to reciprocate what you do for him; so get him involved in the chores! You both want a peaceful home don't you?

You can get more out of a happy man than a disgruntled one; who would much rather spend his time in a pub or with his other girlfriend. (Remember: Chapter 2!). If you cannot get this balance right; then you might be better off living apart from your boyfriend or even husband. Some couples actually find this works better; because they see each other only on their own terms. Give it a thought, if you are having problems maintaining the balance in your relationship; before it gets out of hand.

8. Financial blackmail & bribery

Another way a man can mentally rape you; is by financial blackmail. This method is usually used by fathers over their children; and well-off men to control their girlfriends or wives. It is a shame that real financial equality is yet to be achieved for the female; even in the so-called advanced countries. How many women have ceded to a partner's diverse sexual and other intolerable demands; simply because she needed money from him for one thing or another? For example; a woman who might not enjoy anal sex or fellatio might put up with it...for the promise of a designer shoe or a new kitchen! The price is not really important; because even a million dollars is not enough, when her very soul and self-esteem has been violated. Men are fully aware of the connection between money and a woman feeling good. Some have been known to batter their women; only to apologise later and take her shopping to make her 'forgive and forget'. A few dresses later; and she is actually smiling! *'He must still love me'* she concedes; and promises herself to do better in the future, not to annoy him. Some women even believe that a beating shows that he *'cares'*! What is it about shopping; that suddenly makes a woman feel better? We've all heard of women going to town on a man's credit cards, just to teach him a lesson; as if a shopping spree will heal a broken cheekbone or smooth over his adultery! The willingness of women to accept all kinds of abuse in exchange for financial rewards; is more widespread than they will ever admit. Showing off in front of her friends she gushes; *"Look at this nice dress my man bought me!"* What she will not say; is what she has to put up with to get that dress off him. Men have long salved their consciences with gifts; because they believe they can get away with anything, so long as they keep her happy with financial incentives.

Some men like to control the domestic funds, so that you have to beg him for every cent; and getting money out of him always has strings attached. This is because they think they can curtail your movements; if they keep you on a tight leash. If he behaves like that; you will have to put on your stubborn hat and refuse to do anything, if he is not ready to pay for it. How much is the work you do in the house and the time you save him worth? Imagine how much it would cost him; if he had to hire a cook; a cleaner; a washing woman; a driver; a nanny; a psychiatrist to listen to his problems; security for the house etc. (There was once a survey which valued a woman's housework at about $200,000 a year!). If he refuses to budge or gives you only a tiny increase by claiming *"I am not a bank!;"* then it means he is trying to play smart. You may therefore have to do the same and inflate the costs; so that you can save money for yourself, to be quietly siphoned away for a rainy day. He claims he has no money; but I bet he buys rounds of drinks for his pals in the pub, without batting an eyelid! Ask him pointedly how much he makes; and then shame him by deriding the amount you receive from him. To get money out of your man; you just have to make a nuisance of yourself and nag him into submission. Don't ever be afraid to put him on the spot; and make sure everything boils down to the measly amount of cash he gives you.

1. He wants you to do all the housework and pay the bills etc; yet will not give you enough cash to do the job properly. *("I cannot work under such conditions. I'm going on strike.")*

2. He often quibbles about the amount you spend on the house. *("Why don't you do the shopping yourself and find out what things really cost!")*

3. He complains about the quality of food you are providing. *("If you want good things to eat; you have to pay more.")*

4. He wants to know why the house is never clean. *("I don't have time to clean, when I'm running around town trying to find food bargains; because you refuse to pay up...!")*

5. He does not like the attire you are wearing when he is taking you out. *("Maybe if you bought me some decent clothes and shoes; I would be able to dress to your approval.")*

6. He is looking for some nookie... *("Sorry, I'm too tired; and my feet are aching with all the walking around I've had to do today. Can you massage them for me...?")*

The best way to defend yourself against financial blackmail is obviously to have enough of your own money; which in some cases is almost impossible. Being financially independent is not so easy; because true equality in the workplace has not yet arrived to all females. Having lots of money of your own; does not necessarily make you independent. This is because you never know who your friends are; and paranoia could set in. You will then have to put your trust in your man; who could easily bleed you dry by mentally raping you to such an extent that he will make you feel guilty for not buying him anything he wants. Why bother working; if he knows you can provide him with everything? He will tell you how to avoid the leeches and try to keep you away from your best friends; because he will feel they are enjoying the money he should be spending! He will alienate you from everyone and you will find yourself trapped; because he will make sure you cannot do without his advice. Finally, because it is a rare man who is happy basking in the shadow of his wife's glory; he will at some point be jealous of your success. He could then become so embittered and disgruntled; it will affect your relationship. A simple favour asked of him, will reverberate like a command; and every argument you have, will boil down to how rich you are. *"Just because you've got money you think you can order me around like a slave"*; that is if it does not drive him to depression, drink or into the arms of another woman. You therefore have to set your own standards; and try to be with someone who is of equal wealth to you. For the majority of women however; the man is still the breadwinner in the family because he makes more money than her. She is thereby reduced to having to ask him for cash; and wishing she had married someone richer!

If you marry a man for his money; you should be aware that wealth always comes with hidden conditions, which are not laid out in the marriage vows. The richer the man, the more likely he will mentally abuse his woman; because money makes one emotionally lazy. He will try and buy his way into her heart and out of her anger; with bouquets of flowers; expensive perfumes; gourmet dinners; designer clothes; delicious chocolates; exotic holidays and priceless jewellery. How romantic! But I bet most women would prefer a sincere and heartfelt; *"I love you and I'm so happy and grateful to have you in my life"*. Many wives of rich men become lonely; because he is too busy making more money to care what she gets up to, thinking the platinum card he gave her will solve all her problems. Abandoned, bored and reduced to spending their days shopping, attending fashion shows and indulging in beauty treatments; no wonder there is a high rate of infidelity and alcoholism in their midst!

Most rich men will make you sign a pre-nuptial contract. This is a good thing because, although it is meant to protect his money from you; it can also guarantee you a certain amount, when things go wrong. You will know exactly where you stand; so it is up to you to thrash out every tiny detail to your satisfaction, before signing on the dotted line. You should try and agree exactly how much money you should be given; in the event of things going wrong. You will also need money to run the household and a personal spending allowance (to be increased yearly with the rise in inflation). You should also insist on money to start a small business or charity for yourself; because it will give you a bit of independence and a sense of self-worth. Putting yourself on a sound economic footing is important when you sign a pre-nuptial; because the man may think he does not owe you anything more, since you have already screwed him! You will therefore find it hard to get any decent day-to-day 'operational costs' from him.

With your parents, you have to be more careful; because they are not sleeping with you. (I hope not!) Although one can assume they genuinely love you; it is on their terms and not yours. They might try to tell you what to do. If you don't comply; the only weapon they have, is to write you out of their will. The biggest bone of contention between father and daughter; is her choice of boyfriend/husband. Girls are likely to argue with their mothers over 'trivial things'; like the choice of clothes; sex; alcohol; drugs and education. Children often refuse to listen to parental advice; conveniently forgetting that they have been young before and are probably giving the benefit of their own past experience. Depending on what you have to lose; you might be better-off listening to your parents because they have most likely seen it all before and only want the best for their kids. Many girls have followed their hearts; married the man of their choice and have been disowned by their family. The problem with this is; if the relationship does not work out, you will have no one to turn to. Once a man knows you have burned the family bridge and gave up everything for him; you will be starting the relationship off with a severe imbalance. Make no mistake; he will take advantage of you later on. Is any man worth losing the warmth and love of your family?

A lot of men have no respect for women; and believe every woman is a whore, each with a different price tag. If he does something wrong; then a bunch of flowers or a box of chocolates may not be enough, but a new car or designer attire splash-out in several top stores might! It seems everything has a price; and money can smooth over any cracks, crimes or misdemeanours! Have you ever wondered why there is so much misogyny in the world? Women have to be true to themselves; and that is the only way to put a stop to financial bribery. If someone has really insulted your integrity or reputation; then no gift in the world should be able to buy your forgiveness...unless it comes with a sincere apology. If something hurts, it does no good at all pretending otherwise; because he will never learn his lesson and he will hurt you again, in the same way. The same sense of anger and injustice you feel when you have been sexually betrayed; is how you should feel when something, however small, is not right. The strength to refuse his gifts until a genuine apology is returned; is necessary. Otherwise; men will continue to do and say things to you that will hurt and then buy you off when it gets out of hand. Once your man realises he cannot buy you out, blackmail or bribe you; then you will find his attitude changing because you would have destroyed one of his most potent weapons.

9. Abuse of your feelings

Mental rape of your feelings is a subtle process; which, once it takes hold of you, is almost impossible to completely get rid of. Like its physical counterpart; it is very difficult to prevent something happening, if one cannot spot the signs as they come along. We all have feelings; which can and will be hurt, if we are not careful. A bruise will heal; but how do you heal a wounded pride or an assault on your femininity? As tough as you can be; it would still hurt, if someone came out and called you *"a whore"* or *"a fat ugly bitch!"* in public. You may have a well-timed riposte; but you will not be in a good mood! When a man gives you a nice hug and says; *"Of course you're not fat or ugly. You are beautiful, intelligent and sexy. You should take no notice because she's just jealous of you"*; you may find yourself on stage two of the last chapter. This time he may not have to physically rape you, because you will probably give yourself freely to him; simply because you are convinced he cared about you in your hour of need and you fell for him. It would be easy for him to abuse your love for him; because he knows what makes you tick. He will put on his charming act whenever necessary; allowing you to be hooked on him emotionally.

How about the guy who tells you he loves you; and you end up falling for him? He gets to sleep with you and then dumps you; because all you were to him was an easy conquest. Although after a certain age, most women will not fall for the *"I love you"* syndrome; there are very few women who have not had this particular form of betrayal thrust upon them, because it is a part of growing up. Nevertheless, it is a severe abuse of a woman's feelings; perpetuated by men of all ages all over the world, because there is no law against it. It is therefore up to you not to fall for it; which can be very difficult when your heart is fighting your brain. Sadly for many women; when a man tells her how beautiful she is, it is what she wants to hear. Praise and flattery are clothes, which fit best on a woman! When such compliments are heaped on her; they worm their way into her subconscious and she starts believing them. She finds herself looking more favourably at the person who showered her with the acclaim. Human nature you might say; but it sets off a chain of subtle emotions, which lead up to emotional dependency and mental abuse. How often have you heard a woman say, *"Oh he was such a nice gentleman when I married him; but he seems to have changed for the worse."* Sweetheart; he never 'changed'. He has always been the same; except when you first met him, he showered you with accolades because you were his new toy. His flattery clouded your judgement; and you did not see the signs until it were too late.

Because of centuries of male domination, women still have an inferiority complex; and that is why a woman is flattered when a man calls her *"intelligent"*, or *"beautiful"*. Yet; the same woman will claim sexism, when she is told she has *"a tasty pair of tits"*. She feels that type of compliment is demeaning; and the suitor will have no chance with her! Smart men have quickly learnt to flatter a woman for her mental; rather than her physical attributes. The bumbling idiot who says you have *"a cute arse"* or *" sexy legs"*; is nowhere near as harmful as the clever one who praises your intelligence. Such a flatterer is probably after something, which may not necessarily be a loving relationship; so you have to be very careful. The first few seconds after a woman receives flattery or praise that she enjoys; is when she is most vulnerable to the next move. This could be more flattery or an invitation to get to know him better; ending up in her being date-raped or conned out of her money.

Kindness is the way such men move in, when they want to get something out of a woman. He will be sweet, kind, considerate, charming and a real gentleman. He will only move in for sex, if you pursue it; because he only wants your money, not your body. It will be very hard for a woman to take; if someone she thought so *'loving and kind'*, could be so callous. *"There must be a mistake. He would never do this to me"*. She would be so deluded, that she may never recover from the deceit; meaning she has been well and truly mentally raped. Taking money from you; is not the only reason he might be nice to you. After all, you may not have any; but don't think you are safe, because he may want to make money out of you. You may be working in a bank; or have connections to information he might need to sell to some of your company's rivals. Industrial espionage is now extremely common; because of the sheer competitiveness of trying to sell new products in over-saturated markets. Some men are clever womanisers; and are specifically used by companies to target women in sensitive positions in certain companies. Be very suspicious when a stranger tries to be nice to you in a bar or on the street; because you never know what he is up to or where he has come from. If during the polite chit-chat, the topic moves to where you work and what you do; you must try to change the subject and let him know by the tone of your voice that the subject is off the agenda. If you are drinking, never talk about your work; because an innocuous comment might open a can of worms. Not only could you lose your job; but you could be breaching certain codes of ethics and you could be arrested for conspiracy.

The more polite a man is, the more the suspicion that he really does not like women; but is only being nice, because it is politically correct to do so. In the company of women, men will never say what they really feel; but catch a group of males sitting together in a bar without a woman in sight and their true characters will surely emerge...after they have downed a few drinks! The sheer sexist and misogynistic jokes and comments, that can emanate from their mouths, when men are grouped together; are best not repeated here. *"I'm all for equal rights and equal pay for women..."* is the type of statement that men, backed by 'savvy' politicians, will spout when there are females within earshot; because that is what they assume women want to hear. Yet, not much is being done about 'equal rights'! If that is what men really believe; how come women are still being treated badly, by having opportunities denied them and paid less for the work they do? Not even 10% of those who are in charge of the top 100 companies in the world; are women! Some women who have seen through this guise and refuse for example, to accept a seat from a man on a bus, allow him to carry her bags or open a door for her; are quickly branded as rabid lesbian feminists and short-shrifted. Sadly; the majority of women do fall for the politeness con and are easily fooled. *"What a nice gentleman..."*. If you think about it; it is actually very patronising for a man to feel he has to change his natural behaviour and be extra polite, because there are women around. Like the way children are treated; some men act as if they believe women don't know how to think or fight for themselves and decisions must be made for them. Isn't this is a clear abuse of womanhood? *"Ladies first"* is just an excuse for men to check out your shape, legs and buttocks; as they walk behind you! *"Just joking; Tigress. Honest!"*

Once you recognise that there are only two main reasons why a man will take an initial interest in you; then you will be able to defend yourself from any possible rape situation. They come in all kinds of disguises; but the two reasons are sex (he wants to fuck you) and finance (he wants to make money from or out of you). Beware of the so-called harmless men who like to take you out; without asking for sex in return. They are much worse than the pest who is honest enough to tell you directly, he wants to fuck the living daylights out of you; with no strings attached! Believe it or not; a beautiful or an intelligent woman on the arm of a man, can be of great advantage to him in certain circles. He may not even try to sleep with you; but will reap the benefits of your being with him. He will then drop you when you have served his purpose. Even someone who is gay; may not yet be prepared to come out of the closet and will enjoy being seen with a female, just to make a gay lover jealous or appear 'respectable' to certain business associates, to promote his own prospects. Both of these examples, are rapes of your personality and intellect; which one could argue is as bad as the physical rape, because the man will most likely get away with it.

You should never feel you owe a man anything for his generosity. If for instance, you go to a restaurant and he wants to pay for the dinner; let him! (You can always use your money for the hairdressers! *"Terrible aren't I?"*) Just make sure you buy him a round of drinks when you go to the pub afterwards; so that he does not feel short-changed. There is no need to be rude or over-bearing to prove a point with a man; because you can be just as effective by using your wit and charm. If he thinks he can get into your pants, just because he bought you dinner; then you have to put him in his place, without completely cutting him to shreds. Embarrass him nicely, with something like; *"I'm sorry; but I'm not that kind of girl. I just wish you had told me sex is what you were really after, when you invited me out. I could have saved you the trouble and expense. Do you want the money back for the dinner you bought me?"* You are a woman; so I'm sure you can think of an even-better response! It can be good fun watching him squirm, when you have hit a raw nerve; because he will try to fib his way out of it and dig a deeper hole for himself.

When a man asks you out for the first time; your antennas should be out, so that you are not taken advantage of. The opportunist who gets one over on you by saying, *"Sorry, I forgot my wallet at home; can you pay for the dinner and I'll pay the next time"*; is harmless compared to the one who says, *"I know a good way we can make some money"*. (It is always his ideas and *your* money!). The prevalent attitude of trying to prove she is as good as any man; often gets women into trouble. Why she would want to be as good as a man beats me; because there are not that many good men around. Women have to realise that it is their femininity that makes them strong; not their masculine traits. Because she tried to act tough; many women have been fleeced by unscrupulous men, who wine and dine them pretending to have money...and then go into a business venture using her money. **"Show us your money and let's do some real business!"** Not to be outdone; she delivers her money and he disappears! The minute any man tries to worm his way in by proposing business; your guard should be up. Unless you are a businesswoman, who really knows the ropes; you should never do any business with anyone, man or woman.

Human nature tends to be sympathetic to the one who appears wealthy. If someone walks into a bank looking for a loan of a million pounds; the bank manager will be curious as to what kind of business deal he or she is doing and will listen to the proposal. Go into the same bank manager, looking for a loan of a thousand pounds; and you will be lucky if the clerk has time for you. There are men who are experts at preying on weak women; to seduce them, gain their confidence and then siphon all their cash away. It is not that difficult; because they make the women believe they really love them. They turn on the charm in the beginning; and then disappear into the sunset when they have cleared her bank account. It can be so embarrassing, the woman may be too ashamed to tell even her closest friends that she has been duped; and she may never recover from the deceit. This feeling of betrayal and having been 'used and abused'; is also mental rape. There is nothing the law can do about it; because she 'willingly' divulged the details of her bank accounts. He can only be prosecuted if he stole her money; not if he was 'given' the cash, after she herself withdrew it from her account. She only did it because she was so much in love, she would do anything for him; which is a clear abuse of her feelings.

The only way to stop yourself being used by men; is to constantly make them aware that you know what they are up to. You have to make an inquisitive nuisance of yourself; by always questioning his motives. If you keep quiet, he will think you don't know or care; and will continue doing it. If a man asks you out; don't be afraid to ask him point-blank, *"Why do you want to take me out?"* Although it can take the romance out of the offer; it will immediately let him know that you are not stupid. If he cannot give you a straight enough answer; you should politely decline the offer. If you are rich, it could be your money or your contacts; and if you work in a sensitive job, it could be industrial or marketing secrets that he is after. Even if you have no money; he could be using you as a stepping stone to one of your work colleagues, who will have more to offer him...like your boss or the owner of your company. He will probably spurn out the usual platitudes about how beautiful and attractive you are etc.; but that does not answer the burning question: *'Why does he want to take you out?'* Once you prove too stubborn to fall for his lines; his real character will surface. At this point, most men will probably give up; which should be okay by you, because it is obvious his motives were not genuine. Even when you are in a relationship with a man, you should never abandon this stubborn inquisitiveness; because it will be easy for you to catch him out, if he is lying to you. It will keep him on his toes and stop him treating you as a soft touch; which means he will have to be honest with you, because you deserve nothing less.

Self-confidence is what you need to prevent mental rape taking a hold on you. You must be aware of who you are; and convince yourself that you are special to yourself. You should take no notice of what anybody says about you; which means treating all praises and insults exactly the same...with indifference! A sense of humour is paramount; because making jokes and learning to laugh at one's own expense, is a good sign that you are tough and will not be taken advantage of. When a man praises you or asks you to do something for him, he obviously has a hidden agenda; so don't be scared to put him on the spot. Even if you are wrong, don't be embarrassed; just keep on doing it. As time goes by; it gets easier to weed out the fraudsters and becomes part of your character. After a while; nobody will mess with you because they will realise it is who you are and you won't change. When you catch him out; there is no need to get annoyed. Just ride along with it; and accept that men being men will definitely try their luck...until they hit a brick wall. You should always remember the cut-off point described in the last chapter; so that even if you want to be with him, you know exactly where you stand and how far you will allow him to go.

10. The workplace

If you are not living with a man; the chances are you will be able to avoid most of the excesses. But it is not only boyfriends or husbands who can abuse your mind! Bosses are also well known for all kinds of mental bullying. This can make it unbearable, because you could easily spend a third of your day at work; whilst the threat of losing your job is always there. Even though in most companies, there are unions to protect you; it is a brave worker who refuses to make her boss a cup of tea, because it is not in her job description. If a boss at work is kind to you; be aware that there is always a subtle string attached, which may not be sexual. He may be nice to you in order to win your confidence. You will slowly find yourself becoming his eyes and ears in the workplace; feeding him titbits about what goes on behind his back! You will do anything in order to please him; all because he is so generous to you and you feel safe with him, since *"he never tries it on with you"*. You might think this will do your promotion prospects a world of good; but that may not happen. This is because promoting you might move you away from him; and he needs you in your present position to do his dirty work for him. As a result; you will definitely lose the trust of your work colleagues. They will undermine whatever you do; and may even try and set you up, in order to get you sacked.

You have to be very careful how you deal with this scenario. Once you start giving your boss information; it will be very hard to stop, without incurring his wrath. Right from the beginning; you have to mind your own business and feign ignorance any time you see something. *"What did so and so say about me the other day when I disciplined him?"* This should be answered by, *"Sorry, I wasn't really listening; although he did look a little unhappy. I don't normally pay attention to what is going on; because I have so much work to get through."* This is a nice way of revealing absolutely nothing; and will let him know you will not be easily used. If he says, *"Let me know if you see or hear anything..."* Just say *"Okay boss!"* He will get fed up trying it on with you; when he realises you never seem to 'see' or 'hear' anything. Never ever tell anyone (including those you think are your friends) what is discussed with your boss or about any illegal endeavours you might be involved in; because they may also be on his favour roster and will go back and tell him. A workplace can be a beehive of intrigue, factions, gossip and backstabbing; so it is best to stay clear of such activities. Once you fall out with someone in the office; he or she then becomes an enemy who knows things about you that could get you disciplined or dismissed.

Women on women bullying is also a sceptre that rears its ugly head, more often than most females in the workplace will admit; to the point that a lot of women prefer to work under a male than a female. With a male you can keep things under control, if he steps out of line; because you have the protection of the law on sexual harassment. What do you do when one of your own mentally rapes you? For example; if a man calls you a *"sexy bitch"* you can report him and he will be severely reprimanded. What would you do if you are black and a black female boss calls you a *"lazy coon and a trashy bitch"*? Report her for racism and sexism? You would not be doing yourself any favours; and she could easily ruin your promotion prospects. All female bosses are smart and intelligent; (they did not get the job by being stupid) but can also be very devious and cunning. They definitely know how to make anyone's life a misery! Crossing a man is nowhere near as dangerous as annoying a woman boss. If a female asks you to make her a cup of tea or type something for her, (that is not part of your duties) you might think it does not seem as bad as when a man asks you; but they are both equally degrading.

If your boss asks you without a *"please"*, then you have to bite the bullet and do it; because it would not be fair to embarrass him (or her) in front of the staff. He may be unaware he is abusing his powers; if he has been doing it to other staff members, without protest. You should therefore use a little tact and go to him/her privately and politely state that you do not appreciate being a tea lady/errand girl for anyone, because it is not in your job description; so you will not do it again. If you later feel like you are being victimised; don't be afraid to go to an industrial tribunal and make a complaint. There will always be slight abuses and excesses in all companies. If you have a problem, which could be anything from hygiene and working conditions to sexism and the pay structure; never be afraid to get together with your colleagues and make your voices heard by the relevant authorities. The more women stand up for themselves and each other; the quicker the cancer of mental rape in the workplace will be eradicated. However; it would not be wise to cause friction where none exists. If by making cups of tea or running errands for your boss, means he or she cuts you a lot of slack in other departments; (turning a blind eye to certain infractions like surfing the Internet; arriving late/leaving early; gossiping etc) then use your head and don't rock the boat. A happy working environment is mutually beneficial to everyone!

At work you will always get the opportunists who seem so occupied with 'personal problems', they never have the time to finish their work; and are always asking others to do work favours for them. *"Can you photocopy some files/type this letter/complete the spreadsheet or data base for me?"* The most common requests at work are; *"Can you bring me back a sandwich from the deli when you go out for lunch?"*; *"Can you make me a cup of tea?"*, *"Can I have one of your biscuits?"* and the popular *"Can you lend me some money and I'll pay you back when I get paid?"* Although they seem like pretty innocuous requests; you will be regarded as a soft touch, if you continuously agree to do such favours. You should reply any request, with a look of utter disgust; *"I beg your pardon?" "It would help if you said please. I will do it for you this time; but it is a one-off and you owe me"*. Make sure everyone around you hears you and stick to your guns; so that they also don't think of trying the same thing on you. If he or she ever asks you again, even weeks later; you should remind him or her of the last time you did them a favour and what was agreed. If they do not wish to return the favour; you will have to 'disown' and never do them any more good deeds, even if you have to refuse them a biscuit. With money; it would be better for all and sundry, if you spurn any requests for a loan. This is because you will either not get the money back when it was promised; or you will be repaid in dribs and drabs. Once he or she finally pays you back; it would be like a licence to keep borrowing more, because the borrower will feel he/she has earned the right to your generosity. Refusing to lend money will leave you open to insults; but don't worry about it. Being known as *"the tight bitch who takes no prisoners"*; means you will be left alone to get on with your work!

Office romances are very common; and often lead to problems and heartache, when there is a break-up. This is because the gossip machine always goes into over-drive. Try to avoid going out with anyone you work with; because it means you are spending too long in each other's company. The chances are the relationship will not survive; because your colleagues will constantly be curious to know what is going on. It will be very hard to avoid talking about each other to your respective friends in the workplace; and they will have to take sides, if you have a particularly bad disagreement. By all means go out for a drink with your colleagues on special celebrations; but be careful what you talk about. You will have to live with what you said; even if you did not mean it at the time because you were probably drunk! We all know what goes on at office parties and how people do stupid things; so you must be very careful you don't fall into that particular trap. Nowadays; all mobile phones have cameras. Even an innocuous hug or kiss with a workmate can end up in your husband/partner's handset/E mail box; sent there by a mischievous colleague. This may not be easy to explain away; if you are already having marital problems!

Finally; every office or company has its Romeos who think they are God's gift to the females in the workplace. They will definitely try it on with you; if you give them the chance! I cannot run your love life for you; but if you sleep with one of these seducers, you will most likely be just a notch on his bedpost and he will quickly move on to the next girl as soon as he has had you. He will definitely tell all the men you work with, how easy you are; and exaggerate your prowess in the fellatio and intercourse department. Every sigh and moan you make when experiencing orgasm, will be replayed in graphic detail when the guys get together in the pub; because that is what men do. You can tell if you have been the subject of gossip; if after sleeping with a co-worker, you find another one of them trying his luck with you. If you even smile at him; it will give the first one an easy excuse to dump you by feigning jealousy and labelling you *"a cheap whore"*. The next guy will then tell you how beautiful you are, restore your self-esteem and then bed you; because you think it's a good way of getting back at the first guy for dumping you. Many a naïve girl has fallen for that trick; where they end up being bedded by almost all the guys in the office. Even though she will try to convince herself she is the one in control, who has *'had all the men'*; it never quite works out that way in reality. Being the 'office slag' is never something to be proud of and always backfires; especially when the girls start to shun her, in case she goes for their own men outside the office. For your own reputation, dignity and self-worth; try to avoid sleeping with those you work with! If you love sex that much; I'm sure you can find enough men to 'shag' outside of your workplace!

In order to avoid mental rape of any kind in the workplace; you have to treat everybody equally. If someone pushes you, you will surely have something to say; so any hint of being taken advantage of, should be buried right there and then. If something does not feel right; you should do something about it at the very beginning, before it is too late. You have to see the signs coming; and knock each one back so hard that the perpetrator will think twice about trying it with you again. If possible; do your best to keep your home life away from work. Don't discuss your problems with your work colleagues, unless they really are your friends outside of work; in which case, you can talk to them at home instead of the workplace. Office gossiping should also be avoided; because the *"...he said... she said"* syndrome always leads to trouble. Someone jealous of your influence in the office or after your job; will be only too delighted to accuse you, even for something you have not done, just to embarrass you. Once your work colleagues cannot get through to you and know nothing about your private life; they will have nothing of substance to gossip about you. Be friendly but not over-familiar, because as we all know it leads to contempt; and never repeat what someone tells you. Get on with your work in a professional manner; don't allow anyone to talk you into breaking any rules and keep a respectful distance from everyone. As a result; they will be forced to respect and be honest with you. Your behaviour will always be noticed by your bosses; because maintaining your respect and dignity is one of the true hallmarks of someone who can be trusted. This means you will be a strong candidate for promotion!

I have outlined most of the problems you are likely to face at home or in the workplace; from the partners and colleagues in your lives. Obviously, each relationship is different; so you might experience certain difficulties, which I have not specifically covered. I hope however, that I have put you in a stronger frame of mind, which will allow you to spot the signs that could hurt you; and to deal successfully with each situation when it presents itself, so that you are happy and satisfied with the outcome. The most important thing to remember is to value and respect yourself; and make sure others do the same. Otherwise; you will have to either distance yourself from them, or teach them a lesson they won't forget in a hurry! Some women are clever enough not to fall for the tricks used by men; but there are an awful lot who are conned into believing their men really care for them. The sheer mental bullying they experience is worse than any real beating; because the scars may never heal. A man might try to bully you physically, if he finds out his mental tactics are not working because you are standing up to him; so you have to be prepared for the onslaught. You will have to leave him when it comes to that; but it would still be nice to get some form of revenge or parting shot before you leave! When a situation is very hard to get out of; it becomes an impossible situation, calling for drastic measures. These will be described in Chapters 14-15.

"Come on Tigress; together we will make sure nobody pushes you around!"

Chapter Six
Armed Robberies – *"Why me"?*

I hope you took in the last two chapters on rape. I also hope none of you reading this book will ever have to go through any of those ordeals. Rape however traumatic, may not be the worst thing that can happen to a woman; because looking down the barrel of a gun with her life in danger in armed robbery and other life or death situations, could be worse. Moreover; nothing ever compensates for the fear and mental anguish she has to deal with for the rest of her life. If you ever have to face a perilous predicament with a weapon and live to tell the tale; the quality of your life will change for ever and you will no longer be the same person. The attacker does not need to physically hurt you, to 'kill' you. If after an attack, you are left in such a state that you cannot go out without looking over your shoulder and even the harmless bursting of a balloon by a group of kids makes you jump in fear; then you might as well be dead because your life and the relationship you had with friends, family and partner will never be the same again.

Armed robbery is any attack on a person where the perpetrator uses a weapon to deprive the victim of anything; which may also include her self-confidence. In the past, it used to be considered cowardly to attack a defenceless person; and weapons were for the lowest of the low. Sadly, those times are gone and nowadays only a naïve person does not keep some sort of a weapon at home; in case of trouble. There will always be the threat of murder in all armed robberies; mainly because they are perpetuated by those who are so scared of the outcome of getting caught, they will usually kill in order to get away. The tendency of the victims to fight back, by placing the value of property above that of their lives; is another factor that makes armed robbery so dangerous. They occur all over the world; and even though they are doing their best, the police cannot stop it completely. When a child is born, he is not an armed robber. Social conditions like poverty and lack of a decent education coupled with jealousy, greed and ambition; are all contributing factors to this type of crime. As long as there is a big gap between the rich and the poor; there will always be armed violence. It obviously goes much deeper than this; and only an experienced criminologist or psychologist would be able to give you all the answers. I must therefore stress that this book cannot stop crime. All I am concerned is that it never happens to you!

I go to work every day and I hope you do too. Nothing we say or do, will stop an armed robber from going to do his job; which is basically what it is and probably the only one he knows. To the victim, armed robbery is the worst thing anyone could do; but to the robber, he is just going about his business. The fact that it is illegal will not stop him; because he feels he is doing the right thing, in order to survive and look after his family. The joy on a child's face when he or she is given a new toy; makes how the money was obtained to buy the toy, almost irrelevant. Opinions can be quite sanctimonious in that people believe something is wrong, only if they do not agree with it. The bank clerk quietly fiddling the accounts entrusted in his care; the millionaire evading tax; the politician receiving illegal kickbacks or the civil servant embezzling thousands of euros could all jump up to vilify the armed robber; even though their own actions may have hurt and ruined a lot more people. Even a drug dealer will tell you that he is providing a service to the community; because there would be no supply without demand! This means that there are those who will rob you and not lose any sleep over it; because they feel they have been hard done by in life and are hell-bent on revenge against those they perceive as 'having it all'. Regrettably; this perception often leads to the wrong people being robbed. A woman driving an expensive car could easily be a target; even though the car may be on hire-purchase and she may still be owing money to her bank.

It is no accident that the majority who do armed robberies are those who have been to prison before; and have therefore lost their sensitivity to a victim's suffering. There are a lot of convicts in prisons, as a result of simple crimes like fraud and petty theft. Inside however; they are able to learn the tactics of serious criminal endeavours from international crooks. By the time they come out; they might decide that there is more money in armed robbery than in cashing stolen cheques or picking pockets...because nobody can resist a gun! They can also learn where to buy weapons; from well-connected hardened criminals. By the time the petty thief is released from jail; he is a potential hard drug dealer, serious fraud artist, dangerous robber, callous murderer and big-time smuggler. The criminal world could be his oyster when he is freed; because he will find out that his friends and family have deserted him, he has no money, little prospect of a job and nowhere to live. It is no wonder that many criminals re-offend within weeks or even days of their release from prison.

Through the contacts made whilst incarcerated; he could get to work for an established criminal network. There are sophisticated robbers who will not rob themselves; but will use the many ever-willing thugs at their disposal, to do the jobs for them. Uneducated; with nothing to do and possessing little or no money...why not earn a few grand by robbing a bank/factory or snatching a car for your employer? With a weapon; he will be able to shoot all opposition, including the police...and will have a chance to get away! The police in many countries are so badly-equipped that some don't even have bullet-proof vests; thereby putting their lives in constant danger. It is no surprise that they have been known to run away; at the slightest threat to their lives! How can they be expected to fight armed robbers; when sometimes the robbers are better equipped than they are? As a result; when someone is a victim of armed robbery, he or she is left to fend for him/herself. Even if the police do arrive; it is always when the damage has already been done!

Many robberies are carried out on seemingly innocent victims; but are they really innocent? Just pick up a newspaper and you will read about armed robbers attacking such and such a person; and people will ask, *"Why would anybody want to rob and murder her? She was such a nice person; a pillar of society etc"*. Whilst reading this book; somebody somewhere is getting robbed or even murdered. This is because there will always be those who feel aggrieved that the wealth of the country has not filtered down to them. A lady in a flash car or living alone in a mansion; is a reasonable target for a disgruntled and disaffected youth with a grievance. Thankfully, the amateurish robberies are on the decrease because the police usually know who they are and can easily apprehend them; even though it would be after the event. Nowadays, most robbers tend to choose their victims; making it a lot safer than before. It also means that if you are robbed by a professional; it has to be your fault!

Out of the many rich women in the world; why does an armed robber pick on a poor defenceless female to rob? Sometimes it is just bad luck; because they get drunk/high and go out to rob someone, without caring who it is. However; at least 90 percent of the time, a robber knows exactly why he is robbing a particular person. *"Oh God. Why me?"* (By the way, if God loves everybody; then He/She also loves the armed robber and therefore, cannot take sides. *"Why me?"* could also be *"Why not me?"*) We deserve what we get is more practical; and accepting responsibility for your life, family and property is the first step. Always being alert; by taking the right precautions and observing a set of rules will go a long way in preventing an armed attack on you. Let him pick on some other person and not you! Money/valuables; owing/swindling/upsetting the wrong people; showing off your wealth; and not being security conscious. These are the four main reasons why someone would use a weapon to rob you and cause you maximum pain.

A. Money/valuables

There is so much corruption and illegally earned profits circling around that can obviously not be put into a bank. This means there is a lot of money and valuables hiding inside certain people's homes; making it easy for any crook with enough information, to gain access to these unaccountable riches and use a weapon to rob them. With women becoming more and more financially solvent; murders and armed robberies on females are on the increase in many countries. Money is the root of all evil; so please be serious about what you do with it!

1. You should be aware that some people buy art, gold and diamonds etc as a way of washing suspect money; which means they cannot declare them to the tax man. They therefore have to stash them at home or in clandestine safety deposit boxes. If you cannot keep valuables in a bank; then the source must be questionable. If you are robbed; there is nothing you can do and

the money will be lost for ever. Many victims of robberies have failed to report certain items stolen; in case the police ask too many questions!

2. The police are also wise to the fact that some art/jewellery robberies are deliberately arranged, in order to get the insurance pay out; which then becomes legal money. If you are involved in illegal activities; think long and hard about how and where you keep your money. The insurance companies and the tax authorities are getting smarter by the day!

3. If someone, however innocuous he or she might seem, knows you have money or jewellery at home; then there will one day be an attempt to rob them. You should therefore never divulge too much information on what valuables you have inside your house; even to your best friend. He or she may not be your best friend for ever; and it is those closest to you that have the knowledge and opportunity to do you most damage!

4. If armed robbers take the trouble to come to your house; it is always because of reliable information they have received. To deny the existence of what they have come for; could spell the end of your life. You therefore have to decide whether your life is worth the price of the valuables or the money they are trying to steal from you. Nobody wants to go to prison for the next ten to twenty years or face execution; so if you resist, they will have to kill you, in order to get away! Chapter 16 will show you what to do when armed robbers actually break into your house.

B. Flaunting wealth

Showing off is regarded by the have-nots as blatant confrontation, which could easily get you robbed or even killed; so you should do your best not to parade your wealth. In the Third World, driving a *Mercedes Benz* would be regarded as flaunting your wealth; whereas in the developed world, a *Rolls Royce* and serious jewellery might attract the same attention. The lesson is the same. You should never flaunt what most people in your area do not own and have no legal way of obtaining; because they will definitely try to take it from you. If you are wealthy and you are robbed; very few people will feel sorry for you. They will pretend to sympathise, but will be laughing inside; because it makes them feel better. Wealth provokes envy; which, if not curtailed, becomes jealousy. Many a crime has been committed because of jealousy!

1. You should never rub it in during an argument that you are richer and therefore 'better' than the person you are arguing with; because it will breed a hatred for you. Depending on his or her state of mind; it can also produce an insatiable need for revenge to *'teach you a lesson you will never forget'*. Arrogance coupled with an overbearing and condescending attitude; will always make you enemies! This is simply because it is much easier to hate than compete with you; especially when you act in such a conceited manner...backed by your obvious social status and wealth.

2. You may be a nice rich lady who donates money to all your favourite causes. How nice! But do you have to let the whole world know, by having an interview and photo session with your local newspaper/radio/television station; or by telling all your friends about it? Why not donate the cash quietly? If you flaunt jewellery, throw money around at parties or splash out on shopping sprees in high-brow boutiques; there will be those who wish they had all that money. Since you obviously have too much of it; they might go as far as make plans to take some of it. This narcissistic trait in some people to publicly enhance their credentials; has been the bane of many victims of armed robbery.

3. If you own a private plane, yacht or expensive car; make sure the money used to buy them, was legally earned. It would not be pleasant to have the taxman after you; because he will take it all from you! Never drive a big car around at night; because you will attract the robbers lurking around the car parks and lonely highways. What is wrong in going out in a taxi? The anonymity makes it a lot safer! If you can afford an expensive car, then you should have a driver/bodyguard; so that your car is never left on its own. Why not move to a more affluent area; where your big car would not attract so much attention and the police react much quicker to distress calls? I know this may sound a bit extreme; but in many towns, the police don't always come to your aid quickly enough!

4. If you own a mansion; there will be someone nearby who also wants one and is not prepared to wait for ever. He may not rob you; but will rob someone else and you would have indirectly been the cause of someone else's misery! This is unfortunate and not much can be done about it. There is no point in having money; if you cannot spend and enjoy it! However, you can limit your chances of being robbed; by not being perceived as showing off. This means living in an area which reflects your status; and having friends who are richer than or of equal wealth to you.

C. Debts, swindling and offending

Owing large sums of money and refusing to pay, blatantly swindling people and treading on the wrong toes in certain businesses; are the quickest ways to find yourself at the end of a vicious attack. There are not as many armed robberies in the world, as there are women. The chances of it happening to you are minimal, if you live a peaceful crime-free life without cheating or offending too many people; and if you don't owe anyone a large amount of cash.

1. If you make a promise to pay a debt then make sure you pay it on time; and if you cannot, you should explain and always keep the channels of communication open. If you run or hide away, then you are inviting trouble by making the creditor look like a fool; and he/she will be forced to teach you a lesson. Violent methods will most likely be used to make you pay up; and they will not go away until you do. Crying to the police will not help you; because you are legally in the wrong, by owing the money. You can still be sued for it; even after they have beaten you up!

2. A crook that rips off his company or dupes money from business associates, while stepping on a lot of toes; becomes rich enough to build a huge mansion and ride around in a *Rolls Royce*. Why wouldn't he attract jealousy and outrage from those law-abiding and therefore, less fortunate citizens? What goes around comes around; and he could be a candidate for armed robbery by his criminal contemporaries. The police always know who the big millionaire crooks are; and have been known to wash their hands off a killing and label it 'unsolved'. Another crook off the streets; means one less for them to worry about!

If you rip someone off in an illegal activity; you will get what's coming to you and it will be violent. So please be careful!

3. Arguing with a business partner or somebody as rich and powerful as you; is not a wise thing to do. This is because she or he will have the financial means to set you up; in order to 'discipline' you. Arranging armed robbers to break into your house or attack you in your car is not so difficult! In business, jealousy amongst the rich is common; and armed robberies leading to murder can be arranged, without the perpetrators ever being caught. Even if the police arrest the murderer, he may not even know who financed the killing; as it may have been a pyramid contract, where the order is handed down through several people.

4. Inevitably; most acts of violence are as a result of money or adultery. I don't know how your sex life is; but try to stay away from someone else's husband or partner because a woman hell-bent on revenge, is very hard to stop. Women tend to take things personally; and if she feels she has been wronged, she will make sure you suffer. Armed robbery cannot be ruled out; because it does not cost much to hire a thug! If a man comes on to you and you find out he is married; you should drop him, until you have real proof that he has finished with his wife. If necessary; phone or go to his wife to ask her! She will probably insult you and tell you to get lost; but at least you told her. This means that if you continue with her man and nothing happens, then it must be okay; because she will definitely let you know if it is not! If she asks you to leave her man alone; then you had better do so, or incur her wrath! There are many men in the world. Do you really need to go in for a man; who obviously belongs to a woman who could cause you problems? Men will always chase after a skirt; so it is really up to you to be strong and resist...if you don't want trouble.

D. Security

The rich are much harder to rob because they can afford the expensive security systems needed to keep the 'riff-raff' away; so those less financially fortunate are increasingly being robbed and are often viciously attacked. You have to be security conscious; in order to prevent armed attacks on yourself or your property. This means; thinking like a robber! Even if you do not have a lot of money; you can still be practical and deter anyone from robbing your house. Once you don't owe any serious money; you are not sleeping with anyone's husband and no information has filtered to the underworld that you are keeping money at home; then the chances are, the professional robbers are not going to bother with you. All that remains now; is to make it difficult for the amateurs or opportunists to rob you.

1. You should always check your gates, doors and windows; before going to bed. Unless you are expecting a friend; do not answer your door for anyone after 11 pm. Any time you leave your house to go anywhere (even for a few minutes); you should make sure everything is locked securely, if nobody is at home. If you are living in a house with a garden; keep the back door locked at all times. Thieves usually sneak in the back way; knowing that people habitually forget to lock the doors or close the windows! You will have to fast forward to Chapter 8 for more tactics; which will help you to protect your home.

2. If you are the type of person who keeps valuables in the house; you have to make sure they are insured against robberies as well as fires. The premium would be high, but worth it; because the more valuable a thing is, the more you have to make sure it is not stolen or destroyed. Expensive legal jewellery is best kept in a bank and fakes made; so that you can still show off at the ball or theatre. Many rich women are already doing this.

3. Ring the police if you hear any strange noises or see anyone lurking around your house; as they may be casing your place for a future attack. Even if it is a false alarm; the arrival of the cops will let them know that you are on the police radar. Don't forget to visit the local police station and make friends with them; so that they can put a face to your address. If the police know you personally; they will respond much more quickly to your future damsel-in-distress calls. A nice thank you card/present for the station at Xmas will do you no harm.

4. Do not allow strangers into your house at any time; especially those who claim they are coming to do a survey or sell you

something. If your intercom rings; be kind, but firm. *"Sorry I cannot open the door because I am in the bathroom." "No, I am not interested in whatever you have to offer".* If he or she persists; then a volley of abuse would send the message loud and clear. *"Fuck off, before I call the police; and don't come here again. I can see you on my CCTV!"* (Even if you don't have a closed-circuit system, he will not know that; as the cameras can be very small).

5. If anyone in uniform from the electricity/gas company wants to read your meter etc; you should refuse him/her entry, until you have asked for their name and number and verified it by ringing the company to make sure he/she is the one they sent. There have been cases of robbers pretending to be police; so the same verification rule should also apply to the cops!

6. If you regularly deposit amounts of money to the bank (from a shop for instance); try to vary the routes you take. When you do things the same way each time; it becomes easy for anyone to study your movements and know exactly when to strike.

7. Every business premise is different in size, location and value. If you own a shop or company, it would be wise to hire a reliable well-known security firm to advise you on what precautions to take; in order to deter robberies. Make sure everything is insured and keep your payments up to date. After that; the same precautions should be taken as with your house and only those you trust should have access to keys and code numbers to alarms etc.

8. If you must go out in your car; lock all your doors and only stop for a police check point. That means saying a big *"No way"* to hitchhikers, damsels in distress, roadside breakdowns and any other attempt to stop you when you are driving; day or night.

"Sorry to be so cynical Tigress; but the world has truly changed and it is always better to be safe than sorry. You only have one life; so keep it safe from those nasty armed robbers!"

Chapter Seven
Outside your home... How safe?

In this ever more demanding world, you must be mentally and physically fit to survive; because as I always stress, self-defence is really about defending yourself from any problem or adversity. The issue is not what to do when you are physically attacked; because by then it will usually be too late. Before that happens; there are many things you can do to avoid trouble. You must always strive to master (mistress?) what to do; long before the attack. It should be automatic and instinctive; otherwise you will not be able to defend yourself properly. This chapter will deal with how best to defend yourself outside your home; whether in a shop, an office, on the street, in a restaurant or any place where you will be in contact with people who do not know you. Self-defence outside your home involves your making sure you do not give anyone a chance to believe they can get one over on you. I will give you some guidelines; so that you can adapt some of them to suit your situation and the laws in your country. Things are a lot safer than they used to be, with more visible policing and ubiquitous street cameras; but that however, will not stop an amateur thief. Some of them are so young, they could rob you right in front of a police officer; and then dare him/her to chase and catch them! Also; you may travel to a foreign land where the cops might not be as efficient as the ones you are used to. Don't think it can never happen to you!

The minute you leave the sanctuary of your home; you are basically exposed to whatever fate will throw at you. From the wolf whistle to actual bodily harm; people may come to your aid in certain situations. But realistically; what happens to you while you are out, is your problem and yours alone. This means you will have to take things seriously and be your own self-defence. Relying on the police could be a little risky; because they are usually 'over-worked/under-staffed'. They may not come to your aid in time and will only show up when it suits them...always after the event! If you have the attitude *"I deserve what I get"*; you will be in a better frame of mind to deal with and even laugh, when certain things happen to you. Out of millions of people in your country; why did the bag snatcher or robber pick you to steal from? Why did the rapist choose you to rape? Why did the waiter/shopkeeper ignore you and forget to serve you; when it was obvious you were first in line? How come you can never see the boss of an establishment and his/her people keep telling you he/she has gone out; when you have only just finished talking to him/her on the phone? These are questions you must ask yourself and not curse the bag snatcher, rapist, waitress or rude receptionist; because 90% of the answers should always lead back to you. You can leave the rest to God; who I believe, only helps those who help themselves!

1. Shopping/Bag snatching

Let's take bag snatching for example. You wake up in the morning and you put on a dress, make-up etc. You get into your car and drive into the town centre. You park your car and get out to do the shopping. Where is your money? In your bag! How are you dressed? Magnificently! How is your make up? Immaculate! Who are you walking with? Alone, or with your lovable brats! What shoes are you wearing? High heels! What car did you come in? The latest convertible! How are you walking? Normally! Why? Professional thief's dream! Maybe he even lives near you and knows that every Saturday you go shopping and come back laden with food to feed your brood. He believes you must carry lots of money on you; in order for you to do that much shopping. He is well aware that your brats are a handful and your attention will be on them and not on your bag. He knows you always overdress, even though you are only going shopping; which means you are more interested in what you are wearing than the contents of your bag. He is probably hanging around the car park; watching how you get in and out of your car and laughing at the way you put down your shopping to look inside your bag, searching for your car keys. By the time you drive off; he has in his mind several ways he can snatch your bag. Although it does not mean he will snatch your bag; as many women have broken the rules for years, without any problems. But when it does happen and you are honest with yourself; you will realise that somewhere along the line, it was definitely your fault. You can get away with anything for a long time; but it only takes you to be caught out once and your whole world could come crashing down. As Sod's (Murphy's) Law ominously suggests; *"If it can go wrong...it will!"*

Never go shopping by yourself outside your area; but if you have to, remember to let a friend or relative know where you will be. Were something to happen to you; it is important that someone has an idea of your last movements. While walking in town (even in your area); always walk on the outside of the pavement, when turning a corner around which you cannot see. This is because if someone were waiting for you to snatch your bag; you will have a better chance of seeing him and screaming for help before he can attack. Mind your own business and walk with an air of confidence, without being ostentatious; all the time keeping fully alert that you are carrying a bag. If you are using a mobile phone, pushing a child in a baby-buggy or meet a friend and start talking; you should keep a tighter grip on your bag and make it obvious you have a firm grip on your belongings. Your strong body language lets the potential thief realise it would be too much hassle to try and rob you. In a strange way; there is always a sign that tells him who to strike and who not to touch. You have to remember that the thief doesn't want to get caught; so he will generally only go for something, if he feels he can get away with it. If you need to ask for directions, go into a shop; because to do so in the street would let that person and anyone else within earshot know that you are a stranger and ripe for picking. Be extra careful when walking past a group of kids; because they may try to snatch your bag as a dare or a joke. If you see a police officer and are suspicious of someone following you; don't be afraid to report him.

Dress simply and vary your shopping times. Although your job may make this difficult; it is not impossible because weekend and evening shopping are becoming more popular. Never keep lots of cash in your bag, for obvious reasons. What are credit and shopping cards for? If you are carrying a lot of money; use one of the pouches that clip around your waist and keep it out of sight. You can always go into the 'Ladies' of a department store to remove some of it and put it into your bag. It should be just enough to pay for your shopping; so that anyone watching can see you used up most of your money in the shop. If there are two of you; it is that much harder for a bag snatcher to ply his trade. It is next to impossible to snatch money from a money bag tied around your waist and invisible to the public. You can then carry a cheap bag around your shoulder; but there should be nothing valuable in it. Valuable means so much more than money. Passport, driving license and other important documents are more valuable than cash; because it is such a hassle to get them replaced.

If you can afford an expensive car; then why not have a male friend, brother or even driver come with you? At the very least, he can help you control the kids and carry your shopping! Finally, when you get into a taxi; try to watch the meter so that with time, you will always have an idea what it will cost you before you arrive at your destination. Get the money ready before you get into the car; so that you do not have to open your bag to start searching for the cash after you get out. This is because anybody could pounce and snatch your bag as your back is turned, whilst paying the driver. This way, even the driver will not know how much money you are carrying; and will not be able to relay any useful information to the criminal underworld about how rich you are or how easy it would be to rob you when you next go shopping. Always pick a taxi that can be held accountable when something goes wrong; and never take an independent taxi with someone already in it, if you don't know the person. All registered taxis are safe enough; because the driver knows he can be reported if he misbehaves, or if something happens to you under his care. Stay safe!

2. Dressing/Male attention

Ignore wolf whistles or amorous comments, if you cannot see the person doing them. Never stop to look around; wandering where the voice came from. Many a bag has been snatched in this way, by teams of two. One calls you, distracts your attention for a second; and the other snatches your bag. If however, you are able to see the person and you know him; then all well and good. Most ladies enjoy a bit of banter, praise and flattery; if they are in the right mood! If you don't know him; give a short courteous smile without being flirtatious and he will acknowledge that you are nice but not to be messed with. If he comes up to you with the usual chat-up nonsense like, *"Hi Sexy; you're so pretty, I'd like to take you out etc"*; try to be amiable, *"Thanks! You're kinda cute too. Sorry; you're too late! Someone got to me before you. I'll let you know when I'm divorced!"* Joke with him, giving him a wrong number if necessary; in order to smoothly get away from him. (You can always say you've lost your mobile; if he bumps into you again.) Even though on some days, you might be in a bad mood; you should always make an effort to be polite outside your home because a smile will take you a long way. Never be rude to anyone, if you don't have to be; as more often than not, it leads to insults and possibly violence. If he were to be carrying a weapon and in the wrong state of mind; this could result in your injury or even death...all because he being a man, had his ego bruised when you snubbed him or were rude. With the economic situation on the downturn in many countries; there are a lot of people carrying personal and mental problems and the slightest slur could set him off. You might come across him again even weeks later; and he could be harbouring a grudge against you.

Being a woman; you probably have nice expensive clothes, high heels and handbags at home. Sadly; you should not use them during shopping trips and other excursions where you may be deemed to be carrying a lot of money on you. This is because it will send a message out to any bag snatcher that if you are robbed; you will not be willing or able to run after/fight back, in case you damage your attire. If you dress simply in town (flat shoes/runners, trousers/long skirt, and Tee shirt/cardigan), you might not get any pleasantries or wolf whistles from men you don't know; but the 'blow' to your self-esteem would be worth it, as you will unlikely be targeted by the thieves as well. Try not to show off your legs or body; even if they are nice. Save that for the parties or restaurants where you will be amongst people who you know and respect you; and will therefore be able to protect you. We all like to be appreciated; but the world has changed where flaunting your sex is now deemed a prelude to molestation by undesirables. Women know men will be casting amorous glances in their direction; that is why some dress accordingly and unconsciously show off when walking. Unfortunately, this behaviour always suits a thief's script; because while she is busy wiggling her hips, she may not be able to react quickly enough when someone bumps into her and another cuts her bag off her shoulder or snatches it from her hand. She screams *"Thief!"* but she is not actually sure who stole her bag. She shouts hysterically; at the same time trying to control her kids. A few sympathisers come to her aid. The bag is eventually found. She looks inside; but it is definitely empty. This above scenario is obviously used for effect; but there is a small lesson in there somewhere for everybody. People do get robbed in broad daylight; and it is up to you to make sure you close down the possibilities of it happening to you.

The way you dress goes a long way to determine the kind of person you are; and what you want people to think about you. If you go out to town in a see-through dress; are you not inviting trouble for yourself? It means you are an extrovert and would like to be noticed. All well and good; you will be noticed as you intended. Some might go further and shout comments, rude or otherwise, at you. Others might come close and touch you. Worst of all; you just might have someone following you all the way home to know where you live and then bide his time to strike...for daring to arouse his sexual feelings! He may not strike that very day or even that week. It may take him months for him to find the right opportunity; especially if you use the same route every day and a fascination for you develops. He will one day pluck up the courage to talk to you; and if you snub him, the anger will boil up. When he does strike; don't start crying, *"Oh, I didn't know him. I've never seen him in my life!"* We live in a free society; and no one, least of all I, has a right to tell you how to dress. But I repeat; *"the world has changed and there are a lot of 'nutters' out there!"* The decision is entirely yours!

3. Witness to a crime

If you see any criminal activity happening like a bank robbery or someone breaking into a car or house; never ever get involved, because it could get you killed. You can be of much more help by quietly calling the police; or taking the picture of the thieves with your camera phone. If they have not seen you, then stay where you are and take as much detail as you can; especially the facial features and the number of their getaway car. Many gangs are heavily armed and most robberies are calculated; because the perpetrators have usually gone to a lot of expense and planning to pull it off. They will certainly not think twice about killing someone who gets in the way of their escape. As a woman, you are not expected to fight a man on his terms; so there is no need to be ashamed of yourself because you could not do more to help. If you see something that looks like a simple car theft or break in; you should still keep well away. You could probably scare him off by shouting *"Thief!"* but once again; it is best to quietly call the police. In many Third World countries, a thief would be lynched by the crowd; because once the word *"Thief!"* is shouted, everybody in the area will down tools, chase him and beat the shit out of him! His only safe place will be the police station! Crowds have been known in certain parts of Africa to catch a thief and kill him by driving a six inch nail through his eyeballs; or trapping his arms by putting a rubber tyre around him, pouring petrol over him and setting him on fire! In some Moslem countries they will still cut off the hand of a prolific thief; in order to deter others. In the so-called civilised societies, this is seen as 'barbaric'. One must wonder which system is better; as thieves and robbers blatantly ply their trade in most 'advanced' countries.

If the car/property being broken into or robbed is yours; the instinctive reaction is to rush in and have a go! This is okay if you are with a man, because any man worth his salt will challenge the thief if he is unarmed; and the two of you could then deal with him. (It would definitely be worth a few hugs and kisses from you!). However; if you are alone, do not try to fight him. It would instead be better to clandestinely call the cops; because depending on how far gone he is with the robbery, shouting will probably not stop him. The problem with being a woman in a robbery situation is; the thief will not take you seriously. Men are brought up believing they can easily beat up any woman. If you try to stop him, he will be obliged to fight back; and even though you might be a judo or karate expert, there is no guarantee that you will not get hurt badly. This is because he could also be a good fighter; as many thieves have grown up in the rougher areas of a city and are therefore seasoned street combatants. No car/property is worth six months in hospital on a life support machine. Call the police and give them the details of your car and it will be found within days; because most stolen cars are used for a specific purpose and then dumped somewhere. If you are insured against damage and theft, then you have nothing to worry about; because nowadays it is difficult to sell a stolen car. Also; new preventive systems are around, making it much harder to steal a car or break into a property…so try to make sure yours is well equipped.

People blame the police for unsolved crimes; but they are not magicians and need information in order to combat crime. If for instance, they were told the valid facts concerning the movement of a woman from the time she left the house to the time she was last seen, including the number of the car she was last seen in; don't you think it would make it easier for them to find out who raped, robbed or murdered her? I am not a police officer; but I do feel sorry for the difficulties they encounter. A policewoman investigating a rape and murder of one of her sex; must be very traumatic. We should blame ourselves for giving crime a chance to take place, by not reporting any suspicious thing we see or feel; and for not taking enough precautions. We are responsible for each other in our own circle of friends; so you should make it a point to make sure those you care about are safe, by keeping in regular contact. Although some crimes like drive-by shootings are dangerous; they are not impossible to stop, if we reported all suspect behaviour to the police or the person we think the behaviour could affect. This will give him/her a chance to stop a crime before it starts. For example; if you think those youths loitering outside a shop could pose a danger to the shopkeeper, then tell him/her and let them decide what to do. If something bad happens; it will always feel worse if you found out there was something you could have done about it, but failed to do so, usually because you felt it was none of your business. Obviously, there are deeper reasons for crime; but why not give this paragraph a thought?

4. Going out…

We are now going to look at how you can defend yourself in certain situations when you go out. I probably do not live in your town or country; which means everything I teach is a guideline, which you must adapt to suit your situation. You therefore have to make sure that you feel comfortable with what you are doing; and if you don't, then you should make some adjustments. The idea is your complete mental and physical self-defence; so that you can live to a respectable old age, injury free…with your property, reputation, integrity and anything else that you care about, intact and untarnished. Never go out for walks or on a night out by yourself! (*"I'm sounding like a worn-out record, aren't I?"*) But I have to stress the importance of having company wherever you go; and the more people you go with the better. Men will never admit it; but a pack of six to eight women walking down the street is an intimidating sight and they will keep their comments and hands to themselves. No man likes to be at the receiving end of the acid tongues of women in a group! Obviously, if you live in a small town and everybody knows you; then you are in your environment and it is safe enough to go to the shops or visit a neighbour on your own. It is still advisable to tell someone in your house, where you will be. If you live alone; then make sure someone always knows how you are. A phone call a day to a friend is not very time-demanding; so that the day he or she does not get a call from you will signal something is wrong and they can come to your aid. If you live in a big city; it is much safer to go out with somebody. If you have to stray outside your area, make sure you keep your mobile phone handy; to let someone know you are no longer where you said you would be. If you are the type that insists on wearing alluring attire; then for your own sake, go with a friend...preferably a male if you are going out at night and a female if it is in the daytime.

If you are going for a walk in secluded woodland; try to go with someone. If the area is known to you and you prefer to walk with your dog, then it would be more fun to alternate the times and routes you take; so that you never do the same thing two days running. Although it is rare; it has been known for women to be attacked and raped on country lanes and behind thick bushes in desolate areas. This kind of attack is only possible if the attacker has watched the victim and studied her movements; so that he knows exactly when to strike without getting caught. If you are with someone; it makes it a lot harder for any molester to trouble/attack/rape you. If you stick to public paths frequented by others; you will in time become greeting friends with those who go for walks at the same time as you. This in itself becomes your self-defence; because anyone watching you will realise that one scream from you will alert them. Keep your mobile phone handy and wear shoes you can run fast in; just in case you have to report a crime on someone else and have to escape from the perpetrators. Make sure you obey the rules concerning animals because not all of them are comfortable around humans; and there is a possibility you could be attacked by an angry bull, if you stray into private farmland. You could also be prosecuted for trespassing; so keep an eye open for signs, because ignorance cannot be used as a defence in a court of law! If someone comes up to you with the regular chat-up lines; you have to use your feminine guile and keep him at bay. You should never make it too easy for him by giving away sensitive information like where you live/work or your phone number; because you don't really know him. All potential rapists appear charming at the onset; so it would be better to be firm and tell any suitor: *"Sorry to be rude; but I prefer to walk with my dog..."* and move away from him. The next time you go for a walk; change the time and route so that he doesn't 'accidentally' bump into you again. If you like him; you can arrange to meet in your local bar for a drink, later on during the week. You could then bring your friends with you; so that you can all put him through a typical fearsome female interrogation process. Only if you are satisfied; should you allow him, one step at a time, into your life. Who knows? He may become the best thing that has ever happened to you; but it always pays to be cautious.

Your self-defence outside your home also means being accountable to those you care about. This is because if something happened to them; your life would be seriously affected and a part of your soul will die. It seems very utopian, but if we all loved each other and took some kind of responsibility for those close to us, then we would care enough to want to be sure nothing untoward happened to them; by taking pains to protect each other. Mobile phones with cameras and hand-held computers that can send Emails in a split-second; what is so hard about taking the picture of the car and that guy your sister left with? How arduous is it to send a text message to your friend; to let her know you are okay, the morning after a night out with a man you had met in the bar? I bet if you suspected your partner of having an affair; you would want to know his whereabouts, twenty-four hours a day! You have to value your man enough; to ask him exactly where he is going, when he will be back and what route he is going to take. It may annoy him at first; but once he gets used to the fact that you care about him, then those questions will not seem so petty. However; he also has a right to ask you the same questions. They may seem inquisitive; but if something were to happen to one of you, the other would be the only person who could help the police solve the crime. You therefore lie at your own risk. If for example, you have a boyfriend he does not know about; you obviously cannot tell your partner where you are really going. In such a scenario; you must have a friend close enough to confide in as to where you are at all times. Someone has to back you up; in case your partner starts asking awkward questions!

Most people take going out for granted and just walk out of their houses or get into their cars and zoom off. Nobody really knows where. You might read in the papers a few days later; of a dead body, found riddled with bullets. You have not seen your husband or his car for a few days. He has not even rung and you cannot get him on his mobile. He normally disappears for days at a time on 'business', but always returns with (guilt?) presents for you; so that 'dead body riddled with bullets' cannot be him. Meanwhile the body lies in the mortuary unclaimed for a few days or even weeks. The robbers have disappeared with the car. You go about your daily routine. A few weeks go by and eventually, you go to the police to report a missing person. Finally, they find his body in the mortuary. Now comes the identification horror. *"It's him!"* you scream. The cops politely ask if you could furnish them with any details as to where your husband was going, when you last saw him. You don't know. You mumble something about him going out on business. Where? You don't know. The police ask you to claim the body and tell you they will let you know of any further developments. Another crime unsolved. This scenario is played out around the world, more times than you can imagine; so always assume it could happen to you and act accordingly. It is not paranoia; just playing safe in a dangerous world.

When you go out, try not to get so drunk you cannot function properly; because too many things can go wrong and you will definitely be taken advantage of by opportunistic men. I once saw a woman sitting on a pavement, drunk out of her mind. All of a sudden, she started peeing on herself. Not very ladylike! A taxi driver told me that it is mostly drunk women who vomit and urinate on the back seat of taxis. I will sympathise with them because it is not always easy to find a toilet in town. Men by nature have no qualms about peeing anywhere; but it takes a brave (drunk) woman to bare all and piss in the gutter, in front of strangers. To do this would be an attack on your femininity, dignity and reputation; which is not really good self-defence! Apart from the abuse and wisecracks you will get from equally drunk men; how would you like to be arrested for urinating on the street? It would make headlines in your local paper; with maybe a nice snap taken by someone with a camera phone. The picture of you peeing could even show up on the Internet; whereas, if a man were caught, it would not be news. Think before leaving a venue, if you have been drinking; because a bladder fills up very quickly when alcohol is imbibed.

The little things are the most important when going out. Life can be cruel at times; and the day your insurance or road tax runs out, is the day the traffic police will see fit to stop you! Is your cell phone charged enough to last the time you are out? Does anybody know where you are going? Are you carrying enough cash; so that you don't have to depend on anyone? Will there be a toilet where you are going; so that you don't start looking for one when you are caught short? The shortage of and lack of hygiene in public conveniences makes this an important issue; especially when most pubs and restaurants frown on people coming in to use their toilets, without buying anything. Using your lavatory at home before going out may seem like common sense; but who can honestly say they have never been in town and have suddenly needed to find a toilet quickly? Can you imagine bursting to use the loo; and you are suddenly accosted by a nuisance who tries to chat you up and keeps following you? What of the drop-dead gorgeous guy you've got your eye on in the department store? Looking for the ladies room in the store will mean losing him; because he would be gone by the time you got back! Have you ever had a fight or an argument when you've got a running stomach? Hilarious talking about it; but not so funny if it happens to you!

5. Public relations…

(a). Reception

Remember when you go into someone's reception area, café, shop, restaurant or office; to be courteous to those working there. Try to respect the fact that he or she might be feeling ill, having problems or suffering a bereavement; each of which will not put him/her in a good mood. Have you ever tried smiling; when you have a severe tummy, ear or toothache? How about if you have just been unceremoniously dumped by your man for a younger model? Although one is not supposed to bring one's problems to work; there are some difficulties, which make this impossible. It would therefore be in your favour to keep that in mind; whenever you walk into someone's territory. Even though the customer is 'always right', you should never get angry or argue with an employee who is rude; but rather make a complaint through the right channels, by asking to talk to the manager. If he/she is conveniently absent; you must stay calm. When you get home; phone or write a letter outlining your disgust with the treatment you received. This should be followed up, the next time you go there. If you don't get an apology or any satisfaction; then leave and never go back. You probably have better things to do with your time than to pamper to an ignoramus! It would be their loss when they lose your custom and the patronage of all your friends. If the insulting treatment you received is really serious (racial, religious, sexual, misogynistic); you should seek legal counsel about suing the culprit and putting the frighteners on him/her, because that is the only language a bigot understands. Throwing your weight around might solve your problem temporarily; but you may end up becoming a marked woman. This in turn will hinder your next visit; because he/she will use delaying tactics to make sure you don't get what you are looking for. Politeness and patience is the key. Once people don't get the impression you are being pushy; you will find they will do a lot more for you. If it is a place you will be frequenting; then a nice compliment as you leave, will work wonders for the future. Surly or rude; you will need the receptionist, shop keeper or waitress on your next visit. A friendly smile will let him or her understand that nothing will faze you; and their attitude will change. It is human nature for someone to feel he or she is the king/queen of their castle; so don't give them the chance to throw their weight on you!

(b). Shop

All shop keepers have one purpose and that is to make you spend your money; so be careful when you are told things like, *"this item would be perfect for you Madam..."* or *"why don't you try this dress/shoe in a different colour?"* etc. Having someone with you, will help keep you in check; so that you don't go over-board and buy things you have no real use for. Make sure you only remove money from your bag, if you are going to buy something and not change your mind at the last minute; so that you are not left standing, talking to the shopkeeper whilst holding a wad of notes in your hand. It will alert any potential thief; who could easily wait till you leave the shop, follow and then rob you. If you are using a credit card; make sure the transaction is done in front of you, so that you know exactly what is going on. Taking your card away from you, could open a can of worms; whereby your number could easily be copied and sold to crooks, who could quickly make up a replica card and clean out your account. Even if you are insured against card theft; it will not do your credit rating any good and could easily hamper any loan application you might seek from your bank. Don't be over-friendly with the shopkeeper; because he/she is only being nice to you, in order to make a sale. If he starts flirting with you; it is just a ploy to make you part with your money. It does not necessarily mean you have a chance with him! Even though he may genuinely fancy you; he most likely loves his job more and will not be prepared to lose it by 'fraternising' with a customer. If a shop employee is rude to you; then the same tactics should be used as with any other public sector worker. Report him/her to a higher authority; or sue the shop, if the treatment you received warrants it. You must never receive a hurtful insult and let it slide; because the culprit needs to be taught a lesson, before he/she goes and does it to someone else. Show him/her that you are one 'bitch' who will not be insulted, patronised or pushed around; without a fight!

(c). Restaurant

There are obviously certain situations whereby you must dress magnificently and carry enough money, in order to protect yourself; like going out to a fancy restaurant, theatre, fashion show or top-notch party. Again, it is better not go out alone. You should also have your transport (taxi, limousine or a date who can drive and does not drink) pre-arranged; so that you don't have to walk too far in your high heels. If your bag is snatched; you will not be able to fight or run to catch the thief! Dressing magnificently means wearing something noteworthy (expensive or unique); being neat and immaculate with perfectly manicured hands, exquisite coiffure with just the right amount of make-up! (I can hear you saying... *"What does he know about women and their dressing/make-up?"*). The answer is, *"I don't!"* but like most men, I would find it hard not to fawn over a woman who is looking a million dollars. Human nature tends to gravitate kindly towards the women who look elegant and stylish. Being beautiful helps; but without class, style or grace, it does not mean much. If she makes an effort; any woman can look fantastic and be treated like a queen!

Waiters/waitresses always appreciate class; and that is why stylish women continuously get the best tables. If you want to be treated well in a restaurant; you must start off well in the employees' eyes! As you enter, do not be a bossy-boots; but take your time and allow them to find you a suitable table. If however; the place they have chosen for you is not to your liking, then politely say so. You should never throw your weight around, shouting for the manager; as that would betray your upbringing and your fancy clothes will mean nothing. It will also alienate you from them and they might relay their anger to the cook. He/She in turn might decide to put too much salt in your food or dilly-dally with it completely; and you could be waiting a long time for your meal. *"That will teach the bitch!"* Never be rude to a waiter/waitress and always tip handsomely; if you have every intention of returning to the same restaurant. If the food is good; try to compliment the chef by way of the serving staff. If the meal is disgusting; never betray your dislike for it. Either you eat it quietly; or leave the food, pay your bill and never go back there again. Discreetly complaining is okay; only if you have been frequenting the establishment and are on first name terms with the chef or waiters. But if you are not; it will do you no good to kick up a fuss. Chefs are notoriously prickly to any criticism of their craft; and have been known to spit in the food and mix it up out of spite, before serving it...and you will never know! Sommeliers actually enjoy showing off their knowledge and advising on which wine is in season and which goes best with your food etc. You should therefore never pretend to know all about wines when you don't; because you will be quickly found out and labelled a nouveau-riche know-all parody, who drinks and talks rubbish. I don't believe you deserve to be the butt of waiters' jokes; whilst wearing your expensive dress and jewellery! Unladylike!

(d). Office

As a modern woman; you will sooner or later have to go into a man's office, either on business or to progress in your chosen career. We all need people in influential positions, in order to get ahead! This makes a woman vulnerable to underhand tactics by some men; who will use their positions to crush her to the point that she will become so desperate she will do anything for the man, she believes can help her. The laws on sexism prevent men from acting so blatantly, as to demand sex on a quid-pro-quo basis; but some will use clever and subtle tactics to achieve the same result. *"There's a party tonight where I can introduce you to some influential people..."*, or *"Why don't we go for a bite to eat; so that we can go over your figures and projections for your business plan..."*. This is because he believes she will be more susceptible to his advances in a convivial atmosphere, where he can show off his industry connections; which obviously, she can only get to through him. In such a scenario; many women will agree to the invitation, because making money and career gratification is still more important than personal relationships. Her partner will just have to learn to live with it; or lose her! If she refuses his solicitation; he will suddenly act like she doesn't exist, by politely getting rid of her with, *"Thank you Madam; I will be in touch after I have talked to a few people..."*. She will then find that he is never in, whenever she phones his office. De rigueur; he will try the same tactic on someone else, because clearly, such a man is not looking for any long-term relationship but is using his position to subjugate the fairer sex.

Before going into any man's office; you should always let a good friend know where you are going and to phone you on your mobile at a given time. You can have her wait conveniently for you in the car park or a nearby café. You can use her as an excuse to escape; in case the meeting does not go to your plan! Never go with your boyfriend or have him waiting outside for you; because any man, who agrees to do this, is a pimp in disguise. He obviously knows he will be a beneficiary, to whatever you gain by going into the man's office. If he is not acting like a pimp; he could get jealous and start imagining all kinds of things going on inside. After all; they do have couches…! There will be a strain on your relationship and you will start arguing over trivial matters; especially when business with the man you went to see, starts eating into the time you normally spend with him. It is difficult I know; but if your relationship with your partner is important, you should stay clear of such modus-operandi. It would be better to look for less ambitious or more predictable jobs; which will not take up so much of your time. Business is best left to single women who are answerable to no one; because few men are emotionally strong enough to handle the competition.

Sometimes you must dress well and go alone, in order to be successful in whatever you are doing; and you definitely do not need men tagging along. If you are beautiful and are going to see some 'lecherous big-shot' in his office; you will not get what you want by having a man by your side. It might be better to go with an equally drop-dead gorgeous girlfriend; because if he is in a horny mood, he will find it much harder to try it on when you are with another girl who could be a witness to any lascivious moves on his agenda. If you are lucky and your friend is that way inclined; he might prefer her instead of you and that way, everyone goes home happy! (*"Sorry Tigress; just being mischievous!"*). To get what you want from this type of man, who most likely has a wife and kids at home but still prefers the 'younger chicks'; you have to let him think he will get what he wants from you, (either sex or to make money out of you) while you remain determined he won't! Wearing nice expensive attire and acting in a friendly but professional manner, will tell him you can look after yourself and are not in desperate need of money; so that you will be able to get down to some serious business. If you feel he is looking for sex and wants a date before granting you what you came for; you are better off politely telling him you will see him about that another time. You should then make an excuse and leave his office; because you cannot get something after sex that you could not get before! If he calls you back; then it means he understands you will not be kowtowed and he will treat you with a lot more respect. Your business plan will be treated on its merits and will most likely succeed; if only to hide his embarrassment. If he lets you go easily; then it means you would not have got what you wanted anyway, without the sex. You are better off looking for someone else to help you!

If you really need something whereby no one else is in the same position to help you; then you must give him hope that if after you have got what you want from him, you might go out on a date with him! Flirt and be nice without going too far and always maintain your sense of humour; because he is a man and all men will try it on in one way or another with a woman. It is natural; therefore you have to learn how to 'swerve, bob and weave' without actually getting caught. It is an art many women are good at; so it would be in your interests to perfect it, in order to survive in what is still a male-oriented business world. If however you either fancy him or you think that is the only way to further your prospects; then go ahead and make his day. Always remember that it is your decision and your personal business; so there is no need to tell even your best friend, in case it comes back to haunt you one day. Prostitution appears in many forms and sometimes you have to weigh your options and take your chances while you can. You would not be the first or the last; because as a means to an end, it has worked with many a woman who are now in lucrative positions they would never have got to, had they not done the 'right thing at the right time' in their careers!

(e). Public transport

Going by train is generally comfortable and safe, except on weekends, where the carriages may be crowded and you may come across supporters on the way to or coming back from a sports game. They are likely to be loud, drunk and singing bawdy songs, which may offend you; so telling them to keep the noise down will only make matters worse and you could be teased or insulted. Fights have been known to break out amongst rival supporters; so it would be advisable to avoid travelling by train on weekends. Don't try to dodge paying for your ticket by hiding in the toilet; because there is an inspector who comes around to check and knows all the tricks. If you are caught; you will be fined far in excess of the value of the ticket. The chances of being molested and attacked on a train are slim; so once you get a seat, just put on your *I pod* earphones, get stuck into a good book and you will be left alone to enjoy the journey. Try to keep your eye on your luggage; because anybody could steal your suitcase when the train stops at a station. There are certain popular brands of suitcase which are used by thieves; whereby they will get onto a train with a suitcase full of old clothes and put it with the rest of the other passenger's luggage. When the train stops, they will 'accidentally' pick up the wrong suitcase and walk off with someone else's belongings. If they are stopped, they will pretend they don't speak your language; and it would seem like a foreigner made a genuine mistake because of the similarities between the two suitcases.

The underground trains are the same all over the world, in that it is true survival of the fittest; and if you are not careful, you will be swept along in a tidal wave of physical discomfort. It can become very crowded during the rush-hour with people moving quickly to and fro; making it easy for pick-pockets to ply their trade. Although there are closed-circuit cameras in all stations; it is not really a deterrent, because the thief knows he will be able to snatch a handbag and escape before the police arrive. Even if he is caught; he is unlikely to be jailed, because pick-pocketing is still seen more as a misdemeanour than a felony. Always mind your own business and keep focused on your destination stop. If you pay too much attention on other people; you will lose concentration on yourself and your belongings! By all means fight for your seat and having got one, don't bother getting up; unless you are feeling charitable towards a pregnant lady or a senior citizen and would like to give it to them. If it will make you uncomfortable; be stubborn and don't allow anyone to bully you into moving up and squashing you. It is unlikely anyone would attack you in a crowded carriage; but when standing, try not to give any lecherous rat an excuse to rub his erection against you. Men love it during a crush because there is no room for you to move away; and the movement of the train will give him a lovely sexual thrill! Give him a nasty look to let him know that you are aware of what he is doing; and you won't stand for it. You can 'accidentally' stamp on his toes when the train shakes and then smile sweetly, while telling him *"Sorry!"* The crime rate is a lot higher at night; so you should never travel late alone. If you are in a carriage with some suspicious looking youths; it would be better to move through to another carriage or get off at the next stop and wait for another train.

Going by bus is routinely safe during the day; and since most bus services have reasonable closing times, you are unlikely to have any problems in the evenings either. However; if you don't like noisy or boisterous teenagers, you should avoid taking a bus around school opening and closing times. If it is a double-decker bus; sitting downstairs close to the driver will save you any hassle from troublesome kids. If the bus is too full, the driver will not stop; so you can wait for the next one, which means you will usually get a seat. If you are carrying shopping bags; keep an eye on them, if you have to stand in the aisle for a few stops...just in case someone helps himself to some of your groceries! If you are a senior citizen or pregnant, you are usually entitled to a seat; so don't be afraid to ask a young male to vacate his seat for you. Few would refuse; or they risk condemnation from all the females on the bus. If you are going home alone at night and you do not feel safe because there is a 'dangerous looking man' on the bus; you should move and sit by the driver. If you suspect the man may get off at the same time as you; ring a friend or a neighbour to meet you at your bus stop and walk with you home. On longer journeys; going by coach is probably the most dependable form of transport, but is also the slowest. If you want an enjoyable and comfortable trip; where you can leave and arrive on time, view the beautiful countryside, make several stops at popular tourist locations and reach safely at your destination...then the coach is the way to go!

Because of its sensitive position as an entry and exit point of a country; an airport is generally very safe. There are closed-circuit cameras, security personnel and plain clothed police officers everywhere; and anybody causing trouble will be quickly apprehended. If someone bothers you; all you have to do is raise your voice, *"Please leave me alone...!"* and a security person will come to your rescue. This also means that you should not cause trouble by yelling and abusing the ticket desk for a delayed flight or try to exceed the excess baggage rule; because the airline officials will not change their mind. You will be branded a nuisance; embarrassed by the security staff and insulted by the other passengers in the queue. Don't try to dodge the smoking ban by sneaking a quick puff in the toilet; because the cleaners will report you. Most importantly; don't carry anything on your person which you know to be illegal (weapons, drugs, excess money). If caught; you will be arrested, questioned intensively and possibly prosecuted...inevitably missing your flight. Once you are on-board the plane; be on your best behaviour and obey the instructions of the cabin crew. Don't get too drunk and make a pestering nuisance of yourself; because you will be handed over to the police when the plane arrives at its destination...ruining your travel plans and your reputation.

On occasions, you might go on a ferry or a cruise ship. These are very safe; in that there are lots of closed-circuit cameras and security on board. It would therefore be unwise to cause any trouble; because you will be arrested when you arrive at your next port of call. Due to the high-alert state of emergency at all air and sea ports; the police and security personnel take a very dim view of troublemakers. You may not be treated well and may be man-handled! With the modern phenomenon of terrorism; it is understandable why we all have to go through rigid security checks. Sometimes the police are deemed to have exceeded their powers; so be warned! In all public transport systems; you have to remember that you are on government property and the full force of the law will come crashing down on you, if you are perceived as a threat to the safety and security of the other passengers. Millions of people do it every day with very few nasty incidents; so there is no need to be unduly worried about travelling. Nevertheless; you should still keep your eyes open, mind your own business, move away from anyone you feel is bothering you and report any suspicious activity to the authorities...and let them deal with it!

(f). Double-dealing

If you are in a relationship and you want to go out with somebody else on a date; then why go to the club where your boyfriend frequents? Couldn't you have chosen another place to take your secret date? A lot of fights have been caused because a boy took out a certain girl, paid the gate fee for her and bought her drinks; only for her to see her partner/friends and abandon the guy she came with. If you do that; you are asking for trouble because your man will definitely come and talk to you, just to show the guy you came with that even though he is with you, he the (ex?) boyfriend is still the boss. If you try to ignore your boyfriend; you risk a bust-up and he might try to assert himself by asking you to dance. The guy you came with will try to defend you. A fight, during which you will definitely be hurt, either emotionally, physically or both; will ensue. If you agree to dance with him and you spend too long on the floor; the guy you came with will be annoyed. He might come up to you on the floor and ask you (pull you?) back to sit down. If you refuse; there will be a fight! It has been known to happen that the guy who came with the girl, demanded compensation from the boyfriend for all the money he had already spent on the girl! This included his petrol cost, restaurant bill, gate fee, drinks he had bought and the time he had spent that evening; before he would let her go! He being much bigger and stronger than the boyfriend, won; and the latter paid up to get his girl back. I can imagine what he would have done to her when they got home! She didn't make a good job of defending herself because her loyalty should have been with the person she came with; or made it clear to him that she was already in a relationship. If you feel you are liberated and value your independence; you should go out with female friends, pay your own gate and drinks and then you can do whatever you like, because no man can claim they 'own' you for the night. Men have always had a financial advantage over women and that is why some females still allow men to buy them drinks; even though they have enough money on them and have no intention of taking things further. This is understandable because men are by nature protective and possessive and they will always feel they have to look after a woman; even if she is built like a tank or is a ball-crunching millionairess. Things are changing, but not quickly enough; because most men are slow to realise that women are quite capable of looking after themselves. Sorry ladies, that's the way things are at the moment; so please be careful when accepting anything from any man who is not your partner.

You should never get into anyone's bad books unnecessarily; because thoughts of revenge lurk in everybody's mind and some will stop at nothing till they achieve it. If you owe money; you should obviously not go anywhere you think your creditor will be waiting for you. If you want a peaceful life; it would be better not to owe any money! Ignorance of the law is no excuse; so if you don't want trouble from the police, you find out what the law is and obey it! If you don't want any hassle from your landlord, Electricity Board, Water Corporation or Telephone Company; you should obviously pay your bills. It would be a shame if thieves broke into your house in the middle of the night; and you couldn't call the cops because your phone had been cut off! If you are working or pretending to be an invalid and claiming money off the State; you will sooner or later be found out and the damage to your reputation can never be repaired. If you default on a bank loan; you will be put on a debtor's list and will find it impossible to get credit from any other financial institution. If you don't want problems with your partner/husband; then you have to be honest and stay faithful. Don't flirt or keep two or three lovers on the go; because this always leads to trouble! There are certain everyday situations which, if abused, will be dangerous and detrimental to our well-being; but it seems some women thrive on this and live from day to day, without caring what happens. There is always an effect to every cause (what goes round comes around) and when you double-deal you will one day be found out; so why complicate your life by doing things you know will give you problems? Only you can answer that question for yourself!!!

6. Driving

(a). Accidents

First and foremost, you have to understand that we all have bad days; when we are ready to scream and shout, and in some cases, hit anyone who annoys or looks at us in the wrong way. Always assume every driver is in a bad mood; and do your best not to antagonise anyone on the road. With the high price of petrol and modern traffic congestion making driving so stressful; it is a safe bet to assume that the street is not the best place to find a happy person. Drive carefully and stick to the rules of the road; which also mean being polite and not driving aggressively. Even though you are confident of your vehicle skills; you should never assume that everybody else drives as well (badly?) as you. Always keep your eyes open; because accidents usually happen when both participants are not paying attention. If you cross someone or do something silly on the road; then a gentle wave or a quick flash of your headlights/hazard lights is accepted as an apology. If you are in eye contact; roll your window down and apologise. A simple *"Sorry"* with a smile and some feminine charm; will be enough to cool most people down and prevent their temper levels rising beyond control. If you dismiss his/her feelings; you run the risk of turning a reasonable person into an animal. Most men have not got a good opinion of women drivers; even though statistics in many countries show that women are actually safer drivers. This is good for you; because it means you can get away with a lot of malpractices on the road that a man would not. With a woman driver; you have to be careful. If your smile and feminine charm are not genuine; she will quickly see through you and it may annoy her even more! After waving to her; you should avoid eye contact, keep driving and thank your stars that you cannot hear the delightful names she is calling you!

If you scrape a vehicle and know it is your fault; never drive away thinking you will get away with it. The chances are; someone will have noted down your car number! A visit from the police will follow; and you will be charged and presumed guilty for running away. It would be better to quickly find a safe place to stop the car; come out, apologise and exchange car numbers and addresses. Either offer to pay for the damage; or assure him/her your insurance company will deal with it. If the damage is minimal; it might be better to give him/her the money to repair the car. If it is serious; then you have to keep your mouth firmly shut, wait until the police arrive and let them handle it. If you are not sure it is your fault; never ever apologise for an accident. Wait for the police to decide that! If you reverse into a car and there are no reliable witnesses; you could claim that he/she drove into you! Once you say *"I'm sorry"*; it becomes an acceptance of guilt and you might be biting off more than you can chew. You could be fined, banned from driving for a few years or lose your licence completely. Always remember not to drink or take drugs and drive. If it is shown by a breathalyser that you have been drink/drug driving; any accident would be deemed your fault and you could even be jailed. Once they know you are intoxicated; *"But officer, he drove into me!"* will not wash with the cops and they won't listen to your pleas.

Now let's suppose we are dealing with a male lunatic on the road. You have scraped his car and thought you could get away with it. He stops his car and comes out with a face like thunder. If you are near a police station and you can drive off without crashing into another car; then do so, as soon as he steps out of his car. You had better be quick; because he will definitely get back into his car and chase after you! Drive into the police station and report the incident; giving the cops his car number and explaining exactly what happened (the truth please). The police will know what to do, if he is lurking around nearby; and the chances are, he will accept defeat and drive off. Don't think he has forgotten; because he could still report you for scraping his car. Luckily; you would have already told the police the truth. They will contact him; and that should be enough to prevent him doing anything to you...even if he does see you again. If you are driving and feel you are being followed; you should drive straight into a police station and report the car number to them.

If you cannot drive away because you are stuck in traffic and he comes ranting and raving to your window; don't be scared, because he probably only needs an apology. Roll down your window and be as sweet as pie; which I know you can be, if you really need to. Damage limitation is best for you in this situation; so apologise for scraping his car and offer to pay for the damage, if it is minor. If it is serious; you have no choice but to call the police and pray that your licence, road tax and insurance are up-to-date. It is embarrassing for many women to be involved in a traffic argument; so park your car on a side road and come out and exchange details in a civilised way, away from too many prying eyes. The apology is most important; because many people find it hard to say *"sorry"*. If you feel the accident was not your fault, then there is no need to apologise; but you have to find another way to cool him down. To forgive and forget is not easy; when the fender of his brand new motor has been scratched and he is already in a bad mood from something else that happened earlier in the day. Don't joke about it. Be nice and sympathetic to him, and who knows; you could even end up becoming good friends, (lovers, wedding bells?)...not impossible!

(b). Road rage

The aggressive behaviour by a motorist in response to the actions of another road user; is what is commonly known as road rage. If it happened to you; could you handle it on your own? Are you sure? Could you deal with an irate ignoramus who deliberately rams your car; and then comes out to threaten you, claiming it was your fault? What if he punches a hole in your window and grabs you by the throat? An angry man will not care; even if you are in the middle of town. He could do a lot of damage before the police arrive. Although that is an extreme case, they do happen; and any frightening situation would be hard to deal with alone. You are supposed to feel safe in your car; but in a road rage situation, the car can actually make you defenceless. There is nowhere to run; and if your windows are rolled up, nobody will hear your screams. If you drive off; he will get into his car and chase after you, which will make your situation a lot worse, if he catches you. It is rare to find a female 'road-rager'; but not impossible. If you come up against one; you can give as good as you get and this means squaring up to her, if necessary. You will surely know how to handle any lip she might threaten you with, as most women do; but if she is bigger and tougher than you, treat her like a man and call the cops. If she touches you; sue her for assault!

If you see anyone being attacked in a road rage incident; use your cell phone and call the police. Getting yourself involved is not good self-defence! Stay in your car and don't try to have a go; because you could be tragically hurt. Sadly; the person being attacked might be at fault because he might owe a large sum of money and is receiving his comeuppance. It could also be part of a criminal war; which has nothing to do with you. If you see anything dangerous happening on the road; then mind your own business, call the police and keep moving. Very few people are beaten up for no reason at all! The mere fact that anyone could be so blatantly attacked; means there is far more to the situation than warrants your intrusion. If the attack is on you; it is generally because you did something on the road without apologising, as described earlier on. This idea that you can do what you like and 'sod the consequences'; is what is most likely to rankle someone enough to teach you a lesson. If you see anyone following you after you have traded insults; then you are in trouble and you should drive into a police station. He obviously has time on his hands and will follow you home if necessary! You should have apologised! Naughty girl! Now he is after you. *"Help! What shall I do? I don't know where the nearest police station is!"*

If he is really angry; then stop your engine, come out of your car and try to diffuse the situation. Staying in your car is dangerous; because he will think you are trying to fob him off and his anger will increase. He might break your window and grab you. You can phone the police; but by the time they arrive, he might have already smashed your windscreen or damaged your car out of frustration. The flying bits of glass could easily blind you. If you come out of your car and the situation becomes uncontrollable; you can treat it like any other attack, by running away screaming and shouting for the police. Don't try to physically fight him; because you could lose and be severely hurt. Button your lip; unless it is to try and calm him down. Trading insults will make him angrier and he might 'lose it'. Remember; the law is on your side in that you could sue him, if he dares hit you. There will usually be enough witnesses in the traffic for him not to physically attack you; but to be safe, don't do anything to aggravate the situation. If he pokes you with his finger or pushes you; then collapse in a heap on the ground, making it seem far worse than it really is. Start shouting and crying; and you can attract all the sympathy in the world. You scraped him and you tried to run away; but he still has no right to touch you and he will be prosecuted when the police arrive. It's still good to be a woman! Road rage is very common; but it could be a thing of the past, if more people learnt to accept when they are wrong and apologised. As in all walks of life; politeness is the key to staying safe on the road...so take good care, please.

(c). Safety Measures

Your safety is paramount anytime you go out. You must therefore treat your car as an extension of you and part of your self-defence; because whatever happens to your car whilst you are driving, will affect you. The police can also stop you for many things you might consider trivial, like speeding or using a mobile phone;

which could land you in trouble and your car seized from you, ruining your whole day. You are supposed to keep both hands on the steering wheel whilst driving; which means you are technically breaking the law if you open a drink, peel a banana or eat a sandwich! Did you also know that you can be stopped by the police in countries where there is a smoking ban in public places, for smoking in a company car; because it constitutes a place of work? When was the last time your car had a check-up? Are all the lights working? Are your tyres in good condition? When did you last have an oil change? Has your insurance or road tax expired? Have you got enough petrol to take you where you are going; so that you don't end up in the embarrassing position of having to push your car to the nearest filling station? Speed cameras are everywhere in most modern cities; and once they photograph your car speeding, the police will have your number plate on their computer. This means they will also have the name and address of the car owner. This will open the door to other infractions in your family; like unpaid parking tickets, bank loans, credit card bills and criminal records.

How good is the security on your car; in order to prevent or delay a break-in or theft? Whilst driving; keep your door locked and the windows rolled up enough not to allow someone to put his hand into your car and snatch your handbag. Some thieves have even been known to blatantly open the door and steal a handbag, whilst the car is waiting at the traffic lights. There is no way you would be able to stop your car, get out, chase and catch him; so keep any valuable item out of sight, either in the boot or on the floor under the seat. Make sure there is nothing valuable in view inside the car when you park it. A thief will take the risk of smashing your window in order to steal something he likes; and will probably escape before the police arrive. If you enjoy music in your car; try to ensure the system is either one that cannot be removed easily or the type you can remove yourself and hide away as deterrence. When buying a car; talk with the seller about the security features and have them upgraded, if necessary. It makes no sense spending a lot of money on a car that can easily be broken into and stolen. If you can afford it, you should join a reliable automobile organisation in your country; so that you can call them, if your car breaks down in the middle of nowhere. Although they will never admit it; these organisations respond a lot quicker to women, especially if you say you are alone, than they do with men. You might as well take advantage of their bias in favour of the fairer sex!

If you cannot be bothered to join an automobile club; then it makes sense when going out, to have a trusted man with you to help...in case you get into trouble. For example; if after an enjoyable night out, you had a puncture on your way home or your car was snatched by robbers as you were about to get in; could you fix the puncture on your own or physically defend yourself from the attack? Do you really need that kind of hassle? Having a solid, tough looking man with you, will deter any troublemakers from bothering you; and even a car thief will most likely look elsewhere to steal one that will give him less trouble. In a situation such as a puncture or the breakdown of your car in the middle of nowhere; very few people will stop to give you a hand. The only help you will receive; will be from opportunistic men, who will probably use your plight to their advantage. Instead of helping you fix your car, they might suggest; *"Why not leave the car here and let us take you home? We can find a mechanic in the morning!"* or *"It's a bit late in the day, but I will try and phone for help; so it would be best if I stay here with you, until it arrives!"* Meanwhile; you, your car and your 'guardian angel' could be standing on the side of a deserted motorway, in the cold or rain! In the middle of the night; you can bet anything that the only 'tools' he will want to use will be his own. How romantic! As a safety measure; you should always have the phone number of a man (brother, cousin, platonic friend) you can rely on, who will leave whatever he is doing and come running to your side when you call in distress. Kind, uncomplicated men with no hidden agendas are hard to find; so if you know one, be nice to him and never forget his birthday. You will need him one day!

7. In a crowd

Let's take the following scenario. Mary and Jack had just broken up a five year relationship. Actually, Mary still loved Jack; but had to ditch him because of his womanising. To cut a long story short; they met by chance at a party with their different dates and for a time, everything was fine. They said *"Hello"* to each other and mingled into the crowd. Halfway through the party; Mary realised she could not stand the sight of Jack openly kissing his date on the dance floor. Jealousy showed up the worst in her and she walked up to Jack and poured her drink all over him. She knew that Jack, being the gentleman, would not fight back; and he didn't. What Mary had not bargained for however; was that Jack's date was a real tough cookie and she slapped Mary. Jack tried to stop her to no avail; and Mary got the beating of her life. Mary's date stood speechless; because he had never realised his love was like that and obviously still hankered for her ex. Jack quickly left the party with his date; probably thanking his stars that he and Mary were no longer together. Mary lost her man and got beaten up in the process. She had got it all wrong. She had hoped to embarrass Jack in front of people and got the worst of it. In any situation where there is a crowd like a party; you have to use tact and mind your own business. You cannot misbehave and do things you would like to do; because it could upset or offend someone you don't even know.

If you arrive at a party and you feel there will be problems, either by your presence or that of somebody else; you must talk to the host or hostess and explain why you have to leave. If they insist that you stay; then do your best to avoid the person whom you had not bargained on seeing. If you sense someone trying to cause trouble; (your rival or enemy might 'accidentally' step on your foot while dancing; or if it is a man, he might rub himself against you pretending to dance and believe you can do nothing about it because of the sheer embarrassment it might cause) then you have to decide whether to retaliate and ruin the party for everyone else, or ignore him or her. The wisest thing of course; is to ignore the mischief-maker and move away to another part of the house. If she/he follows you; then you know they are out for trouble. You should therefore report them to the party-giver and explain the situation; so that if a fight does break out, it would not be your fault. If you still feel uncomfortable; then make your excuses and leave. It would seem like a victory for the one annoying you; but in reality, you defended your dignity and self-esteem and walked out with your head held high. Everybody will by then know who irritated and forced you to leave; and that person will not have a pleasant evening. If he/she follows you out of the party; then you must call the police. This 'overreaction' in calling the cops; will let him/her realise that you are serious and will not tolerate anything like that in the future. The police will not arrest him/her; because they have not actually done anything to you, except annoy you. He/She might call you a "*crazy bitch!*" Excellent! They will henceforth leave you alone or face the consequences. If certain behaviour is going on, which you do not approve of (drug-taking; alcohol excess; boisterous antics and sexual misbehaviour); the sensible thing is to make your excuses to the party-giver and leave. The worst thing to do would be to take the moral high-ground and complain or try to get the participants to stop their 'bad' behaviour. In their happy and intoxicated mood; you will most likely be ignored, branded a party-pooper or laughed out of the place.

Always play it safe in a big crowd like a football/rugby/basketball match or music concert; and go with a group of friends. Trouble can easily break out at a sporting event, especially if the result goes the wrong way for certain people; so you will feel much safer when there are more of you. Even if you are in a smaller venue like a women's handball game, where the majority of the spectators are women; you should not go alone. Always sit in the section of the team you support and never abuse the opposing team's supporters; because a faction of them might get angry, and cause crowd trouble. Try to leave before the end of the game or long after most people have left. Don't insult anybody; especially as regards their team, race, religion or country. This is because such insults bring out an instinctive reaction to defend one's honour and avenge the slur. You could be seriously hurt; because with the added adrenalin of the baying crowd, it would be easy for anyone to over-react and attack you, with the intention of maiming you. At a music concert; there will definitely be people who are intoxicated with alcohol or drugs and will be talking and behaving in ways you may not be used to. To make matters worse; they might be concealing weapons on them (knives, knuckle-dusters, bottles and possibly guns). Very few venues have metal detectors or conduct body searches on the paying customer! Go with the flow and don't get angry or into an argument/confrontation; which means you must move away from anyone you feel will pose a danger to you. If the music does not live up to your expectation; try not to publicly disparage the group or any of its members.

There will be hard-core fans who might take it personally; and you could have a serious fight on your hands!

Before you pick anything in an out-door food market; make sure you want it, pay for it politely and leave. With their fluctuating profit margins; to get your money back would be next to impossible. To start yelling at the seller could land you in trouble; because any marketplace (or big shop) will have a bunch of thugs affectionately called 'security', ready to come to the aid of their employer. All the security in the area will fight for each other; so to cause trouble will not do you any good. Most shop owners are on first name terms with the police around their area; so you really don't stand too much of a chance if you are labelled a troublemaker. The word *'Thief'* shouted indiscriminately; still causes sadistic excitement in a lot of people. Some could take the law into their own hands and harm you; simply by branding you a thief. The burden would then be on you to prove you are not. Even when the police arrive and you are later shown to be innocent; the damage could have been done and your reputation sullied. The shop owner's shop is like his/her home; so a shopping centre or supermarket is not the place to cause trouble or be a victim of it! In the excitement of shopping; it is very easy to forget yourself. Many a woman has had her bag or purse stolen; when she nonchalantly put it down, in order to examine a potential purchase. Some women have even managed to lose their children in the crowd of a shopping centre; because the child was obviously left unsupervised and wandered off. If you go with a good friend, keep your eyes open, your hands firmly on your belongings and mind your own business; shopping can be an enjoyable experience.

In any crowded place; forget about being branded a coward and always walk away from an argument/confrontation, because it is too dangerous. If you are in a fight with some woman and her friend kicks you or even stabs you; you cannot really prove who inflicted the damage on you, because there would be so many people around. Even if you know who did it; you could be outnumbered by her friends and be severely injured. We still live in a barbaric world; where people are beaten up, stabbed and killed just for being who they are or for looking at someone in the wrong way. Although it is rare for a man to physically attack a woman in public (because he would never get away with it); there is a growing trend of women-on-women attacks, which the police are finding hard to deal with. There is also the modern phenomenon of girl gangs who walk around large towns and bully people, just for the fun of it. Unfortunately, they usually pick on vulnerable targets; like women walking alone, minding their own business. This means your greatest threat in a crowd, will come from one of your own sex; so you have to treat everyone equally and keep away from those you feel could be a threat to you. If you are walking through a crowd; be as polite as you can, using the words *"excuse me please…"*, *"sorry"* and *"thank you"*, in order to get to where you are going. If you see a gang of youths walking towards you; try to avoid them by crossing the road, walking into a shop or moving out of their way before they get to you. If one of them bumps into you or steps on your toes; it would do you no harm to apologise, even though it was not your fault. They could be using it as a well-rehearsed pretext; to start an argument with you, knock you over, steal your belongings and run away! Don't give them that chance; because you might not be fit or fast enough to run after and catch them!

8. Abroad

Some of the points I make here, may not apply in your own or other 'advanced' countries; but there are over two hundred countries in the world. With the falling price of air tickets; it is likely that you will one day travel to a country you have never been to before, is nothing like your own and are therefore not aware of its do's and don'ts. When you travel abroad, the chances are you will not know many people; so you will have to take extra precautions or you will get unstuck and endanger your health or even your life. Try to take all necessary inoculations and get insurance cover for health, flight delays and accidents. Carry any medicine you may need with you; and if possible, always buy a ticket which can be changed to another day at short notice. If you miss your flight because you were held up in a police station trying to bail out your friend who got drunk and ended up in a scuffle; then you will have to buy a new one-way ticket home, which would be expensive. Try to learn as much as possible about a country, before you go there; because knowing its etiquette will endear you to the locals and make you friends. This always comes in handy, if you ever find yourself in trouble abroad; because even the police will treat you more sympathetically, if you make a positive attempt to explain yourself or apologise in their language.

When going out abroad; always carry your passport and make sure your visa has not expired. Don't expose too much money in public; and hold tightly onto your belongings, when pushing yourself through a crowd. When you go in for the visa; ask the embassy for the do's and don'ts of their country and any important phone numbers like the police/ambulance. Urinating in public, eating snakes or burping after a meal might not be okay in New York or London; but in some places, this is quite acceptable. Don't turn up your nose at anything you see and if you don't like something; just pretend you never saw it! If you are asked to sample some exotic dish you find abhorrent; either refuse politely or taste it, without making a big deal out of it. It is their country and their customs; and nobody forced you to come there! You will however; make a lot more friends, if you embrace their culture. Many countries suffered at the hands of colonialism; and some of the locals can be very touchy when a 'Westerner' comes and behaves in a superior manner. Be very careful with the English language, because some countries don't speak it; and the locals may get angry when you act like they are the ones at fault, for not understanding you. The French, Spanish and Portuguese speaking countries have a genuine fear that the English language is taking over the world; and theirs will one day be wiped out, if they are not careful. You might therefore find some nationalists refusing or pretending not to speak English; and forcing you to converse in their own language. If you first make an effort with their lingo; you will find that they will be friendlier and try to speak yours. Please avoid the condescending cliché, *"Do you speak English?"* It doesn't go down well in many places!

In all big cities abroad; you have to have your wits about you and play it safe with your security. Don't make it obvious you are carrying money on you. If you need local currency, try to change it in your hotel before you go out; or else, go to a licensed foreign exchange bureau or a bank. Avoid the black market; even though they might offer you a little more. If they cheat or give you counterfeit notes; there is nothing you can do about it. Going to the police will be pointless; because without a receipt, you have no proof of exchange. There are usually lots of police around, but they probably don't speak English; so trying to explain what you have been robbed of, is not the easiest thing to do. Being a tourist, you will stick out like a sore thumb; so there is no use pretending to blend in. Use it instead to make friends, by taking an interest in everything; and you will find the locals will be happy to help you. Even though they might find you amusing; keep smiling and never be rude with someone, just because he or she does not think or behave like you. Most importantly; try to make sure you have an idea of the local customs. If you get on the underground train in Sao Paulo, Brasil for instance; it can be a daunting experience, if you don't speak Portuguese. Everybody is in a hurry and they will quickly know you are not a '*Paulista*'. A man's front is not allowed to touch a woman, when standing in the aisle on a bus or subway train; just in case he gets sexually aroused and prods her with his erection! You have to stand facing the windows, so that buttock touches buttock; whereas in Europe and the United States, people stand anyway they feel like. This means a girl might end up face to face with a guy with the most appalling breath and body odour; and a satisfied smirk anytime the bus or train goes round a corner! On some subways abroad, pickpockets abound; so you have to be careful and make sure you are not being followed. You will usually find bootleggers, counterfeiters, quacks and religionists trying to sell you their wares; but you must ignore all of them. There is nothing they will sell you that you cannot buy legally and safely from a legitimate shop.

When you are going out abroad, the chances are you will need a taxi; so find out how much you are supposed to pay, before you get in. A lot of taxis in Third World countries do not operate with a meter. They will try their luck with you and there will be no use arguing after you get to your destination; because the chances are, you will not win. You could even end up in the cop shop; since most drivers have friends in the police force. Whatever price you are told; you should offer to pay about a third of it. After a bit of haggling; (great fun) you will agree on a price that makes you both think you are getting a good deal! Even those with meters in their cars, have been known to 'fix' them; so try to take a registered taxi who can be reported, if something goes wrong. By all means argue and fight for your rights, if you feel you have been cheated; but in a situation where you are going to be roughed up because of fifty cents, it is better to let the cheat have the money. Environment! You are not on your local high street where you know everybody. You are in a much stronger position; if you have the exact amount of money with you and do not require change. Most of the time, you will prevail; because he will not waste too much time with you when he could be making money elsewhere. Never take up important, sensitive or personal conversation with the driver. Stick to frivolities like the weather or handsome young studs and forget about religion and politics. Some drivers are paid informants; and will quickly report you to the authorities for some offhand remark about their human rights policy or their tyrant of a leader. When you are taken to the police station; you will be questioned, warned and will probably have to pay your way out, at best. At worst, you might spend a few uncomfortable nights in a cell and then deported; that is, if your country has diplomatic relations with the one you offended. It is not worth the hassle. You are on holidays!

Never go out alone; (*"Where did I hear that before?"*) but talk to your hotel staff who will tell you where to go/not to go and all you want to know about a particular destination. They will be able to find you a reliable guide to show you around. Just remember that you will be expected to pay for all the food, drinks, transportation and entrance fees to any museum or club; whilst he or she shows you around! It would be worth it, to guarantee your physical and monetary safety. Never get into a taxi at night, if there is already someone in it; and if possible, pay him not to pick up anyone else. Always keep an eye on the road and make sure the driver is going the way you have been informed. If you feel uncomfortable with the route and the length of time it is taking to get there; tell him you want to get off, pay him and look for another taxi. During the day, it is not too much of a problem; but at night, it can be frightening if you don't know where you are going. If you visit a friend's house; make sure the driver knows he or she has taken the car number of any taxi you leave their house in. This way he will not dare rip you off; knowing that your friend knows the city and will be able to trace him, if something happened to you. Just a precaution!

On long journeys to remote parts of a country; try to take a plane. If you cannot afford one, then go with a reputable bus company and make sure you find out what you can about the area you are going. This is because it may be completely different from the city you arrived in and may even speak a different language, even though you are in the same country. In some areas, armed robbers abound; so it makes sense not to travel long distances at night by car, in case you have a breakdown. If you have to go by car; don't stop if you see someone else who has broken down, especially if it is a pretty young girl trying to flag you down. It could be a trap; whereby some thugs will jump out of the bush when you stop. They could seriously harm you before they steal your car and money; and in some countries you could even be kidnapped for a ransom! The high-jacking menace so prevalent in certain countries a few decades ago is now almost non-existent and nowadays there are very few crashes; so planes are statistically safer than cars. Although the ventilation system is conducive to the spread of common diseases like flu and colds; I have never heard of rape or robbery on a flight! You may notice that certain rules like those concerning the hand luggage, excess baggage, smoking and seat numbers may not be taken as seriously as those in your country. If you have any fears or problems; don't hesitate to tell the air-hostess. I'm sure you can deal with the most annoying chat-up lines by pretending to sleep or not to understand what the boorish oaf is saying! You can always ask to be moved; if you are stuck next to a loud snorer, foul windbreaker or an inquisitive nuisance! If the plane is full…tough! You are stuck with him for the length of the journey. Have fun!

Going out in your area is generally very safe because you will usually have people who can come to your aid or call the police in case of trouble; but everyday there are attacks on women, some of them extremely unpalatable. Most of these can be avoided, if you observed a simple set of rules. If you love yourself and everything to do with you; please be careful. It still makes unpleasant headlines when any female is attacked, raped or robbed. The downside of equality is that some men now see women as the 'enemy' and are reluctant to come to the aid of a woman in trouble; unless they see in it an advantage (usually sexual or financial) to themselves. All this means you must be responsible for your own safety; and keeping out of trouble is the best way. Instinctively, all women have a natural self-preservation ethic where they are able to deal with undesirables in their own inimitable way; and so long as it works, who am I to change that? The most important thing is to put your self-worth above everything and do all you can to protect it. If something feels wrong then it most probably is; so you should do something about it! Don't allow yourself to be bullied; but you have to use tact and never make decisions if you are angry. Walk away, if you find yourself about to lose your temper with someone; and leave the area if you think it is unsafe. All you need to do is be vigilant and not leave any obvious chinks in your armour for someone to take advantage of; and you can feel perfectly safe outside your home.

"Dear Tigress, we are now going to prepare ourselves to protect our home. Believe me; it is not as easy as it seems!"

Chapter Eight
Is your abode a fortress?

A woman's home is her castle. It is where she feels most comfortable and she can do anything she likes, without having to worry about whether anybody is looking at her or disapproves at what she is doing. She can wake up in the morning, forget to comb her hair, leave off her make-up and walk around naked. With all this wonderful freedom; have you ever thought that the greatest danger to your life could be right there in your home? If you visit your local hospital, what you see might shock you; because many of the most appalling accidents occur in the home! In an age when many houses are protected like fortresses; how secure is your own? The fact that your windows are barred and you have five locks on each of your doors does not necessarily mean you are safe. How easy are those locks to open, either by you or a potential thief? After locking the doors at night; where do you keep the keys? In the event of a fire; is there a way you would be able to get out of all the security apparatus you have installed? More importantly; will your young children have the sense to get out by themselves? Many have been trapped in their houses, blinded and knocked out by the smoke; before being burnt to death. This is because the occupants were so security conscious; they could not unlock the numerous locks in time to escape. Others have died; simply because they had no idea that oxygen fuels all flames and opening certain doors during a fire will only make things worse.

1. Young children

Since most young children cannot act for themselves and need a constant eye on them; it is really up to the parents/guardians to make sure nothing untoward will happen to them in the home. Otherwise, it would be regarded as negligence; which could have dire consequences. Depending on where you live; you could have the police or 'child protection' services interfering in your family. In our politically correct world; neglecting a child means exposing him or her to any possible physical, emotional, sexual or mental harm. You therefore have to be careful, because there are people who will not mind their own business; and will not hesitate in reporting you to the police, if they feel you are not looking after your children properly. This means that you could leave a child in your car for a few minutes, while you run into a shop to buy something; and then be accused of neglect by a stranger, who may call the cops and have you arrested. You will be treated as a criminal and your child could easily be taken away from you. Is the house too hot or too cold for the children? Is there enough air in the room as they are sleeping? Are you feeding them properly? Do you smoke, drink or take drugs anywhere near them? If a thief breaks into your house in the middle of the night; could he harm them without your knowledge? Are there any dangerous appliances around the house, which they could stumble upon and hurt themselves? You could be asleep when your child may decide to go and eat something in the middle of the night; spills hot water on herself or trips and cuts himself badly. A lot of blood could be lost by the time you can get help. What if the child chokes on something or starts vomiting uncontrollably; do you have enough knowledge of First Aid, in order to save his/her life before the ambulance arrives? Is he or she being exposed to incest or paedophilia with a family member, inside your home? No? Are you absolutely certain? These may all seem like frivolous or rude questions; but they do need to be asked. If your child became ill, injured or was in any way abused, as a result of the conditions inside your house; it would affect you in more ways than a simple trip to the chemist or hospital. Finally; you can unwittingly be sentencing your child to a life-long torment, bullying and teasing...simply by the name you give him or her. For example, if your surname is Davis and you name your child Simon Timothy; his name will be Simon Timothy Davis. This sounds innocuous enough, until you realise the initials are S.T.D; which could also mean 'Sexually Transmitted Disease'. Technically, you should be accused of gross negligence or even child abuse; because all the teasing and bullying your child will experience in school, will be down to your name choice. Can you live with yourself, if your child is beaten up, injured or shunned like a leper; simply because he or she has a 'funny name'? A child is part of your self-defence. His or her needs must be even more of a priority than your own;

which means never leaving them open to the possibility of harm. Those, whose children have died, will testify that it is a tragedy; which will scar you for the rest of your life.

There was a story a few years back; about how a young man came home drunk one night and staggered into his kitchen. The lights did not work; so he lit a match and the whole place exploded. He was burnt to death; as he had left the gas stove on! Stupid as he was; these things do happen. Therefore; it is imperative that you teach your young children what to do and not to do with fire, electricity, hot water, knives and strangers. Make sure they are aware of any possible dangers, by explaining why certain things have to be done to ensure their safety; by using a similar worse-case scenario story as an example. If you simply tell them to do or not to do something; they might petulantly ask you *"Why?"* or forget completely. It would help them understand better; if you used a previous incident of what could happen, in order to make your point. Although it is common sense that you do not light a match if you smell gas; your kids may not know, unless you show them it has happened to someone else before. You should never assume they have been taught something in school; and take it upon yourself to teach them about safety measures. It is better for your child to say, *"Don't be silly Mummy. Of course I know I shouldn't touch electricity when my hands are wet!"* than for you to take a trip to the casualty department in your local hospital. It would not be funny to lose your children to the child protection services; through sheer negligence. Carbon monoxide has been called the 'silent killer' because it is odourless; so occasionally let the experts come in and give your house a check-up for leaking gasses. Buying a book or taking a short course in First Aid should not be so difficult (two thirds of young mothers in the UK and the US have no knowledge of First Aid!) and it will always come in handy. Why not give your house a 'clean sweep' just before you go to bed each night; by checking the doors, locks, electrical appliances and making sure the kids are still breathing. If you love your children; then you don't need me advising you what to do!!!

2. Fire safety

In a society where armed robbers and break-ins abound; it is imperative that you feel safe in the only place where you are free to do what you want. At the very least; you should make sure all your windows are secure from outside entry by thieves. Your doors should be locked at night and each resident must have a key to the front and back doors kept safely somewhere that is easily accessible; so that in the event of a fire, one is not left looking for a key to get out. If you rent an apartment; there should always be a smoke alarm that works and a reliable fire exit. If there is no smoke alarm; you should not move into that accommodation. Report the owners to the housing authorities! If you own your house; then the burden is on you to make sure you adhere to the basic fire safety rules. I'm sure your local police/fire station will be happy to provide you with leaflets and advice on how to prevent fires; and what to do, if one breaks out in your house or area.

Leaving nothing to chance; always make sure the gas container/cooker is switched off before going to bed and instil in your young children not to use it at night. Smell the cooker just to make sure there is no gas leakage. Check that all fireplaces have guards. Sometimes the coal can spit out and a burning piece could land on your rug; starting a fire when you are somewhere else in the house. Before going to bed; all electrical appliances must be switched off and the plugs removed from the socket. Keep children away from matches, boiling water and anything to do with fire. If any of them were to receive first, second or third degree burns; it would also hurt you because your life would not be the same, if something you cared for was damaged or destroyed. Keep a couple of domestic fire extinguishers in the house, just in case. We all know how slow the fire brigade can be, due to traffic congestion on our roads; so why depend on them? Had one been a little more vigilant; most fires could easily have been put out, before they got bigger. It is hardly fair to expect the fire brigade to quickly put out a fire that has been raging for a few hours and save your property.

If the lifts in your apartment block are not reliable; occasionally use the fire escape and time yourself how long it will take to get you and your family out of the building safely. This is called a fire drill and is performed in all institutions. Why not personalise one for your family; so that they all know exactly what to do and more importantly, what not to do? Could you jump out of a second/third floor window, in order to escape a fire; knowing that you would at the very least, break both your legs? How do you know? Can you imagine being badly burnt in a fire; all because you were too scared to jump out of the window, in case you broke your precious legs? If you know in your heart that you will be too petrified to break a window and jump down from an upper floor; then you should either live in a bungalow or make sure there is a reliable fire-escape route where you live. Failing that; take extra precautions to be certain a fire cannot start in your house, while you are away or asleep...by turning off all appliances and keeping the smoke alarm up to date. You will never be able to live it down or sleep soundly at night, if someone died in your house of smoke inhalation; all because you were too lazy or absent-minded to keep your fire safety techniques up to date. In any fire, things you love will be destroyed; so you have to know exactly what is valuable and irreplaceable to you. Although certain things like furniture and equipment might be expensive, they can be replaced if they are insured; but your body and life cannot. It is therefore most important to save the lives of your family; and not waste time trying to save your property. It would be helpful, if important documents like passports, computer memory sticks and bank details are all kept safely in one place; in order to make them easily retrievable on the way out of the house.

Finally, there is the deliberate fire or arson; which happens more often than we think. Some people have been known to deliberately set fire to their own property; in order to claim the insurance money for a complete refurbishment of their homes. If you are going down that road; I advise you to tread carefully, because the police and insurance companies have over the years become very experienced. They can easily find out if a fire was started deliberately; so you will be prosecuted, as well as lose your home. Others have been victims of malicious attacks and have had petrol bombs thrown through their letter boxes; simply because they chose to live in the wrong area or were of the wrong religion, race or colour. Unfortunately; these things do happen and there is not much the police can do, without prior information. Before moving to a certain area; try to extract relevant information about the environment from your estate agent and the local police. If you are Moslem; it would not be wise to move into a wholly Christian area or vice-versa. If you are from a particular country that is a historical enemy of or at war with another race; then for your own peace of mind, it would not be prudent to mix in the same housing estates. If you are white; settling in an all-black neighbourhood could cause you problems. If you are a young, party-loving black lady; moving into an area predominantly full of white senior citizens will not be conducive to your lifestyle. Although moving into areas where you will be in the minority, does not mean someone will burn down your house; it could happen. There are always a few exuberant youths who think it is good fun to cause trouble; and what could have started as a mischievous prank, could end up as serious arson.

3. Burglary

Now we come to the other main threat to your home; burglary. Breaking into peoples homes and stealing valuables is a lucrative way of life for certain crooks who have mastered the art of entering a house without being caught. They are only able to do this when you allow them to do so; by leaving doors and windows open, keys in obvious hiding places or by letting people you don't know very well inside your house, so that they see what possessions you have and send the message out to their partners in crime. A burglar does not want to be caught; so he is most likely to come when you are either asleep or not in. The summer period is the most lucrative time for them because that is when most people go on holidays. He depends mostly on a victim's carelessness; rather than take the risk of forcefully and recklessly entering a place. He may pose as a handyman or a friend, in order not to alert suspicion from the neighbours; until he locates his entry point. He will then enter the house, steal whatever he can carry and leave as quickly as possible (20 minutes on average). He is unlikely to carry a gun; but might have a knife, syringe, spray or knuckleduster, in order to threaten anyone who tries to stop him. He will usually wear a balaclava, hooded jacket or some other disguise like a wig or glasses to conceal his face; so that he is not easily recognised. He may also wear gloves; in order not to leave any fingerprints. He will probably have a friend with him, as a look-out or as a driver; so that they can make a quick get-away. If he knows you are asleep upstairs; he will quietly do all his stealing downstairs. There are even some specialist thieves who will break in, steal your car keys and then drive off with your car. The vehicle will then be used in a crime, sent abroad to be sold or dismantled and the expensive parts sold off. You may not even notice your car is gone until you are ready to go out! If he is aware you are not in; he will definitely try the master bedroom and the sitting room, especially in the cupboards and drawers. All thieves believe that is where most valuables are kept! He will most likely steal something he will be able to carry easily and will fetch a reasonable price; like a digital camera, lap-top computer, jewellery or mobile phone. If he has a van waiting nearby; he may take your flat-screen television or sound equipment. And if he has reliable information; he will dispossess you of your valuable art and cash. Many burglars are junkies looking for something to sell quickly; in order to get money for their next fix. They may not care if they make a mess of your house; so long as they can get what they want and get out before you can apprehend them.

If you hear a suspicious noise coming from another part of your house in the middle of the night and you are sure it is not the cat or the dog; you should call the police and voice your suspicions, before letting the thief know that you have heard him. If you are alone in the house; stay where you are and lock yourself in the room, until the police arrive. Surprising a thief doing his job will make him panic and he may have to hurt you badly or even kill you; because he might feel he has been recognised. Only if there are at least three (brave) men in the house; should they take the risk and go down with baseball bats, golf clubs or some other weapon to challenge the thief. Your family must be valued more than any property; and that is why it is not worth risking their lives for the sake of a television or the car in your garage. Be friendly with your neighbours; as this would give you a 'third eye' watching over your house whilst you are out. A good neighbour will be able to help when you travel; by keeping an eye out for unwanted visitors, putting on and off the lights in the evenings and generally giving the impression there is someone still living there, until your return. If you want to cancel your milk/newspaper orders, then do it about a week before you travel; so that anyone watching your house will not know exactly when you are going away. It would be better for you to get a friend to take you to the airport, instead of hiring a taxi to pick you up from your home. This is because the driver will know you are travelling; and in a friendly conversation, you might let slip the length of time you will be away. It would be very easy for him to reveal the information to any burglar friends he may have; in order for them to rob your house whilst you are gone. Every police station has a booklet for its neighbourhood-watch program, which gives advice on first-aid and how to protect your home and those of your neighbours against thieves and fires. Go and get one for yourself and don't ever be scared to walk into a cop shop to voice your security fears; because they are duty bound to investigate. They are used to false alarms; so it is better to be safe than sorry! It will scare off anybody you suspect has been watching your house, if he sees you going in with a policeman; because he will realise he has been noticed and the chances are, he will disappear!

Wow! So you've bought a new music centre or the latest flat-screen television. Do you have to tell everyone? Don't you think that every time you blast your sound, people might be able to hear it and some may wish they had a system as good as yours? Isn't it possible someone might just be crazy enough to try and steal it from you? Apart from the noise you make from your sound system; how else would anyone know you have one? So you can afford ten air conditioners in your house, one for each room. Doesn't it occur to you that some people do not have any and are sweating it out in their hot studio or bed-sit? You have three cars in your yard and every year you change them to the latest models. Did you know that the majority of people in most countries cannot even afford a bicycle, let alone a car? Ask yourself if you really need three cars; and if you do, did you earn the money legally in order to have been able to afford them? Have you paid your taxes? If the answer is *"Yes"* to my last two questions, then go ahead and have ten cars if you wish; but you have to be able to protect them because someone somewhere will be envious of you. The best thing to do now is move to another area where three cars in your garage will be no big deal; and you will fit in well with your upwardly mobile neighbours. If you do not want to move because you love the area you live in; you will have to make sure all your valuables are protected and insured against burglary. Jealousy is such a powerful force that if your wealth and profile is much higher than those living around you; there will sooner or later, be an attempt to rob your house...so be prepared!

You should try things out first, just so that you are at peace in your own mind that if something did threaten your way of life; you will be able to save yourself, your loved ones and your property. Otherwise; you will never know what you would do in certain situations! This does not mean you should be stupid and try out things, which are either humanly impossible or too dangerous for you. Deep down we are all aware of our capabilities and limitations; but it feels so much better when we are certain. For example; you can time yourself to see how quickly you can get from your bathroom to the car, in case you hear someone trying to drive off with it. If you know you don't have it in you to run naked out of your house to chase a car thief; then always make sure your car is safe whenever you come home, by activating the alarm system. You could be in the shower when the thief strikes; and you may not have the time to dry yourself, dress and then run outside to stop him. If you kept a phone in the bathroom; you will be able to call the police quickly, if you ever felt threatened whilst you were indisposed. The theft of your car or property would feel a lot worse, if you knew there was something you could have done to stop it but failed to do; due to laziness, shyness, embarrassment or sheer stupidity.

4. Security tricks

If you are scared or worried about intruders, then make sure they cannot get into your house or apartment at any time, day or night; by keeping your doors and windows firmly locked. Fitting burglar alarms and closed-circuit cameras with warning signs around the house will be a useful deterrent. Some cameras will be able to record months of footage; which can be stored on a computer hard-drive and retrieved at any time. This will enable you to piece together exactly what happens in and around your house every day; even whilst you are out of the country. There are some expensive systems that have thermal imaging; which allows them to 'see' in the dark, without the intruder knowing that he has been spotted. A loud voice will then blast a warning to the intruder to leave the premises immediately or the police will be called. This is usually enough for the thieves to quickly run away; because they have no idea how many people have seen them. There is another system which fills a room with thick smoke, as soon as it is broken into; so that the thieves will not be able to see anything. This will let them panic and run away; without taking anything. Although no lock is completely burglar-proof; the five-lever mortise locks are the most reliable for the front and back doors. If you have sliding patio doors; they should be locked at the top and the bottom. There should be visible locks on all the windows; so that the thief knows that the only way he can get in would be to smash the window. Because this would attract too much attention; he is unlikely to risk it! If you cannot afford a high concrete wall around your whole property; the back of your house should be surrounded by a high fence, hedge or bushes. This will block a potential escape route and make it much harder for the burglar to sneak in. The front of the house should have a low wall, fence, hedge or bush; so that the front door is visible. This way, anybody walking down the street can see if someone is trying to break in and alert the neighbours or ring the police. Leaving a car in the driveway will tell the burglar that someone could be in; and also serve as a deterrent. Under no circumstances should you leave your car keys hanging in the porch, hallway, kitchen wall or anywhere it can be seen; because it will tempt any thief who breaks in, to steal your car. When not being used; all tools, ladders and garden furniture should be kept safely and out of view, preferably in a shed with secure locks. This is because they can be used by the thief to enter the house. If you are travelling; cancel all newspaper and grocery deliveries (or get a neighbour to collect them, if you are not going to be away for too long). If you allow them to pile up outside your front door; it will tell any burglar that you have travelled and are ripe for easy pickings!

Nowadays, by connecting to the Internet; you can use your lap top computer or mobile phone to view your house through your closed-circuit system, even if you are miles away. For a reasonable fee, you can even have a silent alarm system connected directly to the police; so that they will be able to rush over as soon as your house is being broken into. Try to store a record of the serial numbers of all your valuable property on a CD or memory stick kept safely; so that even if your computer is stolen, you will not lose valuable information. Keeping photographs of things like expensive paintings, antiques and jewellery; will help the police in tracing them, if they are ever stolen. Keep all valuables out of sight with curtains or blinds; so that a passer-by cannot see inside your living room from the street and possibly alert his criminal friends. Children's bedrooms and kitchens are useful places to hide valuables because those are the last places a thief will search; and more than likely, he will not have enough time after rifling through the sitting room and master bedroom. Air conditioners should be fixed, so that they cannot be easily moved; because thieves have been known to crawl through an air conditioning hole, in order to get into a house. Having a ferocious dog that barks at the slightest unusual noise it hears; will serve as an effective deterrent against burglars. Just make sure it is trained to refuse food from strangers; in case it is poisoned or drugged by an insensitive thief.

When going to bed at night, always leave a couple of lights on; just in case anybody has the idea to rob you because he thinks there is no one at home. If you go out in the evenings; you should leave a prominent light on inside the house and keep the radio/television on, if you will not be away for too long. You can buy special lights with timers; so that they come on and off intermittently around the house. If possible, have closed-circuit cameras hidden around your living room, front/back doors and garage; to secretly film anyone who breaks in while you are out or asleep upstairs. Even if they are disguised, this can still help the police arrest the burglars; because most of them are known to the cops through previous encounters. Those unknown to the police; will sooner or later slip up by robbing someone else in the same manner and will be caught. These are all simple tactics, which are ignored by so many people that what I am saying is either a necessary education or a stern wake-up call. Depending on what you have to lose; the cost of all the security tricks would probably be only a fraction of the value of what you are protecting. With a little imagination and love for your home; you should be able to come up with simple and effective ideas to keep your house safe and unattractive to burglars. If in doubt; you should visit a shop that sells security equipment and they will be able to wise you up on how to prevent the latest burglar tactics!

5. Business premises

If you own a company, office or a shop; the same attention to detail in your security must be applied to make sure it is also safe from thieves. If your business premises are very large with many employees; it might be better to bring in a professional company to oversee your security, so that you have some insurance against thieves or in-house crimes like pilferage and embezzlement. After that; you have to make sure you don't do anything to encourage an attack from an irate customer. Most bosses in sensitive positions always have several buffers before anybody can get to them; but this does not mean they will be safe on the way home or in their house. Never put off an angry consumer or patron by making promises you think will make him or her go away and leave you alone; because that tactic may backfire on you. It will deposit a sour taste in the mouth and revenge cannot be ruled out. If he/she is seriously deranged; they could easily follow you from work, in order to find out where you live. They can then make plans to teach you a lesson with burglary, arson or physical attack. Most companies know that they will lose money when they present shoddy products or make false promises to the public. Your self-defence requires you to be honest in business; or you will damage your reputation and possibly lose your life.

If you do not cheat anyone or owe money; always deliver on your professional promises and adhere to an ethical moral integrity, then nobody will think of coming to your business premises or home to harm you. Treating everyone with respect sounds so simple; but how many times have you felt cheated or insulted by someone, in the name of business? This is because people tend to protect themselves and their business, without realising or caring who gets hurt. They would rather lie, fob you off or even insult you; rather than admit they are wrong. Being wrong means they would have to apologise; thereby losing face and possibly money through compensation. The fact that you may be a law-abiding citizen and have so far decided to ignore such abuses and outrages, does not mean that if you did the same to someone else, he/she will be so accommodating. The world is full of good and bad people and there is no safe way of predicting how someone will react to being cheated or offended; so try not to deliberately take advantage of people in your professional and private life. Your home is your sanctuary and possibly the only one you have; it would therefore be folly to unnecessarily invite trouble to your doorstep.

6. Strangers

Most burglaries are a result of specific information targeting your home; which means someone told the burglars what was inside the house, in order for them to be interested. The informant might also have divulged important info; like when you are most likely to be out, where the valuables are kept or which windows and doors are easily opened or broken into. Are you always allowing strangers into your home for a cup of tea and a chat? People can come into your house and in less than a minute, know exactly what you have there that is of value to them. They can then make plans to rob you at a later date. They will find out what kind of locks you have on your doors, who would be inside the house at a particular time and whether that person would be able to stop them or not; and then tell the experts to come and burgle you, for a share of the profits. They might watch the house for weeks or even months before they strike; and you can bet that when they do, they will clear out everything of value. This is because they would have known exactly the time you will be away and how long for. Even though statistically, the majority of burglars are males; a female can easily be used to garner the information needed, in order for the men to commit the burglary. There is also what is known as the 'distraction burglary'; whereby one person will use an assortment of excuses to distract you, whilst his/her accomplice sneaks into the house and quickly steals something from inside your house. For example; a man may come in posing as a plumber or electrician and tell you there have been reports of a water shortage or an electrical problem in the area and would like to check your water/electric system. As he is fiddling about with your equipment; the accomplice will do the actual stealing whilst you are occupied watching the 'plumber/electrician'. Even if he is on his own; the thief may politely ask you to go upstairs and turn the bathroom taps on to see if they will affect the kitchen water supply. As soon as you go upstairs; he will steal something and disappear. He may even be so bold as to ring your doorbell and ask you for a pen and paper to write down an address. As soon as you go in to get him what he needs; he will snatch whatever he can and disappear before you return. You may not even realise your money, handbag, laptop computer, mobile phone or car keys are missing; until you need to use them...several hours later! Although most distraction burglaries are targeted at the elderly; they are increasing being used on anybody who is alone in the house...especially females because it is assumed they are not strong enough to fight back and are so kind-hearted they will be easy to convince with a sob-story!

Never allow anybody you do not know well (male or female) into your house, even for a glass of water; and always keep your doors locked because robbers have been known to walk up to an unsuspecting house at any hour and use a weapon to get what they want. If someone knocks on your door; you should speak through the intercom and give him/her the information, whilst they are standing outside. If you live in a house; you should open the window slightly and talk to them from inside. If you have to open your door; please make sure it is attached to a chain so that he/she cannot push themselves in. Be honest and tell them you cannot let them in because you don't know who they are. If they use the *"May I please use your toilet..."*; the *"I've lost my way; could you direct me to..."* or the *"I've had an accident and I need to use the phone etc."* excuses convincing you to let them in; you should threaten to call the police, unless they go away. This means not allowing any repairmen, meter readers or other officials in; until you have rang the company they claim to be representing and checking their identity cards. Anybody who is genuine will not object to waiting whilst you check up on their credentials. Although this seems a little paranoiac; you have to remember that it is people who rob and burgle. Things cannot go missing by themselves; so you have to be very strict and sometimes unfriendly, in order to deter strangers from entering your house. How many times have you read in the papers that a nice, friendly lady was burgled or robbed at knife-point? Without being over-insensitive; I would say it was her kindness and generosity that allowed callous thieves to take advantage of her. If people know you always keep your front door open and welcome anyone in for a cup of tea and a chat; sooner or later, someone will rob you.

Once you have been burgled; your name and address will be bandied around the criminal underworld or possibly sold to other crooks to try their luck. You might have let in strangers hundreds of times over the years without problems; but it only takes one burglary or robbery and your self-confidence will be shattered for ever. Please be careful!

7. Friends/flatmates

If you live alone; you are safer because no one can undo what you do and you can take personal responsibility for your own security. If you lock the door at night; the chances are, it will still be locked in the morning when you wake up. If you leave a knife in the drawer; it will stay in the there, unless you take it out. Your friends are your friends and they only come to your house to see you. Living with other people is the problem; because they will have friends who are not your friends and therefore, have no loyalty or love for you. Most burglaries are a direct result of insider information and this is easily possible when you allow friends of your friend into the inner sanctuary of your home; which means they also become privy to your domestic secrets. By hiding under the umbrella of your friend; they will be coming in and out of your place at will. This brings an opportunity to garner information about the security, lay-out and what valuables are worth stealing. Imagine a scenario where you are sharing an apartment with a good friend. You go out to visit your mother and come back home, lock the front door and go to bed. Your flatmate comes home much later after a night out with some of his friends, for a few more drinks. The pals leave in the early hours and in his drunken stupor, your flatmate forgets to lock the door of your apartment. One of his 'friends' notices this, sneaks back in and steals something; before disappearing with the perfect alibi that he left the apartment with the rest of the gang. All hell breaks loose in the morning when you wake up. *"Who could have stolen my D V Dees and where's my mobile phone"*? Is that all? Count yourself lucky girl…it could have been all your valuables!

Your flatmate/friend may be totally unaware of what bad acquaintances he/she has; and therein lies the problem. He/She could easily have at one time or another given the keys to the apartment to any of his/her friends, who in turn could have quietly made a copy. This would still be in their possession; even after your flatmate has moved to go and live somewhere else. If you have a flatmate; it would cause problems in your friendship, if you try to control who he/she can or cannot bring into the apartment. Ground rules will therefore have to be laid down right from the beginning; so that if something goes missing, you both know who should be held responsible. This may mean educating him/her to think like you and take personal responsibility for where you are living; because if he/she is only going to be staying with you a short time, they are not going to care about security. On the whole, sharing an apartment is safe enough; and the most likely problems you will have with co-tenants will be untidiness, eating and not replacing food from the fridge and not paying their share of the rent on time. It would serve you well to remember that it is still your home and if something is stolen, it is a painful experience; especially if the theft occurred because you were being kind to a friend, by allowing him/her to stay with you.

8. Boyfriends/lovers & one night stands

With boyfriends and lovers; the biggest problem you may have with them, will be their taking advantage of your love and generosity. If you are involved with one who is not on the same financial footing as you; then you are asking for trouble. Once he 'gets his feet under the table'; it will be very hard to get rid of him...simply because he is sleeping with you! He spends most of his time in your place, eats up all the food in your fridge, borrows your car and increases your phone bill; but doesn't contribute to your household chores or expenses. If you dare grumble, he will charm his way back into your good books; and a few orgasms later, you would have forgotten what you were complaining about! In this case, the man is clearly taking advantage of the woman; which is not conducive to the female cause. With more and more women earning bigger salaries; there are now certain men who live off their women and are actually proud of it. It can be a lucrative career choice for those who are too lazy to look for a job; with free sex thrown into the mix! He can spend all day on the golf course, whilst she is out at work and then make sweet love to her when she comes home; because he knows what makes her tick! Sadly, the women involved in these predicaments see nothing wrong with this arrangement; because they believe giving pocket money, food, clothing etc is a way of keeping the control and the 'love' of their boyfriends. Somehow they never contemplate what would happen, if these men were to meet someone richer; who was prepared to give them even more enjoyment money. What of a worse case scenario; where she loses her job and stops earning as much money as he has become accustomed to? Do you really think he will stick around and feel sorry for her?

The biggest mistake you can make with such a man; is to give him the keys to your home. This is because if things turn sour and you demand your keys back; there is no guarantee he has not already prepared for such an eventuality, by making duplicates. Your home is your sanctuary; so you have to be very careful who you allow inside to share the comforts and secrets with you. If he has a home of his own; then you can relax in the knowledge that he is not planning to move in. You can thereby keep the relationship under your control by letting him in, only when you choose to. However, you have to be wary of anyone who suggests moving in with you; because it means he obviously has an agenda. Don't be afraid to put him on the spot. *"Why do you really want to move in with me…?"* If he claims it's because he loves you; is he prepared to share the household bills and chores with you? Will he give you your own space, when you want to be alone? (Separate bedrooms?) How much is he earning? What is he bringing to the relationship that can make your life better than it already is? When you are in the first flush of love; it is very easy to jump in feet first and suggest moving in together. This might be okay; if you are both young, starting out together and life is still an exciting adventure. If you have already built up a certain lifestyle and worked hard for what you have; do you really want to bring in someone who could ruin it all for you? Granted you may have to take a leap of faith with some men; but it would be wise to wait till he has shown a high level of commitment to you. It is imperative for you to know in your heart that when the chips are down, he will never let you down or abandon you. The best way to do this is to give the relationship an extra six months/one year after you have decided he is the one for you, by not revealing your decision; but rather watching out for the signs described in Chapter 5. Good men are thin on the ground; so if you do find one…don't let him go. Mould him to satisfy your needs!

Sex is definitely an important part of a relationship; but without love and respect, it means nothing. A man, who is prepared to take your money without offering anything except sex in return; is nothing more than a gigolo. He will definitely stick around, only as long as it suits him! You may be richer than your boyfriend and pay for everything; but wouldn't it be nice if he took you out once in a while and paid with money he had earned himself? If you are giving him money and he decides to buy you a birthday present; then you might as well have bought the gift yourself! Your self-worth deserves for you to be treated as a human being with feelings; and not just as a cash machine for him to plunder. As explained in an earlier chapter; having more money than your partner, can lead to mental rape. He will make you feel guilty when you are not pulling your weight in the financial department! He will use the sex you so obviously love, as a weapon against you; by refusing to sleep with you until you see sense and cough up the cash. If you are losing money to him every time you come home from work; then you might as well be working for him. This means your home is not really yours; because it is also his. You are definitely not safe; because his next option will be to steal from you. To get rid of him; will probably mean paying him off with a hefty sum of money to get out of your life. You will then have to change your locks and phone number; but that may not stop him 'dropping by' one day when he runs out of the cash you gave him. *"I've missed you so much...".* You will not be a happy bunny!

Although it may seem like a good idea at the time; but taking a one-night stand home is probably the worst thing you could do, as far as your security is concerned. Yes; he is handsome, sexy and presses all the right buttons in you. Sleeping with him may seem the natural way to go; but what happens after the sex? If he is not up to scratch in the coital department and you don't really want to see him again; how do you get rid of him? He now knows where/how you live, your phone number and a few other things about you and your house; which under normal circumstances, you would not have divulged to anyone so easily. Although men have been doing it to women for years; nowadays a one-night stand is not the sole prerogative of men. Some women are very good at dumping their men after having their 'wicked-way' with them. I implore you to be very careful before going down that road; because some men can be very cruel with their revenge tactics. *"Don't call me, I'll call you"* may get rid of him temporarily; but what if you don't call and he decides to get in touch with you? How long can you fob him off before he gets pissed off and comes to your house; or worse, hangs around outside like a love-sick puppy? Since you don't know him well; how do you know how many criminal contacts he has behind that flattering smile of his? By jilting him so abruptly; he might feel he has been sexually used. He could easily give information to the underworld to have your house burgled; just to teach you a lesson. Since he will not break in himself; you may never cotton on that it was he who organised the burglary. The best thing to do is to make it clear from the onset that it is a one-night stand. Take him to a hotel; so that he never knows where you live. Don't give him your phone number; so that the lines are drawn very clearly in the sand. After the sex; be very business-like and ask him to leave as agreed, so that he will not feel you have done him a disservice. Don't say you will call him; when you have no intention of doing so. Refuse his phone number, if he gives it to you; so that if see him again, it will only be by chance. You should avoid sleeping with him a second time; because there is a risk of one of you falling in love with the other and the love not being reciprocated!

You have to understand that any woman who takes a strange man to her home; usually does so after having had a good time with him in a club or bar. This means alcohol or drugs may have been consumed; and that is why she is able to make such an 'error of judgement'. In her drunken/drugged condition, she may forget about practising safe-sex and catch some unpleasant (incurable?) sexually-transmitted disease; not to talk of an unwanted pregnancy. After the intercourse; she may fall asleep and will be unaware what the man may get up to in her house, when he goes to the toilet or makes himself a sandwich/drink. It has been known to happen that a woman has woken up the next morning to discover the man she brought home the night before has disappeared; taking most of her valuables with him. It is not up to me to tell you who you can or cannot bring into your home; but you have to be very careful because by doing so, you leave yourself open to being date-raped, drugged and robbed. He may not even physically take anything; but could gather information to be used later, like your credit card/bank details and whatever is worth stealing from your home. Even if he is not a thief; he may, after admiring the set-up in your house, decide it would be more profitable to slide his way into your life. Before you know it...bingo! He is your boyfriend, spending your money! I hope you can now appreciate that keeping your home safe involves a lot more than just locking your doors. You obviously know your house better than I do; so using this chapter as a guideline, you should be able to make a few adjustments to what you already have in place and make your abode even safer than it already is.

"Keeping your home safe is one thing Tigress, but how do you keep yourself safe from people? The next chapter will enlighten you."

Chapter Nine
People! – Can you trust them?

People come in all shapes and sizes and from all walks of life; which means there are good and there are bad people and some with a little bit of both in them. We all need people in our lives and therefore, we are bound to get hurt by those we put our faith and trust in; who end up abusing and taking advantage of us. Being female; the chances are you will get hurt a lot more. This is because most of the laws of the world were made by men for the benefit of men; without much thought to the female. Although things are slowly changing, you will find that old habits take a long time to die. One has to admire the female; because if men had to put up with what women have endured over the years, they would not be able to handle it with such stoicism. Patronising men; sexism; misogyny; bullying partners; lack of equal pay and hindrance of promotion prospects in the workplace are just a few of the things that make it hard to be a woman. Amazingly; they take it all on board without serious complaint, while some of them even manage to smile and laugh through their predicament! Even after all that; some women have to look after the children, the husband and the household. We have all heard how women are able to juggle several balls in the air; but it is a myth conveniently peddled by men that women are better at multi-tasking than men. Women have been well and truly convinced that they are better at it; and this takes the pressure off men, who can guiltlessly pass the majority of the work on to the females in their lives! In many ways; true equality has not yet fully arrived for the female. This is because men are still dictating what women should and should not do; with the oldest trick in the book, flattery. *"My wife is a wonderful cook and she's so good with the kids…I don't know what I would do without her!"*

1. Patronising men

Kindness and being friendly is not always a good thing; because it is seen by some people as a weakness and they will try to take advantage of you. As a woman, you therefore have to be very careful and suspicious, even when someone is being polite or nice to you; because there is always a hidden agenda. Even if a man offers you his seat on a bus or helps to carry your bags; you have to realise that it is a subtle way into your life. Out of the assistance comes conversation; followed by a possible exchange of phone numbers and a date you may never have wanted! This is all because you felt gratitude for his help and could not refuse his kind offer of a 'quiet drink' in a café or bar; making it harder to get rid of him. Although it is 'nice to be nice', sometimes you have to be tough to stop people taking advantage of you; by putting your foot down as soon as it happens, and not later. If some stranger offers to help you with anything you can handle yourself, it might be better to refuse; so that he has no way into your life, unless you want him to. This would still be unadvisable because you really don't know who he is or whether he has been following you for days (weeks?); and has chosen the perfect moment to move in, by helping you carry your bags. People have used this very female kindness to dupe and belittle unsuspecting women; whilst some females have been insulted because they were a little too forthright for their own good. Because saying *"Yes!"* to a favour and getting rid of a pest in a nasty way when he offers to lend a helping hand, can become problematic; the safest option would be to shun all offers and get on with your business. This obviously includes refusing someone who wants to buy you a drink or offer you his seat on the bus; if you have no intention of taking things further. You therefore have to learn the art of saying *"No!"* with a smile and using a plausible excuse to let him understand that there is a limit to how far you want him to go; so that he does not get too angry and embarrass you by publicly insulting you. *"Thanks for your kind offer; but I'm a working woman, so I really don't mind buying my own drink/standing/carrying my own bags. I'd love to stay and chat to you but I have a few family problems and I need to be alone to collect my thoughts. Sorry!"* You should then conclude the conversation by keeping a straight and serious face, the way only women know how to when they are not interested; because that will put the final nail into his attempt to coerce you!

Knowing who to be nice to and who to put in their place; is an art very few women have been able to master. This brings us to the 'Yes' people! From the car mechanic and the shop assistant to the bartender; there are always men who should know better, out to get 'one over' on a woman with flattery and a patronising attitude. This is because they think women are stupid and have got more cash than sense. *"Yes Madam, I can fix your car for you; but it will need a new crankshaft which will cost $€£..."* *"Yes Ma'am, the dress looks nice on you; but wouldn't you prefer this other one, which would look even better..."* (More expensive?) *"Yes Sweetheart, I know what you are saying and I never said you were drunk; but it was only a ten pound note you gave me for the drinks, not a twenty..."* Many husband and wife jokes are based on the poor henpecked man being forced to say *"Yes Dear!"* just to get some peace from his nagging wife. The problem is, a lot of women like to insist they are right; and men have learnt that to get anything from a woman, all you have to do is agree with her! This gets women in more trouble than they are prepared to admit; because having laid down a certain point of view, they find it hard to back down and look silly in front of men.

For example; a woman takes her car in to a garage with her defences already up. She brings the *'I will make sure he does not cheat me'* attitude with her and displays an air of importance; even quoting parts of the car she knows little about, but thinks the mechanic will believe she is an expert on cars and dare not rip her off. So, what does the mechanic do? *"Yes, Madam; you are right about the crankshaft but the carburettor is dirty and could do with a clean".* She may know what a carburettor is; but how will she be sure whether it needs a clean or not? Not many women will be prepared to dirty their fingernails and fiddle with the engine, just to prove the mechanic wrong. If she dares say, *"The carburettor does not need anything. I only had it cleaned last week...!"* the mechanic will put Plan B into operation and disconnect something, so that the car will not start. When she is not able to tell him why the car will not work; he has then got her exactly where he wants and can now turn her self-importance into a tidy profit for himself. *"I told you the carburettor needs to be cleaned and I'll change the oil for you as well"*. Meanwhile, in order not to be outdone; the woman, who would by now be fed up, will either tell him to get on with it or take her car to another garage. The mechanic there might do the same thing; because there are so many tricks they use that even men are not safe!

Similar and even more devious tricks are used by all men who are hired to do jobs for women; so please take your time, when you hire anybody to do a job for you. Be careful of the men, who try to use their smiles and charm to lull you into a false sense of security. They are the ones who will compliment your beauty; and call you delightful names like *"Darling" "Love"* and *"Sweetheart"*. Always ask him to give you the names and numbers of any previous jobs he has done in your area; so that you can ring up and find out if he did a good job for them. If after checking his credentials, you do allow him into your home; never pay any money before the work is completed to your satisfaction. If possible, you should write up a contract detailing everything you expect from the job; including the time he is to start and finish work. This should then be signed by both you and him. There is usually a seven-day period after signing a contract; which legally allows you to change your mind. All 'special offers' are not legally binding; unless they are explained in detail and you are given the seven-day time limit to accept or decline. Beware of any man who says, *"I'll give you a good price Darling..."* or *"Trust me; I know what I'm doing...!"*

Remember; you are inviting a stranger into your house. He might be able to relay precious information to his criminal friends to come and rob or burgle you at a later date! This means you should never leave him alone to do the work. If you are too busy; you should get a neighbour, relative or family friend to watch over him, while you are away. Keep an eye on him in stages, as he is doing the job; and don't be afraid to ask pertinent, practical and intuitive questions like, *"How come the screw on this side of the shelf is different from the one on other side...?"* or *"Where is the receipt for the new washer you bought to fix my tap?..."* or even *"Why is the door still squeaking? I thought you said you had fixed it?"* It will let him know that even if you know nothing about the mechanics of the job, you are not stupid; so he will be less likely to try any of his tricks on you. There have been cases where roof tiles have been painted over, and passed on as new; instead of being replaced. This is easily possible, if you are not watching him! A driveway is supposed to take at least a few days to dig up and do up; but you could be conned into paying extra money, when told that it can be done in a few hours.

As long as women try to out-smart men on their territory; they will forever be duped by the "*Yes, Madam*" brigade. If you know nothing about a car; you should be honest enough to admit it and be nice to the mechanic, by treating him with a little respect. A friendly smile, a little harmless flirting or good old-fashioned banter; will get you a lot further than playing Miss Know-all. *"My brother is a mechanic and I must admit I know nothing about cars; but I'm sure you can do everything and fix the car for him. He'll soon be back from his holidays!"* This subtly lets the mechanic know that whatever he does, you have ways and means of having his work checked out; and if he values you as a customer, he should do a good job. Even if you are an expert on cars, it would serve you better to pretend you are ignorant; so that you can catch him out, if he tries any underhand tactics. If you are happy with his work and see him in a pub one day; buy him a drink! It will work wonders when you next bring your car in to him! The so-called 'little men' (mechanics, bartenders, shop assistants, odd-job men, lowly employees etc), are all protectively-proud of their jobs and often feel under-appreciated; so when you walk into their domain with an air of self-importance, it is human nature to bring you down a peg or two. He wants to show off his art or skills to you; and there you are, trying to undermine his few moments of glory. A shop assistant immediately springs to life when you genuinely ask for advice on things he/she is selling. When you come in trying to give them your own haughty opinions and suggestions; it does not go down well. In order not to lose a customer; they would rather get their own back with *"Yes Madam"* and fleece you. In order not to look stupid after trying to look important; you may end up spending more than you originally intended!

Certain stereotypical beliefs still exist; like if a woman is blonde she must be dumb; beautiful means she's as delicate as a flower; tough and strong looking makes her a lesbian; the businesslike and intelligent need a charm offensive and sexy with lots of make-up means she is 'up for it'. All these notions have put men in a quandary as to how best to treat a woman; and many end up saying the wrong things, in a patronising way. It is therefore up to you to immediately set the record straight, when someone says or treats you in a way that undermines your self-worth; because if you don't, he will continue doing it to other people. This also means you should not patronise others; because you may end up being insulted, which will not be good for your self-esteem or reputation. On the whole, women tend to have a more understanding insight into the feelings of others than men; and that is why you will find that men patronising women, is much more prevalent than vice-versa. This is obviously due to the 'weaker sex' attitude men seem to carry around like a millstone around their necks; making them believe every female is a damsel in distress who needs protecting, and saving her is his prerogative. Sadly; many men have not yet got into their thick skulls that the modern woman is more than capable of looking after herself. By patronising her; it rather makes him look stupid and ripe for being taken advantage of! This is the main reason why a man receives very little public sympathy when he is duped by a woman; and is often laughed out of court. If he had not patronised her and treated her like a brainless child who needed nurturing; would she have been able to get through his defences and rip him off? As long as you keep to your inherent female instincts and treat yourself and others with respect, you will have no problems at all with patronising men; because they will have no starting point from which to operate.

2. "I'm as good as any man…"

Women have taken such great strides in all walks of life that there is nothing of any real significance that men do, which women are not also doing. This has put men on the back foot and it has now become like a competition; with women striving and often succeeding in outdoing men on many fronts. The only exception would be in traditionally male preserves like football/rugby/basketball/baseball and ice hockey; where the men would most likely do it better and will fight any female encroachment on their territory. Female athletes are often complaining that male sports players get more publicity and money than the women; some of whom are as skilful as the men. This is obviously because the men started most of the sports being played today. Comparatively, women only just came into professional sports; so competing with men on their own terms, will most likely end in failure. It does not help the female cause when the best female reporters and journalists seem more interested (earn more money?) in covering the men's game than in supporting their own; and you see more women watching male matches than the female ones! The half-empty stands in most female sports events tell the story better than I can. Like any business, sport favours the one who comes first; and that is why of all the popular sports, it is only female tennis players who make relatively equal money to the males. This is simply because they have been playing the game as long as the men and attract equal crowds; but even they had to fight hard for many years to break the status quo. However, because the women still play the best of three sets as opposed to the men and their best of five in the Grand Slam events; there will always be those who will treat women tennis players with derision and contempt and believe they can never be as good as the men.

Women doing things because the men do it, is seen as the easy or lazy option; whereby they are using the laws on equality to take advantage and jump on the male bandwagon, without having paid their 'dues'. It has been a source of bemusement amongst many men who cannot see why a woman often strives to prove she is better at a 'man's job'; rather than start up something of her own. That is the major factor why there is a resistance whenever a woman tries to do something men have been doing for years; resulting in a reluctance to actively support or pay her equivalently for her efforts. If women could invent a popular sport that is only played by women; then the tables will be turned. As it stands; even games like netball, which is played mostly by women, was invented by men as an offshoot of basketball! This just emphasises the point that women have to get together and support each other, the way the men do. There is undoubted female talent in the world; which remains untapped and unutilised. This is because the females who are in a position to change things, are not doing so. Until then; be prepared to play second fiddle, if you continue in sports and jobs that were invented and mostly performed by men. I do not want to put you off your favourite pastime or profession; but you have to be patient and accept that things will change eventually. A woman can still make a very good living from sports or many other jobs; but regrettably, not as lucratively as the men. Did you know that the Girl Guides is probably the only major organisation that does not allow boys to join? Imagine how powerful women would become; if there were more businesses and industries owned and run by only women!

In many an office or working environment, you will see the women working hard in a subliminal effort to show they are as good as or better than the men they are working with; and in the majority of instances, actually succeeding. Employers have realised the usefulness and benefits of the female workforce and often use praise and flattery to make her feel important; resulting in an increased effort on her part. *"Well done Mary! That was a good job you did...!"* is a common and typical compliment women receive in almost every working location from their male bosses; yet rarely are her efforts reflected in her pay check. This allows the men to do less work and laugh all the way to the bank; because his pay slip will be better, or at the very least, equal to that of the woman breaking her back in order to prove she is as good as a man. Even though there is an economic downturn in many countries, and a large number of women are happy to have a job at all; it does not mean you should be short-changed. You deserve to be paid equally with the men, for the work you do. Once you have accepted a job; try to find out what everybody else in your sector is earning. If there is a discrepancy; don't be afraid to (politely) approach your boss and voice your concerns. Get together with all the women in your company and compare notes; so that you will have a viable case, if you are taking the industrial tribunal route. The worst thing to do is to sit and do nothing. Employers (male and female) are paid to save the company money; so it will suit them to pay you less for your efforts! Believe it or not; there is a law on equal pay for equal work! It is routinely abused because few women are prepared to fight over the discrepancy; which is sometimes very little and hardly worth disputing. If every woman in a company downed tools because of unequal pay (however small); the subsequent bad publicity will quickly make the employers come to their senses. Once it becomes an accepted practice for women to demand equal pay and are prepared to fight for it; only then will the practice cease.

A woman will gain more respect from a man and more money from her employers; only if she can do something a man cannot. You will therefore find that it is ideas that make you rich; not the amount of work you do. In that respect; if you have a good business idea, you should try and branch out on your own. Any bank or tycoon will be more than willing to finance your dreams;

if they see in it, a decent profit for themselves. In order to compete in what is essentially still a man's world; you have to play them at their own game. Be inventive, keep your cards close to your chest and go for it girl; because when it comes to a good idea, sexuality does not come into it and you will definitely receive your rewards. More and more women are now climbing quickly up the corporate and business ladder; simply because they bring something to a business that a man cannot, like feminine charm, clever intuition and simple ideas that work. Women on the whole; are more in tune with human nature and approach problems in a more sensitively practical way! If you are in a working environment surrounded by males; don't just accept your predicament. If you want to get ahead; you should try to make a difference for your company. As a woman; you definitely have something different (better?) to offer, which the males may not be able to see. It would be a sheer waste of talent, if your femininity remained un-utilised. Many smart bosses know that in order to broker a successful deal, they always include a woman in the negotiations; because she can usually 'feel' if the deal is good or bad for the company! Although no one likes to admit it; a charming, clever and beautiful woman in a room full of stuffy men in suits, still has the desired effect of ever-so slightly 'softening' them up for the kill! The toughest business negotiations are usually between two women; because neither will be prepared to back down without a fight. That is when the claws come out and the sparks really fly!

In certain public places like a nightclub/bar, where there are men around; you have to be aware of the fact that as a woman, a lot of male eyes will be on you and this can make you a little self-conscious. It is therefore important that you be yourself and retain your dignity by not showing off. Unfortunately, there are some younger women who arrive in groups for celebrations, parties or hen nights; and then play to the gallery, in order to impress the men. They will shout, get drunk, make a thorough nuisance of themselves and hopefully get thrown out; because that is what happens to the male lager lout equivalent. Some will go up to the bar, instead of waiting for the waiter and yell for their drinks; thinking she will be served quicker and attract an equally drunk male suitor. The bartender thinks, *'I'll show her, the loud bitch!'* He serves her and waits for a *"Thank you"*. Not forthcoming; he bides his time till she gets even drunker and gives her less booze and more water in her shots. He might even 'forget' to give her the change, until she goes away; because bartenders are experts at standing their ground in disputes over change. Inevitably; the woman will give in rather than look stupid in front of the men she was trying to impress with her rude and brash attitude. This 'laddish' behaviour in women so glorified in the tabloid press because a few celebrities pretend to do it; is actually detrimental to the reputation of women.

You have to protect your dignity when you are in the company of males; because trying to act like them only makes you a laughing stock. The only interest you will attract; will be from seedy, lecherous men looking for some quick sex! This is okay, if that is your way of life; but certainly not good for your reputation, femininity and integrity. You have to realise that as a woman; you are already very special. There is no need to prove anything to any man; because it is your differences that draws his affection and guarantees his respect. Every human being in this world came out of a female womb; so the love and respect for females is inherent, unless proven otherwise. Why ruin it for yourself by trying to be something you are not; and behaving in a manner, in complete contrast to your sex? Instead of striving to be 'as good as a man'; you should act in a way that will make men strive to be as good as a woman! Real ladies operate impeccably, with confidence and charm; because they know how to get what they want with the minimum of fuss and probably don't need my advice! Don't forget; it was the corruption and malpractices of the banking and financial institutions that led to the collapse of the world economy a few years ago. Did you notice that there were *no women* amongst the 'fat-cat' leaders blamed for the collapse; which tells you that if women were in charge of our finances, they would do a much better job! It is no accident that in almost every household, it is the wife who decides how the family money is spent; and things usually go wrong when the husband thinks he can do better!

3. Sexism

In nature, the male is usually the hunter who goes in search of a female mate; and it is no different with human beings. This is why every woman has, at one time or another, had to deal with rude come-ons; cheesy chat-up lines; annoying wolf whistles; cruel oppression and blatant discrimination because of her sex; otherwise known as sexism. It all goes back to the fact that men still believe a woman is the weaker sex, who cannot think for or protect herself. Therefore, men must make decisions for her; based on what they believe a woman should be like. To be treated differently because you are a woman is a modern day scourge, which has not yet been eradicated; and it is has now become up to the individual woman to make sure it does not happen to her. Sexism will not go away; because those who are guilty of it do not believe or are not even aware, they are doing anything wrong. It is how you deal with people that will determine how you are treated by them; and a man can only be sexist to you, if you allow him to get away with it. The crude man on the building site who calls you *"...Love/Sexy..."* or the drunk football fan who tells you to *"...get your kit off..."* in the stadium; should not be taken seriously and can even be dismissed as an imbecile who does not know any better. Whereas, the businessman or white-collar worker who says something demeaning to your sex, should be quickly taken to task; before he spirals out of control. The more intelligent a man is, the more you have to realise that his sexism is likely to be deliberate; and he should know better. He therefore has to be stopped immediately in his tracks; because such a man is more likely to be misogynistic and needs to be put in his place or he will continue doing it.

Sexist wisecracks from men come in so many different forms, that only you will know how to handle them; depending on how you are feeling at the time. On the whole, most women know how to put men in their place with a quick-fire retort; because when it comes to shooting from the lip, few men can withstand a verbal onslaught from an angry or a clever woman pretending to be angry at some wisecrack. A sense of humour is usually enough to get you through the day, because most wisecracks are harmless; and even if they are painful, (usually when they are true!) you should try to ignore them. For example; if a man calls you 'fat' and you know you are, then don't get mad. He might be doing you a favour to take a closer look at yourself; and maybe eat less or use the gym a bit more. You should always have a confident attitude; *"I know I am fat; but you are ugly and I can diet!"* or *"I don't give a shit what you think, you asshole; 'cause I like myself the way I am. More of me for my partner to love!"* because they will definitely stop, if they feel they cannot upset you. Although it is not politically correct to tease those 'less fortunate' than ourselves or to use sex to judge/describe a woman; make no mistake, it does happen. You therefore have to learn how to deal with it; because ignorance is a difficult thing to fight and re-educate. *"Wow! Check out those tits!"* or *"Nice ass sexy!"* is seen as degrading by some women; but it is impossible to stop an ignorant buffoon from talking like that, because that is how he is. You also have to respect the fact that a thing is only 'wrong', if you do not agree with it; but you also have no 'right' to prevent freedom of speech. Every woman has something she will or will not tolerate; and this might be different from what you find acceptable or unacceptable. Some women are pleased when a man tells her she has *"nice tits!"* or a *"sexy bum!"* This means; a man can go through life making 'sexist' remarks and will think it is okay, if nobody complains! To confuse things further; there are quite a few women who find sexist men and their politically incorrect comments like, *"Women should stay at home and take care of the kids"* and *"Women have small feet so that they can stand closer to the sink to do the washing up!"* very appealing. They often fall for the 'bad boy syndrome'; because their unpredictability makes them more manly and exciting!

A sense of self-worth is important; so that you do not get upset when things go against you. If you have a problem with your confidence; I'm sure there are a lot of self-help books on the market you can check out. You could also go and talk to a professional; because you are definitely going to face sexist remarks in your every day life. It is therefore imperative you do not allow them to affect you. However, if you are in a public place and someone says or does something you find offensive or demeaning to your sex; you obviously cannot laugh it off. Were that to happen; you have to be brave and tell him off right there and then, by yelling at him. *"Who the hell do you think you are, you piece of shit. You have no right to talk to any woman like that!"* or *"Get your filthy hands off me you pervert. I am not a piece of meat for you to grope. You pinched my bum!"* Don't worry about going all out on him. There is nothing he can do to you in front of so many people; without getting arrested for molestation! The embarrassment will most likely stop him in his tracks and the chances are; he will slink away, rather than get into a war of words with you. Just watch out for the opportunistic men who will come to your 'aid', by telling the man to leave you alone; in the hope of scoring some points with you! You may get rid of one pest; only to be replaced by others who, although pretending to help you, might be just as hard to escape from. With them, you have to be a little more tactful in 'appreciation' for the help they gave you; by politely getting rid of them. *"Thank you for your help. I'm okay; don't worry I can take care of myself. No, I don't want to go for a drink with you to calm my nerves. Bye!"*

Sexism in its many forms will not go completely away from the workplace; unless women working together are prepared to stand up for each other, in order to eradicate the cancer. Most letters sent to companies still begin with *'Dear Sir/Madam'*; even though the one receiving the letter will most probably be a woman. Women more often than men, are usually the ones in the firing line of a company; in the form of secretaries and immediate bosses! This kind of sexism is difficult to eradicate because it is still universally assumed that women occupy fewer positions in the workforce. If you do receive a letter like that; it would be deliciously poignant, when replying, to boldly state your name with the pre-fix *Ms. Mrs.* or even *Madam.* I don't believe the person will repeat the mistake in the future; if he wants to stay on your right side! If the sexism is so outrageous, it leads to your being sacked or treated unfairly in your place of work; it then becomes a case of sexual harassment. You will have to go for the jugular, but in a clever way; so that you hit the perpetrators hard in the pocket by suing them. There is a law on sexism; which very few women evoke, because it is either too problematic or might bring too much trouble to them. Sadly; you might not get the support you need from your female work colleagues because they have their own interests to protect. You therefore have to use your head; by slowly and painstakingly gathering enough evidence to make sure you win your case. The more evidence you can gather; the bigger the compensation you are likely to win! Keep a diary of everything that happens to you over a period of time, like six months. If you are being routinely teased, harassed and abused because of your sex; you should sneak a tiny tape recorder in to record all the horrible things said against you. There is some very convenient recording equipment on the market (easily concealable on your body); which can allow you to audio/video everything going on around you. Once you feel you have enough damaging evidence; you should see a lawyer who specialises in such matters. More than likely; your employer will push for an out-of-court settlement, rather than go to an industrial tribunal and all the negative publicity that comes with it. Reporting someone to the authorities may seem like a triumph; but you could become a marked woman and be shunned or teased even more by his friends in your community. Paying some kids to scrawl filthy graffiti on your walls and strew rubbish all over your garden; are ways they can continue with their sexist offensive and deliberate intimidation, without your being able to identify and report the culprits. If the compensation is big enough; I would advise you to leave the company and look for another job. If possible; move from the area you are living in and get away from the bad memories!

Most women already know how to deal with their own errant men. Do not hate a man for being a man; because he is yours and only you can do something to change him. If you find out your man is one that goes around 'degrading' or teasing women (including you); then you have to 'educate' him. Be firm, but use tact to correct him; because he may genuinely believe it is okay to make sexist comments or pinch a female bottom in private or in public. In a funny way; you will be judged by others (especially females) by the way your man behaves in public. If he is a rude sexist buffoon; people will look at you as either a willing collaborator of his behaviour or a stupid ostrich with her head buried in the sand. They will then blame you for not keeping him under control! Instead of retiring to your shell and moaning to your friends; try to do something about him. If you don't; there might be a load of willing rivals who love a challenge and would be delighted to have him, sexist comments et al. Most men will change; if they see you are genuinely upset by their behaviour and it is affecting the relationship. Don't be afraid to let him know how you feel; but still love him despite his faults. Good men are hard to find; but they are all fallible. You know why you chose him; so do your best to keep him that way. Good luck!

4. Dating…

Truthfully; we cannot exist without people. Life would not be worth living, if you were the only person in the world. Loneliness can be so boring that some women resort to Internet chat rooms and dating agencies. Although many people have had varying degrees of success with blind-dating; it is not really a good idea, because too many things can go wrong. This means you really must have your wits about you! When you meet a man for the first time; he will obviously be out to give a good impression of himself by exaggerating or outright lying, which may not be his true character. He may also be a very shy person and may cover up the shyness with blusterous behaviour. All this means that you should not believe anything a man tells you on a first date, neither should you instantly dismiss them; but rather keep an open mind. If you ask the right questions; his barriers will slowly fall and you can get to know the real person behind the façade, which could be exactly what you are looking for. The safest forms of blind-dating are the ones set up for you by close friends; because you will have ways and means of checking up on his background and character. He will most likely not try anything bad on you; because he will not be able to get away with it!

(a) The Internet

The modern phenomenon that is the World Wide Web has opened up many possibilities for interaction with other people, while remaining relatively anonymous; through the social networking sites. It is this anonymity that makes it exciting and good fun; because you can be whoever you want to be and nobody need know the truth, if you don't want them to. Unfortunately; the inherent curiosity of the human being can actually make Internet dating the most dangerous form of socialising, as soon as the boundary of anonymity is crossed. Once you become cyber friends with someone, the next step is to get to know more about the person; and sooner or later, you will want to meet up for real. This is not only very dangerous for children; but also for you as a woman. This is because when you do meet up with him, he will definitely be on his best behaviour; and you might fall for him to the extent that you will want to meet him again. You might then end up in his house and encounter the same problems and dangers as described in the earlier chapters on date rape and mental rape. I would therefore advise you to stay anonymous and never cross the boundary to go out of your way to meet up with someone. Of course, there is every possibility that your cyber pal is genuine; but what if he isn't? Do you need to put yourself in unnecessary turmoil and possible danger, in order to find out?

There are several recognised social sites that require membership and a password. These are probably safer because the site is responsible for vetting each member. They may be better for you, if you need to satisfy your curiosity of meeting up with strangers who are into the same things as you; because you will have ways and means of seeking redress, if something were to go wrong. I realise you are your own woman; so I cannot tell you what to do and who you can or cannot see. But if you are insistent on meeting up with someone you met on the Internet; I implore you to arrange for him to come to your area and never go to his town. Always meet up with him in a public place like a well-known café or bar, whose owner you are familiar with; and if possible, have a friend with you so that she can also give you her insight into your new friend. It will take a few innocuous dates like that, before you can accurately assess and be comfortable in your own mind whether to go ahead and continue seeing him. If it works out for you then I will be happy. There is nothing worse than putting your love and faith in a man and being let down; simply because you failed to spot the signs, until it were too late.

Finally; there are certain sites which are convenient fronts for paedophile rings and other high profile illegal hurly-burly. You should avoid these; because you could get yourself into very serious trouble. The subsequent exposure by the tabloid media will most likely ruin your reputation for good; even if you were found not guilty in a court of law. This exposure could open a can of worms with your safety; because there will definitely be those who will feel so aggrieved, they will try and take the law into their own hands.

Being exposed as a paedophile, prostitute, arms dealer or terrorist; could easily end up with your house being vandalised, your children targeted in school and your being hounded out of your area. Please be careful; because the Internet is still a relatively lawless hive of activities. Every site you visit leaves a link; which the police can easily trace through your service provider. You should always watch out, if your cyber friend suggests visiting a 'cool' site you know nothing about. It could be on the police antenna; and it will be very difficult to prove your innocence, if you are caught up in something unpalatable. If your neighbours see the cops smashing their way into your house and leaving with your computer; you will not be able to stop the harmful gossip that will follow. Ultimately; there is no smoke without a fire!

(b) Dating agencies

All major dating agencies have one thing in common and that is, they genuinely want to see you succeed with your date; because they charge money for their services and every success means more kudos and more customers for them. This means they will require as much information about you as possible, in order to build up your profile and help you find a compatible mate. It would therefore be in your best interests to tell the truth with whatever you allow them to know about yourself. If there is something embarrassing or confidential that you don't want them to know; (criminal record/debilitating disease/illness/financial situation etc.) it would be better to say nothing, rather than to lie. This is because it is what you tell them that they will use to compare with other men on their roster; so that they can arrange a suitable date for you. A good dating agency is relatively safe because they have ways and means of checking up on their customers; in case something goes wrong. If you are ever beaten up, date raped, robbed or insulted; you will be able to report him to the agency and they will be able to furnish the police with enough info, in order to apprehend him. However; you still have to keep your wits about you by meeting him in your area and checking him out properly with a friend over several dates...before making up your mind whether or not to allow him into your life. This means; you must not let him know where you live or work, until you are truly ready. If you both fancy the pants off each other on the first date and you absolutely 'must have him', then take him to a motel/hotel for your frolics; so that you can treat it like a one-night stand, in case he turns out to be a damp squib in the coital department. This way you won't have him bothering you in the future; because you can tell the agency, *"Can you find me someone else? This one didn't work out!"* They will formally inform him of your decision; which he is legally bound to adhere to or face prosecution for molestation.

(c) Speed-dating

This is a relatively new form of dating; where you are given a certain amount of time (about three minutes on average) with a man to find out a little about him before talking to the next 'applicant'. Most of them are run in true chivalrous style by allowing the women to stay put on their seats; whilst the men move from table to table. This in effect means you are the one doing the interviewing! You then tick the required boxes on a form; and if there are enough corresponding ticks between certain people, they will be put in touch with each other and are then free to arrange a real date. This mode of finding out about someone; is designed so that you don't get bored talking to the same person for too long. Since you are required to pay a gate fee to the organisers as soon as you enter; they will have made their money before the game starts. This means they are not really too bothered who wins and who loses! Few applicants tell the truth; and some say certain things just to shock and see the reaction of the person in front of them. It is held in a convivial atmosphere; so you can always go up to the one you really do fancy, as soon as the questioning is over and use conventional methods to 'chat him up'. Speed-dating is safe enough and can be a lot of fun; so long as you don't take it too seriously. It is better if you go with friends; so that you are not pressured into going off with someone on a whim, simply because you 'like him'.

(d) How do you get rid of a boring date?

You are on a date sitting with a total idiot who is boring the pants off you, and you want to get rid of him; but at the same time, you do not want to hurt his feelings. *"Why the hell did I agree to go out with him?"* Poor pitiful you! If you make up a silly excuse *"I've got a tummy ache and I'm not feeling well…"*, you will defeat the purpose of trying to look good in front of him; because he will know you are lying and will not respect you for it. The best thing to do is to be honest. *"You are not really enjoying this are you? Neither am I. You know what? I don't think we are getting anywhere here; so I would like to go home."* Don't make any promises you would not want to keep; because it may come back to embarrass you. *"Why don't we hook up next week instead?"* will not work well because he may hold you up to the promise; and he will then become a nuisance whom you will have to be rude to, in order to finally get rid of him. Some women will rather sit through a boring meal with a suitor and finish the date; rather than tell him the obvious that he has no chance with her and never will! For others, it seems it is so important to remain friends; they would rather endure an evening of garrulous chit-chat, instead of walking out on a date. Never be shy about your feelings; because they make up who you really are at the time. If that upsets a boring date, then it's a case of, 'Tough shit!'

Once you have told him you want out; get up and head for the exit and never dilly-dally or hang around for him to talk you out of it. *"Why don't we go somewhere else instead and you will feel better."* Men can be so stupid and stubborn at times; they will refuse to take subtle verbal hints from a woman and are unable to read her body language. *"She's just playing hard to get. The ice will melt soon!"* If you are not interested in him where you are; how will going somewhere else change your feelings for him? Pretending you like a man because he is paying for the dinner is not a good idea; because he may start plotting his own revenge on you (drugging/date rape?). He will easily know you are pretending, when you laugh at all his jokes and act very friendly; yet your body 'freezes', as soon as he comes anywhere near you. This 'freezing' is an involuntary nervous reaction; which very few women can hide successfully. The minute a man holds your hand or tries to kiss you, it's like your soul telling your body *"I can't do this!"*; while your brain is saying, *"Come on, we've got to get through this. Just go along with it because he can be useful to me in one way or another!"* As smart as you think you are; your soul cannot lie because it is made up of 'who you really are'. Somehow in the realm of metaphysics, the soul of the man will also sense that something is wrong. Sooner or later, you will give the game away; and you will wish you had been honest in the beginning by not accepting a date with someone you obviously have no feelings for. If a man insists on taking you out; let him understand that you are going out as friends and 'nothing more'. Offer to pay for half the evening; so that he does not feel you owe him anything for his expenditure. Do not change your mind; or he will never take you seriously when it really matters...like refusing him sex. You can always arrange another date, if you end up liking him. Honesty really is the best policy in everything you do!

5. The Police

Every country has a set of rules designed to ensure the smooth running of its way of life and to protect its citizens; without which there would be total anarchy. The police are the ones entrusted to make sure we don't break the law; and if we do, ensure that we are punished through the courts by fines; suspensions; community service and prison sentences. For a woman; the police are the only people she can trust to protect her, without having a hidden agenda. They are duty bound to help you; and are covered by a system of checks and balances to make sure they don't over-step their powers. Although it might not be in their interests to admit it; the police also have an institutionalised empathy towards women, children and senior citizens. This means, they will help you much quicker than they would a man! If a woman is raped, beaten up, robbed or makes a domestic violence report; she will receive an immediate response, whereas a man may not be taken so seriously. This 'weaker sex' attitude and positive bias is actually a good thing for women, so should not be criticised; because without the police, men would literally get away with murder. The fact that the police will most likely believe a woman's story over a man's, unless proved otherwise; has kept a reasonably tight leash on a lot of men from using violence on the females in their lives. If you are ever scared of a man or frightened of any situation; then the police are your safest bet. No man in his right senses will continually causing trouble for a woman who has already made a report to the police. Although exaggeration by using tears, tantrums and over-emphasis are tools used effectively by women who want to make sure the perpetrator of her abuse is quickly brought to book; it does not mean you should abuse this preferential treatment. It could easily backfire on you, if the police realise they have been taken for a ride! Once you have lost their trust by lying or 'crying wolf' too many times; it will be very hard to get it back. Finally; you have to remember that without the help of the public, the police would not be so effective. If you see any crime being committed or anybody being mistreated; don't be scared to make a report to them. A quick call, photo or video shot via your mobile phone will be most helpful in nailing the culprits; and more importantly, the police will always protect your identity and give you all the support you need.

(a) The Police Station

Make no mistake; there are female criminals in every society, some as callous and dangerous as the men, but luckily, not as many. As a woman; I will therefore give you the benefit of the doubt and assume you are a law-abiding citizen who will probably never be arrested or charged with a crime. Just in case you find yourself in the clutches of the law; there are a few simple rules you must observe, if you want them to help you and treat you seriously with respect. Since as a woman, you already have their de facto sympathy; the most important thing to remember when entering a police station either as complainant or defendant, is to be polite and TELL THE TRUTH. The police are not stupid and deal with dangerous, lying criminals every day of the week! As a complainant; any story you give will have to fit in with the facts and have a reasonable chance of conviction, before the file will be sent to the Prosecution office. It is there that they will decide whether to allow it to go to court or not. If you have been conned or attacked; then the law has to take its course. The person who caused the offence will be arrested; but not necessarily punished. The police can only charge him; but will then have to leave it for the courts to decide the outcome. If you say someone raped you; it has to be proved in a court of law. It is no use blaming the police; if the judgment does not go your way, due to a lack of evidence. If you claim a man hit you and there are no signs of bruising or cuts; it will stand little chance of success because the police will have nothing of significance to go on. Nevertheless; as a self-defence tool, it is still useful to report any threat or aggression on your person. The aggressor will at the very least be given a harsh reprimand and a severe warning to keep away from you. This will in turn, limit the chances of him coming back to threaten or rough you up.

As a defendant; you will most likely be questioned aggressively and then put into a horrible cell. It would be best to show a little humility and answer their questions politely; and they will realise you have a bit of class and treat you a lot better. If you are on a really serious charge like murder/manslaughter, robbery, grievous bodily harm, serious fraud or drugs; it would be advisable to say nothing and wait for your legal counsel to arrive. He/She will advise you what to do. The chances are, you will be refused police bail and will be locked up until you appear in court the next day; where another bail application can be made. You have to remember that the police are human beings, working under severe stress and stringent guidelines; in order to fulfil unrealistic targets, keep their political masters happy and the media off their backs. If one of them is already having personal, family or marital problems; the last thing he or she needs is you play-acting and giving them a hard time with a holier-than-thou attitude, by pleading innocence when you were caught red-handed. Believe me; the police in every country have to be admired for the amount of bullshit they have to put up with on a daily basis! Yet, they are not officially allowed to get angry; even though they probably feel like hitting some of the defendants and have been known to do so!

As a woman; if you cause trouble, they will send a tough, hard-bitten, 'seen-it-all' female officer to deal with you. She might not be so accommodating with any troublesome tactics you try to use to deflect them from your alleged crime! Angry policewomen are much more fearsome than their male counterparts; so I would advise you not to annoy them because they are female like you, and can get away with treating you a lot worse. Unfortunately, if you have committed a crime; there is nothing much you can do with the way you are treated in a police station...so long as they do not use physical force and injure you. They will shout, threaten, delay any food, drink or phone call requests and give you all kinds of worse-case scenarios; in order to try and make you confess and shop your co-conspirators. You should always remember that they cannot force you to talk; and only a judge and a court can decide your fate. All I can say is; if you know you are guilty, it would be best for you to come clean and play the 'damsel-in-distress' card because you will be treated leniently. Most judges are all too aware of the hardships women have to undergo, in order to look after their children. More often than not; it is a man she is in love with, who convinces her to commit crime!

(b) The Courts

If the police feel you are guilty; you will be sent forward for trial. This means you will face a judge for sentencing; and a jury, if you have pleaded *"Not guilty!"* In the case of petty crimes like shoplifting, credit card fraud or small drug possession; your lawyer will argue your case for you, but at some point, he/she might realise you are fighting a losing battle and will advocate leniency. This will be based on the fact that you are a woman who was pushed into crime by either a cruel and obsessive lover, a desperate need to take care of your children or to fund a drug habit. This line of defence will give the judge a convenient excuse to suspend your sentence, if it is a first offence; or give you a 'short sharp shock' minimal custodial sentence, to teach you a lesson. Judges don't enjoy sending a mother to prison, unless the crime is serious or she is a habitual criminal; because they have to think of her mental balance and the effect it will have on her young children. Whereas with a man; throwing him into jail is the usual option, because of a high likelihood of him re-offending.

If you have been on bail prior to your trial; you will have been aware of the trial date. This will give you a chance to collect good character references from any professional friends you may have, like doctors, lawyers, civil servants or politicians; and this will help the judge in determining a lesser sentence for you. Dress neatly and above all, show remorse; because judges are experts at taking one look at you and deciding your fate through your body language. Any sign of recalcitrance, conceit, pride or aloofness could add a few extra months on to your sentence; and could even be the difference between going to prison and getting a suspended sentence. You are a woman, and the legal system is already stacked in your favour; so if something goes wrong and the book is thrown at you, then it has to be your fault. This can only mean; the crime was too severe, you annoyed the police during the interrogation process or you showed a despicable attitude in court, which the judge could see through. She/He may therefore decide to teach you a nice lesson for your behaviour; and there is no better place to bring someone down a peg or two, than incarceration. The police could also relay the information to the wardens that you are 'trouble'; and you would be starting your sentence off on the wrong foot. Welcome to prison! You are here for the punishment, not the nourishment and your problems may be just beginning!

(c) In Prison

Finally, if all else fails and you are convicted by a jury and/or sentenced by a judge; you will be sent to prison. Not the nicest place for any woman! You will be handcuffed and taken in a van to a female prison, where you will do approximately one third to two thirds of your sentence before being eligible for release. On arrival, you will be taken to a reception where you will be told to remove your clothes, so that they can be searched for drugs, money or weapons; before they will allow you to wear them. Your body cavities (mouth, anus and vagina) may be searched by a female officer wearing rubber gloves; if they suspect you are hiding drugs in them. You will then be taken to your dormitory or cell; which you will have to share with other girls. Just pray that you get on; because the other girls can make your life a real misery with teasing, intimidation and subtle physical bullying. Stories of butch lesbians attacking newcomers are greatly exaggerated. The prison officers keep a tight reign on what goes on; and unless you are that way inclined, you will not be touched. There is however, a lot of drug-taking in all prisons; which the authorities are forced to publicly deny but allow it to go on. This is because it keeps the inmates quiet and happy; causing fewer problems for the staff. It would be better for you to avoid accepting drugs when offered; because you can easily get hooked on them and may not always have the money to pay. That is when you may end up being coerced to smuggle in contraband like mobile phones from visits and give sexual favours to your debtors; or risk being beaten up.

Prison life can be very boring; but the quicker you accept your situation, the better it would be for you. You should therefore try to keep busy by finding something useful to do; and the time will pass quickly enough. However, you should never forget that it is wardens who run a prison; so it would serve you better to be polite and not cause them any trouble. Although they are there to look after the convicts; they do not take kindly to rude and obnoxious behaviour and can make your life very miserable, if you do not make an effort to fit into their regime. Although the food is bland, it is reasonably wholesome; and there is free medical treatment, in case you get sick! There are lots of educational/vocational courses available in all prisons; so it is up to you to make use of the hours, because it is important you do not come out feeling like you have wasted your time. Every prison in every country is different in that, it is the current inmates that make up the atmosphere and conditions. You could have a relatively happy time; if you connect with like-minded girls you can have fun with. It could also be an unhappy experience; if things happen outside the walls which you have no control over and can do nothing about...like a serious illness or death in the family.

Compared to the men, few women ever go to prison; but it is good to know what the process is...just in case it happens to you! You can technically be jailed for seemingly innocuous crimes; like non-payment of fines or sudden out-of-the-blue incidents like dangerous driving (It is not so difficult to accidentally knock somebody down in your car and kill him/her) or fighting (If you push someone who falls, hits the head on the pavement and dies; you will be jailed for manslaughter). Try to be law-abiding and pray it never happens to you, because incarceration can ruin your life; especially if you end up in a prison abroad where you have no friends or family to visit you, and do not understand the language. Even going to prison in your own country, can be a very testing experience. You will lose many of your friends, who will want nothing more to do with you. Others will have made all kinds of promises to keep in touch and even visit you. Don't be surprised, if they fail to do either; because it is very easy to forget all about you. It can be quite a shock to realise that life goes on regardless; meaning, you are not as important to your friends as you thought! The good thing is; you will finally know who your true friends are and realise that prison is not a nice place to go. This will hopefully make you a better person; so that you never go back there again. Freedom is a privilege we take too much for granted; and only when it is taken away from us, that we understand how valuable it truly is.

There are some good people in the world that will not go out of their way to demean your femininity; but as a woman, you have to let them prove it to you. This means; you should never trust anyone until you have known him/her properly and are happy to allow him/her into your life. This book is meant to put you into a frame of mind which will help you make your own decisions and deal with any adversity in a way that will satisfy you. Remember: your self-defence concerns everything you care about!

Dear Tigress; lurking in your midst are some unscrupulous bastards who are prepared to fleece and con you of your worldly possessions! Read on!

Chapter Ten
Beware of the Conman

Throughout this book, I have discussed defending yourself against many things. As you may have noticed; most of what I say, is plain common sense. The problem with the word 'common' is; nobody wants to be classed as common, as there is a certain amount of inferiority attached to it. People like to believe they are 'better than common'; and therein lies one of human nature's greatest foibles. We think we are so smart that sometimes we become stupid and disappear up our own backsides! The nicest people in the world are the ones with very little money and even less ambition; doing things purely out of the goodness of their hearts. Many women fall into this category; and regrettably, their kindness is often taken advantage of by unscrupulous conmen, out to make a 'quick killing'.

1. Confidence tricks as an art form

(a) Pressure sales

From door-to door salesmen to dishonest advertising and pyramid sales; we are constantly bombarded by people trying to make money from us. These dubious practices have become so ubiquitous that a law was finally passed in the United Kingdom in 2008, banning what is known as 'pressure sales'; which occur when you are forced into parting with your money by unrelenting pressure. We have all at one time or another, had to deal with unwanted mail and people knocking on our doors trying to sell us things; while refusing to go away until they have made a sale. Unfortunately; women are seen as a soft touch by these unscrupulous men. This is because in the past, many have been duped into buying things they did not need; mainly for the seller to go away and leave her alone! All this means that it is up to you to make sure you are not ripped off; by not falling for any pressure sale pitches. Earlier on; I explained how you should not allow anyone into your house to make a pitch to you. The same attitude should be applied to television advertising, Internet sales and cell phone attractions; because they all apply different kinds of pressure on you to part with your cash. For the same reason; you should be extra careful when going to any financial institution for advice because they are beholden unto their shareholders and are out to make money from you. They will exert tremendous pressure on you to sign up to any deals they have on offer; like loans, credit cards, mortgages, health and accident insurance. All the power is in their hands, if you are unable to keep up with the repayments; and you could end up losing everything. The recent world-wide banking crash was as a result of banks offering too much to their customers; who were in turn unable to repay them!

Mobile/Cell phone operators are notorious for high roaming fees, selling contracts without explaining in detail what they entail and for quickly cutting you off when you are late paying your bill; so that you will have to pay a 'reconnection fee'. They make it easy for you to sign on but difficult to leave; and you may end up paying a hefty 'disconnection fee'. They may also allow you to make free calls after a certain time, but fail to say the calls are only free if you call someone on the same network; thereby charging you more for calls made outside their network. It is also important to remember that if your mobile phone is stolen; the phone company is not obliged to tell you that your handset is being abused by the thief...even when the calls exceed your normal call activity. This means you could be charged for all the calls made by the thief; if you do not immediately tell them to block your phone in the form of an Email and a recorded phone message, so that there is a time-and-date proof of having made contact and reporting the theft. Other tricks they use in lucrative collaboration with product companies may include charging premium price phone-ins for talent shows on television. There are also dubious competitions where you are told you have won a prize; but in order to claim it, you will have to ring a premium price number. They will then keep you waiting on line for several minutes before you can claim your prize; which is usually a cheap holiday or digital camera. The money they receive for the calls more than makes up for the prizes they give away because nobody seems to actually win the main prize; which is usually an enticing bank-breaker in the region of €50 000. With the proliferation of multi-media gimmicks like ring tones, games, music videos, Emails, sex chat-lines etc; there is tremendous scope for ripping off anyone who buys a cell phone and craves the latest add-ons. Although things are improving as government legislation catches up with the mobile phone operators; you should be very careful when signing any contract with them.

Travel agencies and holiday clubs, in conjunction with the airline companies they represent; are notorious in selling what they have to offer, without explaining in detail exactly what you will get for the money you pay. They will never tell you that legally, there is a fourteen day 'cooling-off' period; which allows you to change your mind and get your money back. They always seem to cover themselves around the unreadable jargon in the contract! A flight may be advertised at a certain cheap price; but by the time you actually board the plane, you could be paying up to ten times more. They will conveniently fail to tell you about the 'hidden costs' like the check-in fee; administration costs; credit card charges; luggage fees and airport charges. Did you know that if an airline loses your luggage; they will only reimburse you for the weight, and not for the value of the contents of the suitcase? This means you will have to take out a separate insurance policy for your valuables; backed by receipts and photographs. Holiday clubs will show you a nice colourful brochure of the country and the place you will be staying in. By the time you arrive at your destination; you could find that you are in a horrible accommodation, with a leaking roof, no running water and insects crawling in your filthy bed sheets. You will then have to use your own money to hire a plumber or buy insect-repellent! More than likely; you will move yourself into a hotel and put an unnecessary dent into your holiday expenses. When you arrive back home; the agency will have a convenient excuse and a smooth 'apology' for your holiday from hell; but to get compensation out of them would be next to impossible. It would be in your best interests not to pay any money upfront to any agency that offers you a 'cheap holiday'; unless they can offer you a written guarantee, which should be clarified...by a solicitor, if necessary! As with banks and car hire firms, who are also guilty of similar subterfuge and known for hiding behind the small print in their customer agreements; it would be more prudent for you to go with the biggest and most well-known operators in your country. This is because they have more to lose by cheating their customers; so you will receive safer and fairer, though not necessarily the best, treatment.

Pyramid sales were very big in the early Nineties but have all but died out; because people seem to have seen through the disguise and have realised that only the founders make the real money. Nevertheless; different forms of pyramids have sprung up and you may still get Internet 'deals' telling you that you can make 'lots of money' by selling products for certain manufacturers. 'The more you sell the more you make' is the usual mantra; but you may have to pay a registration or membership fee for the privilege of selling the products. Just as quickly as these companies spring up, they may disappear or go out of business; and you would have lost any money you paid to join the group. Just ask yourself the question, *"Why do I need to do this?"* and if you cannot find a good answer; don't do it. Whenever anyone wants you to sell things for him/her; you have to have the attitude that you are being used. Unless you are gaining something worthwhile; it would be advisable not to do it. Since you cannot earn much unless you sell a lot; you should realise that there is a discrepancy, and it is most likely a confidence trick akin to slavery. If you have an Email address; you will probably be bombarded with all kinds of deals. These should be immediately deleted before reading them. Once the senders realise you are not responding, they will stop; but others will probably step in to try their luck. Most in-boxes have ways you can filter your mail and keep the junk mail out; but if you are still having problems, get in touch with your service provider to only allow Emails from those in your address book to come through.

Every country has an Advertising Standards Board to check the veracity of what a company purports its products can do. Although television adverts are not classed as pressure sales because they are not so blatant and they do not actually 'force' you to buy a product; they are all but in name, as the pressure is subliminal. Since every woman has access to a television and watches it more than the man; most advertisements are aimed at women. This is because it is assumed that they do the most shopping; since they shop not only for themselves, but also for their family. You will therefore find that many commercials raise the profile of women and tend to degrade men by making them look stupid or at best, frivolously-minded; with beer, sports and car adverts. After centuries of male subjugation; many women will be secretly pleased with this turn of events and may shout with glee… *"About time women were made to look better than men…!"* That however, is a clever ploy by the marketing men to make women feel good about the advert; which means they will watch it with more interest and be subtly hypnotised by the product and most likely go and buy it. Since most companies are controlled by men, they win…again; because they know how to make you part with your money! If a product is good, no one can stop you going out to buy it and there is no need for an advert; but if you honestly ask yourself how many products you have bought because you first saw it on an advert, then you will understand what I am saying.

Remember the famous slogan, *"Diamonds are a girl's best friend…!"* and you will realise women are still being conned by men on a daily basis; and it seems to be getting worse. According to the advertisers, a slim woman is more attractive than a fat one; beautiful is better than plain; models and singers are more famous and make more money than many intelligent, hard-working lawyers, doctors or teachers; the bigger your breasts the more chance you will have of landing a part on some reality television show; so what do many women do? They go for breast enhancement and all kinds of plastic surgery; in order to make themselves 'more appealing' to men. I could go on and on; but I believe my message is clear that advertising is here to stay and so long as women remain spurious and show a lack of confidence in themselves, men will always have the last laugh. There are no easy answers to this, because I cannot tell you to stop buying products. I hope however, that I have now made you aware of what is really going on in this world where women have been made to believe they are 'equal'; when in fact, they are still singing the tunes composed by men. Next time you buy a product, try to make sure you are doing it for yourself and not to please anyone else; because the pressure sale is the biggest con of all.

(b) Hole-in-the-wall scams

There are several forms of theft, all supposedly originating in Eastern Europe; involving the 'hole-in-the-wall' Automated Teller Machines (ATM). The most common one, popularly known as 'skimming'; happens when thieves use glue to fit a false front with a tiny camera on the machine. As soon as a card is put into the machine; the information is quickly downloaded to a remote computer. The camera is positioned in such a way that it can then record a user tapping in the personal identification number (PIN). A new clone of the card can then be made and used to clear the account. There is also 'shoulder-surfing'; which happens when the thief leans over your shoulder to read your PIN, as soon as you punch it in. He then follows you and finds the right moment to mug you and steal your card; which he can then use to clear your account. Another method is the 'loop'; whereby the thief inserts a plastic clip into the cash machine slot that traps your card as soon as you put it in. He then comes to you as a helpful bystander and suggests that you put in your PIN again, in order to release your card; which he can easily memorise. When nothing happens; he will suggest you go into the bank to complain. As soon as you go into the bank; he removes the clip, steals your card and disappears to use your card elsewhere and clear your account. Finally, there is the 'door skimming' method; where thieves put up their own card reader on an ATM. When you insert your card; it reads and retains the information. The thief then directs you to another ATM, claiming the one you have just swiped is faulty and uses the shoulder-surfing method to read your PIN. He later goes back to remove his card reader from the first ATM and disappears to clone your card and clear your account.

From the above examples; you can see that thieves are becoming more professional and sophisticated. This means that new methods are constantly being invented! You therefore have to be on your guard, whenever you are using an ATM. If you have children in tow and carrying a load of shopping; it is very easy to forget about keeping your eyes open, when using an ATM to withdraw money. You have to treat your money as part of your self-defence. If your account is cleaned out; it could ruin you, if the bank deems it your fault and refuses to reimburse you. Always keep a hand over the numbers as you punch in your PIN; so that the shoulder-surfer cannot read it. Before using it; give the front of the ATM a few hard taps to make sure it is not false. If it feels suspicious, don't use it or say anything; but rather go into the bank to report it. If your card gets stuck in the machine; you should stay where you are, until you can send someone to quickly go into the bank to report the problem. Anybody who comes to your aid is most likely part of the criminal gang behind the loss of your card; so you should refuse all offers of assistance and insist on waiting for a bank official. If possible, try and alert the nearest police officer; who will make sure nobody can retrieve your card, until a bank official appears. Since banks have closing times; you should never to use an ATM at night. This means you have to make sure you have enough cash on you when you go out in the evenings. Just think of it as a necessary inconvenience that can prevent a greater calamity; like everything else in the real self-defence!

(c) Credit card theft

This is probably the most common form of theft; and happens more often than we realise. Never ever reveal your personal identification number to anyone; not even to family members or your best friend. They are the ones likely to know certain details about you, like your mother's maiden name, your date of birth and address; which are some of the security questions asked by most banks! The info can be used to obtain a new card by ringing up the bank, declaring the card stolen and receiving a new one. Always ring the bank to cancel your card, if it is ever lost for more than twenty-four hours. It can always be re-activated; if you ring and tell them it has been found. This would be a safer option than not doing anything about it; because the insurance will cover you for any discrepancy in the bill. If you ever go into a shop or restaurant, never give your card to the shopkeeper or waiter to go away with; otherwise you won't be able to keep an eye on the proceedings. It would be very easy for them to take the card away, ostensibly to check it out; make a copy of its details and then bring it back and watch you punching in the PIN. In a restaurant, you may have had a bit too much wine; so you will not be so observant. Before you get home; a copy of your card could be in circulation. Pick-pocket thieves are always on the look-out in shops; to see what you do with your card after you have made a purchase. They can then follow you outside and steal it from you. He may even have an accomplice in the shop that will provide him with your PIN; after watching you punch it in. With thoughts on the 'lovely dress' you have just purchased; you may inadvertently put the card into your pocket to pick up your shopping. Because many women keep their credit cards with their money in a purse inside their bags; it is imperative you hold tightly to your bag, whenever you are in town. It can easily be snatched from you while you are carrying bags of shopping or trying to control your kids.

Some people make a good living by obtaining a card and then using it to pay the debts of another. Once that debt is paid; the bank may increase the limit, which they will use to pay off another debt and obtain another card in a lucrative merry-go-round. Other scams involve ringing the bank to say a card is stolen or lost and then making sure the credit limit is used up just before making the report; so that the expenditure can be blamed on the thieves. After a short investigation; the bank will reimburse the card-holder because they are covered by the insurance. Those types of scams should not concern you, if you are not involved in them; because they are the bank's responsibility and each one has its own checks and balances to deal with the threat. I must warn you that if you are one of those involved in credit card fraud, to be very careful because the police and the courts in every country are beginning to treat it seriously; which means you could easily be jailed, if you are ever caught. There are so many credit card scams going on however, that even if I explained them to you; new ones will be devised within months. They all have one thing in common in that they can only work when the con artist has details of the card; which means they have to in some way obtain the card. If you don't give yours away; you will be safe! It would be better for you to only go out with the card you will be using and not carry so many of them in your wallet, in case it is stolen. It will cause you a major headache with the banks, if all your cards are stolen at the same time; simply because they were all in your bag when it was snatched. Credit cards were invented as a convenient alternative to cash. Treat yours with respect and don't let any of them out of your sight; because it could have dire consequences for you.

(d) Identity theft

This is when a thief steals any document which has your name, date of birth or address on it like your passport, driving licence, utility bill etc.; and then uses them to obtain other documents in your name, by pretending she is you and committing all kinds of criminal mayhem. You may never know what is happening; until the police knock on your door and ask you to accompany them to the station, accusing you of crimes you know you did not commit! If you live in an apartment block for instance; a thief can gain entrance into the building by going in when someone living there opens the main door to go out. Once inside, he can go through the mail; which is sometimes left on a table or on the ground just inside the door for the residents to pick up on the way into their respective apartments. Any official-looking envelopes like those containing bank statements; will be stolen and the information used to get into your bank account, or to clone a credit card in your name. From then on, items can easily be ordered on the Internet and a lot of your money spent, before you notice the discrepancy; usually on the arrival of your next credit card bill. This means you should be extra-careful with your credit card on the Internet, by using it only on recognised secure sites which can guarantee security; otherwise don't do it! If you are using any social networking sites, try to make sure no unauthorised person can get into your home page; by keeping it locked with a secure password. An identity thief can garner enough information about you from your site, and then make up a new profile; using your name to do business and con other people around the world. He will also have access to your Email address book and could cause trouble for your friends by pretending he is you. There has been a recent rise in the influx of foreigners into many American and Western European cities; and this has given identity theft greater importance. Their methods are becoming more and more devious; like using the names of dead people from cemeteries to procure birth certificates. These can then be used to help illegal immigrants obtain 'legal' documents like passports and driving licences.

For your own peace of mind; make sure the arrival of your mail is secure. This means you should make a report to the relevant authorities; if for example, your bank statement or utility bill fails to arrive at the normal time. This is because it could have been stolen; and the quicker you find out, the easier it will be to put a halt to any untoward occurrences. All important documents should be safely hidden away in your house; so that even your friends or flatmates don't know where you keep them. Anybody could be a thief; as it is those closest to you who will have the best opportunity to steal from you. There are people in the criminal world that will pay for identity information; so there will always be those who will betray their friends, in order to make some quick cash, without the slightest feeling of guilt. Identity theft is such a cruel, ruthless crime, that I would not wish it on anyone; especially if the crimes committed in your name, are those you would not be capable of committing, simply because they are so destructive. It is a horrible feeling to realise someone is out there pretending to be you; with access to your money. If your savings are stolen; your life could be in ruins, as very few insurance companies will cover you for your own stupidity. There are some banks which will sell you identity fraud insurance; even though they are liable to reimburse you anyway...unless they can prove you have been negligent. It is very difficult to get a bank to pay you back; because they will find a way to make it your fault! Fortunately; identity theft cannot work on you, if you pay attention to your paperwork and documents. It would therefore be in your own best interests, to shred or burn anything that you have no more use for; and not leave them lying around to be taken advantage of.

(e) Simple scams

There are some conmen who will ring you up; pretending they are from your bank or phone company. They will tell you they have discovered certain discrepancies in your account; and would like to verify, if you are really the person they are talking to. They will then ask you to give them your bank details, including your password or PIN; so that they can continue with their 'fraud investigations'. Once they have your details; you might as well kiss your money goodbye because they will definitely clear out your account. This means that if anybody rings your house; you should never disclose any information to them. If they claim to be from your bank; you should ask them for their name and number and you will come to the bank in person, to sort out the problem. Others will use advertisements in local newspapers, to entice you with ways you can make money from home; but they will first ask you to send a little money (about $50) for the 'privilege' of joining their group. Once they receive your cash; you might receive a small starter-pack and then you will not hear from them again. This is because they will be using untraceable mobile phone numbers! This obviously means that anyone who asks you for money upfront has to be suspect; and you should never do it. If they ring your house; ask them to give you the name of anyone else in your area that is on their books, so that you can check up whether they are genuine or not. They will most likely hang up! There are also the cleverer ones who will call you up as soon as you buy a new mobile phone, and offer you cheap insurance; claiming they have permission from the phone company. You might believe them! How else would they know you had just bought a mobile phone? The answer is simple; mobile phone companies operate with phone numbers in block form. If the conmen buy a phone; all they have to do is ring up all the numbers around their own digits. They will soon find someone else who had just bought a phone and pull a fast one. Once they sell you the insurance; you will find out it is worthless when you lose your phone and are expecting to be reimbursed with a new one! This means that you should never do any kind of business with anyone who rings you up. Always insist on going in person to their office; so that you can put a face and a location to the transaction. There is one other trick where they will advertise a health product on the Internet and claim it is for free. However; you will be asked to give them your credit card details in order to pay for the post and packaging. A few days later; you will receive the product in the post and then keep on receiving the same product every month. You will then find that you have been exorbitantly charged for a year's supply of the product on your credit card! It will be impossible to get your money back because they will claim you signed up for a year's supply and only the first sample was free! There are many more scams all around us; so try to keep your wits about you!

(f) Investment fraudsters

Not all of us are used to dealing with large sums of cash. It is also possible you could receive unexpected sums of money; in the form of a lottery win; tax breaks; pension funds; inheritance windfalls; insurance and redundancy payments. It is very easy to 'lose one's head' and get so over-excited, you could become the victim of an investment fraudster. Once you tell anyone about your good fortune; you leave yourself open to those who would like to relieve you of some of that money. You could be swamped with self-appointed advisers; who will try and tell you how to best invest your windfall. Before you listen to anyone; make sure he/she is listed by the financial regulator in your country and allows you to see a copy of their indemnity insurance policy. This will give you some guarantee that in an unforeseen eventuality, you can get most of your money back. Secondly; never believe anybody who tries to entice you with outrageous profit margins. If they are that good; then everyone would be doing it and therefore, why does he/she need *your* money? Finally; you should never make out a cheque to any individual, who suggests an investment to you. If he/she does not have the backing of a reliable institution you can pay the money to, and be able to monitor the movement and safety of your investment; then why the hell should you trust him/her? How would you get your money back, if he/she absconds or dies? Personal guarantees mean nothing; unless the money is lodged in a reliable escrow account, backed by a reputable firm of solicitors! Please remember that, if anyone suggests anything to you that seems too good to be true; then it is obviously a scam and you should never get involved by letting greed take over your senses. You have been warned!

(g) Loan sharks

The recent world-wide recession affected so many countries, that there was a serious shortage of money inside the financial institutions; making it almost impossible to get a bank loan. Loan sharks and money lenders filled the vacuum by lending money at exorbitant repayment rates. As a result; many families were destroyed when the borrower could not pay back on time. This was because a lot of the money borrowed, was earmarked for certain businesses; which in turn, failed to yield the expected return. This put tremendous pressure on the affected families; who ended up arguing over their inability to live in the style they had been used to. Luxury items in the homes had to be sold; in order to pay for basic necessities, like food and the children's clothes and school fees. There were even cases of marriages breaking up;

because husband and wife were unable to cope with the stress of downsizing! Borrowing money is never a good idea; unless you have a legitimate plan on how you are going to pay it back. Because you are so desperate for the cash, you may sign any repayment plan; in order to get your hands on the loan. You may also be deluded into believing that you will be able to pay back the money, in the time allocated. When you don't pay back on time; the value of the loan goes up and you may end up having to pay more than double the original amount. The problem with borrowing money from a loan shark is the tactics they use to get their money back, if you don't pay. Legitimate money lenders can obtain a court order, to seize your property; so that they can recoup their investment. The loan sharks will use threats and intimidation to force you to pay; and you may end up borrowing from another shark, in order to pay back the first loan. There have been cases of people having their legs broken or even killed; when they have been unable to pay back a loan. I cannot tell you what to do; all I can do is warn you to beware of loan sharks! If you have to borrow money, try to do so from within your extended family; otherwise, you will just have to cut your coat to suit your tail!

(h) Religious conmen

Religious conmen exist in every country and usually prey on vulnerable elderly women; because there is a belief that they are more pious and therefore more susceptible to religious trickery. Every Christian believes in God, Jesus and the Bible; yet it is by invoking this famous trio that some unscrupulous conmen manage to convince people to part with their hard-earned money. Others prey on your ignorance by pretending to pray for you. They will even join a church service in order to look for victims; or follow a woman around town and approach her when she is alone. Check this one out. A man accosts you and says he is a stranger from out of town. He pretends he has lost his way and is looking for a certain church. As he is talking to you, another man comes up to him and asks what the problem is; and proceeds to tell him where the church is, before you are able to. *"Thank you my son"*, says the stranger; *"May God bless you. Praise the Lord! Correct me if I am wrong, but your wife gave birth to a boy this morning and you are coming from the hospital; are you not?"* "Lord have mercy, it *is true. How did you know?"* shouts the man, whilst kissing the stranger's hand. A third man will appear and say; *"Are you not Father So & So from Such and Such Church...the one who has power to heal the sick and the dying?"* The stranger accepts the praise and proceeds to bless the two sycophants. Meanwhile; you are standing there looking at this farce, completely stupefied. Believe me; the fact that you even stayed that long to listen to them, means you have been subtly hypnotised. You will be either robbed of your possessions, or you will find yourself giving him money for his blessings!

Anyone who approaches you, preaching the gospel, is probably up to no good; even if they are wearing the outfit/uniform of a church. Since you do not really have the time to check whether he is genuine or not; it would be better to smile politely and get away from him as quickly as possible. *"Sorry, I'm in a hurry. Goodbye!"* If any recognised religious organisation requires donations; I'm sure they know how to get them. Harassing people in the street is not their way! If someone accosts you in the name of Jesus, then tell him you are a Moslem and keep walking; and vice-versa, if a Moslem tries his line on you. It really is no one's business what religion you are. There are reputable mosques and churches all over the world; where you are able to worship your Allah/God safely. This also means you should take care not to join cults and other 'organisations', which don't have a proven track record for honesty. Find out about any group before you join them, in case they are not legitimate; because you could be bullied into parting with a lot of money or belongings. Be very careful and remember to educate your children against joining clubs, without consulting you. There are lots of crooks masquerading clubs and charities as fronts for illegal activities; such as money laundering, drug dealing and prostitution. (See Chapter 16).

Wherever you are; you will have to be extra vigilant around Christmas, Easter and Bank holidays. These are the times when we all like to relax and enjoy ourselves! The urge to acquire money at all costs for the holidays; lets victims fall easy prey to religious conmen. Some will lead you to their 'church', pray for you and then ask you to bring some of your most prized possessions. Others are more callous and criminal in their dealings. The following scenario is a good example. Because of a shortage of transport around the festive days; you may get into an unlicensed taxi. The next thing you know; the driver has to check his tyre pressure at a station, before taking you to your destination. You will then be joined in the taxi by a 'friend of the driver', who will barrage you with quotes and psalms. Since most people have problems; he will use your suffering to tell you things like your mother-in-law (nobody likes their mother-in-law) is the one responsible for your plight. If you say you don't have a mother-in-law; then he will quickly change it to your aunt or other relative. He may even give you an alcoholic potion to drink to 'cleanse' you of 'impending evil spirits'. This potion is actually a drug to make you more docile and receptive to whatever they have planned for you. You will find that he will even drink some himself. (He has obviously taken an antidote). If you are not careful; you could be taken to some obscure place and raped, robbed or even murdered. Since there is a long waiting list for body organs in many countries; your body parts could be quickly sold on for transplants.

(i) Voodoo

In some countries; the sale of body parts is still rampant and allowed to continue by their governments, who turn a blind eye because many in the upper echelons of power believe in the use of them. There is a widespread belief in some Third World cultures that you can make money or attain high positions of power by offering human beings as sacrifices. They even believe that eating certain parts of the human body will appease the 'spirits' or 'gods'. You see; before a victim is chosen, they already know he or she is gullible because they may have watched him/her for some time before striking. By killing a victim; they believe the 'gods' will be happy and lucrative money-making abilities will pass on to them. There are also some who drink human blood and collect human skulls; while offensive acts like female circumcision and the ritual deflowering of virgin girls are still integral parts of many cultures. These beliefs with their different names like 'juju', 'macumba', 'witchcraft', or 'voodoo' have been going on for centuries in every country; and although most governments have supposedly outlawed the practices, they still exist in many parts of the world. There was a time not so long ago in West Africa, whereby if a chief of a tribe died, his henchmen would go and cut off the heads of anybody they saw; so that the chief would not go into the afterlife alone. I would not like to say whether the practice still exists or not, because those killed are dispensable; so it is hardly likely to be reported. It is murder, plain and simple; which still exists in its different forms in every country!

Instances of spouse abandonment (where Asian and African wives in developed countries are tricked back home with duplicitous tales) are now commonplace. *"My father is ill; so why don't we go and visit him...?"* She flies off with her husband; is treated very badly by his relatives and finally dumped. She is then unable to return because her passport would have been destroyed; with all means of finance and communication cut off. The husband will return with stories of how his 'evil wife' ran off and abandoned him; paving the way for him to ensconce another woman in her place. Bridal kidnapping (where teenage Asian/African girls are forced into marriage abroad) also appears to be on the increase; even though most 'advanced' countries have outlawed the practice. When abroad; take nothing for granted, don't go anywhere alone, ask about the safety of any place before you visit there and report any suspicions to the police. Although you may believe some of these practices involving voodoo and religious conmen could never happen in your 'modern' country; they can easily be imported to a place near you. A perpetrator is not going to change his beliefs when he moves to another country! Each year people go missing around the world and are never found. Have you ever wondered why?

(j) **Third World Scams**

Man is greedy by nature; so there will always be someone who will fall for any money doubling con trick. The notorious scams nicknamed '419', which originated in Nigeria; have been used to dupe thousands of women around the world. It is very simple and comes in many forms. The most popular is the one where you will receive an Email or a letter in the post telling you that someone from a Third World country has a few million dollars he wants to get out of his country; but due to certain government regulations, he is not able to. If you could be so kind as to allow him to transfer the money through your bank account; he will give you 20% of the money. Once you reply their request; you will be told to keep it a secret because the money involved is huge, in excess of ten million dollars. The greed in you will figure that if you allow the transaction to go through using your account; you will be two million dollars richer. Once you give them your account details for them to transfer the money; they will clean out your account. They will try and get your PIN from the bank by using the info you have already given them and pretending they have forgotten it. If that does not work; they will blatantly ask you for your PIN and your mother's maiden name. By then; you will be so consumed with greed that you would do anything to get the two million! A similar trick can be used by sending you an official looking E mail that you have won the Spanish Lottery (probably the biggest in Europe) and they need some money (about €3000) to process the papers. Once you send the money; they will disappear and use the same trick on someone else. They normally send thousands of Emails every week; so if they are able to fool one person a day, it will work out to over a million tax-free euros a year!

Other tricks involve finding (mostly) women who used to live in a Third World country. They will then pretend to be a solicitor's firm from that country and send you a letter to say that a certain person had died and bequeathed you several million dollars. They will claim they are ready to process the money and will even send you documents to sign. Meanwhile; they need to grease a few palms *("Government bureaucracy is very slow; so if you would be kind enough to send us ten thousand dollars, it would make things move quicker!")*. There will always be 'problems'; which means they will systematically ask you to send them money, until you get fed up and start asking questions. That is when they will suddenly disappear with the amount they have already conned from you. Some have been known to fly a victim by first-class to the country; treat him/her lavishly and then dupe them. There was one case where a man was flown to Nigeria and introduced to the 'oil minister'; in whose presence, he signed the 'appropriate documents' allowing him to export oil out of the country. He was even on-hand to witness the shipment he had paid for, being loaded onto a ship. When it arrived at its destination; there was no oil on board! Needless-to-say; the crooks escaped with millions of dollars of his money. 'Mule recruitment sites' are springing up all the time on the Internet; trying to recruit people to launder illegal money through their accounts, for a commission. The websites are professionally built and look so enticing and legitimate; you could be sucked into the scheme, if you are not careful. Once you give them your account number; they will find a way to empty it. Don't be greedy; it will cost you!

There is one trick where they can turn stone into gold before your very eyes; by dropping it in a bowl of water. Once they have got your attention; they will ask you for money to reveal the trick. When you do try it; the stone will miraculous become gold. They will then tell you to put it into your pocket and go home; before removing it. By the time you get home; you will find that the 'gold' is a piece of stone and you have been conned out of your money. There is also the machine that prints money. This involves them coming to you with a machine, which looks like a small photocopier. They feed in the paper and it prints perfect hundred dollar bills. They will then give you one of the bills and ask you to go to town and spend it; whilst they wait for you. On your return, after having verified with a bank that the note is genuine; your greed will take over because you have actually seen a machine that prints real money. They will do it a few more times; till you have seen it print about $1000. They will then offer to sell you this machine for a 'reasonable' amount like $100 000. You quickly pay up and they leave; after telling you not to print too many at once, or your friends will get suspicious where you are getting the money from. The trick to this is very clever; because they actually put about $20 000 of real money into the machine. Therefore, it will continue 'printing' until the $20 000 has run out; which could take several days or weeks. By then; they would have well and truly disappeared with five times their money in profit.

These scams emanated from the Third World countries; but with the world getting smaller through the Internet and more and more people travelling to and fro, these habits can easily filter into different continents. You can take a man out of a country; but you cannot remove his habits. Someone who wants to kidnap a bride; abandon his spouse; con; drug; rob; rape or murder a woman and drink her blood or steal her body parts; is going to do so, wherever he may be. Please take your self-defence seriously!

2. Counterfeit

Counterfeiting is a serious problem which the police in most countries have only recently begun to take seriously. We have all heard about counterfeit money, CDees or DVDees; because those are the type of cases that regularly appear in the news. You may have also heard about illicit alcohol and cigarettes; otherwise known as bootlegging. Automobile parts; electronic equipment; credit cards; traveller's cheques; coins; concert tickets; designer clothes; perfumes; jewellery; organic foods...even houses! Anything can be counterfeited! You therefore have to be very careful; or you will be conned into buying something that is not genuine, which could result in your monetary misery, incarceration, illness or death.

(a) Automobiles

The stolen car business is extremely lucrative and occurs in most developed countries; whereby cars are stolen and shipped abroad to be sold in Third World countries. Others are quickly dismantled and the parts sold off separately. You therefore have to be very security conscious to protect your car against theft because the insurance companies will not pay up when a car is stolen; if the theft were deemed to be your fault through negligence. You should never buy a car off the Internet because they are advertised by using photographs of the cars. These pictures will obviously show the cars off in the best light possible. When you add this to the 'reasonable asking price'; it is very easy to believe you are getting a good deal and buy the vehicle. Once you have paid for the car; it would be next to impossible to get your money back. It could even be stolen; and the papers you will be given to cover the registration, will be fake. If you are one day stopped by the police; you will be arrested for driving a stolen vehicle, although it will be 'registered' in your name! Even if you are buying a car from a dealer; you should take your time because it is an investment you are making on your future and possibly your life. If something goes wrong with it as you are driving; you could crash and lose your life. Once the car leaves his/her premises; most dealers will deny any responsibility for the car. This means; you should never pay for a car without having seen it; driven it; or double-checked by a knowledgeable mechanic you can trust. Always buy from reputable agent-dealers who specialise in the make of car you want to buy; because they can give you a cast-iron guarantee of a few years, against anything going wrong after you have purchased it. A car may look good to you; but it could be an accident waiting to happen. The tyres could very easily be counterfeit; as could the break pads, shock absorbers or even the brake fluid! Only an experienced mechanic will be able to know if every part of a car is genuine. Always compare prices with other cars of the same model and if the price is too low; you should be suspicious and not buy it. Finally; you should beware of people who claim they can sell or buy a car for you or put you in touch with the seller or buyer and then charge you a fee or a commission for doing so. Why entrust someone to do something you can quite comfortably do yourself?

(b) Electronic Equipment

Electricity kills! For that reason; you should never buy any second-hand, cheap or stolen electronic goods...even if it is from a friend. If you have children in the house; you will be able to appreciate the possibilities of things going wrong. Who do you blame, if your child gets an electric shock from a faulty product and dies? Every electronic appliance in your home should be of genuine quality; which means, you should always buy from a reputable shop that will give you a guarantee against any defects. It is always important to have a way of knowing who is responsible when things go wrong with anything you buy. You have to be aware that every single piece of electronic equipment can be copied and counterfeit models made. Although the Far Eastern nations are usually blamed for this; they are frequently being assembled in the developed countries because they will not be subjected to custom checks and import duties. The labels put onto them will also be faked so that they appear genuine. They are then advertised in local trade magazines and the Internet; because they make it easier to attract people looking for a bargain! The only way to avoid any future problems; is to buy from a shop that is a legitimate agent of the company making the piece of electronic equipment that you want to buy. Most of these have signs outside the shop, stating which manufacturers they represent. If in doubt; you should always ask them in the shop which companies they are agents for. You should then ask them what would happen if something went wrong with the equipment you are about to buy. If they are not able to give you a minimum one year guarantee, whereby they will accept responsibility and replace the faulty product; you should look elsewhere to make your purchase.

Having bought your electronic equipment like a television, musical system or computer; you may be tempted into buying cheap copies of original CDees, DVDees or the many computer games on the market. This mode of purchase is very popular, especially to teenagers; because they quickly get bored and are always looking for something new but don't have the money to continue buying new products. Although it might seem innocuous and less dangerous to buy a computer game, CD or DVD; you are nevertheless breaking the law because the products are not genuine and have not been assessed and passed by the National Trading Standards Board of your country. You could be arrested for buying counterfeit goods; if you cannot show with a genuine receipt, where they were bought. The same goes for downloading computer software, games, films and music from illegal sites on the Internet; or sharing files with your friends. If you knitted a jumper; baked a cake; wrote a television script or a book; and someone sneaked into your house and took any of those items without telling you. How would you feel? That is exactly how the authorities view illegal downloading from the Internet. You are taking something that is not yours to take and circulating it amongst your friends. I'm afraid it is stealing; plain and simple! If you are caught; you will be fined far in excess of what you took. If you don't want to get into trouble; it would be better to download from legal sites and pay for it, just as you would do if you went into a shop. The authorities are getting smarter by the day and very soon, nobody will be able to get away with illegal downloading! Be good!

(c) Credit cards, Traveller's Cheques, Notes, Coins and Tickets

Thousands of credit cards are stolen every year. This has made it a very lucrative business for crooks; because it is still treated as a white-collar crime and does not incur a harsh jail sentence. Counterfeits are usually made of the stolen card; even though the hologram on the copy will never be as good as the original. This does not worry the counterfeiters because with the name, expiry date and number of the card; they can still make purchases on the Internet and from unsuspecting shops. Once you let your card out of your sight to make a purchase; the details can quickly be copied, before it is handed back to you. If yours is stolen; you must make a report as quickly as you can, because the banks are notorious for passing the blame on to the card-owner. They will usually claim you were negligent in allowing the card out of your sight; or for giving your PIN away. If you discover purchases are being made with your card, even though it is still in your possession; do not cut up or throw it away because it can still be used to show the bank that you were not the one using the card. By keeping the receipts of all the transactions you make with the card; you can prove to the bank that you were elsewhere when the stolen card was illegally used. If a transaction is done on the Internet, using your card; the banks will treat it as a private matter and may not recompense you. Over 20% of victims do not get their money back from the banks! Although legally, the banks are liable for recompense on Internet transactions; they know the police are not too interested in following them up and will delay repayment as long as possible. Many people cannot remember their PIN; so they tend to write it down in all kinds of careless places. If you write your PIN down in a diary which is kept in your handbag with your credit card; you will look very stupid when your bag is snatched from you by a thief. For that reason; the banks are probably right in blaming the card-owner whenever thieves manage to get hold of someone's PIN. Because a PIN is usually only four digits; it would be advisable to memorise it. If you are very forgetful; you should write it down somewhere at home, maybe inside a favourite book on a shelf with lots of other books. Even if your house is burgled; the thieves are unlikely to steal your books or magazines. A PIN does not mean anything to a crook; if it cannot be connected to a card!

There are also a lot of fake traveller's cheques on the market, especially in the Third World countries; so you have to be very careful how you obtain them. If you are caught trying to cash a counterfeit traveller's cheque; you will be arrested and charged! This would not be so funny, if it happened to you in some backwater of a country! All travel agencies will deny issuing them to you; if they are later found to be counterfeit. The safest thing to do is to insist that the bank, foreign exchange bureau or travel agency you get them from; stamp their logo and address on the back of each cheque. This way; it can be traced back to them in the unforeseen eventuality that you are arrested for trying to cash them. If they refuse to put their stamp on the cheque; you should go elsewhere to buy them. Once you have received them; you should keep them safely, so that they are not stolen. Once a thief is able to forge your signature; he or she will be able to obtain cash for it. If the traveller's cheques are worth a lot of money; the crook will get a fake document made in the name of the cheque, in order to cash them in a foreign country with less suspicion.

We have all heard about counterfeit notes. Fortunately; the media always warn the public, whenever there are many of them on the scene in a country. This is usually enough to put everyone on high-alert and drive the suppliers elsewhere with their contraband. They are normally of the higher denominations of the major currencies; like the Dollar, the Euro, the Japanese Yen and the British Pound. Recently; lower denomination counterfeit notes have been frequently found in the systems of several nations because they are easier for the crooks to get rid of. The quality of these notes is sometimes so good that once they are concealed amongst genuine ones, they even deceive some less-than-vigilant bank tellers! Nightclubs are notorious for giving counterfeit notes in their change; because the barmen correctly assume most customers will not notice them in their drunken stupor under the kaleidoscopic lighting effects. You can be arrested if you are caught with counterfeit notes; unless you can prove where you got them from. It is therefore imperative you make a report to the police, stating all the facts; if you are ever given them. Unfortunately, you may not get your money back; but it will help the police to trace the source because they may already be in the process of building a dossier on the crooks suspected of issuing them. If you immediately notice counterfeit notes in your change; you should loudly insist that they change it. The embarrassment will usually make the shopkeeper give you another note! If he or she refuses; then, stay where you are and ring the police. Even if he/she refunds your money; you should still go to a police station and tell them that you believe the shop is giving out forged notes. The cops may not immediately do anything; but your report will go on file. A few more similar reports against the shop and the owners will be in serious trouble!

In every country; a possible 5% of all coins are counterfeit. Because of their relatively low value, when compared with monetary notes; very few people bother to check to see if their coins are real or fake. The crooks who deal in counterfeit coins; usually target small towns and villages, where the residents may not be aware of them. You can usually spot a fake coin, if you make the effort; because the metal used in them is never the same as the original. There will always be something different about the imprint, the weight and the alignment that should make you suspicious. The best way to find out how to spot counterfeit coins is to go into a bank or police station and ask them. They will usually have some samples and give you advice on what to do, if you are given a dud coin. Some shopkeepers will pass off their fake coins onto unsuspecting customers; as very few shoppers have the time to check their change when carrying a lot of shopping. If you are given a counterfeit coin in your change from a shop; don't be afraid to reject it and insist they give you another one. If it happens to you on more than one occasion from the same shop; you should make a report to the police because it could be the tip of the iceberg of a major counterfeiting operation.

Please be very careful when buying a ticket on the Internet or from anybody outside the venue of a concert, show or sporting event. Before any major event; illegal sites are likely to appear and offer 'cheaper tickets'. Most of these start selling months in advance of the event taking place. In a rush to get one before they are sold out; one can easily be conned into buying one off the Internet from a site purporting to be selling legitimate tickets. If someone came up to you on the street and promised you a ticket for something taking place in 'a few months time'; you would not hand over your money, would you? For that reason; you should never to buy any ticket off the Internet, unless it is from a legitimate site. You can find this out by ringing the venue and asking them exactly how to go about obtaining a ticket; and how to tell a fake from an original. If possible; you should go in person to a designated ticket seller and buy the ticket. If they are sold out; try to be philosophical and accept that you will miss the show. Going to the event without a ticket; is not a good idea because there will be touts operating outside the venue and you may be conned into buying a ticket at an exorbitant price, which may not even be genuine. Apart from being refused entry; you may be arrested, if the gang selling the tickets are under police surveillance.

(d) Designer attire, perfumes and jewellery

Without sounding too sexist; I will safely assume that most women like wearing nice clothes, preferably with a designer label! There is therefore a huge demand for attire; which look like the original, but cost a great deal less. Since many women subconsciously dress to attract members of the opposite sex; they will happily wear counterfeit clothes because most men cannot tell the difference and they will still receive the appropriate compliments. Some clothes are sold with labels which are similar to the original but may have a slight difference in the spelling or the logo of the manufacturer. These are legal to wear because they are not pretending to be the real McCoy! Once a counterfeit article of clothing is sold with a label purporting to be an original; it becomes illegal and you could be arrested for wearing it. The Trading Standards officials in most countries are always on the look-out for people selling counterfeit clothes; so please be careful when any item of clothing is offered to you at a cheap price. I will however; tell you that women are very clever at spotting an original from a fake! If you are wearing counterfeit designer clothes, pretending to be an original; don't look too pleased with yourself because the men may not notice but there will definitely be women sniggering behind your back!

With perfumes; you have to be more careful because you are applying the stuff to your body. The fake ones do not have the original formula and will therefore not have the correct ratio and percentage of ingredients in them. They all contain artificial colouring mixed with an alcoholic base and have not gone through a recognised testing procedure. This means they might have some chemicals in them that could damage your skin or cause an allergic reaction, which could end up killing you. Go into any big city and you will see people out to make a fast buck; by selling fake perfume, using the names of the original manufacturer. These petty crooks will quickly disappear as soon as they see the police arriving. They will never tell you the perfumes are fakes; but would explain that they are selling them cheaply because they got them direct from the manufacture by cutting out the middleman. The problem is; some of these perfumes smell nice enough and only an expert will be able to tell the difference. Because original perfumes can be quite costly; it is very tempting to buy anything that smells nice and costs a lot less. You have to recognise that if something goes wrong and you end up damaging your skin; there is nothing you can do about it because you will not be able to prove who sold it to you. Although it is more expensive; I would advise you to always buy your perfumes from a recognised shop that will give you a receipt. If you cannot afford it; why not prod the man (men?) in your life to buy them for you? It is in a man's interests to make sure his better-half looks and smells nice!

Fake jewellery is also omnipresent because most people cannot distinguish them from the original. There have been cases of 'gold chains' leaving green stains on the skin of the wearer because they were not really gold but probably copper. Diamonds are easy to fool people with, because by the time the buyer goes to find out its worth; the sellers would have disappeared. Since genuine jewellery is usually too expensive for most people; selling a fake makes sense, so long as the seller tells the buyer that it is not real. Like everything else; it would be best to buy all your jewellery from a recognised jeweller, so that you receive a certificate of authenticity from the shop. If any jewellery is offered to you cheaply; it means it is a counterfeit and I would advise you not to buy it. You could be arrested; if you cannot prove with a receipt, where you bought it. If you want to buy something that is not too expensive; there is replica jewellery available in some shops. They look like the genuine article, do not pretend to be real and you will receive a receipt for it and told exactly how many carats it contains. Anything from 18 to 22 carats is regarded as real gold; because pure 24 carat gold is too soft to be effective in jewellery. With diamonds; an international carat has now been standardised to about .20 grams. If you own jewellery and would like to know its value with the hope of selling; it would be best to go to a recognised jeweller to have it checked out because they have the correct scales to make an accurate assessment.

(e) Food and Drink

The most dangerous form of counterfeiting has to be with food and drink; because once it goes into your stomach, there is not much you can do and your body will be at the mercy of whatever was used to prepare the stuff. Once there is a demand for a certain kind of food; it puts the crooks on high alert to counterfeit and sell it cheaper. Organic foods are the biggest victims of this; because many people are obsessed with 'healthy eating'. Once the word 'organic' appears on the packaging; it will be bought with the belief that it contains 'no artificial additives'. Meat, fish and poultry are usually advertised as organic; which means that they have been fed and bred in 'the best conditions possible', before being slaughtered. Since you cannot be there to see for yourself how they are being bred; you will have to put your faith in the shop selling the product. This means you should only buy your food from the well-known supermarket chains because they have it in their interests to make sure their foods are genuine. If you buy your food from a small shop; it is possible the owner may have bought his products from a 'middle-man', in order to get them cheaper. The label may look genuine but the actual product may be a fake. With all foods; the satisfaction is more mental than physical. If you believe something is organic and it does not make you sick; you will continue eating it! Only a food scientist will be able to tell exactly how many chemicals the food contains! The biggest problem with food sold in shops; is with its longevity. Foods which have long passed their 'sell-by date' are regularly sold in shops across every country. The sticker bearing the date can easily be removed and replaced with a new one; allowing the product to stay longer on the shelf. If you get food poisoning; the shop in question will deny it and your own kitchen hygiene standards will be blamed.

Restaurants; take-outs; pubs; bars and cafés; could all be guilty of cooking and serving food in unhygienic conditions; because only those working in them, will be aware of what really goes on in the kitchens. Cockroaches; mice droppings; badly washed cutlery; filthy pots and pans etc.; have all at one time or another, been discovered in small and some well-known establishments. If you add this to the personal hygiene standards of the staff working in any place (some people will go to the toilet and others will blow their nose with their fingers and then go on to touch the food, without bothering to wash their hands). Although there are officials who go around inspecting the shops, restaurants, eateries, bars and cafés; they usually rely on complaints from the public, before launching a serious investigation. Even if you get a bout of food poisoning from a restaurant; your complaint will not be taken seriously, unless many others also complain. Like the shops; all eating establishments will deny they are responsible for your illness! The only thing you can do in such a situation; is to preserve the tainted food and take it to a police station and they will direct you to the relevant authorities. If you go to a doctor to examine and show that you are indeed sick from what you ate; you will have a strong case to sue those responsible. Since food is based on faith and trust; it would be safer to do your shopping and only eat in places where you are familiar with the owners or the workers. If something goes wrong with the food; you will at least be able to know who to hold responsible. As a 'valued customer'; they are unlikely to mess you around and will make sure what they serve you is genuine. (Fingers crossed!)

With drink; it is harder to tell which ones are genuine because once you open the bottle, very few shops will admit to having sold you that particular bottle. If you get sick from alcohol; you will not be taken seriously and might even be accused of 'being drunk' or 'nursing a hangover'. This means your illness will be blamed on the amount you have drunk…and not on the quality of the alcohol! There is not much you can do about this; except to make sure you only buy your liquor from licensed establishments because they are unlikely to purchase bootleg alcohol from unreliable sources! Many nightclubs have been guilty of serving cheap alcohol in popular bottles; because most people will be too intoxicated to notice. If you suspect that your alcohol does not taste the same as what you are used to; do not be afraid to protest loudly to the barman who served it to you. If he tries to be clever by denying it; you should ask to speak to the manager/owner. He/she will probably offer you a free drink as compensation; which is a sure sign that something is going on. Pretend you are satisfied; get in touch with the Trading Standard Authorities and don't go to that club again. The officials may not do anything immediately; but a few more similar complaints and the club will be raided by the police. All their alcohol will be seized and taken to a laboratory for analysis. If found to be duping the public with counterfeit liquor; their license will be revoked.

(f) Property

For many people; the biggest investment they will make in their lifetime, will be buying a house. Some will prefer to buy a brand new property, instead of an old house; because they assume there will be fewer problems. I have to burst your bubble, if you believe that a brand new house is always better than an old one. You see; with an old house, you know there will be problems and you will have to spend some more money to do it up to your satisfaction. With a new house; it has never been lived in before and therefore you will not know what inconveniences are lurking in the not-too-distant future. Many new properties are built with the same architectural plan and the same set of workers; which means the builders may 'cut corners' through familiarity by assuming a job is finished, without checking properly to see if they have missed anything. Two identical houses may be built on opposite sides of the same street and will have different problems to deal with the inconsistencies of the weather. Brand new houses look good on the outside; but the problems usually begin a few years after you have bought the house and moved in. This gives the building company the perfect excuse to blame the problems on the way you operate the house. These problems usually involve shoddy insulation than can cause draughts, dampness and coldness; weak plumbing that lead to the breakdown of your water system; loose tiles falling off your roof; dangerous electrical wiring that can give you a nasty shock and hasty installation of household appliances that break down long before their guarantee. If you take a thermometer into each room; you might find there is too much of a difference between the upstairs and the downstairs. This will tell you that the coldest rooms have not been insulated properly. Anything under 18° centigrade will be considered too cold to live in, without adequate heating. During a cold winter; you may not be able to use a room that is too cold unless you keep it constantly heated. Imagine how high your heating bills will be; through no fault of your own!

Because there is usually a ten-year guarantee for new houses; you might believe that the Housing Board in your country will be able to help you with any problems and get them fixed for you. Sadly; most of these Boards are not independent bodies and are usually employed by the building companies they represent. This means they may not be so thorough in their appraisals and you will have to pay for the repairs yourself because they will claim the houses were okay when you moved in. As a result; the only thing you can do when buying a house; is to pay for your own expert to check it over before you hand over any money. You should then get an additional written guarantee from the building company, ratified by a solicitor; that they will fix any major problems for you within the ten-year period. If they can't do that for you then I would advise you not to buy the house and look for another one. It is too much money to throw away on verbal guarantees.

Time-share apartments can also be a problem because most of them are bought by people who will use them for holidays and do not live in the country where the apartment is situated. The laws governing property may be different to those in your own country and this means you will be at a disadvantage in any disputes with the agents. Pay-offs and fees charged for simple services are normal in many countries and you might find yourself in a minefield when trying to sell your share. You could easily be charged a fee for them to advertise the property and you may end up being shunted from pillar-to-post in a bid to get you to lower your asking price. You may even be offered an alternative property instead of a refund on your money! If you add these 'inconveniences' to the problems with the apartment itself, which may not live up to your own standards or expectations; it could prove to be an insurmountable headache. You should never pay money upfront for any fees because they are supposed to be taken out of the sale price. As in buying property anywhere; it would be better to check out the time-share apartment yourself and then get an independent expert to give you his/her view, before buying it. I hope you can now appreciate how easily you can be conned when buying or selling a property that is outside your comfort jurisdiction.

(g) 'Rogue Traders'

In every country; there are people who pretend to have qualifications and go around offering services to people for payment. Fake certificates are easily available on the Internet and anybody can claim to have the qualifications for anything! You can imagine how dangerous this can be for women who go for beauty treatments and medical examinations. If someone claims to be a qualified plastic surgeon and puts a framed certificate on the wall of the clinic; very few people will ask or bother to check if the certificate is genuine or up-to-date. For years; backstreet abortionists used to operate, without the authorities finding out. Although the situation is now a lot more controlled with unannounced checks on most public establishments; no one can say for certain that there are no more 'rogue traders' in our midst. Before you put your life in the hands of anyone; it would be advisable to do your homework and check up on the establishment in question. You can get a lot of information from the Internet; but it would also be more useful to find out from the relevant association if he/she is a bona-fide member and has not been struck off. Every group that deals with the public; doctors; dentists; solicitors; accountants; real estate agents; beauty therapists; car dealers; gym instructors; teachers; restaurateurs etc. all belong to one society or another. If you feel someone is doing you a disservice; you have to report and have him/her investigated, otherwise they will continue duping the public for profit. A good example would be; the rogue traders setting up companies on the Internet to deal with wills and testaments, by offering a cheaper alternative to a solicitor. Whenever you want to expedite your will; you should always deal with a reputable solicitor specialising in such matters, even if it is a little more expensive. This is because solicitors have a world-wide indemnity; which means that even if the person handling your case dies, you will be able to get someone else from the same company or even from a different firm of solicitors to continue the task for you. Legally; other companies purporting to handle wills, may not be regulated. This means; if you are ripped off, it will be almost impossible to get your money back. They can do this by pushing you to give them power of attorney in handling your assets after you die. They can then help themselves to your money; before informing your relatives of the amount you have bequeathed to them. They will then charge you a hefty commission for the privilege!

All salespeople believe they will be able to convince their target to make a sale. Sadly; women are usually on their radar when it comes to 'easy pickings'. Because of society's inherent condescending attitude towards the female; I implore you to put your nice personality aside and become a 'stubborn bitch', whenever anyone tries to make you part with your money. The sooner you do this, the better; because once a salesperson realises he/she cannot break down your barriers, his/her attitude will change and you will get a better deal. For example; car dealers do not always tell the truth when they offer financing for a vehicle and will try to get you to buy the car immediately, with enticing deals. Never sign any finance documents on their premises; because it always pays to be suspicious whenever someone tries to rush you into buying anything. Ask them to post their offer to you; so that you have time to think about it. By doing so; you will be legally entitled to your country's equivalent of the 'Distant-Selling Regulation'. This will allow you between a minimum 7and a maximum 14-day cooling-off period; in case you change your mind. If you go into a hairdresser for the first time; ask the one doing your hair how long she/he has been doing people's hair and what qualifications they have. If they get annoyed or try to fob you off; it means they are not comfortable with your 'impertinence' and they probably have something to hide. You have every right to refuse their service and either ask for someone else or go elsewhere. It is no accident that the best hairdressers are the ones who have been with the same customers for years and have earned their trust! The same attitude should be used on anyone who wants to do anything for you. Once they start the job; they will expect to be paid, regardless of how unsatisfied you are! Imagine going for a 'boob job' and you are left scarred; simply because you did not check up whether the one performing the operation was legally qualified or not. Certificates on the wall mean nothing without the expertise to back them up; and you may be left counting the cost to your health for the rest of your life. Remember; rogue traders can only ply their trade if we let them!

3. Christmas: Season of goodwill (or is it?)...

Once a year, comes Christmas and New Year; known as the season of goodwill and glad tidings. For many people however, Christmas is a curse; a season never enjoyed, let alone remembered fondly or looked forward to. Millions are still starving, despite it being a season of plenty; and even in the 'advanced countries' of Europe and North America, there are those with nowhere to go and hardly any decent food to eat. Despite all the lows, Christmas is still a high point in the lives of most Christians; and they are determined to enjoy it at all costs. If you don't know what Christmas is and have not felt how life changes; just take a look outside or visit some of your friends and you will notice a change of décor in their living rooms. All major shops and many streets will be decorated and carols can be heard from loudspeakers. Christmas cards will be everywhere and there will be a general feeling of goodwill. Your boss will actually smile at you; even though you will not be doing as much work as you usually do! Even normally strict traffic wardens and on-the-beat police seem friendlier! They are more understanding and allow some things to slide; if they are not too serious. Rather than apprehend a drunken yob who vomits or urinates on the pavement; the cops will give him a warning and advise him to go home. On any normal day; the yob would be arrested! Even with those arrests that are documented by the police; nothing will be done about them until after the New Year because the courts will be closed for holidays.

On Fridays, it is a common sight in most government establishments to see a clerk telling a customer to wait till after the weekend; so forget about trying to do any business in the days before Christmas and the New Year. This means you could be waiting two weeks before things get back to normal. This very goodwill is what clever and not so clever crooks use to dupe and deceive their victims. Student gangs wander around unchecked; even by police checkpoints. Many crimes are committed around Christmas and most are not reported; because there is a popular belief that nothing will be done about them. Read the papers and they are full of hard-luck stories about the elderly being routinely robbed and violated. When a load of joyous singing merrymakers arrive in town and are walking down the street; their very happy mood is infectious and if they are not causing too much trouble, the police might just tell them to cool down. They might not even be bothered to take them all to the station for a body search. Yet; they could very well be armed and using the Christmas spirit to beat up people for their enjoyment, or rob some unfortunate widow alone in her house.

Drink and drugs are everywhere at Christmas; with fake alcohol brewers having a field day putting their booze into respectable bottles. Pubs and bars have been known to water down the spirits; because in their quest to get even drunker, few people ever notice. Bogus drug manufacturers bring out all kinds of shoddy medicine, knowing that people will drink and eat more; therefore they will have all the side effects of doing so like hiccups, vomiting, stomach aches, diarrhoea, constipation etc. You name it; and there will be a drug for it, which has not been approved by the medical board. There will be people knocking on your doors trying to sell you all kinds of things; many of which are probably stolen or counterfeit. You might think you are getting a 'good deal' because of the low price; but there is always a reason why anything is sold cheaply. You are unlikely to be given a receipt; so if you buy a cheap electronic appliance which ends up electrocuting you, there is nothing you can do about it. Dubious charities will all be vying for your money with inventive hard-luck stories; some even using their children as bait to make you feel sorry for them and give them more money. Beggars, pickpockets, credit card scammers and every kind of thief are ever present; because few take extra steps to defend themselves. Everything I have written about previously; applies even more so at Christmas time because people are less vigilant, friendlier and very careless. It is as if the spirit of Christmas takes over and you are not yourself for a few days! Take note of this, even if you do live in a 'developed' country; because the conmen have many tricks, which differ from country to country. Never think you cannot be conned. A trick can originate in one country; and when it is too well known to have any success, the perpetrators will take the same trick and adapt it to another country.

Christmas is a time to enjoy oneself; but there is a limit to everything. Have you prepared yourself for the fun and games, the eating and all the other things that happen at Christmas? How fit are you to face the energy-sapping all-night parties? Parties mean drinking, letting oneself go and having a 'good' time; despite everything else going on in your life. People tend to believe it is okay to get excessively drunk, overeat, say and do things they would not normally do; if they were in their right minds. *("After all; wasn't Christ born at Christmas? It's definitely a cause for celebration!")* Date rape is rampant; but who really cares? When both man and woman are drunk; who is actually raping whom? A girl can easily be raped; because being drunk, she would only feebly resist a man's advances. A man could also claim he was taken advantage of; because it would be very difficult to prove who did what to whom, where, when, how or why! It's only the next morning during the hangover that it might dawn on the woman what had actually happened during the night; but by then, it might be too late to effectively report the matter to the police. Imagine waking up the next morning after the office party in some strange bed; with five other naked male bodies (co-workers?) lying beside you. Just thinking about what might have happened; could have a serious effect on you for the rest of your life. How do you begin to decipher what was done to you? Don't forget, these are your colleagues at work; so which one of them do you report for rape? Can you live with the winks, nudges and innuendoes that will surely surface around the office grapevine? Going to the police around Christmas time, might prove futile; because they receive thousands of reports for much more serious crimes, like murder. You will probably be advised to forgive, forget and put it down to experience; because the inconsistencies in your story would not stand up in court. The cops do not take a sympathetic view on anyone who gets drunk!

Statistics show that there are more car accidents around Christmas, than other holidays. Death on the roads increases because people insist they can drink and drive; when they obviously cannot. Since everyone around is also drunk; there is no one to cause a sobering effect. If your boyfriend is drunk; then don't let him drive. If he insists on driving; then don't go with him. Take a stand! If you are going to a club; then why take the car? What is wrong with a taxi? If you really must drink to get drunk; then stay at home. If you don't know a person well; why go to that 'party' with him? Don't bother going out to a club or a party at Christmas; unless you are with people you trust and know very well. It is a season of joy and happiness; so don't let yours be made miserable and traumatic because you failed to observe a few simple rules. In order to be safe in town whilst doing the shopping; you have to be rude and mind your own business. Do not even waste time talking to people you do not know. If you are able to say *"No!"* with a smile; then do so. The minute you are accosted; you should quickly start walking away and he will be at fault for following you! If you stand still; he can put his charm to work and getting rid of him will be a little harder. Keep walking when you say, *"Sorry I'm a little busy. Another time; maybe"*. If he persists in following you; *"Look, I don't want to be nasty; but if you keep following me, I will call the police"*, should do the trick.

Beware also of the salesmen who come to your house. Once you let them in; they will be able to see what is inside and what kind of locks you have. They could then get their burglar pals to break in when you are out. If you have house-help or children; you should educate them in no uncertain terms, never to talk to or open the door to strangers. Conmen are everywhere and are not averse to using children to get to the adults; but they can only go as far as you allow them. Christmas just makes it easier for them; because people are in a joyful and therefore less security-conscious mood. Before going to bed after the Christmas party in your house; make sure all the alcohol, glass and knives are put safely away, the electrical appliances are switched off and there are no broken pieces of glass lying around or liquids left spilt on the kitchen floor. In the morning; you might still be asleep in a drunken stupor when your kids go into the kitchen to make themselves breakfast. If there is an accident or a fire; you will not be able to help them in time. Every year in the United Kingdom alone; there are over 80 000 Christmas-related accidents in the home. Be careful!

The tricks are too many to put all into this book; but the point is that they do exist. It would not be good self-defence on your part; if you were conned out of all your life savings. It would hurt more than a physical beating! If you are offered money you have not worked for; the chances are it is a con. If someone wants to do business with you, using your money and his/her 'ideas'; then you should never do it. If you buy anything off the Internet; it could be a counterfeit of the original and you will not be able to get your money back. It is still much safer to buy any item from an accredited shop; which has a permanent location and can be held accountable, if something goes wrong. It is always advisable to learn your consumer rights when dealing with any company; because once they have taken your money, it will be almost impossible to get it refunded. Any business transaction should be done through a reputable solicitor and papers signed, so that you know where you stand and there is some insurance you will get your money back; otherwise DON'T DO IT! This means you must never shell out any money; unless you are very sure of what you are doing. If you are one of those who go around conning people; just remember that you will be caught one day! *"If you break the law…the law will break you!"*

So my dear Tigress; what do you do with your family and friends? They are the ones who can harm you the most; as the next chapter will reveal.

Chapter Eleven
With friends like these...

There is a saying that you make your best friends before you are ten years old, which is not actually true; but there is a point that your oldest friends are the best. Everybody needs people who they can trust; and regrettably, it is this trust that ultimately becomes your downfall. Women (God bless them) are loving and trusting creatures; and are often taken for a ride by friends and lovers. When a woman is in love, she gives her heart and soul. Nobody blames her when she becomes a victim of a ruthless conman of a boyfriend or even a family member. When a man gives everything and is taken to the cleaners by a woman; he is ridiculed and called an idiot! Not really fair; but that's just the way things are! This book is about self-defence for women; so I will only deal with things from a female perspective.

1. Keeping secrets

We tend to give away too much information to total strangers and friends; who then end up knowing certain things about us and can use this knowledge to do irreparable damage. Why should you tell your neighbour that your husband gives you a cheque every Friday for X amount of money? Why do you have to bring her to your bedroom to show her what you keep there; or that you plan to steal your husband's money, because he has done such and such to you? Do you have to tell outsiders your marital problems? So what if your husband is a skirt-chasing flirt? Need you tell the girls in the office? It is such 'harmless' information and tittle-tattle, that could end up with you in an embarrassing situation. Gossiping, however interesting, should be shunned because what you say to someone in confidence will definitely be repeated elsewhere; completely out of context. It may even be exaggerated to such an extent that by the time it comes back to you, you will seem like the culprit. There is more to the saying *'women cannot keep a secret'* than they will admit. A woman is usually prone to sharing many attributes with her friends; from kindness to money, gossip and secrets. She will generally confide in another woman; before she will tell a man. If you have valuables which are not insured, and you tell someone; then you can only blame yourself, if they are stolen. We are surrounded by people from all walks of life and diverse upbringing, so we have to be very careful in the way we deal with friends and neighbours; or we could be punished, just for trusting someone. It takes years to know a person well. Even then; you will find that it is this very familiarity, which one utilises for one's gain. It is those closest to you that are most dangerous; as there is a Judas in everybody's life. You will not be crucified; but the damage to your self-esteem, confidence, reputation and bank account could be incalculable. "*Et Tu Bruté?*"; sighed Shakespeare's Julius Caesar, as he lay dying…

Do not interfere with a quarrel between a woman and her man because they will inevitably kiss and make up; and they will both end up blaming you for taking sides. Likewise, you should never divulge any of your personal life's secrets to anyone, even your best friend; because she may not always be your number one. Best friends usually turn out to be the worst enemies; because of something very petty. A perceived insult, an argument, a quarrel or repeating elsewhere, something told in confidence; could easily become a betrayal of trust. What is said or done between you and your husband is your affair; and no one else's. I realise that many women find it hard to keep quiet on certain things; and must tell somebody. One should refrain from such habits because they are detrimental to your well-being; and may come back to haunt you, when the situation changes. If you were told someone you knew was having an affair with another woman's husband and you repeated the salacious gossip; it will have your imprint on it. Should the story prove not to be true; you may be the one saddled with spreading the gossip. You will thereby lose the friendship and trust of the one who told you and of the people involved in the rumour. Do not give away any information, unless absolutely necessary; so that even friends cannot know enough about you to harm you, by repeating the info elsewhere.

Some lonely rich women tend to have no one to talk to; so they end up confiding their secrets to their drivers, cooks, bodyguards etc. This is not a good idea; because the day they get 'itchy feet' and want to leave, they will also take your secrets with them. They could easily harm you by giving vital information about you to others; who would then be in a strong position to do you severe damage. If certain things are stolen without any sign of breaking and entering; then it is what is known as an 'inside job'. This means it was planned, though not necessarily executed, by someone known to you; and possibly living with you. Don't be over-friendly with anybody working for you; like nannies, baby-sitters, house-help, drivers and anyone else with access to your house. Familiarity always breeds contempt! They must never be allowed to know where you keep anything important or of high monetary value. Be kind and fair, but slightly aloof; or they might see it as a sign of weakness and take advantage of you. Even after many years together; domestic employees have been known to walk out of the house with all their employer's valuables. Always keep your bedroom door locked and only allow it to be cleaned when you are present. If you have to go out, leaving a hired help in the house; please make sure you have everything of value locked up. You should also keep a portfolio on all your employees; so that you know where to find them, in case they run off with the family jewellery. Before anyone begins to work for you; their home, parent's home, immigration status and other relevant information should be your priority. It might therefore be better to use a reliable agency, when looking for someone to work for you; so that you have some insurance against anything going wrong with the employee. If you can afford a hired help, you should be able to afford to hide a security camera in the house; in case he/she steals anything or mistreats your children, whilst you are away! If you ever find a nanny becoming too familiar with your husband or son; it would be better to let her go, before she seduces him. The cases of hubby running off with the nanny are too numerous to mention! You can usually tell if a nanny is having an affair with your husband/son by her body language. She will behave like the cat that got the cream and will become increasingly self-assured. She will start making decisions about the house, without consulting you; and may even be rude towards you, if you dare challenge or criticise her.

With your husband, it would be advisable to keep a few secrets from him, like how much you have in your account or how much you earn; unless he comes clean with his own affairs. Most men are unlikely to do so; because it is in their nature not to let women into every facet of their business. Just as you would not like him to read your Emails, open your letters, listen in on your phone calls or pry into your mobile phone address book; there are some things that should be secret. This is because they could be used to harm you if things go wrong in the marriage. You are unlikely to receive as much alimony, if he knows you are richer than he is; so you should always keep a secret account that no one knows about, purely as a guarantee. Anything can happen; even in the most 'blissfully happy' marriages! How would you like to find out he has been giving his cash away to his extra-marital girlfriends or spending it on prostitutes and drugs? By the time he divorces you; there might not be anything left for you and the children. Since it would be hard to stop him spending his own money; you have to protect yourself by having a secret stash…just in case! By all means open a joint account that you can both use for the children and household expenses etc.; but keep your financial matters close to your chest. The last thing you want is for any man prying into your affairs and telling you how to spend or even spending money you have worked so hard for.

2. Family members

Because of their closeness to you, family members are the ones who could hurt you the most; so you have to be careful with what you allow them to know about yourself. Don't divulge where you keep your money to your children because they have been known to steal from their parents. They may also tell their friends, who could convince them to 'borrow' the money, forge your signature on a cheque or use your car when you are out. It is the way a parent treats his or her child in the beginning that will determine what kind of person he or she grows up to be. If you spoil your child by giving him or her everything; then he or she will grow up expecting nothing less. If for some reason, you do not give him or her money that they have become accustomed to; then he/she will seek other ways to obtain it. When a teenage son sees all his friends driving cars, whilst he has only a bicycle; the next step will be to borrow one of his parents' cars. With a car, comes a need for money; and since he is still in school and the girls are becoming more demanding, what does he do next? He watches his parents like a hawk; till he sees a familiar pattern. Once he finds out where they keep the money, he will steal it; regardless of the consequences. Many children believe their parent's property is their due and may not regard it as stealing! Children have been known to physically attack their parents during arguments; yet, if you hit your child, you could be reported to the authorities. This causes a moral discrepancy, which many parents don't know how to handle; allowing their children to walk all over them. They are therefore powerless when a child is rude, obnoxious or downright dangerous. For instance; the mother might get angry with her daughter because she does not get the respect that she, as the mother, believes she deserves. The daughter being younger and probably prettier; thinks her Mum is picking on her because she is jealous of her lifestyle and won't let her do what she wants. An argument starts and one of them says the wrong thing and Wham! A slap is thrown, usually by the mother; but quite often by the daughter! It is very easy to 'lose it' and yell at or even hit your children; which could make them hate you and plot ways to get you back by stealing huge sums of your money. In the most extreme scenarios, there have been quite a few successful attempts by children to murder their parents in order to get the inheritance they feel they deserve; as happened in the 'Menendez case' in America.

As loveable as they are normally; children can also be the most dangerous enemy a woman can have. This is because her unconditional love refuses to spot the signs of discontent and leaves her open to all kinds of danger; from theft and extortion to violence and murder. The first step in defending yourself against attacks or thefts from your children is to raise them properly and teach them to value certain things in life; by not spoiling them, no matter how rich you are. Love has to be tempered with strict discipline from an early age; so that they grow up into well-rounded adults, knowing right from wrong. By teaching the boys how to do traditionally female tasks like sewing buttons on shirts, ironing and housework and showing the girls male-orientated pastimes like how to fix a puncture in a car, faulty plumbing and other DIY tasks around the house; you can make them independent. This is imperative; so that when they go out into the big bad world, they are not held domestic hostage to their lovers or partners. Many parents already know this; by making sure their children are brought up equally and are not treated differently, because of their sex. This obviously means that if Mary does the washing up, then so should John; and if John helps Daddy in the garden, then Mary ought to as well. Even if a child does not want to do something; every mother has her ways of convincing him/her! I do believe that if you explain the reasons why a child should be self-sufficient, he/she will do it; because nobody likes to beg anyone to do something for them. However; male children should always be brought up to respect their female siblings and treat her equally, so that she can stand up for herself. This will make her mentally tough; so that she will not spend her life trying to impress or outdo men and get ripped off or beaten up in the bargain. It is very important to instil in your male children; a sense of equality, loyalty and obligation to the female. Otherwise; they may become the kind of men who go around fleecing and degrading women. For every lady who is raped, beaten up, ripped off or abused; there is a culprit whose parents should hang their heads in shame at what their son has become. No baby is born bad!

Amongst other family members like cousins, uncles, aunts etc.; jealousy is the greatest threat. This means you have to keep them at arms length; so that they don't use what they know about you, to harm you. This can cause a real dilemma. If you are richer than them; you have to either keep completely away or be generous, if you allow them into your life. If you are less well-off; you cannot be too intrusive or you may be treated like a parasite. Family members might be guilty of taking you for granted; because when they ask a favour from you, they never expect a refusal. They may even end up hating you; if you cannot give them what they want! You therefore have to learn the trick of replacing a refusal with an alternative generosity. For example; you may refuse a cousin a loan of some money but surprise him/her with a monetary birthday or Christmas gift, of the same amount that was asked of you. This way; the loan becomes an acceptable celebratory gift. More importantly; he/she will realise you are not stupid and you do not give loans which are unlikely to be paid back. This will prevent them ever asking you again for money! Although you are unlikely to be harmed physically by a family member you are not living with; the gossiping and backbiting can still cause a lot of damage to your reputation. *"Who does she think she is? Because she's got money/married a rich man; she doesn't want to know us anymore. We were there for her when she had nothing...!"* are not very nice things to hear about yourself. Sometimes you have to take a step back and surprise them with unexpected acts of kindness; to let them know you are still part of the greater family. In times of despair, you will need your relatives to support you; so a little affection and letting some of your wealth and good fortune go around them, is not a bad thing. Being a pariah to your family members can be a very lonely existence and you will have no buffer against the antics of your husband, boyfriend or partner. Once he realises you have no one to turn to; he will take advantage of you and try to control your life. Finally; you should never abandon your family or good friends you have known for years, just because of some new lover whose only claim to fame is, he gives you multiple orgasms! Your relatives and friends will always be there for you, long after he has gone; so be good to them!

3. Misogyny

Misogyny is the hatred of women; and I am happy to risk controversy when I say, every man in this world is guilty in one way or the other of misogyny. This is because all over the world, men are feeling the female backlash; which comes in many forms. Deep down, all men are protective of women and believe the 'weaker sex' syndrome; which means he feels superior to her because he is stronger. When a woman prevents him from fulfilling his ambitions; he will resent it. Whether it means she gets the job he was going for; gets custody of the child instead of him; sues him for divorce and wins a hefty pay-out; lies to the police about him to get him into trouble; or many other instances where a man is made to feel second rate; the thoughts going through his head will be misogynistic. Every man has at one time or another felt the force of the female and wishes he could figuratively 'strangle' her; but realises there is nothing he can do, because female power is here to stay. A man will say he is all for equality and *"...it's good to see a woman 'doing well' etc";* but this is only so long as it does not affect him. Will he still feel the same way; if a woman is promoted above him in a gender bias situation? Granted he may be upset, even if a man is moved ahead instead of him; but there is something really damaging to the male ego, when it is a woman who prevents him realising his cherished aims and ambitions. Political correctness has made sure he will not publicly vent his anger; but privately, you can bet anything he will be seething. *'Damned that bitch! She must be fucking the boss!'* Is that not slightly misogynous? Doesn't it say in the Bible that thoughts, words and deeds can all be equally sinful? Unfortunately, there is still a world-wide deep-rooted belief that women are somehow less capable than men; and are often grouped together with children. *"Make sure all the women and children are safe..."* is always used by the police and emergency services during fires, floods, accidents etc. Although it is nice and honourable for the men to think about protecting the women and children; that attitude somehow stops women from being taken seriously. If they constantly need men to protect them; how are they ever going to be allowed to stand up for themselves? The world seems to forget that women have proved time and time again that when it comes to the crunch, they are very capable of physically and mentally standing up and being counted. There was once a time when they said women could not run the marathon, do the pole vault, climb mountains or sail around the world!

I challenge any man to say there is no institutionalised misogyny in the world and I will say he is a liar; because of the following: rape; marital beatings; unequal pay; deliberate hindrance of education, employment and promotion prospects; treated as sexual objects for male gratification; forced marriages; female circumcision; purdah; bridal humiliations; illegal abortions; desperate prostitution and honour killings are still going on and men are sitting there pretending there is nothing we can do to prevent them. By nature; a woman is the most wonderful, loving, inspirational, hard-working and kind-hearted of all God's creatures. Every man should be really ashamed for all the suffering women have had to go through over the centuries; and yet, did nothing about it. We all spent our first moments of life inside a female womb; arrived into her loving arms; sucked on her juicy milk-filled breasts; and for the most part, were nurtured, fed and looked after by a woman in our formative years. Yes, everybody has/had a mother; and yet we repay the female with the suffering they are receiving the world over. How then can any man stand up and say he is not misogynistic; when he is doing nothing about the global female plight? We talk about 'equality' for women; so why are we allowing them to go through hell? Have we so quickly forgotten what our mothers did for us? Even though there are obviously bad and cruel women in the world; you will probably find that they were not born cruel. Circumstances, most likely created by disloyal men in their lives, turned them like that; in order to pay men back for all the hurt they had received. Misogyny? Men have a lot to answer for and owe the female one gigantic apology for past and present humiliations. For my part; I hope through this book, I am doing my bit for the female race.

I will now get off my soap box with a reality check and tell you what you already know; and that is, misogyny still exists. What do you do about it; so that it does not affect you unduly? We still live in a relatively politically correct world; which means the misogyny will not be blatant. Nobody will stand up and shout, *"I hate women!"* You therefore have to make sure it does not openly happen to you; by making a big fuss and knocking the perpetrators back so hard, they will not think of trying it on you again. There is no law against 'hating' women because there is still freedom of thought; and so long as the thought does not become action, it should not worry you. As a woman; I am very confident you have the verbal ammunition to put any man who tries to take advantage of you, in his place. But you have to go one step further and stick up for other females. If you see an injustice on a woman by a man; you should stick your nose in and tell him off. This is because she may not be aware that things being said or done to her; are in any way misogynistic. It would be better for the woman or man to tell you to mind your own business; than for you to say nothing. You may very well have sown some fruitful seeds in her head; which will get her thinking long after you have gone! She may eventually realise the veracity in your words; so that she does not allow it to happen to her again. If for example, you are on a bus or train and you see a pregnant or elderly woman being teased or jostled around by some youths; don't be afraid to tell them off for their lack of compassion. You could even suggest to them to give up their seat for the lady instead of making fun of her. You will be surprised that they will do as you ask; rather than face embarrassment from the other passengers or a tongue-lashing from you. Whereas, if a man had poked his nose in; he would probably be ignored or even threatened and insulted! On a wider scale; leaving wrongs for men to right, has so far been proved to be a bridge too far because of their self-interest and overall ignorance about a woman's feelings. This means women have to use their undeniably substantial electoral vote against all politicians who refuse to accept the importance of the female; because the only language a politician understands is power. Threaten to take it away by voting him out of office and you will see a drastic change in the status quo. There are already laws in place to protect women; but they do not go far enough. The more they fight for even the smallest injustices and make a thorough nuisance of themselves on men to make sure they cannot move a misogynistic inch without being taken to task; the quicker the curse of misogyny will be eradicated.

4. Racism

Racism is another modern day evil that needs to be eradicated. Before I go any further; I would like to say that even if you are a white woman, you can still be a victim of racism...depending on which country you are living or visiting. There is no child under five years old who is a racist; because they don't see and react to people by the colour of their skins. This means that racism is learnt as the child gets older; mainly from the parents and school friends. Like misogyny; racists are very hypocritical and may not openly show it, but will keep it in their hearts. This makes it worse; because it is like a cancer waiting to explode. *"I'm not a racist; I even have black and Asian friends..."* is a common mantra. But the true test would be; if you are white and a black man/woman wanted to marry your daughter/son. Would you not have some reservations; especially for their future children, who would be of mixed race? People believe racism is calling a black person less than delightful names like *"Nigger!"*, *"Coon!"*, *"Wog!"*, *"Black bastard!"* or anything that has connotations of the word 'black'. That would be too simplistic, because the black American rap artists sometimes use the word *"Nigger!"* as a term of endearment in their songs; but would probably be offended, if a white person used the same word on them. This is because they have a history of racism, far worse than any felt by most other black people in the world; and any sign of belittlement of their colour will most likely open up festering slavery or civil rights wounds. A Moslem may not be so annoyed at being called names; but would be angry, if you offended their religion. Whereas those of African and Asian descent, born and bred in Europe; have a different mentality. They believe racist comments are borne out of ignorance and have their own way of dealing with them; not with anger but with nonchalance, stoicism or equally hurtful verbal ripostes. They are even able to make self-effacing jokes about their colour; which has the potent effect of dismantling a racist comment. Two opponents of different race may even end up becoming friends or having a drink together; whilst continuing the racist verbal jousting in a humorous mood!

Racism goes a lot deeper than just calling someone names based on colour; because it is the attitude that makes it so deplorable, yet impossible to subvert. This means that it is the intention that makes something racist. If you are black and your white best friend calls you *"black bitch!"* in a friendly way; you will most likely let her get away with it because you know your friendship transcends any verbal sniping and she is just joking. Whereas, if someone you did not know said the same thing to you in the town centre; you could report him/her to the authorities and sue for racism. A Pakistani Moslem will not be happy to see her child marry an Indian Hindu; likewise an Israeli Jew might ban his/her child from marrying a Palestinian Arab. An African might be happy to see his/her daughter marry a white man, if it means an improvement in the financial and social position of their child; yet the white family the black girl is marrying into, might regard her as a money-grabbing impostor or social climber. How would you feel if you are white and a black girl seduced and stole your husband from under your nose? Would you not have a slightly racist opinion of black women, either vocally or in your thoughts? For years, black women have been complaining that black men prefer white women to them and still don't have a high impression of white women; often giving them names like *"white trash!"* and *"cheap, easy pussy!"* The people involved in each of the above examples would probably tell you they are not racists! It does show that everybody has a threshold which, if crossed, will unleash the dormant and repressed feelings inside; making it all too obvious that if you are a racist, you can never change and it is fear of the law and political correctness that prevents most of us from venting our real feelings.

The only advice I can give to you would be to be true to yourself and be honest enough to admit that if you are a racist, there is nothing you can do; because it is impossible to change from who you really are. You have to realise however, that racism is wrong on so many levels like legal, social and personal. You will therefore have to live with it and learn to curb it; because the world has changed. Just like the great strides achieved by the women's movement; racism is on the way out, albeit slowly. You cannot turn back the tide of progress! If your child wants to marry someone of a different race, which you don't approve of; you have a right to state your reservations but not to prevent the happiness of your child and the spouse. They are obviously of a different generation to you and will therefore have different attitudes to colour from you. If you feel like insulting someone with a comment based on the colour of their skin; remember that you could land yourself in big trouble with the authorities. You may even face a backlash from others of the same skin colour, who may have witnessed your verbal assault and may take it upon themselves to avenge the slur; possibly by violence. Social and economic deprivation of Blacks and Asians has made them very sensitive to any slight or insult. It can easily be seen as rubbing salt into a festering wound and regarded as racist; because they are already angry at the daily injustices they are experiencing. On many occasions, they are forced to encounter racists; who use all kinds of ingenious ways to perpetuate racism. For example, a black person may go for a job or enquire about the sale of a house; but will be told it is not available, with the smooth excuse, *"We're sorry; it has just been taken. We can put you in touch with another agency if you like"*. They will never say it is because he/she is black; because that is against the law. Blacks and Asians are often targeted by the police, simply because of ethnic profiling; which unfairly links Blacks to crime and Asians to terrorism. This form of clandestine racism is on the increase; and there is very little the law can do about it because it is so difficult to prove.

Also, there are those who do not understand the sensitivities of others and may act in a racist way; out of ignorance, not vengeance. For example; a nightclub may have a 'no hats/caps' policy and will have to bar a Sikh wearing a turban, or face the wrath of all cap-loving clubbers. The Sikh will see the barring as racist and insensitivity to his religion or beliefs; and may go home, having a low opinion of whites...inadvertently turning him into a potential racist. Like sexism; racism is still prevalent, even though there are laws against it. If you are a victim of public racism; you have to make a report to the authorities. The guilty party will face charges; most likely culminating in a financial punishment. If you are facing it on a daily basis; it would be wise for you to gather evidence with a concealed video cam or tape recorder, in order to have irrefutable proof against those responsible. The resulting bad publicity and fines; will send out a message that one cannot insult anyone publicly because of skin colour, and get away with it. If the insult is private like over the phone or face to face, without any witnesses; you will have to use some typical female verbal counter-attacks and hit the insulter where it hurts most, by striking at his/her self-esteem or dignity. Such personal insults are usually borne out of a disagreement, owing money or stealing a lover. *"You black/white bitch, leave my man alone!"* could be riposted with *"Shouldn't you be telling that to him? I had to fight him off me last night!"* If she dares say: *"You liar! He was with me last night!"* You should hit back with, *"Ooops! Sorry! It must have been this morning. He always comes to me after you go out! It looks like he prefers my black/white snatch to yours!"* I'm sure you can think of something even more hurtfully poignant!!!

5. Taking advantage

In Chapter Four, I dealt with ways and means of avoiding date rape; by stopping a man getting to certain stages, if you did not want him to sleep with you. Now supposing you do sleep with him and everything is rosy. You are in love and he makes you feel good, every time he is with you. It is possible but very rare, that you can have a relationship without problems. There is also a saying that 'love is blind'; which means you will not notice little things going wrong. Once a man senses you are madly in love; he will start taking you for granted. It is a slow and subtle process; which very few can feel or see coming. It may begin with something small; like him forgetting to say *"Good morning"* to you or kiss you good night, as he normally does. Because you are so blindingly in love; you will start forgiving him for things you consider petty. For example; he is late for a date and arrives with a big smile on his face, but no sign of an apology. By the time he hugs and melts you in his arms, you would have forgotten to ask him why he was late; because you don't want to appear pushy or that you are 'nagging' him. An off-hand remark in public really hurts you; but you brush it off with a smile and even make excuses for him in your mind. *'He must be drunk; otherwise he would not have said that!'* After giving you a good lovemaking session; he really is king of your jungle and can do no wrong. You will not even mind when he goes into your purse and 'borrows' some money for his taxi fare home or a few beers with the boys! Like a drug, you tend to remember the 'high' of the orgasms and forget all his blatant faults; because you are subconsciously looking forward to the next multi-orgasmic fix.

You can tell at what stage a couple is when they are walking down the street; by their body language. When a man has his arm around a girl's shoulders and she has her arm around his waist; then they are most probably in love. When he has his arm around her and she does not reciprocate; then it means he wants to tell other guys she is his girl and they should keep off, but she obviously does not feel the same as he does! When she grips hold of his arm or around his waist and he does not do the same; then she is 'clinging on' and for one reason or another, does not want to lose him. He is then in the position most men dream of; a beautiful woman clinging to his arm, while he appears to be calling the shots. You can actually notice the gloat of arrogance on his face! A lot of rich men are often in this position; where it is obvious the girl is after his money and definitely not his looks. But it still makes him feel good! It can get so bad that the girl is like a child walking with the mother; whereby she takes two steps for every one of his, just to keep up with him! He is supposed to be your boyfriend/lover, yet something is wrong; because he is not treating you right. When he first met you, he was considerate and kind; but now, he is only nice to you when he wants something from you. The sex is still good, but now there is hardly any foreplay; and he does not hug and hold you afterwards like he used to! By the time a woman realises this; it might be too late. She will be so much in love that she will only have two choices. Put up and shut up or dump him! Female complaints are many when it comes to men; but allowing it to reach a point where you are not happy with him, is definitely your fault. Men will slip into a lazy routine very easily; if they are not stopped. Relationships are not easy to maintain at the best of times; and it is usually the woman who is left to keep the candle burning.

All 'imbalances' in a relationship must be crushed right at the beginning; before they are allowed to foment and propagate. His real character usually surfaces when he has finally slept with you; and he realises he does not have to do any more running, in order to continue sleeping with you. From then on; it becomes a burden to maintain the 'perfect man' image he sold to you when he first met you. *"He used to bring me breakfast in bed and cook for me; and now all he does is snore and break wind in bed!"* is a common complaint. If he was looking for sex when he first met you; then it is only natural that he will be nice to you. After the sex, if there is nothing else he wanted you for; cooking you breakfast in bed will seem like feeding a whole army and he will find it very hard to do that...even if it is only once a week. If he stops making you breakfast in bed; ask him (nicely!) why he has stopped! The chances are; if you insist, he will do it. With you as 'dessert'; he will jump quickly to cook it for you! You may have to compromise to just at weekends; but once agreed, you should never let him get away with it, although he may need 'reminding' every week. If he misses a weekend; it will be much harder to get him to do it the following week. What happened to all the lovely flowers, expensive gifts and delicious chocolates he used to buy you; when you were courting? Don't let him escape! The price of a reasonable box of chocolates is less than two pints in the pub; which he would gladly buy for a stranger he had just met and got chatting about sports or politics to! If you knew how much a man can waste in a pub; then you would be demanding a lot more from him than you now do!

A man will always be charming, kind and polite at the start of a relationship; until he gets what he wants. He will then become comfortable and over-confident of his hold on you. From then on, you may find yourself playing 'catch-up'; always running after him and doing things just to please him. Today he may take only a few dollars out of your purse. Tomorrow…who knows…maybe a few thousand? Many a woman has been made bankrupt by a charmer she fell in love with. If he borrows even one dollar from you; the next time you see him, ask him for it back...even if you don't really need it. If he makes a promise to you; follow it up to make sure he sticks to his word, otherwise you will never know when or whether to trust him again. If he breaks a small promise without recriminations; he will have no qualms about breaking a bigger one. This will let him know that although you are in love; you are not dumb. He will think twice before he takes money from your purse again. *'You cheapskate!'* Let him think what he wants. At least *'fool'* won't be one of them. Respect has to be earned; but keeping it takes a lot of hard work. The minute you feel something is not 'right'; don't be afraid to let him know. If he is late for a date and you don't like it; there is no use pretending otherwise. If he cracks a joke at your expense in public and you are not happy; then smiling will only make you feel worse. Either crack a joke back at his expense; or wait till you get home and then deal with him. Kissing and making up must still be accompanied by a severe warning to him not to repeat what he did; or you will react in a nasty way, like dumping him. Mean what you say and say what you mean! The worse thing to do, is to pretend it never happened and forget all about it; because it will continue and the 'jokes' will become more ribald. You might end up being the butt of all the jokes any time you go out together; and even when he goes out without you, he will continue making jokes about you to his mates in the pub! Where do you think all those horrible anti-women jokes are told? Certainly not in front of women! After a few pints; he might brag to his friends what a good blow job you give and confide that you always enjoy swallowing his sperm. *"Why do you think her complexion is so good?..."* amidst raucous laughter. Next time you go out with him to the pub and everyone is smiling at you; it may not be because you are such a lovely lady!

Apart from boyfriends and lovers; close friends can also take advantage of you because they will assume the friendship means you cannot refuse a favour or request. Even though they are not sleeping with you; they will attempt to use the friendship as a form of blackmail. *"Can I borrow some money from you and I'll pay you back tomorrow"*. If tomorrow comes and you say nothing; he/she will assume you have more than enough and don't need the money. *('Why else would she give me the money; if she needed it?')* Before you know it; enough time has passed by and you could forget all about it. It then becomes much harder to ask for the money back; without risking the break-up of your friendship. You could also go out with a friend and end up always being the one paying for the drinks; because he/she is constantly broke. Others might borrow things from you without permission and never return them. They will deliberately take you for a fool; because they think you are too nice/stupid to see through them or say anything. It might get to the point that even if he/she has got money, they will not reveal it; because they have become used to your kindness and largess. Finally; there will be the callous, self-confessed users who will tell you they are only with you for what they can get. This is because they believe that by being honest; they don't need to pretend and have nothing to hide. In some ways; this is quite endearing because such people will call a spade a spade and will not be afraid to tell you off when you do something wrong. All users are charmers who will make you laugh and have fun with them. That is their way of compensating for the fact that they never have any cash; or have any intention of repaying you. If you are aware of their unwillingness to contribute, then all well and good; but you have to ask yourself whether these are the kind of friends you want to keep.

In order to get rid of them; you will have to decline certain outings with a simple but obvious excuse like, *"I'm too busy to go out tonight!"* or *"I don't have any money on me; so we'll go out if you can pay for me!"* More than likely, they will find someone else to go out with and 'sponge' off; which should suit you fine, because it will save you money! Different friends will have different uses for you and will try to use you for their own selfish ends; which makes it very difficult to know who is a true friend and who is not. Short of setting up tests for them to pass or fail; how do you assess whether or not your friend is taking advantage of you? A sure sign would be to ask them to do you a favour; like a loan of money. If they make excuses; then you can also use the same excuse, when they ask you for a loan. It is almost impossible to find a real friend, who is not out for all he/she can get from you. The survival instinct of all human beings means we will always do what is best for us, and people are just stepping stones to our ultimate aim; which is our happiness. If you can accept that imperfection in our genetic make-up; then you will be able to accept people for what they are and not get too upset when someone is deviously or blatantly trying to take advantage of you. A friend who never has money and always depends on you to foot the bill, may turn out to be the one who is there for you in your hour of need; like when your partner dumps you for a younger model and you need a shoulder to cry on! But then; he/she might not stick around during a crisis (arrested/convicted/incarcerated, serious illness, death of your relative etc.). We all have our faults and our uses. If you dump every person who you feel is taking advantage; you may end up being a very lonely lady. The best way to go about assessing a friend is to be honest, and always let them know when you don't like certain things they are doing; by insisting you will not entertain the behaviour any longer. Many will fall by the wayside and will not contact you again; when they realise they cannot stand the fact that you are 'on to them' and are unwilling to change to suit them. However; there will always be one or two who will last the course and become more honest with you, by confessing their own frailties and will accept and love you for who you are. They are the ones you can safely consider true friends, who will be there for you when you need them; through thick and thin.

6. The plunderer

Beware! When a man is nice to you; it is not always to get between your legs. There are certain men who go out of their way to fleece women; and treat ripping off females as a lucrative professional pastime. They have been known to be generous to a woman, to let her believe he has money; and then fleece her when he has won over her love and trust. If you are lonely, it can become very difficult to refuse a date; and that is why the con artist usually goes in for lonely widows, single ladies or rich women whose husbands are always out of town. He is intelligent; polite and charming; listening more than he speaks; offering you advice you want to hear; complimenting/flattering you; and will make no initial attempt to sleep with you. A lot of women will find this kind of attention so intoxicating; they might start divulging personal and crucial information about themselves or their family. This she should never do; because he will use this info to rob her or quietly empty her bank account. Some women suddenly become rich by chance; by winning the lottery or being the beneficiary of a will, following the death of her husband or a relative. These are easier to rip off; because they did not work for the money and they don't immediately know what to do with it or whom they can trust. Even the rich, astute, hard-nosed businesswomen who know the value of money, can be ripped off; because they are always looking for ways to make more money and through greed, can be conned by 'a simple idea'. Don't ever think it cannot happen to you; but rather say to yourself, *"It has happened to many women; but I will make sure it never happens to me"* and always be on the look out. The sea is full of sharks and the plunderer is the most dangerous of them!

If for instance, you frequent a certain bar; a man could watch you for weeks and build a mental dossier on you, in order to assess whether you are rich enough for him to bother with. When a man slides up to you in a bar; he may already know you are worth a lot of money and you are a lonely woman in search of company. He will be so nice that you will start treating him like an old friend; and before you know it, you have told him your boiler or car needs fixing or something just as frivolous. Of course, he will know how to fix it or know someone who can do it cheaper for you; and hits the jackpot as soon as you invite him into your home. If you are not rich; then you can safely assume he is only after your body and it will be up to you how you deal with him. Every woman has her own reasons for wanting to sleep with a man; but you should never let your lust cloud your instinct and judgement. All men know that it's the little things like kindness that most women appreciate; and a good con artist will be the nicest person you could ever meet. He will hold doors open for you, hug you frequently, hold your hand in public and act the perfect gentleman. He will pay attention to your every move and always say the things you want to hear; like how beautiful you look. Once he knows you love being praised; he will do it ten times a day, if necessary! For most women; it is like a dream come true. This type of smooth behaviour is what you should beware of; because it is a dream. When you wake up; he may have already walked off with your life savings!

As I stated before; although it is an ego booster, all flattery should be treated with indifference. A simple straight-faced *"Thanks for the compliment"* will be enough to let him know that you are not easily moved; and more than likely he will stop. This will tell you that he is not serious; because it takes a strong and potentially genuine man to keep on complimenting you, when you act like you are obliviously rude to his flattery! It can be very difficult for a woman; but when you fall for a man, try to keep a big part of you to yourself. Don't give away everything; because life is full of changes. Once you are aware of that fact; you will realise that the nicer a man seems at first, the worse he will turn out to be in the end. High standards are impossible to maintain for a long time! It is much better to meet the honest man, who tells you right from the start that he is broke; so that you go into the relationship, with your eyes wide open. At least; when he asks you for money, you know you won't get it back! He may have other qualities to compensate for his lack of finance! How much is an extra inch worth? (*Just joking!*)

It is really none of my business how you conduct your relationships; but before you allow a man to get too close to you, try to find out his financial situation. This is because there are several subtle ways he can put himself in a position to fleece you. He might start by 'borrowing' little amounts of cash from you; and when there is no resistance, he will progress to scrounging bigger amounts. He might even pay you back the smaller amounts and win your confidence; in order to borrow more. He might then come up with a 'business plan'; which usually involves his ideas and *your* money. You might then start trusting him implicitly; by allowing him access to your bank account or giving him your credit card PIN. You might also find yourself indirectly buying his love and attention by giving him presents; and he will begin to believe you love and need him so much, you cannot live without him. He might then start having a few serious 'financial difficulties'; with the intention of extracting a huge loan from you. *"Could you lend me some money...I will pay you back etc."* It is very rare he will pay you back; especially if he is sleeping with you. You will then find it hard to get the money back from him; without it seeming like you are ungrateful for all the love he has been showering on you. If you become too intransigent; he will just walk out on you and will never pay the money back. If no papers were signed; you will not receive any legal joy from the police either. The worse thing to do is to keep the relationship going, in the hope that you will get your money back; because he will sense this and use it to extract more of your goodness/stupidity. One day he will tell you he is going on a business trip; but never returns. You check your bank account and find out it is empty. The shock; upon realisation that you have lost all your money to such a smooth operator, will be more painful than a physical attack.

If you refuse to give him the money, he may use emotional blackmail; which comes under many disguises. Because you are in love and don't want to lose him; you will find yourself giving him what he wants, just to keep the peace. He can starve you sexually; by suddenly being 'tired', when it comes to sex. Instead of delaying his orgasm to synchronise it with yours; he will deliberately satisfy himself and then roll over to sleep. You will realise something is wrong with him; because that is not how he usually makes love to you. Forget about him 'licking your fanny!' You don't deserve it, you tight-fisted bitch! *'What could be wrong with him? Could it be because I did not give him the money?'* Clever girl! How did you know? You will find yourself giving him the money in double-quick time. When you do that; he will suddenly 'remember' how to perform cunnilingus to perfection! You are finished, if you succumb to sexual blackmail; because he will have no qualms about using it, whenever necessary. He is curt and answers your questions with *"Yes" "No" "Maybe"* or *"I don't know!"* Whereas before; *"Darling"* and *"Sweetheart"* would be generously interspersed in his lively conversations with you, he now appears rude and bored when you have something to say. Like a child; he will sulk because he did not get what he wanted. It is then that he will think seriously about dumping you and finding himself another lonely woman; who will give him what he wants. He will do this by using you for your connections and ideas; and then moving on to the next woman up the ladder. She will most likely be someone you know; because you once let slip that she was the managing director of a company and was also unattached and worth a lot more than you. Once he has broken into your circle of acquaintances; why would he bother with the 'secretary', when he can go for the boss herself? When this happens, don't be sad; because it could so easily have been worse. You should however warn his next conquest what he did to you and that he is obviously after her money; which is why he left you for her. Be aware that your friend could be at the stage you were at when you first met him, and may not listen to you; because he will definitely use the same charm offensive on her.

Playing the pauper is the best way for you to see whether he will last the course; enabling you to trust him, or see if he is out to 'screw' you. If you start telling him how much trouble you are in with your bank and the house is about to be repossessed, followed by other tales of financial woe; he will quickly exit your life, if he feels you are more trouble than is worth his while. You will soon find out if the compliments still flow as easily from his tongue; after you tell him you are bankrupt because your last boyfriend had walked off with all your money! To save face; he will be nice to you for a few more days and then disappear 'on business'. You won't hear from him again; because he will be off to look for some other 'stupid bitch' he can fleece. Although this might be humbling for your ego; it would have saved you a lot of future despair. Playing the pauper sounds easy; but it isn't. If your house is full of valuable antiques and paintings and you tell him you are broke; he will not believe you. You have to play the part as well, for at least a month; if he sticks around that long. A week is usually long enough for a con artist to know if he can get anything off you or not. If he suggests selling some of your paintings or other valuables to raise money; then tell him you dare not. You can explain that the bank knows exactly what is in the house, and you are about to lose everything; unless you can come up with some money. If he still tries to convince you he can sell them for you; refuse him without hesitation and ask him to leave, or you will call the police. Such a character is either a crook or has crooked connections; and either way, you are better off without him. If he offers to lend you the money, ask him for a big amount; like 50 000 dollars. If he is really serious; he will write you a cheque. Collect the money and pay it into your account. If the cheque does not bounce; then you know he is the real deal and not a broke con artist out to milk you. You can then return the money and tell him you don't need it after all. (I hope you will return the money! Or should I write another book: *'The Real Self-defence for men against unscrupulous women'?*)

We all have aims, ambitions and dreams in life and will do what we can to achieve them; even if it means upsetting a few people along the way. What women fail to realise is that for men, more so than women, that dream is paramount; and they will go to much greater lengths, in order to fulfil this ambition. You may just be a stepping stone to his lofty aspirations; and he will have no qualms about trampling all over you to get there. With the plunderer, love takes a back seat to ambition; and this can make him very ruthless, selfish, cruel and cunning. He needs to get to something or somewhere, as quickly as possible. You can buy the car for him and come along for the ride; or he will find someone else with a bigger, better, faster and more comfortable ride than yours. A woman is usually happy, loving and being loved in return; and even though some women are obviously ambitious, it is usually secondary to love. Even if a woman is successful, she still yearns to be loved and adored; and that is why many well-off women are so insecure, they easily fall for the plundering con man. Don't forget that there is also the evil type, who will rob you of your jewellery, cash and other valuables; and then vanish without a trace, after he has murdered you to cover his tracks! Sorry; but if you read the papers, you will find that these things do occur. This book is only trying to make sure it doesn't happen to you; by taking your self-defence seriously enough to acknowledge all possibilities. The world has changed to the point that many women are now making serious money, very quickly. There are some who have not yet learnt how to keep hold on to it, because they allow their hearts to control their heads; thereby enabling the plunderers to ply their trade. Please make sure you are not one of those unfortunate, gullible statistics!

7. Success through fame or wealth

Recent statistics have shown that the more successful a woman becomes; the more likely she is to divorce her husband. This is because the man tends to resent it when her wealth or fame outstrips his; whilst she is less likely to accept being the one to do the household tasks, which means, he slowly becomes the 'skivvy' in the relationship. Her success also means she does not have as much time to spend listening to his problems as she would have, had she been dependent on him for money. It does not matter who you are; because success through fame and money will always equate to power. She might find herself 'telling' him what to do; as opposed to 'asking'! Even if she uses the polite words *"please"* and *"thank you"*, they will still resonate like a no-option order; because at work where she is the boss, she does not tolerate anyone disobeying her. She brings this power home and unconsciously portrays her work status on her family life; which could easily lead to arguments and problems with her husband. Because of this power; she may become intolerant of any dissent shown by her husband and will easily have the confidence to leave him and consult a divorce lawyer. With money; she doesn't need to put up with anything she doesn't like...and that includes the man in her life! Successful women are becoming much more circumspect with their own money and have realised that if they are wealthier than their spouses, they will have to pay out alimony to them; in the event of divorce. This means it is more financially viable not to marry at all; and cheaper to have a baby with a partner, than walking up the aisle. All this economic independence is a welcome modern phenomenon; because for centuries, women have had to play second fiddle to the men in the lives and one has to wonder how they managed. Now that the shoe is on the other foot in many relationships; most men cannot handle the disempowerment and this has led to the rise of misogyny and the lack of empathy towards the female.

Nowadays; a woman does not need to be too rich, in order to decide to ditch her husband. Once she is making enough money to support herself; she may decide to go it alone and do without the hassle of having a man tagging along, telling her what to do and cramping her style. Financial security may be useful for a woman; but one should never envy the rich woman. This is because the richer she is; the harder it is for her to maintain friendships. Even her girl friends can be as devious as her male friends! Everyone wants a piece of her; and no one will even ring her up, without asking her for a favour. Any refusal of a request; would most likely end up in her being criticised and probably hated. It would be nice, if she were rich enough to make all her friends' wishes of come true; but most wealth is an illusion. Very few women are as rich as people believe! A pop star might sell millions of records; but could still be declared bankrupt. The public and her friends may see her as rich; but if she signed a bad contract or did not write any of her songs, she will most probably end up broke when the hits stop. She however, has to continue the charade that she has money; because she is always seen on television or gossiped about in the tabloids. A businesswoman may run a successful enterprise; but she may have silent partners or may be owing money to the bank. Although everyone thinks she is rich; she really isn't as comfortable as she would like to be. With both these examples; when a friend asks for a favour (usually money), she cannot say she is broke (who will believe her?). She therefore has to invent all kinds of elaborate excuses for refusing the loan; thereby gaining a reputation of being a bitch who does not remember her friends. In sympathy with the rich woman; she has been conditioned to believe everybody is out to con her. She will start listening to her entourage instead of her friends and family; whose love and respect she will slowly but surely begin to lose. In the end; estrangement is a foregone conclusion and a by-product of her success. There is always a price to pay for fame and fortune!

There is a tendency for women who are successful to look after 'number one'. This is understandable; because it is never easy for any woman to make it to the top of any profession. When she does get there; the relief and determination to stay there, completely overwhelms her and she may forget about everyone else. It takes a lot more hard work than it would for a man; because she has to defeat existing prejudices against the female, by men who will not think twice about putting deliberate obstacles in her way. More than likely, she will have to toe the male line until she is in a position to create her own independence; and even then, she might still be answerable to her bosses, who will most probably be male. She will then be accused of 'sleeping her way to the top' by jealous men, who have been overlooked in the promotion stakes. The male ego finds it hard to accept that she might actually be smarter than him; and deserves her promotion! Women in the workplace are deemed to be much more loyal and hardworking than their male counterparts; and many smart bosses are realising this. This has resulted in the recent explosion of upwardly-mobile females; who will stop at nothing to achieve success for themselves and their company.

It is a natural trait of the human being to be attracted to wealth and success. The problem is; these rich women start believing the hype and lose all their old friends. Very few celebrities are able to keep their feet on the ground in the beginning, because the rise to stardom is usually very quick; based on a high profile promotion, hit record or a major film. You will notice that the longer she has been a celebrity; the more likely she has 'grown up', accepted her situation and become a nicer person. In the beginning however; it is not easy. She will be called all kinds of names; 'impossible diva' being one of the nicer ones! The wealthier or more famous a woman is; the more suspicious of everyone else she becomes. Inevitably; she will have someone she has to trust, in order for her business or career to function properly. Having lost her family and friends; she starts taking advice from her business partner, manager, agent or lover, who will all contrive to make sure she has no real friends to confide in. They are all obviously riding on her gravy train and stand to lose if the gravy stops pouring; which means, the fewer people around the 'goldmine', the better. She turns more and more to her boyfriend, who will reassure her that he loves her (her money?); and will always tell her what she wants to hear. In such a scenario; the lover usually wins because the manager and agent are on a percentage of her earnings. It would be easy during the 'pillow talk'; to plant seeds into her head that they are 'ripping her off' and that she doesn't really need them! He promotes her feeling of paranoia to his advantage; and she then becomes indebted to him. The next step is for him to propose marriage to her; which she will usually accept, because she really does not have any close family and friends left. The problem with this is that he will know things about her, she may not want the world to find out; and she easily becomes a prisoner to his affections. There is not much she can do in this situation; because to get rid of him will cost her a lot of money, even with a pre-nuptial agreement. She suffers in silence; or may even turn to drugs and alcohol to dull the pain of loneliness.

If you are a wealthily successful or famous woman; there is not much I can tell you. You are unlikely to be mugged or robbed; because you will be cocooned from every day life in your mansion, limousine and high security office. You are probably already aware of so-called friends coming to rip you off; and have adequate precautions in place to protect yourself. However; even though you may have a good manager, a hard-working agent, an honest accountant and reputable lawyers working for you; it would serve you better, if you studied accounting and kept a hands-on approach to your earnings. If you did that; you will not have too many problems, because those working for you will be aware that you know what is going on and will not be able to cheat you. Remember; an accountant is only good, if he/she has no financial difficulties. Otherwise; he or she may start embezzling small unnoticeable amounts from your earnings, over-invoicing your receipts or 'accidentally' forgetting to pay in your taxes to the revenue office. When you are subpoenaed to appear in court for evading taxes, don't act too surprised; because no one will believe you did not know what was going on. The other problem with being wealthy; is the lack of real protection from your boyfriend or husband...especially if you met him soon after you became rich. He will expect to be the main beneficiary of your new-found status; and may not take kindly to any refusals to his requests for 'pocket' money or loans for his 'wonderful' business ideas. Many celebrities have ventured into businesses they had no expertise about, as a direct result of subtle coercion from their loved ones; mainly to keep the peace in the household. Needless to say, most of these ventures have ended in failure; simply because the celebrity did not have the time to devote to them and has been 'ripped off' by business partners. You will have to be cautious and treat him like a plunderer; until he can prove his love, loyalty and devotion to you. Of course, he makes love to you beautifully and adores you; because he is after all, singing your tune for his supper. If you are aware of this and he has signed a pre-nuptial agreement; then who am I to ruin your fun? The devil you know etc.; because if he does not help you spend your money, then someone else will! Despite all the problems success can bring; at least you can deal with them with a roof over your head, a car in the garage, a full stomach and not worry about how your medical bills or children's school fees are to be paid!

It does not matter how you achieve your success; but once you do, wouldn't it be nice to share the secrets of your ascendancy with other females? I'm sure there will be many who would like to emulate you and transfer your formula to their own endeavours! The world needs more rich and successful women because that is the only way men will be forced to sit up, take notice and respect the fairer sex. As things stand now; only the rich and famous women are given any kind of deference. The other females are seen only as far as their usefulness, beauty or sexual attraction to men goes. With more women able to make a difference; it will not take too long for all prejudices against the female to be finally eradicated. It is important for men to realise what every woman already knows; that the female is an integral part of this world and should no longer be ignored, or there will be severe consequences. If you are one of those lucky ladies who has achieved success in your field; please use your fame, wealth and influence to encourage, help and motivate the female race because it is obvious the men are either unwilling, or unable to. Good luck and well done! You are an inspiration to women all over the world.

8. Blackmail

Sooner or later, all wealthy women will have problems with their lovers/husbands, business partners, manager, agent or anyone else they are close to; and will therefore be susceptible to blackmail. Before she became famous or wealthy, she had a past; which nearly always comes back to haunt her when she makes money, gets a high-flying job or becomes famous. In her 'meteoric' rise to success; she would have left many friends behind. Some of them would have become jealous of her fortune and angry because they feel she now thinks she is better than them. She may start receiving phone calls from people she knew in the past; demanding money, or they would reveal 'all the dirt' from her past. This can be very traumatic for a woman who has a vested interest in what the public or her business partners think of her; because her new 'squeaky clean' image is most likely in direct contradiction to what the blackmailer is about to tell the whole world. Once someone knows too much about you and you don't treat him or her properly; the desire for revenge may become so strong that blackmail is a leading possibility. Ex-boyfriends of female celebrities are known to regularly run to the tabloids; to sell stories of how 'sluttish' she used to be. (The more sex and drugs involved, the better the chances of the betrayer collecting a huge sum of money).

Everybody is susceptible to blackmail, if they have something to hide; which would greatly alter their way of life, were it to be revealed. If you are two-timing your husband and someone found out and threatened to tell him, unless you paid a certain amount of cash; what do you do? What of the threat from organised crime? *"We know you are making money and we want some of it or else...We know where you live and where your children go to school!"* If you have done something criminal and someone threatens to tell the police, which would put you in prison for years; what then? All threats should be reported to the police. Anybody who really wants to kill you or break your legs, would do so; without a threat. The police can legally tap your phone, watch your house, or secretly follow you around and have the blackmailer apprehended; the next time he or she contacts you. Make sure your closest friends also know what you are going through; so that, if anything were to happen to you, they would be able to help the police and have the guilty party arrested. If you know who the blackmailer is; then you might think it would be okay to turn the tables on him or her, by getting a few friends or thugs from the underworld to warn him/her off you. I must counsel you that paying someone to 'get rid of' a blackmailer might seem like a good idea; but it is not legal. It will definitely put you into more trouble than it is worth. This is because the guy you paid to do a number on your blackmailer; could also blackmail you and force you to pay for his silence. You would then have to look for someone else to silence him; and whoever else he might have confided in. It is a vicious merry-go-round; which you can never win. So I'm afraid the police are your only bet! Blackmailers are high on their list of undesirables; so rest assured, they will do everything they can to catch him or her.

Never ever pay money to a blackmailer; because there is no guarantee that when the money has been spent, he or she will not demand more. Be strong! Record all your phone calls and make the blackmailer aware that the police know who he or she is. The chances are, the phone calls will stop; because the blackmailer is probably more frightened than you are! He/She will definitely make mistakes; which will enable the police to quickly apprehend him/her. If the threats continue from other sources like organised crime; you have to seek police protection. They will give you the best advice; because they are the only people who can legally help you. In all probability; they will know who the blackmailers are, by their modus-operandi and will arrest them. This will send a strong message to the underworld to leave you alone and you will not be bothered again. If the blackmail is for something that you did in the past, which you got away with but could put you in jail for a long time and ruin your life if it were revealed; then I'm afraid you have three unpalatable choices. Come clean with the cops; pay up; or **** the bastard! Depending on the crime; the third option will probably seem the most tempting! I must advise you that using one crime to solve another; is like digging a deeper hole for yourself. Nothing stays hidden for ever. One fine day, you will surely pay for your crimes; so think very hard, before going down that road!

Honesty and truthfulness can disarm any blackmailer. If for example, you have been unfaithful to your husband and you are being blackmailed; then you have to tell him immediately, in order to stop the blackmailers in their tracks. It could spell the end of your marriage; but, not telling him will entangle you in a web of deceit, lies and intimidation, which will be impossible to get out of. This will make it so much worse for you when he eventually finds out; as he surely will. Be super calm and explain why you did it; and don't be afraid to end the relationship, if he will not 'understand' and forgive you. You only have one life; and you have to live it the way you want to! He can climb aboard your ship and sail with you; or you will sail alone. Once you know who you are, refuse to deny your past and are not afraid to tell the world; then nobody can blackmail you, because you have nothing in your life you are ashamed of. This is what ultimately determines a tough lady, who will not be messed around with. You may think you are successful, in control and can deal with men at any game etc.; but can you handle the truth, especially when it hurts? If you are famous and have something lurid to hide about your past; why not tell the tabloids first and make the money yourself, instead of letting some toe-rag mess you around? By giving the fee to charity, it will send the message out that you were not motivated by financial gain and you are no longer the person you used to be; meaning, you have well and truly 'changed'. It may make the news for a few weeks and then it would be forgotten. With new stories making the rounds every day; no paper will be interested in your past for long.

9. Infidelity

(a) Only a fling!

There comes a point in any relationship, when one or both partners feel like the love they shared has grown stale; and maybe, an affair would spice things up. As a woman; you will every day come across handsome 'fuckable' men, from all walks of life. While most women have their own way of resisting the charms of these men; sometimes the lure proves too irresistible and you may decide that you 'must have him'. You know you are married and you know it is wrong; but there is something about sexual attraction that no amount of integrity, willpower or loss of reputation can prevent the lure to 'fuck the living daylights' out of a man you fancy the pants off. Usually, the woman will sleep with the man and she will either; decide he was not as good in bed as she had dreamt; realise it is wrong because she is already in a relationship; or, with her lust fulfilled; she will no longer be attracted to him and will end it, as quickly as it had started. She returns home to her partner and usually, that is the end of the matter; except she forgets that it might happen again, with another lover. Sooner or later; the cat will be let out of the bag because she will become careless.

If you are unfaithful once or twice, decide it is not for you and stop it in its tracks before it becomes an affair; then it may be wise to behave like most men and say nothing. Telling your partner, whom you have obviously decided you still love; would just cause unnecessary trouble and anxiety for him. He may forgive you, if it is just a 'weakness of the flesh' moment; but that could be because he is no saint in the straying department either, and is forgiving you just to assuage his own conscience. Why take the chance and ruin everything you have? If you were smart enough to use a good contraceptive and check that you have not caught a sexually transmitted disease; your man need never be any the wiser. Just make sure the stud you had the fling with, is okay with your putting a halt to the liaison. If he falls in love with you, he may cause problems for you; whilst your husband will definitely suspect something is not quite right with you. Few men will accept a woman ending a liaison after just one 'shag'. This is because it is a blow to his ego; and he will believe his sexual techniques were not good enough for her. He would therefore try again to sleep with you; if only to make sure he comes out on top, with an 'improved performance'. If you refuse; he may threaten to tell your hubby. Were that to be the case, you will have to come clean with your man; otherwise you will be susceptible to blackmail, and all the dire consequences that go with it. A fling is always a risk. Please be careful!

(b) Affairs

If you are one of those women, who take things further and decide to have an affair; you have to realise that it is a guilty secret, which will one day be found out. It would most certainly spell the end of your relationship; so it would be better for you to be honest and state boldly, *"Darling, I'm having an affair!"* It is an extreme admission, but it is the truth. If you lie about it, trying to appease and accommodate his feelings; you will both suffer because the guilt will overtake you and he will know by your body language that things are not what they should be. Once you are honest and truthful; he will get the message that this is who you are and nothing is going to change, unless he does. If he cannot be more loving and pay you more attention; then obviously, there are others who will. Telling him you will never do it again will not wash; because the lingering doubt will always be there. Never apologise for fucking outside your marriage. How can you be sorry for infidelity? The sex with your lover was great wasn't it? Or are you now sorry because your extra-marital lover dumped you; and you've suddenly remembered you have a husband? No; you did it because you wanted to, and nobody forced you. Even though you may later on regret what you did; apologising does not mean it will not happen again…and again. Would you buy an apology from your husband, if he 'screwed some tart'? No? So don't expect him to buy it either. Be tough! Give your reasons in a clear controlled manner and say you are only prepared to stop…if he changes. He might get angry, start shouting and call you all kinds of names; but if he dares hit you for being so brazen, then you will have to walk out on him. This is because he is hitting you for being honest, and may do so again; since the thought of you in bed with someone else, will never leave his conscious mind. If you change your character on his account; it will always come back to haunt you because you are being forced to go against your soul. The root cause of your infidelity has to be sorted out, before anything can be achieved; so you should never ever compromise for anything less than whom you are. Every man should take note of the fact that the decision to stray from her marriage; is never taken lightly by a woman. It only occurs when something is not right in the relationship and her soul is really hurting.

A man however, can be unfaithful; even when there is absolutely nothing wrong with his woman and he still loves her. He may just be bored and looking for a bit of excitement and adventure; and decides to go in for a one-night stand. He will never tell her, and nine times out of ten, she will never find out; unless it becomes an affair. If you feel there is a lull in your relationship; you have to do something to spice it up. Don't ever be afraid to challenge him at the first sign that something is wrong; and do your utmost to correct it. If you find out he has slept with someone and you feel your integrity is more important than his faithfulness; then be prepared to leave him, even if it means losing your financial security. It really is up to you how to handle a philandering partner. It all depends on how well he treats you; and whether he is discreet and does not flaunt his extramarital affairs in your face. If he guilt treats you like a queen, and proves to you in many other ways that he loves you; then his indiscretions will be easier to forgive (never forget) and you can extract more out of him. It is a question I cannot answer; since I do not know how your relationship functions. The true test will be your feelings. If you cannot bear to touch him after he has been unfaithful, and your soul is hurting; then nothing can change that and you should apply for a separation or a divorce. Never stay with a man just to please him, or for the sake of the children; because you will all be unhappy. Which would you prefer? A possessive man; who gets angry, shouts and hits you for daring to smile at any other man except for him...but does not cheat. Or a philandering husband with a heart of gold; who would not dream of physically hurting you or the children? Sometimes you have to make do with what you have, and mould him to suit your needs; because it is almost impossible to find the 'perfect man'.

(c) Experimentation

Some couples like to experiment with sex toys, porn movies and even 'threesomes' or group orgies; to try and spice up their relationship. Unfortunately, these methods rarely work; because the body and mind can quickly become desensitised. If you are losing your natural attraction to each other; a vibrator, a dildo or sexy lingerie will only work temporarily and paper over the cracks in your relationship. You will soon find yourselves going to greater lengths to better the last performance; culminating in videoing yourselves in the sex act or joining a swingers group. Wife-swapping, 'threesomes', orgies etc. all look exciting in the porn movies; but one fact is conveniently forgotten. What if you are more attracted to a third party than to your own partner? Or more to the point; how would you feel if your man decides the wife-swap woman is so much better than you, that you have never seen him so excited? How come he never has such a big long-lasting erection, when he makes love to you? Believe me; it will hit your self-esteem so hard, you may never recover and you may lose your attraction for him. Anytime he tries to make love to you; visions of him screwing that woman will fill your head and will be a certain passion killer.

Stories of wife-swapping going wrong because one of the partners falls in love and starts seeing the other person behind the partner's back; are so ubiquitous, it is definitely a disaster waiting to happen. With orgies, the sceptre of a sexually transmitted disease might rear its ugly head; and to make it worse, you will not know who gave it to you. This is because those present will definitely deny it; if you asked them a few days later. Even though orgies are omnipresent; very few people would like to admit that they are involved in them. Before they start; everybody will claim they are 'clean'. *"I only went for a check-up last week and I have a clean bill of health!"* Unfortunately; a week is a long time in the swinger paradise. Anything could have happened between his check-up and sleeping with you! If your relationship is good; why would you want to join a swingers group? The only way it will work is; if your relationship with your partner has reached the point of no return, whereby you interact better as friends than lovers and there is no feeling of jealousy on either side. In which case; why are you still together?

10. Female Fun

(a) Toy boys

Some financially secure women go in for toy boys; which are lovers who are much younger than they are. So far as the law is not broken; it's a case of 'whatever turns you on!' There are obvious problems, if the age difference is too big; but on the whole, love is what really matters. If he does not abuse you physically or emotionally and does not take advantage of you; then, who am I to say what is right or wrong? Obviously, if you are thirty-five and are sleeping with a seventeen year old boy still in college; you will incur the wrath of his parents and could be shunned by your community for 'cradle-snatching'. You could also be damaging the boy emotionally. No orgasm is worth a visit by the police! However; older men have been going out with much younger women for so long that it has now become an accepted practice and no one bats an eyelid. He may even be praised by other men; *"the lucky bastard. He must be rich!"* Nobody blames the girl for deliberately using the 'old fool'; who can probably only 'get it up' for a few minutes at a time. In the ratio of time spent sleeping with the wrinkly old prune and the money she can make out of him; she has a very good deal indeed! Modern prejudices mean that if a woman is with a younger man; she will be under enormous scrutiny, (usually by other women) for signs of disharmony. *"Are they really in love or is he using her?"* He on the other hand, might feel embarrassed because he has no excuses for being with her; except for her money. Because of his relative youth, vis-à-vis hers; he will be under tremendous pressure from friends and relatives to justify his position. *"You've been with her for some time now; and what have you gained from her? She must be loaded; so use your head and get something off her, before she throws you out with the garbage!"* He will either have to show he is in love, by publicly displaying his affection for her (which would be difficult, if he does not really love her); or he has to show some trappings of financial gain, in order to keep the rumour-mongers quiet.

There are two types of toy boys; those who are financially okay and can look after themselves, and those who have very little money and are dependent on the female for almost all expenses. With the first example; there are usually very few problems because they are usually in love. Nowadays; there are quite a few young men who prefer the wealth of experience and sexual maturity of the older woman! It's an amazing modern phenomenon that there are so many intelligent, beautiful, youthful and energetic women in their forties, fifties and even sixties-plus. Some of them are so much in demand; they have to keep the younger men at bay! If you fall in love with a younger person, and he is also genuinely in love with you; then all I can say is: *"Congratulations! You've certainly got what it takes!"* However, as revealed in the section on the 'plunderers'; you have to try and find out his financial status, before allowing yourself to fall head-over-heels in love. This is because the love he 'shows' for you and the financial security he claims to have; could all be a very good pretence and he may turn out to be a very clever conman, out to fleece you. Even though he may have been turned on by your sexual expertise in the beginning; he could be like any other student and would want to move on, once he feels there is nothing more to learn or gain from you. The richer you are, the longer he will be prepared to play the pretence game; until he can extract a hefty amount out of you. He can do this; either by blatantly asking for it, or simply stealing it. He will feel it is his 'due' for having to make love to you; when he could be with someone younger! It is at this point that your self-esteem could take a severe knock. This is because you probably believed he 'loved you for being you'; and suddenly, you discover that he was only after your money.

A toy boy is younger than you; which means his youthful exuberance may push you into re-discovering your own youth. You may start doing things with him that may seem exciting and fun, but could easily lead you into taking advice from him and venturing into unknown territory; simply because you are in love. *"I've got this brilliant business idea…!"* You may therefore have to use your greater experience in life to rein him in; and refuse most of his 'brilliant' suggestions. By telling him that you are not really interested in doing business, buying him a car or loaning him money; you will be able to see if he still sticks around. If his interest in you drops, then be thankful; because you would have sussed him out before he could do any real damage to your bank balance. Even if he continues seeing you, be on your guard; because the refusal could prompt him into planning other more devious methods to rip you off. To save yourself any headaches; I advise you to assume all toy boys are either after your cash or your connections and unless he can prove otherwise, you will have to defend yourself in every way possible. Your own self-worth depends on his proving he deserves your love, kindness and largess; otherwise you would be doing yourself a great disservice. This is because his own youth and ego will make him believe, he is the one doing you a favour by being with you. Although you may not be the suspicious type, and like to put your trust in people until they let you down; I feel you should reverse the process because after a certain age, it would be very difficult for a woman to recover from financial deceit. Imagine losing your life savings or money you have worked so hard for; to some young man who tricked you into believing he loved you. You can almost hear the gossiping in town; *"Serves her right! What was she thinking; screwing a man half her age?"* Not very funny is it?

The second example of a toy boy; is where she is a 'sugar mummy' and literally gives him pocket-money and looks after him. Different problems will arise in this situation. He will see her as a convenient meal ticket and will do all he can to keep hold of her; by faithfully sleeping his way into her heart! She may become hooked on his youth and sexual prowess; and may be emotionally blackmailed by him, to the point that he will only perform well after she has bought him an expensive present. Because he is not really in love and is doing it for the money; there will be pressure on him to 'sing for his supper', by always being at her beck and call. Since he is not pretending to be wealthy in order to win her affection; he will try and extract as much as possible out of her in the financial department. It could be to such an extent that unless she is very rich; she will not be able to keep him for too long. The beautiful clothes she buys him, the exotic trips abroad and the expensive restaurants they eat in; are usually for her benefit. It is important for him to always look good; because it allows her to go out with him on her arm, with beaming pride. It will not take long for him to figure that he is the one being used; and that is when he will start asking her for money. They will usually be little amounts at first; graduating to much bigger requests, immediately after making love to her. That is when she may be at her most satisfied; and therefore, most vulnerable and amenable to his calculated demands! If she refuses;

she will find him becoming more and more emotionally distant. He may even start claiming he is 'busy'; whenever she needs some loving! In the end; she will find herself making him financial promises, just to see him. Once he realises this; then she is in trouble because the relationship will turn to blackmail. At this point; she has to make sure she is ruthless and does not allow her emotions to interfere with her decision to get rid of him.

If you go into a toy boy liaison with your eyes open; then there should not be any problem. I assume there will be no emotional attachment on your part; and you will be able to extricate yourself from him, when you get bored. Although easier said than done; some women are able to play the toy boy at his own game. They do this by using him as a sex toy and buying him a few things to keep him quiet; and then getting rid of him when he starts being 'difficult', by professing his love or asking for unrealistic favours or money. Once you know what you are doing; then the next step is to keep a clean bill of health. You have to make sure he uses a prophylactic and take extra precautions; so that you cannot accidentally get pregnant. Nevertheless; you should still get yourself regularly checked out for any sexually transmitted diseases he may have given you. You have to understand that because of his age and lack of finance; there is really not much of a future in this type of toy boy romance. You are both in it for what you can get out of it; which in your case would be some sexual fun and games in the autumn of your life. For him however; you are only a meal ticket and he will probably be seeing other women, apart from you. He may even be in a relationship, possibly with the consent of his girlfriend; since any money he makes from you, will be shared with her. If he contracts any infections from his other girls; he will carry it back to you. I don't think any woman deserves to be infected through no fault of hers! As a mature woman; contracting a venereal disease may prove more complicated than you realise, because your body may not be as strong as you would like to believe! Having a toy boy seems like fun; but when things go wrong, all the blame will be heaped on you and leave you with a lot of egg on your face. As the older one in the relationship; people will always say you should know better than to entangle yourself in such risky liaisons. Please be careful; because an orgasm lasts a few minutes at most...but a ruined reputation is for ever!

(b) Sugar Daddies

The sugar daddy is different from the toy boy; in that, the younger woman is the one being looked after by the older man. Because the man is usually much older than the woman; it will seem to her like heavenly bliss at first because he can give her the financial security and emotional support, lacking in boys of her own age. However; many men who go in for much younger girls are control freaks and like to have their own way. That is probably one of the reasons they find it hard to deal with the mature woman! A beautiful young girl on the arm of a wrinkled old man; is the ultimate in male chauvinism. He uses his financial muscle to make the girl do his bidding; which could include all kinds of 'exotic' sexual practices, his wife or any mature woman would not go in for. He is the envy of all his friends and business associates; and behaves like the king of the castle. Indeed he is! What about the girl? There are only so many dresses and gifts he can buy for her; before she gets bored with them and starts looking elsewhere for her own thrills. A classy restaurant is no substitute for the fun of an all-night rave with the boys and girls she grew up with. What might seem like good sex at first; turns into a chore when she realises what she is missing by not being with people of her own age. He will try to keep her away from her friends; simply because they pose a threat to him. He will obviously not fit into her crowd and will not be oblivious to the smirks and jokes cracked at his expense, by younger people. Increasingly, he will become so paranoid that jealousy will rear its ugly head; and he will become more controlling and impossible to live with. This is because he is afraid she might fall for someone her own age; and will not be sufficiently confident of his pulling powers, to know whether he can get another young girl to stay with him and do his bidding, the way she can. Wealth can be so intoxicating, that he might still be able keep her with what amounts to bribery; but it will be so obvious to everybody that she is using him that he will age dramatically! When it gets to that stage; she may not care about him and may eventually leave him, in order to find herself someone else…most probably richer!

Being the mistress to a sugar daddy is no bed of roses. He most probably has wife/children at home, whom he still loves; and will therefore be unwilling to leave them for you. He will buy you exquisite gifts, put you up in an expensive apartment and even buy you a flash car. He will give you everything, except what you really want; which is his genuine love and affection. Unfortunately, he could also dump you when he gets bored with you or if you become too possessive; as you surely will, the longer you stay with him. When he does get rid of you; don't be surprised to find out that the apartment and the car he 'bought' for you will be repossessed because they are most probably still in his name. From all this; you have to deduce that a sugar daddy is like other men...only more dangerous. Because of his money and connections; he could treat you very badly and get away with it! If you are that way inclined; just remember that most sugar daddies are not stupid, but rather very ruthless. He will be aware you are only in it for the money; so he will give it to you, so long as you toe his line. He must have worked hard for his money and probably trod on more than a few toes to get to where he is now. Although he may be generous and kind to you; never ever make the mistake that you can outwit him. If you make him angry; his revenge might be more than you can handle...with violence not being ruled out! There is no yardstick to gauge him; so all the precautions you would normally take with men must also apply to him...only more so. He could be nice; he could be cruel; he could rape you; he could be the greatest lover you've ever had; he could beat you up; and he could be the best thing that could have happened to you, in terms of setting you up in business or introducing you to the right people in your line of expertise. You may get the easy one you can manipulate with your sex; or the ruthless one who will take no shit from you. Keep your wits about you and just accept him as a bit of fun; where you can make some money and move on. To think it is any more than that; will leave you open to emotional heartache.

As a young woman; I'm sure you know what you want from life. If using a rich fool to get to where you want to go, is what it takes; then go ahead. Be aware that the chances are, no good will come out of it; and therefore, it has to be a means to an end...and nothing more. After having his wicked way with you for a certain amount of time, and has refused to commit his love to you; it is only fair that you gain something from your time with him. You should therefore be upfront and ask him to help you make money;

as opposed to asking him for money, which he may be reluctant to give you much of. If you have a good business idea; you will be more likely to get a legalised loan out of him because he knows he will make a profit out of it. Rich men can be quite stingy with their cash. If he refuses for example, to put the apartment or the car in your name; then you have to be aware that he is no fool. He will make sure you don't con him; so don't try. Play it dumb and enjoy the attention and the gifts; but make sure you save any money/valuables you get from him and hide it away for a rainy day. You have to assume that he will one day dump you; because you are probably, nothing more than an acquisition. In business terms; this means you are expendable, when you have outlived your usefulness! Apart from money; older rich men also have good contacts in other wealthy entrepreneurs and famous people. If you are smart; you can use him as a stepping stone to further your career. By mixing with the 'right crowd' who are the movers and shakers in your country; you can build up an enviable portfolio of contacts, which would not have been possible without your sugar daddy! Sooner or later, you will meet the man of your dreams; who is handsome, younger and most importantly, rich enough to look after you in the style you desire.

Although I have generalised; there are obviously exceptions to the rule. I am sure there are lots of couples who have found happiness with a big age difference. But you must understand that these are rare and special people; who had to work very hard, in order to fight against existing prejudices and still succeeded against the odds. In the world of self-defence; you go with and not against the odds! If something can go wrong; it generally will one day. Better to be safe than sorry!

(c) Gigolos

A gigolo is basically a male prostitute, normally hired through an escort agency. He has become more popular amongst the rich businesswomen; who don't want the hassle of a relationship or an affair with a man. She pays a man to take her out, escort her to events and sometimes make love to her; for a pre-arranged fee. A percentage of the fee (around 40%) goes to the agency and he gets to keep the rest; and anything else he can extract from her. This means that if she takes him out; all the expenses like dinner, drinks, taxi fares and gate fees will be on her head. If she is happy with his performance, she will normally arrange for him to come again (excuse the pun!); because most women prefer to keep the same partner. For a sexual release; hiring a gigolo is okay because there are no emotional ties. Most of them know their way around a woman's body; and are willing to follow her instructions, in order for her to achieve a decent orgasm. They may charge more for 'extras' like cunnilingus, anal sex or unusual sexual positions that may turn her on; but will most likely refuse any requests for masochistic violence like whipping, bondage and artistic rape (acting out a rape scene with the man).

The only thing to watch out for when hiring a gigolo; is your security. It is therefore better to hire your stud from a reputable escort agency; which is able to vet its employees. Don't tell the agency your real name and always take him to a discreet out of town hotel for your sexual liaison. This way; he does not know where you live and does not get the chance to see what is inside your house. One day he may stop working for the agency; but may still remember your address. If he falls on hard times; he might come calling! He may blackmail you, if he knows your real name; or could even arrange your house to be robbed, if you will not play ball with him. Even though he will claim to be 'clean'; it is better not to take any chances. Make sure you use a contraceptive and he uses a fortified condom! If you catch an infection, it can get very nasty; with the agency denying their employee could possibly have given you a sexually transmitted disease. This means you must have caught it off someone else! You may then be counter-accused of infecting him; and possibly sued. Needless-to-say; your reputation will be bandied around town and sullied. The secrecy you were trying to achieve by going for a gigolo will be destroyed. Please be careful!

11. Pressure persuasion

Statistics have shown that many women who go into crime; do so as a direct result of persuasion by their partners. It does not necessarily mean that women are not capable of committing crimes of their own accord; because they are every bit as capable as men in that department. However; you will find that there are hardly any crimes committed by women, which have not been done first by men who were in the position to teach her what to do. The point I am making is that, it is very easy to do something for your man; if you are in love! For that reason; many callous men have no qualms about using their women to break the law for them. They will use pressure, in order to convince the women to do their bidding; by giving her no room to refuse. They can do this through threats, emotional blackmail or sexual bribery; which is easy, if he knows what really turns her on. *"When you get back from the job, I'll have a nice surprise for you. Good luck; I love you!"* Credit card fraud, drug couriering, shoplifting and prostitution are the main crimes committed by women. In each case; you will find there is a man lurking in the background pulling the strings...too cowardly to do the job himself. Women strung out on drugs, often commit crimes in order to fund their habit; but who first introduced them to drugs? Their lovers! What about the desperate women going into prostitution; simply because they have been left to fend for themselves and look after their children by the absent father? One could argue that, had the man done the decent thing and looked after his woman and children; would she have decided to sell her body? The rise in female suicide-bombers shows that there is no limit to what a man can get a woman to do; out of duty, loyalty or love. Yes; men have a lot to answer for, in the descent of females into the quagmire of deceit, crime and even terrorism.

'Keeping up with the Joneses' is another way a man can get you to do things for him, including breaking the law; by using pressure persuasion tactics. Your upwardly mobile neighbours have just bought a new car or seem to 'have it all'; so your man tries to make you jealous, by harping on about how beautiful the 'woman next door' looks in her new dress or fantastic hairstyle. You will soon find yourself trying to look as 'good' as your neighbour; by dressing better or spending more at the hairdressers. If you are well-off; then there will be no problem because you will be able to afford to keep up with your neighbours. What if you don't have enough money and he keeps going on about *"How I wish we could afford to live like them etc.?"* It will be only a matter of time, before he comes up with an idea or illegal plan to make some money. He obviously wants you to play a part in whatever he has organised; otherwise he would not have told you and would have done it himself. Many criminally-minded men have the misguided belief that a woman can get away with a crime, much easier than a man; and even if she is caught, the punishment will not be so severe. They then use this 'illogical logic' to convince their better-halves to go along with the scheme; in the name of love. They usually forget that using his lady or anybody else to commit a crime for him; makes him the mastermind and he will receive a much harsher sentence! The police have 'wonderful ways' of making a suspect reveal the ring-leaders; and there is no guarantee the woman will keep her mouth shut, if she is caught. Any man, who is prepared to put you on the firing line, while he stays safe in the background; is of the lowest of the low and you would be better-off without him. If you are in financial difficulties; his idea for you to commit a crime to earn some money, may become very appealing. I will warn you that if you go along with him; you will have to shoulder some of the blame and you will not escape punishment, if you are caught!

This 'pressure persuasion' is not confined to couples in the poorer sections of society. Ambitious businessmen have been known to convince their wives to 'be nice' to an influential client, in order to clinch a deal; as explained in Chapter 5. Although in this case, no crime has been committed; it is morally worse because if he is ready to pimp his wife, then he will be able to make her do anything. Some men will bring in the boys to eat, drink, gamble, watch pornographic films which are demeaning to women and make a total mess of the living room; whilst she is forced to sit through the raucous behaviour, without saying a word. She will then have to clean it up when they have gone; all because he has convinced her that such behaviour is okay. He may even tell his pals, *"Don't worry about the mess; my wife is cool. She doesn't mind!"* Although you may say she doesn't have to do what he tells her to do; I can bet that there is no woman alive who has never done something just to please her partner, simply because she loves him so much she will do anything for him. The most common thing women do for their men is lie for them; even though they know it is wrong. *"Oh, my husband is not in, he just went out"*; in order to get rid of an unwelcome visitor or phone call. Instead of demanding from the husband why he doesn't want to see the visitor, she just lets it slide or buys his lies; even though he could be owing money and indirectly putting the whole family at risk of repercussions. Despite all the lies she is telling for him; he will still have the nerve to make demands of her. For example, he says: *"I don't want you seeing that friend of yours again"*; so she breaks off contact with her friend because she knows it will annoy her man, if she doesn't. *"You are putting on weight, you need to go on a diet!"*; and she immediately joins a gym and starves herself because she knows she will appear more attractive to him. This urge by a woman to seek the approval of the man she loves; has made women do unspeakable things which were they to look back at, would make them cringe in horror, embarrassment or shame. *"Did I really buy that expensive dress just to impress him...?"* What about that 'sordid' sexual practice he once convinced you to try; when you were either too much in love or too drunk to know or care what you were doing? *"If you really loved me; you'd do it for me...!"* I need not go on because I believe you understand what I'm getting at!

Somewhere along the line in a relationship; there is always a 'transfer of power'. This is when the woman unconsciously allows her man to dictate to her what she should or should not do. It can work both ways; but for the purposes of this book, we will assume it could happen to you, so that you are aware of it and be on your guard. In the beginning of a relationship; you might be so much in love that you may not see it coming, until it is too late. It may start off innocuously enough; with him convincing you to change your mind about something. *"That coat doesn't look good on you. Why don't you wear the blue one?"* You then find yourself doing as he asks; in order to win his approval. Before you know it; he is telling you what to do with different aspects of your day. *"How come you were late back from work today?"* Once the power has been transferred; it will be very difficult to get it back. *"I told you we were going out this evening; why aren't you ready?"* Once he is used to your taking his 'advice'; he will in effect, be running your life. If you then try to challenge his decisions; it will lead to arguments and cause a real threat to the stability of your relationship. It is at this point that many women make the mistake of 'giving in' and basically doing as they are told; in order not to rock the boat and have some peace in the household. You might even find yourself tip-toeing around him when it comes to things you feel will annoy him. Like a child; you might hide just to eat your favourite chocolates because he has told you they are fattening.

Talking to your friend on the phone; you quickly tell her you will call her back and hang up, as soon as you hear him coming because you have to get his dinner ready!

All men believe they should look after the women in their lives; so there will be times he will try to take over the running of the relationship. There are certain things a woman will voluntarily hand over power to her man; simply because she assumes he knows more about it than she does. If the car breaks down; a thief breaks into the house; something heavy needs to be lifted; or some piece of machinery needs to fixed; the woman might even be relieved not to have to take care of it. The problem arises when the line is crossed and he starts 'interfering' into your individuality. *"Why are you wearing so much make-up?" "Why do you watch all that rubbish on the telly? "Why do you spend such a long time in the bathroom?"* The minute you change any aspect of your comfortable behaviour simply because he told you or does not like it; the transfer of power is complete and you are doomed. From then on, the pressure persuasion becomes so much easier; because it is operating from a platform of acquiescence, already achieved from the minute he first told you to do something and you did it, without question. However; I must stress that it will not be easy to win your independence. You may have to sometimes refuse to do something, even though it might seem like an every-day request; simply because he told you to do it and did not ask you nicely. *"Make me a cup of tea, will you?"* should be replied with, *"Sorry, I'm busy; why can't you do it?" "Why are you wearing those high-heels? I told you I hate them."* should be quickly riposted with, *"Tough. I like them! I don't go around telling you how you should dress, do I?"* This type of 'stubborn' attitude portrayed early on in the relationship; will put the brakes on any attempt to take over your life and will go a long way in preventing pressure persuasion. The quicker you let him know 'who you are' the better!

You have to realise that you are first and foremost, a unique individual. It is important that you keep your identity separate from his; in order to create a balance in the relationship. The fact that you love your man does not make him your owner and definitely does not mean he can tell you what to do. Obviously in a relationship, there has to be a certain amount of give and take; but when you know something is wrong or against the law, why do it just to please him? Many women are easily coerced or manipulated into changing their minds and going against their better judgement; by their men. There are also some tough women; who are real battle-axes and will never do what they don't want to do. This proves that it is possible to refuse a request from the one you love. You therefore have to learn how to say *"No!"* with a straight face; so that he realises the topic is closed and not up for discussion. He will be upset the first time it happens; but eventually, he will realise that when you don't want to do something you won't…and there is nothing he can do about it! He may sulk, use the silent treatment and in extreme cases, may beat you up; but the answer should still be a resounding *"No!"* If he does resort to hitting you; then you have to walk out on him and only return with severe conditions. These will have to include threatening to tell the police and all his friends what he has done to you and why; unless he issues a grovelling apology. He has to understand that you have certain principles, which you refuse to breach; and if he wants a war, you will give him one! At this stage, most men will realise they have been beaten; and a new respect for you will be born.

I cannot tell you how to live your life or conduct your relationships. I only want you to be aware that *all* men will use a woman for their own ends, if they are allowed to get away with it; and they will use all kinds of subtle and devious ways to achieve it. Whereas, if you stand firm and don't keep changing your mind; he will realise you are a woman of principle and he will not be able to take advantage of you. He will therefore be forced to treat you as an equal partner; which is the way all relationships are supposed to be. Stay strong!

12. Betrayal

We all need friends and few can live without one. Like Julius Caesar, Samson and Jesus Christ before us; betrayal is as old as the bible and history has proved that those closest to us are most likely to do us the most damage. This means, it is not only men you should be defending yourself against; but women as well. I have refrained from denigrating the female in this book, because of the title; but some of your own sex can be as bad, if not worse than, the men. Sleeping with your man behind your back is probably the most common form of female betrayal. Who do you blame? He should not have done it; but it is very difficult for any man to resist an attractive woman, who is determined to sleep with him. To make it worse; if your friend is sleeping with your boyfriend or husband, you will probably be the last to know! The actual sex act comes a poor second to the feeling of betrayal and disgust you will feel when someone you considered your best friend, shared secrets together and promised to keep off each other's lovers; has broken the sacred vow and done the unthinkable. Once it happens; you have to decide whether you can live with it or not. It will be hard to sleep in the same bed with your man; after he has slept with your best friend. That feeling of disgust will erode your mind and you can go crazy; so it would be advisable not to put yourself through such an awful torment. You will have to think seriously about ending your marriage/relationship; because there is no guarantee they will not repeat the betrayal. This book is here to help you defend yourself; which is impossible after the event!

What makes someone who purports to be your friend; end up being a wolf in sheep's clothing and betray you? The reasons are many and the answers very indecisive. Every man is different; and each relationship has its peculiarities, ups and downs. To blame your friend or your man for the betrayal; may be missing the point. You therefore have to look inwards at yourself and accept that it could be your fault; because that is the only way you can learn from it and make sure it does not happen again. Information spread loosely is what a friend can use to get 'one over' on you; so you have to be very careful what you tell your friends. Could it be you bragged about what your boyfriend could do in bed; to such an extent, that your friend wanted to try him out? There must have been a few signs between them; like a glance, smile, look or touch, which you failed to notice because you trusted them implicitly. This just goes to show that you cannot leave a man and a woman together in the same room, for any length of time. There is bound to be a bit of chemistry; which could be the initial spark that eventually leads to them betraying your love and trust. Maybe he is just a randy rodent, who cannot keep his prick inside his trousers; in which case, you either have to raise your own sexual appetite to match his own, or convince him to go to a sex addiction clinic for help. Failing that; you should end the relationship because if you really don't enjoy sex as much as he does, you are always going to have problems with his cheating. You won't be able to comfortably sleep with him; because you will be wondering who he has been fucking, or what diseases he may be carrying. He will use your coldness as an excuse to go on cheating; by indirectly blaming you. He may even sleep with more of your friends; some of whom may be delighted to go one up on you. It is also possible you starved him sexually and treated him like a child, who had to beg you just for a bit of loving; whilst your friend was happily willing and able to give him what you could not, or refused to. Marathon sex? Sado-masochism? Fellatio? Bondage? Anal sex…?

All stable relationships are based on trust; but it would do you good to keep your eyes open for little signs, that can alert you to the possibilities and prevent things getting out of hand. For instance, if you feel there is unacceptable flirting between your man and your friend; you should talk to them separately and let them know you have noticed what they are doing. You might be accused of being paranoid, amidst their denials; but that is usually a sign that there is something going on. You should refuse to touch him until you are convinced in your own mind there is nothing between them; because sooner or later, they will slip up and make an irrefutable blunder. By refusing to sleep with him; you will be able to tell by his reaction whether he is getting his jollies elsewhere. If he is nonchalant, when before, he couldn't go more than two days without badgering you for sex; then it is obvious he is not horny. This is a sure sign that he is sleeping around; possibly with your friend. You will probably notice that she does not come around to see you as often as before you confronted her. You cannot keep a twenty-four hour guard on your man or your friend; and when someone wants to do something, you cannot stop him or her. Your soul cannot lie; and something inside you, will always alert you to the obvious fact. You just have to be philosophical and accept that they are sleeping together. If he repulses you so much, you cannot bear for him to touch you; then the only option is to dump the lecherous bastard and cut off all communication with your 'friend'. They are welcome to each other!

Stealing from your purse when you are not looking; telling lies about you; going behind your back to spread gossip and innuendo;

revealing a secret she had sworn never to tell anyone; and other less than delightful things a friend can do to you; can make it really difficult for anybody in life. With friends like these; you really don't need enemies! Try this for a test. Are you prepared to die or go to prison for a friend? Of course not! So what makes you think your friend has to keep away from your boyfriend; or will not reveal a secret you told her in confidence? A person will only do something; if it suits him or her. Once you realise this; you are well on your way to defending yourself against the hardest attack of them all...betrayal by your 'best friend'. There is no need for paranoia. Once you accept that a human being is fallible and everything is possible; then you will not feel so hurt when it does happen. Real secrets should be kept close to your chest. If you tell your 'best friend'; there is no certainty she considers you as her 'best friend' and may tell someone else. Before you realise it; everybody knows your secret, without your knowledge! If for example, you have embezzled your company of thousands of dollars; then you are asking for trouble if you tell anyone, unless you share the money equally with that person, who will have to be as crooked as you. Besides; you never know when he/she will have a pang of conscience and report you to the manager or the police.

It is better to do business with someone you hate; because the lines are firmly drawn in the sand. Each person knows where he or she stands; and they will not dare try anything, in case of retaliation. With a friend; everything is based on faith. We all do things because we want to; so unless a gun is put to your head, you cannot say you were forced to do anything. A person is your friend because he or she wants to be; but they all have their reasons. The only way not to be hurt by a friend; is to be honest, tell the truth and never expect anything from him/her. The truth will ensure gossip and innuendo does no harm; because once you can accept who or what you are, nothing anyone says will have any effect on you. Anything that will cause you discomfort or anguish should not be discussed with anyone. Health problems should only be between you and your doctor, who is under the Hippocratic Oath; and is therefore not permitted to reveal your health secrets. Believing that all men are potential betrayers; will make sure you are never surprised when your boyfriend is unfaithful. Expecting him to believe in the same ethics of fidelity and honesty as you;

may be a step too far for most men. It does not mean all men will be unfaithful; but don't be astonished or upset, if it does happen. He is only human! Enjoy the moment with him and don't think too far ahead; because it may never happen!

"Keep your faith in the human race Tigress; because there are still some good people in the world...like me!" (Smile!)

Chapter Twelve
Children: How safe are they?

At what age is a child, not a child? For the sake of this chapter; I will assume that a child is no longer a child at the age of 18. Before then; children should be in school, which ought to be a safety net in a child's life for his or her protection. If a child is not in school or plays truant; then serious questions should be asked of those who are supposed to be looking after his or her welfare. If any child is bullied, molested, attacked, injured, kidnapped or killed; it has to be the fault of the parents or those under whose care they have been entrusted. After school; the parents or guardians should do their utmost to make sure they are out of harm's way and return home safely. Nowadays, there are sexual perverts, child molesters and kidnappers lurking in our midst; as well as the usual bullies and daylight muggers. I therefore feel children should be taught self-defence in a way that will enable them, from an early age, to spot the dangers they may come across as they grow towards adulthood. Emphasis should be made on how to spot the signs that may lead to trouble; because modern attacks are more about brain than brawn. This Goju *real self-defence* ethic should be drilled into the child from an early age; to make him or her understand that self-defence concerns not only themselves and their property, but also the family's reputation. If your child is injured; it will be more painful for you than if the injury had happened to you. Eventually, the child's own gut instinct will feel what is right and what is wrong; and the parents can sleep easily, knowing that he/she will not do anything stupid before the age of eighteen. After that; one has to assume that he or she will do things by choice, so they must be warned that there are consequences to every action!

1. Potential dangers

Just as every parent warns a child about the dangers of crossing a road, staying out late, sexual activities, drugs, drinking and smoking; they should also warn the child about other potential dangers. These are the threats, which may not immediately cause them problems; but if not stopped in their tracks, would definitely lead to problems in the future and could result in serious injuries, incarceration or even death. This can be done with weekly question and answer scenario games with the child, making them more difficult as he/she gets older; in order for the parents to be assured in their own minds that the child is clever enough not to be easily fooled into trouble. These games can be fun and become part of the family routine; with appropriate rewards given for interesting, innovative and safe answers. They are usually simple questions starting with: *"What would you do if..."* The earlier you start this the better; so that by the time the child is about ten, he or she should be able to tell the difference between good, bad, right and wrong. The game will also help them not to be afraid to talk to you about things that have happened during the day; and how they coped with them. As they get older into their teens; you can hit them with the more difficult scenarios concerning drugs, sex and crime. The answers to all the following questions should be evident and drilled into any child by the parents; who should always take into account the area they live in, the laws of the land and the mentality of the people. I could answer the questions for you, but I won't; because even though the answers are obvious, every child is different and it is really up to you how you handle yours.

(a) You are walking home from school and a man starts talking to you, asking you where you live and what your name is; then offers you a sweet?

(b) Someone you don't know offers you a lift, when it is raining?

(c). A school bully steals your bicycle, I Pod or mobile phone etc?

(d) Your best friend dares you to go into a shop to steal some sweets?

(e) You see a thief beating someone up or stealing a handbag from a woman?

(f) You find yourself being teased and bullied in school?

(g) Your school friends find a way of cheating for the exams and ask you to join them?

(h) *Someone knocks on the front door at your home and you don't know who it is?*

(i) *You see a thief trying to steal your parents' car outside your house?*

(j) *You are wrongly accused for something in school; but you know who the real culprits are?*

To the more difficult:

(k) *Your pals offer you cigarettes or drugs and then tease you when you refuse?*

(l) *A girl/boy in school fancies you and wants to have sex with you?*

(m) *You got yourself or made someone pregnant...?*

(n) *You accept a ride in a car from your friend; who then tells you the car is stolen?*

(o) *Your best friend has committed a crime and the police ask if you know anything about it?*

(p) *You know someone is selling drugs or alcohol to some of the kids in your school?*

(q) *You catch a sexually transmitted disease from one of your school friends?*

(r) *You are asked to join a gang; knowing that if you refuse, you will be ostracised?*

(s) *Your friend invites you to an 'illegal' party at his home; while his parents are away?*

(t) *You are attacked and beaten up on the way home by some thugs?*

(u) *Your girlfriend says she loves you; but you find out she is sleeping with someone else?*

(v) Your boyfriend has been sleeping with your best friend?

(w) Your boyfriend/girlfriend is embarrassed and ashamed to be seen with you?

(x) Your boyfriend is so possessive he won't let you have any friends?

(y) Your boyfriend beats you up...

(z) Your boyfriend wanted you to have sex. You refused and he forced you.

By taking the idea I have given; you can use your own judgement to ask different types of questions and devise a way to teach them how to protect themselves from these threats, so that you can sleep a lot easier at night. The most important thing to make them realise and never do to you; is tell lies. This means they have to be taught that before you can trust them; they must be honest. If for instance in question *(d)*, he or she says they will not steal and later on you find out they have been stealing; then the anomaly must be stamped out immediately with your own form of disciplinary measures, before it is allowed to foment as he/she grows into adulthood. By telling you the truth, (in question *(o)* he/she will most likely refuse to 'snitch' on their friend to the police!) even if it is not what you want to hear; it will make you aware of his/her way of thinking. You will then be able to give sound legal and logical reasons why their way is not the right way to go. With all children; you cannot just tell them something and expect it to be done. You have to convince them with indisputable facts, figures and previous examples; so that they have no chance to out-manoeuvre you with their 'cheeky-smart' answers! Failing that; you have to let them make their own mistakes, if the consequences will not be too serious (Incarceration, injury or death). Sometimes the gloating *"I told you so...!"* (Which can easily apply to questions *(m)* and *(q)*) can be quite satisfying for a parent; when a child learns the hard way that the 'old fogies' are usually right!

With the last five questions; it is evident they are serious enough for you to leave no stone unturned to find a solution. Teenage physical and mental abuse is rampant; and very little is known about it because the children are not ready to talk about it. The obvious solution of leaving the culprit and reporting him to the authorities; is often the last thing a child will do. They are too young to know how to deal with mental abuse or even know when it is being used on them; so they will need a strong mature shoulder to cry on. It is important you do not unduly criticise them and always offer a solution they will be comfortable with; otherwise they will clam up and you will get no answers from them. With the girls; there is the added fear of physical abuse, which will be difficult for them to cope with. *"He says he loves me; yet he beats me up and won't let me have any friends!"* Such a scenario is difficult enough for an adult; but for a teenager, it can be traumatic. If she comes home with her face battered and bruised; she may not be willing to tell you who did it to her and might even say she got into a fight with some girls, or was beaten up outside the school. What if he forced her into having sex; when she was not ready (Rape!)? What would you do? As the parent; you would have to weigh the pros and cons. Your daughter may be so besotted with her boyfriend; she could end up hating you, if you do the obvious and call the police on him. What if you are good friends with the boy's parents? They might accuse your daughter of 'leading him on'; and the friendship you had with them will be broken. Word will spread around your area; with both sets of friends taking sides to ostracise the boy and the girl. To make matters worse; she could go back to him because whatever attracted her to him in the beginning, will still be there and he could charm his way back into her heart. Finally; what if your son is the one who abused or raped his girlfriend? Could you call the police on your own child? I realise I cannot tell you how to run your household or bring up your children, because they are your responsibility; and trying to tell teenagers what to do, even in their own interests, cannot be easy. I'm sure however; you can appreciate that there are a lot of potential dangers lurking around for every child. It is therefore, in your own interests; to make him/her aware of them and make sure they do not bring trouble on themselves and the family.

2. Disappearance

Every year thousands of children go missing in cities and towns around the world. As a woman, if your child disappears; it is probably the most heart-wrenching thing that could happen to you.

The uncertainty makes it even worse than a death; which has some form of closure attached to it, and can at least be accepted as part of life. Not knowing where the child is; who he or she is with; what is happening to them; and whether they are dead or alive; are just some of the horrible thoughts that will prey on your mind. You therefore have to instil in your children from an early age, to always let you know where they are and with whom; so that you are confident they are safe. As a family; if something happens to any one of you, it will affect everybody else. Once it becomes a habit to let you know where they are at all times; the habit will stay with them throughout their teens and they will realise that they are not alone in the world. The chances of their going missing will greatly diminish! Although this sounds like common sense; you have to admit that there have been times you have not known where your children were, even if it were only for a few hours. Be honest; and make them aware that it worries you when they go missing. Insist they always carry their mobile phones with them when they go out; even if it means having to top up the credit for them! School and bank holidays are the main times children can go missing. This is because in the post-school excitement; they tend to forget about safety and hang out with their friends. Some may even go for long walks on their own, to 'reconnect their thoughts'! Halloween with its bonfires and fireworks can make this seem even worse; because you might fear they have had an accident and been burnt by an exploding firework. Although most times it is perfectly safe; the day a child does not come home when you expect them to, could become the worst day of your life because anything could happen to them. Teenagers could be tempted by peer pressure to get themselves drunk; take drugs; have unprotected sex in dingy alleyways; get into fights; or commit petty crimes like vandalism, shoplifting, joyriding in a stolen cars and burglary; thereby not returning home when they are supposed to. Add this to the threat of drug dealers targeting their wares at children; sexual molesters; rapes; robberies; prostitution; religious cults; terrorist groups; kidnappers; murders; and you will realise that losing your children, even for a few hours, can be a horrible experience.

I can understand if you are a little bit quizzical; because you cannot keep an eye on a child for twenty-four hours a day. A simple text message from your teenagers to say they are fine or they have moved from the place where they said they would be; could be the difference between a sound and a sleepless night for you. You may have to lay down the law or nag them when they get home; if they ever forget to keep in touch as promised. When you act like you don't care; it can easily become a lost cause and they will forget completely. If they ever do go missing; you may not realise until it is too late and the damage has been done. By having to let you know where they are; it can keep them out of serious trouble because it would be hard to get up to mischief, if they are not given the time to do so or if they know you will surely find out. The minute you realise there is a break in the pattern of keeping in touch with you; it should alert you to the fact that something is wrong and your child is up to something. You should tackle it immediately he/she returns home! If necessary; you should wait up for them to confront the problem, as soon as they walk through the front door. This is because you will most likely spot a few behavioural and appearance clues; which you will miss if you wait till the next day to discuss what they had been up to. If they react in a rude or un-cooperative manner and tell you to *"mind your own business…!"*; the alarm bells should start ringing. It means he/she is already doing something they know is either not good or against your express wishes (drugs/alcohol, petty crime, illicit sex). You must find out what is going on; before whatever he/she is up to, becomes something serious. There is no point locking the stable door after the horse has bolted!

Since every mother loves her children and often cannot/refuses to see where and when they are going wrong; I can only advise you, based on the assumption that your child is normal, intelligent and willing to listen and take your advice. There are obviously difficult kids who will not do as they are told and will go out of their way to cause you maximum distress; by disappearing and not bothering to show up for hours, without an explanation or an apology. If you are faced with such a situation; you should never be held hostage to his/her antics. It might be in your best interests to ask a police officer to come and give the child a few harsh facts of life that could save him/her from getting involved in crime and ending up in prison. Finally; a child may deliberately go missing by running away. With such a scenario; there will be psychological factors involved, which I am not qualified to answer since I do not know your domestic situation. I do advise however, to seek professional help if your child shows early signs of mental illness, violent behaviour or unhappiness; so that the problem can be nipped in the bud, before it gets out of control. If a child with mental problems like autism or schizophrenia disappears; he or she will not be able to cope with the obvious dangers they will surely face. You have to realise that if they do go missing; the police can only work from the last place they were seen or where and when their last phone/text message was sent. This could make a big difference in tracing them. Nowadays, there are tiny, ingenious tracking devices you can make your children wear as a bracelet/necklace/watch or have connected to his/her mobile phone; so that you can use the Internet to locate the area they are in. This can be very useful if they have been abducted or lured somewhere by a stranger.

3. Strangers

Don't allow your pre-teen kids to go alone on the bus, train or for walks. With the nearby shops; you should go with them at first and time yourself how long it takes to go there and back. If they have to go and buy something; you can warn them that you are timing them. This means, they should ring if they bump into a school mate on the way and are delayed; because any friend could easily convince them to change plans and go off somewhere else. Going to and from school safely can easily be arranged by taking and bringing the children back yourself; through parent car pools; school buses; or having the children walk together in a group of friends. They should also be taught never to accept anything from a stranger; because things may not be what they seem. A friendly face could turn out to be the most dangerous! For example; a bar of chocolate can be spiked with a drug like LSD, or something more dangerous, to hook the child as soon as he/she eats it. The 'high' will enable him/her to look very favourably on the stranger; who would probably have arranged for them to meet again. The next day; the 'nice gentleman' will show up with his 'acid chocolate', which made the child feel so 'good'. Within a week, this stranger will be friends with the kid; and could easily lure him or her to his house for some paedophile sex. The poor child would be too high or too weak to do anything about it; and then too ashamed to tell anybody. It will then become 'their little secret'. Sadly; you may be the last person to find out.

There are so many sophisticated tactics and weapons (like knockout sprays), that it is better to drill into all children not to talk to any stranger, or go anywhere; unless there are at least three of them.

Children should never be taught that they can beat up grown-ups; because they can't. Even if the child is learning boxing or the martial arts; he is unlikely to be warned that hitting anyone could get him into trouble with the police. How do you explain to a ten-year old child who has been taught in his self-defence classes to kick his attacker in the groin or punch him in the nose; and make him understand that you are not really allowed to do it to anyone? If a stranger comes up to him and asks for the time; legally, he has not committed a crime. For the child to attack the stranger, simply because he has been made to believe that all strangers are bad; will one day back-fire on him. There is no guarantee the child will come out of it without injury; fatal or otherwise. It would be best for him/her to shout/scream and run away to report the matter; however harmless or gentle the man might have seemed. Any attempt to offer them anything, follow them or ask them to go anywhere; should be rebuffed and reported as quickly as possible to the first police officer they come across. If they see anything strange or dangerous; they should never interfere but report it immediately to an adult in authority (anyone in uniform, working in a shop/office; otherwise known as safe-strangers). The 'molester' may only get a caution from the cops; but if it becomes established that any attempt to solicit a child, would be universally reported, then it would greatly reduce the attempts by these molesters.

Once the child realises that a stranger only becomes dangerous when he crosses the line by speaking to him/her or following them around; then he/she can feel perfectly safe in town or anywhere else outside your house, so far as he/she is not alone and has some way of communicating with you, every couple of hours. *"Mummy, I'm fine. Stop fussing!"* is better than hearing nothing at all. It has to be the fault of the parents and the child's school; if they fail to educate him/her on the evils of child sex; prostitution; pornography; kidnapping; or alcohol and drug taking. How can you convince children to refuse gifts from strangers, especially sweets; when you as the parent, are not giving them those simple pleasures? I do not advocate spoiling them; but they have to learn to only take things from you and never from anyone else, except a family member. In the end, it all boils down to how well a child is brought up; which I am afraid is down to the parent. There is something wrong in a situation, whereby a child is willing to accept sweets from a stranger; simply because the parents have banned him/her from eating them. Sweets may only be the tip of the iceberg. It can apply to anything the child cannot have and feels shy, embarrassed or afraid to do in front of the parents; because they have tried to convince him or her it is bad for them.

A child should be allowed to be a child and not become an extension of the parents' beliefs and prejudices. If for example, a parent is a vegetarian or against junk food and forces the child never to eat meat or chips; then he/she is going to eat them without the parent's knowledge and could easily be enticed by a stranger to the nearest fast-food joint. The same goes for money, video games, toys and even outings (bowling alley, cinema, football matches etc); which the parents cannot afford to give the child. If he or she knows there is something they cannot get at home, which is always available at a stranger's house; it will not take long for the stranger to become his/her 'friend' and introduce him/her to his way of life. The child may then start lying to you, claiming he/she is at a friend's house; when in actual fact, they are having fun at a stranger's house and may even phone to tell you they are okay. It would therefore be in your own best interests to try and make friends with the parents of your children's friends; so that you can be sure they are always where they say they are. More importantly; you will know they are safe. Hopefully, they will not be spoilt rotten; because it could provoke unfair comparisons between your household and that of your children's friends. *"David's Mummy allows him to use the Internet, so why can't I?"* or *"I had chocolate ice cream at Mary's house...!"*

4. Peer pressure

Just as adults will rob an easy target; children can also be materialistic enough to steal and rob from other students, who are perceived to be rich and 'have it all'. A lot of well-off parents like to give their children the best of everything; from clothes to toys and food. It is as if their kids are some form of status symbol; and the better they are showed off to the world, the better it looks on the parents! As soon as these children arrive in school looking like they are richer than their classmates; they immediately stick out like a sore thumb and will become targets of envy. Even the quality of the food in their snack boxes can be a dead-giveaway; and the child will have 'friends' coming up to him, as soon as he/she arrives in school. They all want to sample the smoked salmon and cucumber sandwiches; because it is better than the crisps, fruit and cheese most students are saddled with! As a parent, you must try to let the child blend in with his or her environment; which means you must not spoil them, unless they are going to a school attended by other rich kids. By allowing him/her to carry the latest gadgets that their friends cannot afford; it will alienate him or her from them and create juvenile jealousy, which can lead to bullying and stealing. Whilst walking to and from school; he or she will be noticed by everybody else as a rich kid and attract the not so juvenile elements of a society. They might beat him/her up; while robbing any money he/she may be carrying. Children have had bicycles, *I-Pods,* watches and cell phones snatched from them; by teenage gangs marauding through the town, with nothing better to do. If your children own expensive things; it would be much safer for them to keep the gadgets at home, away from prying eyes. They can wear the smart, fancy gear, only when they go out with an adult; when they are unlikely to be robbed. If you also tell them not to brag to their school mates about what they have at home; they will not be pressured into bringing the gadgets out of the house to school to prove that they are not lying.

Peer pressure becomes very dangerous when it is used by close friends of the victim; because the subtle threat of losing their friendship will make him or her go to greater lengths, in order to fit in. Stealing from the teacher's bag, cheating at exams and playing tricks on the weaker and 'geeky' students; are just a few of the mischievous things your child could be doing, as a result of peer pressure. If he/she is not caught; you may never find out what your 'sweet son' or 'darling daughter' is getting up to in school. Pressure can easily be put on a child to part with valuables; because he or she wants to fit in with the crowd and become popular. The child will give things away; because he or she thinks the parents are rich (stupid?) enough to replace them. He or she may even tell lies; claiming the gadget was dropped and broken, misplaced or stolen…when in actual fact, it was given away to school mates through intimidation or bravado. Again; this is the fault of the parents who spoil the child by buying him or her expensive things, without instilling into them, the value of money. A rich parent may be so busy; he or she may have lost all sense of monetary value and may not be aware of the damage such expenditure is doing to their children. Buying the child a $100 pair of the latest sport shoe; probably means nothing, when the parent is involved in multi-million dollar business deals! On the other end of the scale, if you are not rich enough to buy your child the things he/she craves; he/she may become one of those who go around bullying other kids to part with their possessions. A fine balance must be created; whereby you have to educate your kids against the temptations they are likely to face (shoplifting, stealing from school friends/family members) and the grave consequences of such actions.

The only way to avoid your children becoming victims of peer pressure; will be to take an active interest in their lives, so that you know exactly what they get up to. If for instance, there is a popular mobile phone ring tone doing the rounds in the school; your child may put one on his or her phone, without reading the small print on the offer and will most likely be charged more than expected. You may then end up having to pay the bill for something your child did; just because everyone else was doing it. By asking him/her how they got the 'nice' ring tone; you will be able to see if your child is a follower or a leader. You could then advise them accordingly, that everything in this world costs money; and if they want to be the 'coolest kid in school' with all the latest gadgets, then they will have to earn it. Don't buy them expensive things; and always make them do chores around the house to earn the pocket money to buy any of the gadgets they crave. If they have had to work their socks off for a bicycle or cell phone; I cannot see them losing it or having it stolen. If per chance they are robbed; I can guarantee that they will give you the names of the perpetrators, with ease! If you buy them a watch and they return from school without it; you must immediately ask them where it is. If they spin you a story that it has been 'lost' or 'stolen'; an appropriate punishment must be given, like making them do some work around the house to earn another one. If they realise that you always seem to notice everything about them; they are less likely to lose things or give them away. If you feel they were bullied into parting with certain items; then you will have to inform the school to find out what happened, so that the culprits can be brought to book. If your children know you will look out for and not unduly criticise them; they are more likely to confide in you. A strong relationship will develop; making it extremely unlike they will become victims of peer pressure.

5. The Internet

With the advent of the World Wide Web; many children (some as young as six years of age) are hooked on the social networking sites and can easily fall victim to a pervert pretending to be someone of their age. He befriends the child; who then begins to trust his/her cyber pal more than the parents, under whose roof he/she is living. It seems incredible; but these perverts can divulge a lot of information from the child. All it takes is an argument between you and your child; and he/she will feel unloved enough to confide all to the cyber pal. A relationship develops; and the child could leave home to go and meet his/her new friend, without telling anyone. What happens between them, sexual or otherwise; may never be revealed by the child, who sees this new friend as a realistic substitute to the parents. The pervert easily convinces the child that there is nothing wrong with what they are doing. He will then set about convincing the child that he/she does not need you; because you are holding him/her back. This intimacy makes it easy to ask him/her do things for him; which may even include stealing from you. Even more dangerous; is when the pervert is rich enough to be able to buy things for the child. This means you could find yourself being marginalized; because everything he or she needs will be supplied by the Internet friend. Since there is no such thing as a free lunch; the pervert will obviously want something in return! You may never find out what is going on; until it is too late. Mentally and emotionally; you would have lost your child for ever. The above scenario, is obviously extreme; but make no mistake, it does happen. Many a woman is now counting the cost of allowing the Internet in her house!

You would not want your children out on the streets on their own, talking to strangers; so why do you think it is okay for them to go on the Internet alone? In some ways; having them using the computer at home, is better than wandering the streets and getting up to mischief.

You should therefore, try to learn as much about the Internet as possible; because it will make it easier for you to know what your children are doing. You can then advise them of the possible dangers of giving away too much personal information; which they may not be aware, can be used against your family. There are quite a few useful Internet security companies; that can be used to deny access to certain sites, which are inappropriate for children. There are also ways to use a timer to automatically cut off the computer; whenever you feel they have had enough (usually two hours). You can even put a password on the computer; so that your children will have to seek your permission to go on the Internet. There are certain ways you can read your children's Emails to make sure they are not making contact with people you have never heard of. You can see which sites have been visited during the previous month or more; by checking out the history. Any file that has been deleted should be in the recycle bin, which will give you the time and date it was deleted; and this will give you an idea who did it. If you find the history has been deleted and the recycle bin is empty, when it wasn't before; then be very suspicious because whoever was on the Internet, obviously did not want anyone to know where he/she had visited. There is special software available; if you really want to retrieve the deleted history. Failing that; it would not be too expensive to bring in the experts to check out your computer and they will be able to tell you exactly what your kids have been up to. You can then warn or discipline them; depending on what they have been getting up to!

Although you may not approve of 'eavesdropping' on your kids; it may be in your own security interests to do so...until you are sure they can be trusted. If they get hold of your credit card number, they can order things; and you may not find out until the bill arrives. There are many scams, fake products for sale and get-rich-quick schemes on the Internet. Out of simple curiosity, a child can easily be tricked into using your credit card to pay for something; thereby giving the number and expiry date away to the scam artist. Children can also be careless enough to give away their real names, home address and phone number when they join a social networking site. If they forget to lock it with a password; it could enable the identity fraud experts to use the information for their own nasty ends. When you realise that there are sites which sell identities for as little as $100; others where you can hire a hit man; buy drugs; pick up a prostitute; find the answers to certain exam papers; learn how to make bombs; buy guns; commit suicide and many other salacious activities; you will understand that the Internet is the modern equivalent of the old lawless Wild West. Anything is possible; and not the safest place for children! Having said that; there are however some interesting, salubrious sites that are useful for youngsters. It is therefore up to you; to make it your business to keep an eye open, whenever your kids are on line. It is important to be secure in your own mind; that nothing untoward is going on, which can harm your family. They are part of your self-defence!

It would be better if you make sure your children share the same computer at home. It should be in an open place like the living room; so that no one is on it for too long and the whole family can see what is going on. This should not be a problem if nothing untoward is occurring. It will also enable you to monitor their reactions and behaviour when they are on the Internet; or immediately when they come off it. This is because their behavioural patterns may change; which should alert you that something is wrong. Many women (and even more men) allow their children to have computers in their bedrooms. This conceals any problems your kids may be experiencing; simply because you cannot see or know what is really going on. If they are victims of Internet bullying or in contact with perverts; it is your right and duty as a parent to know what is going on. Be very aware that if the kids cannot get past your 'security measures'; they might decide to use the Internet at school instead. Some children are so smart; they are able to bypass any safety measures the teachers may have installed on the computers. It is also very possible that the school head has no idea the kids are so computer savvy, they are able to download Internet porn in the school! Go into any reliable computer shop and the salesperson will be able to tell you the names of the best security software. You can then talk to the head of the school; so that you can be sure the security features on the school computers are of the 'unbreakable' variety. Although the software is easily available, they are naturally a little expensive; so some educational institutions will be reluctant to install them. Please make sure their carelessness does not cause any problems for you. Your children are minors; and you will ultimately be the one who will have to take the blame and clear up the mess when things go wrong. There is no need for panic; just be a little more vigilant!

6. Bullying, teasing & gossip

School children are often bullied by cruel text messages or Emails. Physical bullying is outlawed in all schools; so this form of attack is the viable alternative. It is very difficult to catch the culprits, because most of them use pseudonyms. A false rumour circulated by text; can be so devastating to the victim that he or she may never recover. Children in their 'innocence' can be very cruel to each other; without realising the psychological implications. A bruise will heal, but a mental scar will not; and will fester in one's subconscious for a lifetime. One can now appreciate how beating someone up physically, could soon be a thing of the past; because of the criminal charges they would incur. Mental and subtle bullying is more popular, because the law has not yet caught up with this type of offence; and it is not seen as serious wrongdoing by the perpetrators. Some teenagers have become victims of the 'happy slapping' craze; where bullies gang up on and slap him/her around with the palm of the hand (so that they don't leave any bruises for the teachers to find out). Others are stripped naked and their clothes soaked in water. They are then laughed at, while they run around trying to retrieve the clothes; which are thrown from one perpetrator to another. These scenarios are then filmed on a camera-phone, circulated by text and posted on the Internet; for the viewing pleasure of the world. Although it might seem like harmless fun to the culprits; the result can be devastating to the victim. There have been several recent cases of sufferers, committing suicide!

The parents of those involved; may be too self-absorbed in their own lives to care what their kids are doing on a daily basis in school or on their computers at home. As a result; whenever a parent is told that his/her child has caused trouble in school; there is a feeling of surprise, shock and horror...followed by strong denials. *"My boy/girl would never do that. There must be a mistake!"* If the child is a victim of bullying, teasing or gossip; the first reaction of the parents, is to blame the school. They may verbally or even physically attack the parents of the student giving grief to their child. No one ever stops to think that it could be the fault of the victim; and by affiliation, his or her parents. You see; a child is only bullied, teased or gossiped about in school, because he/she is different from the others. If for example, the child is from a wealthier family than the others; they will try to take advantage by getting things off and forcing him/her to share the wealth with them. When that is not forthcoming; they may resort to bullying (stealing/damaging things belonging to them), teasing (name calling, false accusations) in a way to make them ashamed of being from a rich family and gossiping (unfounded rumours, malicious lies). The same methods will be used; whether the child is poorer; cleverer/more stupid; weaker/stronger; prettier/uglier; timid/shy/brash; and therefore, does not 'fit in'. Jealousy is usually the root of this mistreatment; because it is much easier and safer to bully, tease and gossip, than to physically attack the victim. However; physical attacks will occur, if the victim decides to fight back by attacking one or more of the tormentors. They will then gleefully report him/her to the teachers for the attack; culminating in his/her suspension or dismissal. This now goes on record as the victim's fault; when all he/she was doing, was reacting to the mental torture. Therein lies the seriousness of teasing and gossiping; because the authorities never know what is going on, until there is a reaction. This usually comes from the victim; who becomes so fed up that he/she may feel the only way to make it stop is with a physical attack. Since there is no proof of the teasing; the attack now becomes the 'cause célèbre' and the victim is punished. Hence; the parents' utter surprise, indignation and anger!

The problem is; there is nothing you can do about your child being teased, bullied or gossiped about...unless he or she tells you. Many children are too scared, shy, afraid or ashamed to tell anyone; because of the consequences. 'Snitching' to teachers and parents is seen as a sign of weakness by all students; and the bullying will get worse. I am afraid, as the parent; you will have to keep your eyes open and take a personal interest in your children's lives, in order to know for certain, whether they are victims or perpetrators. As soon as they come back from school; watch out for any physical changes like rumpled clothes, scratches, bruises etc. and don't just assume he or she got them from playing. Also; keep an eye open for any changes in their behavioural patterns. Uncommunicativeness, sullenness, rudeness, crying and temper tantrums are all signs that something is wrong; so you have to find out exactly what it is. You know your child better than anyone; so you have to use all the tactics in your arsenal, to try to get to the bottom of it. All women know when their children are lying; so if that happens to be the case, you have to be a little 'sneaky'. If this means looking into their mobile phones when they are asleep, to see if there are any incriminating messages or photos; don't be afraid to do so! Read their Emails, talk to the friends, teachers and siblings; in order to build a picture in your mind. This will tell you much more than the child would!

There is new technology available to protect children from mobile phone bullies. It involves special software being downloaded onto the child's handset, through the phone number. A copy of any message sent to the child will be transferred onto the parent's own mobile; before the child gets it. The parent is then able to read the message before the child does; and then choose whether or not to allow him/her to see it. The parent will also be able to see where the message is coming from and can then decide what to do about it. This may prove unpopular with the child; because it is akin to reading his/her diary. It is therefore up to the parent to convince the child to go along with it; otherwise, just do it without telling him or her! If the mobile phone was bought by you for the child; it would be registered to you and therefore, there is nothing illegal in snooping on what is in effect, your own phone. Although it might seem a little underhand when you break into your children's privacy; you have to understand that whatever happens to them, will affect your family. More than likely, you will be blamed for being a bad parent; so you have to do 'whatever it takes' to protect what you love. Every country has security services who legally/illegally spy on people, who might be a threat to national security; which looks bad when they are caught, but still goes a long way towards keeping a nation safe from its enemies. So, in the 'interests of your family's security'; you have to take it upon yourself to find out what your kids are up to…just don't get caught!!!

Once you find out your child is being bullied; you have to ask him/her exactly what is being done and why. If it is something you realise is your fault (buying the child expensive things to take to school) or the 'fault' of your child (rude, obnoxious, too intelligent, arrogant etc.); then you have to try and fix it by giving him/her advice on how to mix with other children. However; if the problem is definitely from the other kids in the school, you have to make a report to the teachers to try and find out who is doing it. You have to be tough and make sure they are ready to fix the problem; or you must threaten to go to a higher authority, like the educational body the school belongs to. If the school is being intransigent (many head-teachers will deny the presence of anything, they feel would be detrimental to the school's image); it would be advisable to remove the child to another school because it means the school may not try to catch the culprits and the bullying/teasing/gossiping will continue. In case you do find out; you should never confront the children who are bullying your child. They will tell their parents and you could have a child molestation charge on your hands! To make it worse; the parents whose child you accused, could come and insult or possibly attack you for daring to threaten their 'darling son/daughter'. The father may only tell you off, because you are a woman; but the mother will not be shy about physically attacking you. For some reason; mothers are more aggressively protective of their children than fathers!

If your child is a perpetrator; you have to let him/her know that you are aware of what is going on, but are not pointing fingers. You can then explain that it is wrong for your family's reputation and against the law. If you spell out the consequences (which could be anything from your own form of punishment, to suspension or dismissal by the school, to criminal charges being laid upon them); most children at this stage will listen and stop what they are doing. To them; it is just 'a bit of fun' as a result of peer pressure! However; if you sense that your child has not stopped the instigation; you can emphasise your seriousness by asking a police officer to come to your house to talk to him/her. They have impressive ways of convincing any minor, what it means to be arrested and sent to prison! If your child will not listen to the police; then I am sorry to say, he is on a slippery slope and may end up joining a gang, being jailed or killed, before he is twenty-one. It would therefore be advisable to seek professional help from experts in child psychology. You have to be aware that over the years, experts in many countries have come up with all kinds of theories for child misbehaviour; which usually blame the parents, for something that happened to the child in the past. The 'solutions' they propound will not work; if a child is determined to go down the criminal route. There is nothing anyone can do about this; and you may regrettably have to let him or her go into the big bad world to learn life's lessons the hard way. You can only do your best for your child; and if that is not good enough, don't beat yourself up!

7. Gangs, weapons and fights

(a) Gangs

What starts off as a group of kids playing together in school; could easily end up with them walking around after school and getting up to mischief. Once the youths start hanging around together on a daily basis, they are in theory, already in a gang; which means, it is only a matter of time before they get into trouble. It may start off with loitering around corner shops, listening to music; and through simple boredom, could lead to playing practical jokes on innocent bystanders, frightening old ladies for fun, shoplifting and mugging. If they are not caught; they could slide into serious crimes involving drink, drugs, money and weapons. Gangs (any group consisting of three or more youths) can be a frightening sight as they walk through a town; especially if they are intoxicated with drink and drugs. There is a feeling of owning the street; which means, anyone who gets in their way will be insulted, threatened, bumped/pushed out of the way or assaulted. Daring to argue or fight them; may culminate in a severe beating or even a stabbing. With the recent rise in all-female gangs; it is not only groups of boys one should watch out for, but also girls...who can be just as upfront and vicious as their male counterparts! Gangs will never go away; because as soon as the police break up one with their 'stop and search' tactics, another one will take its place. They are getting smarter by not carrying the weapons on them. They will have them hidden in certain places along the routes they frequent; so that they can easily be retrieved, if there is a fight with a rival gang.

Being in a gang means they can easily become fearless and dare each other to do more and more outrageous stunts. If your child is weak-minded and a follower, as opposed to a leader; he/she may be used in committing misdemeanours and/or serious crimes that the ringleaders in the group will be too smart to do themselves. Students have been known to attack their teachers or beat up other students; and one must wonder whether such acts of violence are of their own accord or as a result of 'earning their spurs' with the group or gang they belong to. With all students; there is a need to feel important and be respected by their peers! They will tend to move around in groups; which in effect, becomes their protection against other groups in the school. The rivalry between the different groups in the school could either see them form several 'mergers'; or try to outdo each other with the clothes they wear, the music they listen to, the latest gadgets they own, the colourful language they use and the things they get up to. The 'baddest' or 'coolest' gangs will be the ones that can get away with the most outrageous or illegal acts; which will most likely include sex, drink and drugs. In school for example; if the most powerful gang is walking down the corridor, they expect the other students to move out of the way. They will expect to be first in any queue and will push everyone else out of the way to get there. They could bully the weaker students into parting with their food, money and mobile phones. They will grab a student into the toilets and 'discipline' him or her for disrespecting them; just because he/she looked at them in the wrong way or said something they did not like. They could also go as far as 'gang-banging' (several boys having sex with one girl) a willing female student; because they know it is her way of fitting in. Because they are held in such high esteem in their schools as a result of their tough profile; it is easy to transfer this behaviour to the outside world, where they believe the same rules apply. It will not take them too long to realise that on the streets, they have to be even tougher to rule the roost; because there are rival gangs vying to control the same street or turf. The next obvious step is to arm themselves, so that they can feel safer; in order to intimidate and frighten anyone who gets in their way.

If you find out your child is in a gang, there is not much you can do if he/she is over eighteen, except warn and advise; because legally, he or she is responsible for his/her actions. For the benefit of this chapter on children; I am assuming your child is less than eighteen years of age. This means it is your business and responsibility, how he or she behaves. Since most gangs start off in schools; it would be better if you were aware of what your child gets up to in school, outside of the school report. A child with straight 'A's'; could still be a gang member, bullying other students without the teachers' knowledge. Because of the likely repercussions; it is rare for a bullied student to report the bullies! The relief at knowing that their child is very clever and intelligent; usually blinds most parents from seeing or accepting any 'imperfections' in him/her and will not bother to scrutinise his/her behaviour, so long as the grades are good.

It is therefore imperative you take an active role in your children's lives; otherwise you may live to regret it. Take some time off at least once a week, and talk to them about school, their problems, tears and fears; keeping a mental note on what they say, whilst watching out for certain signs. Rudeness or arrogance are dead-giveaways that he or she is used to getting their own way; and have brought the lofty behaviour home with them. It also means they have already been put on a pedestal by their school mates; and more than likely, they are gang leaders. Since you are unlikely to receive any bad educational reports; you will have to take it upon yourself to find out if everything is as good as the teachers are making out. You have to remember that most teachers are over-stretched and underpaid; so it is natural for them to feel their job is done, once they have taught the students enough to make the grade in the exams. They are not really interested in the students' behaviour outside the classroom, so far as it does not affect the grades; because that is how they are judged by the school and the parents of their students. Once you pinpoint things you are worried about; you will have to voice your fears to the head of the school and find a way to curb the mentality. You may also have to enforce your own brand of discipline; to dispel the gang culture from their minds before it is cemented into them. Once they reach the age of eighteen; it may already be too late!

(b) Weapons

Weapons, especially knives; have recently been the bane of many modern societies, whereby several youths have been brutally stabbed to death. Even though knives are illegal; many youths (boys and girls) from disadvantaged areas carry them, as a means of protection. They assume everyone else has them; and thereby feel they are putting their lives at risk, if they don't have them. Most of these knives are regular kitchen knives; which can easily be bought in many shops. The rest are readily available on the black market; to anyone who really wants one. Any knife wound can be fatal; and even if the victim is saved in hospital, the mental scar and fear of a repeat stabbing will never go away. To find out her child has been stabbed to death is one of the most traumatic things that could happen to a mother. She will never forgive herself that she could have done something about it; if only she had paid more attention to the child. I sincerely sympathise, if your child has been a victim of a stabbing; but if he or she was under eighteen, it should have been avoided. I hope what I am saying here will prevent someone else being stabbed. You see; nobody gets stabbed without a reason and unless the attacker is caught, you will never know why he or she did it. Even if caught; the perpetrators tend to use 'self-defence' or the lame, *"It was an accident. I didn't mean to do it!"* as an excuse. With the right lawyer to defend them; they could be back walking the streets in a few years. Meanwhile; the victim's family are left to endure lifelong anguish, desolation and pain. Apart from knives; there are an assortment of other dangerous weapons, like syringes; clubs; knuckledusters; whips; meat cleavers; martial arts equipment (sword, nunchaku, sai, tonfa); and guns; that could easily fall into the hands of your child. It is therefore imperative for you to keep a watchful eye on your children and advise them; while they are still young enough to take your advice. If you leave it too late; it would be almost impossible to alter their mindset. Take a walk to your local police station; and they will give you a very good idea of how safe or dangerous your area really is. If you rely on sensational newspaper reports, you might think there are stabbings all over the country; which is never entirely true. On the other hand; the politicians will try to convince you by 'massaging' the statistics that things are under control and not as bad as they seem!

When a child starts having problems at school; it is up to the parents to spot them and try to solve them with the teachers. Otherwise; professional advice must be sought. If he or she is being bullied at school for instance; he/she might become introverted and shy, turning him or her into a loner. This means, there is a likelihood he or she will prefer to do things alone; and this will obviously include walking around town on their own. He/She could easily become a prime target for more bullying; from the many gangs moving around the streets, looking for someone to pick on. On the opposite end of the scale; if a child is brash, rude and obnoxious or a walking temper time-bomb, he or she will definitely end up in an argument in town. Depending on his/her stubbornness; it could easily lead to a fight and a stabbing. In any town; word spreads fast via photos, text messages and Emails amongst students of different schools. A candidate for bullying can easily be targeted; even by those he or she has never met before. The same advice I previously gave about never going anywhere alone or letting a stranger know where you live; should apply even more so, to your children. If they bring a friend home; you should make it a point to ask the friend for the parents' number and ring them immediately, to let them know their child is with you. This establishes a contact with them; so that if something happens and the kids get into trouble together, you will be able to meet up and discuss your mutual problems. Allowing children to roam the streets in the evenings or at night, is bordering on neglect; because too many things can go wrong. Even if he or she is not stabbed to death; there is the threat from strangers; paedophiles; drugs; alcohol; fights; unprotected sex; petty criminals; organised crime etc. Need I go on?

Since it is mostly youths who carry knives; there is every chance that your child could be one of those who has one and may have already terrorised someone with it. Unless the police make an arrest; you may never know. You have to keep an eye on your children and watch out for little signs like; lying/refusing to tell you where they have been, the state of their clothes when they come home, breaking any curfew you have imposed on them and the friends they mix with. If you are not happy with their suspicious behaviour; don't be afraid to 'nose around' their bedrooms when they go out because they could easily hide a knife or another weapon there. If they are living under your roof; you have to protect the reputation of your family and make no apologies for the tactics you use. However; if you do find a dangerous looking weapon in your child's bedroom, you will have to use tact. If you confront him/her and seize it; he/she may go underground and start hiding future weapons elsewhere. The problem would not have been solved; plus the fact that you will probably lose any trust he/she has in you. The best thing to do is to wait till the child goes out, and then see if the weapon is still there; and if it isn't, then you know he or she has taken it with him/her. You would then have two choices. Either wait up till he/she returns home, and then confront him/her; or call the police to your house to take the knife off him/her. The cops would then deliver a severe warning that he/she is on the police radar. This means they could be arrested and jailed; if they are ever caught again with a weapon. For every person who is stabbed on the streets; there is someone responsible who could have been stopped by those closest to and most capable of doing so…the parents or guardians!

Although as a woman, you are unlikely to be stabbed on the streets; you could be threatened by one as a prelude to a robbery or mugging at your front door, or as you are getting into/out of your car. If you try to fight back; you may be stabbed out of panic, before the thieves make their get-away! You can avoid most of the mugging pitfalls by following the advice I gave in a previous chapter. Since you will not always be with your children; you have to warn them that carrying knives, leaves them open to retaliation. You should also advise them that it would be much safer to keep their eyes open when going out; never walk around alone and to stay away from certain areas. They should avoid talking to strangers, report any suspicious behaviour they see and observe the basic safety rules of going out. If you have time; take them to a hospital and let them see for themselves, a few victims of stabbings and shootings. They may not be aware just how dangerous weapons are; and that being injured could ruin a person for life. Every person who is stabbed will have friends and relatives who will be out for revenge; so the danger is never-ending. If for example, your child is with a friend who ends up stabbing someone; he becomes part of the attack. Even if he is not charged by the police; he will have to keep looking over his shoulder, when going out. This is because some families will stop at nothing, in order to exact revenge; which may be far in excess of what happened to the member of their family. In other words; a non-fatal stabbing may end up in the murder of the alleged perpetrator and anyone else who was part of the incident. This in turn, puts your whole family in danger of reprisals. If someone, obsessed with revenge against your son, cannot find him; he may decide to go for someone else in your household!

On top of all that; there are now laws in many countries, against carrying knives. Your child could easily be arrested and charged with offensive behaviour; even if he/she does not use the weapon! There is also a relatively new unforgiving piece of legislation, called the *'Joint Enterprise Law'*; which was first introduced in the United Kingdom and is making its way around the world. Put simply; it says that the police will be able to prosecute anybody involved in a crime, even if he or she was not the one who specifically committed that crime. Imagine your child is with a group of friends and there is a fight with a rival gang; whereby someone ends up getting stabbed and killed. Everyone who was there during the confrontation, antagonisation or coercion and did nothing to prevent or intercede in the violence; will also be charged with the murder! Doing nothing also means; knowing that the perpetrator had a knife on him and was not reported or persuaded to leave it behind. Although this law seems unfair at first glance; it is the surest sign that the authorities are taking gang violence seriously, by putting the burden of responsibility on those present during the incident. Even though many kids will not be aware of this law; there is no excuse for ignorance! If your child is in any way involved in any criminal behaviour; you could have the police breaking down your front door and your whole family being treated like violent criminals. He/She could be jailed for something they 'did not do'; and end up with an unwanted criminal record. At the very least; he/she will be expelled from school, whilst your family will be shunned and pilloried by your neighbours. Once your kids realise that any of the above situations could easily happen to them, even if they are only carrying weapons 'for their own safety' or 'having a laugh'; something in their brains might register for the good. If you cannot keep your kids under control; it might be wise to seek professional assistance because when they reach the age of eighteen, they could already be on the slippery slope into crime.

(c) Fights

Sooner or later; every child will get into a scuffle in school or even at home. Thankfully; these are usually broken up by the other students, the teachers or members of the family, before too much damage is caused. The problem with fighting is; some kids believe it is the quickest way of sorting out problems or arguments. If a child starts throwing temper tantrums at an early age; many parents will let him or her have their way, mainly to get some peace. That is the worst thing to do; because the child will grow up believing that, yelling and threatening behaviour gets you what you want. He or she will quickly find out when they go to school, that it does not always work; and will get into fights, probably on a daily basis. This could result in their being labelled a troublemaker and excluded from activities, suspended or even expelled. Once a child wins his/her first few fights easily, and realises he or she is handy in combat; he/she might start believing that is the best and only way to solve all problems and difficulties with other students and even their friends.

This belief in their prowess could continue into the teen-age years and over-spill into public life; with threatening behaviour or actual physical attacks on people they have any sort of altercation with. *"Shut up or I'll beat the shit out of you!"* will win many an argument in town; especially if the thug uttering those threats looks mean and dangerous enough to deliver on the promise. A group of teens walking down the street would probably scare anyone; and every sensible person would move out of the way to let them pass. However; there will definitely come a time, when he or she will come up against someone as stubborn or combative as he/she is and a fight will ensue, with one or both participants getting hurt.

As explained in the chapter on night clubs; no fight is ever completely won or lost, because of the possible repercussions and the damage to reputation and property. If your child beats up someone, he/she might feel victorious; but it could be the beginning of their (and by default) your family's problems. Anyone of you could be attacked while walking down the street, or at home! If your phone rings and then hangs up when you pick it up; how are you going to feel? What if your doorbell rings in the middle of the night; yet no one is at the door when you open it? What about; a brick thrown through your window; faeces smeared over your front door; or your house set on fire, through your letterbox? These are all feasible ways the victim's friends and family can get back at you. Can you afford the medical bills of your child and/or the person he/she hurt in a fight? Can you raise the money to pay a good lawyer for your child; to defend him/her against charges of assault from the victim? How would you like your child to go to prison for threatening behaviour, manslaughter or murder? This is easily possible because; one punch from a silly argument could knock the opponent down, allow him to hit his head on the pavement and die. The possibilities of things going wrong in a fight are so numerous, that the sooner you warn your children against fighting; the better.

All aggressive behaviour starts from childhood. Although I would not like to tell you how to control your children; I have to stress that it is in your future interests to find the best way to curtail such behaviour, as soon as it occurs. Please contact a child psychologist or buy books on the subject; if you are having problems. Encouraging your children to get involved in sports (especially the team ones like football, rugby, basketball, volleyball, handball or hockey); will help expunge some of the excess energy he/she may be harbouring. They will also let them realise that losing and winning is part of life; and therefore, differences need not necessarily be solved by fighting. Group activities like the Scouts and the Girl Guides, are useful in teaching the child different skills; which will be beneficial to them throughout their lives. Enrolling your child in a boxing or martial arts club would be advantageous; because of their physical, mental and spiritual benefits. They will quickly calm down any aggressive tendencies of the child; and he/she will become much calmer and more aware of his/her own mortality. They also teach discipline and respect for each other; which will help the child defend him/herself by restraint, as opposed to aggression…just in case they do get into an altercation, through no fault of their own! More importantly; the pugilistic sports will teach the child that they cannot win every fight, because there is always someone in the club and in the big bad world, who is tougher and stronger. I have to stress that they will have to be doing the fighting arts for quite a long time; before they will feel physically and mentally confident enough to handle a street confrontation. Although a martial art will greatly help a child defend him/herself against children of a similar age and size; it cannot solve the safety problems for them because their greatest threats will always be from adults. Kids should be taught to always report any form of aggression against them to someone in authority, rather than take the law into their own hands; because it is very unlikely they can physically beat up grown-ups. Once your children realise from an early age, the consequences of fighting, especially the possibilities of revenge and criminal procedures; they will calm down and you will not have to worry when they go out!

Please be aware that it makes no real difference if someone is a martial artist or boxer and is not supposed to fight. Your child might still get into a fight; simply as a matter of honour or principle. He or she might be pushed into a corner, where the only way out would be to defend his/her pride. For example; if a boy is with his girlfriend and she is insulted, he cannot stand there and do nothing. If a girl feels another girl has 'stolen' her boyfriend by using lies; she might decide to get her own back, by beating the culprit up. The same goes for insults against the family or against a girl's femininity; because to do nothing will leave him or her open to continuous teasing, until they 'snap'. Even though they may come off worse; all children will at some point fight, if their money or valuables are being taken off them by bullies. Most boys will fight if their mother, sister or female friend is insulted. *"Your mother/sister/girlfriend is a whore…"* will send any boy into a fit of rage; so if you find out your child has been fighting, please don't reprimand him or her until you know all the facts. There is something rather endearing, to know that your child was prepared to break your rules about fighting; in order to defend your honour. You can then quietly explain that what he or she did was courageous and bold, but does not make it right; even though you are proud of him/her for defending your family. Boys will always be boys; so don't bet on it that it won't happen again in the future. The 'weaker sex' mentality of men is instinctive. Every male child will feel the need to defend the females in his life; even though they may be older, bigger and tougher than him! I'm afraid that's just the way the cookie crumbles; so don't knock it too much!

8. Intoxicants

Finding out your child is taking/smoking drugs or drinking; is every parent's worst nightmare. The realisation is usually sudden; and few parents notice the signs, until it is too late. Alcohol and drugs are here to stay; so you have to understand that sooner or later, your child will experiment with one or both of them. Fortunately; statistics have shown that most children start using drugs and alcohol after they are eighteen; which is the best one can hope for. You therefore have to educate your children as early as possible, and alert them to the dangers of intoxicants; so that they have a responsible attitude to them, as they grow into adulthood. One day you will have to let your children go; especially when they go away to university. The campus is where many kids start experimenting; because it is one of the first symbols of their independence. After being 'trapped' at home all their life; it is only natural for them to enjoy themselves, without having to answer to their parents!

A. Cigarettes

The world has finally come to realise what every doctor has been saying for years; that cigarettes cause lung cancer and other smoke-related diseases. Although certain measures like; increasing the price;

putting them out of reach from children in the shops; removing the vending machines; banning smoking in public places; shock advertising and printing health warnings on the packets have been tried; they have still not stopped people smoking. The anti-smoking lobby has been pulling its hair out in desperation, trying to convince governments to ban them altogether; but to no avail. The main obvious reason why cigarettes are still ubiquitous is; because they are still one of the biggest sources of tax revenue for any government. However; this financial windfall ceases to be of any benefit, when you realise that more money has to be spent on the health service to help those afflicted by cigarette addiction. The cigarette manufacturers are clever enough to know that there is always a new generation ready to start smoking; because the youth will always try anything that they have been told, is bad for them! Coupled with the fact that, many Third World nations are smoking more than enough to make up for their 'loss' in profits from the developed countries; the cigarette companies are still laughing all the way to the bank.

This harsh reality means you have to take it upon yourself; to educate your children from an early age, about the dangers of cigarette smoking. It does not help the cause, if the parents are smoking in front of the children; because kids will always pick up on what they see around them. If you are a smoker; please try not to do it in front of the children. In school; it is very likely that through peer pressure, some kids will hide away and smoke but will not tell their parents. Since nearly all children know that smoking is bad for the health; it means they are only smoking for fun and will probably give up when the novelty runs out. Nevertheless, if you notice your children are smoking; you have to put your foot down by cutting the pocket money until you are satisfied, they will not spend it on cigarettes. Just telling a child that cigarettes can cause lung cancer does not really work; because the disease is associated with much older people, who have been smoking a long time. The threat will not register emphatically enough in a fit and healthy youngster; who believes he or she will live for ever. You should try to emphasise more on the knock-on effect of cigarettes; and what it can lead to. This means you have to find a way to link it with alcohol, drugs and sex. On the school peer pressure ladder; smoking is known to be a forerunner to alcohol. This in turn leads to drug experimentation and ultimately, to promiscuous sexual behaviour; with all its complications. The sooner your child understands the link to these potential dangers the better; so that they are not forced to find out for themselves, the hard way.

B. Alcohol

Once the child starts smoking; the next step will definitely be alcohol. This is probably a child's greatest danger; because it is legal, and is the cause of so many future problems. According to certain statistics; nearly half of all murders; 80% of all fatal car crashes; and nearly 50% of sexual infections; are caused by alcohol consumption. If you include almost all verbal insults; many work-related accidents and under-performance; teenage joyriding; rapes and wife-beating; you will realise the seriousness of alcohol. Most governments are in shameful denial, when it comes to the evils of alcohol. This is because it is, along with cigarettes, a lucrative source of tax income; which they are unwilling to forego. The cartoon of the angry, fed-up wife with the rolling pin in her hand, waiting up for the husband because he went out drinking; may seem like a joke. But it hides the awful reality of domestic abuse; which is mainly caused by alcohol. How many women have lain in bed; wondering what their men are getting up to when they go out for 'a quick pint'? How many have had to endure his drunken gropes, foul breath and shouting; as he staggers into the house looking for 'bit of nookie'? Imagine how many women have been hit by a drunken man; and then forced to acquiesce into having sex, with the threat of further violence. It doesn't bare thinking how many wives are experiencing so much mental torture whenever the husband gets drunk; that they find it easier to quietly open their legs and let him have his 'selfish way', just so that he will go to sleep and she can get some peace. The reality for many women is so painful, that society would rather not talk about it; and only the most obvious cases of domestic abuse are ever reported.

Domestic abuse is not the sole domain of the working and lower classes, but also of the professional middle-class and the rich upper-class; as explained earlier on in this book. However; because alcohol removes inhibitions, it is possible that many men are not even aware how badly they behave when they are drunk. Once they are sober, they act normally; allowing the wife to forgive his behaviour, by blaming it on the drink. As a result; nothing is done to address the issue because both man and woman may not see it as a problem. Women are not immune from alcoholism. It has been shown that many of them drink quietly at home. If she does not behave badly in public; one may never know! Go into any bar, pub or restaurant on a Friday or Saturday night; and you can see that there really is a national alcohol problem in many countries. When the bars close; youths will cause trouble on the streets, vomit/urinate on the pavements and swig cans of lager/bottles of spirits. The 'sensible' ones will head home and continue the drinking there! This makes it impossible to determine how much people really drink; thereby hiding the true statistics and allowing any government to conveniently sweep the problem under the carpet. Nothing I say; can change the mindset of someone over eighteen years of age, who enjoys drinking and does not think he/she has a problem. I cannot force a wife to come forward and seek help against an abusive or violent husband; because alcohol, like everything else in life, is a matter of choice. Knowing one's limit is the key to enjoying it; as opposed to abusing it!

Since every woman knows the evils of alcohol; it is imperative that you teach your children what it can do to a person, when it is abused. Most alcoholics began drinking from an early age; which should set the alarm bells ringing for any mother, if she finds out her children have started drinking. Alcohol is everywhere, with even the supermarkets selling it; which means, one can drink all day if one wanted to! There is a proven link between alcohol, drug taking and the loss of inhibitions. This in turn, leads to easy sex; unwanted pregnancy; and sexually transmitted diseases, which are harder to detect in females than with the males. Try not to allow your children to stay out late with friends; because the scope for getting into trouble is much greater, than during the day. Whilst walking around the streets in a group; they can have access to alcohol by asking older friends or relatives to go into a liquor store to buy the drink for them. They will then put the alcohol into soft drink bottles and sit in parks or abandoned building sites, getting drunk; before looking for trouble to cause. Criminal behaviour in youths starts with getting drunk; losing their inhibitions and then daring each other to do the most outrageous things. This can easily lead to starting unnecessary fights; deliberate damage to public property; muggings; shoplifting; breaking into cars and joyriding.

Teen-parties are also places where kids get drunk. Even if there is no alcohol on view; there will be those who will sneak some into the party, resulting in boisterous and indecent behaviour. Most times, this goes 'unnoticed' by the adults present; because they want to appear 'cool' in front of the kids, and not be party-poopers.

A child will most likely start drinking, as a result of peer pressure in school; after having tried cigarettes, without the parents knowing. It can therefore be a shock when you find out. You will have to take a sharper interest in your children; from around the age of twelve. You may even have to search through their bedrooms, when they are out; for hidden bottles of alcohol! You can also smell their breaths when they come home, or smell their clothes for alcohol spillage when they put them out for the wash; until you are certain they have not fallen into the alcoholic trap. Once you find out they have been drinking; the next step is to enforce your own brand of discipline. This could include withholding the pocket money and finding out who their friends are. You can then inform the parents; and together, you can nip the problem in the bud before it gets out of hand. From then on, you have to make him or her aware that you will be keeping an eye on them; so that they don't have any time or place to drink, without your finding out. They will probably eat a lot of chewing gum; which should be a sign that they are trying to hide the smell! Be aware that it will be a constant battle, as they grow older; because the chances are, they will eventually drink when they are legally out of your control. As with cigarettes; children are not interested in hearing what is bad for their health and it will most likely make them want to try it out. It would therefore be better; if you can drum into them, the evils of drinking. Emphasis has to be lain on the loss of behavioural control and the harm one can do to other people, when one is drunk; especially those closest to him/her. They have to thoroughly understand the possibilities of criminal charges and imprisonment because of bad behaviour. There are available pamphlets in all police stations and several Internet sites; which can further explain the alcohol problem to you. If you have time; take your children to the nearest women's shelter and let them see for themselves, the horrendous physical and mental pain women have endured, because of alcohol and drugs. This will hit home and paint a realistically harsh picture of what you have been telling them about loss of inhibitions and control. This may not stop them drinking; but it will make them aware of the consequences. At the very least; it will make sure that if they do drink, they will do so responsibly and show a lot more respect and consideration for the female.

C. Illegal drugs

Just as alcohol makes a lot of tax money for a government; illicit drugs make no money for the country and as a result, are vilified much more than alcohol. Drug money is probably the most lucrative source of income for criminals; and a means of finance through laundering, of many legitimate businesses. People are more willing to blame drugs for the scourges of violence in a society; because, compared to alcohol, there are fewer drug-takers than alcohol imbibers. It is therefore more convenient to blame someone else's poison for the ills in our society. To malign one and celebrate the other; only goes to show just how hypocritical politicians, sections of the media and society can be. Alcohol and drugs are both bad for you; and cause a lot of different, but nonetheless serious, problems for women. It is therefore, difficult to say which of the two poisons is the more dangerous. Millions of people are taking drugs every weekend, with comparatively very few deaths; and when someone does die of a drug overdose, it is usually highlighted in the press. There are far more deaths due to dangerous driving caused by the consumption of alcohol and far more women being beaten up or raped because of alcohol; which, comparatively very little is written about. It is extremely difficult to stop the drug business; because almost all drugs originate from plants grown in Third World countries. Their silent economies depend greatly on the hard currency they earn from turning these plants into narcotics; which are greedily consumed by the developed countries. A kilo of cocaine in Europe or the United States retails for at least US$40 000; which could set up a family for life in a poor Third World country! It is no wonder that many are prepared to risk jail by bringing the drugs over to a developed country. Until the world economic situation improves, where there is a fairer distribution of wealth amongst the Third World countries; the drug business will remain the easiest/only option of earning some hard currency for their impoverished majority. In the developed world; one must assume it is too late to save this generation from consuming drugs. We therefore have to look to the future; by educating our children in a sensible way.

There are different types of illegal drugs; each having different effects on different people. Heroin, Cocaine, Marijuana, Hash, Speed, LSD and Ecstasy are the main drugs on the market; and they all have their problems. I will highlight them and you can decide for yourself, which drug you feel is the most dangerous to your children; and try to prevent them from using it. Sooner or later, your kids will be in contact with drugs; and once they leave home, there is not much you can do to stop them. The more unbiased information they have about the different intoxicants, the better. It is therefore important; you also understand that most people who take drugs actually enjoy it. They make the user feel 'good'! It is almost impossible to stop someone taking any intoxicant that, for a few hours, makes him or her feel better and more exuberant than they normally do; and helps them escape from the daily drudgery of their lives. Because drugs are illegal; those who consume them will most likely deny it, or do it in secret. This means; you have to keep your eyes open to make sure your children under the age of eighteen are not doing it. Once they are adults and outside your control; they have to understand the consequences of drug-taking because society tends to turn against those who are in any way involved in the drug business. The drug user could easily lose his/her job; go broke; be ripped off their money; be blamed for anything that goes wrong in their lives; alienate well-intentioned friends and family members; end up in prison; be a victim of gangland violence and eventually ruin their health and die; which one could argue, is really nobody's business, except their own. Unfortunately, once any of those consequences start affecting their nearest and dearest; it becomes a big household, and by default, national problem. Since your family and quite possibly your country are part of your self-defence; you have to be concerned when any of your children are on drugs. Please pay attention to what your kids are up to; so that you can nip it in the bud before it is too late. If even one person is abusing intoxicants; it will affect the output of the company he works for, through lateness; laziness; negligence; bad judgement and illness. With enough people consuming drugs or alcohol; the economy of the whole country will eventually be affected. Add the cost and effect those seeking treatment will have on the health service; and you can understand better why drug consumption can be a worry for any government. Like pollution and the environment; you have to be aware because anything that ruins your country will not leave a nice place for your children to grow up in.

(1) Heroin

Heroin is generally regarded as the most harmful drug; because it is physically addictive. Once a user is hooked; it is very difficult to come off it. It is usually smoked in cigarettes or on silver foil at first; and then injected, as the user becomes more addicted. It makes the user feel calm and peaceful, as if he or she is on a nice hovercraft ride; so it cannot be described as a 'high', but rather a 'happy lull'. In the beginning there might be some vomiting, as the body struggles to get used to this alien poison; but because the user will go into the toilet to do it, the family or friends may not even notice what he/she has done. It lasts for a few hours; whereby the user will behave normally and appear in a good mood. As it begins to wear off; he/she will become irritable, edgy and impatient. He/She will most probably smoke some more to achieve the 'wonderful lull' of the previous few hours. As soon as he/she runs out; they will have to go out to look for more. So long as it is obtainable; there will be no obvious behavioural signs that they are on drugs because they will carry on as normal. The problem arises when he or she runs out, and cannot afford to buy some more; because the body will always crave more. The user will most likely get the 'shakes'; commonly known as 'cold turkey'. This is where the body will be physically ill; and it is at this point that the family will realise something is wrong. The user will try to brave it out and deny he/she is using drugs; but will nevertheless ask to borrow some money, without saying what it is for. Refuse to give him/her the money; and they will start stealing from you. As a woman; it can be a horrible experience, when you realise your teenager is on heroin. Your love for the child is so unconditional; you might find yourself burying your head in the sand by denying to yourself that there is a problem. You could even begin financing his/her habit; instead of seeking help for him/her.

If you feel your child is behaving sluggishly, slurring his words, eyes half-closed and has lost his or her appetite; you should search his/her room and look for a syringe or traces of silver kitchen foil with black track lines on them. On finding them; the next step is to confront the teen. Be prepared for his/her vehement denials; so you may have to take drastic steps and seek help from the professionals. Since there is no feasible law to force a child to join any treatment program to wean him/her off drugs; there may be severe resistance. There is a substitute called *Methadone*, which is normally used to wean addicts off heroin; but unless the user is determined to break the habit, this form of treatment will not work. Besides; it tastes horrible, there is no 'happy lull' involved and the user will most likely go back to the real stuff. This is the reason why the best treatment is not only the harshest, but also the most expensive. It involves locking the addict away in a secure environment for several months; and letting the professionals handle him or her, in their own tough, uncompromising way. Heroin addiction is the hardest to break; and unlike other drugs, it only takes one snort or smoke for the user to be hooked. It might be a good idea to take your teenagers to a treatment centre, and let them see for themselves, the horrible effect it can have on a person; so that they never want to try it.

(2) Cocaine

The cocaine high is extremely quick; but does not last very long, before the user will be craving for another snort. At anywhere between 50-100 dollars a gram; it is potentially the most expensive. It is the 'glamour drug', which used to be very popular amongst the well-off; but with so much of it around, has filtered down to the working class and students. Due to its expense; it has become the cause of many forms of crime by those looking for money for their next 'hit'. The reason it is so popular is because it really does make the user feel 'fantastic', talkative and confident; making him/her the life and soul of a party. That is why it is usually taken at weekends; by partygoers out for a good time. It also enhances sexual desire; by making the body extremely sensitive to touch and allows the male to maintain an erection for far longer than he normally does. Many guys use it as a reliable 'foreplay'; because it can make a girl horny and easier to get into bed. The female orgasm is much more intense after she has had a few lines of cocaine! Because of this; a female hooked on cocaine will most likely have a dealer as a boyfriend, in order to get her poison for free. When used 'sensibly', (a few lines at weekends) it does not cause any long term damage to the user; so long as he/she manages to maintain a healthy lifestyle. This means he/she must exercise, eat and sleep properly during the week; in preparation for the weekend binge!

Because of its highly addictive nature; it is very difficult to pay constant attention to one's health, whilst indulging in cocaine and almost impossible to just have 'a few lines at weekends'. Unlike heroin; this addictiveness is more mental than physical and allows the user to crave it, but with a little willpower, can overcome this craving. Sadly; there are not many people with strong enough willpower and therein lies the greatest problem of cocaine. It makes the users so confident that they may start using it every day, instead of weekends; and still manage to go to work. They are then able to convince themselves that everything is okay; and they don't have a 'problem'. It can cause weight loss because it banishes hunger; depriving the body of its daily nutrients. This means; it can easily kill the user, when the body becomes too weak due to the lack of food. It also prevents him/her from sleeping; and can cause paranoia when he/she has not had enough sleep. This in turn; can make him/her behave in dangerously erratic and violent ways. Horrendous assaults can be committed; if the cocaine user feels that everyone is 'out to get him/her'. He/She could easily decide to attack those nearest and dearest to him/her. Because of its popularity; the sellers make huge profits by mixing it with all kinds of substances. Since few people really know what good stuff is; they will always be in grave danger of putting their health at risk. It is very rare to find pure cocaine; unless you live in one of the producer countries, or are friends with an importer!

Because of its glamour and omnipresence; cocaine is probably the most likely drug danger to your children. Once they have left home; the chances are, they will try it. Your only hope is to educate them, as soon as they reach their teens; so that they are aware of what they are getting into. Cocaine has bankrupted and ruined many a life! It makes the user over-generous and enables him/her to be ripped off by friends; because rash business decisions are easily made, when one is 'high' and over-confident. It can also make the user drink heavily; because the alcohol prevents him/her from getting too 'high' and creates a different kind of 'buzz'. Loss of appetite; heavy drinking; lack of sleep; irrational behaviour; violence and sexual deviancy; it is no wonder that cocaine has been the cause of many marital and family break-ups! Your child is unlikely to leave any clues in the bedroom about cocaine use; but if you see silver kitchen foil, ammonia or bicarbonate of soda in his bedroom, then he is probably smoking it in its purest form. (The powder is 'cooked' in the ammonia or bicarbonate of soda to clean it of all impurities. The resultant 'rock' is then smoked on silver foil or glass paraphernalia). This method is known as 'freebasing' or 'smoking crack'; which is more addictive and as a result, more expensive than in powder form. It is unlikely your child will be hooked on cocaine before the age of 18; but after that, who knows? It is a dilemma, I would not wish on any mother. The only thing you can do is seek professional help and hope your child acquiesces.

(3) Marijuana/Hashish

Marijuana (Cannabis) is the most popular drug on the market; because it is the easiest one to buy. Many policemen turn a blind eye when they see someone walking down the street, smoking a joint in cigarette form. It comes from the hemp plant and is not seen by those smoking it as harmful; but rather, 'medicinal' because it is also used in the treatment of certain eye problems like glaucoma. Repeated use may lead to psychological dependency; but some governments have realised that it is probably safer than other drugs. Although it is still illegal; the punishment for possession is not as severe as with the harder drugs. Many Third World countries grow it and it is smoked there, without causing any problems; but rather produces euphoria and relaxation. However; marijuana tends to make the user lazy and dulls the brain. If you have an important job to do, exams to take or a sports game to play; you will lose your edge. It is not expensive; so the user is not going to commit a crime to fund his habit; go bankrupt; crash his car or beat up his wife; as with the case of heroin, cocaine and alcohol. Nevertheless; if you notice your kids are smoking marijuana, you have to remind them of the effect it will have on their studies and the possibility of moving onto something stronger.

Having tried marijuana; it is very likely the user will progress to hashish, which is also cheap and easily available. Hashish comes from the purified resinous extract from the dried leaves of the female hemp plant. It is a hard dark brown lump that needs to be softened up with the flame of a lighter, in order to break off a small piece. It is then crumbled into smaller pieces and mixed with tobacco, before smoking it in cigarette form. It is stronger than marijuana; so smoking too much of it can cause psychosis and hallucinations. Like marijuana; it is also not regarded by governments as too dangerous; but is also illegal. As a result; great profits are still being made by the drug dealers from selling hashish and marijuana. Students should try to avoid hashish, because it can make them lethargic and lose concentration on their studies; resulting in lower grades in school. Because it does no immediate damage to the body; there is a likelihood of smoking too much and getting bored. This may allow the user to think about trying harder drugs. This is the main reason why governments are reluctant to legalise hashish or marijuana; simply because there is evidence that many of those who are now hooked on hard drugs, started with marijuana and hashish.

(4) Amphetamines & hallucinogens

'Speed' is a slang word for Amphetamines. This is a synthetic colourless liquid that stimulates the nervous system; and is usually taken in tablet form. It can have unpleasant or dangerous side effects; like irrational behaviour, paranoia and strong dependency. It gives the user a rush; making things seem to move faster and creates an 'out-of-this-world high'. The 'high' does not last long; so the user is likely to take several tablets in the course of an evening. It cuts the appetite and disturbs the user's sleep pattern; allowing him/her to easily go more than twenty-four hours without sleep. It used to be illegally given to horses to make them run faster! You can now understand that it can raise the energy levels in a user; allowing him/her to talk, dance or engage in sex for hours, without rest. As a parent; you have to be concerned because having uncontrolled marathon sex is conducive to all kinds of venereal diseases. The user will be so 'out of it'; he or she may not care about contraception or be aware how many sexual partners they have. This can easily end up in a rape or an orgy! Amphetamines are considerably cheaper than cocaine; and therefore, more likely to be tried by teenagers before they graduate to cocaine or heroin.

Also taken in tablet form; LSD (lysergic acid diethylamide; sometimes simply called 'acid') and Ecstasy are known as hallucinogenic drugs and are popular with teenagers. They are powerful drugs that act as a stimulant and can produce hallucinations. LSD has been around for a long time. Many of today's grand-parents tried it in their youth; and it supposedly did no great damage to them. It can be dangerous because the user can literally 'lose the mind' and imagine all kinds of things, from monsters and weird colour changes to out of body experiences; from which they may never fully recover. Used 'sensibly', (once in a while in small doses) it can expand the mind; allowing the creative user to add different dimensions to his/her creations. Some of our most popular songs, paintings and inventions from the Sixties and early Seventies; were created when the authors were supposedly 'high' on LSD. Although it has lost some of its appeal; there are still those (mostly discerning university students) who like to experiment by going on LSD 'trips'; to 'expand' their minds.

Ecstasy is more popular than LSD, amongst the youth of today; and is ubiquitous in almost every nightclub or party. It dehydrates the body; which means you have to drink a lot of water, just to negate the effects. It can be dangerous because it is most 'enjoyable' when dancing. Since dancing also dehydrates the body; you can very quickly run out of fluids and damage your heart, liver, kidneys and stomach. It creates a 'rush' of adrenalin, raises the blood pressure and speeds up the heart. It gives the user a nice 'buzz'; which means, he/she may not realise the damage it is doing to the body…and death can easily occur. It is usually taken in nightclubs or dance raves; accompanied by loud (minimum 140 beats per minute) dance music. It is also a stimulus; making it popular for sex. The users can 'go for hours'; thereby creating the same kinds of sexual dangers as amphetamines. Once a user gets used to marathon sex; he/she will want to use it every time for lovemaking. This creates a dependency; whereby any sex without the drug, is not interesting enough to bother with.

There are other drugs of course; including legal ones like painkillers; anti-depressants; sleeping tablets; and cough medicine; which can all produce a 'buzz' when taken outside a doctor's control or above the recommended dosage. The increasingly popular 'herbal highs', sold legally in head shops in many countries; could also be dangerous because no one knows exactly what they do. They have exciting names like BZP (Benzylpiperazine); GBL; Spice; Blow; Magic; Kettamine and Meow Meow; which is enough to entice some youngsters to try them, even though there have been several cases of chest pains, seizures and fatalities! Mephedrone is probably the most famous one; because it caused the death of several people, which was highlighted in the media. Although it has now been banned in several countries; it can still be obtained 'under the counter' and on the Internet. Some have labels on them that say *'not for human consumption'*; so that if someone takes them and something goes wrong, the manufacturers can cover themselves from legal troubles. They are unregulated, with new ones springing up all the time; so it is advisable to stay well away from them. Kids have been known to get 'high' by sniffing all sorts of products like: glue; varnish; paint; petrol; and rotting food; without caring about the damage they could be doing to their health! Even nitrous oxide (laughing gas), used by dentists as an anaesthetic; can produce exhilaration and is the drug of choice by some adventurous teenagers. This just goes to show that if a child wants to get 'out of his head'; there is not much anyone can do about it. It is therefore important that kids have all the facts about whatever they decide to imbibe.

This book is not really a drug manual. There are available pamphlets in all police stations and several Internet sites; which can explain the drug problem to you in more detail, and show you where you can get help in your area. I have only highlighted the most popular; which are the ones your children are most likely to be in contact with. Since everybody is different; it is not my place to say what drugs will or won't do to your child...but only what they could do. There are people who have died from taking drugs; but there are also those who have taken them for years, without any serious problems. This is because they use drugs; as opposed to abusing them! If you have enough discipline to eat very well; exercise regularly; sleep soundly and then indulge a little at weekends; you are unlikely to experience any long-lasting problems. However; if you are not eating healthily; do not exercise or sleep properly; and are smoking or snorting dirty substances (which could have been mixed with anything from crushed aspirin to sugar, salt and rat poison for the powders; and tea leaves, spices, grass or mud for marijuana and hashish); then one line or a few puffs could kill you...especially if you are mixing the drugs. Alcohol, marijuana, hashish and heroin are known as 'downers'; whilst cocaine/speed/ecstasy are all 'uppers'. If you mix any 'downer' with an 'upper'; your heart will struggle between slowing down and speeding up and will be damaged. Too many uppers; might speed up the heart so much, it might cause problems for other organs in the body…and you will die! Mixing two downers like heroin and hashish; might slow down the heart so much, it could stop beating altogether. There is also the high risk of sharing contaminated needles with other users and contracting HIV (Human Immuno-deficiency Virus); which could easily develop into full-blown AIDS (Acquired Immune Deficiency Syndrome). All drugs have the effect of the body getting used to them; which means, you will need more and more in order to achieve the same 'buzz'. This will not do your body or bank balance any favours! They also have the tendency to gradually become the most important thing in a person's life; to the detriment of other necessities like: exercising; washing the body; eating properly; sleeping soundly; paying bills; looking after the family; or fulfilling emotional, sexual and conversational duties with his/her partner. This neglect of one's basic priorities and responsibilities; has culminated in the break-up of many a family, marriage and relationship and is the best reason of all to emphasise that drugs are not good!

Substance abuse is more harmful to children; because their bodies have not yet fully developed. It can easily harm their heart, kidneys, liver and other less obvious internal parts of the body, like the vocal chords and nasal passage; thereby creating complications, later on in life. Therein lies the greatest threat of taking drugs or alcohol. You don't know what they will do to your body; or how long it will take to harm or even kill you! Common sense should therefore tell you; it would be better if you did not take any drugs or alcohol at all. However; life would be very boring and you could become a social outcast, if you refused to mix with people because they drank or took drugs! This means that sooner or later, your children will be in contact with drugs and might choose to dabble; simply because everyone else is doing it. Hanging around the streets; children can easily sniff glue to get 'high'; get drunk on alcohol; or run into contact with drug dealers; who will either sell the drugs directly to them or use them to sell and transport the drugs, for a fee. When a child, used to the paltry pocket-money given by the parents, is suddenly able to double his weekly amount in a day; he/she will not be hard to convince into drug activities. It is therefore up to the parents to teach them at the beginning of their teens, the dangers of drugs; most of which I have tried to highlight, by not leaning too much, one way or the other. There is still some drug-hysteria in the media, fuelled by the anti-drug lobby; which, although well-intentioned, usually backfires. This is because children are naturally suspicious of any doom and gloom aimed at them; and will most likely do the opposite of what the adults say. Many will decide to take drugs; just to see what all the fuss is about! Teenagers are not as stupid as many adults think; and hate being patronised. They are aware that a government's anti-drug stance; could be more to do with the fact that it is not making any tax money from the drug trade than any genuine concern for the health of the populace!

Because drugs are not legal; there is no legislation, safety or control. This makes it very dangerous to dabble or be around people who deal in them. Rip-offs are widespread. Since one cannot go to the cops; jungle justice is always used in resolving conflicts. This has resulted in many murders and unsolved crimes. People are usually killed because they owe money, are giving information to the police or are selling the drugs in someone else's 'territory'. The awful stuff most of the drugs are mixed with, in order to create extra profit; is probably responsible for almost all of the drug deaths. Everyone knows drugs are illegal and could send you to prison for a long time; yet people are still doing it. This just goes to show that the problem is much more serious than we realise; and government policies are obviously not working. There is a strong argument for legalising drugs and putting them under strict government control, thereby taking the business out of the hands of criminals; which would drastically lower the crime rate and fill the tax coffers. However; no government would like to be the first to do so. This is because it would be admitting it has failed, and that drugs are okay for public consumption; which would be highly irresponsible. Considering the damage already caused by alcohol consumption; making drugs legal would probably create uncontrollable mayhem. As things stand; can they really get any worse? Don't blame the politicians for dilly-dallying on the drug problem; because to all effects and purposes, they really do not know what to do about it!

9. Sex, pregnancy, abortions, diseases and homosexuality

(a) Sex

Artificial insemination aside; we are all in this world as a result of sexual intercourse between a male and a female. As natural as breathing, the sex act is unavoidable; and even children as young as ten years old, have been known to be sexually active with members of the opposite (and sometimes the same) sex. To a mother; it could mean sleepless nights of worry, when her children reach the age where they start taking an interest in the opposite sex. Many parents are reluctant to discuss the facts of life with their children; preferring to leave it to the school. Because the students are taught in a group; this can never be fulfilling enough. Every child is different; therefore, his or her individual needs and family circumstances have to be taken into consideration, when it comes to discussing such 'delicate' issues. Also; the way it is taught in most schools, does not take into account the 'sensational feeling' factor. Sex is such a powerful emotion that no amount of lectures and warnings against pregnancy and diseases; will be enough to prevent a boy and a girl in the heat of passion, from going all the way. It really is the responsibility of the parents; to explain the facts of life and what having sex will mean to the family. If your child is having sex; it affects two families. At some point; you will have to bite the bullet and discuss the 'problem', together with the other family involved. You have to be prepared for what to do in the worst-case scenarios of pregnancy, abortion, diseases or possible elopement; if you try to drive the youthful couple apart.

You have to assume you cannot stop children having sex, once they are eighteen; and in some cases, before that age. You therefore have to make sure they have all the information necessary; as regards to pregnancy, abortion, diseases and the expense/responsibility of raising a child. Telling two teenagers in love they cannot see each other; will only drive them closer together and the chances of their engaging in sexual intercourse will increase. Some schools have even started handing out condoms to the students; which might seem from the outside, as condoning sex. Sadly; there really is no other alternative, because explicit and subtle sex is everywhere: in films; on television; in magazines; and with almost every advertising campaign. Trying to convince kids they should not do it; is an impossible ideal! You have to get off any moralistic high horse you may be sitting on; and come down to the level of your children. By discussing sex with them, more as a friend than a parent; you will be able to see exactly where their minds are at. You have to remember that you were once young too; and discussing sex is not the easiest subject to tackle. Many adults, let alone children; are very shy when it comes to this 'taboo' subject! You have to find a way to broach the subject of sex; so that they feel comfortable in discussing things with you. This must be done, even before they get close to the opposite sex; so that when they do, it will seem more like a natural progression than a sudden invasion. You will then be able to sleep better at night; safe in the knowledge that your child will not do something stupid.

(b) Pregnancy

One of the worst nightmares a mother can have; is the one of her teenage daughter getting (or her teenage son making a girl) pregnant. Unfortunately; this continues to be a reality for many women. Pregnancy can ruin the future for both the boy and girl involved, and must be taken seriously by the parents; because inevitably, they will be dragged into the mire. As the mother; you will be blamed by some of your friends and neighbours for not looking after your child. If he or she is still in school; you will more than likely be the principal carer of the baby. No woman really wants to go through or recommend an abortion; which means, the sensible thing would be not to let your child get into such a position. Contraception would seem to be the logical answer against pregnancy. But from the male and female condoms to foams, the coil and the pill; there is no reliable contraceptive that is one hundred percent full-proof. Giving long lectures about pregnancy to teenagers will not stop them from having sex. All kids believe they have all the answers; and so long as he wears a condom, there is *"no way she can get pregnant!"* Most of the time; it will be the boy, who in the throes of passion, will tell the girl anything to get her to cross the line and sleep with him. Teenage boys are notorious for using psychological blackmail to get a girl to sleep with them; and will openly flirt or even sleep with other girls, in order to make the girlfriend jealous. At that age; it is most probably only the girl's first or second boyfriend and she will not be aware of the tactics he is deviously using on her. More than likely; she will do anything to please him, so that she doesn't lose him.

If she does get pregnant; the chances are the boy will deny it and call her all kinds of names, like *"slag"* or *"whore"*. This is mainly to hide the fact that he is too scared to face up to the enormity of their actions. The poor girl will then have to face the anguish on her own. She may be too scared to tell her parents; until they notice a change in her behaviour or in the shape of her body. By then; it will probably be legally too late for a termination. She will be in serious trouble; because she will be forced to tell her parents and name the father. After severe interrogation from his own parents; the boy will finally admit he did sleep with her, but might still try to wriggle out of it, by saying that *"maybe she slept with someone else, as well as me…"* Eventually; the dust will settle and the air will clear...but the facts will remain. She is pregnant and she will be a teenage mum! As delightful as a baby can be; it is still hard work rearing him or her, not to talk of the added expense to the family. Is your daughter prepared to leave school and raise the baby? Can she afford to feed and clothe him or her? Is the father of the child ready to help; knowing that it is the end of his teenage years, as he knows them? Psychologically; she is still a child herself. Will she be able to cope with the persistent demands from the baby; with the crying, nappy changing and sleepless nights? There will be tremendous obligation on her to do the right thing and look after the child, at the expense of her own social life; and she might end up resenting her predicament, or even hating the baby. There are many other problems of course; but I believe I have made the point crystal clear that a teenage pregnancy in any family is not an easy burden to bear. You have to defend yourself against it as much as you can!

All aspects of sex should be discussed with your teenage children; so that they know exactly what getting or making a girl pregnant entails. Without using scare-mongering tactics; you should pick the right time to start the talks, a little bit at a time, so that they are not scared to talk to you about anything they may face, feel or fear. If you have an inkling that he or she might still go ahead and have sex; then you will have to take him/her to a doctor to advise on the best contraceptive to use…even if you have to buy it for them! It would also do no harm to let the girl keep condoms in her bag; because boys are notorious at 'forgetting' to use them. You cannot keep an eye on them twenty-four hours a day; because the chances are, they will sooner or later, engage in sex. There is no need to make things worse; by adding pregnancy to the mix! Once they reach 18; they will probably be outside your control. It would be better if they go into adulthood; knowing all there is to know about pregnancy and its implications. At least you will have done your best; and as a mother, that is all you can do. With pregnancy; all you can really do is hope and pray!

(c) Abortion

When a young girl gets pregnant unexpectedly; she may not want anyone finding out and will try to hide it. She may then think very seriously about having an abortion; but not knowing how to go about it, she may ask her close friends for advice. Getting excessively drunk and vomiting; strenuous exercising; overdosing sleeping pills or cough medicine; are all dangerous ways the girl may try to induce a miscarriage. When that fails, she will inform the boy that she is pregnant; and he, being as scared as she is, will suggest an abortion. Fortunately; the days of the backstreet abortionist are all but gone because there are now strict laws governing pregnancy terminations. This means; she will have to find a doctor to do it for her. Because of her age; no member of the medical profession will do it, without informing the parents and suggesting a series of counselling, to make sure she is making the right decision. Eventually; the parents will realise something is wrong, by her moody behaviour and change in physical appearance. She will then have to come clean with her problem.

It is at this stage that the couple involved and both sets of parents will face a severe moral dilemma. The child couple may want an abortion; but the parents, who are from a different generation, may refuse to grant permission. This is because they may see abortion as the murder of an unborn child. The girl may insist that it is her body; so no one has a right to tell her what she can or cannot do with it. The boy, who most likely thought sex was just having a bit of fun; will realise the enormity of what he has done. He may see his future slipping away and will insist on 'getting rid of it'. On the other hand; the girl may insist on 'keeping it' and the parents will want her to 'get rid of it'…because they don't think the boy is the 'right material' for their daughter! They might believe he will undermine their carefully laid future plans for their girl; and a baby will get in the way, by tying the two families together. In the final analysis; you have to realise that there are two frightened teenagers involved and their interests must take prominence over parental squabbling. One must also consider; what an abortion would do to the health of the girl. There have been cases of young girls not being able to have any more children, after having a termination.

Whichever way you look at it; there are no easy answers to abortion. Even if practically, it is the best way to go; there will always be the religious issue and a moral dilemma. The abortion debate has brought down governments; split families; divided the male and female sexes; and triggered violence against some clinics suspected of performing terminations. It is therefore a question this book cannot answer; because I do not have the moral or legal right to choose for you. The only way you can decide what is right or wrong; is to seek advice from your spiritual and religious leaders; examine your present circumstances; weigh up the future implications; dig deep into your conscience and then do only what is best for you. Just remember that; you will have to live for the rest of your life with your decision!

(d) Diseases

There are quite a few sexually-transmitted infections/diseases or venereal diseases, commonly known as, STI, STD or 'VD'; which your children could easily catch, as a result of having sexual relations with other students. Thankfully; a cure has now been found for all of them except AIDS, which has attracted tremendous global awareness. The most common are probably vaginitis (whitish yellowish discharge from the vagina), gonorrhoea (horrible mucus discharge from the penis or vagina) and genital herpes (painful watery blisters); although syphilis (painful chancres/ulcers) has made a recent re-appearance. Finding out one has caught an STI can be so embarrassing for a teenager, that he/she may not say anything; until it becomes too painful to ignore. He/She might then try self-diagnosis and cure. They will probably confide in friends, each of whom with a different 'idea' on how to cure it; and the parents will be the last to know. As with sex and pregnancy; you must keep the lines of communication open with your children so that they are not scared or shy to discuss anything with you. It is important that you do not get angry or hysterical, when your child comes to you with his/her 'problem'; because they will not trust you with their future problems. Catching a venereal disease is not the end of the world; so be practical and ask your child where he/she believes they got it from. You should then take him/her to a doctor; who will advise you on what to do. All sexually transmitted diseases are cured by a course of treatment; as opposed to a one-off cure. It would be better if both sexual partners were cured together; but it is not always easy to know exactly when the infection was contracted. This means your child will have to abstain from sex and endure continuous check-ups; until the doctor is certain he or she is completely cured.

The main problem with finding out your child has caught a venereal disease; will be informing the parents of his/her sexual partners. You will not be in for an easy ride! They may get angry; deny their 'angel' would ever get involved in sexual activities; and insist your child obviously got his/her disease elsewhere. The stubborn denial of unpalatable truths; is very common with parents, who are too busy to take an interest in what their children get up to. The only thing you can do, if they won't listen to reason; is to stop your child from seeing the sexual partner involved. Sooner or later; the parents will realise their 'angel' has an STD because a venereal disease does not cure itself! An STD is a valuable wake-up call for any teenager; who thinks having sex is just 'a bit of fun'. Once your child is cured; you can explain to him/her that sex has to be taken seriously and respected. If they are not careful; they could easily catch a worse disease, which could complicate their future sex lives. For a girl; it may also affect her ability to bear children. After a severe dose of gonorrhoea or syphilis; I believe your child will stay clear of sex for a long while!

(e) Homosexuality

Although being gay or lesbian does not hold the same stigma as it used to; there are still many people who do not look favourably on it. School children can be very cruel with their jibes when they suspect a student behaves in any way different to everybody else. It is possible that your child may be homosexual; but will hide it from you. Gay sex is probably easier to slip under the parental radar than heterosexual sex; because it is less obvious. If a son brings a male friend home and they go up to his bedroom; most parents will not be too bothered because they will assume the children are playing computer games or talking. Likewise; if your daughter brings her female friend into her bedroom, the last thing you will think of is them engaging in lesbian sex. Whereas, if your child took someone of the opposite sex into his/her bedroom; your alarm bells would rightly be ringing. In many cases, the parents are the last to know their children are homosexual; only finding out long after they have left home, when they return to introduce their partners.

Once you find out any of your children are homosexual; there is no point in trying to change them from being 'who they really are'. The next step is to let them be aware that they will not be in for an easy ride in life; because homophobia is still rife. They will be teased, bullied and overlooked for certain jobs. There will even be people who will pretend to tolerate them; while at the same time, undermining them. Luckily, there are gay communities in every city. It would be better to mix with those going through the same ordeals that will be able to advise and steer him/her through the gay world. Although it might be a shock to the system, if your child is homosexual; there is not much you can do except love, respect and support him/her. They will obviously be going through a hard time in school and struggling with their sexuality. The last thing they need is for those whom they depend on for support; undermining them.

10. Give the youth a chance!

In many Third World countries, children who misbehave are always seriously disciplined; first by their teachers, and then again by their own parents. This is because bad behaviour is seen as a disgrace and a shame on the family name. Beating a child; is believed to be the best way to teach him/her not to repeat a wrong. A child who knows he will be whipped if he misbehaves; will quickly calm down! Rapists, paedophiles and child kidnappers caught in the act; would most probably be burnt alive, after a severe mob beating. It can be argued that this system, although deemed barbaric by the western world, is good; because it works! In the United States or Europe;

most rapists and child molesters get away with it in court. Because it is difficult to prove; there will always be someone who will try his luck! School bullies are usually given ready-made excuses by child psychologists, to cover up for their bad behaviour! Maybe the psychologists do have a point; but it also sends out the wrong message to children that they can do what they want and then blame someone else!

Discipline is very important for a child and needs to be instilled as early as possible; otherwise once he or she becomes a teenager, it might be too late to change his or her way of thinking. To allow your children to get away with certain infractions, may come back to haunt you. Doing something at home; does not mean they can get away with it elsewhere! Parents who try to be 'cool' with a laissez-faire attitude do their children no favours, in the end. They allow the kids to do what they like; without stressing that with freedom, there has to be responsibility. What they do today could affect them tomorrow! They have failed their children; if they send them out into the world with a carefree attitude, where they think they can get away with anything. A child could insult or steal money from the mother; and she will sweep it under the carpet, as if it is what kids do. Some teenagers are rude to their parents; without ever being reprimanded for it. Others could tell their mothers to *"shut up!"* or *"fuck off!"*; yet the women do nothing about it and suffer in silence. No child should be allowed to insult the woman who gave birth to him/her. It shows a blatant disrespect for femininity, which could be carried into adult life and he/she will end up insulting/abusing other women. The fact that a child is a boy or a girl will make no difference on the streets. If they insult the wrong person who is in a bad mood; they could get beaten up or even stabbed to death. In the reality of the big bad world; fights occur because of an insult...perceived, intended or otherwise. Some have been killed over stubborn arguments; and many are beaten up within an inch of their lives, over unpaid debts. Disrespect any woman; and your child could have every male in the woman's family after his/her blood.

You should never allow yourself to be blackmailed by your children. If they feel they can do what they like with you; then they might take the behavioural pattern out into an outside world, which is not so forgiving. If a child takes money from your purse and you do nothing about it, then he/she might feel it is okay to owe money. One day, you are going to have to let your kids fend for themselves, where you will not be there to bail them out. You would have failed them; if you do not make them aware, what is regarded as unacceptable practice. If a child is stabbed or beaten up on the streets; the reason is not so important because the damage would have already been done. It could easily have been for something as simple as hurling an insult or owing money. This should ultimately be the fault of the parents; because it is never okay to steal, owe money or insult people. Had the child been aware of the public behavioural codes; he might not have gone into debt, would have kept his lips buttoned and would not have been beaten up or stabbed. It is therefore imperative for your children to know the importance of the 'preventive apology'; whereby pride takes a back seat to peace. Most times; a quick apology is all that is needed to prevent someone getting angry enough to cause harm and avert a disaster!

Despite everything; one has to admit that not all children are bad. The majority of kids are in fact, very good role models! Go to any school and you will see that most of the students want to learn and pass their exams. They know cigarettes, drugs and alcohol are bad for them; and that teenage sex causes problems. They are polite and do not insult their parents; so it would not be fair to tar all kids with the same brush. As a parent; you have to take a firm interest in what your children want to do and then do your best to support/help them to achieve their goals. When they do succeed; you can proudly say that you have also succeeded! Even if you have no money; you can still use your connections to help your children up the ladder of employment. Most kids are acutely aware how hard it is to succeed in our competitive world. With the right encouragement; they will do the rest themselves! They have brilliant and innovative ideas. All they are asking for is a chance to realise their dreams, by finding a job that they love. If adolescents are doing something they love; you would be very surprised at how hard they can work and how effective they can be for a country's economy. If society continues to hinder the progress of our youth; they will take the law into their own hands and it won't be a pretty sight, because they all have ambitions they need to fulfil. Without adequate help from the adults; the youth are liable to become disillusioned and may use underhand tactics to try and succeed. For every frustrated student with a grudge against government policies; we have a potential criminal in our society! If we give the youth a chance; the world will truly be a better and safer place. However; it all starts as soon as a child is born. It really is the responsibility of the parents and teachers; for whom/what he or she eventually turns out to be.

You may have noticed that throughout this chapter, I have been unwilling to give specific advice on how to control your children. This is because every child is different; and as a parent, you should already have your own methods of disciplining or controlling your children. I do not have enough knowledge of your domestic situation, in order to change that. You will obviously be aware of some of the points I have made; and you may agree or disagree with them. However; I do believe we are in unison when I say children are precious and need to be pointed in the right direction because it is very easy for them to go wrong. I hope that my guidelines have given you a more realistic view of what could happen; so that you can adapt accordingly to your own situation, and teach your children the best and safest way to stay out of trouble. No one says it is easy being a parent! You can only do your best! Good luck anyway!

Dear Tigress; children are not the only ones who need looking after! What about your elderly relatives? Read on!

Chapter Thirteen
Senior citizens – Protect them!

With the standard of living going up in many countries; we are living longer than before and there are now many people over the age of sixty. Regrettably; you are at your most vulnerable when people think you are too old. That is when they will try and take advantage of you! In the Third World countries; respect for your elders is the first lesson taught to children and is carried throughout adulthood. Rarely is a senior citizen robbed or attacked. People rather go to them for advice and to settle arguments; because they are known to have wisdom by experience. Police crime statistics in Europe and the United States reveal that an unusually high percentage of robberies are on senior citizens or those who are physically less able to defend themselves. Some senior citizens who have tried to fight back have ended up dead from the shock; or the actual attack. This shows that not enough is being done by 'modern' societies to protect their elderly. Many of them are physically/mentally impaired and unless they have been involved in tough sports like boxing, wrestling, the martial arts, weight training or rugby for most of their lives; they will not be able to physically defend themselves. They therefore have to learn to protect themselves, with the help of friends and relatives; by using preventative measures.

Many senior citizens (over the age of sixty) lose the will to live, after experiencing a robbery on their home or an attack on their person/their long-term partners. Once the spirit is broken; it is usually the beginning of the end and sadly, death follows soon after. Although an attack or a robbery can contribute to a senior citizen's untimely demise; rarely is the attacker punished for it, because the death is not immediate. It usually happens months or even years after the event; whilst the quality of life they had before the attack, is always destroyed. Every knock on the door or noise in the night; will trigger a panic attack and flashbacks of the original robbery or assault. Assuming you have elderly close relatives who are living alone; they will be part of your self-defence. If they were attacked, robbed or murdered; it would affect you deeply, especially when you later realise that you had not been in touch with them as often as you should have. Although the easy option might be to put your elderly relatives into a nursing home; sometimes the duty of care in those places is not the best. Since you will not be there to keep an eye on their treatment; you may be doing more harm than good. It would be better to have them live nearby; so that you can check their living arrangements and suggest alterations to make sure the home is more secure against thieves, fire and home accidents. We will all become old one day; so the more we understand their way of life, the better.

1. Ageism:

In our youth obsessed society; once a woman hits 40 years of age, she is already regarded by many as 'past her sell-by date'...whilst a man of the same age, is considered as 'still being in his prime'. Even though there are many beautiful and attractive women in their forties and fifties; they are still regarded as 'too old' for employment, in all but the most menial of jobs. This means that in all probability, a woman who is over 40 will be forced to stay where she is. If she left her job; she may not be able to get another one, unless she is headhunted or starts her own business. By the time she reaches her sixties; few people will be interested in her and she might as well not exist! Whether we like it or not; there is still institutionalised discrimination against the elderly (men and women) in many countries, which is unlikely to change any time soon. This is grossly unfair, because there is really no substitute for experience; and we are losing the benefit of their wisdom. Forced retirement; bullying; lack of patience; total disregard for their feelings; and derision of their opinions; are just some of the burdens senior citizens have to carry. Even though there is a law against age discrimination in the workplace; many employers still prefer to hire younger talent. This is because they are deemed more energetic and not set in their ways; which means they are controllable and malleable. If an ageing employee refuses to leave a job when asked to step down; the employer will just make things difficult for him/her by belittling his/her achievements and making them take on demeaning tasks. The employer will then fire him/her, when they cannot do the work properly or quickly enough; by claiming he or she is 'not up to the job'. It can also be hard for senior citizens, having to endure youngsters in their twenties barking orders at them; without any sign of respect for the age gap. Most of them just go quietly when told *"...your services are no longer needed".* Like racism and sexism; people will pretend ageism does not exist and prefer to sweep it under the carpet, rather than confront the issue. It's a case of 'out of sight…out of mind'; because even those who purport to care about their ageing relatives would choose to shunt them off into nursing or retirement homes. As a result; many are not even given the chance to contribute their undeniable experience to making the world a better place.

As a female senior citizen; there is not much you can do about ageism, except report the culprits to the authorities. It can be even more depressing because the ageism could also be tinged with sexism and possibly racism. The problem is deciding which set of authorities to make the report to. Many of those who are supposed to help; might be young enough to be your children or even grandchildren and may therefore not have the empathy needed to get the job done quickly and effectively. Unless you are physically impaired; you should never give up on an injustice against your age. Since most senior citizens do not have the will or energy to fight a long legal battle; it is left to their relatives to make sure they do not have to face any injustices on their own. If you have elderly relatives; try to put yourself in their position. Many of them are too proud to ask for help; so you may have to keep asking them to share their problems with you. Even though you may be very busy; sometimes keeping the lines of communication open is enough for them to feel included in your life. If they encounter any problems; they will not feel shy about telling you and then you can give them some advice on the best way forward towards solving their grievances. Since you may also not know what to do with certain situations; you may have to find out from the Internet about solicitors, groups and organisations which cater towards helping senior citizens and they will be able to direct you. Rest assured; there are committed individuals in many of these groups and organisations who are more than willing to offer their time and advice, free of charge, to right a wrong against a senior citizen. The more reports of injustices that the authorities receive; the easier the problem will become part of the mainstream and create awareness, whereby few people will dare commit any 'atrocities' against the elderly...for fear of the consequences. Only then will the cancer of ageism be finally eradicated from modern society.

2. Robbers & Con artists:

Being old can be a very sad, lonely existence; and to make things worse, robbers and con artists know just how vulnerable the elderly are. If given the chance; they will take advantage with cunning cruelty. The thieves will usually case the house or apartment for a few days; to see who comes in and out of the place. They will quickly find out that most senior citizens live alone or with their partners; with only the occasional visitor. This means their houses will be easy to break into! These crooks are also fully aware that because they are so lonely; most senior citizens are very friendly with everybody and it is extremely easy to win over their confidence. Any house help they receive would be on a timetable basis; where at a certain time on a certain day each week, the same visitor would arrive to do the chores and then leave. Once they know the senior citizen is alone at home; the crooks will try to inveigle their way into his/her confidence with all kinds of tricks. This will most likely include; *"can I have a drink of water please"* or *"my car has just broken down; may I use your telephone?"* Sometimes they will push their way into the house as soon as the senior citizen opens the door; knocking him/her to the ground. Once inside; they will unleash untold damage on the property, if they cannot find the money they are looking for. They may even beat up the victim to within inches of his or her life; if they feel he or she is holding out and refusing to hand over the money. There have even been cases of female senior citizens being tortured and then raped! Needless to say; a lot of attacks on the elderly are from desperate junkies, high on one drug or another, looking for money for their next fix. They are therefore, in no fit state of mind to realise the atrocities they are committing; until it is too late. Regrettably; there are psychologists and apologists who are ever-ready to spout out excuses on their behalf. This has resulted in disproportionately lenient sentences dished out to criminals, for crimes against the elderly. Maybe the gun laws should be amended; so that every person over the age of sixty can keep one at home! If thieves and robbers knew that every 'defenceless' old lady/man had a gun and was permitted by law to use one; they would be a lot more careful, as to whom they pick on!

With the con artists; they are acutely aware that the elderly are not up on the latest technology and will use all kinds of tactics to dupe them of their money. From the door-door salesperson to the Internet fraudster; they will deliberately target the elderly for easy pickings. By badgering the senior citizen; they will prey on his/her fears, in order to make a sale. A simple example would be to sell expensive insurance policies, the latest mobile phones or fast-speed broadband technology to the senior citizen; by convincing him/her that they are necessary modern-day acquisitions. Other scams would be to suggest repairs to the house or garden and then over-charge for the job; which they might not even bother to do properly. If the senior citizen proves a little too stubborn; they could sneak into the garden and deliberately sabotage the drainpipes or smash a few windows. They will appear the next day; blame the damage on the youths in the area and offer to fix the problem. They could even be so devious as to knock on a senior citizen's door with a bag of dead rats and claim his/her garden is infested. They will then offer to get rid of the rodents for a 'reasonable price'! Since most senior citizens do not have the Internet at home and do not know how to do transactions on line; some utility companies are guilty of deliberately charging them more for paying their bills by post. Others will offer 'free' phone services with hidden costs. They will protect themselves in the small print; which they know the senior citizen will never be able to understand or read with his/her failing eyesight. For the senior citizens who do manage to navigate the Internet; there are many bogus charities that use stolen pictures of current tragedies, in order to ask for donations. The elderly are seen as 'soft touches' who are willing to give money for good causes! The recent earthquake in Haiti is a good example; where some of the millions of dollars given to help the country, ended up in dubious bank accounts. If you need to donate money for worthy causes; try to get advice and stick to the most well-know charities that are accountable to their reputation. There are so many scams; I could not possibly put them all into this book. The important thing to remember is that once you are a senior citizen; you should refuse any attempt by anyone to get you to part with your money. The modern world is constantly changing at a furious pace, which you may not be aware of. You cannot trust people in the way you could, a few decades ago! If something looks a little tempting; you should bounce the idea off a few of your younger relatives, neighbours or friends and they will give you a better idea how genuine it is. Everything detailed in Chapters 8 and 10; should apply even more so with the senior citizen. Please be careful!

3. Disappearance:

There have been cases of some senior citizens going missing because they could not remember their way home. Some have simply died at home and are only found weeks later, when the neighbours have alerted the police; because of the *"horrible smell coming from next door…"*. Others have been beaten up, robbed and left for dead; without anyone knowing who they are. They may end up in hospital or the morgue before the relatives can be contacted! The minute they step out of their houses; they are prone to attacks by pickpockets, muggers and opportunists. Kids with nothing better to do; will tease them and steal food from their shopping, in the name of fun. The police cannot be everywhere at once; which means it is up to every senior citizen to look after him/herself. If you are elderly and living alone; you should try and be friendly with your neighbours, so that you can keep an eye on each other. This will enable them to alert your relatives if something goes wrong; you fall ill or fail to return home from a shopping trip or walk. Private security companies paid for by everyone on the street; are useful to look out for thieves and suspicious behaviour in the area. Unfortunately; this can only be a deterrent because they do not have legal powers to arrest or detain a suspect. Although they are allowed to restrain a thief until the police arrive; they have to be careful they are not sued for using heavy-handed tactics.

4. Security:

Nowadays; all criminals have a few nasty tricks up their sleeves and may also be carrying a weapon. It would therefore be folly for a senior citizen to try and physically fight an attacker because he/she is likely to come off worse and be injured or possibly killed. Because senior citizens are very vulnerable to attacks by cowardly rapists, muggers, thieves, burglars and robbers; anybody over the age of sixty should treat self-defence as a means of survival and a way of life. This means they have to be aware of their own vulnerability; avoid trouble and not put temptation in the way of anyone. They can do this by following a set of rules, based on where and how they live; similar to ones already described in earlier chapters. Almost all attacks on the elderly could easily have been avoided; if they had obeyed certain simple common sense rules. Having a dog; secure locks on doors and windows; panic buttons and silent burglar alarms linked directly to the nearest police station; closed-circuit video cameras; caller ID features on your phone set; regular phone calls and Internet video links from friends and family to see if you are alright; will all help to keep you safe and more self-confident, if you live alone. Always leave a light on in the house when you go to bed; and the slightest suspicious sound should be reported to the police. Although it might be expensive to keep your house secure; you have to bite the bullet and do as much as you can because the alternative could mean losing all your valuables and/or your life!

If you are not confident with your security; visit the police station, ask them for safety advice and they will be happy to give it to you. This puts you on first-name basis with the cops! They are more likely to respond quickly to an attack on your property and treat you more sympathetically; if they know you personally. There are also useful neighbourhood watch schemes you can join; where someone will always make sure you and your house are safe. If there are none in your area; why not get together with other residents and form one, by asking the police for advice on how to do so? A phone watch scheme is also good; whereby for a small fee, someone will call you every night to make sure you are okay. When something is wrong; he/she will automatically inform the other numbers on your list (family members or close friends) who will be able to come quickly to your aid or call an ambulance, if they know your medical history. Phone calls to the Samaritans and other agencies will also help; if you feel lonely at night. Never allow anyone into the house for any reason, if you don't know them; even if the person says he/she *"only wants to use your bathroom"*, is trying to sell you something or asking for directions. It could be a clever ploy to see if the house is worth robbing! He may not do it himself; but will convey the information to other crooks, to rob you later. If you have someone who comes in to help with your housework; try to arrange for them to alternate the times, and if possible, the days they come and see you. Any thief watching your house will never be sure whether you are alone or not! Keep your eyes open and your security intact; and you can feel very safe at home.

5. Exercise:

Physical fitness may be reduced; but does not disappear with age. Your reflexes might slow down; but your strength is always the last to go. I cannot imagine any good martial artist ever admitting to being too old. He/She will always be dangerous! Experience allows one to best assess a situation and know how to react to it quickly; in order to preserve one's way of life. It can help afford you valuable time, to get away from your attacker; or delay an assault, until help arrives. Martial artists have been known to train and do amazing things...in their nineties! 'Kata' (physical and breathing dance-like movements, sometimes known as 'forms') is the most popular discipline amongst them. I would never suggest that an elderly citizen can fight and soundly beat someone, thirty or forty years younger; because the chances are, he/she will not be able to. Martial arts will only work for the elderly; if they have been doing it for a long time and are still active. If you are a senior citizen, and for some reason, you don't like or know much about the martial arts; you should still try to engage in regular exercise. Jogging; skipping; dancing; going for walks with the dog; a few rounds of golf; or just horsing around with the grandchildren; will all do wonders for you. A stationary bicycle or treadmill inside the house will also help keep you fit; if you don't feel like going outside. Exercise is a good tonic and helps keep you strong, flexible and agile; which in turn, allows your brain to remain sharp. Check with your doctor to advise on how much exercise your body can handle! If you are physically or mentally impaired and cannot do regular exercise; it would be best if you allowed your doctor or physiotherapist to devise a set of movements for you. If done repetitively often enough; all movement becomes exercise! This book can only generalise on the basis that you are old, but not impaired; because I have no way of knowing your physical condition. Sorry, I cannot be of more help to you.

"Dear Tigress, what do you do when faced with an impossible situation? All will be revealed in the next four chapters!"

Chapter Fourteen
The impossible situation (Part 1)
Battle of the sexes

I will now discuss self-defence against seemingly impossible situations. There was once a car sticker in the United States of America, which came out at the height of the female movement for equality. *<<Honk! If you've beaten your wife today!>>* It was meant to be a joke; but it was closer to the truth, than most women were prepared to admit. Here they were, looking for equal pay; when the very real problem of marital abuse had not been addressed, let alone solved. Financial independence had led to more abuse; because women were telling their husbands to: *"Get lost. I can do what I want now; because I have my own money!"* He would then retaliate with mental abuse, a beating or marital rape; to show her he was still the boss. This ultimately led to divorce and unhappiness on all sides. There is always an underlying battle of the sexes in any marriage. This is usually good fun and is on a give and take basis; where you concede one favour, in order to gain another. However; this battle can get nasty, whereby it becomes a battle of egos. Because the female is more patient and therefore, intuitively smarter and more cunning; she usually wins the war, if not the battle. The man can take the humiliation up to a point; until he feels his manhood is threatened. He may then react in several ways; which are ultimately designed to cause the woman maximum pain. Some will resort to violence; but the cleverer males will do something even worse, by picking up prostitutes, or having emotional affairs with other women. A purely physical affair could be forgiven (never forgotten) by most women; but once he embarks on an emotional infidelity ride, whereby he falls in love, devotes his time/sexual energy and spends his money on another woman, it will hit deep inside her soul. Hatred followed by revenge; will be uppermost in her feelings. She will then be in for a real battle; which she can only win, if she calms down, uses her head and hits him hard where it hurts most. This is usually in his pocket and reputation!

There is always a certain amount of expectancy in marriage; which, when not fulfilled, becomes the root cause of all marital problems and breeds a resentment that quite often leads to break-ups and divorce. You are expected to behave in a certain way; which may be alien to your real character. An abuser of women will not change, because a piece of paper says he must 'love and cherish her'. Likewise; a friendly, outgoing female flirt will not become a timid mouse after marriage, just to satisfy her man. Doing things to please your partner is the cause of a lot of female woes. Women are kind by nature; and although few will readily admit it, pleasing her man is usually uppermost in her list of priorities. However; she may end up becoming resentful if her love, care and affection are not reciprocated. A man expects his wife to behave in a way he likes; and if she doesn't, he will revert to nature, just to prove he is still in charge. A woman expects her husband to protect, provide and look after her emotional needs. When that is not forthcoming, she has no choice but to fend for herself; thereby creating her independence and becoming her real self…which her husband may not agree with! The tense situation will most likely cause friction between the couple; which can only be solved, either by an uneasy truce (which hardly ever lasts) or a leading of separate lives. It is much easier to walk away from a man, if you are not married and there are no children involved; otherwise, it becomes an impossible situation. When you are put into a position, whereby you are at your wits end as to what to do to liberate yourself from the war zone, because you are afraid of causing problems for yourself or others who might be hurt by your decisions and actions; that dilemma also becomes an impossible situation.

If you have any problems with your partner; you are better off talking about them, rather than letting the pain fester in your subconscious. The pain will not go away, until the problem has been solved! This means you have to be patient, assess a situation and talk about it. Only when there is a stubborn recalcitrance in your partner; should you contemplate other possibly more extreme measures, in order to ensure you come out on top. Self-defence is about making sure you win; or at the very least, walking away with your health, dignity and integrity intact. There has to be an understanding; backed by the police if necessary, that there will be no comebacks on his part! This book is not a sex manual and I cannot say I am a relationship expert; but because it is about 'self-defence for women only', I look at things purely from a female self-defence perspective. This means I have to warn you against anything that hurts; whether it is physical or mental. When your dignity, integrity, self-esteem or reputation is damaged; it may stay with you for ever. It can therefore be more destructive than physical pain; which has the benefit of healing over time. Unfortunately, there are no hard and fast rules to solving impossible situations; there are only suggestions! You therefore have to decide for yourself; if any of them would serve your best interests, by following them or not. I will give you several situations, which could lead to unacceptable behaviour by one or both of the parties in a relationship; culminating in a desire to either walk away, or in some cases, destroy one another by violence. This has in the past, led to murder or manslaughter! More than likely; anything I say will have to be 'fine-tuned' by you, in order to fit your situation and environment. No two cases are ever the same; and no two marriages or relationships are ever developed by the same history or geography!

A. THE SEX WEAPON

Impossible situations for a woman usually come about because there is a breakdown in communication with her partner. He starts behaving in a way you don't like. This then makes you behave in a way you know he will not like; in order to 'punish' him for his behaviour. This means the root problem must be fished out; before anything can be achieved. I'm sorry to say, this could be your fault; even though the chances are, you may not be aware you are doing anything wrong. For example; there is a tendency for women to believe that sex is so important to a man, that one of her greatest powers is denying him entry into her vagina or any access to her body. The combative *"Leave me alone. Don't touch me!"* is a common dictum by women, annoyed at one thing or another their partner may or may not have done. Obviously, if he has done something really bad, then you cannot be expected to 'open up', just because he feels like it; but you have to be aware that generally, men need sexual release on a more regular basis than women. To deny it to him unnecessarily, just to punish him; may backfire on you, when he decides to get his kicks elsewhere. It would be much better to tell him in a calm and smooth manner that you do not feel like having sex at that particular moment, but maybe sometime 'soon'; which could take weeks. By doing so with a friendly smile; he himself will know he has upset you. He will then have to come to terms with whatever he has done; by doing his utmost to make it up with you. Using any aggressive manner to deny a man what he believes is his conjugal right; has the effect of wounding his self-esteem and festering in his subconscious. Make no mistake; he will find a way to pay you back immediately, either by violence (hitting you or forcing you to have sex) or by tantrums (rushing out of the house to the pub or to a more compliant mistress). If he does nothing; you should never think he has forgotten. There may come a time when you are looking for sex; and your harsh refusal will come flooding back to him. He may also not to be 'in the mood'; because good sex is more mental than physical. Just as you have to be mentally ready for intercourse; the same applies to him. If he has 'problems' with you; his mental state will affect his physical performance! A man is able to ejaculate in any vagina going; whereas with the female, the conditions have to be perfect, to achieve a decent orgasm. He may roll over and fall asleep, as soon as he has ejaculated; without caring whether you are satisfied or not. This is a form of marital rape; because your dignity and reputation as a woman, has been abused. When a man has sex with a woman, and only uses her vagina as a receptacle for his penis, without any feeling of love and respect for her body and her emotions; then he is treating her like a prostitute, in all but name!

The second way a woman tries to use sex as a weapon; is by never being in the mood, even though he has done nothing wrong. He will put up with it only for a while; before he will be tempted into having an affair with one of his work colleagues, or the ever-willing girls who hang around the pubs and nightclubs. If there are genuine medical reasons why you cannot have sex; then you have to seek professional help. But if it is only because you do not 'feel like it'; then I'm afraid you are being a little selfish and his behaviour towards you will change, whereby he might lose complete interest in you. When a man has not had sex for a long time; he will become 'very horny'. This means; the levels of his sexual feelings will rise, and his skin will become much more sensitive to touch. This is a dangerous state for a man to be in; because even shaking hands or brushing against a female at work, could turn him on to the point that an affair will be just around the corner. He could one day be so aroused, that all sense of decency will go out the window and he may force you into sex; which then becomes marital rape. You therefore have to make an effort to keep him interested in you; by sometimes consenting to sex, even though you don't enjoy it as much as he does. If you use sex as a weapon for too long; you will be playing into his hands because he will use that as an excuse to openly display his newly acquired girlfriends. Mistresses are always ready to listen to the woes of a husband; because they can then do things that they know will please the man. If for example, a husband tells a mistress that his wife hates oral sex and will only have sex in the missionary position; then the mistress will make sure she does what he enjoys to perfection and have the man eating out of her hands. Is it any wonder that mistresses are treated far better than the wife?

It has to be up to you to create the right conditions, so that you can achieve regular orgasms; by 'educating' him, step by step if necessary! Your sexual life will improve greatly, by showing him what turns you on; instead of lying there night after night sexually frustrated, after he has done his husbandly duty and gone off to sleep. To add insult to injury; he might then proceed to break wind and start snoring, thinking he has done a good job! *(...the things some women have to put up with!)* You have to remember that a good and happy sex life is important to your self-esteem and reputation; because if you are not getting enough loving attention, it will put you in a bad mood. This in turn; will affect your temperament, interaction with the people in your life and ability to give the best to your work. Faking an orgasm is the worse thing to do; because it gives him a false sense of achievement. It would be better to use your renowned 'female tact' by gently suggest to him where he is going wrong, and immediately showing him a better alternative; changing positions if necessary. Since foreplay is important to many women; you have to bring it to his attention your likes and dislikes, so that he knows exactly what he has to do. Remember; the thing that turns men on most about women in sex...is the sight of her enjoying herself! It is a real ego booster for a man to see that he is doing a good job; and that is why you should never pretend you are enjoying it, if you are not. All men want to please their women in sex; but if they don't know what to do, how can they ever give her the big 'O'? If cunnilingus turns you on; you have to pinpoint to him the exact spots that bring you to the best orgasms. *"A little to the left...No not there...Up a bit...Ooohhh! Yes, just there!"* You can make it fun by giving him marks out of ten; so that he will always be striving to do a better job. You should also do your bit by brushing your teeth and taking a bath before sex; so that he can see you have made an effort. Most men will 'lick a woman's fanny' without any problem; if it is clean and smells nice. A foul smelling vagina could put him off for ever; because a horrible smell never leaves one's sub-consciousness. The problem is, he may be too polite to tell you exactly why he does not want to indulge in your favourite sex act; and this in turn, will leave you bewildered as to what you have done wrong to turn him off you. Once he sees you are hygiene conscious; he will be obliged to do the same and will make sure his penis is clean enough to deserve your attention. For any man; there is something very beautiful and sexy about a woman who is straight out of the bath/shower and he will be raring to go. Why lose such a precious opportunity?

You can then register your pleasure, by doing 'special things' for him! The quality of a man's sexual performance; is down to the woman to create the right atmosphere for him to function well. Little things like cooking his favourite dinner; being kind and supportive; taking a genuine interest in his work; lots of loving and praise, with objective instead of subjective criticism; all help to make a man happy. When a man is content; he will do anything for you. Physical and mental abuse would be what happens to other unfortunate women. A happy man means a good sex life; because when a happy man is inside you at the point of ejaculation, he will never be more yours! Some women even tell their lovers that they have not climaxed yet, even though they have; several times! This makes him work harder to give you that extra one! A man's solid erection is a precious commodity; so make the most of it while it lasts, because all women know that a flaccid penis is of no use whatsoever! Believe me; a man is very easy to tailor to your needs, so long as you do not damage his fragile ego. Once you make him feel he is sexually useless; he will 'revert to nature'. He will not see you as a partner, but as someone who is always belittling him; and all respect, love and affection for you, will slowly but surely disappear. It is a subtle process; so when you do realise what has happened, it can be quite a shock. You will never be able to pinpoint where it all went wrong! Many women will at this point, try to spruce up their relationship by buying sexy lingerie, exercising, dieting and indulging in beauty treatments etc; in an effort to win back his interest. Unfortunately; such tactics are usually desperate short-term measures and don't last. This is because by then, it may be too late; as his feelings for you may have already changed. For your own self-defence, please remember that as physically tough as your man may be; all men are fragile creatures who function best when the women they love, show how much they need, respect and appreciate them.

Using sex as a weapon could also involve; imposing your femininity on him in such a way that he is made to feel useless and that his 'balls' have been cut off. A man likes to think he should be the sole provider for his family; which nowadays, is most times not the case. Women are now making enough money to look after themselves; so they don't really need a man for financial support, in the way they used to. Every woman likes to feel loved and protected by her man; even if she is earning more than he is. For her, the money is not the issue; whereas love, support and commitment to the relationship are more important. With the man, it is all about money and looking after his family; which he feels a need to protect and sustain, because of the 'weaker sex' syndrome attached to women and children. If he has no money to look after his family; it is as if he has failed. Asking him to do something menial will seem like you are ordering him around; and his resentment of the situation will build up. Slowly but surely, the tense atmosphere will lead to arguments, sulking and possible loss of libido; making him unable to please you sexually, in the way he used to. The frustration could easily boil up and explode into marital rape, violence and affairs. This is because you will also be disappointed, and possibly angry that he is behaving so childishly; and he will be a sexual turn-off for you. Refusing or making excuses not to sleep with him; will be seen as a massive snub. Deep down; he will blame it on his inability to earn enough money to fulfil his husbandly and parental obligations. Even if you do sympathise and sleep with him; it will be very hard for you to disguise the fact that something is not quite right in the relationship. He might even see it as patronising and 'feeling sorry for him'; which does not solve the original problem and probably makes the situation worse.

If you are earning more than he is; it is not a wise move to rub it in. It will hit deep into his self-esteem and dignity; and he may end up resenting you for it. Be practical and help him get back on his feet, if he has lost his job; so that he does not feel useless. Losing a job is one thing; but the fact that he cannot do more to provide for his family, is what hurts a man most. If he is not strong-willed; he may resort to drinking, drug taking, going out and not doing his bit around the house. From then on; he will be on a slippery slope, which can only end up hurting you, when he resorts to violence, marital rape or sex outside the relationship. Instead of making sarcastic comments or showing negative facial and body reactions every time you have to give him money; why not find out what he wants to do? No man enjoys asking his wife for money and I am sure no woman likes giving her man money either! If you are married, it means you are a family; so when something is not going well, you have to fix it together. He may not have your brains, but it does not mean he is useless; because he may be good with cars or fixing things. Why not use your connections and find him something to do; even if it is only a part-time job? If however, he is a no good drunken slob who refuses to work; you may have to bring out the big stick instead of the carrot and let him know in no uncertain terms, how you feel. Get his friends to talk to him! If that fails; threaten to leave him, if he is going to carry on like that! If that does not shock him into motivating himself; then it means you may be too late to change him. You may have to be prepared to carry out your threat; by filing for separation with the intention of divorce.

I know it takes two to tango and he also has to do his bit to make you happy; but you have to use your head, because nature has shown that the female is intuitively smarter than the male! You therefore have to take it upon yourself to slowly mould a man into what you want him to be. The quicker you start doing it in your relationship the better; because most men are not conducive to change. You have to make sure it does not seem like you are bossing him about. All men are suspicious of their women trying to 'change them'; so do it in such a way that whatever you want him to do, will become 'his idea'. You can do this with suggestions, which he will at first reject; but sooner or later, he will trip himself up and then you can 'slide in' your original idea. *"Why don't we try it this way darling; it might be a bit better?"* There are many ways to let your unhappiness register with him; without having to insult or belittle him! Just like no woman likes to be told she is ugly and fat; no man likes to be ridiculed by the person he depends on for emotional support. You know your man best; so use all the ammunition in your arsenal to get him to do what you want. Play the little lost girl! Cry! Sulk! Shout! Threaten! Refuse him sex temporarily! Cook him his favourite meal and then ask him to do something he has been neglecting to do! Restrict the sexual 'perks' he has been used to; until he has done something that has pleased you! Believe it or not; using the stick and the carrot works! Once the end-result is achieved; it does not really matter how you do it! Do anything to make sure you succeed! He is part of your self-defence; and eventually you will find out exactly what works and what doesn't. If he regards himself as the man of the house; why not let him believe that? Leave the family decisions to him until he makes a bad call; and then you can be ever so nice and say, *"Darling, I know you are doing your best; but why don't I have go at deciding what's good for this house?"* You then move into the job; and if you are proved right, he will be more than happy to let you run the household. Like everything else in life; you have to prove yourself and not just assume you are better!

Always give him a little freedom; so that he does not realise you are the one pulling the strings. *"Of course, you can go for a drink with the boys after the match. Don't be too late dear; because I have a special surprise for you!"* He will be thinking of the 'special surprise', all the time whilst he is in the pub; and will rush back sooner than expected. If you are looking your sexiest and most seductive when he returns, and then give him the best sex he has had in a while; he will realise that a drink with the boys is not quite in the same league! I'm certain your 'special surprises' are guaranteed to work their magic! Just remember that a sense of humour is needed whenever you are telling him off; and always do it well after the event, when your anger has subsided. The delayed, *"Sweetheart, I know we made love last night and you were great; but I really did not like the smell of booze on your breath!"* is better than, the immediate, *"Don't come near me; you're drunk!"* That kind of aggressive tone might one day send him to a mistress! Depending on his character and mood at the time; he could even beat you up or force you to have sex, just to prove to you who the boss in the household is.

You should never ever make fun of your man in public, or in front of his friends. Even though he may laugh with you; it could become a festering wound, which might open up violently the next time the same joke is cracked in public and he is in a bad mood over something else that had happened during the day. Once is a joke; the second time, it is not so funny. Continue with your putdowns and you are inviting trouble. One fine day, he will carry the resentment with him back home and explode it in your face, for no reason at all; and it would seem as if you had done nothing wrong, and he lashed out at you. Marital abuse exists both ways. You have to be prepared for the fact that the causes to some of them could be your fault; if you are ever subjected to abuse from your partner. Wives have been known to inflict terrible mental (and physical) cruelty on their husbands. Not much is done about this, because most men would be too embarrassed to tell even their best friends; and would probably be laughed out of the police station. After years of nagging, refusing him sex, belittling his achievements, not allowing him a social life and generally destroying what's left of his manhood; the only thing he has left is his physical strength. The moment he hits or rapes her; then all hell breaks loose and he is the bully who beats up his wife!

Please don't shoot the messenger, because these things do happen; and much more often than we will ever know. If you are a woman who thinks, *"He would never dare do that to me…!"*, keep in mind that the wife is always the last person to find out her man is having an affair; and no man tells his wife he has been seeing prostitutes, who make a roaring day-time trade, especially during the lunch breaks. The fact that you think he has gone to work or dutifully stays at home at night; does not mean he is incapable of sleeping with women outside the relationship. Most violence by men is conducted behind closed doors; and is usually as a result of pent-up frustration that finally boils over, because of something minor. *"How could he do that to me…?"* The problem is, if you keep pressing the wrong buttons he can; and in many households, even the so-called respectable ones, it is still happening. For every woman you see sporting a black eye or bruises and claims she walked into a door or tripped and fell; there are thousands more who refuse to go out until the wounds have healed…so that nobody will realise what has been going on. For every man who rapes, beats up his wife or has a string of affairs; there will always be a lingering suspicion that it could have been her fault because she did not do enough to prevent the tragedy. Everyone knows marital rape and wife-beating are wrong and people will always pay lip service and 'sympathise' with the woman; but no one seems to do anything about it. This is because of the widespread acceptance that it is a private matter; there are always two sides to an argument; or there is no smoke without fire. It therefore becomes an impossible situation; so let's make sure you are not one of those tragedies! Now that I have shown you a few things that could turn your man into a marital rapist, wife beater or a lecherous rat; we can begin dealing with the impossible situations. These mostly occur in marital households; because it is a lot harder for the woman to walk away, when she is married with children and does not have the financial means to set up life elsewhere.

B. MARITAL RAPE

Every man is capable of marital rape. It only takes the slightest rebuke or ridicule to tip him over the edge! It is a slow build-up; and marital rape is just one of the consequences, when he tries to regain his masculinity and heal his wounded pride. Most men are relatively easy going, until you hit a raw nerve; which usually involves subjecting his manhood to ridicule. From then on; any time he looks at you, he will see the person who is making fun of him. It will not take much for him to lose all respect for you; have an affair, beat you up or rape you. A smart man will most likely not hit you; but affairs and marital rape are much more common. This is because the woman is unlikely to tell anyone, except maybe her closest friends. Whereas with a beating; the evidence is there for all to see and will land him in serious trouble. There are so many different forms of marital rape that some women may not even be aware it is happening to them. Once you can accept that it could happen to you; then it would be easy enough to prevent it, if you are able to spot the signs that lead up to it. It is imperative that you put your own self-preservation at the top of your list of priorities.

Chapter 5 highlights most of the mental forms of abuse you are likely to face from your man; and how to deal with them. However; when the abuse becomes so serious that physical or extreme mental force is involved, then alternative tactics will have to be used because it must not be allowed to continue. If he beats you up; refuses to give you money for the household; rapes you; or treats you like dirt; then you have only one option. Alerting the authorities, followed by divorce! That kind of behaviour will most likely continue unabated; unless it is stopped dead in its tracks. In a marital situation, where your husband does not actually beat you; but treats you badly, disrespects and rapes you…what do you do? A slap; followed by apologies, kindness and fantastic sex. Is that better than no sex at all; surrounded by abuse and insults? Tough one isn't it? If you are not on talking terms; do you still have a right to throw him off when he demands sex? Most women would refuse and throw the husband off; which is understandable. But what if he forces you into having sex, without hitting you? It is still marital rape of course; but who will believe you? What do you tell the police? You need some form of physical evidence; in order to be taken seriously. Some women would even tell you how lucky you are; because their men can hardly get their pricks to stand up! If he comes home drunk, whilst you are asleep, and wakes you up for sex; you will probably refuse him. Having lain in bed, thinking of what he might have been up to on his night out; you will definitely be tired and really angry! What if he forces you? You may not fight; but you will be forced into being a passive partner to the act. That is theoretically rape as well! But again; without the bruises, who will believe you? If he comes home with lipstick on his shirt, or other signs of sexual transgression; there will be a quarrel. He may then try to 'tame the tigress'; by forcing you to have sex. You will go crazy not knowing whether he has contracted some form of venereal disease or even AIDS; and passed it on to you. That is serious marital rape; but you can do nothing, without the bruises. What if you go to the doctor and are told you have gonorrhoea or syphilis? That is also marital rape; because you never signed up to the sexually transmitted disease club. You may file for divorce, but your life will be ruined; because sex will never be the same for you again, no matter who your next partner is. Terrible! And you thought a beating was the worst thing he could do to you!

From the above paragraph; you should deduce that marital rape is not only sex without your consent, but also when the consequences are not what you expected. You marry a man because you love him; and hopefully, he loves you in the same way. A few years down the line, and he has become a drunken slob who forces sex on you; which means, he is no longer the man you married. Many marital 'transgressions' like laziness; developing a pot belly; not listening to you; not paying you as many compliments; taking you for granted etc; can be forgiven, passed off as growing older and dealt with in your own inimitable way. Forcing himself on you sexually should never be tolerated, even if you still love him; because it is a violent intrusion into your body and causes irreparable damage to your self-esteem, dignity and reputation. Not good self-defence! Once he gets it into his head that he can have sex any time he feels like it and you will consent to it after a brief struggle, even when you don't want to do it; then you might as well be his whore. He gives you money for the household expenses and fucks you whenever he feels like it! Not very nice is it? Because nature has made sex in such a way that it is the man who penetrates the woman, it is imperative that she gives her full consent and that there is no coercion, threats, bribery, blackmail or physical force involved; otherwise it becomes rape. This means that sex should always be initiated by the woman; either subtly or brazenly. Otherwise; she might be consenting to it for reasons, which she may not be prepared to divulge. Fear of the consequences could be one of them!

What can a wife do to stop a husband/partner from raping her? A rich girl can lock herself in the spare room. But what if you don't have a spare room; and you had to sleep in the same bed? Chapter Four details several ways to stop a stranger or a boyfriend from raping you. When it is your husband/partner, you have to be careful;

as the consequences can be as bad as the act itself. He is your man and not mine. Therefore, I have to sort of mind my own business, by giving you a few ideas; but I have no right to tell you what to do in your own relationship. If you are living separately; you don't have to let him into your house. If you are married however; how can you refuse to let your husband into the house, even when he is drunk? Some women would not bat an eyelid and would refuse to open the door. If you know from experience that he is drunk and will be coming to rape you; how can you let him in? You are better off phoning the police to come to your house, telling them you think there is an intruder outside your door! The cops will arrive and warn him to behave, which should cool him down; so although he will be angry you called the law, he cannot do anything to you that night. What about the next night? He will most likely be harbouring a grudge for what you did; and he could try to force you into having sex. It is not an easy position to be in; because many men believe that the best way to 'show her he is the boss', is to 'fuck the living daylights out of her'! A few orgasms later and your anger will have subsided; and therein lies the greatest mistake made by women with their partners…that of forgiveness.

Although you have obviously not forgotten that he got drunk and tried to force you into having sex; the core problem of his alcoholism and tendency for marital rape has not yet been confronted. This means that even if you have kissed and made up; it could all happen again. You have to put any sentiments aside and talk to him; because deep down, you have to believe there is hope in salvaging the wreckage. *"Darling, did you know that you forced me into sex last night?"* If he tries to be smart with a crude remark like, *"…but you enjoyed it didn't you?"* then your alarm bells ought to ring; and you should realise that your situation is not going to get any better. That kind of man is not going to listen to you or agree to see a marriage counsellor; and is certainly not going to admit to anyone that he is a marital rapist. You therefore have to start planning in your mind for the eventuality of a break-up. You cannot allow the situation to continue; as it is an invasion into the very core of your soul and self-esteem. At the end of the next chapter on dilemmas; I will show several ways you can break up with your husband and teach him a severe lesson at the same time!

There have been examples of women violently fighting back against marital rape; like the story of a woman pouring acid over her husband, as he slept. There have been cases of women pouring petrol on a violent hubby and setting him on fire. Others have been known to drug the husband to put him to sleep; and then throw boiling water on his genitals. Poison him; tell him you have AIDS; or that you are in your period! Be nice to him; then make him a drink and spike it with a strong laxative! Kiss him and bite his tongue off! Throw hot water over him! Fight for your life! Do anything; because your life really is in danger. If he is a violent rapist who breaks into your house, then you obviously have to be ruthless; and such tactics are understandable. If your life is in danger with your husband; then you may have to treat him the same as any other rapist or attacker. If your life is not in peril however; then only you will know what best to do. You can pretend to be nice to him, make him a cup of tea/coffee and put some sleepers in it; so that he will be too tired and weak to try anything. He will go straight to bed and will be calmer in the morning. There was once a film where the heroine cut off the rapist's penis in the bath; by pretending to consent to his advances. Maybe you should keep a copy of the film in the house; and he might think twice about raping you! Subtle self-defence can also be very effective! If you are too drastic and for example, you bite off his sexual organ; who loses? He is your husband; and not some guy off the streets, who broke into your home to rape you. Although he cannot rape you anymore; you could still go to prison, get divorced and be ostracised by friends and community alike. Which man is going to trust his penis in your mouth after that?

There are no real solutions to the impossible situation in marriage…only suggestions! Here are a few of my suggestions; which make sense to me, as a self-defence exponent, but might be too extreme for you. Have a look at them; and if they will work for you, don't be afraid to use them. Otherwise; you may have to seek advice from a marriage counsellor and hope whatever he/she tells you, will succeed. The most important thing to remember is that, you don't have to put up with anything you find abhorrent. There is professional help out there for you; so don't be afraid to seek it. Some women really have to be admired for keeping their errant men in check; because it is not easy trying to balance your love for him with the harm he is causing you! I'm sorry I cannot be of more help. Marital sex is such a private matter, that some women will get offended; when others try to interfere in their love lives. Good luck anyway; and remember to always do what is best for you!

1. You are in bed with your man and he tries to physically force you into sex, against your wishes.

Tell him in the nicest possible way that you are not really in the mood. If he won't listen; lie on your front, cross your legs and wrap your hands around your body. It is almost impossible for him to uncross your legs. If he starts getting aggressive; then get up and lock yourself in the bathroom till you feel he has calmed down. Warn him that you are prepared to go to the police; if he uses force on you again.

2. Your husband has gone out to get drunk; and you know he is coming home to force himself on you.

Prepare for his homecoming by welcoming him at the door in your most seductive manner. Sit him down, by suggesting that he has a drink or a cup of tea/coffee before you have sex. Because he is so drunk; he will not notice when you crush some sleeping tablets into his drink. This will allow him to fall harmlessly asleep; before he has a chance to rape you. You can make love to him the next day when he is sober; if you still have feelings for him. However; you have to start talking to him about his drinking and unrealistic demands for sex. You have to warn him that you are not prepared to put up with it any longer. Don't threaten him with what you have in mind; which would be to leave him and take most of his money.

3. Your man yells at you to come into the bedroom and get ready for him, even though you are not in the mood; but are aware of the violent consequences in refusing him.

Lock yourself in the bathroom and tell him you have a running stomach or you are feeling sick; and then let him hear you coughing and vomiting. If that does not put him off; start crying and insist you are not feeling well. If he continues to pester you;

shout so loud that he will be afraid the children or the neighbours might hear. Be prepared to leave your house and go over to a neighbour's place; only coming back when you are sure he has calmed down.

4. Marital rape has been going on for some time; but you don't know what to do.

When he is out of the house; find time to go to the police and make a report so that they can put it on file. Report him to all his friends and family members and then start making plans to leave him; by arranging somewhere to stay. You then ask the police to charge him for marital rape; and issue a barring order on him to leave you alone. You quickly go and see a divorce lawyer and plan how you are going to get compensation from him; after he has been jailed for raping you.

5. You would like to leave your husband because of his marital rape tendencies; but are scared nobody will believe you.

When your husband is out at work; hide a video camera in the bedroom, positioned so that it can record everything going on. There are some good inexpensive 'spy-cams' that can also record sound. If you don't know how to set one up; you can bring in the experts to install it for you. There is no need to reveal the real reason. They will probably think you are doing it for some kinky sex games; and will not be suspicious. You will then be able to amass enough evidence to take to a lawyer; to cement your divorce and take him to the cleaners. You can also show it to the police; who will not hesitate in arresting him for rape.

C. WIFE BEATING

From childhood; we are yelled at and sometimes spanked or slapped by our parents, if we do something wrong. A two-metre man yelling at a one-metre tall child; is frightening to the child and as bad as actually hitting him/her. Yet; most parents get away with that kind of abuse, where there are no witnesses outside of the family. We are punished by our teachers, if we disobey them; not necessarily with a beating, but most likely with public humiliation in front of the class.

"What kind of an answer is that? You stupid, brainless girl!" and we accept it; because verbal and physical violence on the weak and vulnerable is done everywhere. A child could then grow up into adulthood, believing it is normal to do the same to others put into his/her care. This idea that it is okay to shout, humiliate or beat up someone who is weaker; is often transferred into the marital environment. Many wives have suffered as a result! Women in the Third World put up with a lot more beatings than their European or American counterparts; because the practice has still not been outlawed in many countries. Although this is changing; no one can say it does not exist. Who will listen to a child in Africa or Asia who claims that his father or mother beat him/her? Wives get beaten every day of the week; and not just those who are dependent on the husband for financial support. Most prefer to keep quiet, and not wash their dirty laundry in public. In the so-called civilised world; a woman could be sporting a bruise on her eye and would claim she fell down the stairs! Men who realise that hitting someone in the face, leaves a bruise for the world to see; will instead punch the woman on the arm and then force her to cover it up with long-sleeved attire. Only her closest friends might know the truth; and they would be the only ones most likely to sympathise with her. Women have even been known to run to their parents, as a result of a beating; only to be sent back to the husband, to sort out their problems. Wife-beating seems to be accepted in many societies and there is nothing much one can do about it; simply because it is always seen as a personal matter. The sanctuaries that take in battered women seem to cater more for the lower class of a society. The middle/upper-class women would rather camouflage the problem than become the butt of societal jokes. Unwilling to risk losing the financial and status rewards, by leaving a wife-beater of a husband; they would rather put up and shut up than upset the applecart.

The fact that violence is against the law does not mean it does not exist. There are many women who get yelled at and beaten up; yet do nothing about it. The police and family members are powerless, without a complaint from the victim; backed by physical evidence and validated by a doctor. Whether a man hits you or yells at you; makes no difference to the fact that he has frightened, humiliated and hurt you. This means the situation should not be allowed to continue unabated; because it is a severe attack on your dignity, self-esteem, integrity and reputation. There are women who are cowering in fear from their men, who do not actually beat them up; but will shout, threaten and intimidate them, to the point that he only has to give her a dirty look and she will be shaking with fear. Again; without any bruises, there is not much she can do because no one will believe her. You have to understand that, just because you don't enjoy being beaten up or yelled at; does not mean it is the same for another woman. Believe it or not; there are some women who do enjoy a good shouting match or a beating! They even encourage it from their husbands; because it shows he 'loves her and cares for her'! They would deliberately say something to annoy him; knowing he would turn round and hit her! Some would intentionally flirt at a party to get him jealous; certain that he would beat her up when they got home. One woman claimed that she would obstinately antagonise her husband, so that they would quarrel first, fight and then make passionate love; as he is at his lovemaking best after a fight! This is quite common in marriages; because a truce after a fight has been known to spark up many a couple's love life. The question this book will attempt to answer is: *"What can a woman do against a beating from her husband?"* For every masochistic missus; there are hundreds of women at the receiving end of a husband or partner's fists, who don't ask for it. It really is an impossible situation; so we have to try and make sure it doesn't happen to you.

Physical abuse by a husband is more widespread than anyone is prepared to admit; but the solution rests with you. I cannot really tell you how to deal with your own husband; if you are not ready to face the problem yourself. You should have seen some sign of his character before you married him; but I don't think it is fair to blame you, for what the man you love has done to you. I will however, give you a few suggestions; and you can decide for yourself, whether they will serve your best interests or not. Jealousy, humiliation and control, originating from the inherent insecurities of the abuser; are probably the root causes of spousal violence. The feeling of 'owning you' and fear of 'losing you'; can make him take it a step further by not allowing anyone else to have an influencing contact with you. Jealousy may allow him to beat you up just for looking at or talking to another man; because he equates the contact with other men, as a prelude to going all the way and sleeping with him. As a way of controlling you; he may keep you away from your friends. Any contact with them, will result in a beating; so that you realise he is the one in control. This means you have to do what he tells you; or be in line for more beatings. Most spousal abusers are calculating and clever; turning on the charm when anyone visits the house. They can also be very nice and kind to their wives; and this in turn confuses their women. He yells at and beats her up one day. The next day; he takes her out for dinner, gives her money for a shopping spree and is so kind, she believes him when he says he is *"sorry"*. She balances the good with the bad; and decides to put up with it! The trouble is; he may genuinely be contrite...until the next time. Many women are fooled into continuously forgiving their men. If you see a woman driving a posh car and who seems to 'have it all'; do not be envious because you do not really know what she has to put up with at home!

It is important to realise that if your man is the jealous, controlling type, inclined to yelling, beating and humiliating you; then there is not much you can do about it. He is unlikely to change; so the only way you can keep him from losing his temper and using violence on you, is by not rubbing him up the wrong way. A man beats a woman to prove a point. If the point is not there to be proved; there can be no beatings! This might involve your making sacrifices, completely alien to your true character; which you may not be prepared to do. In such a situation; it is best you get out of the relationship and find someone else, who will allow you to be yourself. If however, you love your man and you want your relationship to work; then you will have to find a way not to make him jealous. This means you have to behave yourself; and gently let him know when you don't like the things he is doing. For a modern day woman with her own career; kow-towing to her man may seem like anathema. Sadly; many women are finding out the hard way, through violence; affairs; separations and divorces; that fighting with a man does not achieve anything. Some have realised that it is much cleverer to play the 'dutiful wife'. This is because she can extract a lot more love and obedience from him; if she sets an example, by not giving him any reason to pick on her. In public; most men want people to think they are in control of the relationship. All you have to do is smile, laugh at his jokes (even if you've heard them before) and be a 'good wife'; so that he remains proud of you! When you get back to the privacy of your home; you can then let him know, if he did something you did not like. He will respect you more; for publicly allowing him to wear the trousers! If you try to denigrate him or challenge him in front of his friends, he may be politically correct and 'pretend' it is okay to be 'under your thumb'; but inside, he will be seething. He will then hold a grudge; which will slowly bubble under the surface until you have a row. He will then react far in excess of what the argument was about. This will surprise and baffle you; because you will not be aware of his underlying anger. All men will do as the wife tells them; so long as there are no witnesses to his 'cowardice'. Through your simple kindness, understanding and common sense; he will realise the priceless gift he has in you. In return, he will do anything for you; which means, you are the real power behind the throne in your relationship!

Make no mistake; all men have a cut-off point, where they will resort to verbal or physical violence. Embarrassing him in public or getting into a competition to see who is in charge, breeds resentment; and he will lose respect for you. As a woman, you have a right to be 'equal partners'; but you also have to understand that, just as no two fingers on the hand are the same, they all have their uses and have to live together side by side! Therefore; a husband and a wife are supposed to complement each other. Competing with each other always leads to problems! Depending on the stubbornness of the couple; it can also end in heartache and the possible break-up of the marriage or relationship. He may not hit you per se; but he could get so angry, he will smash up the house or run off to the pub. He could then proceed to get drunk and take his frustrations out on somebody else; just for looking at him in the wrong way! He is your husband/partner; and only you know what turns him on or off. To voluntarily annoy him; will do you no good at all. If you are in a pub together with friends and you want to go home; a clandestine wink or facial movement to relay your wishes to him, is much better than the authoritative, *"Come on; we're going home...now!"* Ordering him around in public; may make him behave like a child and fight your authority, by either refusing or sulking all the way home. A little snide remark like, *"You are useless in bed"*; will open up a wound, which could have been festering for years. Suddenly, a smile to the milkman or a cheerful greeting to the handsome man next door; becomes a big deal. It could easily start a quarrel; which, if not controlled, could ultimately lead to violence. Adultery, perceived or otherwise, leads to jealousy; which history has shown, people have killed for! You know your man better than I do; so if you enjoy being yelled at, or beaten up before he makes love to you, then no one can do anything about it. If you think it will make things easier for you to do as he tells you; then you should do so. In a funny way, he may genuinely love you; but does not know how to do it properly. This means; it would be up to you to teach him how to love and make you happy. If you are going to fight pride with pride, then everyone loses; and you would be better off living apart.

You should be able to see the signs coming, well in advance; and back off when he is getting heated up and ready to quarrel with you. If you argue with a fool; you only bring yourself down to his level and people won't be able to tell the difference between you and him! Sometimes a quarrel is deliberately started; so that he will have an excuse to get into his car and drive off to his mistress or the pub. If he intentionally picks a quarrel with you; don't fall for it. Play it smart with a simple, *"You are right. I'm sorry"*; (with conviction please!) and that will be enough to cool him down. It will also throw him off-balance; because women usually like to have the last word (a common male belief). Smart husbands do this all the time; averting a fight by agreeing with the wife! It brings the peace and he can then get on and do something else; whilst she is still in a good mood, after winning the 'argument'. (A man winning an argument with a woman; is definitely not a good pre-coital move!) You therefore have to use your head and know when you are being sucked into a fight; by pulling out before it spirals out of control. All men hate a 'nagging bitch'. In a situation where a woman seems to be winning an argument, by getting too personal and insulting; then he has very few choices left. Wham! *"That should shut her up!"* He might even think, *"Sod this. I'm off to the pub!"* or possibly, *"I know a nice girlfriend who would never say that to me. I'll go and see her!"* Either way, you lose; unless you want him out of the house to get some peace and quiet!

A lot of women understandably do not give in easily. Instead of crying after the first slap; they tend to fight back and give as much as they get. This brings out the male instinct in him, to prove he is tougher. He might momentarily forget she is a woman; and hit her as hard as he would any man. Even after a beating, some women will continue to hurl abuses at their men; thereby attracting the neighbours and making a domestic quarrel, the talk of the town. If it comes to the point of no return and he actually hits you; violence for violence is never the solution. The best thing to do after the first strike; is to 'submit' and cry. Few men will continue to beat a woman after she has submitted; because it means he has 'won' and she has conceded that he is truly 'the boss'. You can also run away and lock yourself in the toilet or bedroom until he has cooled down; usually after about an hour. You can then come out, apologise as if it were your fault; and try to make up. Fix him a drink and talk about what went wrong; and then explain gently that you cannot put up with the beatings any longer. In reality, you have not submitted at all; because you can quietly bide your time and pay him back, in so many other ways. You have to first let your unhappiness register with him; so that you have him 'over a barrel', by making him feel guilty for what he did. Under no circumstances, should you allow him to make love to you. If he does not respect your body enough, that he has to use it as a punching bag; then he has no right to enjoy its benefits! Use the silent treatment to its full potential; ignore him and go about your business. Don't do anything for him for at least a week; and more than likely, he will realise you are worth a lot more than he takes for granted. If possible; go and stay with friends or relatives for a while. Don't come back; until he promises in front of his and your friends, never to hit you again. Naming and shaming will make him think twice; before he does it again. He will not be the most popular man amongst his peers at work, or in his local pub; if the word gets out he has been hitting his wife. If you have tough brothers or cousins, then a quiet word in their ears will have them issuing a warning he will be unable to ignore; or he will have to face unpleasant consequences! It is a fact that very few women, who have a close-knit family of relatives; experience physical beatings from their partners.

The next step will be to see if you can solve the problem; and find out why he thinks it is easier to use his fists on you. He may be mentally imbalanced; or he may genuinely not know any other way of dealing with things. Unless you are a kick-boxing or a karate expert; you should not try to fight a man on his terms, because you could be seriously injured. He is your husband; so you must find a way to register your disgust, without resorting to violence. Refusing to cook is not always the answer; because he might decide to go to a girlfriend's house to eat. If you prove too stubborn; he might just kick you out. Of course, you can do the same to him; but depending on what you want from a relationship, kicking him out could spell the end of your marriage. This may seem like a good idea when you are hurt and angry; but you might regret it a few weeks later, when you see he has moved into a girlfriend's house. A trip to the psychiatrist or marriage counsellor may be a good option; only if he will agree to it. You should never force him, because that will make him think he is at fault; which will push his back against the wall and he will dig his heels in. He has to realise that what he is doing is wrong; so you have to find a way to register it loud and clear, without threatening him. You cannot allow the violence to continue; because it could become an addiction. The doses will get bigger and bigger as you get used to them; until it becomes murder or manslaughter. Those who smoke will know that it is hard to stop any habit; which means, if he is used to hitting you to get his way, then he cannot stop. If you don't do anything about it; you could become addicted to the beatings and even expect it to the point that you don't feel 'right', until you have had a couple of insults and maybe a slap! Funny? Not really!

Imbalance at the beginning of a relationship is the root of the problem; because once you allow certain things to slide, they are very hard to correct. Let's assume he is not mentally imbalanced; but still beats you up. If you really feel bad because it is a regular occurrence; quietly find time to go to the police and make a complaint, which should be put on file. Ask the police not to prosecute; until it happens again. In the eyes of the law; you would have done the right thing and not overreacted. Like in the marital rape scenario; get an expert in to install a hidden camera in your bedroom and sitting room, which will record the next time he decides to hit you. You then make sure all his friends and relatives know what is going on; so that word will get back to him that everyone knows what he has been doing. If he dares touch you again after that; quietly go back to the police and press charges, knowing that you have irrefutable visual proof of his abuse. Always act 'normal' whilst you are hatching your plans. Calling the cops in the middle of a fight could backfire; because he will be so angry, he might do you serious damage before they arrive. On this occasion; forget about the children, the consequences and everything else and only think of yourself. It is such a shock to anyone who is arrested, when things appear normal; and he will most likely deny it. This will not work in his favour; because everyone already knows what he has been up to. The evidence on the spy-cam will put the final nail in his coffin. He will most likely be jailed; and you will be able to extract a hefty divorce settlement. Although young children are important; you should never put your personal safety at risk, just so that the father can play happy families. This is because your relationship would be based on blatant falsehood. When the children are older; you can always show them a copy of the video of him beating you up. It is important they understand what their father did; for you to walk out on him.

No marriage is a bed of roses. Physical abuse is bad; but mental abuse can become much worse, as stated before. Wife-beating is an impossible situation; so the final decision will always be with you. You marry a man for richer or poorer; better or worse; till death do you part etc. You know why you married him; so surely, you knew what he was like before you went to the altar? Is what you gain from him, worth a beating? If so; then stick with it and try to remove the causes of the beatings. If not, then leave; but be prepared for the consequences, which although uncomfortable, will never be worse than a broken nose or cracked cheekbone. You will lose some friends and whatever status and lifestyle his job or professional reputation has made you accustomed to; whilst the next man you fall in love with, could become much worse. Thankfully; the modern woman is much tougher mentally than her predecessors and is earning a lot more money. She does not have to put up with anything she does not like! There are probably more pros than cons in marriage; as many couples have learnt how to co-exist with each other and bring up happy well-adjusted children. Most of these couples had to work very hard to achieve what we call 'marital bliss'; which means, it is possible. As a woman; your marriage is also part of your self-defence. Before you marry; make sure he really is your Mister Right and then do all you can to make the marriage work. This means; you will always have to be the smart one in the relationship, by using your head and allowing him his public ego trips. Once you know you are the real boss in the relationship; there is no need to show it off! Many women have managed it; so I'm sure you can! There is some truth in the Tee shirts which say, <*All men are bastards!*> and <*All women are bitches!*>. Once you realise that potentially, all men are bastards; you will have a better understanding of them! You should therefore try to make sure you marry a 'better bastard'; who is acutely aware that you can be a real 'bitch', when you want to be!

D. AFFAIRS

Although it might seem like all doom and gloom with regards to marital rape and wife-beating; you can rest assured that because of the legal problems they would cause the abuser, the chances of your man beating you or raping you in your marital bed are decreasing. Men are wising up to the fact that the stigma attached to a marital abuser, is not worth the hassle; because it could destroy his career and reputation in society and haunt him for the rest of his life. What is more likely to happen, if your man is dissatisfied or feels threatened by your femininity; is that he will stray outside the relationship, by having an affair with a woman whose traits and character are more in tune with his taste. Beauty does not come into it; and many wives whose husbands have affairs, cannot understand why he would choose a less attractive woman. *"What does he see in her...?"* is a common riposte by women who are finding it hard to come to terms with a man's betrayal. The more successful a woman becomes, the more her self-esteem rises and she begins to value herself more; usually to the detriment of the relationship. This means the husband will begin to feel that he has 'lost her'; or that she has become 'too big for her boots'. By imposing her femininity on him and squashing what is left of his male pride; she inadvertently drives him into the arms of another woman. Instead of looking inwards and asking questions of herself that she may be 'at fault'; she will rather gravitate towards blaming him for his 'ingratitude'. *"He does not respect the fact that I'm a hard-working, ambitious woman making lots of money for our family; and he goes and does the dirty behind my back! How dare he?"* One can easily understand the anger and rage a woman goes through; when she realises her husband is having an affair.

Because women have generally not been in positions of wealth, power and authority for as long as the men; many do not know how to combine power with humility. This makes it very easy to carry her status at work, back into the marital home. It takes a brave and understanding man, to 'lie down and die'; when a woman starts imposing her femininity on him. It is a slow process; which usually begins with the tone of voice she uses when asking him to do something. A few months down the line; this can end up sounding like an order or a request, he dare not refuse. From then on, things are done only when she wants; whilst the man, slowly but surely loses his masculinity. Very few women realise it, when they are slowly 'cutting off a man's balls'; and she will never feel like she is doing anything wrong. It is a no-win situation for a woman; because if the man is also successful, he does not want a 'competitor' in the household. He would prefer a more pliant woman, who understands his needs; so that there is a clear distinction between the women he competes with at work and the one he comes home to. If a man is not as successful as the wife; the feelings of insecurity and belittlement will come to the fore, as described earlier on in this chapter. The idea of 'women in control' is a good thing for the female, but bad for relationships. This is because men are not yet used to being under the financial and intellectual influence of women. The smart woman is the one who allows her man think he is the one calling the shots; when in actual fact, she is! Regrettably to the detriment of the wife; the mistress usually turns out to be the clever one, when a man has an affair. This is because he will always give away the reasons why his wife doesn't 'understand him'; thereby handing the control and power over to the mistress. She is then able to keep the man on his toes, and running back to her at every opportunity; conveniently created by her!

In many ways; an affair is more hurtful to a woman than either wife-beating or marital rape. This is because there is nothing she can do to stop her man cheating on her; and there is no law that says he has to love her, the way she wants him to. The feeling of not being 'good enough' for her own husband, can have a devastating effect on a woman; and no matter how much of a brave face she tries to put on it, the betrayal will change her life for ever. If she is not strong-willed; it can also have horrible consequences like depression, alcoholism and drug dependency. It may even promote promiscuity; just to prove, mainly to herself, that she is still desirable to the male. Whichever way you look at it; an affair is a severe blow to a woman's self-esteem, dignity and reputation. She will most likely blame herself; not necessarily for what she has done wrong, but rather for what she has not done or could have done, that would have prevented the affair. Fighting a man is easy; compared to competing with a woman who has stolen your man. Because she is of the same sex as you; she will have no qualms about going for the jugular, in order to hurt you. A woman knows exactly how to go about causing maximum pain to another woman. If she steals your man; the chances are she will not lose any sleep over it! The feeling of superiority a woman feels, when someone else's husband prefers her to his own wife, can be very intoxicating; and she will not put an end to the affair. This means; the fault has to be with the man, for making her feel comfortable with the deceit. In many cases however; the man often 'sees sense' and comes running back to the wife. This usually happens when the mistress starts becoming too possessive; by making impractical demands and giving him ultimatums. *"Leave your wife or it's over"*, or *"We can't continue like this…!"* etc. is usually the wake-up call for the man and the downfall of the concubine. It is much easier to leave the mistress than the wife; where there are financial assets and domestic dependants like children, to consider. In the end; if the mistress feels like she has been used, the man will be open to blackmail. She will definitely threaten to reveal the affair to the wife; and might even demand a financial settlement, to ensure her silence. There is no guarantee she will not tell her best friend; who could in turn, leak it to the wife via the local gossip queen. It can get very complicated and messy! This means there will be no real winners; as he will have to confess his deceit to the wife. The relationship they had shared before, will never the same again!

There are two ways a man can cheat on a woman. Mentally, by falling for someone else on an emotional level; or physically, by picking up prostitutes or loose women, purely for the sex. It usually happens when the woman thinks everything is okay in the relationship. At the beginning of the affair, he will go to great lengths to make sure she doesn't find out; by doing his best to 'act normally' and may even be extra nice to her! This means that deep down, he still loves her and knows that having an affair is not conducive to the relationship he has with her; but still goes ahead and does it. This is unforgivable, even if she does 'forgive' him; because her brain and her heart will be saying different things. There is no feasible way you can take a man back after he cheats on you mentally or physically; unless you are prepared for him to walk all over you, for the rest of your life. Things will never be the same after an affair; because the thought of him inside another woman will be impossible to erase from your brain or your heart. Can you really allow him to touch your naked body; if you know he has been doing the same with someone else, who is probably gloating over you or might even be carrying all kinds of venereal diseases? Although relationships have been known to survive an affair; the chances are, in the long term it will not. Like the leopard and its spots; there is every probability he will do it again! Your soul cannot lie; so whatever caused the affair will always be there. It will be almost impossible to change who you are, in order to satisfy your partner. Because the trust will have disappeared; every time he goes out on his own or answers the phone, will have you wondering what he is getting up to. This will be very difficult to live with! Even though many affairs are short-lived; it is no consolation to you as a woman, if your man cheats on you. Once the damage has been done; the spiritual link you had with him will be broken. It is not something you can sew back together; so you have to prepare yourself for the aftermath of life without him.

1. Mental affairs

As you are well aware; a woman is just as capable of having an affair as a man and is probably cleverer at covering her tracks! The reasons for the affair may be many; but they all add up to the fact that she believes the grass is greener elsewhere. I have to make you aware that a man is also unfaithful; only if he is not happy with what is on offer at home. This may not necessarily be your fault; because some men are natural womanisers and are unable to keep their pricks in their pants! However; if he could get from you, what he gets from other women, it is very unlikely that he will stray! Any man is capable of infidelity; especially if what he gets from the mistress is better or more exciting than the wife. It usually starts with the man complaining to a woman, how unhappy he is in his marriage; because the wife is a 'stubborn control freak', who makes his life a misery with her unrealistic demands and lack of sexual ambition. Add this to the usual falsehood men tell to women, *"We hardly talk; and the fizz has gone out of our relationship..."* etc; and he can always get the attention of any woman who catches his fancy. True to form; this woman will listen sympathetically and store the data so clinically, that by the time she becomes his mistress, she would have well and truly got her claws into him. He will then find it very hard to go back to his wife! Anal sex? *"No problem. I've never done it before; but I'll try it for you!"* Blow job? *"Of course, my darling; that's easy! I'll even give you a nice massage first!"* She will cook for him, tell him how great he is in every lovemaking department and give him so much comfort and sympathy; he will think he has died and gone to Heaven! From then on; he will start spending a lot more time and money on the mistress...whilst the poor wife sits at home, wondering what has happened to the man she married. He is never hungry when she cooks; hardly talks to her and is very abrupt and rude when he does. Even if they do make love; it will be obvious his interest has waned and his erections and ejaculations are not as powerful as they used to be.

Because it is in a man's nature to try and have his cake as well as eat it; he will never tell you he is straying. In the end; you will probably find out, only when it has reached a point where he is so reckless, he does not care whether he is caught or not and is ready to walk out on you anyway. This means; you will have to find out either by accident, or have a way of noticing the suspicious behavioural patterns as they occur. Once he starts having an emotional affair with another woman; he will start spending a lot more time with her, by using his work as an excuse. If the woman is a work colleague; it may be a long time before you find out. The office will legitimately bring them in touch with each other; and they will probably be having sex at work or slipping off during the lunch breaks! If the woman is also married; they will both have an interest in keeping the affair concealed. He is likely to behave 'normally' when he comes home; but if you are clever enough, you will be able to notice subtle changes in his behaviour. The days of hubby arriving home with lipstick on the collar are long gone; because men are becoming much smarter at hiding affairs. They really do not want to be caught out; as the financial implications in a divorce settlement, make it very foolhardy to have an affair. If he makes such a glaring error; it can only mean the mistress deliberately put the lipstick there, with the intention of his wife finding out so that he will be thrown out and fall into her arms. This will tell you that if you see love bites on his body; lipstick on his collar; smell a different perfume on him; find a female handkerchief in his pocket and other 'errors of judgements' like his taking extra care with his dressing and appearance as if he is going through a mid-life crisis; it can only suggest that the affair has been going on for some time. Any change in his behaviour; especially if you know he is lying to you about his whereabouts or where he is going as he leaves the house, should set your alarm bells ringing.

If you suspect your man is being unfaithful; you will have to set a few traps for him to fall into, in order to be certain. The best way to start your attack is to refuse him sex for about a week or two; by claiming you are *"...not really in the mood"*. If he does not bother you for it; then he is probably getting it elsewhere. Even if he is a lecherous rat, who will sleep with anything in a skirt and continues to badger you for sex; you should still refuse intercourse. You should however; continue to sleep in the same bed and watch out for certain signs. When he has not had sex in a while; his body should be very sensitive to your touch. If for example, he is normally very excitable to your hands touching his naked thighs; then stroke him there when you are in bed. If he does not react in the way he should; then he is obviously not horny and may have been having sex with someone else. It is very difficult to hide one's body language; so you should hug him and kiss him as usual, when he leaves to or arrives from work. If there is an 'over-enthusiasm' in his clinches with you when he comes home; then be very suspicious because he could not have missed you that much!

Because you have been refusing him sex for over a week; he will give himself away by going out more; staying out longer; making secretive phone calls on his mobile by pretending he is talking to a male friend; and not paying you too much attention. This means; someone else is attracting his loyalties away from you! Although you are now aware that he is not being faithful to your relationship; you still do not have any concrete proof. To confront him now; will ruin your modus-operandi and he will thwart your investigations by changing his tactics.

Once you know he is having an affair; you have to use reverse psychology to deal with your husband. You need to gather some irrefutable evidence and put yourself in a very strong position; in the event of a break-up. Knowledge is power! What you know more about him, than he does about you; is what will eventually win you this kind of war. Be extra nice to him and don't look for a quarrel; even if you are boiling inside at his deceit. Cook him his favourite dishes and don't do things, you know will infuriate him. If for example; he says something out of character, like he doesn't want you showing your legs off to the world, then don't. Even though you might be tempted to do the opposite to what he wants, because you are angry with him over the affair; you have to be super-cool and smart. He may be trying to assert some form of control or censorship on you; because he will be acutely aware that he is not the only one who can have an affair. The thought of you doing the same thing as him; can bring out the green-eyed monster in him and he could suddenly become over-possessive, whenever he sees you being friendly to any man. This interference in your independence; is another give-away sign that he is cheating on you! His guilty mind wants it to seem like he loves you and cares about you; but in actual fact, it is a sign of his insecurity brought about by his deceit. He could also become irritable, whenever you suggest an outing or doing something together; like staying in to watch a DVD. He will suspect that you know what he has been up to and are trying to thwart his plans, by cramping his style! Your man might even start being overtly nice to you by buying you expensive presents; as if to compensate for his lack of affection towards you. For him; this is the easier option. To show you the 'feely-feely' kind of affection with constant hugs and kisses; would definitely give him away. This is because in his mind, he knows what he is doing behind your back; and you will know something is not quite right, by his body language. If your man is having an affair; it does not necessarily mean these traits will be attributed to him, because every man is different. But one thing all men will have in common; is the inability to hide their guilt for too long. Sooner or later; you will know something is wrong by the way he behaves or tries to behave. The thing you have to remember is; never to alert him to the fact that you know what he is up to. There is still more for you to do!

Things will now get interesting; because you will have to play detective without him suspecting that you are on to him. Check your house phone records; because even though it is unlikely he would use your house phone to conduct his affairs, there might just be a suspicious number on the list, which he may have called by mistake. If he leaves his mobile phone lying around; look into his messages and call register when he is asleep. Do not delete anything; because you don't want him to know you have been snooping. Go through his pockets for any incriminating evidence; like receipts to restaurants, presents, out of town hotels etc. and make a note of everything. Make sure you put the receipts back; so that he does not know you have a record of them. Check the bank and credit card statements as soon as they arrive in the post; just in case there is any untoward expenditure on them. By making a note of the shops, dates and amount spent; you will be able to deduce what he has been doing with his money. Sleeping around behind your back is one thing; but it would be like rubbing salt into an open wound, if you find out he is spending money meant for your family, on her as well. If you feel the affair is a serious one that could end up in the divorce courts; it might be useful to hire a private detective to follow him around. He/She will be able to garner some hard evidence; like the places he takes her, what she looks like, who she is etc. This will put your mind at rest; knowing that you have him where you want. There are also tiny tracking and bugging devices you can plant in his car; so that you can have an idea where he takes her or what he says to her in the car. These tactics will all be useful when the time comes to confront him; so that he has nowhere to hide. You cannot afford to put a foot wrong! Act normally, and eventually your 'kindness and love' will hit him with guilt; making it impossible for him to deny he has been cheating on you.

You should never let him know what you are up to; until you are certain what you want to do. Once you have revealed your hand; you will have no more aces to play and he will be able to find ways and means to counter your accusations. The mistake almost all women make; is to confront the man with the evidence already gathered. This will only serve in pushing his back against the wall. Not only will he deny it; but he may even put the blame back onto you with a multitude of hurtful excuses. *"You are never there when I need you…" "I find sex with you boring…" "Things are not working out…" Maybe I should move out".* He will then start hating you for playing detective and poking your nose into what he believes, is 'his business'. Once he realises you have been snooping on him; things could get nasty. He will definitely take steps to protect himself; in anticipation of a separation or a divorce. He might for example, quickly empty his bank account and put the money elsewhere; so you should always be several steps ahead of him. Go and see a divorce lawyer and let him advise you on your options; so that you are firm in your own mind, the road you are going to go down. This could be separation by throwing him out of the house; break-up of the relationship; ultimatum to return to your fold; or divorce. You can then say to him that you had a dream he was having an affair; and watch his facial reaction. If there is a quick vehement denial, over-the-top surprise or absurd laughter; then it means he is a hard-core liar. You will not get a guilty plea or any remorse from him; even if you do confront him with the evidence! You would be better off divorcing him through the lawyers; because he obviously feels he is doing nothing wrong. If however, he shows signs of nervousness; then it means he is a man who is not really comfortable with cheating on you but is only doing it because he thinks he can get away with it. An ultimatum might be better for him; backed by telling him the consequences he will face, if he does not end the affair. At this stage; you should not tell him about the evidence you have gathered. It will come into good use; if the divorce turns nasty. Your lawyer can then bring out, what will turn out to be your trump card. He will be exposed as a liar in front of the judge and it will win you the divorce and a far bigger slice of alimony.

An emotional affair also means spending time with another woman; even if you believe they are not sleeping together. This is because you can never be certain what they are getting up to; even though he may claim they are 'just good friends'. In a many ways; he is cheating on you, if her priorities are higher than yours. The way he talks about her; the happy facial reactions whenever her name is mentioned; jumping immediately to her defence whenever you say anything less than flattering about her; will all not do any good to your self-confidence or trust in him. Over time; they will set your jealousy juices flowing! The clever 'just good friend' might even become friends with you; so that you might never suspect anything, when he says he *"dropped by Susie's place for a chat and a glass of wine…!"* This kind of subterfuge is a serious affront on your intelligence; because they are using your good nature, to conduct their affair right under your nose. We have all heard about a woman wailing and wallowing in despair; because her best friend or sister had done the dirty and slept with her husband. *"They were at it for years, without my knowledge. I could kill the bastard/bitch…!"* You may not agree with me on this; but you have to treat any female friend of your husband as his potential seducer and defend yourself accordingly. Once they do start sleeping together; it would be too late and you might lose him to her. This is easily possible; if you are either too trusting or too absorbed in your own life to worry about him. It is only when you look back; that you will realise you overlooked certain obvious signs that something was going on. An affair needs a pattern to survive, so that it does not interfere with his everyday life with you; because the perpetrators do not want to be caught and ruin what is going on. You should always confirm everything your husband does; so that you are secure in your own mind that he is telling the truth. Even then; you should occasionally check up on him by 'dropping by' without warning at any location he says he will be at. This will make him aware that he cannot lie to you and get away with it! Let him call you a jealous, paranoid woman, if he likes. It is a sure sign that he is up to something!

He goes to the gym every evening: Have you ever been down the gym with him, to find out if it is really true he goes there; and is not using it as a convenient excuse for his subterfuge? Change the gym with any other location he supposedly frequents; and you will understand where I am coming from.

He works till late at night and comes home tired: How do you know he is really at work? Even if he is; who else works late with him? What time does he actually finish work; compared to the time he arrives home and is supposedly too exhausted to make love to you?

He says he was at a male friend's house: How do you know? The next time he says he is going there; why not insist on going with him? Alarm bells should ring, if he tries to put you off. Let him go and then ring the male friend's house with a convenient excuse and ask to speak with him. If he moans that you are checking up on him; then that is too bad. If he has nothing to hide, he should not be bothered!

He insists that woman and him are just good friends: Invite her for dinner and watch the way they are together. As a woman; you will definitely spot certain facial signs, awkwardness and body language. This will let you know if something is either going on or could easily happen; if the temperature between them does not cool down.

He comes back from a business trip: Ask him who he went with. If he says, with work colleagues; make it your business to find out where they went, whom he went with and what they got up to. If he tries to put you off; then he obviously has something to hide. Did he really go on a business trip; or was that an excuse to shack up with a woman or pick up prostitutes on a boys night out?

Those are just a few examples of how to 'make a nuisance of yourself'; so that he knows you will not just accept everything he says, but will always question his motives. That is how you are; so he had better not deceive you! As I stated earlier on in this book; being inquisitive is a good thing because your husband is part of your self-defence. You have to fight to defend what you have together; even if it means poking your nose into everything he does! It is important he realises you are not stupid or a timid mouse that will lie down and die; and you care enough about him not to let him go astray. Woe betides any woman (or man) who dares entice your man away; because this is one bitch that bites back and leaves permanent teeth marks! Once his friends know you have the *'Roar of the Tigress'*; I can guarantee they will not allow him to go off the handles because they know how dangerous you are. Nobody can escape your wrath; if they entice your man into stupid escapades! If he is a natural flirt who likes the company of females; then don't be too hard on him, if you see him talking to a woman...so long as that is as far as it goes. If for example, you are in a night club and the drink has made him slightly over-excited by the female company on view; then keep your eyes wide open on him. Don't be afraid to intervene by 'butting in' on their conversation, to bring him back down to earth; and to remind the women he seems to be infatuated with, that you are very much around. In many ways; men are like children. They will try anything; because the fun is in getting away with it! You should always lay down your marker and let him have his fun; so long as he knows there is a line he should never cross, if he does not want trouble! It is not so difficult to keep your man under control; if you realise what can go wrong and then react accordingly, by creating a buffer zone!

Since I am not privy to whatever you have going with your other half; I cannot really say any more, except that the final decision will always rest with you. Being cheated on hurts, whichever way you try to dress it up; but living without him may also not be what you want, because he may be good to you in many other ways. It might therefore be more prudent to forgive him; because your very understanding and loving nature will make him see the error of his ways. (He will know he owes you big time, and you can get a lot more out of him; because he has to make it up to you for the rest of your lives!) Please understand that forgiving him must come with a set of conditions, which he may not be able to keep; but might promise to do so, just to satisfy you. This means that you have not solved the problem of his philandering; and there is every chance it will re-occur. If you refuse to forgive (impossible to forget!); then you have to be prepared for a divorce. In some countries; he may take a second wife. This will push you down the pecking order in his affections and financial considerations! If you are financially independent and can live through a divorce and all its social stigmas; then that is your prerogative. You only have one life; so if you feel trapped in a loveless marriage, then you should get out. If it is not working; why continue to punish yourself? The end result is your happiness; so you have to do what is best for you. This is the ultimate aim in your self-defence!

2. Physical affairs

(a). Prostitution

In case you did not already know; I will tell you that the majority of prostitutes do not hang around street corners! Although soliciting and loitering with intent is against the law in many countries; prostitution in its different guises is still very much alive and kicking. Because of its secretive nature; a married man picking up prostitutes is more widespread than most wives are aware of. The more money a man is prepared to pay for the professional escort; the less likely he is of ever being exposed. There are many high-class brothels and escort agencies that operate by word of mouth and don't need to advertise; which means officially, they do not exist. They have a group of girls working for their client list and the men go directly to the prostitute's apartment for the liaison and then leave quietly; satisfied that they have 'got away with it', because the wife is unlikely to ever find out. Anybody who is in need of cash could become an escort or prostitute; even if it is only for one night. It can be a quick way to pay off debt and pay tuition fees; or simply to improve a lifestyle with designer attire and other materialistic goodies. Some of these girls are intelligent, well-dressed, courteous and beautiful; and don't look like prostitutes, in the conventional sense. The man who picks one up is thereby able to convince himself she is not a prostitute; but someone to keep him company. Such women come with hefty price tags; which guarantees their compliance to certain sordid sex acts, their discreetness and confidentiality. Go to any lap-dancing club, strip club, casino or nightclub; and you will see men chatting up the ladies of the night, with the sole intention of sleeping with them for payment. They are legally not allowed to solicit on the premises; but for the 'right amount of cash', they will gladly come to a man's hotel room after closing from work. It is not possible that each of these men is unmarried, free and single! Many will remove their wedding rings and give false names; so that they can screw the girls with a clearer conscience. On out-of-town business trips; many a businessman will hire an escort to keep him company in the lonely hotel room. She will most likely leave before the morning; so even his business friends may not be any the wiser. In this case; he will confidently convince himself he 'still loves his wife'. He will not feel that he is cheating on her; because such men believe picking up a prostitute is just a sexual release and 'nothing more'. When you add those who love the danger of kerb crawling and paying for sex with girls in their cars; and you will realise that however much we like to pretend it does not exist, prostitution is not called the 'oldest profession' for nothing.

Any man can pick up a prostitute if he is horny; because a man's penis has no conscience! A hard-on can arrive at any time or place; and if there is a chance he can pay a girl for a 'quick one' with no strings attached, he will! He will then go about his business in a better mood; as if he had done nothing wrong! By wearing a condom; he believes he cannot catch any sexually transmitted diseases. He will then return home from his business trip with some perfume, chocolates and flowers for the wife; who will be none the wiser. She will be so happy to see him back home safely; she is unlikely to ask him if he 'fucked a whore' on his trip! It is an unwritten rule that most married men have at one time or another cheated and/or continue to cheat on their wives, by paying for sex. It could be on a business trip, a weekend excursion to a sports event with the boys; or just a quick lunch-break fumble in a downtown hotel room. Some companies even lay on boys-only bonding sessions to out-of-town nightclubs; where all kinds of shenanigans are likely to take place. It is like a mafia 'omerta'; because no husband will be prepared to break the silence and confess to his wife, what really goes on when boys get together on a night out. If your man goes on a business trip abroad; it is very common for the host to make the guest feel 'at home', by providing him with an escort to accompany him. This will supposedly put him in a better mood to facilitate the business discussions! You should also be aware that other countries may have different codes of sexual ethics to yours. Many massage parlours and sauna paradises in Third World, as well as some developed countries, offer legal 'sexual relief' to their clients;

which involves masturbating them to ejaculation. Although this is not exactly full-sex and is unlikely to transmit any sexual diseases; if a man likes the hand-job so much, what is to stop him offering the girl more money for a blow-job? She could even come to his hotel room later; and continue from where she started! This obviously means that if your husband indulges in one of these 'luxuries', he would still have cheated on you; but because it was done in a foreign country, there is no way you can find out...let alone prove it!

Because no man will ever tell his wife he has slept with a prostitute; there will also be a strong denial by the wives who believe, *"My husband would never do that to me...!"* In the greater scheme of a marriage, one can argue that sleeping with a prostitute is nowhere near as bad as an emotional affair; because it can easily be dismissed, denied or pretended it never happened. The greatest danger in picking up whores to sleep with, is the diseases a man could pick up and then bring back to the wife. Even if he wears a condom; there is no guarantee he will not catch 'crabs' (pubic lice), genital herpes or the infamous 'swine flu', which he will pass on to his wife. All the high-class prostitutes are tested for AIDS; because it is in their interest to do so, in order not to ruin their business. Unfortunately; nobody knows how many sexual partners they have a day. This means that even though they could be tested weekly for sexually transmitted diseases; it is really no comfortable guarantee! It only takes one 'shag' to catch a disease; so a clean girl on Monday could be an infected menace by Wednesday. In comes your husband; catches something indescribable and then goes home, thinking everything is okay. If you end up with crabs or an infection; there will be an argument, where he will most likely take the moral high ground and blame you for your lack of hygiene. All this means is that you may never find out your man has picked up a prostitute; unless you catch a sexually transmitted disease off him. This is no real comfort to you, is it? You should always let a man know at the beginning of the relationship that if you ever found out he is picking prostitutes; there will be no forgiveness and you will have to dump him. If he tries to be all-moralistic and says *"I would never dream of doing that to you darling"*; it means he is more than capable of doing it. With men; the stronger the denial, the more the possibility of guilt! Although you cannot stop him picking whores; it will instil in his mind that you are aware all men have at one time or other in their lives done so. This will at least make him more careful; if he decides to go behind your back. More importantly; it will put your relationship in perspective with the physical affair. If he is smart; he will realise that what he has with you is more important than paid sex. *(At least with you, the sex is free! Sorry! Another one I couldn't resist!)*

If you think your man is paying for sex behind your back; you have to treat it like an emotional affair and protect yourself by setting traps for him without his knowledge. You will need to gather enough evidence for the time you are ready to confront him; with the intention of leaving him. If you don't jump straight into bed with him when he returns from a business trip, and allow him to make the first move; you will be able to assess how eager he is to sleep with you. If there is no great rush, then he is obviously not horny; and therefore may have already 'got his rocks off' during the trip. It may also mean that because he has slept with someone else; the guilt has made him a little hesitant to sleep with you straightaway. Emotionally; he will not be ready until the guilt has worn off and been consigned to history! Even if he does rush into bed with you; try to apply the same 'horniness test' described earlier, in order to see how his body (feelings to your touch, erection strength and power/speed of ejaculation) reacts to you. If he has already ejaculated in the previous forty-eight hours; the amount of sperm he has left in him will be substantially less than if he had stayed celibate during the week or two that he has been away. Although this method is not full-proof; (he may have had sex on his first night away and then stayed clean until his return, which means he may still have enough sperm left in him to convince you he has not cheated; or he may have masturbated, which might explain his lack of sperm) if you add it to the way he behaves and acts around you as soon as he returns, it goes a long way in determining whether he has been sexually up to no good. Sex with a gay prostitute is still cheating on you! You should also go through his pockets when he is not around; in case he leaves a receipt or a piece of paper with a phone number written on it. It may be the number of a massage parlour or even a call girl! Finally, if you are friendly with his friends; try to use your female tact and intuition by asking certain indirect questions about what they get up to and you will probably be able to piece two and two together and come out with four. Unless you are prepared to follow him around or hire a private detective to find physical proof; there is no other way of finding out your man is picking up prostitutes. Unlike an emotional affair; you will not be able to find the girl, in order to confirm your suspicions. If you feel the doubt is eating into your self-confidence; you may have to hire a professional snoop to confirm or put your suspicions to rest, so that you can sleep a little easier at night.

You will definitely catch your man out; if he sleeps with prostitutes so regularly that he starts making obvious mistakes. This means he is out of control and does not care about your health or feelings. Picking up prostitutes has become an addiction! Once you are convinced that he is a whore-monger; you then have the unenviable task of confronting him with your suspicions. He will most likely deny it; and this means you have to make a major decision. *'Should I stay, or should I go?'* In such a scenario; you will have to seriously question the future of your relationship, because your health and possibly your life (HIV or AIDS are as good as ruining your life for ever) are in real danger. As in an emotional affair; seeking a divorce may not be the best option for you, because other factors have to be taken into consideration. If you stay with him; you would be advised never to allow him to sleep with you, even if he wears a condom. The thought of his body rubbing up against a woman who may have already slept with thousands of clients; does not bear contemplating and you will never be able to mentally or physically enjoy sex with him. To all extents and purposes; your marriage will be over. This will lead to bitterness, arguments and frustrations. As hard as you may try to forget about what he has done; you will eventually end up in the divorce courts or the dissolution of your relationship. Forgiving him, if he will seek counselling for his addiction; is also an option. However; I must remind you that it may not work, because an addiction is part of who a person is. To break the mould; takes a determination and willpower, few people are able to muster. There is every possibility that even after the counselling sessions; he will continue to pick up whores and may then be forced to lie, in order to conceal his involvement. What may start off as a bit of fun with the boys on a night out; could end up as the worst nightmare for the woman waiting at home for the husband to return. For that reason; prostitution has to be taken as a serious threat to any marriage.

(b). Casual sex

Those who are too mean, too broke or too afraid to pick up prostitutes; will try and chat up girls in pubs and nightclubs, with the sole intention of sleeping with them. They will then return to their wives; as if nothing has happened! For many single men; there is a lot of fun and excitement in seeing a new girl at a bar; chatting to her; buying her drinks; and then sleeping with her. For a married man; it has to be a real ego booster to know that he has still got what it takes! There are lots of girls who enjoy one-night stands and are also on a mission to 'pull a fella', whenever they go out; so in many ways, a casual fling is a more obvious threat to a marriage, than either a full-blown affair or prostitution. Although it seems easy enough to blame a husband when he sleeps casually with a woman; there are certain ladies who have no qualms about 'bedding' a married man and pursue them with a zeal very few men are able to resist. When a woman wants a man, she usually gets him; because most men are very weak-minded, when it comes to refusing anything from a woman they find attractive. When a man sitting alone in a bar, sees a woman by herself; just trying to be polite or friendly with a *"Can I buy you a drink?"* scenario, often leads to a lively conversation. This is only one short step away from them jumping into bed together!

On another occasion; a group of guys could be in a pub watching a football game on the big screen and are then joined by equally sports-loving girls to enjoy the game. After a few-too many drinks; the conversation usually turns to sex and the banter becomes frolics. Before you know it; your man could be giving the girl 'a quick one' in the car-park; toilet; backseat of his car; or even an alleyway. He may be even bolder and go to her place to 'finish the job'; because he is certain the wife will not be expecting him home anytime soon. As a wife; you have to be suspicious of any female who enjoys male sports and goes out in all weathers to watch testosterone-filled men running around a pitch chasing after a ball. The attraction of watching fit, strong, tough young athletes doing their thing, whilst surrounded by thousands of vociferous men has to be a sexual turn-on; even though the women involved will probably deny it and tell you: *"We enjoy supporting our team. What's wrong with that?!"* (In that case; why don't they go out to watch the female version of the sport?) After the game; they will head off to the pub and become 'one of the boys', by downing vast amounts of drinks. It will not take much for the women to take their pick of the men on display; and one of them could easily be your husband. When you include the temptations of sleeping with the women in the work-place; (which statistics have shown, is an easy place to have affairs without the wife finding out) you will realise that it is almost impossible to stop your man having a quick fling with a willing and determined female.

Because the casual affair is not seen as a permanent liaison, but more like a bit of fun between two consenting adults, who could both be in long-term relationships; it is more prevalent than many wives are aware. Since most casual flings and one-night stands occur around the imbibing of alcohol and possibly drugs; it never occurs to the participators that they are doing anything wrong, until it is too late. The dangers of sleeping with someone you hardly know; are possibly worse than with prostitution, where the girls are answerable to the brothel they work for. Casual sex with a stranger can easily lead to the spreading of diseases; because your husband can never know how many sexual partners the woman has recently had. If he 'screws some tart' he met in the pub and catches a sexually transmitted disease; he could easily pass it on to you. This is because there will be no time for him to notice what he has caught, before he sleeps with you. A man could also be tricked by a seductive girl and then lured to her house. As they are having sex; the 'angry husband of the girl' walks in on them with (a gun?) a camera, takes their picture and then threatens to beat him up and tell his wife...unless he pays some money. If that were to happen; he can never tell his wife and will be susceptible to blackmail for the rest of his life. Without any receipts; how is he going to explain to her the withdrawal of large amounts of money from his account?

The questions all wives must ask themselves from the above paragraphs are:

1. *'What was my man doing alone in a bar?'*

It is not a good idea for you to allow him to go out alone in the evenings; because the scope for getting up to mischief and keeping secrets from you are much wider. Although you should allow your man his freedom to go out; you should make it a point of knowing exactly where he goes, with whom and what he does when he is out. This would be impossible, if he went out alone. Why not go with him???

2. 'What kind of friends has he got, who allow him to go too far with any girl; knowing that he is in a relationship/married to me?'

It is always a good idea to make friends with the wives and girlfriends of your man's friends; so that you have a circle of feminine bonding you can rely on, when you suspect your man is up to something detrimental to your marriage. It would be next to impossible for your man to indulge in casual sex without your finding out; because sooner or later, one of his friends will say something to his own wife that will give the game away. She will then be able to warn you; so that you can take preventive or affirmative action.

3. 'Should I take an interest in his sport and go with him to watch the game, even if it is just to keep an eye on him?'

The answer is an affirmative *"Yes!"* All men are like children when it comes to sports; because they get very excited with things happening on the pitch, which most non-sporty women would consider petty. This means they are at a disadvantage to the women who follow sports and are very comfortable amongst men of all ages and status. A team scores a goal and your man could easily hug and kiss a complete stranger standing next to him. If that happens to be a woman who is equally excited by the goal; a sexual chemistry could easily develop. This might be hard for your man to resist; simply because you are not there to rein him in. A quick 'fling' to celebrate their team's win is not out of the realms of fiction or fantasy; but very much a modern day reality.

4. 'What does he really do when he goes to work?'

Try to take a healthy interest in his work and if possible, either drop him there in the mornings or go there when he closes; so that you can come home together. This will let his co-workers know that he is very much in a relationship; which will at least make him think more clearly before embarking on a casual affair with a female co-worker. This is because he will never be sure if someone will come and tell you what he is getting up to at work!

5. 'What secrets is he keeping from me?

If he comes and goes from your house without saying where he is going; you have to assume he is up to something and you should ask him where he is going. Your own intuition should be able to tell you if he is lying; which means you have to protect yourself by not having sex with him, until you are sure he is clean. You can defiantly tell him that because you don't know where he has been; there is no way he is getting any 'nookie' from you! He will then have to offer some kind of explanation; which you can follow up through his friends and the places he claims to have been. You are his wife/partner; so there should be no need for secrets, otherwise, what is the point being married or living together? You should therefore consider your relationship options; which should include living apart, where it will be even harder for him to get any sex from you.

"Does my bum look big in this dress?" is a question many women have at one time or another asked their partners; and most men will lie and say, *"No darling. It looks fine!"* This means a man will definitely tell a lie, in order to protect a woman's feelings; so you cannot expect him to confess to a casual affair. It is therefore in your own interests to make sure you do not give him too much of a rope; or he will surely hang himself. In other words; if you want your man to behave himself, then you must keep a firm hand on him without it seeming like you are controlling him. It is almost like the way the police can keep control of a crowd at a football match, by using intelligence and subtle surveillance; without the crowd noticing that their every move is in fact being watched. Once you know exactly what your man gets up to and it is no threat to your marriage; you can relax. Until then; you have to gather enough information to make up your intelligence, which has to be constantly updated. For instance; if he goes regularly to a pub, then go with him a few times and make friends with the waitresses, bar staff, doorman, manager and a few of the regulars. This way; he will know that if he makes a wrong move by trying

to pick up a girl, someone is bound to tell you. Once you have that under control; there is no need to go with him because you are aware of the environment he will be at. He cannot go elsewhere without your finding out; because one of his friends will surely give the game away. If he strays from his location and starts lying about it; it means he has something to hide and you should refuse sex with the usual *"I'm not in the mood..."* tactic. By refusing him sex until you are sure he is 'in good health' through your network of wives/partners of his friends; he will realise that you are one tough cookie and he will not be able to get away with infidelity for long, because you will find out and that would be the end of what he has with you. For most men; knowing in no uncertain terms what they have to lose if they embark on silly escapades, is enough to stop them straying. A man usually slips up when the lady in his life has not taken the relationship seriously enough to spell out the no-go areas and their consequences. *"I will leave you if ..."* is what all men need to know at the beginning of any relationship. Nobody expects you to police your man twenty-four hours a day; and it would be unrealistic to expect him to behave himself, when you are not around. There is however, always a line he should never cross; or else it will threaten your relationship and could even destroy it completely. It is important to make him acutely aware what that line is; so that there is no ambiguity.

If he seems to have lost interest in you; then your alarm bells should start ringing. If he is not horny; it can only mean he has not got enough sperm to spare for you. He might have used most of it on someone else! If you are sure he is not having an emotional affair; then it can only be a physical affair. You have to get to the bottom of it; for your own sake and sanity! Like any crime that is committed; there will always be clues left behind when a man has a casual fling with a woman. This is because it is usually a rush job and may not have been planned. It is important that you keep your eyes and ears open; so that as soon as you have an inkling something is wrong, you start piling up the evidence and prepare yourself for the confrontation. If there is to be a break-up; you have to make sure you come out on top! If you get a chance to do the washing; go through his dirty clothes and smell them for female perfume. Pay attention to the crotch of his underwear for semen stains. There is no mistaking the odour of a woman's vaginal juices; if he makes the mistake of having indiscriminate sex and does not have time to wash. Check his mobile phone when he is asleep; in case there are any revealing messages left on it. Even though casual sex is supposed to be 'no strings attached'; some people find it hard to let go. He might still be in touch with the girl! Talk to the wives/girlfriends of his friends; so that you can set a few traps for him. Amongst men; nothing stays secret for long. His friends will definitely know what he has been getting up to! If she uses her head; one of the wives/ girlfriends can find out for you, without her man becoming suspicious. If one of the men is having casual sex; it could also mean another of the boys could follow suit. It is therefore, in the interests of the wives to get to the bottom of it; before any real damage is done.

Snooping on your man may seem unethical; but in the world of self-defence, you have to put the interests of you and your family at the top of the agenda. Sex outside a relationship is a betrayal of the unity you are trying to build together, and will ruin everything! It is important that you keep a firm handle on what is going on around you; so that when there is a threat to the relationship, you will be in a much stronger position to fight it. This also means that you have to start as you mean to go on; by playing your part in not doing things that will make you a hypocrite. Believe it or not; men also have feelings that can easily be hurt! You should never indulge in any affairs outside your relationship; because he may also have his ways of finding out! Be good and he will be obliged to follow suit!

Battling with the opposite sex can be trying at the best of times! What happens if you are at a loss as to what to do about a loved one; because his behaviour is driving you up the wall? See the next chapter!

Chapter Fifteen
The impossible situation (Part 2)
Dilemmas

As a woman in a marriage or relationship; you are from time to time going to come across certain difficulties and problems with your husband/partner or children, which you are going to find very hard to solve. Because you feel the obvious solutions will not be pleasant; you may end up dithering for so long that nothing will be done about them. This means the problem or difficulty will not go away; simply because you are afraid of the outcome or drastic change in your lifestyle. Dilemmas are usually the downfall of a woman; because her loving and forgiving nature stubbornly refuses to see that something in the one she loves is not good for her well-being. Friends and family could tell her the obvious truth, and she will agree with them; but still cannot get herself to cross the finishing line and put an end to her misery. Many women who suffer in the hands of cruel, selfish, manipulative and domineering men; fall into this category because somewhere in her heart, she believes things will work out in the end. To make matters more confusing; the men involved in this mental and physical abuse can also be very kind, generous and loving...when it suits them. As a result; the woman tends to remember the good times and tries to blot out the bad incidents from her memory. There is a saying; that nobody is all-bad or all-good! No human being is as stupid as he or she appears to be; because people do things by convenience. This means we only act when it suits us; and for that reason, a woman could be accused of 'getting what she asks for'. Unless she herself makes the move to correct the ills that surround her; everyone else is going to mind their own business. Most women who suffer from dilemmas are in the habit of keeping things to themselves. Inwardly, she would be undergoing extreme mental conflict; which ultimately, could destroy her dignity, self-esteem and reputation. The loss of face and shame in the failure to be loved and respected by her man; can be so degrading that she will outwardly pretend that everything is fine, rather than unveil the truth. To tell anyone; would reveal that her 'perfect' life which she prefers people to believe, is in fact, not so perfect after all! When you add this to the fear of losing the lifestyle she has been used to, by becoming a divorcée with less status and income; and the unwillingness to destroy the family by leaving the children without a stable home...one can understand and sympathise the trauma women face with their dilemmas.

I am not in the position to judge or criticise your way of life; because I know you are very capable of making your own lifestyle choices. I will therefore, offer some ways that things can go wrong in a relationship; whereby you could find yourself in a dilemma. However; the solution I give you may not be what will solve your predicament to your satisfaction. In the end, you must do what is right for you and your family; bearing in mind that it is very hard to change from 'who you really are'. This means that whatever dilemma your man puts you into, he is unlikely to change just to please you; and if you change your inherent beliefs and personality just to accommodate his, you will be very unhappy. Personally; I do not believe any man is worth compromising your happiness, dignity, integrity and reputation. But if for example; he is still offering you a fantastic lifestyle; has given you some happy moments; and you have borne him wonderful children, which you are unwilling to forego; then as far as you are concerned, my advice could be wrong. You could probably live with his failures; if he is not harming you physically! This book is one of female self-defence; so I have to assume the problems are with those closest to you and the dilemmas are yours, against him. I can therefore, only show you how to defend yourself against what he is doing to you; because only an expert specialising in mental health and psychological issues, can probably help you save you from yourself. If you are the one with the problem; you will first of all have to recognise and be willing to do something about it, before any professional can help you to succeed. I'm sorry I cannot do more for you!

1. Substance abuse

All substance abuses are unhealthy, debilitating, dangerous and expensive; which means, they are a major threat to a family's well-being and existence. I stated in an earlier chapter that you should always check out if your man is an alcoholic or drug abuser; and if he shows tendencies of not being able to give up, you should not marry him. The main problem with substance abuse is that it can change one's character to such an extent; he/she will do and say things they would not have, had they been sober. Once alcoholism or drug use hits a person; it is almost impossible for him/her to stop, without expert counselling and a drastic change in their lifestyle...in addition to a tremendously strong will-power. Even then; he or she is only one sip, puff, snort or jab away from undoing all the hard work of the counsellors. Those who are into substance abuse; are liable to hate, undermine, insult and even attack anyone for daring to tell them to stop. If your man is a substance abuser; he will never be in his 'right mind'. This means, he will potentially be dangerous to you. He could easily yell at you; beat you up; rape you; or rush out of the house to a more compliant mistress who 'understands' him. You therefore have to seriously persuade him to seek help; before his habit destroys him and the rest of the family. It is a real impossible situation; so you have to also prepare yourself for failure, because breaking your husband's addiction will probably be the hardest thing you will ever have to do. In the end; you may have to leave him, taking the children with you or call the police on him, in order for him to come to his senses.

(a). Alcohol

Since drink is part of many a country's culture; it has become increasingly difficult to judge anyone for their drinking habits. What is too much for one; might not be excessive to another drinker! The wine imbiber might be quick to criticise the beer guzzler; even though the wine probably contains more alcohol than the beer. Beer is associated with the lager lout and responsible for many public disorder problems; whereas wine and spirits are seen as more 'behaviour friendly'. Yet at the same time; most domestic alcoholics prefer wine and spirits! Both of these examples have been known to produce violent alcoholics; except one is deemed more acceptable than the other, because it is done secretly and out of the public glare. This means that there is a lot of hypocrisy associated with alcoholism; and society prefers to sweep things under the carpet, rather than admit there is a national problem. Alcohol is responsible for over half of all domestic violence and almost all car accidents and street brawls! So, what can a woman do when her man starts drinking to excess; and as a result, his behaviour towards her alters? If you are also a drinker; he will not listen to you! In a sensible way, you may also have to stop drinking, if you want him to; because you will be seen as a hypocrite and deliberately putting temptation in his path. You should also be aware that if alcohol has become part of him and is what 'makes him tick'; you could be jumping from frying pan to fire by trying to make him give it up. This is because he will not be the same person without a drink in his hand; and could become more irritable, rude and possibly violent. In the end, you must realise that you cannot do it all by yourself; and it would be wise to either contact the professionals or wash your hands completely off him.

Getting drunk numbs the senses; and your man may not be aware or even care how badly he is behaving. An evening out on the town can easily be ruined by his intoxicated state; whereby he may say and do some very hurtful things to you, without accepting responsibility for them. Although there are women who do get drunk and misbehave; the worst behavioural excesses are usually with the men. This is why you have to keep a wary eye open on your man, when he starts drinking excessively. The following examples are only the tip of the iceberg of male bad behaviour caused by alcohol!

1. You may go out together to a party, where the drinks are free. Your man gets blindingly drunk, starts making a fool of himself and embarrasses you by lewdly eyeing up and propositioning the other women; completely forgetting that he came with you.

2. You go out for a pleasant meal and meet some old male friend of yours by chance. He gets jealous because he thinks the man was trying to 'chat you up'; and starts threatening him to leave you alone. An argument erupts. The evening ends abruptly, when the two men start fighting; causing extensive damage to the premises. The police are called and he spends the night in the cells. He is then hit with a hefty bill (one which in the end, you may have to help pay) for the damage he caused.

3. He insists on driving, even though he is drunk; crashes the car, knocks someone over or hits another car and injures/kills the

occupants. Even if he manages to get home safely; he could easily bring his bad behaviour home with him by yelling at, hitting or raping you because he thinks you 'enjoyed talking to other men'.

4. You arrive home from the nightclub in good spirits, expecting a nice bout of lovemaking. Sadly, he cannot 'get it up' because he has 'brewer's droop'; leaving you sexually frustrated.

5. He gets so drunk, he starts vomiting. Because he is so 'out of it'; you are the one who ends up cleaning up his vomit off your living room floor or having to apologise to your party hostess, for his ruining of her favourite sofa/rug.

First of all; if he is drinking too much, it is unwise to criticise or try to stop him in front of people. He will most likely refuse; and will yell at or threaten you, if you push it too much. It might also make him drink even more; just to show you that he is 'master of himself'. No one, not even you; can tell him what to do! You therefore have to act as if everything is fine; get him on his own and try to convince him to continue drinking at home. By gently offering him 'a better alternative' like his favourite sex act; you should be able to get him out of the party or nightclub before he starts causing mayhem. If he refuses to leave; you have to make sure you stay with him all the time by hugging him or holding his hand tightly, until he is ready to leave. Unfortunately; this in effect, would have ruined your evening! The alternative would have him running riot unchallenged and ruining everyone else's evening; which is not a good idea. As a couple; you may never be invited to future parties and you may even be banned from all the clubs in your area. Word spreads fast against alcoholic troublemakers! If he decides he wants to drive home whilst intoxicated; you must refuse to get into the vehicle and insist on leaving the car and taking a taxi. Get his friends or the bouncers of the club to physically prevent him from driving the car. If necessary; call the police on him, without his knowing it was you who called them! The police will not arrest him because he has not actually driven the car; but they are within their rights to warn him he will be arrested, if he gets behind the wheel in his inebriated state. If he proves difficult; they will seize the keys off him and impound the vehicle. That should sober him up very quickly! Once you get him home, he will definitely be in a bad mood because of your intransigence; so try and coax him into bed. You could also use sex as an incentive or fix him a drink and put some crushed sleeping tablets in it; which will make him fall harmlessly asleep! He probably won't remember how badly he misbehaved; so there is no need to mention it in the morning, when he wakes up!

One of the biggest mistakes most women make; is to offer excuses for their partner's bad behaviour. *"Oh, he was drunk; he's not normally like that…"* Without a doubt; it will happen again! The fact is; just one evening of mayhem could ruin your marriage. This is because you may decide not to go out with him, if he is drinking; by constantly reminding him of the night he misbehaved in public. He quickly promises to behave. Like most women; you give him another chance. He then goes and causes more trouble, when you go out. You are so angry that you ban him from drinking; which puts him in a bad mood and thinks you are nagging and picking on him. *"…But you drink as well…!"* You reply with the dismissive, *"…but I don't get drunk and misbehave…!"* From then on; it is a slippery downhill slope, which will most likely end up with the breakdown in your relationship. This is because you may refuse him sex when he drinks. He will then start seeing you as some sort of 'antagoniser'; who only sees his faults and not his good points. Arguments will follow; and he may end up hurling hurtful insults at you; hitting you; raping you; or cheating on you. He will either begin drinking secretly when you are out of the house; or he may start going out more, so that he can drink in peace. He will definitely meet someone else who sympathises with his drinking; and will most likely sleep with her, since he is not getting any sex from you. Once he starts an affair; he will spend a lot more time with his newly acquired mistress because she will not judge or criticise him for his drinking. Since he is not in his correct frame of mind, due to the alcohol; he may not even care if you find out! You will then be in direct confrontation with his love for the bottle and his mistress. I am loath to say, you will lose this battle; because it will be two against one. Your relationship will effectively be over! Even if he gives up the drink; could you also forgive his indiscretion with the other woman? Somehow, I doubt whether any woman has that kind of patience, understanding and forgiveness in her heart.

You now have to realise that you have a real dilemma on your hands; so you have to assess your situation. Uppermost in your thinking; should be that you cannot and will not put up with his drinking anymore! The dilemma you will face will be that when he is sober, he is fine; and even very sweet towards you and the children. You still love him, but not when he is drinking; so you have to find a way to convince him to seek help. When he is sober; you have to sit him down and explain to him in plain language, things like the monetary cost of alcohol to the family, the hurt he is causing you and the children and what you will be forced to do, if he does not stop. You must sympathise with him that you know it is not easy; but you are prepared to go with him and stand by him, should he decide to seek professional help. Try to use female tact when talking to him; so that he realises there is a problem, which needs to be fixed. It is important he does not feel like he is being blamed; because it will bring his self-esteem even lower than it already is. He may decide to give himself a 'lift', by going on a *"...my wife doesn't understand me..."* type of 'pub crawl booze-bender'; possibly ending up in a casual sex scenario. Alcoholism is such a tough habit to crack that you are definitely going to face resistance. You will realise after a while, whether he is the type who is capable of giving up; or one who will pay lip service by promising the earth but delivering nothing. If he is the latter; then I am afraid you have to use a shock treatment by walking out on him, albeit temporarily, and refusing to return until he seeks treatment.

If he becomes violent or forces you to have sex whilst he is drunk; you have to use the same methods employed in the wife-beating or marital rape scenarios, described earlier in this chapter. You must not beat around the bush and keep giving him chances; because once he starts using violence, he cannot stop. The alcohol will always prevent him from realising what he is doing wrong. It always begins with him yelling at you, for something very simple; like not having his dinner ready on time. From then on; he will find fault with every little thing you do or forget to do. If you dare answer him back with the combative, *"Shut up, you're drunk!"*; he may decide to hit you for criticising his new love, *Ms. Alcohol*. Once he hits you; the next step will be to demand things from you, especially sex. When that is not forthcoming; he will hit you again. If you concede to his demands; then like a child, he will realise that violence works with you and he will not stop. He may end up killing you; because he will never be able to control the amount of force he uses on you. In such a situation; you have to call the police and start thinking of living your life without him. He will most probably be barred from coming anywhere near you; or jailed. If you are looking for a divorce; it would be helpful to your lawyers to hide a spy-cam in your house to film how much he drinks over a twenty-four hour period...just in case he tries to deny he has a drink problem or denies he treats you violently. The camera will record revealing footage of his behaviour; which will give any judge a valid reason to grant you a divorce and substantial alimony. You could also hire a private detective to gather evidence against him. This would be easy; because he would have already made a name for himself all over town. There will be enough witnesses to make your case rock-solid!

If your man drinks excessively, but does not cause you or the children any financial or violent problems; then you do not have any realistic way of convincing him to stop, apart from stressing the damage it could be doing to his body. More than likely; he will not listen to you! People who drink never take health problems seriously, until they find themselves in hospital looking for an organ donor; usually a liver or a kidney. You however, have to take it seriously! If he damages his liver or kidneys to alcohol; then the children will be without a fit father and you will have an invalid on your hands. If he is ill; he may lose his job and less income will be flowing into your household. This means, the brunt of looking after the family will fall on your shoulders! Can the family afford the hospital and medical expenses if he falls ill; knowing that you may have to give up your job and ambitions to look after him? Are you ready for any or all of these possibilities? All these are valid enough reasons to lay down the law on him to stop; or at least, cut down the amount he drinks. Since you know that his situation can only get worse; you have to warn him that if he has not sought help in the next couple of weeks, the relationship will be over and you will be contacting a divorce lawyer. He is being selfish; so you have to think of yourself and the children! If he cannot see that his drinking is hurting you, then it means he loves the alcohol more than you; and just as you would do if he had a woman on the side, you have to kick him out. If he wants to ruin his life; it would be better if he does it alone and should not be allowed to drag the family down with him! Believe it or not; men are not indispensable! It is always better to be without a man; than to have one who continues to cause you problems by undermining your dignity, integrity, self-esteem and reputation!

(b). Drugs

Aside from alcohol; the other substance abuse likely to destroy your family is drugs. Because each drug will have different effects on the user, you have to keep your eyes open for any behavioural changes in your husband; just in case he has a secret habit. The possibilities of drugs destroying your family are enormous; because they all have one thing in common, in that sooner or later, the drug becomes more important to the user than the family. Eventually, whatever drug he is indulging in; will affect his reactions, judgement, priorities and loyalty to you and the children! Although he probably won't rape you because he will be too 'stoned' to even bother making love to you; he may become unaffectionate, lazy, arrogant, verbally abusive and disrespectful to you, without his realising that he is doing anything wrong. Because drugs are illegal; he will have to do it secretly. This can cause paranoia; making him believe that everyone is 'out to get him'. This might include you; because he knows you are against his habit! He will then take unusual steps to defend himself; by hiding the drugs around the house, in places where you are unlikely to look. This is because he believes you will flush them down the toilet if you found them! All this subterfuge will slowly drive the two of you apart; because he will be living a double life and you will be the last person he will confide in. Without your 'nagging' presence and interference; he could make financial decisions, which to his drug-fuelled mind, will seem like a great piece of business but might turn out to be loss-making and send your family into economic ruin. He will most likely take family and personal decisions without consulting you; because his arrogance will assume he knows better. It will be only a matter of time, before one of his druggie associates convinces him to go into a catastrophic business venture. When someone takes drugs, especially the more expensive ones like cocaine and heroin; the sharks amongst his 'friends' will begin to circle, trying to get him to part with his money. They will assume anybody who can afford to spend that kind of money on a regular basis, must have a lot of financial resources! Unfortunately, this money is usually meant for the family; and you may not realise that he has squandered most of his cash, until it is too late. Like alcohol, the things that can go wrong in your relationship when your man is seriously into drugs are too many to mention all of them here; but from this paragraph, you should be able to deduce that whichever way you look at it...it is not good news.

If you are too set against his drug use; he will start going out to friends to do it there. Slowly but surely; you will lose any influence you have over him. Drugs can make the user very talkative and he may reveal all kinds of family secrets to a complete stranger or to his druggie friends; who could one day use his revelations against him. Because he is drugged out of his mind; he will see you as the 'enemy' who does not approve of his habit. If he makes any disparaging remarks about you to other people; he will feel they are your 'just desserts'! There will be nothing sacred in your relationship; and all respect for you will go out of the window. *"The bitch won't let me smoke in the house; and sex with her is boring. She won't even give me a blow-job...!"* It will not be hard for any woman who fancies him and actually approves of his drug use, to get him into bed. She will then have such an influence over him that he will start funding her own drug habit; in return for sex and a gentle ear, which listens to him instead of blocking him. Within a relatively short period of time, you will notice a 'change' in your man. Aside from his drug use; he will also be having an affair, whilst spending more and more time and money with his new love. His suspicious behaviour will be impossible to hide, and he may not even care; because he will have lost all respect for you, due to the fact that he has a 'new woman' in his life. Drugs are such a powerful force, that you will most probably feel jealous of how it 'possesses' your man. Very few women can win, when asking a junky to choose between the drug and her! If he loves you, he will start lying to you that he will give it up; but will most likely continue doing it behind your back. Rather than accept the truth that he is too hooked to give up; he will make all kinds of promises about how he is going to 'change for you'. If he has been taking drugs; he may stay away from the house, sometimes for days at a time, until he is sure you will not notice his bloodshot eyes or has smartened up his unkempt appearance.

When he does decide to return home; he could still be so 'out of it' he will start misbehaving around the house, thinking he is just larking about. This could frighten the children and make you feel very insecure; not knowing what he might do next. For example; because he is 'high', he might decide to lift the children, throw them in the air and catch them before they fall down or chase them around the house. This might seem like fun to the kids; but in the context of his drug use, very dangerous because he will not be in full control of his strength, reflexes or sobriety. He might suddenly get 'the munchies' in the middle of the night, go into the kitchen, cook himself a meal and leave the place in a mess for you to clean up in the morning; that is, if he does not break your favourite china in the process! He may also have been on a drug bender; and will return home so tired that he could fall asleep for days. He will then have to lie to his bosses at work that he is 'sick'; because he has not got the strength to get up and go to work. In the end; he could lose his job completely, when his work colleagues get fed up with his succession of no-shows. He may feel guilty he has been neglecting you for too long and decide to shower you with affection and gifts. This will not impress you; because you know he is not in his right senses! You will then reject his advances and he will feel you don't 'love him'; which will send him down a spiral of more drug use. These, with other boisterous, irresponsible and 'irrational behaviour' too many to mention; are what can make any drug abuse by your man such a torrid rollercoaster for you. No woman can be expected to put up with that kind of emotional torture. In desperation; you might try to find out where he is buying his drugs and then call the police on the dealer. This tactic, although understandable, is never a smart move; because it puts your family in danger of recriminations, if it were ever revealed who alerted the law. Besides; he will most likely know other dealers and will very quickly move on, whereby you may never know where he is getting his stuff from.

As I explained before; a few puffs of marihuana or a couple of lines of cocaine at weekends will not cause any lasting damage. The problem is; very few people have the willpower to limit their drug use to a social level. Sometimes it is better to have a little understanding; so that if he is using a drug and not abusing it, you should not be too harsh on him. If you try stopping him; he will go and do it elsewhere and you will lose him! You have to remember that you are not dealing with a child, but with an adult; and it will be very difficult to tell him to stop or convince him that it is bad for him. He may have been taking drugs on and off for more years than he can recall; and was probably doing it, before he met you! Trying to change his habit to suit you, will cause resentment and he will accuse you of being selfish; especially if you have your own vices, like cigarettes and alcohol. Therefore; the best way to look at it, is to decide whether his behaviour when he is on drugs affects you and the rest of the family in a negative way. Is he rich enough to afford an expensive drug habit? Does he do his chores around the house efficiently, without complaint? Has he got time to play with the children and listen to their problems in a loving way? Does he go to work on time and fulfil his financial obligations to the family? Does he make love to you in a way that satisfies you totally? Is he interested in what you have to say and offer responsible solutions to your problems? Is he affectionate, fun and loving to be around? If the answer is a resounding 'Yes!' to all the above questions, and he does not do the drugs in front of the children; then it means his habit does not affect the family in a negative way. In such a situation, it might be better to let sleeping dogs lie and allow him his habit; and hope he will one day 'see sense' and give up on his own accord, either out of boredom or for the benefit of his health. It is very hard to find the 'perfect man'! A sensible drug user, whose habit does not affect the family; is much better than a non-user who gets drunk, sleeps with women all over town and comes home to yell at, beat up or force unpleasant sex acts on you!

If you are also taking drugs, then this acceptance of his habit will allow him to behave 'normally' and not feel ashamed to do it in front of you; so that he does not feel a need to go elsewhere to do it. However; the problem with both you and your man taking drugs, is that there will not be a sobering effect around the house. This means that things like the needs of the children, the domestic chores and financial management of the family will be neglected; because both of you will be too absorbed in yourselves to care.

Taking drugs will probably mean drinking and smoking cigarettes as well; because marijuana, hash, cocaine and heroin are often mixed with tobacco and smoked. To the untrained eye; it looks as if you are having a quiet smoke and a drink! If you have children; there will be no one to give them the love and attention they need. Slowly but surely; little things around the house will be neglected and go wrong. All drugs will eventually erode into your self-confidence and energy; and before you know it, your temper starts fraying and you are yelling and losing your patience with everyone. One by one; your non-druggie friends will stop coming around. This is because any time they do, it ends in an argument; usually started by your volatile mood swings. All children will pick up on this lack of control; and may even get 'contact high', by inadvertently inhaling the smoke around the house. This would make it very easy for them to grow up without any discipline, not knowing right from wrong; and end up on cigarettes, alcohol and drugs as well. This is simply because there is no one to tell them how destructive substance abuse can be! From then on; they may fall into the teenage traps of gang culture, violence, crime, incarceration and death…all because the parents were so into drugs, alcohol and self-indulgence; they did not have the time to give them the love, care and attention they deserved.

Even if your man's drug of choice is 'only' marijuana, it can still affect the family because it will make him sluggish and lazy; thereby neglecting certain tasks, which at first may seem innocuous enough. This may include not bothering to wipe the dribble from a child's mouth/nose or attend to him/her when they are crying; but could easily lead up to his completely forgetting to pick the children from school or feed them their dinner on time, when you are out of the house. Not noticing dangerous objects around the home like electrical plugs and kitchen knives; are also signs of forgetfulness that could be brought on by marijuana or hashish. With cocaine, the dangers are even more prevalent; because the stranglehold on a user is much more intense and the high does not last so long. This means he will continue doing it for long periods at a time; till the body gets so tired, he falls asleep. Whilst he is indulging in cocaine; he will definitely neglect his responsibilities towards you, the children, his work and even himself. It is mentally addictive; so even if he claims he does not do it all the time, he is likely to spend all his time between snorts, thinking about his next high. This means he will not be mentally alert to take care of the important things in his life; like looking after himself, his work efficiency, responsibility to the children, his domestic duties and affection towards you. If you add this to erratic and possibly violent behaviour caused by paranoia; then you will realise that cocaine is not really such a 'glamour drug' after all. Heroin is probably the one that should cause you the most concern, if your man is hooked on it; because it is physically addictive and you will see your man deteriorate before your very eyes. It is the only drug that the junky cannot hide from; because the effects are so blatantly physical! With cocaine and marijuana the craving is mental; which means it is possible to do them casually for years, without anyone outside the close family or circle of friends knowing. It is almost impossible to give up heroin, without expensive professional expertise; because the user will actually fall ill without it, and will miraculously 'get better' as soon as he/she has a 'fix'. Rather than see their men so miserable without the drug; there are women who will turn a blind eye or even pay for his habit! This is because he is a completely different person once he has taken some heroin; by being more fun, loving, full of life and a better lover. As soon as the 'buzz' wears off; he will be irritable, pathetically feeling sorry for himself, sweating and shaking as if he has a fever. In American ghetto parlance; this is what is sometimes known as *'the Jones coming down'*. It is hard enough for a woman to see her man deteriorate in front of her eyes; but can you imagine how it will mentally affect the children, to see their father in such a condition?

Once your man starts seriously taking drugs and you realise it is affecting your family, you have to immediately make a major decision; whether to put up with it, try and stop it or walk away from him. If you have children; it will be even harder to decide what to do. You must realise that he is not going to stop it because of you. It has to be his decision! You therefore have to sit him down on a day when he is sober and insist he gets professional help; by detailing exactly how his drug use is hurting you, and likely to ruin your family. If he will not listen or breaks promises about giving up, then you have to take steps to defend yourself with the ultimate acceptance that at some point, you are going to leave him; because he will bankrupt the family, end up in prison or even die. If you are not married and have no children; then there is nothing to stop you walking away, whilst you can. There must be better ways to live your life than with a drug addict who refuses to change; or at least, control his usage to acceptable levels! Once you are in a relationship; you have a duty to yourself and your family to protect and defend your interests with a guile, secrecy and determination to win, usually attributed to combat generals. I hate saying this, but if he is abusing drugs in the house; you will have to hide a video camera in your living room to secretly film his domestic behaviour. This is because you need as much ammunition as possible, in order to facilitate a strong argument for your lawyers during the break-up; so that you come out on top. If you can afford to hire a private detective to find out where or from whom he is buying the drugs; you should do so. A few photos and recordings later; you will have irreversible proof that he is throwing money away. The private snoop will know how to relay the information to the police; without anyone knowing you were behind the bust of his dealer. From then on; you should secretly start making plans to move away from him, taking the children with you. You must then get an injunction for a court to freeze all the money in his account; so that he cannot withdraw it, without your knowledge. You can use the argument that you are afraid he will spend it on drugs, to the detriment of the children; and may end up in prison. Once you are away; you have to seek a barring order against him so that he can only see you and the children under supervision. It would be very easy for the Child Protection Services in your country to take them away from you; if they find out you allowed them to live under the same roof as drug abuser!

Leaving him will obviously hurt; so the decision must not be taken lightly. You have to think of yourself and your family; which means, not even the scourge of alcohol or drugs should be allowed to get in the way of your safety and happiness. If that does not shock him into seeking professional help, then you can thank your lucky stars that you are out of his life; because he will never change. Give him a few months before pushing for a divorce; so that your conscience will be clear that you did your best, gave him enough chances to clean up his act and he refused. Even if he does seek help; you should not go back to him until he can prove through the addiction counsellors that he has been clean for at least a year. This probably means your relationship will be over anyway; because you may meet someone else during that time. You are a woman who deserves to be loved and respected by the man you have given your life to; and if he cannot reciprocate the sacrifices you have made for him, then there is nothing more you can do. Sadly; it's a case of *'good riddance to bad rubbish!'* because you are no miracle worker!

2. Addictions

There are many addictions of course; but the main ones that could hit your relationship in a negative way are gambling, cigarettes, sex, gluttony and exercise. They are the ones that can easily become more important than the actual relationship. Since they are not immediately visually harmful to the body, there is a tendency not to take them as seriously as drugs and alcohol abuses. There is also the false belief that the culprit will listen to advice and seek help from the professionals. This can be very soul destroying, when you realise that they are just as difficult to get rid of as substance abuses; because the one involved will always believe he/she is not doing anything wrong. If the threat is not spotted early and nothing is done about it, an addiction could do irreparable damage to your family and your life; because you are the one who is going to end up with the problem and the solution dumped firmly on your shoulders. The most dangerous addiction for you and your family is probably gambling; because of the irreparable financial damage it can do. Cigarettes and gluttony are not far behind; because of the well-known deterioration to one's health. A sex or exercise addict in your relationship will destroy your self-esteem, dignity, integrity and reputation; because he will seek to control you and make you pander to his addiction. Again, for the purposes of this book, I have to assume the problem is with your partner and not you; so if you are the one with the addiction it would be best to seek professional help.

(a). Gambling

With the advent of the Internet; gambling has now become so popular that the politicians are worried at the effect it is having on society as a whole. What used to be a bit of fun in the casino at weekends or on trips abroad; has got to the point where there are people who spend most of their time and money on the phenomenon. When added to the established betting on week-end sports; gambling is now a cancer that is ruining many a marriage. It could be poker or black jack on the Internet; card games with friends; roulette and slot machines in the casinos; betting on dog racing; picking winners on horses; 'get-rich-quick' schemes; or predicting football results. Once money is involved; it becomes an obsession to win, which can turn a normally pleasant person into a monster.

As a woman, you have to be very worried when your man becomes a regular gambler; simply because of the amount of money he could be losing, to the detriment of the family. The addiction could become so serious; that he will even forget he has a family and neglect you completely. He will be so absorbed in the gambling; that he will not bother doing his chores around the house; the quality of his work will suffer; he will have no time for you or the children; and it will affect his lovemaking prowess. The high of winning is so exciting, that it is very easy for him to be sucked into his 'hobby'; without realising that like drugs, it is very short-lived. The depression that comes with losing is enough to ruin any relationship! Instead of saving the money he wins; he is more likely to plough it back into another bet and may end up losing everything. This suggests that he is not doing it for the money, but rather for the thrill of playing; and that means, it has possessed him so much, he will have to seek professional help. Because most of his gambling will be done away from you in gambling dens, betting shops, on his mobile phone or computer; you may never be aware just how much damage he is doing to his bank account...until the bills start piling up. By then; he may have squandered everything!

Like substance abuse; you have to find time to talk to him on a day he is not gambling and explain in no uncertain terms how his gambling is affecting the family. You have to make sure you do not try to dissuade him when he has just won or has just lost; because in either case, he will not listen to you. If he is on a winning streak; he will not see the problem and may even give you money to go shopping, just to prove his point. If he proceeds to pay off all the outstanding bills, then he would have defeated your concerns; because you will have nothing to fight him with. If he has been losing; he may 'agree' with you that it is costing him money and may promise to change. But something inside him will tell him that he is a failure; and has gone down in your estimation of him. He may then proceed to 'put things right' by going back to the gambling world, in order to try and win back what he has lost; so that he can 'finish on a high'. Unfortunately; he may lose again and will be back to the beginning. He will then keep on playing till he wins 'enough' money; which may be a long time arriving. This inability to quit while ahead is what ruins all gamblers. If you want to save your marriage or relationship, then drastic measures will have to be taken by you; because he will certainly not be willing to do it himself.

Telling anyone how he/she should spend their money is always seen as an intrusion into their privacy; so you will have to decide for yourself how much his addiction is hurting your family. If he is so rich that the money spent on gambling is very little in comparison; then you can put it down to an expensive hobby and leave him to it. However; if the children need new clothes; the fridge is half-empty; the school fees have not been paid; and it has been a long time since you had a family holiday or bought yourself a new dress; then you would be justified in putting your foot down, because his addiction is directly affecting the quality of your life. You will then have to start thinking about taking steps to stem the flow of cash out of the family coffers. Because of its secrecy, you will not be able to directly stop him gambling; so the only way is to check the finances. You have to organise a separate bank account for the family; which he should under no circumstances be able to assess. By establishing a direct debit from his account into the family one; you will be able to guarantee a certain amount flows in every month to pay the bills and look after the family. You should also have a separate account for yourself; so that in the event he blows all his money on a bet, he cannot get any more from you. You then try and find out how much he spends every week on gambling; by checking his bank statements when they arrive. If necessary; you could also hire a private detective to uproot his mobile phone records and credit card details, in case he makes bets over the phone or on the Internet. Once you have gathered enough relevant evidence that he is squandering the family silver; you should go and see a solicitor to clarify your position, in the event of a separation or divorce.

Aside from his gambling, you will most probably still love him; so it might be time for some tough love. Don't be afraid to vocally chastise him for his 'lack of effort' in the lovemaking department; even if secretly, you are happy enough with it! *"What's the matter? You never used to be so tired. Are you having an affair? Don't you find me attractive anymore?"* Try to 'nag' him into submission with some typical female chastisements; and keep embarrassing him for the children's needs and household money. *"You forgot to empty the bin last night". "How come you never spend enough time with me/the children? You haven't even noticed that they need some new clothes". "I need to have some money for...".* If he dares refuse your requests; you should use your renowned female battering ram of verbal abuse and snide remarks, followed by the silent treatment and inactivity around the house, described earlier on in Chapter 5. No man is that stupid! Eventually; he will realise something is very wrong and you are not happy. It is only when he asks you what the problem is; that you tell him you believe his gambling is getting in the way of the relationship and you are thinking of going away with the children for a while, in order to assess the situation. If he tries to dissuade you from going; then you have to tell him to seek professional help for his addiction, or you will divorce him. You can no longer live with worrying about the amount of money he wastes on gambling! Since he cannot provide a financial guarantee for the family; any future with him will never be secure and you are better off walking away from the madness. Be very calm; and don't pay any heed if he tries to bluff his way or threatens you. That would be the addiction in him, retaliating in defiance; in order to hide his embarrassment. Besides; your solicitors should have already told you where you stand, so there is not much he can do. He will be acutely aware that a divorce will be very costly for him. Offer to support him; and immediately tell him you are making the appointment for him to see a gambling addiction counsellor. If he stubbornly refuses to listen to you; then you have to be brave and carry out your threat by either moving out of the house with the children or throwing him out. *"Get out! I've had enough of this!"* or *"I'm leaving!"* You should follow this up by getting a court order to keep him away from you and the kids; citing emotional torture and fear for your safety. The official who signs the barring order; will be fully aware that most gamblers end up in debt and start borrowing cash to continue their obsession. Your life could easily be in danger; when the debtors start coming to your house to collect what your man owes them!

If you have no children; you should move out of the house and stay with friends until the divorce. The verdict from the judge should compensate you adequately for your emotional distress; in living with a gambler who refuses to give up his habit. No woman deserves to lie awake at night fearing for her safety; and shaking with fear any time the doorbell or the phone rings. It is better you get out before it reaches that desperate stage; because it will! You really are better-off living alone and determining your own destiny; rather than watch the one you love throwing the family money away. It is not fair to spend your life worrying about a future with no financial guarantees or security; caused by the man you love!

(b). Cigarettes

Cigarette smoking is probably the most famous addiction. Even though it is common knowledge that it causes lung cancer, it has not stopped the die-hards; because they are well and truly addicted. Because death from smoking is never immediate; the smokers do not take it seriously and believe they will stop before it can do any lasting damage. This selfish attitude to continue smoking, to the detriment of everyone else; is increasingly being recognised by some governments, who have now banned smoking in all public places. They should actually take it a step further and ban smoking in front of young children; because they may not be aware of the dangers, and have no recognised way of voicing their fears. If they are uncomfortable with the smoke in the room; they don't even have the option of leaving the house! In comparison to gambling, it does not cost much to smoke; which makes it very dangerous to the health. If someone has been smoking for a long time; then nothing I say here will deter him/her. He/She already knows that it is not good for the health! The most common argument against a partner who smokes; is the damage it could do to him in the long term, which means his quality of life will suffer. You have to look further ahead and realise that it will affect you also; because if he falls ill, you are the one who will have to nurse him. If you are not prepared for the added responsibility to your life; it can come as a big shock to your system. You may have to give up your job and your dreams of career fulfilment, in order to look after him. This will be all the more painful; if over the years, you had consistently warned him to stop smoking to no avail. Why should you lose a promotion in your workplace because of his callousness? Why should you have to play nursemaid to his recklessness? Why should the children suffer because of his selfishness? Why should you put your own health at risk; by breathing his second-hand smoke in your own home?

It is not funny watching the man you love, deteriorating before your very eyes; so if you feel he is smoking too much, you have to take a firm decision not to put up with it. Depending on what kind of life you are already leading; you have to issue an ultimatum for him to quit smoking or you will walk out on him. Although it may seem a bit extreme, leaving a man simply for smoking; if you put it into a larger context, it makes very good sense. If you are a career woman with lots of prospects; why do you want to ruin your life by having to look after an invalid, whose sickness is completely of his own making? If you have children; do you want them growing up, breathing cigarette smoke? Even if your partner/husband does not smoke in front of the kids; his clothes will still carry the smoke. When he picks them up or hugs them; the odour will slowly seethe into their consciousness. This will affect them in the future, because they may decide to smoke as well. As explained earlier; when teenagers start smoking, there is a direct link to alcohol. This is potentially followed by drug-taking, misdemeanours, indiscriminate sexual encounters and full-blown crime. Can you afford the medical bills, for the constant visits to the dentist to clean the stains off his teeth? What if he gets sick; or is diagnosed with terminal lung cancer? What will you do? Do you really want those nicotine-stained fingers probing into your vagina, during lovemaking? Did you know that you could also catch smoke-related diseases from second-hand smoke? Is that what you signed up for, when you agreed to live with or marry him? 'For better or for worse' in the nuptial vows; does not mean he should deliberately destroy your life, just so that he can 'enjoy' his. In self-defence terms; you have to think of yourself and what matters to you. This means; if he does not care about himself...why the hell should you?

This all shows that your family's future is really at stake; even though as he is puffing away on his cigarette, he may not realise it or even care. So you have to protect yourself! If someone lives alone and wants to smoke; then that is his/her prerogative because he/she is harming no one but him/herself. Once other people are involved; then those who do not smoke, have to warn him/her about the consequences. Sadly; most smokers will not listen to anyone who tells them to stop. They always use the well-worn selfish argument; *"I smoke because I enjoy it!"* and that is why I believe a drastic ultimatum is the only way to go. If you walk out on him and he is forced to sit at home alone, having to do all the domestic chores himself; he will have plenty of time to contemplate his folly. He will hopefully realise that you and the children are worth a lot more than the cigarettes. If he cannot see that; then it means he loves the smoking more than his family and you are better-off without him. You should therefore file for divorce; citing irreconcilable differences, emotional torture and the safety of your children's health. The legal system has now recognised the damage smoking can do! Every woman deserves the chance to reach her full potential; live her life happy and free from unnecessary worries. She cannot do so, when she is dragged back by someone who will not listen to what every single doctor and health expert in the world has been saying for years; and that is; *"Yes! Smoking really does kill!"* It can kill the future of your family!

(c). Sex

As you may be only too well aware; there is a lot of sex discrimination meted out to women in all walks of life, none more so than in the bedroom. If a man sleeps with several women; he is lauded as some sort of modern Lothario. If a woman dares sleep with anyone other than her partner; she is branded a 'cheap slut' or 'an easy lay'. If he sneaks away from his relationship and picks up prostitutes; questions would rather be asked of his woman, who might be accused of not doing enough to hold onto her man. If a woman satisfies her lust with a gigolo; she will be chalked down as a ball-crushing feminist who cannot get a man to stay with her because she is 'too hard'. The word 'nymphomaniac' is very derogatory; because it implies the woman has an uncontrollable, 'un-satisfiable' itch between her legs. Whereas 'sex maniac', that usually refers to a man;

implies he has a rock-solid never-ending hard-on, which many women would supposedly give their right arms for!

If you are living with a sex maniac; it is no laughing matter. For a woman; sex is enjoyed most when she is ready for and initiates it. With a man; it is always assumed he can get going as soon as he gets an erection! What do you do when your man can never get enough; and wants it all the time? In the beginning of your relationship; it may seem flattering to be showered with so much attention. As time moves on; there will always be occasions when you don't want sex, but just want to be kissed, held and cuddled. Any form of bodily contact in the form of hugs, kisses or just holding hands; can trigger off an erection in a sex maniac. Somehow, he will need to satisfy his lust! How do you tell him that you really do have a headache; without upsetting or confusing him with your conflicting signals? What if you have a toothache, an earache or even an upset stomach? Can you explain that to a horny man; without sounding like you are making up silly excuses?

Telling a man she doesn't want sex comes very easily to a woman; without realising the effect it can have on him. A lot of men cannot understand that a woman is a human being, not a sex machine; and doesn't always want intercourse! He might be able to put up with it once in a while; but if the refusals are too many, he will suspect that you do not love him or are angry with him for one thing or another. Why else are you always making excuses not to sleep with him? Most decent men will bite their tongue, try to woo you with gifts, pay you more attention and hope that your urge for sex will return. You will however; get some who are not prepared to wait around till you are ready. He will quietly visit a girlfriend whom he has been neglecting for some time; and who is 'always up for it'. The sex maniac will badger you so much that you may give in, just to keep him quiet; so that he can leave you alone, when he has finished. You may even choose to let him fuck you and then hit him later for that 'new designer dress or shoe' you have had your eye on for some time; as some sort of payback for your 'kindness', in letting him have his 'wicked way' with you! This 'pressure sex', as explained before, is subtle rape; since you only agreed to sex because you were backed into a corner. If it happens once in a while; it can easily be dismissed as part of the 'give and take' of all relationships and no harm should come of it. On the other hand; what if it is an everyday occurrence? How many times are you prepared to concede to his outrageous sexual demands? At some point; you will feel that you are being 'used/abused' and your refusals will become much more vehement. This could quickly turn into a serious marital argument; because he could be a sex addict who wants it two or three times a day, every day. If your vaginal juices are unable to cope with the demand; you will become so dry that it will hurt and you may even bleed. Certainly not the way lovemaking is supposed to be! Your rejections will spill over into other aspects of your relationship; and like a spoilt child, he may be reluctant to do things for you. This is simply because the bulge between his legs is dictating his moods and behaviour! If you tell any of your female friends; they may not realise the seriousness of your plight, unless they have been through it themselves. You will most likely get teased into keeping the problem to yourself. *"Wow! Three times a day! You lucky girl! If you don't want him; give him to me and I'll take care of him…"*

You have very few options open to you when your husband is a sex addict. Did you not notice it before you married him? Would you prefer he didn't bother you at all? Should he take on a mistress to satisfy his lust? If the answer is *"No!"* to these three questions; then you have a problem. You love him, you enjoy sex with him, but not that often and only when you are ready; which is a woman's prerogative as the 'receiver' in the lovemaking game. Too many refusals will move the goalposts so far, that he will feel he is the one being persecuted; and you are at fault. He wants sex and you don't; but you still love him. *"Dear Agony Aunt, what shall I do…?"* I am no relationship expert; so all I can do is give you advice from a self-defence perspective. This means you have to find a way to satisfy him; without necessarily resorting to full intercourse. You could try masturbating him to ejaculation; but this will be tiresome on your arm. The more sex a man has; the less sperm he has left in storage and the longer it will take for him to achieve an ejaculated orgasm! Likewise; a 'blow-job' will be hard on *(excuse the pun)* your jaws. This is not really much fun, if you have to keep doing it day after day. Can you give fellatio for more than an hour, without getting bored? You will probably get fed up and tell him to do it himself; that is, if you don't bite it off completely in frustration!

If you enjoy sex three times a day and don't feel like you are being taken advantage of, then you do not have a problem; so you can skip this paragraph. If his insistent sexual demands are ruining the quality of your life; you have to put a stop to it by encouraging him to seek a sex addiction counsellor. If he refuses to go; then you will have to deny him sex until you are ready. This puts him on a cliff-edge; because he will either have to play by your rules or find himself another woman. If he does; it means your relationship will be over and you will have to kick him out, or walk out on him. It may seem an unorthodox way to end a marriage or relationship; but not all women enjoy sex all the time. If the problem will not go away; leaving him is your best option. You see; the penis is like any other muscle in the body, in that, the more you use it, the 'fitter' it becomes. It may reach a point where he has to have sex, in order to feel normal; because the penis needs its thrice-daily workout! In the end; the sex he has with you will not be based on love, but rather on lust. He will only be doing it to satisfy himself and will not care about you. This is not good for your self-esteem, dignity, integrity or reputation as an equal-partner! You are a woman first and foremost; and your vagina is not a playground or a gymnasium for his penis. If he fails to realise this fact; then it means his respect for you has gone out of the window and the relationship cannot survive. You will for ever be 'playing catch-up' and running after him; just to keep him happy! The main purpose of this book is to awaken the 'Tigress' in you! This means you must do things that make you happy and take 'no shit' from no one; not even from the man you love!

(d). Gluttony

Another addiction that could affect your marriage is gluttony and unhealthy eating; especially when your man will pay no heed to you or his doctor. You marry a handsome, fit 'cool dude'; and ten years down the line, he has become an overweight, pot-bellied parody of the man you fell in love with. He refuses to exercise, drinks gallons of beer, stuffs himself with junk food; and then expects you to make love to him and enjoy it! *"There is more of me to love...!"* He lies on the sofa in front of the television watching the sports; with the remote control in one hand, a beer in the other and the snacks within easy reach! He drops the empty cans onto the floor; because he is certain you will end up clearing up after him. He then proceeds to laugh raucously, break wind, fall asleep and snore! He tries to play with the young children; but because he is so overweight, they run rings around him and he ends up pulling one muscle or another! The teenagers in the neighbourhood blatantly tease him by calling him names like *"fatso!"* and *"porky!"* and asking him *"Who ate all the pies...?"* You dread going to the supermarket with him because he fills the trolley with junk; and you can hear the smirks and laughter from the other shoppers! You are ashamed to be seen at social events with him because your friends always ask you what you are feeding him with; indirectly blaming you for the state of his mid-riff and double chin! When you are making love; he has to 'rest' every five minutes because he is completely out of breath. This can be annoying, if you are on the verge of orgasm when he decides he needs a breather! He is so obese; you have to move aside the layers of fat on his stomach, in order to find his penis! (Can you think of anything more frustrating for a woman in heat?) If you are forced to always 'go on top', because you cannot stand the amount of weight he puts on you in other positions; sex will eventually become monotonous and boring. You may even find yourself making up excuses not to sleep with him! One may be tempted to laugh at the above scenarios; especially if they have not yet happened to you! The reality however; can be very depressing for a woman, because the deterioration usually takes place before her very eyes and there doesn't seem to be anything she can do about it. One morning she wakes up, sees this fat lump lying next to her and wonders where it all went wrong. *'What the hell have I done...? There has to be more to life than this...!'* In chapter 5; I stated that if your man is the type who does not look after his health and refuses to exercise then you have to think twice before marrying him. Assuming you do not pay any heed to this advice and marry him; simply because you *"love him!"* You could one day be faced with a situation, which will be difficult to get yourself out of; and you may end up walking out on him to regain your sanity.

Men can be very stubborn when it comes to being told they are overweight, even by a doctor; whilst women are more likely to do something about it. If you are ever in a position, whereby you are not happy with the shape, size and condition of your man; you will not be in for an easy ride. Even if you refuse to feed him any unhealthy foods; there is no guarantee he will not go out to the nearest burger joint, when your back is turned. *"I'm off to the shops to buy a newspaper, Darling. Back soon!"* When he is at work; you can never be able to control what he eats or drinks. He may happily eat your vegetables; knowing that he is already full of chips and fried chicken! If you also eat junk food and are overweight; it would be like the pot calling the kettle *"black"* and he will laugh at any suggestion you give him to diet. Unless there are real medical reasons why your man is overweight; he has no excuse for allowing himself to fall into such disrepair. Nobody becomes fat overnight; as it takes many years of neglect, in order to accumulate such weight excess! You just have to lay down the law and try to encourage him to exercise, even if it means going with him to the gym; which will help to keep you fit as well. If he sees that you are also making an effort, even if you don't need it as much as he does; it will help motivate him because he will not feel as if he is being victimised. You should however, only do it to a point; because he has to learn to keep it up for himself, even if you cannot always be there to push him. You will probably have to offer him some praise, use a bit of bribery and maybe a few 'sexual perks'; if he shows tremendous improvement in his quest for fitness. Once he realises that you are happier when he is exercising; the children are more fun to play with; he feels better when he wakes up in the morning; and most importantly, his sexual prowess has improved; he will not need too much convincing, that exercise is good for him! It will be a slow process; but if you keep up with the encouragement and resist the snide jibes about his weight, the rest will follow. There is no need to tell him what he should or should not eat; because your main goal is to get him to exercise. The fitter he gets, the less likely he will gorge himself on junk food! You can start him off by going for walks together and then graduate to power-walking and maybe cycling; before going into the gym, where there are always qualified instructors to give a helping hand.

If he stubbornly refuses to listen to you; then you have to take matters into your own hand and use whatever tactic you feel will shock him into taking a long hard look at his lifestyle. In a 'cruel to be kind' scenario; you may even have to refuse to make love to him by claiming that the last time you had sex with him, he 'hurt your back' with his excess weight. If you continuously 'pretend' you cannot lift any heavy objects around the house, and ask him to do it for you; he will not have a moment of peace to sit on his butt! You can be even more devious; by deliberately letting out the air from one of the tyres in his car. He will then have to change the tyre before he can go out; which should burn a few calories off him! If he is forced to do a lot more work around the house; it will make him tired and let him realise that he is not fit. If your shock tactics are not working; then you have to be more drastic and threaten to leave him, because he is 'no longer the man you married'. Tell him you want a few weeks away from him to go and stay with friends; go out, have fun and enjoy yourself. Hopefully; during the time you are away, he will take a hard look at himself and realise what it would be like, if he actually lost you. If the possibility of losing you and the children does not move him into doing something about his weight; then you are dealing with a lost cause. Quite frankly, no woman should have to put up with such intransigence; especially if it is affecting the relationship.

It might seem a bit harsh to walk out on a man because he is overweight; but you have to think of yourself and your children. In five years time, such a man will be even worse than he is now; and you cannot be expected to lie down and accept it. Although there is a societal belief instigated by the media, that being thin is better than being fat, and it is not politically correct to label someone 'fat'; you would be a fool to let other people dictate what is happening in your own household. Society and the media will not be there to clean up the mess! There is nothing wrong in being a little overweight; because that can happen to anyone. When it gets to the point where he is dangerously obese and it is affecting your family life; you cannot just sit down and do nothing, because it will come back to haunt you. If he is so unfit and gets injured; it will be you, who will end up having to look after him. Who is going to pay the medical bills and run around for him; if he is forced into hospital because he suffered a heart attack, kidney failure, liver disease, dangerously high blood pressure or diabetes? All of these illnesses could occur because he refused to listen to you; when you told him several years ago that he was overweight! Admittedly, you marry a man 'for better or for worse'; but if he refuses to listen to your warnings, why should you be the one to clean up his mess? What if you are a high-flying career woman; or even an aspiring female with dreams and ambitions of your own? Why should you ruin your future because of him? The days when women put their careers and aspirations on hold, just to satisfy the men in their lives; are all but over. Like with any other addiction; you have to do some tough talking and threaten to leave him, if he shows such disregard for your feelings and warnings. If he dares you to go, because he does not believe you can go through with it; then you will have to leave him. If you stay with him after that; he will walk all over you. I repeat; no man is indispensable! Sometimes it is imperative that you get rid of all the excess baggage and clutter in your life; in order to be free to be who you want to be!

(e). Exercise addiction

There are many other addictions that could affect your relationship; but I do not feel a need to list them all because an addiction for one couple may only be an aberration to another! Exercising for instance; could be seen as an addiction, if your man spends all his time doing it and has no time for you or the children. One might argue that it is a good thing to be very fit; but an exercise addict is never satisfied with his/her fitness and always strives for improvement, even when it is not necessary. This obsession with exercise and 'perfection' can easily filter down to other aspects of the relationship; and he can become very controlling, by trying to tell you how to live your life. It could get to the point where he will refuse to have sex with you; because he believes it will weaken him for his next training session! He will stand in front of the mirror; seeing imperfections in his body, where there are none. He will then decide to work-out longer, to improve. His lack of confidence could get so bad that he will buy muscle and keep-fit magazines; in order to compare himself to the men in the photos. This will make matters worse; because he will exercise even harder, in order to look as good as those in the magazines. Just because he does not eat certain 'unhealthy' foods; he may try to ban you from eating things he does not approve of. Imagine your man banning you from eating your favourite chocolates or cookies! How would you feel, if you are not allowed to eat and drink what you like; in your own house? You could obviously refuse to listen to him. But he could become so overbearing; you might find yourself hiding the chocolates, so that you can eat them in peace. You may even start spending more time with your friends; just to bring some normality into your life! It could get so bad that he may even begin to ask you each day, if you have defecated; and may want to examine your faeces, to make sure you are eating the right foods! This is because many exercise addicts believe defecating twice a day is healthy; and the faeces has to be a certain colour to denote healthy eating! The annoying thing is; all your friends will praise you for having such a fit, healthy-looking man and may even become envious of you. The stark truth is; you will not be happy because his addiction is more important to him than you!

If he is a professional athlete who earns his living from sports; allowances have to be made for the dedication, because he will need your support in order to function well. For many a 'sports widow'; it is no laughing matter when her man is never around when she needs him! It can be a very lonely existence; and to all extent and purposes, they could be leading separate lives. If your man is not a pro-athlete; his addiction to exercise could easily ruin your relationship. Living with an exercise addict could become so stressful; you might feel you do not have a life of your own. Leaving him may be your only way out; because he will not change. Exercising is not seen as a marital problem, in the way substance abuse or gambling is; so you do not have any convincing grounds for a divorce. If he does not beat you up; does not rape you; gives you enough money and physical comforts; you may be accused by your friends of being an 'ungrateful cow' who does not know how lucky she is! If he does not give you what you crave most: - love; affection; and independence to make your own decisions for your body; it will seem like he does not respect you for who you are, but wants you to be a clone of his idea of a perfect healthy woman. Eventually; he will try to make you exercise as much as he does! This would be okay, if you were unfit and wanted to be like him; but what if there is nothing wrong with you? What right has he to tell you how to run your life? You can appreciate that a relationship based on the above conditions will not last long; even if he is the most handsome and fittest man in the world.

His behaviour could become so over-bearing and you may feel so emotionally neglected; that you may contemplate having an affair with a 'normal' man who pays you lots of attention, does not try to change you and allows you to be who you are. He may be so into his exercise regime that he will not even notice how unhappy you are; and you could have several affairs without his finding out! In such a desperate scenario; an affair is not the answer because you will be at fault and he will be deemed as having done 'nothing wrong'. You will be seen as the 'wicked woman' who cheated on her husband. This will obviously not win you any plaudits in a divorce court! You will have to sit down with him (if that is possible) or go jogging with him and tell him you are not happy; so you are thinking of taking a break from him. If he does not act surprised and continues running; you will have to assume that he does not care. This means the exercise is still much more important to him than you. If he stops running to listen to you; then it means there is still some hope in the relationship. You should try to iron out the creases; before they become too rumpled! Relay your concerns in a cool, calculated manner. You have to be firm in your mind that you have had enough and are not willing to back down and be dismissed as a petty neurotic. You are not trying to stop him exercising; but if you feel neglected, then you are not really in an equal-partner relationship. It would be like there were three of you in the marriage; with you fighting a losing battle with his addiction, for his affections. What does any woman do; when she is not the priority in her man's life? That's right! You calmly walk away with your dignity, integrity, self-esteem and reputation; before he completely destroys them. One day he will come back from the gym and you will be gone. If he does not come looking for you; then you will know you made the right decision. Even if he does realise he needs you in the house; he has to be told in no uncertain terms that there is no way you are going to play second-fiddle to an addiction. He has to seek help; before you will contemplate returning to him!

Anything could be classed as an addiction; if he is so obsessed, it dominates his life. This would include obsessions; impulsive/compulsive behaviour; hypochondria; kleptomania; obsessive tidiness; and the two famous eating disorders, bulimia and anorexia nervosa; all of which require guidance from dedicated professionals. Although on a national scale, there might seem to be a lot of people with 'addictions'; most of them can be contained by your own typical female determination and common sense, so that they do not interfere with the smooth running of your family. *"Darling; that's the fifth time you've washed your hands in the last hour. Don't be silly; there are no germs on them. Please get ready and take the kids to school...!"* If you think they are becoming too serious; you have to push him to seek counselling and leave no room for his disobedience, before the molehill becomes a mountain. *"Why do you keep taking the cough medicine, when you don't have a cough? That's it! We're going to see a doctor, right now!"* Since your husband is unlikely to suffer seriously from any of these 'minor addictions'; you should not worry too much about them. If they happen to your children; you have to tread carefully and find a way to get professional help for them. Teenagers especially; are very difficult to deal with. Once they become adults; the addiction will be much harder to control!

3. Crime

There are very few people who have never broken the law! Even a late payment of a fine/debt; running through a red traffic light; or parking in the wrong place at the wrong time; could have the police knocking on your front door. You therefore have to understand that having even a minor criminal record could affect a family in many ways; some of which you may not be aware of, and could surprise you when least expected. There are certain acts known as 'victimless crimes'; like tax evasion, non-payment of fines and insurance fraud (because supposedly, no one gets physically hurt). These are very popular; because those involved are often mistaken in believing that they are not really crimes. With the advent of the Internet; it is very easy for anyone to check up on a particular individual and find out things about his/her past, he/she would much rather have kept secret. If you commit a traffic offence; default on a bank loan; fail to pay a fine; get involved in a wrangle with an insurance company; or avoid taxes; your name will go onto a national database. All financial institutions and interested employers could have access to it; and it could be used to refuse you further credit. Although you may think non-payment of a debt is not a crime; as far as any prospective creditor or employer is concerned, you are not credit-worthy, cannot be trusted and are therefore unemployable. Your family will suffer;

because it means spending longer on the unemployment queue and not getting the mortgage you were looking for!

Insurance fraud is just as serious; and since there are always new ones cropping up, it would be impossible to list them all here. The most popular is the accident claim; whereby ingeniously devious ways are used to get money off insurance companies or the local councils. There is a popular one; whereby someone overtakes and brakes suddenly on the motorway. This allows a large commercial vehicle to crash into him. Because the driving seat of a truck sits so high up; the driver may not notice that it was not his/her fault. Since the trucks are always fully-insured; the fraudster will claim whiplash-injury and receive a handsome pay-out because most of the damage will be to his smaller vehicle. 'Fronting' (putting down an adult as the main driver instead of a younger person; so that the insurance premium will be less.) is prevalent. Arranging a burglary or deliberately setting fire to one's property, in order to dupe the insurance company; is also popular. The 'claim-culture' can be so profitable; you will get people deliberately falling over loose pavements, obtaining a medical report for their 'back/neck injuries' and then using a well-versed solicitor to sue the relevant authorities. There was one case; whereby a quick-thinking man fell off a tree on a farm and broke his arm. He immediately boarded a public transport bus, stood in the aisle and waited for the driver to brake at a traffic light; before throwing himself onto the bus floor. The bus driver was blamed for his broken arm; and he received over €20,000 in compensation! In each of the above examples; the perpetrator may think he is being clever, especially if he is not caught. But his name will go onto one computer or another and will be 'in the system'. Sooner or later; it will come back to haunt him and by default, his family.

Although there are female criminals in any society; the statistics show that the majority of women are law-abiding. The prison population demonstrates; it is the men who are most likely to get themselves involved in criminal activities! If a woman becomes a criminal; it is usually because she was originally coerced or persuaded by a man she loved. This same love could also convince her to turn a blind eye to what he gets up to. Crime is always one of the things that divide the sexes; and can become an impossible situation. On the one hand, you love your man; whilst on the other hand, you do not like his involvement in crime! Probably because of the relatively quick way it is acquired; most criminals are very generous when they succeed in making a lot of money. He may shower his immediate family with gifts and creature comforts; thereby blinding them to the source of his largess. However; very few criminals get away with all their crimes! Sooner or later; they will be undone and whatever they gained, will be swallowed up on fines, legal fees or asset seizure. If your man is involved in any illegal activities; you have to try and dissuade him. If he is caught and goes to prison; it will affect you and/or the children! Crimes like fraud and shoplifting may seem harmless; help pay the bills and provide nice things for the household. The day he is caught; will be the worst in your life, when the police knock on your door and repossess everything in your house for not having receipts. *'What will the neighbours think?'* Nobody will believe you did not know anything about it; and you will be blamed by other women for failing to control your man. It does not even matter if you were not involved. If your man is a criminal; people will look at you in the same light! One by one, your friends will give up on you; the phone will stop ringing and the invites to parties will be thin on the ground. Your kids will be teased or bullied in school; and although your work colleagues will pretend to be sympathetic to you, I cannot see them inviting you into their homes.

With serious crimes involving weapons; violence; intimidation; money; drugs; or stolen property; the consequences are much more grievous and could ruin your life for ever. Your man may also be so deeply involved; he cannot stop his activities, without putting his life at risk. This means you have to make a conscious decision; whether to stay with him or not. If he is caught in a serious crime; the prison sentence will be much longer. You might as well kiss your marriage/relationship goodbye! With the best will in the world; he will not be the same man when he comes out. More than likely; he will be angry, broke and emotionally hardened. Even if he is initially happy to see you; it will not take long before the cracks appear. Whilst he has been in prison; what have you been up to? He will have been going crazy; wondering whether you have been faithful or not. Having been on your own, whilst he has been incarcerated; you would have become accustomed to your independence. You will definitely not allow him to dictate what you can or cannot do! The children will not take too kindly to his orders or ideas on how to behave either; simply because he was not there when they needed him. He may find all this very hard to deal with! A friendly smile to the milkman or a male voice on the other end of the phone line; will have 'conspiracy theories' buzzing around in his head and he may become so jealous, he will be impossible to live with. The evils of marital rape, wife-beating and affairs cannot be discounted!

Even if he decides to give up his criminal tendencies; your patience, love and understanding will be severely tested. He will find it extremely difficult to get a job; and definitely not one, which will offer him as much money as he was used to. You will probably have to support him financially and emotionally; until he gets back on his feet. You have to be prepared that he will be ostracised by the neighbours and his community; so he may end up back in the only place he feels loved, appreciated and respected... the criminal fraternity. The obvious unwillingness of society to forgive the serious criminal; is one of the major factors why he re-offends within two years of his release from prison. She may put on a brave face; but it takes an extremely strong woman who is prepared to stand by her man, against all odds. Nine times out of ten; he will not appreciate her sacrifices. He will see and criticise her faults much quicker than he will praise her undoubted loyalty. Deep down; he will realise that during the time he missed out with her, she has been able to live without him. He may therefore resent the fact that he has lost his influence and her compliance. Is it fair that a woman should have to experience such disrespect and disregard for her bravery in standing by her man; when all others had deserted him?

If your man is into serious crime; you have to assume that one day he will be caught! If you cannot stop him breaking the law; you should always make preparations for his day in court. If he gives you any money; try to save it for a rainy day. Once he goes to prison; the gravy train will stop and you will have to cope on your own. You will have to stash the cash somewhere safe, but not in a bank account; because it can be taken away from you. Many criminals keep money in a family member's bank account; which is not a good idea! The police and the taxman in every country have their ways and means of finding out what is in anybody's account; and can legally seize it, if the source of the money is suspect. You then have to worry about recriminations; in case your man is not honest in his dealings with his fellow criminals. He could be hurt very badly or even killed! Your life could also be in danger, if the crooks come looking for him; because they will assume you know where he is, if he runs off with more than his share of the loot. You should always arrange a place where you can go and live safely; in case the 'shit hits the fan'. A smart criminal will house his family in a different town from where he operates, and then live in a rented apartment; so that if something goes wrong, his wife and children do not feel the backlash. Even though this seems like a considerate move; it may not be what you want...unless you agree with his criminal endeavours. Believe it or not; because of the financial rewards, crime does attract some women! With such an arrangement; you will still have to worry about his safety and whether or not he has another woman on the side. You cannot be with him every day of the week! How would you feel; if he often tells you he is 'on a job' and won't be contacting you for a few days, until it is over? Wouldn't you suspect he had a mistress? When the children keep asking why their father is away most of the week; wouldn't it sound like a worn-out record, when you keep telling them *"he works out of town...?"* I hope you can now deduce that the hassles and worry that will come your way, if your man is breaking the law; may not be worth the money he brings home. It would definitely be better and safer for you to be out of harm's way! If you have children; it would not be fair to put them through the trials and tribulations of their father's criminal activities. This may include losing him to a few years in prison; serious injury or his untimely demise.

Too many things can go wrong when your man is into crime in a big way; and in self-defence terms, it means you will surely be beaten. If he decides that committing crimes is more important than his family; you have to use your head to protect yourself and your children. If he was a criminal before you married or started living with him; then you obviously knew that your life would not be a smooth ride. If that is what you enjoy; then nothing I say, can deter you from staying with him! However; if you are a law-abiding woman who suddenly finds herself with a man hell-bent on committing serious crimes, whether it is armed robbery, burglary or 'simple' bank fraud; I have to advise you to make your plans quietly, with the intention of walking away. The crimes will keep getting bigger; and when he is caught, you will be implicated by association. Unlike other impossible situations, you cannot give him an ultimatum to give up on crime or you will leave him; because most criminals do not have any other way of making a lot of money. He will either, tell you he will stop and then continue operating behind your back; or he will tell you to take a running jump back into the lake you came out of! It would be unwise to shop him to the police; because most serious crimes are committed by more than one person. This means he will have associates, who could also face the backlash of the law; if your man is arrested because of you. You will therefore be putting your life in danger of recriminations from the families of the other gang members. The 'quiet life' you were seeking would quickly become a living nightmare!

This means your decision must not be up for negotiation! You can tell him you are fed up with his lifestyle; so you are leaving him and taking the children with you, if you have any. If you have somewhere to go and live, it would be better to move there; until he realises you are determined and contemplates seriously whether his crimes are worth losing his family over. If he has already made a lot of money; he may decide to give up. But if like most criminals, he loves the 'buzz' of getting away with crimes; then you would have made a good decision, in getting away from him. He will never stop; until he is stopped! With all persistent criminals; the only certainty is that they will one day pay for their crimes. There is no need for you to be around when that happens; because when someone refuses to listen to good advice, it is always better to leave him be to learn his own lessons in life.

4. Work/family life balance

The work-family life balance is one that has puzzled women over the years. Even though only very few of them have managed to succeed in both at the same time; there is still a popular belief that *"women can have it all!"* That is why they strive to work hard in their careers, whilst trying to keep their family life afloat; which may include children. In the end; both career and family life suffer, as a result of the shared-responsibility. In the old days when women stayed at home to look after the household and children; they lost out whilst the men made all the money. This meant that they kept control of their women by operating the purse strings. It would be very unfair to expect the modern woman to do the same; especially if she has something to offer the workforce and her country. If you give up on personal ambition and career fulfilment, for the sake of the family; you may end up regretting it. The country thereby loses out on your talents! A box of chocolates every Mother's Day and the occasional *"I love you"* from your husband and children; will do nothing to soothe the *'what might have been'* feelings you will have eating away at your subconscious, from time to time. It becomes a real battle of the sexes and an impossible situation; when the arguments and guilt feelings of not doing enough for your husband and children, come into play. It is therefore imperative you sit down and think very carefully about what you want; and then sacrifice one for the other. If you want to do both; you must realise it is your decision and not let anyone bully you, one way or the other. Since I do not know how you live your life; it is not my place to tell you how to run your career or family. For both to succeed; they have to be run like a military campaign, with you as the general. It would be too risky to rely on anyone else to do your bidding; as they may have different ambitions. You will have to organise your own contingency plans; to cater for overtime or travelling at work and illnesses or accidents at home. You have to also be able to deal with a jealous husband/partner; who may not be on the same wavelength as you and may desert your ambitions, by not doing enough to help. He may even complain that you don't spend enough time with him. This could open a can of worms; if he decides to find solace in the arms of a willing mistress.

Once you have a plan in your head about your career and how far you want to take it, so that you can guarantee a better future for your family; you must do what you have to do. You must not worry, when others try to make you feel guilty about not spending enough time with your children; because it is the end result that is important. All women love their children and family; but they have different ways of trying to achieve a worthwhile future for them! If a woman spends long hours at work; it is only because she wants to make as much money as she can, so that she can enjoy her later years and create her independence. Isn't that what the men do? They say women can 'juggle several balls at once' and it can be done; so far as you are earning good money, with enough lucrative future prospects to ensure that you can retire at some point, with your ambitions fulfilled. You will then be in a stronger position to give your time back to your family. If you are not always there for your children when they are young; then it would be nice to be there for them when they are teenagers or early adulthood. A child will always need its mother! You will be a much better and happier mum; if you can devote your time and experience to your children, without having to worry about 'what you missed out' in your career. If you are in a dreary nine-five job with very little pay and fewer prospects; then the stress and worry will leave you too exhausted to spend quality time with your children, after work. It might therefore be better to find a way to work from home; by starting your own business. Bringing a child into the world, when you cannot give him/her certain basic necessities like your time, love and physical comforts; is not really conducive to its upbringing.

In most developed countries; there are ways and means to get government-backed support for you and your children, if you are financially strapped. Some companies are finally realising that children are important to a woman; and she has to be happy and worry-free, if they are to get the best out of her. They are therefore willing to help her out with her work hours and offer a certain amount of paid-leave. You should look around and find out exactly what your job can offer, if you do get pregnant; so that you can plan ahead. It is always better to be prepared; because pregnancy is never easy! This means you have to plan things for yourself, changing jobs if necessary; if it will offer better prospects for your career and your pregnancy. If they are both important to you; they should be given equal billing! As you will be only too aware; the lack of money can cause problems in a relationship. It is imperative that you know where your next dollar is coming from! If you have to worry about cash as well as carrying a baby; it cannot be good for your well-being. Even though I sometimes paint a gloomy picture of men; I have to admit that there are some good ones around, who just need a push in the right direction.

Even if he cannot do as much as you want him to around the house; he might be able to offer you enough financial support so that you can stay at home and look after the baby properly. This can make a big difference to your peace of mind; so that you can eventually return to work, refreshed and buzzing with new ideas for your business or company. Don't ever be afraid to lay down the law with your partner, to stop him wasting money. He could easily be blowing cash meant for you and the baby, down at the pub with his friends; whilst celebrating the arrival of 'his' new baby!

Some women are prone to assuming that having a child; will bring the husband closer and make the relationship stronger. I believe this could be a mistake! The relationship has to already be strong, before a child can cement everything together; otherwise, there could be problems further down the line. These will mostly be about the question of loyalty; because there may be arguments over whose career is more important, vis-a-vis the baby. For most men; career ambition is more important than family life. When a man realises one ambition; he usually looks for another to conquer. Women tend not to be so 'greedy'; and are usually satisfied when they have achieved their life-long ambition. If you decide to get pregnant; he will be expecting you to do most of the work and curtail your career, for the sake of the baby. A man will make all kinds of promises before the baby is born; but when he realises the sheer magnitude of work and worry involved, he may renege on his pledges of shared-responsibility. He may even swear that when the kids are older, he will cut down on his hours at work; so that he can spend more time with them, whilst you go back to work. It never works out that way when the time comes! Even though there are some so-called 'new men' who will change nappies at four o'clock in the morning; you will find that any man with a successful career will have little time for such 'trivialities'. You may have to do everything yourself! This may be too much; and you may end up having to employ a live-in nanny. There is no point in having children; if you are not sure your marriage or relationship is going to last. A child can complicate things and breed resentment when things don't work out as planned! If the child is in some way 'deformed', ill or suffers behavioural problems; the man may feel that since the child was your idea, you would have brought an unnecessary complication into your lives.

If he believes you tried to 'trap' him with the child; he might even end up resenting him/her. This means that having a child has to be your 100% decision; so that you are prepared, in case all the responsibility falls on your shoulders.

If you do choose to have children and go to work; it would be best that you have a strong and loyal family support system behind you. You will then be able to give your utmost to your career; safe in the knowledge that your children are being well cared for. Some women may send their children to a crèche or employ a child-minder/nanny. This would solve the short-term care problem; but will do nothing for your self-esteem when the children feel happier with their carers, than they do with you. By way of experience; the grand-parents may be the better option. If they were able to raise you, and you turned out okay; they should have no problems with the grandchildren! You can at least guarantee that your kids will be loved; and taught the difference between right and wrong. However; you have to be careful you do not take your parents for granted. Although they are unlikely to refuse looking after your children, whilst you are at work; physically, they may not have the energy to run after them around the house or play with them in the garden. It may leave them very exhausted at the end of each day! This will not be fair; especially when you are making pots of money. Try to remember to show your personal appreciation, from time to time; by taking them out or funding a vacation for them! Buying gifts may send out the wrong message; and they may feel that they are being used and then bought off with presents. Other family members or friends could also be brought in to look after your children; but you have to be careful they do not get annoyed, that they are being treated like an unpaid child-minder. You may therefore have to pay them the going rate! This is okay; if it allows you the luxury of being able to do your job, with fewer worries. This means the person looking after your children, will have to know exactly what to do; if something goes wrong. Your bosses or work colleagues will not be too pleased; if your phone is ringing every five minutes, whilst you are at work! Installing closed-circuit cameras in your house; can put your mind at ease that the one looking after your child is doing the right thing at the right time.

Women are already facing tremendous discrimination in the workplace; especially those who choose to have children. There is not enough being done to cater for them! As a result; a woman's mind may not be totally focused on her work, if she is worrying about her child. Single mums face even more hardship because the work structure is based on the assumption that all children are products of two-parent families, whereby there will always be someone to look after the child whilst the mother is at work! There are bosses (male and female) who will ask prospective female employees; if they intend to have children and how they are going to cope with the work/pregnancy balance. Although these questions may seem intrusive; you can refuse to answer them and accuse them of gender discrimination, if they do not hire you because of your refusal. However; if you don't tell them your 'pregnancy plans' and still get the job, you will be starting off on the wrong foot. There are many ways your bosses can subtly pay you back! You might deliberately be given extra work; scrutinised for mistakes you might make and denied promotion. This is because they will not be certain of your loyalty. They might be afraid that you will kick them in the teeth by getting pregnant when it suits you; and then demanding maternity leave, with pay. Having a baby is not the problem; but rather the timing of the pregnancy. This can upset a company; if you have to take time off at a crucial period. Even if you have a baby and return to work a few months later; you will find that someone else has taken your place in the workplace structure and it may be very difficult to get things back to how they used to be for you. Other women in the company might shun you; because they may see it as unfair that you are getting preferential treatment, whilst they will have to work harder to cater for your absence. Discrimination against women in the workplace is obviously not fair; but it remains the status-quo for the foreseeable future. It is important you recognise this anomaly and selfishly look out for your own interests; because nobody else will do it for you! Try to learn the law on gender equality in your country; plan your strategy and keep your cards close to your chest, so that you do not lose out in an ever-demanding and competitive working environment.

The world has still not completely understood the value of women to a society; and many are still seen as carers of the home and children. The ones that succeed in their careers are often referred to as 'unfit mothers'; and made to feel guilty for neglecting their children. The stark truth is; many women have no idea how useful and fantastic they are. This is because men are not doing enough to show their appreciation to the women of this world. It makes no sense a man telling his wife, *"I love you and appreciate you…"* and then giving her some flowers and perfume. If this is not backed by action, whereby he actually does something to make her life easier; then it is like kicking her in the teeth! Even though we have an 'International Women's Day' and a 'Mother's Day'; they are both quickly forgotten once the day is over, as women go back to the daily grind of their lives. Even in this modern age; they are still being treated disparagingly because of their sex! You have to remember that, men are like children; in that they will do anything and continue doing it, if they can get away with it. Whereas; the 'forgiving nature' of women, is what consistently gets them taken for granted. This means; the existing affairs of degradation for women will continue unabated, unless they are prepared to fight for their inalienable rights. First of all; a woman is a human being with sensitive feelings. It is wrong for anyone to trample all over them because she will one day be forced to fight back and it could get nasty! Secondly; her brains, skill and intuition are a necessary part of the national equation…without which, a society would be worthless. She should be encouraged to do what she wants to do; and not be victimised for voicing an opinion. Finally; it is nature's way that a woman carries a child during pregnancy. Without children; the human race would die! Getting pregnant should therefore be seen as a blessing; and she should not be ostracised for wanting to have children. She should rather be encouraged and given the right conditions; so that she is happy and healthy enough to incubate and raise them properly. If she wants to work as well as have children; she should be allowed enough time off to do so, (which could be subsidised by the government in the form of tax breaks for the company she works for) until she feels ready to return. Surely, that is not too much to ask?

Although the laws to protect women are slowly improving with time; no woman can say they are perfect. The only way there can be a drastic change for the better; will be for all females to grab the bull by the horns and take what is their due. The originators of the female movement went to great lengths to begin the process towards equality; so it is only right that it reaches its logical conclusion of a real, worthwhile and lasting liberation. Since women represent at least half the voting block in most developed countries; the best way change can be effected is to use her vote and not choose those politicians who do not have any serious empathy towards the female cause. This also means ditching the women politicians who spout female causes; but once they get into power, are out-manoeuvred into supporting the status-quo. These women are forced to toe the line; so that they can keep their token jobs, in the male-dominated establishment. The reason men have held onto power for so long is because they tend to stick together; and will only allow into their 'boys club', the kind of women who will play by their rules. Regrettably; there are some women who are prepared to kow-tow to men for their own advancement. I'm sorry to say this; but too many women in positions of authority and power, are only thinking of themselves. They do not do enough to help other females; and that is why advancement for women appears to have stagnated. Self-defence for women on a national scale; has to be up to all the females in a country to get together and push for change. Politicians will only listen and do what you want them to do for you; if they think they will lose their jobs and the power, if they don't. The fact that many opposition political parties have not cottoned on to this fact and done more for women; speaks volumes. It means; there needs to be a clean sweep of today's politicians and a new generation of far-sighted policy/lawmakers installed. If women ruled the world; there would be far less corruption; free-health service and education; very little unemployment; no homelessness; hunger would be wiped-out; and children would not suffer unnecessary diseases and illnesses. The world could easily afford these 'luxuries'; because with women in power in every country, there would be no wars. This means there would be no need to spend money on an arms race! Isn't that an ideal worth wishing and pushing for?

5. The Break-up

Throughout this chapter and the last one on the battle of the sexes; I have detailed a few of the greatest dangers that could befall a woman and how best to deal with them from a self-defence perspective. I am sure there are other less-obvious dangers, which I have not specifically covered; but by using this book as an inspirational guideline, you will quickly learn to value yourself more! By being in a defensive frame of mind; you will put yourself first and make sure you do not get hurt. Once you are able to spot the danger signs, before they become calamities; you will have no problem in dealing with them! I have also consistently advised you to leave any man who does not live up to your expectations and refuses to change. I am also aware that leaving a man is not as easy as it seems; so you have to be tough and determined. The alternative would be living a life that would not be worth living! However; as much as I would love you to be a superwoman and a real tigress; the decision to leave a man, will always be yours. I cannot do it for you! You therefore have to weigh the options and decide between the worst thing that could happen if you stay with him; and if you were to leave him. There have been many examples of women who suffer terrible abuse from a partner. They take advice from family and friends to kick him out; only to find themselves taking him back. This is understandable; because many people are afraid of change, or the unknown. They really have no idea how they can cope without their partners! When you have been with someone for many years; it is very difficult to prise yourself away, even if the person is not good for your well-being. Even though everyone and every logical reason tells you to leave him; there is something that keeps you from pulling the plug and you find yourself drawn back into his lair. The problem stems from the fact that nobody is all-bad; and even the worst abuser of women, will at times be the most wonderful man she has ever met. This is because; whatever attracted her to him in the beginning never goes completely away. Once he knows what turns her on, or what makes her happy; he will have no qualms about using the tactic to get himself out of trouble. Sex is also a very powerful weapon in an abuser's armoury; because the more intense orgasms he gives a woman, the more likely she will put up with his failings. Most physical and mental abusers are so used to turning on the charm, when visitors come to the house; they even manage to convince themselves that they are doing nothing wrong. As a result; she ends up living in bondage to her man. The only way to break the chains; is to grit her teeth and walk away. Luckily, there are laws that protect women; so leaving a man is not as difficult as it used to be. Even if you have nowhere to go; there are refuges and organisations in every country, which can help a woman escape and stay away from an abusive relationship.

Leaving a man is the easy bit. Keeping him away from you; could be the hardest thing you will ever have to do. Even if you stay away from him; it does not mean he will stop pestering you. Barring orders and the threat of prison; will do nothing to stop a man who is still so much in love that he will stop at nothing to get you back. In some cases; he might decide to do you harm, so that no one else can have you. It is a severe dent in a man's ego; if a woman leaves him, because of his culpability. He will do his utmost to get her back; even if it means dumping her, once he has got her back on side. For most men; it is very important for his ego and credentials that he leaves on his terms! That is why a lot of men who want to end a relationship; will play silly games like not returning phone messages and acting very cold. He hopes the woman will decide she has had enough and tell him she wants out! *"Darling, I think our relationship is not working. Why don't we take a break from each other?"* Perfect! She walks away and he gets the sympathy vote from his friends. *"I did nothing wrong. I was always there for her; and then she does this to me. Boo Hoo Hoo!"*

Someone who is so used to abusing his woman and getting his way with her, through fear and intimidation; becomes very hurt and angry when this power is taken away from him, through the woman's abrupt decision. He is so used to being the one telling her what to do; that for her to make such an independent decision, can be soul-destroying. Revenge will be uppermost on his mind! You must remember that men are also afraid of the unknown. There may be severe resistance on his part; culminating in promises to 'change' or to do anything, to make you stay with him. Realistically; it is impossible to change from 'who you really are'! Even if he does it to satisfy you; it means you will be living under false pretences. A wife-beater can curb his anger and may be able to desist from beating up his partner; but the threat will always remain. This means the woman can never sleep easy; knowing that he could erupt at any time. If you constantly have to tread on eggshells around your partner, in order not to annoy him, in case he beats you up; then your relationship becomes a prison. You would be much better-off walking away!

If he is guilty of any of the aforementioned abuses; then leaving him becomes a little easier. If he rapes you; your face is swollen from a beating; or even if he loves his affairs/substance abuse/addictions/

criminal endeavours more than his family; then the decision becomes very straightforward. It is also possible that you might want to leave him; simply because you feel the relationship has run its course, and you are bored. In such a situation; dumping your man can become an impossible situation, because he will feel he has done nothing wrong. The pressure will then be on you to justify your actions; and you may be made to feel guilty for 'hurting' your partner. The popular excuses; (*"There is no one else involved…". "You've done nothing wrong…". "It's not you, it's me…"*) will do nothing to hide the fact that there is no easy way to leave a long-term relationship. A break-up still carries social stigma; and that is why some women will do nothing, while suffering in silence. On one side; there will be relatives who will try to convince you to stay and 'sort out your problems' in order not to ruin the family name and may even guilt-trip you, by urging you not to disrupt the lives of the kids. On the other side; will be your friends, especially those who have been through break-ups themselves. They will be urging you to: *"Dump the bastard; you're better-off without him…"*) because it makes them feel better that they are not the only social 'failures' in town!

Once you break up; friends of the family will be taking sides and you may find yourself in a social void, shunned by your husband's acquaintances and relatives. Your husband will also feel the pinch and may lose out in the business world; which still regards any separation or divorce as a sure sign that he cannot control his domestic situation and therefore, will be 'mentally unfit' to handle any big business deals. For his own selfish reasons; he may beg you not to leave him and will hate you for not heeding his entreaties. Sometimes it might be 'too late' to walk away; especially if there are children involved or if you have already sacrificed everything for the marriage, making it too difficult to resurrect your career. The problem is; you may not have planned what to do with your post-relationship/marriage life. Even though living alone can be fun; not everybody is cut out for it and loneliness is one thing many women cannot handle with ease. You could therefore decide to stay put in the relationship; whereby you continue it as 'friends' in a brotherly-sisterly way, without the sex. You would then be leading separate lives in the same household, in order not to upset the apple cart of family routine. Isn't that a little sad; if not tragic?

I hope you can now appreciate the pressure you will be under; once you decide to break up. Some women make the mistake of 'sodding the consequences' and walking off; simply because they have reached a real state of fear, despair and exasperation. This always plays into the man's hands. He can make up all kinds of lies and excuses to his friends, why you ran away; and you will not be around to defend yourself. Whatever your reasons for leaving or staying; you have to make sure they are yours and yours alone and that you were not pushed into it by pressure from friends and relatives. In the end; your 'true self' will always surface and you will be very unhappy, if you have made the wrong decision. For that reason; I implore you to treat a break-up as serious business, which requires planning and strategy.

In keeping with the theme of this book; you have to make sure you are the winner in your life. It is imperative that you make the right decision for yourself, in order to win the break-up battle. Make no mistake; if you leave any man, he will be hurt (even if he does not show it) and he will be out to hurt you for hurting him! He will definitely try to win the tug-of-war over the kids; and the tussle over money, property and assets. He will also be out to win the reputation, dignity and self-esteem fight; so that he can salvage as many crumbs as possible, from the wreckage that you caused by leaving him. Even in the friendliest of separations, there is always a winner; and it is the one who feels the most victorious after the event. You have to make sure that winner is you! If you are severely defeated; it will haunt you for the rest of your life, due to the simple fact that you have only one life and you cannot re-live it. It is such a horrible feeling to realise that in absolute good faith, you sacrificed your life and career for some man; only to be kicked in the teeth by him. You therefore have to see well in advance, the possibility of a break-up; so that you can protect yourself. If he hits you, rapes you or is constantly abusing you mentally; it does not take a brain surgeon to tell you that the relationship cannot continue and sooner rather than later, it will all be over. Once you spot any sign of a future break-up, which could even be your suspicions over another woman he may be seeing on the side; then you have to prepare yourself for the inevitable. In the chapter on mental rape; I detailed a few ways to teach him a lesson when he misbehaves. When his bad behaviour goes overboard; refusing to cook for, sleep with or do anything for him, may not work. You will get the feeling deep inside you, that he no longer loves or respects you; therefore, any attempt to come to the peace table, will amount to window-dressing and pretence. You will then be fully aware that it is just a matter of time before the relationship will be over; so you have to be tough and use your head. This means; you have to find a way to keep smiling and don't ever let on that you have spotted the end. You have to make sure this is one battle you refuse to lose!

There are certain steps you should take; before finally kicking him out for good. At that point, you will find that it is the only and most natural thing to do; because all else has failed.

(a). ultimatum

Most bad behaviour can be dealt with by a severe telling-off, or non-participation in his domestic life; as explained in Chapter 5. If you still love him; it would be in your best interests to use these 'softer' ways of registering your displeasure, to see if he will change for the better. This will subtly let him know that you are not prepared to put up with whatever he has done to displease you. It will also give him a chance to make up for his failing; because most men are sensible enough, not to continue annoying the women in their lives. If you feel that what he has done is too serious to ignore; you have to issue an ultimatum to let him realise that under no circumstances, are you prepared to put up with it any more. Once you issue an ultimatum; you have to be prepared to carry it out! If he continues doing the things you don't like; you should always act normally and let him think you have forgotten. You can then begin making your plans for the inevitable parting of the ways.

(b). dismissal

If you cannot bear the sight of him, because of something he has done; (mistreatment, having an affair, substance abuse or crime) then you will be justified in throwing him out of the house. This could only be a temporary measure; because he will definitely come crawling back, begging for forgiveness! Once you have thrown him out; you have to realise that you will have hurt his feelings and he will be out for some sort of revenge. You will have to be on your guard; because even if you forgive him, there is no guarantee he has forgiven you. Any man kicked out of his own house, will have a bruised ego. He will do anything and accept any kind of condition, in order to get back into the house; from whence he can plot his own revenge. If you threw him out because he was having an affair; there is no guarantee he will not have another one in the not too distant future. With substance abuse, gambling or crime; he will most likely continue doing it behind your back. He will thereby be putting your safety at risk; so you will have to make secretive plans for the inevitable break-up.

(c). separation

Once there is a breakdown in the relationship and all respect has gone out of the window; there should be no going back because there will be no trust and you will only be tolerating each other. This will lead to arguments and insults; so you have to start preparing for life without him. For a separation to work best in your favour; it would be better that you are the one who moves out so that you can quietly make plans for the divorce, without any interference from him. However; you should try to gather enough evidence against him, before you do move out. This means; you have to grit your teeth and tolerate him for a few months, whilst making your plans. He may try all kinds of tactics to get you back; but you should use your brain and not your heart. Respect, trust and love, once lost; are hardly ever likely to be regained. No woman should ever have to beg a man to love and accept her for who she is. Separation should always be a prelude for the inevitable divorce!

(d). divorce

Getting a divorce is the last resort; whereby you have accepted there is no hope of a reprieve. You have to make sure you come out of it with your dignity, integrity and reputation intact; as well as enough financial reward, for everything you were forced to put up with. If you are not married, but have been in a long-term relationship; you have to treat the separation with the finality of a divorce. If you feel you have a bona-fide right to the property, or any other assets you may have contributed to; you will have to set up legal proceedings to get him out of the house, so that you can move back in. Otherwise, just cut your losses and go; because arguing over the house, will bring you back into contact with him. Sometimes; you have to pay a price for your freedom, peace of mind and sanity! A man who has been mentally or physically abusing you and cannot stand the sight of; is the last person you want to be in contact with, arguing over who owns what, why, where and how. It would be much better; if you have gathered enough evidence, in order to prosecute him. You can then let the cops and solicitors deal with the nitty-gritty.

First of all; you have to help the law to help you. You need to gather as much evidence as you can, in order to facilitate your case; as explained earlier on in this chapter. Without this; you will be severely hampered in the fight for your freedom and justice. Secondly; you have to be very secretive and not reveal your hand. Otherwise; he will be forced to retaliate by taking steps to protect himself. Even if he has done nothing wrong and you are just bored with the relationship; you have to put emotions aside and think practically about the children; the property; the assets; the money; your reputation; self-esteem and dignity. You have to decide what you want from each of them; and how you are going to go about achieving it. If for instance, you know about his secret off-shore account; then you have to make sure that he cannot siphon the money away elsewhere, in order for you not to get any of it. If you can install a few closed-circuit cameras around the house when he is at work; it will enable you to have some visual proof of his bad behaviour and build a stronger case for yourself. If he arrives from work and starts yelling at you or disrespecting you in any way; the cameras and microphones will capture it. Over a period of a few days; this can paint a very accurate picture to anyone who views the footage that the marriage has irretrievably broken down. Telling a divorce judge that your man doesn't love you; is one thing. But if he saw the unedited footage for himself; you will be in a very strong position. This will help you take him to the cleaners! The same attention to detail must be pursued by you; as regards his bank accounts, property he owns and huge expenditures. You should do your best to obtain photocopies of all the paper trail! When times were good between the two of you; he may have bought you a car, jewellery or even a holiday home. He may have 'forgotten' to put them in your name. Because you were so excited at his generosity, and due to the fact that you were happily married at the time; you may have failed to mention it. All that property will still be legally his; and you will then have to fight tooth and nail to get back, what is yours. If he is a philanderer; he may also be spending money on other women! If you have copies of the receipts and movement of money from his account; it will paint a darker picture of him, in front of the judge who decides how much alimony you will get.

Once you have gathered enough evidence against him for his larger sins; (marital rape, wife-beating, affairs, addictions, substance abuse or crime) you can then make plans for your life without him. You must start by organising where you are going to stay, so that he cannot find you. Only when every bolt has been tightened and you have covered every loophole; should you finally confront him with the immortal words: *"I want a divorce!"* or *"I'm leaving you because...!"* and watch out for his reaction. If he denies your accusations; then it shows he still loves you and is scared of the consequences. You should tell him you will be dealing with him through the solicitors; and then move out with the children, if you have any. Since your mind is already made up; you should not give him any room to try and convince you to change course. He may know a few reliable buttons to press, which will leave you confused! At this stage; you can hand over all the evidence to your solicitor and say nothing to your partner. He will never suspect you have been so clever; and will not have taken enough steps to defend himself. Although many men have now accepted that they will lose a certain amount to the wife in any divorce settlement; it is still a bitter pill to swallow, especially when he later realises, you have been so underhand in gathering evidence against him. You should therefore, not say or do anything to aggravate the situation. You should never jump into somebody else's arms before you have told him you are leaving him. It is very important that you play the 'injured party' role to perfection. Having a lover on the side; will strengthen his hand and it can be used against you in any divorce settlement. Once you have left him; you have to be aware that he will be looking for ways to discredit or hurt you. Having a lover; will have him suspecting you were sneaking behind his back whilst you were together. Adultery or cheating in a relationship creates bitterness. If he does not beat you up, he might do so one day; even long after you are divorced. Many murders are as a result of adultery! The bitter pill he has to swallow, that he was not good enough for you; will anger him. He might make sure no one else can have you; by killing you! The law can only protect you up to a point; because nobody has a permanent police bodyguard! Never underestimate the impact, adultery has on a man's self-esteem and ego. Most top policemen, lawyers and judges are men; so a crime of passion as a result of woman's adultery and 'extreme mental cruelty', will attract a great deal of institutionalised sympathy. He might only do a few years in prison for killing you! That does not help you or your family does it?

Breaking up is something that you really have to put your mind to; in order to make sure you win the aftermath. You need to be able to get on with the rest of your life; without having to look over your shoulder, whenever you go out. Once the divorce is settled, and preferably when he has found himself someone else; only then should you openly parade your new flame, because he is unlikely to bother you. Eventually; you may even be able to see each other in town and exchange pleasantries, without having to avoid each other. However; if you do leave a violent man, make sure it is for ever. It is better to move away from that area; so that he never knows where you are. If you have to meet him because of the children; then you can arrange a public drop-off point and make sure you are never alone with him. The first six months are the most crucial; if he is going to make a last-ditch attempt to get you back. This might include; threatening or following your friends around to see if they will lead him to you. If he does manage to find you; don't hesitate to call the police. You should explain that you do not feel safe with him lurking around outside your house; because your life could be in danger. If the police fail to act; then maybe paying a few thugs to make him heed your wishes, will not be such a bad idea. A broken leg or two will make him see things your way! Some men have to be forced into realising that women are very capable of violence; and will act, either by themselves or by paying someone to do it! If he realises that when push comes to shove, you will hurt him badly and that you have tough guys who will come to your rescue; you will find his attitude towards you quickly changing!

Dear Tigress! A Dilemma is no easy fight to win; but once you realise that the most important person in your life is you, then you will not feel so guilty about doing what is best for yourself. You only have one life to live. Make sure you keep it safe!!!

Chapter Sixteen
The impossible situation (Part 3)
Life or Death

Well, as the saying goes; all good things (and bad) must surely come to an end. Naturally; this must also include your life! Throughout this book; I have covered many situations, except the most serious one. What do you do when you are faced with a life or death situation? The answer is: You use your head and you never over-react! You have to put the value of your life above everything else; because you are of no use to anybody, if you are dead. If you are alive; you can learn from your mistakes, even if it means 'losing out' in certain situations. For example; if you see someone robbing your car or snatching your purse, it would be folly to tackle him physically. This is because; he might be carrying a weapon and you might end up getting shot or stabbed to death. If you are involved in illegal activities and get ripped off; you could easily be killed, if you try to get your money back. It would be best to leave them alone; and get on with the rest of your life. The same goes for; interfering in other people's business; trying to separate fights; gossiping viciously about someone; stealing someone else's husband or owing money. They are all circumstances that will make one or more persons angry enough to hurl insults at, or attack you; whereby you could easily get injured or killed. In each of these cases; death can be avoided if you approach them in a calm, careful manner and realise that there are consequences to every action. You will have a much safer life, if you are able to treat everything you do, as if you are crossing a road; (*'Look left, look right and look left again'*) knowing that you will be knocked over and injured or killed, if you ignore the safety routine. We would all like to live to a respectable old age, injury free; but unfortunately, this is sometimes not possible. The lives of people are often cut short; because of neglect, sickness, sheer stupidity or violence.

If you neglect your responsibilities, like your children; they could easily be led astray into shenanigans like robbery, drug dealing and prostitution. These are the crimes, most likely to cause a risk to their lives and health; whereby you will be unable to save them. If you don't take an interest in your children's lives; they could join a cult, or be inducted into a terrorist organisation. This means, they might as well be dead; because you would have lost them to their new ideology and group of friends. In a worse-case scenario; they could also be kidnapped and killed, if you dilly-dally and fail to come up with the ransom money. This happens; if you place the amount of cash required, above the value of your child's life. Your world will be shattered for ever! If you ignore the security in your house and in your everyday life, by not being observant to your surroundings; it can easily lead to crimes being committed against you. It would be no use complaining after the event; because you might not even be alive! Safety information is readily available in every police station; about what you should or should not do in your area. If you are burgled; you cannot blame anyone but yourself, for giving the thieves the opportunity to invade your home. Even though we all have accidents; if we do not learn from them, they will happen again. Accidents usually occur; when certain basic rules are neglected. It only takes one fatal one; to ruin your life for ever! Sadly; many people are not aware that things they do in their everyday lives, could actually kill them. The fact that it has not yet happened; does not mean it won't! It would be a shame to lose your life, over something that could have been avoided.

With sickness; it is usually a slow build up, before it becomes life-threatening. It may result in your death; if you do not take your body seriously. It is imperative that you go for regular check-ups; so that any impending problems can be diagnosed early enough, to facilitate treatment. For instance; if you study your breasts for irregular lumps, you can defeat cancer before it spreads. With the same spirit; you should try and understand your whole body. If something is bothering you; it would be better to let a doctor find out what it is, before it becomes too late to cure it. Don't be afraid to seek a second or even a third opinion; if you are not satisfied with what a particular doctor tells you. In the haste to treat as many patients as possible, in order to meet unrealistic targets; misdiagnosis has become quite frequent in clinics, surgeries and hospitals around the world. You have a weak heart, a damaged liver or other frailties in your body; and have been told by your doctor to take it easy, cut down on your alcohol or nicotine intake and do more exercise. It would be entirely your fault; if you fail to heed their advice, fall sick, collapse and die. Why should you put your family through the worry, monetary and time-consuming expense of looking after you; when the answer to your health and fitness lies firmly at your door? This may seem like common sense; but if it were so common, there would be far less unnecessary deaths through sickness. This means; there are definitely those who do not take their bodies seriously enough! The whole idea of self-defence; is to defend yourself and make sure you don't come to any harm. Surely that means; you have to make sure you don't harm yourself? *"I rest my case Your Honour!"*

Sheer stupidity can get you killed, if you rush into things without thinking; which is what many people do, when they are trying to get things done quickly or looking for revenge. If getting your own back is so important for you; it would be better to bide your time and plan it well, in order to get maximum satisfaction. Believe it or not; one day, you will definitely get the opportunity to do so! Using one crime to solve another, never works; and will always come back to haunt you. This is why it is always better to let the authorities win the fight for you. That way, your problem becomes more than yours; as there is always more security, when you have others legally fighting your corner. Mixing with the wrong group of people; is another example of stupidity that can end up in an outcome, you are not prepared for. You have to be very strict with yourself in making new friends; and that is why we have the adage, *'old friends are the best'*. You see; allowing someone into your life, also means you have to be prepared for whatever problems he or she may bring with them. You have to be very careful; in not allowing your good nature to lead you into trouble. You therefore have to be ruthless and learn to decline requests from strangers; and not go too far, when trying to help people. For example; someone meets you in town and asks you for directions. It would be better for you to either pretend you don't know, and keep moving; or direct them to the nearest police station. You must not let them monopolise your time; because it could end up in a conversation you were not looking for. Even when dealing with friends; you have to make sure they don't take advantage of you. If something does not feel right; you should not go through with it, even if it means disappointing him or her. If a friend asks you to cover for him with an alibi or keep some stolen property for him; then you become part of the crime and its implications. You could easily be jailed or even killed; because he might have ripped off some criminal associates and you will be on their radar when they come looking for their money. Once you understand that most people will not tell the truth when asking for a favour, because they know the truth will make you refuse the request; then you will be able to decline with a clear conscience, using the simple excuse: *"Sorry; I can't help you because I'm too busy with my own problems..."* or the blunt, *"No, I won't do it for you because I don't like the idea and I will not change my mind; so don't bother trying to sweet-talk me!"*

Violence can rear its ugly head; because some men don't know any other way of resolving conflicts. Ever since the days of the school playground; boys have believed that the winner of any argument is the one who wins the fight. Regrettably; some will carry this belief into their relationships with women. If you have split up with a violent or obsessive man; you have to assume that he is more than capable of looking for revenge, by using violence. You therefore have to take steps to protect yourself; by moving house and changing jobs, if possible. You have to make sure that after leaving that type of person; he will not try and harm you. A jilted lover is also a dangerous one; who might decide that if he can't have you, then no one else should! The safest way would be to arrange where you are going to stay; (the further away from the scene of your abuse, the better) **before** telling him you are getting rid of him. Reporting a man for hurting you, and he ends up in prison; may seem like a victory, but could be the beginning of your problems. What do you do when he comes out of jail? He would have had plenty of time on his hands to think of ways of hurting you! You will not be told by the authorities the exact day he is released. If you are still living in the same house; there is nothing to stop him sneaking up and doing you harm, when you least expect it. Whichever way you decide to get him out of your life, must take planning; so that he cannot come back to interfere with you. You do not want to suffer undue vengeful consequences from his friends and relatives either; so you should never tell any of them where you have moved to. Even if they don't physically hurt you; they could watch your house or car and then damage them when you go out.

If you cannot afford to move or change jobs; you have to keep your eyes open, as soon as you hear he has been released from prison. He is unlikely to harm you, when he sees you for the first time after his incarceration; because he might feel there is still hope of reconciliation. As soon as he shows up at your house; you should take that as a cue and use clever tactics to tell him nicely that you have moved on to a new life, without him. If he comes bothering you at work; you should let your security deal with him, so that he doesn't come there again! If he persists in harassing you; then you will have to inform the police. They will warn him off; but the onus should always be on you to protect yourself, and leave nothing to chance. Having to live your life in fear; is one of the unfortunate consequences you will have to face, if your tormentor is jailed. Even the police may not be able to protect you, twenty-four hours a day! Fortunately; the modern man understands that being dumped is a sign of the times and he will most probably take it in his stride. But you should never underestimate the impact, leaving a man; can have on him. When you have been in a relationship for a long time; it is never easy to let go. If he feels his life is not worth anything without you; he might decide to end it and take you to Heaven with him. It is important you realise this and include the possibility in your plans; when you are thinking of walking away or reporting him to the authorities. It is better to look silly, by being over-cautious; than find yourself in a coffin!

A. Murder and Manslaughter

With all the advice I have given about self-defence in different situations; it is still extremely difficult to fight your husband or child, because of the emotional attachment. This is why it takes most women, a long time to seek help; and it is usually when her life is really in danger. Since you are living under the same roof, it is not easy to prevent it happening; because any attack is usually unexpected. It would be difficult to foresee the first time it occurs; unless you are aware of certain behavioural patterns. The minute a man shouts at you, gives you orders or tries to control your lifestyle; then the chances are, you will one day rebel and refuse to do his bidding. This means; the next step would be for him to hit you! If he is an alcoholic or drug abuser; the chances of him attacking you, will be greatly exacerbated. Any beating he gives you; could very easily become manslaughter or murder! When he finds out his hands or feet are not having their desired effect on you; he may choose to hit you with a weapon. A simple push on you; could result in your falling down, hitting your head on the corner of a table, cracking your skull open and dying. *"I didn't mean to do it!"* would probably be his defence; and he will most likely only do a few years in jail, for manslaughter. That would not help you; when you are lying cold in your grave! The previous yelling and beatings, which culminated in your death, will be conveniently consigned to the dustbins of history; along with your dead body. It is imperative that you study your own family; and watch out for the same signs that could end up in tragedy for you. Even at an early age; a child will show signs of losing the temper, shouting, banging the fists on a table or throwing things around, in order to get his/her way. That is when you should never pamper to his/her demands; but seek professional help. It is important to nip the temper tantrums in the bud; before it results in future violence, which could end tragically for you. Respect for the female, has to be learnt early on in a child's life; because there are far too many examples of physical and mental abuses on women. These could all have been avoided; had the perpetrators been taught right from wrong, at an early age.

If your husband or child attacks you; you only have two choices, knowing that it will most likely happen again. You can put up and shut up; or go to the police and break up your family. A very tough call indeed! Kick a man in the groin; punch him hard in the nose; scratch his eyes out; throw him down or break his knee cap; are all ways of dealing with a stranger, if you know how to fight. What if you don't have any combative skills? Even if you do; how can you poke the eyes out or kick your own husband or violent child in the groin? A smooth functioning penis is the basis of a happy heterosexual marriage; so why ruin it all because of a quarrel, which could be over as soon as it starts? To poke someone in the eye could blind the person; and you will have to live with the guilt and consequences for the rest of your life. How can you do that to the man you love; or to your daughter; because she attacked you for not allowing her to go out with a boyfriend you disapprove of? Could you pour hot water over your daughter; or smash her over the head with frying pan? No? What would you do if she pulled a knife on you; and was about to stab you? In such an extreme situation, where your life is in danger; anything is possible and your instincts will take over. You might even surprise yourself by what you will do for self-preservation! Kill or be killed! If your husband or child attacks you, with the intention of killing you; then you have to defend yourself. This could result in over-reaction and tragedy; when one or both of you gets hurt or even killed. You should always leave a house you are not safe in, and stay with friends; until you feel the situation has cooled down. You should then use a third party, like other family members; to sort out the problem. Never ever move back into the house; unless there are assurances made in front of relatives from his family's side, that he will not harm you. From then on; you should start planning for the inevitable break up. You cannot afford to live in a house where you do not feel safe and you have to keep treading carefully; in case you upset him and he attacks you again. If he is the type of man who does not know when to stop, beats you regularly and maliciously wounds you with the intention of killing you; then you have to use your wounds as evidence and report him first to his family and then to the police, before seeking a divorce. He will definitely do it again one day! You must not give him the chance; by moving away from your area, once he has been jailed.

With violence from a child; you should immediately call the police. A couple of hours in a cell to cool him or her down, with a sincere warning from a stern-looking officer; should be enough. If he or she continues to attack you; then sentiments should be put aside, and you should have him/her arrested and prosecuted. It is always better to be safe than sorry! The courts will more than likely, for a first offence; suggest professional counselling. You would be wise to attend the sessions; because the reasons for his/her violence may be deep-rooted, and could inadvertently be your fault. For example; some children have problems in dealing with divorce and may blame the parent they are living with, for the absence of the other parent from their lives. You would be doing him/her a favour; by making him/her aware at an early stage, that police stations are not the most comfortable of places to be taken. If your child is violent and you do nothing about it; he may grow up using violence on his girlfriend or wife and end up in serious trouble one day. The blame for his behaviour will fall squarely on your shoulders! How many times have we heard people blame their failings on their up-bringing? *"It's not my fault. My parents abused me as a child...!"* You have to put the value of your life, above even that of your violent offspring; because the reasons why he or she attacked you, will not disappear overnight. You cannot afford to sleep with one eye open; in case you are attacked again! The last thing you would want; is to be held to ransom by your children, whereby you allow them to do what they like at the expense of your well-being and instincts as a parent. It would be better if a child's violent tendencies were stamped out early; but if you are in the unfortunate position of having lost control of your teenage child who regularly pushes you around, then shock treatment is the best solution to the problem. If he/she is old enough to leave home; you have to throw him/her out of the house, change the locks on the doors and alert the authorities. He or she will be arrested; the minute they show their face anywhere around your house! A few weeks out in the cold with no one to cook and clean up for him/her; should have a sobering effect. If it doesn't; then forget about him/her and get on with your life! Although a woman's love for her children is usually unconditional, and she is able to put up with many things from them; there has to be a limit, where violence is concerned. If a child, whom you carried for nine months in your womb, turns out to be a violent monster; he or she loses the right to your love. Ç'est la vie!

Women have been known to take the law into their own hands in abusive relationships; by murder or 'manslaughter'. Whilst he is asleep; pour petrol on him and set him on fire; stab him to death; or cut off his penis, if he has been unfaithful! Pour boiling hot water over his face; if he is close enough to yell at you! Hire a hit man to kill him and dispose of his body! These are simple enough methods to get rid of a man! A spell in jail might be preferable to what you will have to go through with him; which in many ways is also a prison. (You don't have to take my advice on this. It really is up to only you; whether you want to put up and shut up, leave him or get rid of him for good!) In the heat of the moment, it may seem like a good idea to hurt your tormentor; but the iron rule of self-defence says that with every action there will be a reaction. This means; there will definitely be consequences, so violence for violence is not a good idea. The law and most of society tends to sympathise with the one who is most hurt in an affray. For example; your man has been systematically beating you up over the years. If you get a gun and shoot him dead; you will be convicted of murder or manslaughter. You may be lucky and get off on a self-defence technicality! Women tend to get the rub of the green in domestic violence cases; but you have to be aware that your life will change for ever. There will always be those who will ask whether it was necessary to go so far; and you will be socially tarred and feathered, as the wicked witch who shot her defenceless husband. What are you going to do against reprisals from his family and friends; who will never accept that the man you killed was a violent bully? Revenge is such a powerful force, that even if you moved away from the area; there is no guarantee that one of his friends or relatives will not track you down. They could make your world a misery; kill you or pay to have you murdered, in retaliation. In effect; the rest of your life will be ruined because you will never be able to sleep easily at night. If you are thinking of murdering the man in your life…think thrice!!! .It is much more satisfying to let the law win the battle for you; so that he is not given any more room to manoeuvre and manipulate your life!

Killing is such a divisive subject; even psychological experts cannot agree wholeheartedly on why someone would choose to kill the one he/she loves. Anybody, even a quiet moody man; could snap at any moment, lash out and end up on a murder or manslaughter charge. Once someone cares passionately about something; there will always be a likelihood he/she will be prepared to go all the way and kill…if this passion is hurt, damaged or they are deprived of it in any way. Women are just as capable of killing as men! You cannot afford to hurt anyone so badly; that he or she feels there is no other recourse, than to get rid of you. If you steal, rip-off or go after someone else's man; you run the risk of hurting him or her so badly, that killing cannot be ruled out. Money; religion; beliefs; family; property; dignity; self-esteem and reputation are the things most people will get passionate about. If you injure, subjugate or destroy any of these; then you are setting yourself up for dangerous reprisals. In a world where there are suicide bombers prepared to kill themselves and many others, in order to make a point; and murder rates going up; there is no telling, how far anyone can go to heal a wounded pride, passion or ego. I therefore insist that the best way to deal with violence is to spot the signs that can lead up to it; and do your best not to upset the applecart. If you are ever in a position where you feel you will be in the firing line; I advise you to make your well-laid plans to get out while you can. There will always be something that makes you feel uncomfortable about someone. You should always rely on your gut instinct and keep a watchful eye open for further pre-signals. Try not to wait till he attacks you; before you decide to leave him! It only takes one punch or strike with a weapon to kill you; or injure you so badly that your life will not be worth living. Be selfish and think of yourself!

B. Kidnapping

In this materialistic world; it seems as if there are many people who want what they haven't got and cannot afford. To be able to buy things, you need money; and some will prefer to take it, rather than work for it! This is why stealing, robbery and kidnapping of the rich; has become such a lucrative tool for criminal gangs, in need of large amounts of quick money. As previously explained; your self-defence concerns amongst other things, those closest to you. If your child is kidnapped; it will probably hurt you more than if it had happened to you personally. The longer you delay, the greater the suffering of your child; so it is really unforgivable to place the value of money over the health of your child. Life is worth more than money! If you have the resources; it is better to pay the ransom and get your child back alive, rather than lose him or her. Since kidnappers are motivated by money; they would most likely have done their homework and they will know that their target has the financial means, before they strike. Refusing to pay will make them angry enough to harm the child; simply to let you know that they mean business. They don't really want to kill a child; but if you try to be stubborn, they will definitely prove a point to you. This will send the word out to their next victims; that they don't play games. Although one might occasionally come across amateurs; (who usually get caught because they keep changing the deadlines, hoping to get the money) you have to take all kidnappers seriously. The longer a criminal gang has been successfully plying their trade; the more professional, ruthless and dangerous they become. You cannot afford to put a life at risk, by messing around with delaying tactics. Kidnapping of a child is a horrible crime that can destroy the cosiness in a family; because mother and father will start blaming each other, for not having kept a watch over the child. Even if he or she is returned safely; the pain and worry the parents will go through, will change their lives for ever. If you are wealthy; it is important you act responsibly and accept that it could happen to you...by taking steps to increase the security of your family.

The mentality of a kidnapper differs from continent to continent and can be influenced by religious beliefs; financial motivation; political bravado; criminal intention and economic desperation. In Latin American countries; kidnapping is rampant and the ransom demand usually so small, that the families quietly pay up without informing the police. As a result; the child is always returned unharmed. Since only the most famous kidnapping cases are ever reported in the media; it makes sense to pay the money and get your child back safely. Once it attracts the press; the kidnappers may become more desperate and will realise they cannot get away with it. They may as well kill their victim! Kidnapping is not an African or an Asian trait; and is almost non-existent in those areas. This is because there is a strong inherent sense of family and local community; and not many people wealthy enough to interest a kidnapper. Those who are very rich; will have adequate security precautions in place, which will involve all the locals in the town they live in. The rich usually do a lot for the local people; so there will always be informants, ready to divulge useful information to them. They will most likely have the police at their beck and call; making it impossible for the local criminals to use kidnapping as a tool of their trade. If any strangers arrive in town; they will be noticed and followed. This makes it extremely difficult for them to spy on a house or hang around a school, in order to snatch a child. In many parts of Africa; anybody caught kidnapping could be burnt alive, after a severe mob beating! There is however, an exception in war-torn Third World countries; where kidnapping is extremely popular as a political and an economic tool. The lawlessness combined with the breakdown in communications and infrastructure; makes it very easy for the kidnappers to keep their victim secretly hidden in terrible conditions. This allows the relatives to feel the pain and pay the ransom quicker! Needing the money for political ends, which will include buying weapons for their cause; they will be more ruthless and will not think twice about killing their victims. They know that they will face certain death if they are caught; and their ruthlessness means, they will most likely get their money.

In the developed world; kidnapping is not so popular. This is because the police have a lot more experience in dealing with the crime; so the crooks are unlikely to succeed. If someone is kidnapped; it will in all probability be a businessman and done by criminals motivated by greed and money, rather than ideology or as a political tool. The businessman's associates will most likely pay the money quietly; in order not to attract any media attention. They obviously have a lot more to hide, and would not want their dirty laundry washed in public. Questions may be asked about their business practices, which warranted the kidnapping! There has been a recent rise in 'robbery kidnapping'; which was used successfully a few years ago in a huge Northern Ireland bank robbery and imitated around Europe. This is where the crooks will hold the wife and children of a bank official hostage in their home; and then force the banker to go with them to the bank to open the vaults. They will steal as much money as they can and then escape; before releasing the family members. This method is very effective; because it can be used on anybody who has access to the cash on a business premise. Once the crooks find out who has the keys to the safe; they will target that person, kidnap his/her family and then force him/her to go with them to open the safe. Since he/she is just an employee; he/she may not be so willing to defend the company, by refusing to co-operate. His/Her priorities will obviously be with their family! He/She will not be as rich as the owner; and will therefore not be expecting such an attack. This means he/she will definitely not have any personal security measures in place! A kidnapper relies on the fact that the relatives will do anything to save the victim from getting hurt; and that is why, kidnapping is unlikely to go away any time soon. Crooks will always find new ways to subject a family to pain and desperation; in order to make money!

If your child or relative is ever kidnapped; you can never be certain who the kidnappers are. It is therefore imperative; you take them seriously, by doing whatever they say. If they tell you not to go to the police, then don't; because they could be watching you. You should try to get a friend to go to the police; but insist to them that you would rather pay the money and get your child back. Although the police are trained not to negotiate with kidnappers or allow criminals to threaten them; they will take your cares and wishes into consideration and instruct you how to go about paying them.

From then on; you should do exactly as they say. They will have much more information on the identity of the kidnappers than you will! They will also know whether they are professionals or amateurs; and will tell you exactly how to deal with them. In order not to alert the child-grabbers to the fact that you have reported them to the law; the police will be able to hide, so that they can witness the pay-off with audio/visual and photographic evidence. They can then use their own methods to follow the crooks and capture them intact with the money. If necessary; they will shoot them dead! Kidnapping is regarded as one of the most dastardly criminal acts; and every member of a city's force will be out to make sure they don't get away with it. The kidnappers will be identified, arrested and punished; whilst the best part is, they cannot be sure who tipped them off to the police. They might even blame each other for the leak; which can save you from future reprisals! It is unlikely that any of their friends will be back to kidnap your child again; because they will assume rightly, that you are on the police radar and therefore, irreproachable.

It is highly improbable that you will ever be kidnapped. If it does happen; you will have to assume that they know exactly why they have chosen you, out of all the millions of women in your country. Do you owe any money? Have you ripped-off any business associates? Have you stepped on anybody's toes with an arrogant and combative manner; in order to get what you want? Does anyone hate you enough to organise such a crime against your person? How did they find out where you live and your daily schedule; making it possible to broach your security? None of these questions will matter; if you have been kidnapped and are imprisoned in a dingy apartment, somewhere in a strange city. Since all kidnappings are different; there is not much I can tell you, except to do as they tell you. If they do reveal why they have kidnapped you; it will probably make sense to comply with them. As soon as they allow you any contact with your family or business associates; you have to let them know you are alive and well. It is important you insist that they pay the money, if they want to see you again. People have an instinctive reaction to resist giving away any money; and may not realise that by doing so, they are prolonging your agony. As in a case where your child has been kidnapped; it would be better to pay the crooks and allow the police to stay in the background, in order to capture them.

The more you co-operate with them, the more the likelihood of their becoming comfortable in your presence and slipping up; whereby you will be able to garner information for the police, once you have been released.

On a very rare occasion, you might be kidnapped by an ex-lover and kept hostage. He loves you so much; he believes that if he keeps you imprisoned, you will eventually succumb to his point of view. Since there is no ransom demand; this kind of kidnap is potentially more dangerous because he will not allow you any contact with the outside world. This means your friends and family may not even realise you are missing; if you are not living with them. Love can make a man do foolish things. He may keep you locked in a room as a prisoner; so that he can have you anytime he likes! Don't fight with him or try to escape. He might decide to kill you and then commit suicide; since he will be going to prison anyway, for the kidnap. If he tries to rape you; you may have to fight him off by lying on your front and crossing your legs. You can then 'concede' to his demands by luring him into a false sense of security; biting his penis off, hitting him hard over the head with an object and then escaping. This modus-operandi, described in Chapter Four; can only work, if you have a good idea how you are going to escape after you have injured him. If that tactic is not possible; the alternative would be for you to play along with him by sympathising with his insecurities and agreeing to love him. Unfortunately; you may have to grit your teeth and sleep with him to show you are genuine. This will help him relax in your presence and will make your suffering a lot less painful. You can then start making plans to be with him. During this time; keep your eyes open for any cracks in his security. This will enable you to figure a way out of your predicament. Once he becomes convinced you are back in love with him; you can persuade him to go on holidays together. You can even suggest booking the flight on line; where you can quickly send an Email to a friend to tell him/her what is happening. She/He will be able to inform the police on your behalf. The Email will allow the police to track the source through the service provider and lead them to the address. If no computer is available; you can suggest he goes to a travel agent to buy the tickets. On his return; he should be convinced you are for real and will allow you to get ready for the trip. Once you are out in public; you can alert a police officer to your predicament. If you take the cops back to where you were being held; there should be enough evidence in place, to convict him of kidnapping and raping you. I am afraid you will have to leave the area you were living in; because he will not be a happy bunny when he comes out of prison!

The police have closed the loopholes in many crimes; which means, only the professional criminals are succeeding in their endeavours. With the tight economic situation in the world; there are some very desperate individuals and gangs in every country, who will stop at nothing to get money. If you are having problems with your teenage daughter and she decides to leave home; kidnapping is a very realistic possibility. It can lead to shoplifting and credit card crimes; prostitution, drug trafficking and illegal couriering of cash from one country to another. If she is coerced with the lure of easy money into stealing; committing fraud; selling her body; or carrying drugs; she has in theory, been kidnapped. 'Mental kidnapping' is on the increase; because the old system of physically dragging a girl off the streets into the back of a van is too crude and will quickly have the police on their trail! Nowadays; pimps and drug dealers have subtle ways they can brainwash girls into becoming sex slaves, prostitutes and drug smugglers. A man and a woman, pretending to be a rich married couple; will meet a girl walking down the street on her own, who appears to be broke and down in the dumps. They will listen sympathetically to her problems and become her friend. They will be very kind to her; until she feels comfortable in their presence and is seduced by their stories of travel and riches. It will not take long for her to ask if she could also make some money; and will 'willingly' agree to whatever is on offer. This could involve flying to a foreign country to bring drugs back; or being used to seduce a gullible man to fall so much in love with her, that he will unwittingly be used as her cover for the criminal operation. The girl could also become a high-class call-girl for rich businessmen on their yachts; in private villas and expensive hotels. When a girl is flown by first-class to exotic locations; sleeps with handsome rich married men and returns home, thousands of dollars richer...she may even forget she is a prostitute!

On the seedier side; the girl could be charmed by the same subtle tactics, into the clutches of a criminal gang. They will give her money, buy her things and take her out; until she becomes indebted to her benefactors. It will then be suggested that she does something to repay their generosity and earn her own way. Seeing the dollar signs instead of the implications; she will be eager to make some money and become as rich as her new friends. Once she agrees to do their bidding; there is no going back. She will then be put under the control of the 'enforcers', who will be using false names. She will have her passport taken off her and told exactly how to behave. She will then be threatened with a beating and shown pictures of horribly scarred and disfigured women, who had dared to disobey them. The girl is now their slave; in all but name! She will be forced into performing degrading sex acts on all kinds of grubby, lecherous men. She may even be having sex, ten to fifteen times a day; with very little protection for her health and well-being. She dare not refuse; because she knows she will be beaten up. She cannot go to the police; because she will not be given the time and space to escape. Besides; she will not know the names of her abductors. Without proof; the cops may not take her seriously! If she is very useful to the organisation; she may be 'rested' from the sex and used to entice other gullible girls to the operation. As a result; she may stay with the gang for many years, because she really has nowhere else to go! Although teen girls are mostly at risk; the same thing could happen to a boy, because male prostitution is also prevalent. A boy will most likely be used to commit the atrocious crimes; like murder and armed robbery. Once the first crime is committed; there is no way of getting out of it, without going to prison. He will not be in touch with his parents; so they will never know that their son has been mentally kidnapped. One day; they may see his name in the newspapers, when he has been caught in a crime or killed!

Kidnapping is so unpredictable and dangerous; it has to be put in the same category as violence and murder. This means; you have to understand the signs that can lead up to it and then use preventative methods to make sure it does not happen to you or any member of your family. Keep a wary eye on your teens; and be there for them, when they are experiencing growing-up problems. Otherwise; they could be lured into a dangerous world, where they will be unable to escape from! If you are rich enough to interest a kidnapper; you should be able to afford the security measures needed against your own kidnapping, or that of your family. Kids are only kidnapped, when the gang has watched a family's movements and lifestyle; and are certain there is a pot of gold for them. As a safeguard; register your young children with the police, by having them tagged. Alternating the routes they take to and from school and making sure they are escorted at all times; will also help keep them safe. The same lifestyle precautions described in the chapter on armed robbery; should also apply to kidnapping. If you show off your wealth; you will make someone jealous enough to try and take some of it from you! If you rip-off a criminal rival; he might decide to kidnap your child, as a way of getting his money back...with interest! If you live in an area where the average income is far less than your own; you will be perceived as lording it over the community. This may annoy some local criminals, enough to try their luck; by kidnapping your child. If the kidnappers realise they cannot get to you personally; then by going for your child, they would have as good as beaten you...without touching you! Once you can understand that there are many ways a person can be beaten; you will take a more responsible attitude to protecting yourself and your family. Knowing how to fight physically is really not that important; unless you are into the combat sports!

If you have any fears or worries for yourself or your family; it would be wise to inform the police. They will be able to advise you on what precautions to take. Be aware that if you go to the cops; they will ask questions and will be suspicious why you think someone wants to kidnap you. You therefore run the risk of revealing things about yourself; which you might not want them to know. If you are involved in criminal activities or have not been paying your taxes; you may not want the police finding out. This means; you cannot go to them for help, if you are really in trouble! That is another good reason why the best way to avoid a kidnapping; is to remove the causes that may lead up to it. If someone really wants to hurt you; there is not much anyone can do. It could be someone from your past, who has held a grudge for many years. He/she may now have the financial and criminal muscle to teach you a lesson; for something you did many years ago. The only thing you can do is to lead an honest life and use your wealth wisely; without being ostentatious. Don't let even your friends know exactly how much you are worth; because jealousy, not money, is the real root of evil!

Those who are closest to you are the ones who can garner enough vital information about you; to pass on to criminal associates. They are also the ones who will be able to reveal information that could be used to hurt you; through jealous gossip and loose talk. It doesn't matter what advice I give you; because there is always a reason for someone to go out of his or her way to cause another person distress. Why would anyone want to kidnap you??? The answer to the question must lie firmly at your door!

C. Armed robbery

If an armed robber breaks into your home and threatens you; then there is not too much you can do about it. You therefore have to look into the reasons why he would want to target your family. How did he know you had money or valuables in your home? Why was yours picked out of all the houses in the area? Either he or they must have noticed you showing off at one time or another, with your expensive tastes; or you simply made enemies amongst the wrong circles. The robbers might also have noticed something about the security of your house; which told them it would be easy to get in. If you offend, or owe a large amount of money to a powerful businessman, a dangerous criminal or a vindictive acquaintance; then nobody can help you. Robbery is one of the tactics such people use to teach someone a lesson and send a strong message; in order to deter others, who feel they can get away with owing money. Since they would most likely hire a professional to do the job, through a pyramid system; it would be very hard for you to know exactly who organised the attack on your property. This means; the ringleader will probably get away with it. It is extremely difficult for the police to stop an organised murder, made to look like a robbery; because there are not enough police personnel around to guard everybody every hour of every day. Luckily; women do not cause as much trouble as the men. That should mean; there are many more attacks on men, than there are on women! Therefore, as a female; the chances of an armed robber deliberately coming to kill you, should be minimal. Unfortunately; robbers like to pick on easy targets. As a result; helpless women and old people regularly have their houses broken into and are sometimes attacked, robbed, raped and murdered. The police usually catch the amateurs; but with the gap between rich and poor getting bigger every year, there will always be cowardly attacks by young criminals. You really do have to appreciate that it could one day happen to you; and take precautions to narrow down the possibilities.

To be safe, however; always try and pay your debts. If you are unable to pay; you should let the person know and keep the lines of communication open. If you say nothing and keep away from the one you owe money to; it will make him or her think you are doing it deliberately and that is when he or she will think of harming you. Don't show off your wealth or divulge sensitive information to anyone; including your friends. Don't be over-friendly to strangers; so that they don't find an avenue into your life and have an opportunity to hurt you. Try to make sure the security in your house is good; with strong locks, secure windows, burglar alarms and if possible, a silent alarm linked to the police station. If you have any doubts at all then, depending on what you have to protect; it might be wise to seek professional advice from a good security company. This can be expensive; but well worth the price, to ensure your peace of mind. Make sure somebody knows where you are at all times; by keeping in regular contact with family and friends. If you hear someone trying to break in at night; quickly make a call to the police, before you try to play the heroine. You would do well to go to your local police station and seek their advice; because they will gladly give you valuable instructions and leaflets on how to keep your house secure. Most importantly; they will tell you how not to behave, if you don't want to attract undesirables to your property. If you throw loud parties every night; leave your car unlocked when you go shopping; are always walking around the town in expensive attire and going in and out of designer shops; then someone somewhere is going to think you have more money than sense and might want some of this expendable cash! A lot of areas have neighbourhood watch schemes, which you can join for a small fee; so that there is always someone looking out for you and keeping an eye on your house. It would be very difficult for robbers to break into a house or steal a car; if every household on a street looked out for each other. They would be noticed as soon as they appeared on the street; and the curtains would be twitching to see what they were up to! The police could be called immediately; if they attempted anything suspicious. Believe it or not; there is a regular robber grapevine, where information is readily exchanged on which streets, houses and people offer the easiest pickings. That is why you will find some areas and people are robbed more than others. Once your house is known as an easy prospect; then you can be sure you will be targeted several times in a year.

If it is within the laws of your country; keeping a gun at home can be useful in helping to make you feel safer. But you also run the risk of your children stumbling across and playing around with it. If the gun were to go off by accident; you will be held liable for the consequences. You could be prosecuted if you point it; even if it is against someone who tried to rob or threaten you in your own house. If you kill an intruder in your house; you could be up on a murder or a manslaughter charge. The laws surrounding self-defence; are at best, very confusing! In the United States; there is now a *'Stand your ground law'*, which started in Florida and has now been adopted by at least 14 other states in America. It gives people the right to shoot intruders who break into their homes and cars; and anybody else they feel threatened by. Although this approach seems to carry the possibilities of things going wrong; there have been relatively very few cases of innocent people being shot for doing nothing. It has actually lowered the robbery and burglary rates of those states! If the criminals knew that everyone had a gun and could use it against any robber who broke in or threatened their security; they might not be so eager to pick on the so-called easy targets of women and senior citizens! In Europe, this is not yet the case; so you have to be very careful. What you regard as reasonable force; may not be the same as the police and you could find yourself in jail. Killing anyone, even in self-defence; leaves you open to retaliation from friends and family of your victim. It is not a healthy way to live; when you have to walk around looking over your shoulder all the time and you shake with fear whenever your doorbell rings!

I have already covered the reasons why anybody would want to enrich himself at the violent expense of others; so let's just say you are confronted with a *"Your money or your life!"* situation. My dears, if you can; just give them what they want and don't try to fight back immediately. It's usually only money they are after; so give it to them! If they have enough money; they would most likely leave, rather than risk the time-consuming task of trying to find enough valuable property to escape with. They know you have it; otherwise they would not be in your house. Don't bother trying to convince them you don't have it; because they won't believe you. You could be signing your own death warrant! You can always get back whatever you lose; but if you are crippled or killed, then what good is that to you or your family? If they come in, without covering their faces; then it means it was planned. The chances are; they are there to kill you, because they would not want you to describe them to the police. In such a situation; there is really nothing much you can do about it. You are obviously being targeted for something you have previously done; which has hurt someone so badly, that they feel your demise is the best thing for you. This is the main reason why it is imperative you do not overstep the mark and upset someone; without any attempt to mend the situation. There is nothing much you can do to stop someone; who knows where you live and really wants to have you killed! In the majority of cases, it is men who are deliberately killed; but recently, women have become bolder in the business world. Some would happily rip-off a rival and tread on as many toes as possible; in order to get what they want! The idea of a woman being murdered gang-land style; is no longer a figment of a scriptwriter's imagination, but a harsh reality. If you are into business; please be careful, because it only takes one bullet to end a life. What you may consider a minor debt not worth paying; could to someone else, turn out to be a point of principle only proved by your murder.

Unless it is a revenge attack; I do not believe an armed robber deliberately goes out to kill a victim. The gun is just an incentive for you to be quick about parting with your belongings; and the killing is only a panic measure, when they realise they have been recognised or the police arrive. Since most armed robbers are as scared as the victims; a sudden twitch of his finger and you will be killed. Nobody can dodge a bullet! Even if he is arrested by the police; he could claim he didn't mean to kill you and might get away with manslaughter, instead of a murder charge. Because one needs a motive for a murder charge to stick; a robber will always claim he was not aware there would be anyone in the house. He was only defending himself when you tried to stop him; and accidentally killed you! It does not seem fair; but unfortunately, that is how the law works. You cannot afford to make the mistake of gambling with your life, in an armed robbery situation. If he has no gun; you could possibly afford to stall him by screaming and throwing things at him. With any armed threat however; (gun, knife, knuckleduster, syringe, club and acid spray) your life will definitely be in danger. It would be folly to try and fight! Whether they are in your house or are robbing your car in broad daylight; you have to co-operate as much as possible and then make a report, after they have gone. Even if they have covered their faces with masks or balaclavas; try not to look too long at them, because fear of recognition will be uppermost in their minds and they will kill you. Once you have been spared and they have gone; you should make a report to the police and give them as much detail as possible. Don't pin your hopes on them being caught; because a lot of robberies remain unsolved. You might get some of your property back; if you have a record of the serial numbers and they try to sell them on. Forget about any money they take; because it would be hard to prove it was yours. If they have stolen a huge amount of cash from you; the police will ask questions about the source and why it was not kept in a bank. Just thank your lucky stars they did not kill you!

In the majority of cases; tragedy can easily be avoided, if we are more vigilant and learn to recognise when something is wrong or does not feel right and then do something about it. There is a very thin line between life and death; and unfortunately, some women are caught in the crossfire by being in the wrong place at the wrong time. For example; a lot of wives do not know or care what their husbands get up. Robbers break into a house looking for the husband, and she gets it instead; because they assume she knows where he is and is covering up for him! Try to take an active interest in your husband's affairs. The 'common sense' advice a wife gives; can go a long way in saving the lives of her family, if he is up to something illegal. Women can instinctively 'feel' when something is wrong; whilst men tend to ignore such signals. You should always let your man know when you don't like what he is doing, and then take steps to protect your way of life; which could be irreparably damaged after a visit by the police, criminal associates or armed robbers. Next time he buys you a new car or expensive jewellery; ask him how he got the money. Be prepared to refuse the gift; if you feel the money used to buy it, was illegally obtained. These things have a way of rebounding on you, when you least expect them to! You should never be afraid to put your foot down, by threatening to leave him or report him to the authorities; if you feel his criminal activities are threatening you and/or the children. If he is jailed or killed; you will be the one who has to pick up the pieces! You will also be blamed by society for not keeping your man under control; and will be left feeling guilty, when you are widowed.

D. Stalking

Stalking literally means hunting; and it is often associated with someone who develops a fixation and then decides to prey on a celebrity. You should however understand that this attraction can occur at any time; and can happen to anyone! As a woman; there will always be something beautiful about you that men (and women) will find attractive. In the same way; you could also find beauty in another human being, that you will find hard to dismiss. Whilst strolling down the street; you might suddenly see a gorgeous hunk of a man, whose vision refuses to leave your brain...until you see someone even better! Most of us are able to contain this fixation to the realms of fantasy, where we might have a few amorous dreams about it; but that is as far as it goes. Because celebrities are seen on television; in films; in DVDees; in newspapers and magazines; it is very easy for them to have admirers, who might go as far as to believe they are in love with their favourite heartthrob. Sometimes this fixation can become so obsessive; that the culprit will start collecting pictures, newspaper articles, posters etc on his or her prey. Sooner or later; this will not be enough and he or she will decide to go and look for the heartthrob, by finding out exactly where the celebrity lives. They may obtain the phone number and bombard the celebrity with nuisance calls. They may even start hanging around outside the house. In some serious cases; they will actually break into the property and steal mementoes. Finally; they will present themselves to their love interest. This is usually when the cops are called in to investigate! For a first complaint; they will warn the stalker to keep away or be arrested. This is exactly what some of them want; because they become associated with the star. From then on; they might blatantly loiter around outside the house, until they are arrested. This will obviously make the papers and they will get their fifteen minutes of fame!

For some celebrities; it is almost an ego boost to realise that someone likes them so much that they are willing to risk prison for their sake. They will refuse to press charges; so long as the stalker promises to leave them alone. For others however; a stalker can become a real nightmare, when he or she starts intruding into their lives and refuses to go away. The danger arrives; when the celebrity decides he or she is too famous to pay attention to the stalker and panics by calling the police at the first opportunity. This can trigger hate, followed by a need for revenge; in a fan. One must always remember that there is not much difference between love and hate in intensity! A stalker could love a celebrity so much that the love could quickly turn to hate; all because of a snub. He/She might then choose to cause damage with hate-graffiti on the walls of the mansion. They might go as far as physically attacking or even shooting the famous one dead; as has happened in the past. If you are a celebrity; there is nothing much I can tell you that you do not already know. I am certain you have your own security measures in place! But sometimes; it pays to show a little kindness and humility to your fans. A simple smile; a wave; an autograph; or replying an Email/letter; can be the difference between someone loving you for ever and hating you. I know you must have heard many times that it is the fans that make you who you are; but it is very true. It is so easy for the fame and riches can go to one's head; whereby that important fact is forgotten! Even though you must be very busy making hay with your God-given talents; you must never forget that it can all be taken away in one split second by a bullet. Not even the most stringent security tactics will be able to save you! Certain smart celebrities will take the time to meet up with the stalker and get into his or her mind; in order to find out exactly what he or she is about. They often realise that most stalkers are harmless and just want a bit of attention. A short friendly conversation; a few free concert tickets; posters; autographs; and pictures; are usually all it takes for the nuisance to be satisfied. He/She will then go away happy; to brag to his/her friends, whilst singing the celebrity's praises!

If you are not a celebrity; it is still possible to have a stalker. This could be much more dangerous; because you will not have a security apparatus in place to protect you. Whilst walking around town; you can never know who is watching you and developing a fixation for you. You therefore have to try and keep your eyes open, whenever you are going home; because that is when a stalker will most likely follow you, in order to find out where you live. From there on; he will be able to make his plans, how he is going to get to know you. Once he recognises where you live and work; he can wait till you are in a café, pub, shopping or anywhere else you will be alone or with your female friends. He will then come up to you; pretending to have met you before. It would not be difficult for him to strike a conversation with you; based on his knowledge of your movements. Your curiosity will find it hard to resist this; especially if he is in any way attractive! Such modus-operandi is often used by men; in order to be able to break the ice for a cosy chat-up. This is usually quite harmless; because every girl has her way of dealing with smooth-talking men. What you should be worried about; is how he knows so much about you. You should be very cool, calm and collected, and keep talking to him; so that you can find out more, to catch him out. If he claims to have met you in a supermarket many weeks ago; you can say something you know to be untrue. *"I remember, you! You were standing in front of me and you said hello to me. I was wearing a red dress wasn't I?"* If he slips up with any of your trick questions; then you know he is lying and he must have been following you. Once you have sussed him out; you should continue the small-talk with him, so that he has no idea you are on to him. At the back of your mind; you should start making your plans how to get rid of him.

In literal terms; he is your stalker, so you should be very careful how you get rid of him. If you reject or snub him rudely; he then becomes dangerous, in that he probably knows where you live and work. He may not take rejection so easily; simply because he has developed a fixation for you and never expected his efforts to result in failure. Once he feels he has got your 'loving' attention;

he will definitely make his move and ask to see you again. This is when any tough male friends of yours become invaluable. If you are in a pub or shop; try and go into the toilet and phone a male friend to come and rescue you. It would be better, if he pretends to be your boyfriend/husband; in order to put the pest's mind to rest that you are off-limits. Using a female to pretend she is your lesbian lover; will work just as well, in case you do not have a male at your disposal. Rejecting a man on your own, may work in the short-term; but there is every possibility that he will not take you seriously and could accost you again in the near future. Having a lover around you; will add credence to your claim that you are unavailable and will finally make him realise that you are not for him. Don't forget; he is still the man who came up to you out of the blue to reveal things about you, without your remembering ever meeting him before. You have to get rid of him smoothly; without giving him a chance to breach your defences! You must always keep your eyes open; especially when you are going home or leaving your house to go anywhere. As you are walking home; occasionally look behind and around you, just in case he is loitering around your abode. Since he is now aware you know who he is; he will not want to be recognised as a stalker! If he does come up to you outside your house; you should be polite but firm and ask him to leave you alone, because you don't have the time for him in your life. If he refuses to go away; you should go inside and secretly take a picture of him through one of your windows. You then ring the cops to let them know there is someone who keeps following you and refuses to go away. The presence of a police squad-car arriving at your house; will finally make him understand that you mean business. His picture will be most useful to the officers; because he might be on their list of regular stalkers. At the very least; they will be able to warn him and even arrest him, if he proves difficult. It is highly unlikely he will bother you again; but that should be a lesson to always keep your eyes open when you are anywhere near where you live. A stalker can only get away with what you allow him!

If you are ever walking around in town and feel someone is following you; the best thing to do is to stop, look around as if you are lost and pretend you have not noticed anything. You should then walk into a big shop; or anywhere with lots of people. If he also comes in to the shop; relay your fears to the security guard. The chances are; the pest will leave the shop or pretend he is there for something else. Under no circumstances; should you think he has gone away. He will probably be loitering around outside, waiting for you to come out; so that he can continue following you to your destination. A smart stalker does things in stages; because he does not really want to be found out. He will follow you until he finds out where you live or work. He will then come back at a later date; when he thinks you have forgotten about him. This is why you should never go home when you are being followed; but rather use any subterfuge you can, in order to confuse and then finally lose him. A good way would be to go to a bus stop, if there are people standing there; take the first bus that arrives, go for a ride and then pick a different bus route back home. If you have some money on you; quickly stop a taxi and direct the driver to take you home. The stalker will not have the time to get into his car and follow you! It seems like a lot of trouble; but ignoring him, could bring you problems, once he trails you to where you live. If you are on your own in town and feel you are being followed; you should walk straight into a police station and tell them what is going on. They are duty-bound to at least take you seriously; and will most likely drive you home in one of their cars. If the stalker is hanging around outside; he will not dare follow you! The presence of the police will also convince him that he has been spotted; and will forget about you for a long while.

The most important thing you should realise when you are being followed; is that he may already know where you live and work. This is because he may have followed you in the past; without your knowledge. You should leave nothing to chance; by changing the way you move around. However; taking different routes to and from work will be ineffective, if he already knows where you live. All he has to do; is wait for you to come home, before accosting you! For the next few weeks; you have to keep your eyes open as you enter and leave your house, to make sure no one is spying on you. You need to feel secure in your own mind that he has well and truly gone away. Everyone living with you should be told of your fears; and a strategy planned to beef up your security. They should not allow anyone to come to your home, when you are not in. Never allow your children to be so negligent; that a stranger could bluff his way into your home, by pretending to be your friend. *"My Mummy is not in right now; but she'll be home soon. You can wait for her if you like…"* is not a good idea! If you have some tough looking friends or relatives; you should let them take turns visiting you regularly. This will let the stalker realise that you are not a frightened little female with no friends. If you live alone; make all your neighbours aware of your predicament and don't allow anyone who is not your close friend, into your house.

If your phone rings out of the blue and you hear heavy breathing on the line; you may have a serial phone pest on your hands and you will have to change your number. If he manages to find your new number; you will have to inform the police. They have their ways and means of finding out exactly where the call came from; and will set a trap for the next time he calls you. You have to take nuisance calls seriously; because answering your phone, lets the caller know that you are at home. He can also tell how frightened you are; by the tone of your voice. The calls will then become more frequent; because that is what gives him his thrills. There are some perverted men in this world! The sound of an angry, desperate or frightened female voice; can be a sexual turn-on for some of them. Such perversions are hard to curtail; unless he is stopped in his tracks, by being caught red-handed by the police. Once he knows you are at home; the next step will be to ring your doorbell with an assortment of excuses, in order to get inside your house. From then on; the possibilities of causing you distress or harm, are endless. You should never allow it to go so far; that you are in genuine fear of your life. Never ever be afraid to call the police; because no woman deserves such treatment from anyone, male or female. Stalking is a very cruel pastime indeed!

E. Miscarriage of justice

1. Wrongful accusation

It is very possible that you could one day be accused of a crime you did not commit; especially if you have been a victim of identity fraud. It could also happen to your husband or any of your children; which will affect you severely. Either way; the priority must be to clear the name of your family, because your reputation is part of your self-defence. A wrongful accusation is as lethal as any physical attack; because a damaged reputation will never heal in the way a wound or injury would. If someone wants to harm you, without touching you; all he or she has to do is spread a vicious rumour against you, accuse you of something you did not do or commit a crime in your name. With clever tact and imagination; he/she will most likely get away with it. Once you are arrested; it would be extremely difficult to prove your innocence from behind bars. You will definitely need all the help you can get! Denying it to the police may not work; because they would usually have enough circumstantial evidence, before they will arrest and charge you. This means; the onus will be on you to prove your innocence! If they came to your house to arrest you; the neighbours will start speculating. You will probably be guilty in their eyes, for every crime under the sun; since they would not know exactly why you have been arrested. Unfortunately; the gossip grapevine can be as hurtful as the actual charge, because mud always sticks. You might find yourself being shunned by the neighbours; with the invitations to functions and parties, suddenly drying up. There is nothing you can do about this; so forget about them and concentrate on how you are going to prove your innocence. If the wrongful accusation is for sexual crimes like rape or Internet child pornography; you will have to do it quickly and effectively. Once the word gets out; you might be targeted by vigilante extremists, taking the law into their own hands. They could target your children; vandalise your property; abuse you verbally; rubbish you on the Internet; or attack you physically and endanger your life.

Whatever you have been accused of; the first thing you have to do is remain calm and co-operate with the authorities. Don't start shouting the odds or protesting your innocence; because it is always seen as a sign that you have something to hide. Listen to what you have been charged with and let the police tell you exactly what it means; so that you know where you stand. You should then ask politely for permission to seek legal advice by ringing your own solicitor; or one from the state legal aid system, if you cannot afford to pay for a legal representative. Once the solicitor arrives; let him or her do all the talking and you will have a better understanding of what the police can or cannot do with the evidence they have. Depending on the severity of the crime; the solicitor should be able obtain a police or a guarantor's bail for you, when you appear before a judge. You can then go home, lick your wounds and draw up your battle plans. Initially; you should keep everything within your household and never discuss the problem with friends, neighbours or relatives. This is because you do not know who was behind the slur campaign or accusation. Even if it was a case of identity fraud; it could still have been initiated by someone close to you! They can do this deliberately, by stealing your documents; or carelessly, by revealing information about you in moments of bravado, gossip and idle chatter. Keeping quiet will be difficult; because people believe if you say nothing, it means you must be hiding something! Remaining silent is imperative; because whoever is behind the slur on your reputation, will not know what you are up to and will therefore not be able to make the case worse for you. It might also make him or her panic and make the mistake of trying to do something else to damage you and get found out; as in the case of vicious gossip or committing a crime and blaming you for it.

Check out websites for consumer advice on miscarriages of justice; and you should find individuals and organisations that will be ready to help you, free of charge. They will also be able to find you a reputable solicitor; who is well-versed in the type of crime you are alleged to have committed. Go to your local media outlet and engage a friendly journalist or radio personality to explain your side of the story; and a newspaper should be able to get a campaign going, to make people aware of your plight. If you can afford it; you should hire a private investigator to see if he or she can come up with anything to help clear your name. They will also be able to find out the reliability of the witness who is accusing you. Even if you know you are innocent; never think the problem will go away on its own...because it won't. If you are found not guilty in court; there will be those who will believe there is no smoke without fire and you just got lucky with the jury. It is therefore imperative that after you have been found not guilty, you do not relax; by using the media to bury the accusation once and for all. You have to make sure there is enough damage limitation; in order for you to rebuild your life in your community and learn to be more careful with whatever you do and with whom you associate with in the future. Good luck!

2. Police brutality

Although it is illegal for the police to use force on a suspect; no one can say it does not go on behind the scenes. Policemen and women are human and they can get annoyed; especially if the nature of the crime is exceptionally repugnant. People talk of police brutality in some countries, by condemning them; but no one ever asks why it exists. The main reason is the frustrations the cops feel; when the law prevents them from using certain tactics to ascertain the truth. If an armed robber or rapist who has terrorised a town, is finally caught; he would naturally get a few slaps and kicks from irate interrogators, if he shows any recalcitrant behaviour. It is the failure to catch such people; that give the police a bad name in the eyes of the public. If a criminal proves too stubborn to crack; the police have a way of doing him over so that they don't leave any tell-tale cuts and bruises. They will then throw him into a dingy cell; whereby no one will feel sorry for him. Nothing can stop a police officer teaching a rude suspect a lesson; because that kind of attitude is what all law enforcers hate. They will make sure they mess him around; before he is able to make that call to his solicitor. He may even find the number he is trying to call is always 'busy'! As evening draws near; he will be refused bail and will be forced to spend a night in the cells, where they can continue with their mental 'games'. They don't even have to touch him! Spitting in his tea; dropping his meal on the floor before giving it to him; running out of toilet roll; leaving his light on all night; peeping into his cell every five minutes; jingling their keys outside the cell door, as if they are coming to let him out; and other simple tactics; can give them a good chuckle!

Being female, you are unlikely to suffer such ignominy; but it could happen, if you are the type of woman who thinks she is tough and throws her weight around. If you are ever taken to the police station for one reason or other; politeness is the key to survival. Even if you know you are innocent; do not start shouting or threatening to report them to their superiors or some 'big shot' you might know. It could make your case worse for you! If you go to report a crime; do not exaggerate and always give the correct facts because the cops are not stupid. If you tell lies or exaggerate; you could end up being arrested for being privy to the crime. People reporting dead bodies on the road from a hit and run driver, have been arrested instead and charged with the incident they came to report; simply because their stories did not fit. There is no use being hysterical about an armed robber; because it will still be treated as an armed robbery, no different from other daily reports. There is nothing you can tell the police; which they have not seen or heard before! Although it might seem like they are being insensitive to your plight; you have to understand that they deal in facts and do not get excited by emotions. They are acutely aware that many crimes are only reported because of self-interest; so there might be an ulterior motive for your appearance at the station. This could be anything; from trying to get an enemy into trouble to trying to deflect the police from investigating another crime you may have committed. For the same reason; some crimes are not reported because the victim has more to hide from the police than whatever he/she has been a victim of and may deny they saw anything, by refusing to name or shame a suspect. Have a little sympathy for the police; because their job is really not so easy!

It is also important to remember that if you go abroad and end up in a police station; their mentality might be different from the police in your country. You have to be on your best behaviour; even if you have been wrongfully accused! Beating up suspects is a normal process in many Third World countries; because it is seen as an effective tool in obtaining confessions from hardened criminals and to coerce them into revealing the whereabouts of weapons, drugs, stolen money and co-conspirators. As a female foreigner; a male officer will not hit you. If you are rude and obnoxious; you might receive a few slaps from a female and then pushed into a filthy, overcrowded cell with a bucket for a toilet...to cool you down. This is the usual tactic to frighten you enough; to allow you to offer them some money to 'ease' your predicament. Once they get money out of you; (the more serious your alleged crime, the more money you will have to pay) the charges will miraculously disappear and you will be freed. If you are rude and are subsequently slapped or pushed around by a policewoman;

there will probably be nothing you can do about it because complaining to a senior officer will only make your case worse. Your embassy will most likely tell you to learn your lessons and take better care in the future. Even though such behaviour is obviously against any law enforcement code of ethics; it is prevalent, because of the poor salaries and conditions the police in those countries are forced to survive on. In some countries; coercing money from criminals, is the only way they can earn enough to feed their children. The feelings of a suspect will definitely be very low on their list of priorities! Luckily; most females behave reasonably well when they go abroad and it is the males who usually get drunk and find themselves in trouble! You might one day have to go into a police station; to rescue your man who foolishly got into an argument leading to a fight. Don't forget to bring lots of grovelling apologies for his bad behaviour with you; backed by sufficient amounts of cash!

3. Torture

If you are ever involved in serious crimes like espionage, drugs, armed robbery or murder and you refuse to co-operate with the authorities; there is a distinct possibility you may be tortured, in order for you to reveal your sources and betray your co-conspirators. In countries which are ruled by the armed forces; the normal rule-of-law is non-existent. Depending on the relationship between your 'developed' country and the one you are visiting; you could find yourself in serious trouble. A simple arrest by the police; might end up as a trumped-up espionage charge and you will be handed over to the army for interrogation, charged and jailed. In such a situation; torture cannot be ruled out! You could find yourself being used as a bargaining tool; whereby the country you have been arrested in, can obtain some sort of reward from your own country, for your release. This could involve a prisoner swap, financial loans or economic benefits; and you will most likely be held for a protracted length of time, whilst behind-the-scenes negotiations take place. When this happens; the media in your country that highlight your case could actually make things worse for you. This is because the country you have been arrested in will be portrayed as barbaric and its prison conditions derided; in a bid to get you deported back home to serve your sentence in a 'better and less harsh' environment. This attitude is likely to annoy the country holding you; and they will dig their heels in by portraying you as a 'major' spy, drug trafficker or terrorist. They will not like to be seen by the rest of the world as a soft touch; kowtowing to the whims of a rich 'superpower'. The 'poorer' country will be acutely aware that if the roles were reversed; it is very unlikely one of its own citizens would be let off a charge and sent back to serve the sentence in his/her own country!

Since it is highly unlikely you will be tortured in your own 'developed' country; you have to assume that going anywhere abroad poses a certain risk. It is always better to do a little research before you travel anywhere! A quick visit to the embassy of the country you intend to travel to; will alert you to any local customs, possible dangers and no-go areas, so that you don't end up insulting the locals and getting into trouble. You see; when you arrive in someone's country, they will assume that you know what you are doing. This is why when journalists are caught and arrested in certain countries, for being in the wrong place at the wrong time; they are routinely accused of espionage and arrested. If you are a tourist walking around with a camera; nobody is going to believe you are not going to send pictures of sensitive locations back to your country. Any photo can easily be manipulated; to make the foreign land be seen in a bad light to the rest of the world. With the advent of the Internet, where pictures can be sent back in seconds; you have to be very careful what you do with your camera! If you go anywhere; make sure you move around with a local guide who speaks your language. He/She will be able to tell you what you are allowed or not allowed to do. Once you have a camera; it will be rightly (or wrongly) assumed that you are a journalist..., which means you could be a spy! If you are arrested in the wrong place, your camera will be seized; you will be interrogated and most likely tortured. It makes no difference, if you are a woman; because there are so many ways to torture someone, without physically harming him or her. Sleep deprivation; hearing the screams of others being tortured in the cell next to you; leaving a bright light on all night shining in your face; not feeding you properly; refusing you basic toiletries and medicine; banning phone calls to loved ones back home; interrogators playing 'good cop' and 'bad cop' with your emotions etc. You will never be the same person; when you are eventually released!

In all Third World countries; you should be wary of thieves, who target the residents in the more luxurious hotels. They will follow the targets out of the hotel and rob or even kidnap them; if the opportunity arises. Also; there are many government informants working in the hotels and driving the taxis. You have to be very careful you do not become a victim of a set-up; arrested, charged and tortured as a spy. This is easily possible with a careless slip of your tongue; by criticising or saying the wrong thing against the country. It would therefore be advisable to always move around in a group of three or more tourists; because it will make it harder for anyone to molest, rob or arrest you, without causing a commotion. As a female, it would be folly to walk around any foreign country alone; because rights for women may not be as 'advanced' as those in Europe or the United States. You could land yourself in hot water; for breaking centuries old customs. For example; in most Moslem countries, a woman is required to cover her head and legs. If you are accosted by a policeman for not wearing a scarf; you will not get people running to your aid, like you would in the 'developed countries'. It does not bear thinking what problems you will encounter; if you dared to wear a mini-skirt and walked around, shaking your hips! The most important lesson you can take from this piece on torture; is that it very much exists around the world. It could easily happen to you; if you do not follow the basic rules of respecting their customs and traditions, when visiting a foreign country. Show a little humility and never think you are better than the people you are visiting; just because you are richer, more educated or more well-to-do than them. Your money, brains or country will not always be able to get you out of trouble!

4. Societal malpractices

If you want the honest truth; I will tell you that the world is not fair. The rich, the intelligent and those in positions of power, really do get what they want and do what they like; because they can. People tend to fawn over and give the benefit of the doubt to those who are rich, have important jobs and/or are lucky enough to have had a decent education. This is because they are able to deceive those who are not so blessed; with the sheer power of their wealth, position and intellect. For that reason; millionaires, politicians and intellectuals will walk over anyone and will even seek to destroy those who stand in the way of their ambitions. The recent world-banking crisis is a clear example of how financial experts used their intellect to commit economic murder. The average person does not have a clue how a financial institution works; yet will entrust their money to the banks, simply because they believe the bankers know what they are doing. For the same reason; politicians have been known to ruin a country's economy, with decisions based purely on self-interest. Some businessmen, who should know better, will do anything to make more money; even if it means that people will suffer and die of health problems when they build a factory in a populated area or excavate a sensitive location, in search of raw materials. Others have attempted to flood the world with shoddy goods; in order to save on expenditure and increase their profits. In the past, we have seen mothers die from complicated pregnancies and babies born deformed; because they were exposed to pollution, caused by one company or another. How many wars have there been; where innocents have been killed by 'accident', in order for the industrial/military complex to test their latest weapons? What about brazenly arrogant politicians, under whose guidance and leadership the voters have put their trust and confidence; only to be betrayed by their scandalous and corrupt behaviour? It does not take an environmentalist to tell us the world is being destroyed by the greed of certain industries and companies who want to make money, without caring who gets hurt in the process. I do not need to give you any more examples; because I believe you already know what I am implying. In relation to this chapter; the way we are going, is a matter of life and death. What happens in your country is part of your self-defence; so you should be concerned.

Money and power are already widely known to have a corrupting influence; but intelligence is the one you should be more careful about, because it can be used to deceive and hurt you in more ways than you can imagine. Ignorance really is a curse; because we tend to put our faith in anyone who seems to know what we have no idea about. That is when we can be taken advantage of! Statistics are often used to confuse and befuddle those who are either ignorant or could not care less; in order for the protagonists to do and get what they want from them. Laws and rules have in the past been made by men for women; when the men have not got a clue what it is really like to be female. As a result; a woman can lose out at work for daring to get pregnant! The idea of maternity leave is to give women the time to recover from childbirth and bond with the baby. But surely, every woman is different; and therefore, the recovery rate can only be determined by the woman herself? The sexual health of a woman is often put in the hands of a male gynaecologist; simply because she has been told, *"the doctor knows best!"* Medical theory is all very well; but how can a male doctor be a hundred percent certain, what a woman feels in her vagina? The same goes for breast implants and other forms of cosmetic surgery; where it is impossible for a male practitioner to know exactly how it will affect her emotionally, when he is advising her on what treatments to undergo. I can only deduce that these males don't really care for a female's feelings; so far as she has the money to pay for the treatment. They can get away with it; because they have managed to convince the female population that they know better! If you really look into it; you will find many other laws and rules that benefit men more then they do women. For example; a rapist or a violent mugger will go to prison and will be freed at the end of his sentence. But the woman will have to live with the trauma for the rest of her life; with no protection against future attacks. Need I go on…???

I would not like to be spurious and say everybody who is rich, intelligent or in a position of power is doing something wrong; because that would obviously not be true. However; money, know-how and power are the three aphrodisiacs that can easily corrupt, whereby someone might believe he/she is above the law and can get away with anything. Even respectable institutions cannot be trusted; because they all have an agenda. A hospital might insist on a certain drug for an ailment; simply because it is on the payroll of the drug company. In their hurry to qualify for bigger grants; hospitals will misdiagnose treatments and send patients home before they are ready. This makes it seem as if they are swift and efficient! Many schools will rush students through exams, without making sure they understand the syllabus properly; in order to feature high on the national league tables. The more students that pass their exams; the better the school looks! A boutique will try to get you to buy a dress, shoe or perfume, by telling you what you want to hear; because it is probably on a commission from the manufacturers to sell as many products as possible! Legal Aid lawyers will try and convince a suspect not to worry unduly about a charge and to plead not-guilty; so that the case lasts longer and they make more money! What about the miscarriages of justice we sometimes read about in the papers; or the corruption and double-dealing, which are conveniently swept under the carpet and quickly forgotten because they are an embarrassment to one government ministry or another? Intelligent people will always use or pretend to use their 'superior' knowledge of a subject; in order to get what they want. Since women are institutionally seen as soft targets; I seriously implore you never to take anything for granted and assume someone knows what he or she is doing. Most people have an agenda and will do whatever it takes, to achieve their goals; even if it means hurting or destroying anyone or anything in their way. It always pays to ask pertinent questions and seek a second opinion from a different establishment; whenever you are given any advice that concerns your welfare. It is very important you are sure in your own mind; that the right thing is being done for you!

The days of women 'lying down to be fucked' are thankfully on their way out; but there are still some females who will put their lives in the hands of men, because they believe the myth that men know best. Although nowadays, we are seeing a few females who are prepared to stand up and fight; it is clearly not yet having a world-wide effect. You just have to make sure it does not happen to you! If for example; a supermarket in your town is selling out-dated food, then whoever buys the food could get sick and will need hospital treatment. This could prove to be time-consuming, expensive and dangerous for the health. This also means; the greed of the food seller could affect not only you, but also your children and anyone else living in your area. It is therefore imperative that you do something about it, as soon as you notice it; and not let them fob you off with the usual excuses. *"The food is still okay for a few days after the expiry date..."* Stand in the supermarket aisle and boldly ask why they are selling expired food. If you say it loudly enough; you will attract enough people to embarrass them to take the food off the shelves. You should not stop there; but make a report to the police and ask them for the address of the Trades Standards Board or Customer Complaints Office in your town. You see; if you do nothing about the expired food and expect someone else to do it, the supermarket will continue to deceive the public by using timeworn jargon and excuses to dismiss any complaints. The same attitude should go for anything you see; that you are certain could affect you or your area. That is the only way greedy entrepreneurs; lazy public servants; rude local councillors; arrogant politicians; shoddy workmanship in public buildings and old fashioned cheats; can be brought to heel. Things will always change when enough people make noises against them; so never be afraid to publicly speak your mind. Thanks to the Internet; there are now many ways you can get justice for whatever ills you notice in society. The good thing is; you will always get others who have experienced the same problems as you. You should therefore try and have the attitude that what happens to any woman could also happen to you; and not let anyone take advantage of your naiveté.

You will obviously, have better things to do; than spend your life finding out who is doing things incorrectly! But if every woman did the same and kept her eyes and ears open; it would be impossible for men to get away with the notion that women are stupid and will believe anything they are told. It is this condescension towards women; that has caused so much misery and hardship for the fairer sex, over the years. We are now in the twenty-first century; and such attitudes should not be allowed to prosper. Men will not bother to do anything against it; because to all extents and purposes, it serves them better for women to be mentally and intellectually subjugated. The battle of the sexes is swinging towards the female; who is now making a lot more money than before and creating her independence. The last bastion for men; is to try and keep control of how society can be manipulated to suit their needs. Nowadays; a woman's biggest threat is not from rapists, muggers or burglars. This is because it is getting much harder for anyone to use violence and get away with it; due to more public awareness, stricter security measures, smarter police tactics and longer prison sentences. Crooks, opportunists and those who are in positions where they can use their money, power, influence and intellect; are the ones you should be wary of. The worst nightmare for any man; is a feisty woman on the warpath, who will take no prisoners. If something is really upsetting you; don't hold back, but feel free to vent your anger! If you think that tactic will not quite do the trick; then like a chameleon, quickly calm down, leave the area and quietly report them to the relevant authorities. I am confident your 'feminine zealous charm' will be able to put your point across convincingly! You could also go to your local media outlets with a worthwhile complaint; and you should be able to get a campaign rolling, to stop any relevant abuses. If a woman really wants something done; she knows how to do it! Never ever be afraid! If women are able find a way to unite and make sure all malpractices do not go unnoticed and unpunished; I believe they will finally earn their cherished emancipation. Right now, they are not quite there; so I sincerely hope this book will give a push in the right direction.

5. Religious groups, clubs and organisations

There are many churches, mosques and religious groups in the world; catering for the different religions. The choice is so wide that sometimes it is very difficult to know which ones are good; and that is why most people tend to follow the religion of their parents. Children are often sent to schools, which support the religion of their family; and grow up with the beliefs and moral ethics they were brought up with. Although most religious institutions have had their scandals and immoral behaviour in the past; they are nowadays under tremendous scrutiny to act properly, treat their converts equally and conduct their affairs in an honest way. Joining a major church or mosque; is still enjoyable and safe! Sadly; because many religious personnel cannot always agree on the true meaning of the scriptures; break-aways are common. New, smaller churches and mosques are springing up all the time; as factions or splinter groups to the original. Religion is something many people take very seriously; so there will always be a religion, or a belief, which will suit everybody. It is also relatively easy for a group to function unvetted and then go underground, when the heat is on them. By the time that happens; they would have gained a lot of lucrative supporters, making it financially suicidal to break up the party. These new organisations are always looking for fresh converts; and have all kinds of methods to draw in vulnerable people. Because the old established doctrines do not appeal to them; there are always those, especially amongst the ranks of the disaffected youth, who are looking for something new to believe in. This makes it easy for someone to be attracted by a movement. Once they have joined; they can be coerced into parting with their cash and property, in order for the group to function economically. The leaders usually make it a point to tell a convert what he/she wants to hear and restore their self-confidence by making them feel like valued members of the group. The Internet has made it even easier to target specific youth groups to get them to join. They will then be used to get their friends to join; by offering them financial incentives.

Because there are so many groups catering for all kinds of beliefs; there is always a danger that any of them could become a cult. There is then a good chance that the followers will be brainwashed into doing anything for the group; including criminal activities or endangering the lives of others. Once someone has been 'brainwashed'; it will be very difficult to get him or her to change their minds. If he or she happens to be a friend, relative or loved one; then you may have lost them forever. In such a predicament; the loved one may as well be dead to you! If you tried to change his/her mind; you will be seen as the 'enemy' and he or she may walk out of your life forever, by joining the group permanently. In the past; there have been cases of crimes, public disorder and group suicides, attributed to cults and organisations, which operated under the radar of the government or the police. Some organisations will indoctrinate their younger members so well; that they might start stealing money from their homes to bring to the group. They would have been told that their parents are the ones holding them back; by not releasing money that is their due. The older members, who are disillusioned with their lives; could also be made to embezzle money from their place of work or transfer large amounts of their savings to the group, in order to satisfy the group leader. Others have been used as fronts for prostitution rings; drug couriering gangs; tax evasion operatives; anti-government subversives and harbouring illegal immigrants. The leaders can be so clever that the majority of the members will never know what is really going on. The more ignorant members there are; the less the chance of being infiltrated by the police or other criminal syndicates. The police can only operate on a tip-off; but will not be able to get answers from someone who obviously knows nothing and believes that his/her group is genuine and could not possibly be up to any harm.

If the organisation is prominent in the community, by helping the youth, the aged and the destitute; the leaders can quietly go about their illegal activities, without attracting any suspicion or flak from the police. A youth club for instance; could be a pick-up-point for a drug gang, who are using the people present playing pool, table tennis or video games as perfect cover. Foreign girls could easily be part of a prostitution racket; whilst using the club as a meeting point. They will be able to pick up their 'punters', or move from there to the destination of their clients; so that they are never seen loitering on the streets. Even a prayer group; can be used to solicit donations for a charity to buy new equipment for a youth club. Any illegal money can then be safely mixed with the legal donations. Let's say for argument's sake; a pinball machine or coffee percolator is bought with the illegal/legal proceeds. The money made out of people using the machines; now becomes clean! The drug gang can collect the legitimate cash; pay their taxes and put the money safely in the bank. Another way is to send the crime cash to a Third World country; in used notes. The money can then be sent back to the organisation, legitimately through a bank; as a donation. The illegal money then becomes legal; because it would be next to impossible for anyone to find out from abroad, how the money was earned. By using a false identity; the name of the donor would also escape scrutiny. Those are just two simple methods; but there are lots of more sophisticated ways, crooks use to launder illegal money through clubs and organisations. You have to be concerned; because the place your loved one goes to, might be one of those being used as a front. If there is a bust and he or she is caught up in it; the responsibility will be on your head. The police will ask why you were not more observant in detecting what was going on inside your own family.

As explained before; this book is about *your* self-defence. If you are one of those women involved in a dishonest group, by taking advantage of people's sensitivities and naiveties; then there is not much I can do for you, except to warn you to be careful. Sooner or later; you will be found out! If it is a man you love, who convinced you to do it; then you should take a long hard look at your relationship with him. You are obviously being used; and your love is being abused! Although there will always be examples to the contrary; I will continuously repeat that it is not in a woman's nature to be criminally-minded, unless she has been convinced by a lover or close relative. I will therefore assume that you are like most females; respectful and law-abiding. If your child, your husband or any loved-one joins any group or club; you should make it a point to talk to him or her about what exactly they do. You should also check up through the Internet and the local police station; so that you can be clear in your own mind, that it is a bona-fide organisation. Watch out for changes in behaviour; whenever he or she returns from a meeting of the organisation. Be especially concerned, if he or she tries to convince you to join the group; because any legitimate group does not use its members to coerce others to join. Never force him/her to leave the group; because they will most likely dig their heels in and refuse. You may have to feign interest; so that your loved one opens up and gives something away. This will allow you to see whether it is a legitimate and honest organisation. You should then go together; to see for yourself, what is really going on. If you feel there is something not right; like drugs being consumed on the premises; a few over-dressed girls loitering around; or some who don't speak the country's language; you should do a little investigation through the Internet and inform the police. Even if you are mistaken, it is better than doing nothing; because you may not be the only one voicing concerns about the establishment. At the very least; it will make the police take a closer look at the place. Who knows what they might unearth in the future?

Since all organisations, groups and clubs depend on money to survive; they may try to prevent you leaving, with forceful persuasion, threats or blackmail. This is because they will lose out on whatever contributions you are giving them. Were that to be the case; you have to go to the police and report them. You should always reveal everything you know; and what your suspicions are. The group may already be on the police radar; and all they are waiting for is a chink in the armour, whereby someone breaks ranks and lets them know what is really going on. Once you have given them the information; try to distance yourself from the situation and let them find their own way to go on from there. If the police ask you to keep your eyes open, in order to bring more information to them; it would technically make you an informant. You would be advised to refuse; because you would be putting your life in danger of reprisals. The police will always protect you, if they feel your life is in danger; but they cannot protect you twenty-four hours a day, every day. Even if they do; you will be living under their rules. This will virtually make you a prisoner and restrict your movements. An exposed criminal gang; will not take it lying down and will try to find out who was responsible for the deceit. I am sure nobody wants to live in constant fear of their lives; therefore, being an informant will not be in your best interests! The law of averages will tell you that, although most organisations will be above-board by doing good things for their community and members; there will always be one or two, which will literally be getting away with fraud, duplicity and brain-washing of its members. They could also be using the group as a convenient front for lucrative money laundering and other less than favourable activities; which may even include, financing terrorist organisations in other countries. Please be careful; whenever you are joining any group, club or organisation. They may be easy to join; but leaving one may prove to be a real headache!

Dear Tigress; as you can see, most life or death situations can be avoided by using common senses and intuition to keep out of trouble. What happens when you have no control over your life and death; simply because there are those who are ready to destroy innocent people, in order to achieve their selfish aims? The next chapter might interest you...

Chapter Seventeen
The impossible situation (Part 4)
Terrorism

In recent years; the world has had to face up to the phenomenon of air rage; hijacking; hostage-taking; suicide-bombs; explosions; high-profile murders; spying; deliberate use of violence; and other jeopardous life or death situations; whereby we are subjected to a wave of fear and uncertainty, known collectively as terrorism. Unfortunately; there is nothing much anyone can do to stop the violence, unless we have prior-information. This however; will have to involve years of painstaking fact-gathering by the government agencies assigned to protect the population. The world is now divided into the developed world and the Third World countries; which could also be called the 'Haves' against the 'Have-nots'. The conflict between these two divisions; is the main cause of terrorism. Because the 'Have-nots' have no way of defeating the political, military and economic power of the 'Haves'; some of them have chosen violence and the endangering of lives to frighten the world, in the hope that things will change in their favour. There are also those amongst the 'Have-nots', whose sole aim is to destroy the 'Haves'; by using religion as an excuse and an effective tool. This is because they see the developed world's way of life as serious imperialistic domination, which threatens to undermine their own existence; whereby they will lose control of their people, religion, language and culture. Although terrorism has been attributed to the countries in and around the Middle-East and the Moslem religion; it is increasingly being used by other groups fighting for independence or inequality, all over the world. It is also used by individuals, looking for attention or trying to prove a point. They feel no one will listen to them; unless they kill a few innocent people or destroy a prominent building! Because in many instances, the perpetrators are prepared to lose their lives in the process; terrorism has to be taken seriously. It can happen anywhere; to anyone at any time!

Modern terrorism could be said to have started in the Sixties; when certain criminal groups used bank robbery and kidnapping for ransom, to obtain funds. Although some terrorist organizations continue to use these tactics; most other groups are given money from people who support their cause. In the late 1970s, the Irish Republican Army (IRA) was assisted by extensive funding from Irish American sympathizers; whilst countries at loggerheads with the United States, such as Cuba and Libya, also helped fund terrorists. The Palestinian terrorist organizations received large amounts of money from petroleum-rich Arab nations that wanted Israel overthrown. On July 23, 1968; a group of terrorists from the Popular Front for the Liberation of Palestine, hijacked one of Israel's El Al airliners in Rome and forced the pilot to fly it to Algeria. This event is generally considered to be the first modern terrorist attack. Since then; there have been several well-known terrorist organisations like the Baader-Meinhof Gang; the Red Brigades in Italy; the Japanese Red Army; the Provisional Irish Republican Army; the Ulster Defence Association; ETA Basque militants; the Puerto Rican Armed Forces of National Liberation (FALN); the Iranian funded Hezbollah; Hamas; Sendero Luminoso (Shining Path) in Peru; al-Qaeda and a few other groups who were at one time related to the Palestine Liberation Organization (PLO). Some of the most notorious acts of terrorism occurred in Europe. This included the kidnapping and murder of Israeli athletes at the 1972 Olympic Games in Munich, Germany, by a Palestinian organization called Black September; and the assassination of Aldo Moro, a former prime minister of Italy, by the Red Brigades in 1978. However; no one was prepared for the new generation of terrorists, who have become more ruthless than their predecessors.

Whereas all the other terrorist groups in the past could be pinpointed by their murder and intimidation tactics, ideology, personnel and headquarters; the Al-Qaeda movement is completely different. It is a loosely-bound organisation personified by the notorious Osama Bin-Laden and blatantly endorsed by the Taliban; a fervently Islamic group, which had been ousted from power in Afghanistan and replaced with a pro-American democratic system. There is no specific headquarters; and their only ideology can be traced back to their hatred of the United States and all things Western. Using Islam as an effective 'us-against-the-infidels' tool;

they are able to draw in supporters who actually believe they must get rid of their enemies because their way of life is damaging the world, whereby they will eventually destroy Islam. Their ultimate goal; is to defeat the United States and all moderate Muslim states, in order to establish a single World Islamic State. Aided by the Internet and with an apparent abundance of finance; they can easily attract sympathy to their cause and collect people who are prepared to kill and die, in order to hurt the 'the Great Satan'. America's apparent disregard for the feelings of the Muslims in Iraq and Afghanistan has increasingly made her enemies in the Middle-East; because her indiscriminate bombing campaigns have accidentally killed and maimed many women and children. Anyone who is prepared to lose his life, whilst taking others with him; will be very difficult to stop. It is therefore important to know a little about the history and causes of terrorism; so that you can at least understand why it happens and have a chance to avoid the areas where violence is likely to explode.

A brief history...

Throughout history; there have always been religious wars and conflicts, involving peoples and countries with different ways of life and beliefs. For years; certain European countries namely Britain, France, Spain, Portugal and to a lesser extent Germany controlled most of the world through their colonies. Although they developed and modernised these colonies, they also looted them of their raw materials and treasures; which one could argue, has been used to form the bedrock of modern European prosperity. The United States arrived prominently into the international fold after the First World War; when they came to the aid of Europe, to halt the German aggression against her neighbours. When Germany lost that war, she also lost her influence on her territories; which then became up-for-grabs and were mostly taken over by Britain and France. The League of Nations was formed in 1920 as part of the war settlement; but because the United States refused to join, it proved ineffective. It did not take long for Germany to rise again through Adolf Hitler. He restored his country's pride and wrested back control of her lost territories; but also made the mistake of exterminating millions of Jews in gas chambers in the Holocaust, whilst the world stood by and watched in horror. Germany and her coalition Italy made another fundamental error of trying to take over Europe; even going as far as Russia, which from 1922, had been known as the USSR (Union of Soviet Socialist Republics) and slaughtering millions of people. Japan, Hitler's ally in Asia, invaded countries in the Far East, including Korea, Vietnam and China; subjecting those peoples to many horrors. Britain was then dragged into what became known as the Second World War; in order to halt the German aggression, which had already taken over France and surrounding countries like Belgium, Luxemburg and the Netherlands and was about to invade England. Because the Germans were so strong; the United States were again called in to rescue Europe. Beginning with the D Day landings in Normandy in 1944; the Allies managed to defeat Hitler and free Europe.

The war finally ended in 1945; when the United States destroyed Japan, by dropping an atom bomb on Hiroshima and a second bomb on Nagasaki. This was in retaliation for a somewhat cowardly and unforeseen Japanese attack on Pearl Harbour. The war was so destructive that the United Nations was born out of the original League of Nations; so that countries could settle their differences without having to go to war. The Yalta Conference of 1945 confirmed the United States, the USSR and Britain as the leading powers in the world; and were forthwith known as the 'Superpowers'. Having won the war; they were the first countries to have control of a nuclear arsenal! However; the USSR, who had suffered the most in the war by losing more lives than all the other countries put together, fell out with Britain and the United States. Under Stalin; she took over Eastern and Central Europe with communism and eventually formed the Warsaw Pact in 1955. The two remaining Allies led by Eisenhower and Churchill, formed N.A.T.O (North Atlantic Treaty Organisation) to bind America and Western Europe together; in defence against the USSR and her Eastern bloc countries. This division was henceforth known as the 'iron curtain'; a term coined by Churchill. The United States agreed to rebuild Europe with her famed Marshall Plan; whilst the power of the USSR was greatly enhanced when she took over the rebuilding of Eastern Europe. Whenever the USSR and the United States disagreed; the rest of the world would be on tenterhooks as to whether they would go to war or not, because they both had enough nuclear weapons to destroy the world. This uncertainty between the superpowers became known as the 'Cold War'. It reached its zenith in 1961 during the Cuban Bay of Pigs missile crisis; when President Kennedy warned the USSR's Khrushchev that he would never allow nuclear weapons to be deployed in Cuba, because it threatened the security of the United States. In the same year; the USSR divided Berlin into two with a huge wall, as a symbol that she would not be bullied by America in Europe. The battle lines were now clearly drawn! Both the USSR and the United States, resorted to all kinds of subterfuge to undermine each other; by using their intelligence units KGB and CIA respectively, to cement their influence around the world. This included campaigns of 'dirty tricks'; and installing leaders of their choice in countries under their influence. Iran and Iraq both benefited from American generosity; whilst Cuba, Libya and Syria received aid from the USSR.

In 1949; Mao Tse Tung and his communist Red Army, which had overrun China during his famous 'long walk' in 1934, took over the vast country. He then made sure the Americans and Russians had no influence over her; by keeping the two superpowers out of China. Chinese leader Chiang Kai-Shek, who with help from the communists, had freed his country from the Japanese clutches; fled with his supporters to the island of Taiwan, because he did not like the idea of communism. He formed close ties with America; who flooded the country with development aid. Taiwan has been a bone of contention between the two superpowers ever since; because China has refused to recognise her. Korea however; became the focus of control between America and the USSR and was divided into two in 1953, after a brief war between the North and the South. American troops were then deployed to keep the peace at the border between North and South Korea; in order to stop the spread of communism southwards. For similar reasons; Vietnam was also divided into two, with the USSR and China having influence over the North of both countries and the United States supporting the South. The difficulties involved in dividing a country into two, with one-half communist and the other capitalist also led to the Vietnam War; when the North tried to overrun the South. Because the United States, under Presidents Johnson and Nixon, had championed herself as the bulwark against communism; she was forced to go to the aid of the South. She suffered so many casualties; it led to antiwar peace movements around the world. She was finally forced to withdraw her troops in 1973; whereby the South was immediately taken over by the North and a single Vietnam country was created. This 'ignominious defeat' stung America badly; because it was seen as a victory by communism over capitalism. In reality; she could not continue a war, which had become too expensive and had lost the support of her own people.

Throughout the Seventies and Eighties; the United States and the USSR divided up the world into their spheres of influence. Britain stood staunchly by the side of the United States. It seemed as if France was still reluctantly in debt to the two English-speaking allies, for rescuing her from Hitler's aggression; and she developed nuclear weaponry of her own, to emphasise her independence. In order not to be left out of the global equation; China also did the same. The five countries with a nuclear arsenal formed the Security Council in the United Nations, each with a veto; which meant that no decisions could be passed, unless they all agreed. The United States constantly criticised the human rights abuses of both the USSR and China; which did nothing, except make the two big powers dig their heels in and dismiss the US as 'decadent and imperialistic'. Even though they both embraced communism; China was not particularly friendly with the USSR...but did not trust America either. There were frequent deadlocks in meetings of the Security Council; because each superpower would use her veto, whenever it benefited her policy and spheres of influence around the world.

Because of America's staunch loyalty to Israel; the Middle-East countries started to lean towards the USSR, who realised that she could easily move into the vacuum created. Since the Middle-East was of strategic importance to the West, because of the amount of oil exported out of there; the United States accepted that she had to quickly find a way to stay friends with the Arab nations, or have them fall under Russian influence. China under Mao Tse Tung on the other hand; because of the negative press she was receiving from the United States, did her best to keep Westerners out of the country and crush all dissidents. President Nixon visited China in 1972, with the hope of normalising relations; but Taiwan was always a stumbling block. In 1979; President Carter chose to break official relations with Taiwan, in order to please China and restore full diplomatic links with her. Despite this rapprochement; the hardliner tactic was continued after Mao's death in 1976, by Deng Xiao Ping, the new leader. This eventually came to a head in 1989 at Tiananmen Square; where the Chinese military killed some of the students demonstrating against the oppressive policies the country was living under. Even though more soldiers than civilians were said to have died on that day; the worldwide condemnation of this massacre and crushing aftermath of all dissidents, eventually forced a policy rethink by the Chinese hierarchy.

In December 1979; Soviet forces invaded Afghanistan in a surprise attack, claiming the Americans were interfering there. The Afghans resisted from their mountain hideaways, by waging guerrilla warfare; and many fled the Soviet advance by moving as refugees into Pakistan. Carter immediately denounced the invasion. He cut off grain exports and the sale of high-technology equipment to the Soviet Union; stopped the debate on the ratification of SALT (Strategic Arms Limitation Talks) and would not permit U.S. athletes to compete in the 1980 Olympic Games in Moscow. The Eastern bloc retaliated by not attending the 1984 Olympics in Los Angeles. Even though they were forced to withdraw in 1988, after suffering too many casualties; the Russians felt they had done the right thing, in order to prevent American expansion into their area of influence. This idea that the Americans thought they could interfere in a country so close to the Soviet Union, yet had in the past refused to allow them to do the same in Cuba; became a very sore point for the Russians. The USSR decided henceforth; that they would never allow America or anyone else to dictate what they should or should not do. This has defined their foreign policy ever since!

Most of The Third World countries, which had recently been granted independence from colonialism; played the superpowers off against each other in order to extract as much aid and weaponry from them, in return for securing their votes in the United Nations. It did not take too long for India and Pakistan, who had both gained independence from Britain after the war; to develop their independent nuclear technology. This happened; despite the fact that they were always at loggerheads and had fought several mini-wars against each other, over the Kashmir region. Once these two

Third World countries had obtained nuclear weapons; it opened the door for other countries to develop their own. 1979 was the turning point; when a coup in Iraq, a former British protectorate, brought Saddam Hussein into power and the Ayatollah Khomeini used his Islamic revolution to overthrow the Shah of Iran, who ended his days in exile in the United States. The subsequent skirmishes and eventual war between these two Middle-East nations; brought the burning nuclear dilemma into the forefront. It was believed by the United States that, were these two warring countries to be in possession of nuclear weapons, they might very well have used them; a prospect which obviously did not please Israel. Initially, Britain and the Americans supported Saddam; until he became an embarrassment they could no longer afford, with his human rights abuses. Iran was constantly under threat from the United States; because of the way the Shah, a prominent Western ally, was overthrown and his efforts at westernisation destroyed and replaced with Islamic law. This included a botched attempt in 1980, to rescue some American Embassy officials who had been taken hostage. For the first time; two oil-producing countries would directly affect the rest of the world, because they could control the price and output of all petroleum products. Their being at war with each other; did not augur well for the 'Haves'! It was at this point; that America pushed the superpowers to agree to the principle that no more countries should be allowed to have nuclear weapons. It seems however, that a clandestine exception was made for Israel; in view of the threat she faced from all the Arab nations that surrounded her.

After the Second World War; the Jews who survived the Holocaust, were given permission by the Allies to settle in Palestine. This was an area in the Middle-East; which henceforth became known as their Promised Land. Regrettably; the feelings of the Arab population, who were already living there, were not taken into account. The neighbouring Arab countries were so incensed; they attacked the new nation as soon as it was proclaimed. In the resulting war; the Jews captured about 50 percent more land, whilst Jordan and Egypt occupied the rest of the region. Several hundred thousand Palestinian Arabs were evicted from their homeland. The majority fled to the West Bank and the Gaza Strip; but more than twenty percent of the displaced Palestinians left Palestine and settled in other parts of the Middle-

East, mainly in Lebanon. They were not allowed to return after the war ended; whereby they attracted tremendous sympathy for their cause. In 1948, the United Nations partitioned Palestine; allocating about half the land to the Palestinian Arabs and the other half to the Jews, to create the new state of Israel. In 1950; the United Nations established about 50 refugee camps for the displaced Palestinians in the West and East banks of Jordan, the Gaza Strip, Lebanon and Syria. This experience of exile shaped the Palestinian political and cultural activity for the next generation; and a proud national identity and fervent hatred for Israel emerged. An umbrella organization of several Palestinian groups, calling itself the Palestine Liberation Organization (PLO), was founded in 1964; and thereafter claimed to be the sole representative of the Palestinians. In the Six-Day War of 1967; Israel occupied East Jerusalem, the West Bank, the Gaza Strip and the Golan Heights. The Egyptians, who were fighting for the Palestinian cause, were later soundly defeated in the Yom Kippur war of 1973. Throughout the 1960s, '70s, and '80s; Israel continuously proved too intransigent for the PLO, which had launched frequent guerrilla attacks against her. When these proved futile; different types of attacks evolved and terrorism became a key element in the Palestinian struggle against Israel.

Ultimately, a movement seeking to reclaim Palestine and end the existence of the Jewish state developed; backed by a variety of Palestinian guerrilla organizations, which had come to the fore at the end of the 1950s and the beginning of the 1960s. These included the Palestine National Liberation Movement (known as Fatah); the Popular Front for the Liberation of Palestine (PFLP); the Syrian-backed Sa'iqah; the Democratic Front for the Liberation of Palestine (DFLP) and the Popular Struggle Front (PSF). In 1988; the PLO declared Palestine an independent state and finally voted to recognize Israel's right to exist. Israel at first; refused to deal with the PLO. But in 1993, after several months of secret negotiations; she finally agreed to recognize the PLO and to gradually withdraw from most of the occupied territories. The Declaration of Principles on Palestinian Self-Rule was signed in Washington, D.C., on Sept. 13, 1993. These peace accords called for Palestinian self-rule to be established in most of the West Bank and the Gaza Strip; over a five-year period, beginning in 1994. The

Palestinian Authority (PA) was created to govern the Palestinian-controlled areas. The Israelis were to withdraw from the Gaza Strip and the West Bank town of Jericho; by May 1994. After another peace agreement was signed in September 1995; Israeli troops began withdrawing from several towns and cities in the West Bank. PLO leader Yasser Arafat was elected the first president of the PA in 1996. Progress towards Palestinian self-rule deteriorated in the late 1990s; and the deadlines established in the 1993 accords were not met.

In 1990; a debt-ridden Saddam Hussein in Iraq used a flimsy border dispute as an excuse to invade Kuwait, take over the oil fields and avoid having to pay his debts. Since he had spent most of his money on the build-up of his military machine; he reasoned that by controlling Kuwait, with the third largest oil reserves, he could help push up the price of oil on the world market. There was also a very real threat that had Saddam taken over Kuwait, he might have gone all the way and taken over Saudi Arabia; thereby controlling most of the Middle-East oil reserves. The United States; an ally of Kuwait and benefactor of the hitherto 'reasonable' oil prices caused by the glut of oil, (supposedly due to Kuwait's over-production) could not allow this to happen. She declared war on Iraq in 1991; with a massive build-up of troops, not seen since the Second World War. A sustained bombing attack, coupled with the freezing of Iraq's bank accounts, amidst unanimous world-wide support (which surprisingly included Russia); finally forced Saddam to withdraw from Kuwait.

Although militarily, Russia still had her nuclear weapons; economically, she could not sustain looking after her satellite states in Eastern and Central Europe. Following the cue of the Solidarity Party in Poland, which forced democratic elections that eventually brought Lech Walèsa to power in 1991; the other countries also became very vociferous in demanding their independence. What began with an uprising in Hungary in 1956, which was ruthlessly crushed by the Russian army; finally ended in 1990, with the fall of the Berlin Wall. This effectively meant that America under Presidents Reagan and Bush Senior had won the Cold War! Like a domino effect; most of Russia's Union of Soviet Socialist Republics also eventually gained their independence, although they kept their economic and cultural links with Russia. True to form; the Russians blamed the Americans for fomenting the dissent in her satellite states that led to their demands for independence, by strengthening cultural, economic and military ties with the Eastern European nations. The influential power of the United States became evident when Russia under Mikhail Gorbachev and his successor Boris Yeltsin, realised it would be more advantageous to draw closer to the United States than to oppose her; especially when the rise of China as an economic, military and political global force, meant Russia could easily be pushed into the background of world power. It is a true testament to Russia's maturity on the world stage; that she was able to put aside her differences with America and play a leading role in the peace negotiations that managed to halt the N.A.T.O bombing of Serbia and ensure that Russian troops would co-operate in safeguarding the peace. Yeltsin also vowed to push ahead with economic reforms in Russia; but shocked the international community by resigning in 1999, due to ill health. He was succeeded by Vladimir Putin, who decided that Yeltsin had gone a little too far in his rapprochement with the United States; and vowed to restore Russian pride. He quickly moved to re-establish bilateral relations with Europe, which had broken down with NATO's military intervention in Serbia; by supplying her with natural gas and strengthening cultural links. He consolidated power by moving against the oligarchs and nationalising Russia's immense wealth; with the intention of making her a world economic, as well as a political power. He was however, against any move by America to amend the Anti-Ballistic Missile Treaty; which showed that the old Cold War suspicions were still ever-present. He had problems with the breakaway republic of Chechnya and former soviet republic of Georgia and was accused by America of human rights abuses; which he chose to ignore because he believed the dissent was instigated by the United States. Putin has obviously decided that Russia will not be pushed around by anyone; and even when he stepped down in 2008 in favour of Medvedev, he was still suspected of being the real power behind the throne! He has now returned to power and has taken over the Crimea with the possibility that some parts of Eastern Ukraine will follow suit. With her dependence on Russian gas supplies, Europe is somehow not in a strong enough position to curtail Moscow's ambitions; leaving the United States as the only realistic nation which can stand up to the Soviet bear.

China underwent a transformation of her own, when Deng Xiao Ping died and was replaced by Jiang Zemin; who decided to break from the past and place the strengthening of the economy above that of ideology. Hong Kong was peacefully reunified from British control in 1997; a sure sign that Britain was warming towards the idea of rapprochement with China under Jiang. This is because it appeared he was relaxing his hardliner control on his people; by undergoing economic reform aimed at increased trade with the rest of the world. Despite being accused of human rights abuses and their lack of a western-style democracy (mainly by the Americans), China has proved herself a force to be reckoned with on the world stage; by quietly spreading her economic might around the Third World countries (especially in Africa), which had felt let down by their former colonial masters. The Chinese have also invested their money wisely around the world; because they have learnt from their history that economic power is now more important than political and military might. The Olympics held in Beijing in 2008, was such a technological and economic marvel that the world had to sit up and take notice; especially when China was one of the first countries to recover from the world recession. Even though the Western media highlighted it in 2009; the twentieth anniversary of the Tiananmen Square killings came and went without any relevant fanfare or trouble. This showed that the authorities had moved on to a new chapter in their nation's evolution; whereby, dissent and demonstrations would no longer be tolerated or even supported by the populace. They are obviously too busy making money!

The millennium began badly when the Middle-East peace process collapsed in 2000; after Arafat and Israeli Prime Minister Ehud Barak were unable to negotiate a final agreement. A second Palestinian uprising; which became known as the Al-Aqsa intifadah, broke out late in the year. The violence intensified in 2002, characterized by an escalating cycle of Palestinian suicide-bombings targeting Israeli citizens; followed by swift and severe Israeli reprisals. Israeli troops reoccupied the West Bank and the Gaza Strip; and at times prevented the Palestinians from leaving the occupied zones. Thousands of Palestinians and Israelis were killed or injured during the intifadah. Because Israel had her own nuclear arsenal for protection; the Arabs realised there was no way they could defeat her, unless they could force America to withdraw her support. This was highly improbable; because of the amount of Jews living in the United States and the guilt Britain and America still feel for sitting back whilst millions of Jews were gassed by Hitler. America was seen by the Middle-East nations, as the biggest stumbling block to their problems; by imposing her will on all who dared to oppose her and siding with Israel, but at the same time, claiming to be a friend to the Islamic countries. Out of this hatred for America's arrogance and apparent megalomania; came a brand of terrorism, which was difficult to pinpoint. This is because they chose to attack the United States, in areas where they were least prepared; or never thought possible. The attack on the twin-towers of the World Trade Centre in 2001 was right on America's doorstep; and made her realise that the threat against her way of life was serious and very real. Finding the culprits for this horrible attack on innocents; consumed the George W Bush presidency so much that he was willing to go to war, to make sure it never happened again.

Saddam Hussein in Iraq became the first casualty; when he was accused by Britain and America of having 'weapons of mass destruction'. He had obviously not learnt anything from the war with Kuwait; as he continued terrorising the Kurds who were looking for independence in the north of Iraq. His cruel and random tactics provoked a humanitarian crisis, abhorred by the rest of the world. He continued abusing his population; and several times, refused to cooperate with the United Nations weapons inspectors. This was seen as a belligerent act; which brought on economic sanctions, followed by American air strikes. In March 2003; President Bush ordered Saddam to leave the country or face removal by force. When he refused to leave; a U.S and British-led coalition invaded Iraq. Saddam, along with his family and closest advisers; immediately went into hiding. Within months of the invasion; a number of the advisers were found by the advancing coalition forces. In July 2003; two of Saddam's sons were killed during a raid on their hideout by U.S. troops. Saddam himself eluded capture until Dec. 13, 2003; when U.S. troops discovered the former dictator in an underground hideout near his hometown of Tikrit. Although armed; he surrendered without a struggle and was taken into custody. He was eventually tried and hanged by the new democratically elected Iraqi government. Even though it was later revealed that Saddam did not have 'weapons of mass destruction'; he did however, use illegal chemical weapons in his indiscriminate attacks against the Kurds. His removal was generally seen as beneficial progress for the Iraqi people; if only the American troops did not have so much control of the country. The United States however, could not just leave Iraq; because they had still not come any closer to finding out who had bombed the twin-towers. They thereby continued the 'War against Terror' into the mountains of Afghanistan; where the deposed Taliban leaders were supposedly holing out. Despite imprisoning terrorist suspects in Guantanamo Bay in Cuba and using cruel torture tactics on them; they have so far failed to catch and destroy the main Al Qaeda terrorists. This is because many of them are said to be hiding in Pakistan; a country which benefits greatly from American largess and regards herself as a partner in the fight against terrorism. At the same time; she has to be careful not to be seen to desert Islam, just to please America. This is a delicate balancing act; which bodes problems in the future. The assassination of Benazir Bhutto, a former prime minister, and the ubiquitous suicide-bombings; has shown that all is not well in the country. Influential forces backed by the Taliban, against the United States; are still ever-present! The recent turmoil in Syria and Iraq has shown that the invasion of Iraq and the withdrawal of American and British troops from Iraq may have both been mistakes because they have created more problems for the populace and peace is still a long way off.

President Obama has sought to ease the tensions between America and the Islamic world; by using rhetoric designed to appease the Muslim community. This is a brave move; which would have been anathema to previous American governments. He has also learnt not to openly interfere in the internal affairs of other countries; as in the case of the 2009 disputed election in Iran. In the name of rapprochement; he has even offered aid to Zimbabwe; despite President Mugabe's mishandling of the economy there. In one famous speech in 2009; the word 'terrorist' was replaced with 'extremist', as he tried to equate the suffering of the Palestinians with that of the Jews. Although well intentioned; this did little to satisfy either group. Being an American; he will always stand accused of pandering to the whims of the Jews! Britain and the United States feel they have a 'moral duty' not to abandon Israel; because they were both influential in allowing the Jews to set up home in Palestine after the Second World War. Little did they realise the panic and pain it would cause the Muslims in the Middle-East! The tough stance and harsh reprisals shown by the Israelis since the War, although reprehensible to some; is understandable. After what happened to the Jews in the concentration camps; they are only making sure they protect themselves, so that it does not happen again. The seemingly cowardly attacks by the Palestinians; is also understandable. Their backs are against the wall; as they have tried many times to defeat Israel, without success. This is why they have resorted to 'terrorist' activities. A few speeches even by a genuine leader as astute as Obama; will not be able to wipe away seventy years of hate, pain and sorrow. Many observers believe that without an independent Palestinian state, there will always be problems in the Middle-East. That however, cannot be possible; unless the Palestinians wholeheartedly accept Israel's right to exist as a nation. Even if there were to be an independent Palestinian state; she would have to renounce violence and would not be allowed by Israel to arm herself. In view of past hostilities; this cannot be acceptable to the Palestinians. The Middle-East problem is much bigger than Palestine and Israel; because it affects every single Jew and Muslim in the world. Until there is a final solution, agreeable to all parities in the conflict; every country could become a victim of the terrorism.

One can see from the above synopsis of world history; that the Second World War was the catalyst that gave birth to what we now call terrorism. The world is a much smaller place because of easier travel opportunities and access to the Internet; which has made the movement of people and the sharing of information much faster. A would-be terrorist can conveniently be recruited on the Internet; trained in one country and used to attack innocent people in another, where he/she will not be known to the security agencies. Those who remember the War and suffered because of it are the ones who are still very influential in world affairs…either personally or through their immediate children. This means that the Holocaust will for the foreseeable future, continue to influence Israel's thinking. The Islamic world will also remember the millions of their people who have suffered because of that initial decision to allow Israel to settle in the Middle-East; which probably seemed reasonable at the time, because of the biblical history relating the Jews to their Holy Land. The problem lies in the fact that there has never been a real, heartfelt and unconditional apology or compensation by the Germans and the major powers of the day; for allowing the killing of six million Jews to take place right under their noses. To add insult to injury; there are some who do not like the Jews and are happy it happened...and some who say it never happened. Delight and Denial of the Holocaust is the main reason Israel is so intransigent and will do anything to protect herself; even if it means the Palestinians suffer for it! The Islamic world on the other hand; has a unique sense of unity towards each other. This is intrinsically linked to Allah and the Koran; and not to a specific country. When one of their own from any part of the world is killed or injured; there will understandably be feelings of hurt and thoughts of revenge. Israel's enemies may come from anywhere in the Muslim world; and for that reason, the 'terrorists' may also target any country that appears to be a friend of Israel.

Terrorism is used when the practitioner believes there is no poignant way to make a point, other than to sacrifice his/her own life, along with the lives of others; so that the targeted nation will also feel the pain he/she went through that led to the terror. One's life becomes meaningless, when he or she has lost all their loved ones; and therefore, every bomb that is dropped by America and every person that is killed in the Middle-East, will be seen by the Islamic world as a death caused by an aggressive force in defence of Israel...one which can never be forgotten or indeed, forgiven. Although America's reasons for going into Iraq may have been well-intentioned; she made the mistake of not taking the feelings and sensibilities of the Islamic world into consideration. Trying to impose one's way of life and beliefs on a different culture; never works! The attack on the twin-towers was just a reminder that there are some very dangerous people in the world; who will stop at nothing to embarrass her. There are millions in the Islamic world, who can never forgive what the United States has done to the Middle-East. Amongst them, will be some who will either seek revenge through terrorism; or use the weak, easily influenced and the vulnerable to do their dirty work for them. Her recent debacle in Vietnam; has obviously not taught America that interfering in the internal affairs of other nations, always brings problems. Her expansionist policy needs to be modified to take into account the history, feelings and sensibilities of others; and to realise that we cannot all be alike. Nations need to develop at their own pace and eventually; the democratic ideals spouted by the United States will prevail. This is because all human beings basically want the same things in life; a free and safe society for their offspring to grow up in. Wake up America! Remember; the Cold War was not won by bombs, but by a gradual realisation that the communist system was not working. Trying to force others to do what you want them to do; will most likely make them do the opposite! Those who have children will readily agree with this!

America's greater might in the media also means that the plight of Israel attracts more sympathy amongst the 'Haves'; whilst the Palestinian plight is seen by the 'Have-nots' as totally unfair. The fact that they are being bullied by Israel is conveniently underplayed by the western media. Although this media is useful in divulging information; it can also be detrimental because it is able to highlight how the 'Haves' have a better standard of living than those in the Third World. Freedom of the press is not available in many countries; and therefore, there are those who cannot understand why newspapers and television stations in the western world are allowed by their governments to write and show what they believe are distorted facts against their country. As a result; the 'Haves' are often accused of deliberately giving bad press to countries who do not believe in their way of life, thereby portraying the Islamic world as 'backward' and uncivilised. This would naturally cut deeply into the national psyche of any country, which is proud of her traditions and history. This is especially poignant to those who were victims of colonialism. Most of them still believe their countries were exploited by the colonial powers who despite their abundance of riches; have done little to compensate their former colonies. This gives potential terrorists the ammunition to hate those who seem to have it all; whilst the rest of the world is ridden with starvation, disease and poverty. It is not so difficult to convince someone who has little prospects for his or her future; that their problems are caused by the 'Haves' led by the 'Great Satan' America! Although it is sometimes convenient to disparage the United States; one must never forget that she twice came to Europe's aid, when called upon in two world wars. Without America; Hitler would have won the Second World War and the freedom we all take for granted might not have been possible! She therefore feels a duty to make sure it never happens again; even if it means installing army bases in Germany and trying to do the same with the former Eastern bloc countries. The American people are also the most generous when it comes to helping nations in need with aid; and highlighting the suffering of indigenous people in war-torn and destitute areas, through their high-profile documentaries, films and music. Indeed, their way of life is copied and admired all over the world; so credit should always be given where it is due. Well done America; the world loves you really! It's those 'gung-ho politicians' giving your nation a bad name; with their imperialistic policies!

For similar reasons of respect and taking the feelings, culture and history of others into consideration; both the Russian and Chinese hierarchy should listen a bit more to their people. A happy population, which is given enough freedom to pursue its dreams; will not resort to terrorist activities that undermine the government! Undeniably, there will always be some who advocate violent upheavals; but they can easily be contained and stopped in their tracks, if they have no backing from outside or support from inside the country. Chechnya is a sore point for Russia; as is Tibet for China. They have both accused America of interfering in their internal affairs. They fervently believe that if they don't take a stand; the United States will railroad them into submission. This is understandable; because in the past, they have all been known to blatantly interfere in the internal affairs of each other's countries! America should therefore learn to back off; and allow the Russians and the Chinese to solve their own problems. Believe it or not; both nations are acutely aware that something has to be done and do not need to be told or intimidated. Trying to force independence in areas where one has no personal experience of their history; can easily be interpreted as deliberate interference. This will then be rebuffed and a tit-for-tat scenario will emerge; whereby the superpowers will frustrate each other, when they are most in need of each other's support. After the 9/11 attacks on the world Trade Centre, there were parts of the world that were actually rejoicing; and others who proffered lukewarm condolences, whilst secretly glad that America had received her comeuppance. Surely; that is a horrible state of affairs for any country to endure? How can a nation that does so much good around the world; be so hated? Change is inevitable in any society; and draconian measures aimed at curtailing the civil liberties of a country will only delay but cannot stop the inevitable movement towards individual independence. Understandably, history has played a major part in the way the superpowers view the world; but the day is fast approaching when the War and its aftermath will be consigned to the dustbins of history and a new generation of leaders will emerge. They are the ones who will surely see the bigger picture; that a world where individual liberties are safeguarded and all countries are treated with genuine respect for their points of view and way of life, is the only way to go. This is because far bigger problems involving over-population, climate change and the state of the environment are looming menacingly on the horizon and will need the co-operation of all nations to address them.

In the immediate future; Britain and America will continue to stick together in major decisions and conflicts, because of their common history, cultural similarities and the English language... which is fast becoming the international language. They should therefore be honest and be able to tell each other when and where they are going wrong; instead of only criticising countries, who do not agree with them. The powers-that-be should listen more to the truthful voices in their media who are the mirrors of society; and realise that bad policies give the country a bad name. In the end; it is their innocent citizens travelling abroad who suffer and not the politicians. The lessons from the Cold War and their inherent distrust for each other will continue to undermine American and Russian politics; even though they are good at pretending they like each other! If these two superpowers worked more together, instead of trying to undermine and accuse each other for their hiccups; they will realise that a peaceful world without suspicion is a far safer and cheaper option. Money earmarked for defence and war can be used for the betterment of their country! The 2010 agreement in Prague, whereby Russia and the United States agreed to reduce their nuclear warheads by one third over seven years; is a good sign that the two superpowers can work together, if they really put their minds to it. However; it did not go unnoticed that they will still have enough weapons to destroy the world ten times over! The powerful emergence of China will be treated with caution by the other superpowers; because it was the nonchalance of Britain, America, Russia and France that allowed Hitler's megalomania to get as far as it did. To their credit; the Chinese have realised that their non-interference in the internal affairs of other nations, has given them the time and freedom to expand their economy. Although their apparent lack of democratic ideals has been roundly criticised; their belief in a strong economy will help them ease slowly into a free society that will be envied by every country. In another fifty years; China will probably be the most financially stable nation in the world!

France is a proud nation; which has still not quite got over the embarrassment of twice being rescued by Britain and the United States, during two world wars. She also sees her language being slowly but surely overtaken by English, as a world lingua-franca...even in her former colonies. She has been known to disagree with the United States and Britain; as a matter of principle and to safeguard her independence. She is at the forefront of the European Union with Germany; so a third war inside Europe is now extremely unlikely. A stronger Union will also be in a better position to counter apparent American interference in Europe. This will allay the fears of Russia; who have long disliked the presence and increasing influence America is having on the former Eastern bloc countries. Regrettably; there are still a few nationalist movements around Europe, fuelling the racism fire. This threatens to undermine the safety and integrity of those regarded as foreigners; sometimes simply because of their religion. Once the Union is able to integrate immigrants from other countries and treat them with respect and equality; the threat of terrorism will recede. The Islamic world should also realise that respect cuts both ways; and do more to appreciate the customs of the people, amongst whom they are living. The Europeans have done a lot to accommodate other cultures, in order to move Europe towards a truly multi-cultural society. It would therefore be appreciated; if more immigrant Muslims would try to integrate and obey the laws of whichever country they have chosen to make their new home. Although a lot still remains to be done in Europe; there seems to be a 'stagnation of integration' in some countries in North Africa and the Middle-East, where their refusal to adapt to the times is beginning to cause problems for the ruling hierarchies. The Internet has now opened the eyes of many and the swift movement of views and ideas has recently been used effectively to overthrow the powers-that-be in Tunisia and Egypt and caused serious disruption leading to revolt in Libya. This led to the easy decision by NATO to help the anti-government forces overthrow the regime of Gadhafi with a sustained bombing campaign condoned by the United States. This movement towards freedom and equality, nicknamed 'Arab Spring', is likely to keep on spreading in the Arab world and their unequal treatment of women will be the straw that finally breaks the back of the Islamic male hegemony. The future of the world remains is in the capable hands of the superpowers; who must find a way to include the Muslim world in any decisions they make concerning our planet and this will go a long way towards curtailing terrorist activities in the world.

India is another country which, like China, is awakening from her slumber and will play an increasingly influential part in world affairs; both economically and culturally. She has had her own problems with terrorism; and has usually blamed Pakistan for them. She should recognise however; that with such a huge population, the difference between rich and poor is still too great. Something will have to be done to close the gap, before it leads to more terrorism or even a full-scale revolution; which will have nothing to do with Pakistan and the Middle-East crisis. Australia is a beautiful and popular country; which, because of her economic and historical links with Britain and the United States, has chosen to back them all the way. Although loyalty is an admirable trait; it should also bring with it, a sense of responsibility to tell her allies where they are going wrong. By wholeheartedly backing the invasion of Iraq for instance; she might easily have been tarred with the same brush by potential terrorists. These might even come from her indigenous population; because there are some aboriginal descendants who are not entirely happy to have had their land snatched from them and still be treated as 'second-class citizens'. Japan is one country that has to be admired; and proves that it is possible to let bygones be bygones. How a country that was so devastated by two nuclear strikes in 1945, was able to pick herself up off the floor and become a world economic power in less than fifty years; is a wonder to behold. Although she has not forgotten what America did to her; she has learnt to forgive and become a useful ally to the United States...who to their credit, helped rebuild Japan after the war. If Japan can forgive and befriend her attacker; then surely, all is not lost in the Palestinian crisis?

I personally believe the path to peace in the Middle-East must start with a genuine and heartfelt worldwide apology and compensation by Germany to Israel, for the Holocaust; and then a public acceptance of responsibility by Britain, the United States and Russia for sitting back and allowing it to happen. Israel must then find it in her heart to forgive them; because to be fair, the protagonists of the War are nearly all dead and it is a new generation that is now in charge of those countries. Once Israel is able to forgive; the ball will then be firmly in her and the Palestinians' court, to forgive each other for their past atrocities. The Palestinians must try and be big-hearted enough to realise that is too late to remove Israel from where they are. Although since the late 19th century, there had been a gradual settlement in Palestine, of Jews escaping persecution in Europe and Russia; after the Holocaust, it became more of a mad rush, which the Palestinians were not prepared for or willing to accept. Without the Holocaust; the Palestinians would have had more of a chance to get used to the gradual arrival of Jews into an acceptable area envisaged by the Balfour Declaration of 1917. A workable two-state solution would have been in existence today; without all the heartache! Both countries must accept that they need to recognise each other's right to exist and live peacefully where they are; for the sake of their children's future. Even the die-hards on both sides must surely realise by now that the problem is costing too many lives and going nowhere. At the moment; it seems as if the United States is doing all the work to find a lasting solution to the crisis. This is not fair; because it leaves her open to accusations of interference and favouritism towards Israel. It really needs the united active support of all the superpowers, in conjunction with the Islamic states; so that the Palestinians feel as if they are also part of the solution, instead of the feeling of exclusion they are currently undergoing. Since the idea of forming two separate states, poses too many security questions and will put both sides on a war-footing of suspicion; why not join them together? A one-state solution, where freedom and religion of the individual is enshrined in the constitution and both Israelis and Palestinians are given an equal amount of seats in a democratically elected Congress or Parliament; is not as far-fetched as it sounds. If it is financially and militarily backed by the superpowers; the extremists on both sides would quickly realise that they have been defeated by a greater force...the love of peace! With her commendable religious freedom, there are already Muslims living safely in Israel; and intermarriage is accepted. This means there are some people who have both Israeli and Palestinian blood in them; and there are Palestinian Jews and Israeli Muslims!

The Union of Palestine and Israel or 'Palisraelestine'! Now there's a thought! The land they have been fighting over would henceforth belong to the Union; which means there will be no more settlements or forceful removals and everyone will be housed. With their dignity restored; the Palestinians would be less likely to look on the Israelis as the enemy! If all the women on both sides of the equation decided they were tired of the fighting and killing and seriously 'leaned' on all the males in their lives; it would not take too long for the men to realise that they are destroying their future with the conflict. With female support; health, education, the economy and the environment would be given the priority they deserve. A new generation will emerge; where the children of both religions will go to school together and learn each other's customs and language. The 'them and us' mentality would disappear; because they would be sharing one country and one economy. Without the fighting; the standard of living will definitely increase and the terrorists will not have a strong-enough platform or the support to cause trouble. Obviously in the beginning, the Israelis will have more control of the political and military machine; but that would not bother the average Palestinian who is more interested in a peaceful place for his/her children to grow up with a comfortable roof over their heads, healthy food in their stomachs and a good education. With a feasible democracy in place; a president of Palestinian origin will eventually emerge. This will take far less than the sixty or more years that has already been spent fighting a war neither side can win. President Obama did it in America, where few thought it was possible to have a black president; and even the IRA was able to disarm and join the peace process in Northern Ireland. South Africa has managed to dislodge apartheid; whereby both whites and blacks have forgiven each other and are proud to call themselves South Africans, in a multi-racial society. Exclusion from the political process is one of the main reasons a group will resort to terrorism; and those already in power should do well to remember that!

The Arabs in the Middle-East are obviously not as stupid as they are sometimes portrayed; and will continue to use oil as a weapon, in order to extract as much as they can out of the 'Haves'. They are acutely aware that the oil will not last for ever; and that the non-Islamic world is only friendly to them, because of it. There is even a strong suspicion amongst the Arabs that the Americans only invaded Iraq, because they wanted to make sure the oil did not get into the wrong hands; and their accusations of 'weapons of mass destruction' were just a convenient smokescreen. The Islamic world also knows that the Jews will always be the Americans' priority; and they will continue to arm Israel, so that she can defend herself. This is because there is no guarantee that there will not be another Holocaust; should some Arab extremists have their way. The recent attempts by Iran and North Korea to blatantly go ahead with their nuclear plans, despite obvious condemnation by the Western nations; is a sign that the world is changing. Countries are not ready to kow-tow to the double-standards of the superpowers that do not want to get rid of their nuclear weapons; but are insisting no one else should have them. Having seen what has happened to Iraq and Afghanistan; Iran obviously feels insecure, due to the fact that one of her leaders, Ahmadinejad, has made his anti-Israeli views patently clear. She is under constant threat of upheaval, caused by the 2009 disputed election result; which she has blamed the United States and Britain for. With North Korea; the population is strictly controlled by a leadership, which still remembers the horrors it faced from Japan during the War and the aftermath of the division of Korea. She probably suffered more than the South; who were supported by the United States and have since become more prosperous. The vocal threats by the United States for North Korea and Iran to disarm; will only make things worse, because no one likes to be publicly threatened. They will just play to the gallery and dare America to do her worst! It also puts some members of their population at risk;

because all totalitarian regimes are fond of arresting and detaining, without charge. It would be easy to accuse anyone of being a western spy; have them jailed, tortured and possibly killed. The United States should realise that 'quiet-diplomacy' involving all the superpowers and the nation in question; is the best and only way forward, in this modern age!

The Iranian/North Korean 'audacity' has given many Third World countries like Venezuela, Bolivia and Zimbabwe the confidence to do only what benefits them; and not what they are told by the bigger nations, who have profited from their natural resources. The fact that many African and South American countries have not done enough to criticise these 'renegade nations' and have left it to the United States to go it alone; means there is probably a quiet admiration for them for having the guts to stand up to America and Britain. Money has now become the weapon of choice by the 'Haves'; because a country that receives tremendous aid and a decent share in the profits made out of her, will be unlikely to rebel. There seems to be a dash for giving aid to the African nations; which could prove to be detrimental in the long run. This is because it could be seen as a way for the developed world to salve their consciences for slavery and colonialism; which is patronising, to say the least! The 'Haves' must realise that many of Africa's problems arose from the way France and Britain partitioned the continent to suit themselves; separating tribes and in some cases, families. They then plundered the continent of much of its wealth; which many in Africa still believe has not been fully repaid! Although they also developed much of the infrastructure; they left behind nations who are now so impoverished that many are running to Europe for a 'better life', so that they can earn enough to send money back home to their families. The immigration problem of Europe; could therefore be seen as some form of payback for colonialism! It could also pose a terrorist threat; because many of those arriving illegally into Europe; are destitute, desperate and angry. It would not be difficult to convince them into crime or criminal damage; that ultimately harms the country they are in. Africa has now woken up to the fact that she has been ripped off in the past; and now wants a bigger share of the world economic cake. This is why we are increasingly finding that they would rather do business with the Chinese; than their former colonial masters, Britain and France. Being portrayed as beggars in need of aid is likely to annoy the Africans; because they are capable of looking after themselves, if they are given a fair price on the world market for their raw materials. The corruption on the continent, where politicians siphon money away to western banks, will soon be a thing of the past; as the younger generation realises that what has been going on is harmful to their country. An African terrorist threat could come from the poor; against the corruption of the rich, who are helping foreigners loot the wealth of the continent. The recent bombings in Kenya suggest that Africa might now be seen as a soft touch by the terrorists; who can achieve the same devastating results without the difficulties of trying to plan a bombing campaign in the developed world.

Terrorism can happen to any country, where there is a silent majority who feel marginalised and shut away from the processes that run the country, with no way of enjoying some of its wealth; like those with undemocratic dictatorships, family sovereignties and military rule brought about by coup d'états. It can come to those countries that blatantly support one nation to the detriment of another; like Britain, Australia or Canada did with America for the invasion of Iraq...or for the way America appears to actively support Israel more than she does the Palestinians. It can also arrive from minority groups trying to break away from a country they feel they don't belong to; due to their historical, religious or cultural differences. Examples of this are the separatist movements in countries as diverse as Spain; Turkey; Sri Lanka; Peru; The Philippines and Colombia. Finally; it can happen to individuals who try to impose their wealth and power on others and expect submissive surrender from those who already feel cheated by their poverty. Terrorism is a horrible turn of events for any country; and politics aside, a nation has every right to defend herself. One cannot put too much blame on the United States in Afghanistan or Russia in Georgia or Chechnya; for the tactics they have been accused of using to fight. In the heat of the moment; one can easily be consumed by passions of revenge, in order to seek out and destroy those responsible for one's misery. To sit down and do nothing against your avowed enemies; will be seen as a weakness and give confidence to others to try their luck. It is only when one takes stock of a situation; that one can understand that people just want to feel included. When the greed in the human being tries to take everything to the detriment of others; then anger and jealousy can lead to terrorism. For some; death is preferable to the status quo! I have constantly stated that once something has happened, it is obviously too late; therefore, it is better to try and remove the causes that lead to terrorism...rather than suffer the consequences. It really is very difficult to see an attack coming!

1. Air Rage

Air rage is when someone gets angry or bored and causes trouble on a flight, by invading the space of others; and is usually caused by too much alcohol consumption. It can be quite frightening for the other passengers; especially when the air crew are forced to refuse him (or her) any more to drink. The troublemaker then goes on an abusive verbal rampage; by shouting, threatening or making a thorough nuisance of him/herself, to the discomfort of the others on the flight. It is almost impossible to know a person's mental state or physical health; which means it could be classed under terrorism, because 'air-ragers' have been known to attempt opening the door of the aircraft in mid-flight! The behaviour could also turn violent because it could be the beginnings of a suicide attempt; whereby some recent incident in the culprit's life has made him/her decide to kill him/herself in mid-air by smashing up the plane. The passenger's safety and comfort are always uppermost in the minds of the air crew; and therefore, any sign of abnormal behaviour will be considered a threat to the aircraft and treated accordingly. Luckily, all air crew are trained to deal with air-rage; and the pilot would quickly radio ahead to the next airport. Whoever causes any trouble on a flight will be arrested as soon as the plane lands! There is always an in-flight closed-circuit camera monitoring everything going on in the cabin; so the air-rager cannot deny his/her behaviour. Pilots will refuse to fly or will even return to the airport if there is a troublemaker on board who starts playing up before the flight is due to take off, or has only been in the air a few minutes. The crew also have it in their power to physically restrain someone and handcuff him/her to their seat until the plane arrives safely. Needless-to-say; causing trouble on a flight is not a good idea!

Most rowdy incidents occur during chartered flights for stag parties or sports events; whereby you have groups of people who have had too much to drink and are intent on having 'a good time'. It can be quite amusing watching a drunkard stagger around the plane talking rubbish, trying to chat up the women; because he can liven up an otherwise boring flight and will eventually talk himself to sleep. For some strange reason; women are very patient and always seem to have the time to listen to silly chat-up lines used by men when they are drunk! If it happens to you on a flight; don't be afraid to use a swift retort of your sharp tongue to send any drunkard who bothers you, sheepishly back to his seat with his tail between his legs. If you are having problems; just report the troublemaker to the air crew and let them deal with him. The airhostesses know exactly how far to let a drunken passenger go before reading him the riot act! If anyone you are travelling with gets drunk or is drugged up to the eyeballs; it might be better to postpone the flight or else, keep an eye on him and make sure he does not leave his seat during the flight! Being a woman; you will be judged by other women on how you keep your man under control. Allowing him to get drunk and make an idiot of himself on a flight; will not earn you any brownie points!

2. Hijacking

A major threat to airline safety comes from hijacking; sometimes referred to as skyjacking. In hijacking a flight; terrorists will seize control of the plane and use specific demands to get what they want, in exchange for the safe release of the passengers and crew. This is a simple tactic, which usually works; because the safe return of the passengers is uppermost in the public's minds. No one wants to be responsible for their deaths, by not conceding to the demands! This is usually money, but may also be a request that the plane be flown to another destination where they will be able to escape extradition; or that their comrades be freed from certain jails around the world. However; in the deadliest cases, the terrorists will deliberately explode or crash the plane without warning. This happened on Sept. 11, 2001; when suicide terrorists simultaneously hijacked four commercial airliners in the United States. They flew two into the Twin-Towers of the World Trade Centre in New York City; and one into the Pentagon in Washington, D.C. The fourth crashed near

Pittsburgh, Pennsylvania; after the passengers had tried to wrest control from the hijackers. About 266 people were killed on the planes; whilst many more died in the buildings and on the ground.

The first known case of skyjacking happened in Peru, in 1931. It occurred for the first time in the United States in 1961; when a commercial airliner en route from Miami to Key West, Florida was forced to fly to Cuba. There were about 50 hijackings worldwide between 1958 and 1967. This figure increased four-fold between 1968 and 1970; when there were nearly 200 hijackings. In the Eighties and Nineties, this figure fell dramatically. The reduction was credited to the improved use of detection devices like X-ray machines; extensive passenger security checks; well-informed security personnel; trained dogs to sniff out explosives; severe punishment for violators; and a determination by governments not to grant sanctuary to the planes. A notorious incident of this period was the 17-day hijacking of a flight to the airport in Beirut, Lebanon in 1985 by Hezbollah, a militant group associated with the Iranian leader Ayatollah Khomeini. The use of plastic bombs that could be detonated while an airline was en route became possible in the mid-1980s. Such a bombing occurred in 1988, aboard a Pan Am 747 that exploded over Lockerbie, Scotland; killing all 259 (mostly American) persons on board and 11 on the ground. This was later attributed to the Libyans, who were made to pay compensation to the victims; whilst the perpetrators were eventually jailed. One of them, Al-Mehgrahi; was famously released early from a Scottish prison in 2009 and returned to Libya because he was dying of cancer. This caused tremendous anger in the United States; because Britain was seen as condoning the release, in order to open up lucrative business opportunities with the Libyan government. Although there may have been some truth to this accusation; he may have been released to avert a terrorist threat, which would have been likely, had Al-Mehgrahi died in prison.

Although all airline crew are trained to deal with certain dangerous situations including hijacking; the volatile nature of it makes it almost impossible to predict the outcome. This means one has to wait and see what the demands are; and hope that the hijackers do not want to die. I pray it never happens to you, but if you are ever in a plane that is hijacked; there is not much you can do, except keep quiet and do as you are told. Never cry; whisper; talk; shout; insult; look at them in the eyes; or dare them to do their worst; because they have probably taken one drug or another to give them the courage to go through with the task. They would definitely be prepared for a worse-case scenario; where they will have to blow up or kill the pilot and deliberately crash the plane. If you are allowed to use the toilet; never try to be clever by using your mobile phone, or play the heroine by attacking them. They could kill you as an example to anyone else who thinks he/she is smart! Sooner or later, they will be forced to land; and once they have relayed their demands to the authorities on the ground, you can be sure that all will be done to get the passengers out safely. One can never be certain which plane is safe, once you climb aboard; so you have to leave it to the police, secret service and airport security to protect you. This means; the more information they get from the public, the easier it will be for them to stop a hijacking before it occurs!

3. Hostage-taking

This is a type of kidnapping used by terrorists to create a big impact; in order to attract enough media attention to draw attention to their cause. With kidnapping; it is usually kept quiet because money is the main reason. With hostage-taking; the demands may be political, whereby they could seek publicity or effect a change in the policy of the government whose citizens have been taken. Like hijacking; the hostage-takers may also demand the release of some of their comrades from prison, before they will free their victims. It is high-profile people who are usually taken; and the American Embassy officials held hostage in Iran in 1979 is perhaps the most famous of this type of crime. This happened when President Carter permitted the exiled shah to come to New York City for medical treatment. This angered the Iranians under the Ayatollah Khomeini so much that a mob broke into the American Embassy in Tehran and took everyone hostage. The Iranian captors wanted the United States to send the shah back to Iran to stand trial for crimes against the state; but in response, Carter froze all Iranian assets in the United States and banned trade with Iran until the hostages were set free. The Iranians refused to change their demands; and five months passed without any progress. In frustration, Carter decided on military action; and a team of commandos was sent to fly secretly to Tehran to free the hostages in April 1980. The action was aborted when two of the rescue aircraft collided in the desert and the commandos had to be withdrawn. The last hostage was eventually released in 1981. This debacle ruined Carter's re-election prospects and he was defeated by Ronald Reagan in the November 1980.

Recently, there have been several journalists taken hostage; mainly for political reasons. Even though behind-the-scenes negotiations involving the paying of a ransom and agreeing to other lesser demands, have managed to free some of them; there have been other cases where the hostages have been gruesomely killed and the bodies dumped for the media to find. This naturally causes world-wide outrage; and gives terrorists the courage to continue with the tactic. This is because they are able to convince themselves that when any of their own people are unjustly killed; the western media does not give them the same coverage. This seemingly unfairness in favour of the western nations, is a very effective tool in recruiting would-be hostage-takers; in order to seek revenge against citizens of certain 'unpopular nations' who visit their country. Hostage-taking is a fact of life. You therefore have to take this into account, whenever you travel anywhere; because there are certain countries, usually around the Middle-East, North Africa and parts of South America, that are at loggerheads with the western nations. These are the places where it would not be safe to go; unless you stick to the rules. These would obviously include not going anywhere alone; staying in safe hotels and not saying anything that is likely to inflame the local population.

If you are not a registered journalist; you should never try to act like one by snooping around with a camera and asking questions likely to arouse suspicion. Apart from being taken hostage; you could be arrested on trumped-up charges of spying. It is imperative you find out the political situation from your ministry of foreign affairs; before going to any country. You should also ask the embassy when you go for the visa; for advice on what you should not do, where to stay and even what inoculations to take...so that you don't catch some awful disease. If you are going anywhere to film; make sure you have permission to do so and always organise your trip with a local company. This will give you the security of knowing that you have people in the country that will care if you ever go missing. They will also be able to protect you; by providing officials to go around with...so that you don't get problems with the locals. Not everyone likes to be filmed or interrogated; and if they cannot speak your language, violence might be used to show their displeasure! Those who are taken hostage are the ones who do not stick to the rules; wandering off alone, staying in places where there is not enough security and do not tell anyone where they are going.

Finally; there has been a recent rise in piracy around the Indian Ocean. This is where pirates board a cargo ship along certain routes and seize hold of the crew and cargo. They will then look for a ransom from the owner of the ship; which is usually paid because the value of the cargo is always much more than the money requested. This mode of terrorism happens when the rule of law has broken down in certain coastal war-torn countries like Somalia, Ethiopia and Eritrea; where banditry is prevalent. This is a very convenient area around the horn of Africa; because the ships have to pass by to get to the Suez Canal, which was built to save ships time when they sailed through the Mediterranean on their way to Asia. Because the pirates know it would be too costly for the ship to take an alternate route all the way around South Africa; seizing a cargo ship and demanding a ransom has become a very easy way of making money. The armed pirates move around in fast motorboats and then board the cargo ship when it is dark. They are then able to take the crew hostage without any fear or feelings of guilt; because they believe the ships should pay their poverty stricken areas some sort of tax for using their sea for business. Although they have on several occasions been foiled by navy ships and killed; their success rate is so much greater that this type of terrorism is likely to continue being a lucrative source of income for some time to come. On occasions; the pirates have been known to seize private boats and kidnap the occupants. They will then demand ransom money from their families. This is an effective tactic; because their plight will be highlighted in the media and this puts the government of the victims in a quandary. If the politicians don't try to negotiate their release; they will be seen as uncaring and become unpopular. If the victims are killed; it could lose them the next elections! If they pay the ransom for their release; they will be opening the gate for more pirates to attack ships belonging to their country. Although most governments say they will never negotiate with the pirates; it often happens that a ransom is quietly paid and the victims are released!

If you own a cargo ship; you will have to take the threat of piracy seriously enough to beef up your security. This will most likely involve posting armed guards to travel with the ship and making sure your radar equipment is accurate enough to spot the speed boats a long way off in the dark. This will enable the crew to frighten or fight them off as they approach your ship. Being in the middle of an ocean; it will always take too long to radio for help to arrive. Other tactics include; pouring oil or hot water on the pirates as they try to board the ship. In the name of self-defence, they may have to shoot first and answer questions later; because if they don't kill the pirates, they will board your ship, terrorise and kill your crew. Although the cost of arming and insuring your ship might be prohibitive; it will probably be only a fraction of the value of the cargo. The only other alternative would be to look for a different route; which may not always be feasible or profitable for your company. If you enjoy sailing; you will have to accept that there are certain areas in the world where you should not sail and do your best to keep away from them. It would be wise to visit the ministry of foreign affairs in your country and they will give you a more accurate picture of the no-go areas in the world.

4. Suicide-bombing

This form of terrorist activity is potentially the most dangerous because the perpetrator knows he (or she) is going to die anyway; and is therefore prepared to take as many people as possible to the pearly gates. The suicide-bomber will strap explosives around his/her body or inside a bag he/she may be carrying. He/She then walks unassumingly into a crowd of people, either in the open air or in a building; and detonates the bomb. The idea is to cause as much damage as possible; in order to create major media impact. Once it hits the world-wide news, then his/her aims will have been achieved; because the agenda of whichever group was responsible, would be highlighted. The suicide-bomber has no qualms about who dies in the explosion; which means innocent people will definitely be blown up, and the more the merrier! There are many young men who are ready to become suicide-bombers; because they believe they are donating their lives to a greater cause and will receive their reward in the after-life. There are also women who have lost loved ones, directly or indirectly through the bombings and occupation of America and her allies in the Middle-East; and are looking for revenge. Because their lives have been decimated; these women are ready and willing to die, believing that they are going to join their loved ones in paradise. They would most likely have been paid in advance; so that they are content their children will be looked after when they are gone. They will make peace with everyone they have had disagreements with, say goodbye to their family and friends; and will then go and stay in a safe-house. On the day of the bombing; they would probably be given certain drugs to get them in the right mood so that they do not think of changing their minds at the last minute. The fact that there are people ready to blast themselves to pieces; means suicide-bombing, although selfish and dangerous, is actually a very brave thing to do. Every nation should rightly be concerned; because there are some who are angry enough to go through with it!

The areas with the most prolific suicide-bombings are Iraq, Pakistan and Afghanistan; where initially, foreign soldiers were targeted. When that modus-operandi became too difficult, softer targets like market-places were blown up; because there are usually a lot of people milling around. Although most of the suicide-bombing has been as a direct result of the pro-Israeli policy of the western powers and their apparent lack of support for the Palestinian cause; more Arabs have actually died in the explosions than Israelis, Americans or Europeans. The death of any westerner is always highlighted in the world media; whereas the Arab casualties are usually demoted to footnotes in the news. As a result; the intensity of suicide-bombings is ever-increasing and more people are dying with each blast. The bigger the casualties; the more likely it will make the world-wide news! The 2005 bus and underground suicide-bombings in London received more publicity than all the other suicide-bombings in the Middle-East; and even though relatively few people died, (52 killed and

700 injured) the global impact was huge. That such a devastating attack was able to take place in a major European city; shook the British to the core. They realised that terrorism was not just an American problem; but could happen to any country. The fact that the bombers were British-born made it all the more poignant and dangerous; because it meant the enemy had made serious inroads inside a relatively secure country.

It is for this reason that some governments have introduced anti-terrorism laws; in order to fight the unseen enemy. The human rights activists have declared these laws to be an invasion of privacy; because they involve monitoring our movements and snooping into our lives by eavesdropping on our phone calls and reading our Emails. Although some security experts believe this will help; it can also be seen as an excuse to turn a country into a 'Big Brother' surveillance society, where there will be no freedom and the powers could easily be abused. There is no law that will be able to stop the suicide-bomber; because once he or she decides to go through with the suicide, there is not much anyone can do about it. Even without strapping a bomb to the body or carrying one in a rucksack; someone could easily go on a shooting spree, kill as many people as possible and then turn the gun on him/herself. This has occurred quite a few times in several countries, over the years. It is therefore in the best interests of any government to value the lives of the people in their country. This means, if necessary, a softening or even a complete U-turn change in its foreign policy; in order to limit the threat of a terrorist attack. Although there will always be a few who will want to cause trouble; it would be much harder for them to garner finance and support, if the major causes of terrorism are removed. Until the day arrives when we can all breathe a little easier; every population must do their bit to help the security agencies in their country to snuff out an attack before it occurs. We all have to learn to keep our eyes, ears and feelings open! Any anomaly in someone's behaviour, which appears suspicious or dangerous, should immediately be reported; because each report will be treated seriously, with confidentiality. The security agencies have their backs against the wall and cannot do it alone. The honest truth is; they really do need all the help they can get!

5. Explosions

The planting of bombs in a location in order to cause an explosion; has caused untold misery and killed many innocent people over the years. This mode of attack was made popular in the Seventies; when the IRA used it against British targets in its attempts to end British rule in Northern Ireland and to unite her with the Republic of Ireland into one independent Irish nation. Their idea was to blow up prominent buildings; in order to frighten the British Government into taking them seriously. They would sometimes telephone the police in advance; in order for them to clear the area before the bomb went off. On other occasions, there would be no bomb; but a hoax call would be made just to create panic and fear amongst the populace. Although other terrorist groups around the world have since replicated this tactic; it has recently been more the handiwork of the Al-Qaeda movement, which has recruited thousands of members around the world. This means that explosions could occur anywhere at any time! Among the explosions attributed to the group are the bombing of the World Trade Centre in New York in 1993; the detonation of truck bombs against U.S. targets in Saudi Arabia in 1996; the killing of tourists in Egypt in 1997; the simultaneous bombing of American embassies in Nairobi, Kenya, and Dar-Es-Salaam, Tanzania; and the suicide-bombing of the U.S. warship Cole in Aden, Yemen, in 2000.

Explosions are different from suicide-bombings, in that the perpetrators do not need to get hurt and are unlikely to be caught in the immediate aftermath; because the bomb could easily be detonated from afar. It could also be the handiwork of renegades, soldiers of fortune or men with military expertise; who are disgruntled with their unappreciated existence and have decided to sell their knowledge to a terrorist network. In order to blow up a building or a vehicle; the bomb has to secretly be put into place. This would involve keeping a watch on the area for months in advance; in order to find the right time to plant the bomb, without being detected. It will in all probability mean that it cannot be done alone; and several people will have to be involved in the financing; planning; purchasing of materials to build the bomb; and execution of the operation. It would therefore be almost impossible to stop a bomb going off; if the authorities do not know where it is located and have not been told when it is going off. This naturally puts at risk; any country whose governments have been lambasted by terrorist groups. Russia, Sri Lanka and Spain (to name only a few) have been recent victims of bombing campaigns by separatist groups; as have most countries in the Middle-East. These populations somehow learn to live with the fear that when they leave their houses in the morning to go to work; they may not return home in one piece!

The job of detecting where there might be a bomb is extremely difficult for the police, security and intelligence agencies; and that is why in some countries, martial law with a curfew is imposed on the population. This supposedly makes it harder for undesirables to move around at night; but it does little to restrict their movements during the working hours, when they are still able to do what they like, by mingling with the population. In Britain; there have been calls for everyone to carry an identity card and to make it much harder for foreigners to enter the country. The problem remains that not all terrorists are foreigners; and anyone with a little expertise can make a home-made bomb, which could kill several people. If a single person is killed from a bomb; then questions will be asked of the security agencies about why they did not catch the bombers, before they could act. They are in a real dilemma! Like other forms of terrorism; the only way for the security agencies to catch the culprits is to have prior information and stop them before they can act!

6. High-profile Murders

This is when terrorists assassinate politicians or businessmen they either dislike for their lifestyle, their policies or for some statements they have made; which the terrorists feel are hindering their cause and putting them in a bad light in the public's consciousness. By killing them and taking the credit for it; the terrorists can then highlight their cause and the powers-that-be might start taking them seriously. The businessman Hans-Martin Schlyer, who was kidnapped and killed in Germany by the Baader-Meinhof Gang in the Seventies; and Aldo Moro, the politician described earlier in this chapter; are both examples of terrorist high-profile murders. Even though most rich businessmen and politicians are aware of the threat from the kidnapping of their families and attempts on their lives; it would be almost impossible to stop an organised assassination by terrorists. This is because these things are well-planned and involve watching the movements of their target for months beforehand, in order to study his/her movements. Once they have got that in place; the next step is to hire someone who is prepared to die, to do the killing. They do this by paying him in advance; so that he knows his family will be well-looked after, if he is killed or has to go to prison. The killer will then make sure he does the job properly; because he has no personal worries. He will have been indoctrinated into believing that what he is about to do, is for a just and greater cause. He will also be aware that; having already been paid, if he 'chickens out' and refuses to do it or goes to the police then he will be found and killed anyway...that is, if they don't harm his family first!

The only way this kind of murder can be stopped; is for the police or secret services to have prior-information, so that the suspects can be arrested before they act. This obviously involves someone breaking ranks; either by not being paid enough to keep quiet or by having a pang of conscience. All police and secret service agencies have a network of informants working for them; and that is how so many would-be high-profile murders are nipped in the bud. Unfortunately; it involves a lot of painstaking fact-finding and detective work, to keep in tune with terrorist activities. It is therefore up to the public to open their eyes and report anything they hear, witness or feel; however trivial, to the authorities. I have to reiterate the importance of women in this; because if a husband, brother, father or boyfriend is involved in a high-profile murder, the women in the lives of the organisers will surely have a clue what is going on. Even the best businessmen and politicians have enemies and could be assassinated; but would you like to be the partner or wife of the man who is involved in an assassination that rocks a nation to its foundations? I leave that question for you and your conscience to answer.

7. Spying and Sabotage

A person will attempt to betray his country; if he feels his country has in any way betrayed him. He could do this by spying on his country and sending the information to another country; in return for money or future asylum. Once you are working in a job and are privy to sensitive information; you are obliged to adhere to the official secrets act of your country. If you are caught betraying the faith and trust, you will be charged with treason and jailed; or in some cases, executed. What most of us see or hear as terrorism is the violence; because that is usually the end-result, where the damage is caused. What few of us realise is; no terrorist activity can take place, without planning and detailed information. In order to blow up a building, for example; one has to know exactly when it would be best to do so; how the building was constructed; how strong it is; how many people would most likely be there at a particular time; and the damage it would do to the prestige, fear and sensitivities of a government etc. With all this information; the terrorists would be able to devise the right strategy to cause their intended level of destruction. This knowledge is normally provided by someone who is ready to betray his/her country for a reward; or as a means of revenge against the ruling government. This person is technically a spy; and if caught, can be prosecuted for treason. If the terrorists want to assassinate a certain public figure; his/her movements and whereabouts at a particular time will have to be known to the assassins. This means he/she will have to be betrayed by a close associate or friend; who will pass on vital information to their contact. This betrayer is also a spy; and is guilty of treason. Without the betrayal; the high-profile murder would take much longer to succeed...or may not even be possible! Since the ringleaders of a terrorist attack are rarely caught; the instruction given by a spy is invaluable and necessary. The attack can then be planned in such a way that the assassins will have an easier job; without being able to divulge any useful information, if they are arrested.

Every government has specific agencies to tackle spying; and rely on information provided by a network of informants who infiltrate every fabric and facet of its society. It is such a delicate and dangerous job; that all kinds of tricks, like double agents and disinformation are used to confuse the enemy into revealing its hand. In the past; this has been very useful in keeping a country safe and arresting those trying to overthrow a government. Terrorism has now made their job a lot harder because a planned attack can take years to put into place; and could involve ordinary people who are outside the radar of a government agency. It is very difficult for any agency to keep tabs on all of its people; without prior knowledge of their intentions. As a result; sabotage is increasingly being used by terrorists. There is no need to overthrow a government; when the country can be brought to its knees by sabotaging certain sensitive locations! Blowing up railway lines; exploding bombs in cars parked near schools, stadiums, police stations or army barracks; poisoning food and putting it on supermarket shelves; spreading dangerous bacteria through the water supplies etc; are all tools used by terrorists to create panic and fear in the population. Throw in a few vicious rumours of impending doom and gloom; and this will enable the people themselves to get fed up and vote out the 'offending' government. It could also distract the security agencies into over-reacting with the gradual or sudden erosion of civil liberties. This will in turn, make the ruling government unpopular enough to make enemies; who will be only too happy to aid, abet and organise more terrorist activities!

8. Illegal Strikes, Riots, Looting and Rape

Terrorism may be classed as; any act that is perpetuated, in order to hurt a country for any reason. This will obviously include illegal strikes, rioting, looting and rape. By organising a strike; law and order is undermined and sometimes breaks down completely. More importantly; it gives the enemies of a country a chance to infiltrate the workforce and spread mayhem, designed to eventually bring down a government. Terrorists are becoming more sophisticated in their planning and have realised that blowing up anything is counter-productive; because public sympathy is more likely to go against them. They are now using the Internet; rumour; disinformation; and fear of an uncertain financial future; to cause impatient agitation in the populace. For example; if a big public company hears that some of the workforce are going to be made redundant or that their wages are going to be reduced, it would not be difficult to push the unions into going on an illegal strike. As soon as the government caves in to their demands; the terrorists will realise that striking can cause mayhem. If it doesn't cave in; it will be accused of high-handedness and abuse of power. From then on; it is a simple matter of infiltrating other workforces and instigating more strikes to inconvenience the population. Once the majority of the people are annoyed; it will be only a matter of time before the government is voted out of office!

A riot is another act of violence; which can be instigated by terrorists, using the local people. The accidental killing of a local citizen by the police; the mistreatment of someone because of sex, race, religion or proclivity; and the passing of an unjust law, which hurts the majority; can all be perceived as an injustice. This is enough for a clever instigator working for a terrorist organisation, to organise a riot; which if not stopped, could lead to the injury and death of innocent people. Once the police are called; their tactics in containing the riot will be used by the protagonists as examples of police brutality. This accusation will be enough to anger the rioters to move up another level into looting and wilful destruction of property. From then on; it is like a domino effect, whereby a riot could spread from one town to another and more police will have to be brought in to contain it. Once the scenes are captured by the media; the images will be flashed around the world within seconds. This then becomes a propaganda coup for the terrorist group; because they will be able to recruit more people inside the country to continue their fight against the government. The images can also be conveniently edited and shown on the television of any nation that wants to convince its own populace that the grass is not always greener in the developed countries.

Rape of innocent women is normally used by terrorist organisations in Third World nations fighting a battle inside their country; in a bid to topple the government. By raping the women; it strikes fear into the local people, who will then be forced to support the terrorist group. This normally happens when rule of law has completely broken down and the government is not strong or popular enough to police the whole country. Although rape gives a bad name to the terrorists; it also ruins the government's reputation because it will be seen as unable to control the country. Sooner or later; there will be a coup d'état by members of the armed forces, in a bid to restore law and order. This obviously leads to more killings, sabotage, pillaging and rape on both sides; because the military are notorious for their violent tactics in attempting to instil order. Eventually; world opinion against the mistreatment of women will be so loud that the government will be forced to enter into negotiations with the terrorists. The mistreatment of women as a tool of war has been going on for centuries. What is happening now in some the Third World countries; is something that used to happen in the developed world! It is horrible; and the world should be concerned. We all know it is going on; yet not much is being done about it. It is however; a clear example of how far terrorists are prepared to go, in order to achieve their aims.

As you can imagine; skyjacking; hostage taking; suicide-bombs; explosions; high-profile murders; spying and sabotage; illegal strikes, riots, looting and rape; are all terrible crimes, which take careful planning and time to organise. This means there will be people who will either suspect or know what is going to happen and yet do nothing about it; either through fear, loyalty or acquiescence. I will have failed with the purpose of this book; if I do not beg you not to get involved in any terrorist activities. If you know anyone involved or about to get involved in it; you should please do the decent thing and report them to the authorities. The future safety of the human race really is at stake; and cannot be allowed to be destroyed by those whose ideologies and strong beliefs overcome their consciences and their value for human life. Blaming the Muslims for all terrorist activities is too simplistic and grossly unfair, because the causes run much deeper; as I have tried to explain in this chapter. It is therefore the responsibility of everyone not to elect governments; who stubbornly insist on policies that anger the majority and inflame the sensibilities of the minorities. Those who are marginalised and ignored are the ones who have no other way of having their voices heard; and will most likely resort to terrorism!

What can we do?

I apologise for what seems like a digression from the theme of this book, with this chapter on terrorism; but since your country is also part of your self-defence, I feel it is important that you are aware of everything that could harm you or your children. If for example, you have a little knowledge of recent history; you will know why it is not useful for you to arrive in France and start speaking English, expecting them to do the same. This is because there will be those who will be offended enough; not to offer assistance, when you most need it. You will also know why you should not to go to China and disparage them for their Tibetan policy; or arrive in Israel spouting the Palestinian cause! You will nod your head and understand why Iran and the United States have not been friendly since 1979; and why there is no American Embassy in Iran. You will even smile at the posturing anti-British antics used by Mugabe in Zimbabwe; because you will understand why he is behaving like that and why the British government is so against him. Freedom is a privilege; which we tend to take for granted and assume everyone else is the same. That attitude is insensitive; and may be deemed arrogant by those less fortunate than ourselves! If you are British or French and go to a poor Third World country wearing an expensive Rolex watch, looking like you have more money than sense; then do not be surprised if you are robbed, injured, kidnapped or killed. That country may have been a former colony; and still feels the wounds from when the parent country took advantage of much of her wealth. For the same reason; the Slave Trade is still a sore point amongst many black people. There are some who believe Britain and America have not officially apologised wholeheartedly; or compensated enough for the disgrace. Even the tone of voice used by a White person on a Black person; could be regarded as a racial insult and may put your safety at risk in certain countries. You should therefore try to read a little or ask the embassy about a country's history and culture before you visit it; and always remember that the world is a much smaller place than it used to be. There may be people of different origin, race, religion, culture and financial circumstances living in your midst; so even an off-the-cuff remark could upset someone enough to harm you irreparably. This is the main reason why terrorist activities are sometimes used by citizens on their own country; simply because their loyalties are more for their origin, beliefs or religion than they are for their country of residence. If they do not like the way their government conducts its policies; then they might feel the best way to highlight their hate is to destroy something where innocent people are likely to get hurt.

Since terrorism is a fact of life, which will not go completely away unless there is a drastic shift in the policies of many countries; you have to assume that it could happen and do your best to help protect your country. I presume it is where you live and would like your children to grow up peacefully and safely in! It is therefore imperative to report anything you see, hear or suspect, however trivial, to the police and let them handle it; because they will know what to do. Even an anonymous tip via a phone call; could be the difference between saving many lives, or not. It is always better to be wrong than have a death on your conscience! Believe it or not; the police tend to take women very seriously when they report a crime. This is because they are less likely to exaggerate or keep quiet; whereas men are more aware and fearful of possible reprisals and would more likely mind their own business or even deny they saw anything. You would be surprised about how people can give things away; even with what is considered normal every-day behaviour. 'Casing a joint' is the most common suspect behaviour; so if you see someone acting suspiciously around a building or a car, you should pretend you have not seen him and ring the police from a safe distance away. If you are on a bus or at a train station and you see a package or suitcase unattended, you should not touch it; but you have to tell an official in uniform and he or she will take the problem on from there. It might not be a bomb; but it could be drugs, guns or even proceeds from a crime that someone forgot or left deliberately for a criminal accomplice to pick up. If you touch it; you could be endangering your life or charged by the police with being involved with whatever the package contains. If you see a crime anywhere; there is no need to confront the suspect and put your life in danger. By alerting the first police officer you see; you will have done more than enough to possibly averting a tragedy. Many nations have had their fair share of terrorist activities; which could have been avoided, had someone who knew about or suspected it could happen, done the decent thing and alerted the authorities.

As a woman; you may not realise your importance in the greater scheme of your country's safety. I will tell you now that women hold the key to solving almost every crime or terrorist activity. Since most criminal endeavours are performed by men; they will obviously have women in their lives that are in position to influence their thinking and have enough evidence to report them to the authorities, if they are involved in activities that could harm the country. For every highjack, hostage-taker, assassin, suicide-bomber, serious or petty criminal; there is a wife, girlfriend, mother or sister who knows what he is getting up to. She is therefore in the unique position to dissuade or stop him in his tracks; before he can harm others! How would you feel; making love to a man who has just blown up a building or vehicle and killed hundreds of innocent bystanders? Could you live with that on your conscience? In every relationship; the woman has her own subtle ways and means of getting her man to do certain things. A man always knows when his better-half is unhappy; by the way she behaves towards him! It would therefore be very difficult for a man to pursue terrorist activity; if the woman in his life is vehemently against it. Yes, the sex will be different; because spiritually, the two souls will not be able to unite in sexual harmony! It will hit his conscience hard, when he looks at his wife and children in the eye and sees what he could lose because of his ideological intransigence; which is leading him to perform atrocities that will harm innocent people. He will then have to make a choice between his family and his ideology. If he chooses the latter; then it is as good as saying the relationship is over. The best thing to do would be to leave him and report him to the authorities! If you are the type of woman who believes in and is involved in terrorist activity; then there is nothing I can say to you that will change your mind. If like most women, you want a peaceful, safe environment for yourself, your children and future generations; then you have to place the safety of your country, even higher in your list of priorities, than the man you love. This means you may have to make the most difficult decision in your life and report your man to the authorities; if after trying to dissuade him not to go ahead with whatever atrocity he is about to undertake, you realise his obsession is more important than the love he has for his family. The police can keep your anonymity; so that he will never know it was you who gave him away. It is a tough call; but you have to remember that by reporting him, you could be preventing a tragedy and saving many lives.

Although it may sound unpalatable; but you have to take a healthy interest in what your man gets up to. The late nights and shifty behaviour may not mean he has a lover. He could be involved in something much more sinister! If you confront him and he refuses to talk; then you have to take matters into your own hands and do some investigating of your own. Never think your man's affairs are none of your business; and bury your head in the sand. If he is ever caught; you will find it hard to say you knew nothing about it. You could even be charged with aiding and abetting terrorist activity; whereby your house will be flooded with police, looking for evidence. Needless to say; the life as you know it, will be in ruins and your children will be targeted and teased in school. Imagine what the nosy neighbours gleefully looking on, would say! With salacious gossip; one can never tell the difference between innocence and guilt! Keep your eyes and ears open when his friends come and visit; especially the ones your instinct has told you are a bad influence on his behaviour. You know your man and how he behaves; so if this changes in an odd way when his friends are around, then it means he has something to hide. You should do your best to find out what they are up to! Talk to him and find out where his head is at; and if he goes out a lot, you should insist on going with him. If he refuses or tries to fob you off; you will definitely know something is up. If you are financially solvent; you could hire a private detective to study him. If not; you can use a friend of yours whom he does not know very well, to follow him one evening and find out where he goes. You will then be in a better position to know what to do. The rest will be up to you and your conscience; but I can tell you that the best thing one can do for one's country, is to help keep it safe from its enemies within.

Whew Tigress! Sorry for being so blunt; but terrorism really is a horrible crime on the human race and we all have to do our bit to make sure our countries do not suffer from it.

Chapter Eighteen
The real self-defence is common sense

1. What does this book mean for women?

The Real Self-defence *'for women only'* is all about the prevention rather than the cure; which is only possible, if you are aware of what needs to be prevented. The idea is that the defender (woman) is usually the wronged party, fighting for her rights in a male-dominated world. It is therefore necessary for me to portray the male as the 'baddie'; so that you learn to take decisions for yourself and not depend on what any man tells you. Finally; it is also to remove the prevailing beliefs that all attacks done to a woman are physical. Obviously, not all men are bad; but I have the firm belief that every female has the intuition to decide which advice reflects her situation and react accordingly. What this book does; is tell you what can go wrong with men and will hopefully make you mentally tough enough not to take 'any shit' from anybody...man or woman. Although the title *'for women only'* may seem a little sexist at first glance; it is a necessary evil because too many women are experiencing unfair discrimination and attacks, solely because of their sex. It is important that women have something for themselves that will make them aware of how dangerous anyone can be; if she lets her guard down. A lot of the advice given in this book can also apply to men; but women are more receptive to the idea of self-protection and are more likely take on board anything that will keep her and her family safe. On the other hand; men seem to have the attitude *"I don't need anyone. I can take care of myself!"* If a man will not listen to me; he might listen to his better half! After having read this book; I hope you can now appreciate that there are much worse ways to hurt a female than simply hitting her and that she has to constantly be on her guard against being taken advantage of. I have done my best to cover as many aspects as possible that a woman needs to defend herself; and even if I have missed a few topics, this book will put you in the right frame of mind to do what is right for you and hopefully allow you to instil it into the minds of your family!

This book highlights certain basic rules in life; which if you do not follow, will always end you up on the losing end. You will have to use your common sense and imagination to adapt what I teach to suit yourself; so that you are never in a position whereby you will be attacked, used and abused. Most women are attacked because they either leave their guard open or are unaware of the potential dangers; and this allows the attacker to succeed. A man attacking a woman goes against a fundamental rule laid down by nature; which says that because a woman is a potential child-bearer, she is vital to the survival of the human race and therefore needs to be protected, respected and cherished. This rule is frequently abused because the modern woman is now much more than a child-bearer; and has become every much as competitive as the modern man. It is this conflict between the sexes that is the main cause of women not being treated with the respect they deserve. Simply put; men feel threatened because women are now seen more as competitors to male hegemony, than as carers and nurturers. For that reason; a man will have no qualms about hurting a woman to get what he wants. It is therefore important that as a woman, you are aware of this threat and be on your guard. It also means that you should not deliberately antagonise people; because anyone is capable of attacking a woman, even though it is wrong to do so! 'Wrong' here is a deceptive word because if for example, you owe money and you are attacked; you cannot claim to be the wronged party. Even if you win the legal battle for the attack; the debt still remains and your attackers will be back for it! If you insult or hurt someone; you have to be prepared for revenge because very few people are attacked for doing absolutely nothing. The lunatics; who run around the streets jumping on innocent people are few, far between and easily dealt with by the police. What the police cannot prevent; is the cause of an attack. If you steal someone's money and you are attacked by a gang of thugs; there is not much the police can do, except arrest the suspects. You on the other hand, could be in hospital fighting for your life; and even if your attackers are jailed, your injuries will not heal any quicker! So although you are a woman; you have to recognise that sometimes you can be in the wrong and do your best to correct it. If you quarrel with a friend; go over and apologise if you can, because life is too short to keep looking over your shoulder. Trying to recognise a potential physical or emotional attack long before it happens, is the key to a peaceful life; and hopefully, this book will help you to think twice before you do anything.

Most men mistakenly believe that any self-defence tactic by a woman; will not work on them. This has to be good for women; because the element of surprise is firmly on her side. So long as men have this 'weaker sex' perception; the advantage will always be with her. Women can be very vicious when they have no other choice; and it would do men good to observe this fact. There are a lot of things a female can get away with, in the name of self-defence; which a male could not. Biding her time and taking a man 'to the cleaners'; is just one easy way a woman can get her own back in a messy divorce. A petrified scream in the middle of town will bring all kinds of people to her aid. A man will find it very hard to escape an embarrassing accusation by a woman; because most people will believe her, unless proven otherwise. In public; it would be difficult for a man to get out of a loud accusation like, *"Get your filthy hands off me! You touched my bum, you pervert!"* or *"Leave me alone. Stop following me or I'll call the police!"* Well-timed tears of distress can get you all the sympathy you need; and whoever is troubling you, will have to find a very big hole to fall into! We all love to criticise the police; but women should be thankful to them because they do not take kindly to attacks by cowardly men on women. Run into any police station, if you have a problem; and the greater your distress, the quicker the response by the cops! It is still good to be female; if you know how! I am sure most of you have an instinctive arsenal of tactics you readily employ to steer you through the minefield of a day. This book not only emphasises that fact; but also shows a few more ways to help you stay safe.

Try not to abuse this 'privilege' by making false claims; or the pendulum will swing and the men will fight back. Use it wisely to your advantage! If things were to change dramatically; you could find some lechcrous pest who has been annoying you all evening, suing you for 'emotional and physical distress', after you slapped him. How would you like to be accused of raping a man because you dragged him off to bed; when he preferred to be having a drink with his mates? Right now; he would be laughed out of the police station. Were the law to be changed where equality was interpreted to the letter; it would not be so funny for the fairer sex! I can see the men queuing up at the police station. *"Officer, I would like to report an intrusion by Ms. Beautiful on my privates. She had no right to touch my penis without my permission. I then became aroused and she seduced me. Now I am so much in love with her that I cannot stop thinking about her; and it has affected my work. I have just been fired! I am going to sue her for compensation!"* Impossible? Don't bet on it!

2. Goju Real Self-defence is the modern way to go!

As you may have already gathered after reading this book; the real self-defence is not about fighting, but using your head to get yourself out of nasty situations. It is highly unladylike to fight on the street and be branded a thug; so you have to learn to win the war, without fighting. One can never really win a fight because: if you beat up someone and in the process, cut your hand, ruin your favourite dress and finish up in the police station, court and prison; that is not much of a victory, is it? Are you fully-insured against injury? Who will pay your medical bills? What if the person you beat up, sues you? What if he or she has family who will seek revenge for beating up their 'favourite' sister, brother or cousin? Are you prepared to look over your shoulder for the rest of your life? Have you got the guts to answer your doorbell after beating up someone? So for all you women who think you are tough and can beat up any female and some males who cross you; remember, it is not so easy to win a fight! Although you have to be reasonably fit to do most sports; self-defence has so many variables, you should never think you are useless if you are not tough or fit enough. It is all about feeling confident within yourself to take on any situation in a calm or if need be, not so calm manner. The girls who can turn a life-threatening situation to their advantage are the ones who will rarely face any trouble. Mental strength and determination are much more important than physical attributes in a fight; and this means you have to be even more determined to get away from your adversary, than he is in beating you up. There are no rules to street fighting; and there are no rules to self-defence. Anything you feel will work in getting you out of a nasty situation, is allowed in the real self-defence; but it is also common sense, which means you have to use your head. There is no point in harming someone, if you don't have to; or if you will not get away with it in court. Never ever be afraid to go to the police for protection, if you feel threatened; so that you have a head start on anyone you think may harm you.

You need common sense and resoluteness to be able to be good at the real self-defence. You have to convince yourself that you can and you will get out of whatever some idiot tries on you; leaving nothing to chance. If for instance, you see a madman coming menacingly towards you and you know you cannot deal with him; then you have to run away as fast as you can, screaming to safety. If you are at a party and do not feel safe because drugs are being openly consumed; you should make your excuses and leave. If you join in just to be 'cool', get high and participate in an orgy; there is no point feeling sorry for yourself the next morning, complaining to people that you were taken advantage of. If someone offers you a lift and you know he is drunk, then why go with him; even if he is your friend? Being your friend would only make it harder to tell him, *"No! I don't want sex with you!"*; were you to get caught up in an embarrassing situation at his house. This would only infuriate him because of his close acquaintance with you; and being drunk, he would not care or even 'remember' what he did to you. If you stop a taxi and don't like the look of the driver; you should trust your instincts and take another one. If in a club, someone starts bothering you near closing time; why not make an excuse, pretend to go to the toilet and disappear? These are just simple examples of how you can defend yourself; without knowing how to fight. There are many more ways of course. I have however, sown the seeds; so the rest is up to you, depending on who you are and where you live. The love of yourself should be uppermost in your thinking and always have faith in your instincts. If something feels wrong or dangerous, then it most probably is; and should be avoided. If you are badly injured or lose your life; where would you get another one?

Few women will enjoy doing push-ups on their knuckles or kicking a punching bag. Try to poke a man in his eyes and miss; and you are in serious trouble. You might as well be fighting two men; because he will be so angry he could kill you for trying to blind him! What if your attacker also knows a few martial arts techniques? Could you fight a Black Belt who is out to get you by any means? Nowadays, everybody knows a trick or two. The skinny looking guy snatching your bag; could also hurt you very badly, before going off with your possessions...if you try to resist and fight him. Why take the chance? Isn't it better to avoid such horrible incidents? Unfortunately; it is the female who is in most need of protecting herself, because the male will always hunt for the female. This is the main reason why she has to be able to defend herself in any way she knows how; ways which are never taught in fighting clubs. If a man realises you are learning the martial arts; he will use different tactics, which you may not have been taught how to defend yourself against. It takes many years for someone to become aware of all the possibilities of an attack; and even then, new ones are always being invented. This means a tactic taught in training, may not work; and that is why this book has not shown any.

As far as the real self-defence is concerned; you have to take full-responsibility for your own protection and not expect anyone to do it for you. Ultimately, you live or die by what you do; so you have to play by your own rules, in order to ensure your safety and longevity in life. Self-belief is what you need to make sure you do not fall into the trap of believing the fiction, which says that men are stronger than women; therefore, a woman has no chance against an attack by a man. It is your life that you are protecting; so you have to plan your own strategy. A man will scorn at a woman doing self-defence; but if he knew she was the one making the rules in her self-defence, his tune would quickly change! Because everyone is different and no one is invincible; my only aim is for you to avoid trouble and prevent it from starting. This book is a guideline and an eye-opener; but you still have to assess whether it will work for you and take bits and pieces of everything I teach, in order to mould a self-defence strategy applicable to you. Two women will read this book and each will come out with different ideas, ways and means on how to defend herself; hence, the title of this chapter. This first-of-its-kind book has hopefully opened your eyes to many things; some of which you probably already knew but perhaps never realised their importance or effectiveness.

3. The top 50...

Here are fifty self-defence tips to help keep you out of trouble and danger.

1. *You are living alone and you don't feel safe.*

(Make sure your doors (especially your back door) and windows are always locked. Keep in regular contact with family and friends. Don't invite anyone into the house; unless he or she is a close friend. Keep at least one light on in the house; even when you are asleep. If self-defence to you means having a gun at home, then keep one if you have a licence for it and you feel it will make you more confident; especially if you live in the middle of nowhere. Just remember that if you point a gun at someone, you will be breaking the law and could still be prosecuted; even if you don't fire it.)

2. **Keep your eyes open.** *"Those kids standing on the street corner; why are they always there when I come out of the bank (shop)?"...*

(Change your routine! Arriving at different times will confuse them, if they are watching your movements. You may occasionally receive a few insulting comments or tough guy looks as you walk past them; but don't fall for it and always ignore them whilst going about your business. Many towns have nowhere for teenagers to play after school; so more than likely, they are just bored and looking for some excitement.)

3. *"I don't like the look of that man standing in my way"...*

(Smile politely and keep out of his way, or better still; cross the road to avoid him! If you have no choice but to go past him; always be polite. Smile; say *"please"* to ask him to move and *"thank you"* when he has done so. He could be looking for an argument; which will give his friends hiding nearby the chance to attack and rob you.)

4. *"Why is that guy getting beaten up by that gang? Shall I go and help him?"...*

(Sadly, this is not a good idea! Call the police and start yelling at them from a reasonable distance to leave him alone. Try to remember what they looked like, when the police arrive. If you have a camera phone, discretely take a picture of the assailants; in order to help the police apprehend them later.)

5. **You are in a nightclub and a man you fancy gives you the 'come-on' look.**

(Be careful! Give him a few minutes to make sure he is not with anyone, before moving in. The girlfriend may have gone to the toilet and he could be trying to make her jealous. If she is the jealous type; she will verbally or physically attack you! You might tear your dress, ruin your hair, break your watch and get thrown out of the club; trying to defend yourself. Is any handsome stud really worth fighting over?)

6. **You are in bed with a man and just when he reaches the point of no return, you change your mind and ask him to stop; but he tries to continue.**

(Lie on your front, cross your legs tightly and tell him you are not feeling well. Start coughing, allow saliva to drip out of your mouth and pretend you want to vomit. If he still won't stop; stick your fingers down your throat to induce a vomit or pee all over yourself. That should cool him down! This situation could easily happen to any woman and become a rape scenario; so please pay attention to Chapter 4.)

7. You are driving along a lonely highway; and a beautiful girl appears on the side and flags you down for a lift.

(Male or female; I would advise you to keep driving and not to pick anyone up. It could be a ploy; with the friends hiding in the bushes to rob your car. If however, she appears dishevelled and in distress; you should ring the police and give them directions for them to pick her up. It sounds a bit cold-hearted; but the world has changed. Even if you picked her up; she could still attack you and rob you off your money. If it is a man; he could easily threaten and then rape you. You were obviously on your way somewhere before she appeared. Stick to your original plan. It makes life so much easier!)

8. You are driving along a road and you see a nasty accident.

(In some countries; you are obliged by law to help. Do what you can to comfort the victims, if you have knowledge of first aid; but only after you have called the ambulance and the police. Make sure it really is a nasty accident; and not a set-up used by thieves to make you stop and then rob you of your car and possessions! If you do not feel safe then don't stop; but phone the police and ambulance anyway.)

9. You are driving along the motorway and you see a car broken down with the occupant flagging you down for help.

(You should forget about stopping and keep going. You might feel guilty for a few minutes; but the alternative of being attacked or robbed doesn't bear contemplating!)

10. You are walking down the street and someone 'deliberately' bumps into you.

(Quickly tighten your grip on your handbag, in case it is a clever mugger's ploy. If your belongings are intact; then apologise with a smile and keep moving. If your watch is missing; quickly grab hold of him and yell *"Thief"*. The embarrassment will probably make him drop your watch. If however, he does not drop the watch and he is big and strong, then shout for the police but don't try to fight him; because he may also be carrying a weapon. Make sure you have a good description of him to give to the police.)

11. You are eating in a restaurant and the food is not to your satisfaction.

(Be polite if you want them to change it for you; but it is advisable to quietly pay up and inform them on your way out that you will not be returning, due to the bad service you received. It might embarrass them enough to change their attitude for future customers!)

12. You are walking around a town not familiar to you.

(Try to do your best to look like you know what you are doing, because thieves are very good at detecting easy targets; which are normally those perceived to be strangers in town. Make sure your belongings are safe enough not to be easily snatched from you; and remember to walk on the outside of the pavement when walking around a corner...in case someone is lying in wait for you.)

13. You are sitting at a bar having a few drinks and you need to go to the toilet.

(Unless you are with close friends, it is advisable to finish your drink before leaving your seat. You can always buy another one when you return. It is very easy for someone to spike your drink while you are away. The date-rape drugs are not only used on women for rape. You can also be drugged in order for your money, cell phone or credit cards to be stolen!)

14. You are in a nightclub and a pest won't leave you alone.

(Try to politely warn him to go away. If he refuses; have a quiet word with the manager or the security men and they will give him a few words of warning. This is why it is important to be polite to the doormen when you enter a club and tip them on your way out; because you never know when you might need their help!)

15. You are walking alone in town and you notice someone obviously following you.

(Walk into a big shop and try to leave by a different entrance/exit. Whilst inside; you can relay your concerns to the security staff of the shop and ask them to direct you to the police station. If he is still following when you come out of the shop; you should walk into the police station and report him. If you see the police on the street; don't be afraid to convey your concerns to them. However, I hasten to add that it is always better to go out with a friend; as going out alone raises too many security issues.)

16. Someone knocks on your door trying to sell you something.

(Talk to him/her through the intercom, window or the door. Never allow him or her into your house; for whatever reason. Tell them you are not interested in buying anything, unless you really are; in which case, ask for the name and phone number of their company. You should then tell them to wait outside; whilst you ring to confirm if they really work for the company and have its permission to knock on people's doors trying to make a sale. If they refuse to give you their names; tell them to go away or you will phone the police.)

17. Someone knocks on your door and wants to use the toilet or drink some water.

(Unless you have a few tough friends in the house with you; it is advisable to refuse with a plausible excuse, without opening your door. *"Sorry my toilet (water system) is broken. I have just rung the plumber and he is on his way to fix it."* Once inside; he could be looking to see if you have anything worth stealing later on. He could also attack you or threaten you with a weapon as soon as you open the door; and then steal your money or valuables. Better safe than sorry; even if it means being unkind!)

18. A friend asks to borrow a big sum of money.

(Only lend what you can afford to lose, without inconveniencing you or your family. Most borrowers are so desperate for the money; they will tell you anything, in order to get it. Once you give the money; the chances are, you will not get it back on or before the time promised. The borrower always assumes you have more than enough; that is why you were able to lend it to him/her. Trying to get money back from a friend; has ruined many a friendship! You are better-off lending money to a casual acquaintance, than to a friend. Remember the saying, 'familiarity breeds contempt!')

19. A friend wants to go into business with you; but has no money to invest.

(All joint-business ventures should be in partnership. This means the investment should be shared equally; unless you are prepared to go to a lawyer, in order to draw up a tightly binding contract that gives you shares equivalent to your investment. Since he/she has no money; it means it is effectively your business, if you provide the cash. This will never work; and will create animosity because he/she will feel it was his/her idea in the first place. I would advise you to decline; unless he/she brings the same amount of money as you, to the table. If you have too much money; you are better-off putting it into shares in reliable blue chip companies! Being ripped off will probably hurt more than being beaten up; because the mental scars never heal when a friend cheats you. If you don't go into business with him/her; you should never go behind his/her back and do the business yourself. It would be tantamount to stealing his/her ideas and he/she will hate you for it. Depending on how successful you become, using his/her idea without him/her; murder or maiming cannot be ruled out. Jealousy and greed bring out the worst in the human being!)

20. You have heard that someone has been badmouthing and gossiping about you.

(The worst thing to do; is to physically confront the culprit because more than likely, he/she will deny it. Keep your dignity and slowly try and find out the facts by telling him or her, what you have heard. Never get angry; and make a joke of it, if necessary. It is not difficult to see if he or she is lying; and then slowly break off contact with the culprit. Stop phoning; and always insist you are busy whenever he/she suggests an outing or get-together. They will soon get the message that you don't have time for them.)

21. You are a victim of a road rage lunatic who comes out of his car to threaten you.

(Stay in your car; roll up the windows and keep the doors locked. If you get out confronting him; he may be armed with a knife and could hurt you badly. He is unlikely to attack you in your car because there will be too many witnesses in the traffic and the chances are, someone will call the police. Allow him to shout as much as he can; and then roll down the window slightly and offer him a simple apology. Don't trade insults with him; because that would lead to violence. If he is yelling at you from his car; just ignore him and continue driving. If he follows you in his car; you should drive into the nearest police station.)

22. You are a victim of nuisance calls on your phone.

(The chances are; it could be a friend playing a prank. Stop answering your phone; unless you know who is calling you. If they conceal their number; then it is obvious they do not want to be found out and may get bored, if no one answers the phone. If they leave any threatening messages; then you have no choice but to change your number, if it is a mobile. On a fixed line however; you can lodge a complaint with the phone company and they will be able to trace the call or contact the police, if the calls are seriously threatening. It is easy to get call blocking features on your phone; so don't hesitate in having them installed.)

23. You are being pestered for your phone number or address.

(It is not everybody you would want to give your phone number or your address to; especially if you think he is out to fleece you. You may have to be honest and tell him you don't give your number out. Depending whether or not you will see the person again; it may be better to give him a wrong number or the number to the local police station. If he rings and a police sergeant answers the phone; he will get the message! In case you do meet him again; you can say that you sometimes do reconnaissance work for the police. If he has any ideas of ripping you off or bothering you; they will be quickly dispelled!)

24. A serious fight has broken out in the nightclub.

(Most fights start with raised voices or a heated argument. If you hear a loud fracas close to you in the club; then you should be mentally prepared to leave. Check to see if your possessions are safe; then make a mental note of the nearest exit door and how you are going to get there in the event of a fight. The minute the fight starts; move quickly towards the exit door, in case of flying glass. It would be advisable to report any suspicions you have to the manager/security staff; who can come and calm the argument down before the fight begins.)

25. You are walking down a street in town and you see a man rushing menacingly towards you.

(The chances are; he is running away from someone or something. He may have just robbed a shop and is desperate to get away; so quickly cross the road or step into the nearest shop till he has passed. Never stand in his way or try to play the heroine and tackle him; because he may be armed. Ringing the police to voice your concerns; could very well be counter-productive. Do you really have the time for several trips to the police station to give statements and then appear in court as a witness; if he were to be arrested and charged with having committed a crime? Sometimes it is better to just mind your own business!)

26. You are involved in a minor car accident that is clearly your fault.

(In any accident, tempers will rise; which could turn into a fight, if both parties refuse to accept responsibility. An accident usually occurs when both parties are not paying attention; but since you banged into his/her car, it is technically your fault. If you know it is your fault; it would be advisable to quickly apologise and offer to pay for the damage you caused, if it is not much. Otherwise; you will have to exchange details and inform the police and your insurance company. Show a little consideration for the welfare of the accident victim; in case he/she might need hospital treatment. Complete disregard for his or her health will only inflame matters and fisticuffs could easily ensue. Be extra sympathetic, if it is a woman whose car you smashed into; because being of the same sex, she will have no problem with fighting you. There will be several male drivers who will be only too happy to see two women come to blows; and then play the 'concerned citizen', by 'rescuing' both of you!

27. You are involved in a minor car accident that is clearly not your fault.

(You have to assume the person who hit you, will not admit fault; so to accuse him/her will only make matters worse. He/she could have reversed into you and still claim you drove forward and hit him/her! If there are witnesses; ask for their details, in case they will be needed. You should then phone the police and wait for them to arrive. Make a note of the car number and if you have a camera phone, take his/her picture; just in case he/she tries to drive off. It will make it easier for the police to trace him/her! Even if he/she offers to pay for the accident; make sure you get the name, address and phone number...as well as the details of the car. Never lose your temper or try to touch/fight him/her; because he/she could turn round and accuse you of assault. This would put you in more trouble than he/she is!)

28. If you have been drinking.

(You should never drive if you are drunk! If you get involved in an accident, it will be deemed your fault; even if it wasn't. If you fight, you will probably lose; because your balance and speed will be affected. You are more likely to get into an altercation because your judgement will be impaired and you might feel an insult where none exists; leading to an argument and a fight. Men will know you are drunk; and they will assume you will be easy to fuck. This will raise their confidence levels and they will definitely try their luck! Thieves and opportunists will all believe they can take advantage of you. I will never tell anyone never to drink; because it is socially important to many people. It is crucial however, to know the amount your body can handle; and when you are over the limit, you should go home to cool off. If you are going out to drink; never go alone and one member of your group should stay sober, in order to keep the others in check. Before you drink; make sure you have eaten properly. Alcohol on an empty stomach is destructive to the body organs like the liver and kidneys; and you will get drunk much quicker. You will then end up doing and saying things you might later regret!)

29. If you have been taking drugs.

(If you are already taking drugs; then nothing I say will change your mind. Likewise; if you are not into them, then you are obviously aware of the dangers. Because drugs are regarded by society as unsociable; those who take them will usually pretend they don't. Different drugs have different effects on different individuals; and like alcohol, they make the user socially obnoxious to those who are not in the same intoxicated mood. Whether you do or not, is entirely your business; because some people can handle them better than others. If you have to take drugs; it would be wise to stay at home, where you won't be a nuisance to others. That is how many a fight starts! The same rules apply as they do with drinking; except with drugs, they are also illegal. You therefore have to be careful not to be seen taking them in public; because you could be arrested and charged. Be warned! If you see someone taking drugs in the toilet of a club; it is advisable to mind your own business and keep your eyes away from her. She may not be in a correct frame of mind (some drugs can cause paranoia in mentally unstable over-users) and may aggressively insult, threaten or even attack you; thinking you are going to report her to the management or the police.)

30. Talking business with strangers.

(Never talk business in public with a stranger; because he/she might pick up information which could be detrimental to you or your company, if he/she repeated your conversation elsewhere. Industrial espionage is very common; so you have to be careful when someone approaches you in a bar or on the street and acts overtly friendly. Before you know it; you could be having a few drinks and a nice conversation with him/her about what you do. If you are involved in any suspect activities; be aware that the police use plain-clothed informants to garner information for them. That handsome man at the bar might be a plant for the police, organised crime or big business. Trust no one! Always go out with friends; so that you can have a safe, comfortable conversation.)

31. You wake up in the middle of the night and you hear intruders in your house.

(Since you are not sure how many there are or whether they are armed or not; it would be better not to confront them. Keep very quiet and lock yourself in the room you are in and then quietly phone the police; but don't come out of the room until they leave. Never keep any real valuables where they are likely to be found. It would be useful, if you had a silent alarm and surveillance camera hidden outside and inside the house; so that you could give the police a visual description of the intruders. The chances are; the cops will know their names by comparing their modus-operandi to other burglaries in the area! This will make it easier for them to be apprehended, charged and prosecuted. The questions you have to ask yourself are: *"Why did they target my house?" "How did they get into the house?" "Which of my friends or relatives knows about the valuable contents of my house?"*)

32. You are confronted by a burglar in your house and he is armed.

(There is no guaranteed way to fight someone who is armed. Remember; he may also know how to fight! If he is brandishing a knife; you may be able to pick up a chair to keep him at bay...but it is still not worth the risk. Since he is alone, you can try talking to him to leave; but if he proves obstinate, you should start shouting and try to attract the neighbours. He may panic and run away; but if he doesn't, you should run into a room, lock yourself inside and then phone the police. However; if he is carrying a gun, you must do as he says. Give him what he wants and pray he will be satisfied and leave. Since guns are illegal; he will probably be wearing something to cover his face. More than likely; he will not harm you, if you don't fight him. Sadly; he may have to kill you, if he feels you have recognised him and will go to the police. This is because he knows it will result in a hefty prison sentence for him. Ask yourself the same questions as in No. 31.)

33. You are taking a shower and you hear someone robbing your car outside.

(There is not much you can do; because by the time you get dressed and rush outside, he may be long gone. Are you prepared to run outside naked and tackle the thief? What if he is armed? Start yelling from your window and hope it attracts someone; otherwise you will have to hope and pray the police will find your car. There are certain impossible situations that could happen to anyone; and this is one of them. The only way to avoid your car being robbed while you are inconvenienced, is to make sure it cannot happen; by locking your car and activating a full-proof alarm and immobiliser whenever you park anywhere, even for a few minutes whilst you go shopping.)

34. You are about to enter your house when you are confronted by a man with a gun.

(This is another impossible situation. I'm afraid you will have to do as he asks; because he is either a junky desperate for money or somebody who knows exactly why he has targeted you. Either way; he will kill you, if you give him no choice. Do everything he says, give him exactly what he asks for and keep your eyes away from him; in case he thinks you will recognise him in the future. He knows your house and the time you arrive home; and has obviously weighed up the pros and cons, before coming to attack you. This should tell you that he is serious; and trying to fight him will result in your death or severe incapacitation. If you are lucky enough to escape with your life; you should take the confrontation as a severe warning. If you know why you have been targeted; try and quickly settle any debts and problems you have. Your attacker could be a hit man hired by your business enemies and may return at any time; since he knows where to find you. The police will not be able to protect you for ever! Herein lies the importance of being honest in your business dealings; don't insult, cheat or rip off those who are financially able to do you harm!)

35. You are about to enter your car when you are confronted by a man with a gun.

(Car-jacking is another impossible situation that could happen to anyone. Most professional thieves will not rob a car when there is someone inside. You have to assume that it is probably someone who has just committed a crime and is desperate to get away; or a teenage joy rider and the gun is more than likely, not a real one. I'm afraid you will just have to give up the keys and let him take the car; because in his desperation to get away, he may hurt you badly. Although your property is part of your self-defence, it is lower in priority to your life; so it is better to be safe than sorry. Since he is not a professional thief; he will definitely dump the car when he has used it to get to where he wants to go. Make a report to the police. Your car will be found; and the insurance should pay for any damage caused to it. The best way to avoid the threat of car-jacking is to park in reliable and secure parking spaces covered by closed-circuit cameras; and not try to park in cheap run-down areas, just to get free parking. If you are in town; you should pay for your parking and walk to where you need to go. Before you park; keep your eyes open for any layabouts prowling around the area. If you do not feel safe; then move away and park somewhere else. Don't forget to activate the alarm and immobiliser; so that the car cannot be stolen whilst you are away. A sticker on the car, stating that it is alarmed and protected with an immobiliser; is a useful deterrent.)

36. You are on the dance floor in a nightclub and someone deliberately stamps on your foot or keeps bumping into you.

(Try to move away from where you are dancing to another part of the floor; because he may be a harmless over-exuberant drunk, who does not know what he is doing. If he follows you; then you know he is deliberately trying to cause trouble for you. If you retaliate; it could lead to an argument or a fight and you will be thrown out, causing you embarrassment and allowing someone else to move onto the guy you had your eye on! Leave the dance floor and report him to the security staff; and they will warn him. Make sure he is not lurking around outside, when you leave the club. If you are afraid; then talk to the security staff and they will find you a taxi home.)

37. You are sitting in a taxi and he is taking a route unfamiliar to you.

(As soon as you notice the problem; relate it firmly to the driver that the route he is taking, is not the one you know. If he insists on going his way;

politely tell him you would like to get down from the taxi. Take a note of his registration and car number; pay him off and find another taxi. If he refuses to stop, then you know he is up to no good; so let him know you are going to ring the police from your mobile. Open the car door if necessary; to let him know that you are prepared to jump out. That should make him stop; because he knows someone would have seen you opening the door and may alert the police! This is why you should only pick registered taxis whenever you are returning home from a night out. The police can trace the driver and the car, if he misbehaves or something goes wrong.)

38. A fire breaks out in your home.

(If it is possible; find out where the fire started and close the door to keep it contained in one area. If you can put it out with buckets of water or a fire extinguisher; then do so. If not; you should ring the fire brigade and then take steps to get your family out as quickly as possible. Remember; the smoke kills much more often than the fire itself! If it is a major fire then you may have to think of drastic ways of getting out; which may include jumping out of windows. In an apartment block; there should be a fire escape and a siren to warn other residents. Forget about your property; unless it is possible to get important documents out. You may not have time to save anything else! Once the smoke gets into your lungs; you will not have the strength to escape. Have your house regularly checked out for carbon monoxide poisonous fumes that may be leaking from your electrical circuit system. Check the smoke alarms and replace the batteries in them on a regular basis. Turn off all appliances before you go to sleep. With fires; the prevention is always better than the cure! Ask your local fire or police station for advice on fire prevention and they will give you the necessary pamphlets, detailing the dos and don'ts. Stay safe!)

39. You arrive home to find your house has been burgled.

(Ring the police immediately and don't touch anything until they arrive; in case the thief has left some clues. There is nothing you can do after the event; except to make sure it never happens again. A burglary is painful because it feels as if you have been physically violated; and depending on what was taken out of your home, the mental damage done to you may never heal. This is why I stated in an earlier chapter that modern self-defence concerns your property as well as your physical being; because a thief will feel he has beaten you, if he manages to steal your property. Attacking you physically, is too much trouble and leads to a much harsher jail sentence. This way he gets one over on you and makes money selling your valuables as well! Burglaries rely on information from a reliable source. Someone obviously knew you would be out; so ask yourself these questions and do something about them! *"How did the thieves get in?"* Who else knows what valuables I keep at home? "Who is the latest friend I allowed into my house? If you have not been burgled before; the newest arrival into your sanctuary of friends should be suspected! Otherwise; make sure you have not annoyed one of your trusted friends! Give the police as many details as possible; but don't expect the items to be found. I hope you have kept the receipts and insurance papers for all your valuable items! One more thing...Change your locks!!!)

40. If your child is kidnapped...

(If you are rich and powerful; then the quickest way of beating you, is to hurt those closest to you. Kids are only kidnapped; when the gang has watched a family's movements for a while and know there is definitely money to be made. Many wealthy people around the world have had their children abducted. Most pay up the ransom without informing the police; because one of the kidnappers' demands would be not to tell anyone, or the child will suffer. Life is worth more than cash; so if you can afford it, you should always concede to the kidnappers' demands. The longer you dilly-dally, the worse the suffering of your child! They know you have the money; so why pretend you don't and let your child suffer needlessly? Always pay up first; get your child back and then let the police know as many details as you can obtain. If you allow the police to hide in order to witness the pay-off, then so much the better; because you get your child back in good health and the kidnappers will be caught. The police can arrest them later on; after following them to their hideout. This way the kidnappers may not suspect you had anything to do with their arrest; otherwise they may come looking for revenge. If you are rich enough to interest a kidnapper; then you should be able to afford the necessary security to keep your family safe!)

41. You have been arrested for fighting and taken to the police station.

(Fighting equates to violence! The police always hold a dim view of anyone who fights in public places; even if you were fighting in self-defence. You may still be angry from the fight; so the first thing is to calm down and do as you are told. Don't argue or shout at them; never play the innocent victim; never threaten to report them to their superiors; and never brag about the 'people in high places' that you know. The police are used to dealing with troublemakers; and it will only make things worse for you. Most police personnel are underpaid and overworked; so if you are looking for sympathy, the police station is not the place! Remember, you are perceived to have done something wrong; so be polite and listen to exactly what you are being charged with and only answer when spoken to. It is only after you have been granted bail or thrown into the cell, should you politely ask to phone someone who can come and help you; like a friend, a solicitor or your embassy. Police stations in most countries are not the nicest places in the world and you might be thrown into a filthy cell with other troublemakers; where you could easily be beaten up by other prisoners or in some cases, the police themselves.)

42. You are at a football match or other event where a fight or crowd violence erupts.

(The important thing is to get away from the area as quickly as possible; because the normal rules of behaviour do not apply. Shield your eyes with your forearm and find your way out of the mêlée before you get seriously injured; as there could be bottles, knives and sticks flying around. If the fight has nothing to do with you; then it is advisable not to be around when the police arrive. As soon as you arrive at any venue; make sure you know exactly where the exits are and how you are going to get there quickly in an emergency. For your own safety; you should leave the venue as quickly as possible after the event. In the case of a football match, there has probably been a winner and a loser; which means one set of supporters will be sad or angry and the other happy. There is no need to stay around for the ensuing action; as both sets of supporters will move onto places where alcohol is served. Arguments leading to fights between rival supporters are very common; even long after the game has finished. If you drove to the venue; it is advisable to leave a little early to avoid the rush at the end of the game. This is because the traffic will be congested; and the pickpockets will be on the lookout for easy pickings!)

43. You are in a public place like a café, nightclub or on a bus; and someone starts looking for trouble, claiming you have taken his/her seat.

(If you are in a café; it is better to call the waiter or manager to diffuse the situation. In a nightclub; it could lead to a fight where you could be injured by flying glass, before the security men can reach the scene. It is therefore better to get up and give him/her the seat; if gentle persuasion will not work. It could be a ploy to start a fight; so that his/her friends can steal your valuables and disappear in the mayhem! It is never worth fighting over a seat because you could be thrown out and charged by the police with destroying the club's property; which will prove very expensive for you. On a bus; if you feel outnumbered by his/her friends then it is advisable to get up and give him/her the seat. You can also complain to the driver/conductor; if there is one nearby. There are usually other passengers who will be helpful witnesses for the police on most public transport systems; so the chances are, he or she will not attack you. You could always brave it out, if you have the time for a verbal confrontation; but like everything else, it is better to avoid trouble where possible. Keep your ego in check; allow him/her their little victory and look for another seat!)

44. A friend owes you a large sum of money and refuses to pay.

(Unless he/she signed legal documents to that effect; there is not much you can do about it. Do not use violence on him/her because it will be used as an excuse never to pay you; and you may even be reported to the police.

Because he/she is a friend; it would be unwise to hire some thugs to get your money back. The thugs will demand a big cut from the money; and it can get messy because your friend will become your enemy. He/she may know things about you that could hurt you in the future! Patience is the key; but whatever happens, the friendship and trust you had together will be broken for ever. The safest thing is never to lend money to a friend, unless you are prepared to write it off; and never lend money to anyone, if you are not completely financially solvent. It is better to explain to your friend that you cannot afford to lend him/her the money; even if you lose his/her close friendship. A real friend will understand!)

45. You are accused of stealing from a shop; when you know you are innocent.

(If it is a reputable shop; it would be advisable to say nothing, until they have told you what you have stolen. Since you are innocent; the stolen article will not be on your person...so they have no case. Depending on how embarrassed they made you feel; you can report the shop to a citizens' advice bureau and sue them for defamation of character. In a dubious shop in a Third World country; it is probably a ruse to fleece you off some money and they may even 'claim' they found the article on you. You therefore have to stand your ground and insist on calling the police. In most cases, they will back off; but if they don't, it is better to go with the police and ask to phone your embassy. At times like this; you may as well pay the police some money to let you go and put it down to experience. If you keep insisting on your innocence; it could drag on for days or even weeks. In most countries the burden of proof is on the victim; so you will be locked up, taken to court and then fined or jailed. Meanwhile, you will be liable for your hotel charges; because your things will still be in your hotel room. Finally; you may miss your return flight home and lose the money on your ticket! Whenever you go shopping outside your environment; it is advisable never to go alone. With two or more of you; it is much harder for a shopkeeper to frame you and for the police to bully you.)

46. You have accidentally knocked down someone in your car.

(In most Third World countries, you could be badly beaten up and possibly killed by the mob; especially if the victim is a child and you have killed him or her. If you are in an African country; you should not stop but keep driving straight to the police station and hand yourself in. If you stop and stay in your car; the mob will destroy the car and may even set it alight with you inside! If you come out of the car to tend to the victim; you will be manhandled by the mob and easily killed. In Europe and the States; you are required by law to stop and not desert the scene of a crime. If you drive away and you are later arrested; you will be charged with murder because, only the guilty run away! You will therefore have to stop, come out of your car and phone for an ambulance; and then wait for the police to arrive. You will be insulted by other motorists; but you won't be lynched. Be prepared to go to jail for manslaughter; or be sued for reckless driving. If you have been drinking or taking drugs; your case will be so much worse!)

47. You are talking to a man in a nightclub and a girl comes up to you and tells you to leave her "boyfriend" alone.

(It would be advisable to do as she says and walk away; but watch the boy's reaction. If he says nothing; then you know they have something in common and they may have issues, which have nothing to do with you. To interfere; will definitely lead to a fight because the girl is already jealous and angry with him. He may be using you to get back at her! If he rejects her and asks you not to go anywhere; then you should try and talk some sense into her that the man is obviously not interested in her. Be prepared for a fight because she may be drunk; which is probably why she is being so unreasonable. If the man wants you; he will definitely try and prove a point to her that whatever they had before, is over. If she attacks him; I'm afraid you will have to be the perfect lady and walk away. No man is worth the hassle; even if it means he may not talk to you again! Remember the saying: *"There are plenty of fish in the sea!"*)

48. You are being held hostage in your house by a lunatic with a gun.

(In such a scenario; there is nothing you can do except do everything he says. Never try to escape; because in his state of mind, he may kill you and then kill himself. Keep talking to him; unless he tells you to shut up. Try to find out what he wants and why he is doing that to you. Be sympathetic; and if necessary, agree with whatever his grievances may be. He may only want a listening ear; and by being his friend, he may realise his folly in kidnapping you. Don't even think about calling the police; because even in his demented state of mind, he will be able to sense you are against him. If your phone rings; ask his permission before answering it. Don't talk in code and don't raise the alarm; because you will be putting your life in danger. Time is your ally in such a situation because he may eventually get bored and will be inclined to let you go; if he knows nothing will happen to him. If he is a thief; just give him whatever he asks for and he may decide to take it and go. Once he is gone and your life is safe; you can then call the police and give them his description. You may have to move out of your house, until he is caught and jailed; because he may come back, if he feels you have betrayed him to the authorities. Impossible situations are never easy!)

49. You are caught up in a skyjacking scenario.

(Although skyjacking is now decreasing; as a result of better security, police and customs patrols at all major airports...they could still happen! This is one impossible situation, which can never be blamed on you. Every flight you take; there is a risk of a lunatic on board who may not even be a terrorist, but could hijack the plane for his own selfish purposes. Short of not travelling to high-risk areas, where the security is either lax or suspect; there is nothing you can do about this. What you should not do; is play the hero and tackle the hijackers because they are obviously prepared to die before they embark on such a high-risk adventure. They may be wired up with a bomb; whereby one small mistake will blow up the whole plane. Don't use your cell phone to alert a loved one on the ground; because any sudden movement will be seen as a threat and they could shoot you as an example to the other passengers. If they pick on you and ask you to do something; you just have to obey. Not doing as they ask; will put yourself and the other passengers at risk.)

50. Suicide bombers and stray bullets.

(Knowledge about the country and area you are in and about the current political and economic situation there; is the only thing that could help you avoid suicide bombers and stray bullets. With suicide bombers; you can reduce the risk by staying away from countries at war with an occupying army...like some in the Middle East or parts of Asia. Crowded areas in the big cities in the super-power countries are also dangerous; because the bombers have no other way of beating them except by targeting innocent victims and causing as much damage as possible. If you are walking through an economically-deprived, gangland or drug-infested area; you increase your chances of being killed or injured by a stray bullet, because there are always turf wars going on. This is why it is important you know where you are going, especially in foreign countries; because you could easily stray into a dangerous area and be attacked, robbed or even lose your life. Most places in the world are safe enough; but there is always the unknown factor one can do nothing about. Nothing I say can help you; if you are blown up or hit by a stray bullet! Being at the wrong place at the wrong time can only be attributed to fate; because nobody can be prepared for things they have no way of influencing. *"Good Luck and pray to your God it never happens to you!"*)

You have to remember that the above scenarios are basic common sense advice and are what I consider the safest ways to keep you out of serious danger. However; you have to read between the lines and rely on your gut instinct, whilst using whatever advice I give you, only as a guideline. Every situation is different; and it all depends on who you are and where you live. For example in No. 7; I tell you not to pick up any damsel in distress, whilst driving to your destination. You may disagree; and in certain areas you could stop to pick her up without any problems. In No. 16; I advise you not to allow any salesmen into your house, without checking their identification with the company they are claiming to work for. This obviously also applies to anyone coming to read your electricity or gas meter; even if they look official and are wearing the company uniform. I can only deal with what could happen and advise you with the words, "*If it can, it will!*"; a version of Murphy's Law, which ultimately means anything is possible. We are all intelligent enough to assess a situation and react accordingly; but it is always better to be safe than sorry because you can never undo something, once it has already happened. Instinctively; the human being is kind-hearted and will usually help someone in distress. Regrettably in our modern society; this kindness has been abused and is seen as a weakness, to the point that no one is completely safe. Lives and reputations have been destroyed through trying to help a fellow human being; and by sheer carelessness. Once you are aware of the possibilities of things going wrong; only then will you be able to develop a cynical and selfish attitude to life and only think of yourself; your family; your property; your dignity; your integrity; your self-esteem; your reputation and your country. In short; protecting the things you care about...***the real self-defence***! Believe me; nothing else matters!

"It has been a real pleasure writing for you Tigress; and I hope this book will empower you to become the woman you deserve to be...loved, respected and above all, safe and happy. Thank you, and good luck! I love you all...I really do!!!"

PS. *"I'm still young enough, free, single and ever willing to mingle; if you are!!!"* (Smile)

Goju
xxx

Appendix

Goju (real name, Danny Gwira) is the Founder and Chief Instructor of the survival systems **African Goju; South American Goju; Gojurobics**. He started his combat training with boxing and fencing in 1962 in the UK. He continued with Judo; Jujitsu; Tae-kwondo; Shotokan; Chinese Goju; Kempo; Kyokushinkai and Wadoryu. He became a professor of Martial Arts Education in 1987, after studying at the University of Martial Arts and Science in the USA under the tutelage of Grandmaster Ron Van Clief. He is the owner of the *Martial Arts Institute, www.africangoju.com; www.africangoju.net; & www.gojurecords.com.*

WHAT IS AFRICAN GOJU & SOUTH AMERICAN GOJU?

African and South American Goju are survival systems based on reality and common sense. They were originally developed because what one country perceives as self-defence may be different from another; and therefore, it all depends on who you are and where you live. Although it started in Africa; it quickly expanded to other nations and both systems became known simply as *Goju*. There are now over 7000 students in Ghana; Nigeria; Cameroon; Ivory Coast; Liberia; Upper Volta; Angola; Kenya; Botswana; South Africa; Zimbabwe; Australia; the Philippines; Bangladesh; China; Hong Kong; Russia; Switzerland; Holland; France; Germany; Portugal; England; Northern Ireland; Eire; Portugal; Canada; the United States; Brasil and Bolivia. It is not only taught as conventional martial arts, but also as a philosophy; through books available on the website. Goju is my attempt to teach the psychology and philosophy of self-defence, based on one's way of life. Very simply; you fight to win, using any effective way to make sure you do! Every individual has a twenty-four hour day. You know what you do for a living, where you normally go and the possibilities of getting into trouble. You then have to use your imagination to prepare yourself accordingly; relying on the principle that things will go wrong, only if you allow them to. Can you behave yourself after drinking; so that you are not taken advantage of? Could you physically defend yourself in a fight? If you go into a nightclub; do you know the owner? How would you cope, if trouble exploded? What of a burglary, whilst you are sleeping or in the shower? Is your car/house safe against thieves? How secure are you at work; in case of an attack by an irate customer? How smart are you; in order not to be taken in by a con man? How would you handle mental/physical abuse; betrayal or infidelity? It is this attention to detail that makes Goju different from other disciplines and can easily be adapted to suit whichever country you live in. The same philosophy was used in preparing this book for the modern woman!

In conclusion, Goju is: *"The art of knowing how, where, why and when to fight or not to fight; knowing whether or not you can win and get away with it, defending your body, family, property, dignity, integrity, self-esteem, reputation, and country in the process. The ability to withstand both mental and physical pain, when coupled with extremely effective combat techniques; makes Goju the most realistic and potentially dangerous system in the world."*

WHAT IS GOJUROBICS?

Gojurobics is a form of aerobic dance exercises in which self-defence moves are used, whilst moving around to the beat of simple catchy music. Great fun! The moves are described on the song **Doing the Goju Dance.**

Here are the lyrics to sixteen songs, which I hope will help you to feel good about yourself and stay strong. If you prefer to hear them with music; the CD or download of each song is available from my website: *www.gojurecords.com.*

1. THE ROAR OF THE TIGRESS ©
© (Dublin: 29/08/10)

When I say 'No'!…I do not mean 'Yes'.
And I don't take!…orders from no one.
That goes to show!…I could not care less.
It's obvious I!…am my own woman.
I earn lots of money…Got a big house and car.
Has to be a special person to hook me.
Most men are scared of me…They dare not go too far.
Because they know what I'm like when I'm angry.

I've got the Roar of the Tigress inside me.
That really means nobody…controls me.
I have great pride in my femininity.
That's how I want every…woman to be.

So important!…for any woman.
To try and keep!…her independence.
Do what you want!…As much as you can.
In your own time!…It surely makes sense.
Don't take me for granted…or I'll eat you alive.
Capable of doing more than you expect.
I've got brains in my head…Energy zeal and drive.
And I deserve to be treated with respect.

<<Leave me alone!…I'm on my own!
You can't force me!…To go with you!
I am happy!…In my body!
Why can't you see?…I don't need you!

I am wired to all your tricks!…Your chat-up lines make me sick!
I'm not attracted to you!…I won't go to bed with you!
Take your filthy hands off me!…or you'll feel the wrath in me!
I'll show you I've got, the roar of the Tigress!>>

Remember: Many women in the past suffered in order for you to enjoy what you have today. Don't stop till you reach the top! Don't take any shit from nobody! It's good to be a woman!

2. POLITICALLY CORRECT GIRLS
© (Dublin 15/05/08)

Ever since women got their equal rights…the men are all confused,
Because they've realised…we do not need them.
We are now strong enough to stand and fight…won't be used and abused,
Cut them down to size…give them problems.
We have the law on our side.
They can't stop us now.
They don't have no place to hide.
We will show you how.

We are real politically correct girls!
We are out to put men in their place.
We are real politically correct girls!
We're the new face of the female race.

If your man tries to throw his weight around…just tell him to get lost,
And prove to him you're…more than capable.
You have to be prepared to stand your ground…don't quit at any cost,
If he dares touch you…he's in trouble.
Don't be scared to call the cops.
Be a divorcee.
You'll surely come out on top.
With alimony.

We must all get together and unite…it will make us stronger,
And there is nothing…we cannot achieve.
They'll have to accept we are in the right…it is now or never,
We'll have everything…if we believe.
Our passion is now aroused.
We are very hot.
Next stop could be the White House.
Who says we cannot?

Remember: Women comprise over half the world population. If you stick together the way the men do; the sky is the limit.

3. CAREER GIRL
© (Dublin 17/09/08)

She works so hard every day…in order to earn good pay.
That's the basic condition…in any profession.
She don't care who she upsets…what she wants she always gets.
She's got no time for romance…
She is very ambitious…she won't stop till she's the boss.
Any time there is a test…she's always the best.
All the men are scared of her…that's because she's so clever.
She puts them all in a trance.
…Many girls are just like her…
…They will never depend on men…
…Her whole life is her career…
…A great example for women…

She is what you call a ca…ree, er girl.
She don't need a man in her life.
She wants to get to the top of her world.
She won't sit at home to play…wife.

She's not yet found a soul mate…'cause she never goes on dates.
She's got her own car and home…and she lives alone.
In this male oriented world…life is tough for every girl.
She does the best that she can…
Unlike other young women…she's put off having children.
She says she will wait until…her career's fulfilled.
Hope she don't leave it too late…or she'll end up full of hate.
When she can't get any man.
…Career girls are everywhere…
…To them it all makes perfect sense…
…They know how to conquer fear…
…Call it female independence…

Remember: Go for your dreams and ambitions Girls! Men are not the only ones who value their careers!

4. BISEXUAL BEING
© *(Dublin: 2004)*

Well it's a crazy world 'cause there are some girls,
Who can't find a man to go out with.
They would sit at home fuming all alone,
While their souls slowly rot and perish.
Well I ain't one of those kind of girls,
Who'll sit at home all by myself.
I'll go out and bag myself a man,
If I can't get one I'll get a woman.

I'm a bisexual being, a true love machine,
I need love like anybody else.
A hetero woman, can still be lesbian,
I love men and I love girls.

Well I'm a bisexual being we all know what that means,
I can go one way or the other.
I love sex with a man as much as a woman,
I'll even take them both together.
'Cause I'm so tired of hanging around,
Waiting all year for the perfect man.
If I really feel like getting down,
I'll make love with whomever I can.

I'm a bisexual being, a true love machine,
I won't keep my body in a shell.
In these modern days, it's okay to be gay,
With me you can never tell.

Remember: Always be proud of who you are.

5. ON SOLID GROUND
© (Dublin: November 2004)

At first he was such a dear, he was so compliant,
Anything I'd ask he'd do to make me happy.
He really made me feel on top of the world…
The cracks began to appear, when I got pregnant,
He did not seem to have any interest in me.
It was so obvious he'd found another girl.
In my delicate condition, nothing that I could do,
If I let it worry me, I'd risk a miscarriage.
Just 'cause I acted, so very cool,
that did not mean that, I was a fool…
I won't let no one, man or woman,
I won't let no one, ruin my marriage.

My love was built on solid ground,
I won't let my man mess around.
My love was built on solid ground,
And now he's found…
A love so strong, it can't be pushed around.

As soon as I had baby, the battle began,
He looked so surprised did not think that I knew.
I told him I was looking for divorce…
It was either her or me; he had to choose one,
He'd lose the baby there was nothing he could do.
He broke down in tears and was full of remorse.
Been married for a long time, been through thick and thin,
There's no need to spoil it all, by being unfaithful.
I had to show him, just who I was,
And now he knows that I am the boss.
My love was built on, such solid ground,
And that's what makes it so beautiful.

Remember: A man has to be reminded that there are some things you cannot allow him to get away with; and you will fight tooth and nail to protect your dignity and integrity.

6. YOU HAVE NO CHANCE!
© *(Dublin 13/11/08)*

Are you so blind, that you just cannot see,
When a girl is not in the mood for love?
You might just find, you've met your match in me.
I'm afraid you don't excite me enough.
I've already…been hurt before.
The last thing on my mind is to get involved.
Don't be silly…don't be a bore.
Leave me alone and the problem will be solved.

Stay away from me…I'm warning you.
I'm not interested…in your romance.
There's no telling me…what I should do.
That is what I said…you have no chance.

If I told you, what my last boyfriend did.
You will see why I feel the way I do.
The time is due, there is no closing bid.
I don't have it in my heart to love you.
Impossible…so don't bother.
I'm sure you're man enough to find someone else.
You'll be able…to discover.
All over town there are lots of lovely girls.

Remember: It is always better to be honest and upfront with a man. It can save you a lot of hassles. If you don't like him...give it to him straight up!

7. TO BE FREE
© (Dublin 20/09/08)

Woke up this morning…thought I was dreaming.
A nice feeling came over me.
First time in my life…no longer his wife.
And it made me very happy.
I still cannot believe…I am now divorced.
I am finally free from him.
I don't have time to grieve…no time for remorse.
I can now do things at my whim.

To be free…it's so nice…to be free.
That's the way things are supposed to be.
To be free…it's so nice…to be free.
Married life was never good for me.

He used to go out…come home late at night.
As drunk as any man could be.
He would curse and shout…looking for a fight.
And then try to make love to me.
If I dared to refuse…It made no difference.
He would beat me till I was sore.
Sheer marital abuse…it did not make sense.
And I could not take anymore.

Had no choice but to…apply for divorce.
It was granted immediately.
I will start anew…get things back on course.
He's not allowed to come near me.
What I had to go through…was very serious.
And I felt that it should be shared.
If it happens to you…just be courageous.
Divorce him, no need to be scared.

Remember: The more women stand up and speak out about abuse; the better! If you are unhappy, get out while you can. You are still a woman. You can get anything you want!

8. TAKE IT ON THE RUN
© (Dublin: 20/04/10)

I have just had the biggest escape of my life.
Don't even know what I ever saw in that man.
It was so bad, a marriage of sheer stress and strife.
I was an incredibly unhappy woman.
The beginning of…the rest of my life.
I am glad to say…things will get better.
I have had enough…of being his wife.
And as from today…it is all over.

Take it on the run…Gonna have some fun.
It's now me me me…I'm finally free.
Take it on the run…Justice has been done.
I've got my divorce…My life's back on course.

I would rather, not tell you what he put me through.
I got fed up I just could not take anymore.
Now or never, I did the best thing I could do.
And I can't think why I did not do it before.
I took the plunge and…applied for divorce.
Emotional and…mental cruelty.
His sexual demands…were obtained by force.
One can understand…it was not easy.

<<I'm gonna achieve…things I missed out on.
Going to parties…dancing with the boys.
I still can't believe…he is really gone.
I'll do what I please…now I have a choice.>>

Remember: Freedom is a state of mind. Have fun with your singledom; but be careful you don't jump from frying pan to fire! There are many wolves in sheep's clothing!

9. THE HEROINE
© (Dublin: 21/11/09)

It just had to happen some day…a girl who had the guts.
To do something that all women…have long been dreaming of.
For so long men have had their way…no ifs no whys no buts.
Forcing their wives to have sex…in the name of love.
For better or for worse…the famous saying goes.
It does not bear thinking…what some women go through.
Marriage can be a curse…insults rape slaps and blows.
Enter the heroine…it was long overdue.

This is the tale of a woman…who'd had enough of his love.
When she was raped by her main man…took a knife and cut it off.
Picked up the penis skin…threw it in a dustbin.
Oh what a heroine…victory for women.

The husband is a six-foot hunk…he is so big and tough.
When such a man says he wants sex…there's not much she can do.
One night he came home late so drunk…and forced her to make love.
What would you have done…if it had happened to you?
Years and years of abuse…had to be the last straw.
It was surely no sin…she was fighting a war.
It made the front page news…he can't rape her no more.
She's now the heroine…she has opened the door.

<<*This has scared all the men…they now have a problem.*
It's hard for them to win…the law is on our side.
They will never know when…it could happen to them.
Thanks to the heroine…they've got nowhere to hide.>>

Remember: Before you do a 'Lorraine Bobbitt' make sure it really is the last resort. It might be easier to call the police at the first sign of abuse and don't let it get this far. Take care!

10. MODERN MISTRESS
© (Dublin: 2004)

He comes to see me, at his own convenience,
That's because he still, loves his kids and wife.
And just because of, his own guilty conscience,
Gives me everything, just to be part of his life.
I am under no illusions,
He won't leave his wife for me.
He gives me the best love sessions,
I can't ask for more really.

I'm just a modern mistress,
He treats me like a princess.
Wife doesn't know about me,
That's just the way things should be.

He likes to show off, with me to all his friends,
He's so proud of me, takes me everywhere.
He says he loves me, because I am different,
He does things with me, with his wife he would not dare.
I always tell him he's the greatest,
And cook him his favourite food.
That's why a man has a mistress,
Someone who makes him feel good.

He's bought me a car, gives me lovely presents,
Holidays abroad, and the best restaurants.
He's installed me in, a plush modern apartment,
So that he can come, see me whenever he wants.
I know it can't last for ever,
I'll have my fun while I can.
So that when it's all over,
I'll find me another man.

Remember: Ultimately you are responsible to yourself. Do whatever makes you happy. Using a man for your own ends is not a bad thing; but it would be best if he weren't married!

11. GOOD TIME GIRLS
© (Dublin: 10/03/10)

One can see them…strutting down the street bold as brass.
Intelligent…sexy and oozing so much class.
Shaking their hips…and flashing their smiles at the men.
They're what we'd call…cute sophisticated women.
Loud and boisterous…more than capable.
There is nothing…they cannot handle.
They like their guys...tall rich and handsome.
They are friendly…but they are not dumb.

Good! Time!...Good time girls!…Without
A! Care!...In the world!…Flaunting
Sex! Is!...Natural!…They're just
Good! Time!...Good time girls!

In the night clubs…they're the ones always on the floor.
With sexy moves…you may never have seen before.
They've got money…can afford to do what they want.
Having a ball…to them that is what's important.
They're the envy…of every woman.
'Cause they know how…to get any man.
So exciting…full of zeal and zest.
Liberation…at its very best.

<<Good time girls are…known around the world.
Some prefer to…say they are bad girls.
They are only…out to have some fun.
They do not cause…harm to anyone.>>

Remember: It's good to be liberated and have fun; but please protect yourself! Venereal disease is not good self-defence.

12. WHO THE HELL ARE YOU?
© (Dublin 22/10/08)

Woke up with a headache…this morning.
I went out last night with some friends.
Having fun on the make…and drinking.
This good-time madness has to end.
I feel as if I've…been hit by a truck.
Who the hell is this guy inside my bed?
Been roasted alive…I can't pass the buck.
This is not really what I intended.

Who the hell are you?…get out of my bed!
I do not want to know what happened last night.
Who the hell are you?…get out of my bed!
If you refuse to go…there will be a fight.

I think it's better if…you went home.
Besides I don't even know you.
This is no lover's tiff…please go home.
There is nothing else we can do.
It's been a mistake…I feel very sore.
We were both drunk and these things do happen.
For both of our sakes…we'll just say no more.
And I hope I never see you again.

Remember: Too much alcohol is bad 4 U and leads to problems! Moderation is the solution!

13. YES, I'M GUILTY!
© (Dublin 28/09/08)

The telephone rang…it was my husband.
Calling from the police station.
Sincerely he hoped…I would understand.
He was in a bad situation.
He'd been caught, committing fraud…and they thought.
It was an extremely serious crime.
Well of course, here was cause…for divorce.
He'll be going to prison for a long time.

I don't care what other people say.
I don't care whatever they will do to me.
I will stand by him in every way.
Because I am the one who's really guilty.
I'll do for him…the best I can.
He is my one…and only man.
Yes I'm guilty…Oh so guilty…Yes I'm guilty…
Of lo o-o ooo o-o…ving him.

This is such a blow…to my whole ego.
I should have stopped him from doing it.
I feel I'm the one…who should have been done.
It's something I'm not proud to admit.
I'm guilty, as much as he…don't you see.
I knew what he was getting up to.
Now he's in jail, refused bail…I have failed.
Honey you know I'll never abandon you.

Can't explain why I'm in love with him.
Can't explain why I refuse to let him go.
Stranger than any song book or film.
Loyalty is what makes the love garden grow.
Together till…death do us part.
He'll always be…inside my heart.
Yes I'm guilty…Oh so guilty…Yes I'm guilty…
Of lo o-o ooo o-o…ving him.

> <<No need for me…to cry or shout.
> I'll wait for him…till he comes out.
> Yes I'm guilty…Oh so guilty…Yes I'm guilty…
> Of lo o-o ooo o-o…ving him>>

Remember: Sometimes love means telling your man what he does not want to hear. If you suspect him of doing something illegal and you don't like it, keeping quiet is not the answer. Warn him before it is too late. Visiting him in prison is not fun for you or the children!

14. HOUSE HUSBAND
© (Dublin 07/02/08)

Dirty clothes in the wash…nice clean sheets on our bed,
Remember to feed baby…and rock him to sleep.
Try not to leave it late…change him if he gets wet,
Make sure that you give the house…a very good sweep.
Don't forget to…throw out the garbage.
If the phone rings…just take a message.
Prepare dinner…and do the shopping.
I won't be back…until the evening.

I go to work and…make the money,
While he stays at home…and slaves for me.
I wear the pants and…he understands,
He's my very own…house husband.

When he first lost his job…what a blow for my man,
He used to feel so guilty…I felt so sorry.
But he's proved that a man…can do what women can,
He does the housework so well…now I don't worry.
I take over…during the weekends.
While he chills out…with some of his friends.
They are so cool…they never demand.
The reasons why…he's a house husband.

Whenever he needs it…he borrows cash from me,
It is a small price to pay…for our piece of mind.
Till he gets on his feet…that's how it has to be,
I love him ever so much…he's one of a kind.
Role reversal…it is nothing new.
We're just doing…what we have to do.
Love and marriage…they go hand in hand.
He's happy to…play the house husband.

Remember: You really can have your cake and eat it. Some men actually enjoy being used and abused! Makes a change doesn't it?

15. THE DEVIL I KNOW
© (Dublin: 24/11/09)

He's put on so much weight…tells me there's more to love.
He does the things I hate…and then says life is tough.
Goes out and comes home late…partying with all his friends.
It can get so bad sometimes…I think it is the end.
Some days he can be okay…and he makes me happy.
In his own delightful way…I know that he loves me.
Like a kid who loves to play…but he will never cheat.
I'm sure he will change one day…from his head to his feet.

It may seem like a curse…but it could have been worse.
And I don't think I can let him go.
I count myself lucky…that at least he loves me.
It's better the devil I know.

He might as well be dead…he hates to go to work.
Drinking all day instead…he's just a lazy jerk.
He farts and snores in bed…God knows what he dreams of.
And he is always asleep…when I want to make love.
Whenever I get angry…he feels very guilty.
He then says he is sorry…never meant to hurt me.
With sad eyes he looks at me…as if he is in pain.
But there is one guarantee…he will do it again.

Remember: The grass is not always greener on the other side! It is better to keep the one you've got; if there is a chance of teaching him how to love you properly.

16. FEMALE INDEPENDENCE
© (Dublin 14/03/08)

A woman should not have to…depend on a man.
That's why we have come to do…everything we can.
We must think of something new…and very quickly,
Or we'll just say goodbye to…real equality.
If we sit on the fence!…we will go backwards instead.
It's on our own conscience!…if we don't shout it out.
It don't make any sense!…the way women are treated.
Female independence!…is what I'm talking about.

Female Independence!…we will put up a fight!
Female Independence!…because we know we are right.
Female Independence!…Women in the whole world, unite!
Female Independence!…that's what we call equal rights.

Women can do anything…that the men can do.
Without us they are nothing…they don't have a clue.
It's so discriminating…we deserve our due.
They could give us everything…if they wanted to.
We've all worked very hard…to get where we are today.
Now we are on our guard…they can't fool us no more.
They have played their last card…they have nothing more to say.
We will claim our reward…they'd better open the door.

How many women are there…in all the top jobs?
I don't think that it is fair…we are being robbed.
Anything we try to share…they just fob us off.
I now say they should beware…we have had enough.
We're not here for the ride!…they must take us seriously.
We've got nothing to hide!…that's why we will succeed.
Our faith has not yet died…we're determined to break free.
A kick up the backside!…is exactly what they need.

It is important for your dignity and self-worth not to have to depend on anybody. That way you become the mistress of your own destiny and nobody can tell you what to do. I really hope this book will achieve this for you.

© All songs written by *Daniel Gwira. (Danny Gee Goju)*

www.ingramcontent.com/pod-product-compliance
Lightning Source LLC
Chambersburg PA
CBHW051123230426
43670CB00007B/648